THE ỊZỌN
OF THE
NIGER DELTA

Edited by

Ebiegberi Joe Alagoa
Tekena Nitonye Tamuno
John Pepper Clark

Onyoma Research Publications

ISBN: 978-978-8195-00-9

Published in 2009 by
Onyoma Research Publications
11 Orogbum Crescent, GRA Phase II
P.O. Box 8611, Federal Secretariat Post Office
Port Harcourt, Rivers State, Nigeria

E-mail: kala_joe@yahoo.com
Website: www.onyoma.org
Mobile: 0803-308-3385

Cover design by:
Diseye Tantua

Maps drawn by:
Mr A.S. Okoro, Cartographer

Printed by:
Doval Ventures Limited
12 Ohaeto Street, D/Line
Port Harcourt, Rivers State
0803 307 5443, 0803 309 7988

Word Processing:
Rachael Ekejiuba, Inainkemi Nicholas

Type Selection and Layout:
Jigekuma Ayebatari Ombu
at Hisis (Publishing) Ltd · Port Harcourt

0803 300 4589 · 0805 743 6265

CONTENTS

MEMBERS OF THE IJAW HISTORY PROJECT COMMITTEE

1. **Ebiegberi Joe Alagoa**, PhD (Wisconsin), JP, OON, FHSN, FNAL. Emeritus Professor of History, University of Port Harcourt: Chairman.

2. **Tekena Nitonye Tamuno**, PhD, DLitt (London), FHSN, FNAL, fni, OFR, CON. Emeritus Professor of History, former Vice Chancellor, University of Ibadan; President, Bells University: Member.

3. **C. A. Dime**, PhD, Professor of Philosophy, Edo State University, Ekpoma, first President, Ijaw National Congress: Member.

4. **Nkparom Claude Ejituwu**, PhD (Lagos), Professor of History, University of Port Harcourt: Member.

5. **Nicholas A. Frank-Opigo**, B.A (Ibadan), Chief: Member.

6. **B. A. Obuoforibo**, PhD, Reverend Canon: Member.

7. **Zebulon Bire Agbede**, Surgeon: Member.

8. **T. O. Onduku, Chief.** [Represented by Preye Onduku Esquire]:Member.

9. **Tam Fiofori,** Film-maker, Photo Journalist: Co-opted Member.

10. **John H. Enemugwem,** PhD (University of Port Harcourt), Sub-Dean, Faculty of Humanities, University of Port Harcourt: Secretary.

Secretariat:

11. **Inia Ibufukama**: Accountant

12. **Rachael Ekejiuba**: Computer Operator

13. **Esinkuma Nyananyo** and **Bomo Nyananyo**: Computer Consultants

CONTRIBUTING AUTHORS

AGBEGHA, C. Budonyefa. Mr. Agbegha teaches English at the College of Education, Warri, Delta State.

AGORO, Saviour Nathan A. Dr. Agoro teaches Theatre Arts at the Niger Delta University, Wilberforce Island, Bayelsa State.

AKPOGHOMEH, Osi S. Akpoghomeh is Professor of Geography, and Dean, Faculty of Social Sciences at the University of Port Harcourt.

ALAGOA, Ebiegberi Joe. Alagoa is Emeritus Professor of History, University of Port Harcourt.

AMA-OGBARI, O. C. Dr. Ama-Ogbari teaches history at the Niger Delta University, Wilberforce Island, Bayelsa State.

AMGBARE, Eva Ogbozimo. Miss Amgbare is member of the Ijaw Peoples Association, London.

AMINIGO, E. R. Dr. Mrs. Aminigo teaches in the Department of Microbiology, University of Port Harcourt.

ANDERSON, Martha. Dr. Anderson is Professor of Art History, School of Art and Design, New York State College of Ceramics at Alfred University, Alfred, New York, U. S. A.

ASUK, Charles. Mr. Asuk teaches history at the University of Port Harcourt.

AYUWO, Jones G. I. Mr. Ayuwo teaches linguistics at the University of Port Harcourt.

CLARK, John Pepper. Professor Clark is Chairman, Pec Repertory Theatre, Lagos and Funama, Kiagbodo, Delta State.

DAMINABO, I. E. Mrs. Daminabo teaches Geography at the Rivers State College of Arts and Science, Port Harcourt.

DEREFAKA, Abi A. Derefaka is Professor of Archaeology, University of Port Harcourt.

DEVONISH, Hubert. Dr. Devonish is Head, Department of Linguistics, at The University of the West Indies, Mona-Kingston, Jamaica.

DUNU, J. B. Mr. Dunu teaches in Ogbe-Ijoh, Warri South-West Local Government, Delta State.

EJITUWU, Nkparom Claude. Ejituwu is Professor of History at the University of Port Harcourt, and Fellow of the Historical Society of Nigeria.

ENEMUGWEM, John H. Dr. Enemugwem, Historian, was Associate Dean of the Faculty of Humanities, and Head, Department of History and Diplomatic Studies, University of Port Harcourt.

ETEKPE, Ambily. Dr. Etekpe teaches Political Science at the Niger Delta University, Wilberforce Island, Bayelsa State.

GBENENYE, Emma. Dr. Gbenenye teaches history at the University of Port Harcourt.

GREEN, Eldred Ibibiem. Dr. Green teaches English at the University of Port Harcourt.

HARRY, Otelemate G. Dr. Harry teaches linguistics at The University of the West Indies, Mona-Kingston, Jamaica.

HOLLOS, Marida. Dr Hollos is Professor of Anthropology at Brown University, Providence, Rhode Island, USA

IGOLI, Timipa. Mr. Igoli is a graduate student of history at the University of Port Harcourt.

IKPORUKPO, C. O. Ikporukpo is Professor of Geography, University of Ibadan; currently serving as Vice Chancellor, Niger Delta University, Wilberforce Island, Bayelsa State.

JAJA, J. M. Dr. Jaja is of the Institute of Foundation Studies, Rivers State University of Science and Technology, Port Harcourt.

KARI, Ethelbert E. Dr. Kari teaches linguistics at the University of Port Harcourt.

KARIBORO, Joseph. Mr. Kariboro is Administrative Officer, Rivers State Liaison Office, Abuja.

KOROYE, Seiyifa. Mr. Koroye teaches English at the University of Port Harcourt.

KOWEI, F. A. Mr. Kowei teaches at the Comprehensive High School, Igbobini, Ondo State.

KPONE-TONWE, Sonpie. The Rev. Dr. Kpone-Tonwe teaches History at the University of Port Harcourt, Faculty of Humanities, Port Harcourt.

LEIS, Philip E., Philip Leis is Professor of Anthropology, Brown University, Providnce, Rhode Island, USA

NDIMELE, Ozo-mekuri. Ndimele is Professor of Linguistics at the University of Port Harcourt.

NWALA, Ugwulor Eugene. Mr. Nwala is Director of Chieftaincy Affairs in the Rivers State Ministry of Local Government and Community Development, Port Harcourt.

NYANANYO, B. L. Nyananyo is Professor of Plant Science and Biotechnology, University of Port Harcourt,

OGUOKO, Benaebi Benatari. Mr. Oguoko was Secretary-General, Ijaw Peoples Association, London.

OKARA, Gabriel. Okara is Doctor of Letters, *honoris causa*, of the University of Port Harcourt.

OKONNY, M. P. Dr. Okonny is an educationist in Port Harcourt, Rivers State.

OKOROAFOR, Stanley. Mr. Okoroafor teaches Archaeology at the University of Port Harcourt.

OKOROBIA, Atei Mark. Dr. Okorobia was Head of the Department of History and Diplomatic Studies, University of Port Harcourt.

OLALI, S. T. Mr. Olali teaches history at the Niger Delta University, Wilberforce Island, Bayelsa State.

ORJI, Kingdom. Dr. Orji is of the Humanities Department, Rivers State College of Arts and Science, Rumuola Road, Port Harcourt.

OWEI, B. J. Mr. Owei teaches at the Ijaw National High School, Arogbo, Ondo State.

SOKARI-GEORGE, Gamaliel. The late Sokari-George taught history at the Rivers State College of Education, Rumuolumeni, Port Harcourt.

SORGWE, C. M. Rev. Dr. Sorgwe teaches history at the Niger Delta University, Wilberforce Island, Bayelsa State.

TAMUNO, Tekena Nitonye. Tamuno is Emeritus Professor of History, and former Vice-Chancellor University of Ibadan, Oyo State; and President, Bells University, Otta, Ogun State, Nigeria.

UBI, Otu A. Dr. Ubi teaches history at the University of Calabar, Calabar, Cross River State.

WARIBOKO, Nimi. Dr. Wariboko is the inaugural Katherine B. Stuart Associate Professor of Christian Ethics at Andover Newton Theological School, Newton Center, Massachussetts, U. S. A.

WARIBOKO, Waibinte. Dr. Wariboko teaches History at The University of the West Indies, Mona-Kingston, Jamaica.

WILLIAMSON, Ruth Kay. Williamson was Professor of Linguistics University of Ibadan and University of Port Harcourt. She died on the 2nd January 2005, and was buried at Kaiama, Bayelsa State, Nigeria.

LIST OF FIGURES

LIST OF PLATES

LIST OF TABLES

LIST OF APPENDICES

PREFACE

On the 14th August, 2004, Chief Diepiriye Simon Peter Alamieyeseigha, JP, Governor of Bayelsa State, inaugurated the Ijaw History Project Committee to run the Ijaw History Project, in the presence of the Executive of the Ijaw National Congress.

In his letter to the members of the Committee, the late Dr. S. A. Bobo-Jama, National Secretary, Ijaw National Congress, invited the Committee to

"…write a comprehensive single compendium harmonizing as much as possible the existing individual contributions …".

According to the National Secretary, the Ijaw National Congress conceived of the Ijaw History Project as

"…not a self-glorification project but one of self re-discovery which is a basic ingredient in our quest for self-actualization".

Governor Alamieyeseigha confirmed that the project for a global history of the Ijo people had been recommended to him by an Ijaw Interactive Assembly comprising representatives from all parts of the Niger Delta.

The Committee set to work without delay. It has received the cooperation of the government of Bayelsa State during its periods of stability. Dr. Goodluck Ebele Jonathan, Deputy Governor to Alamieyeseigha, gave the Committee absolute support when he became Governor and later Vice President of Nigeria. Neither Alamieyeseigha nor Jonathan sought to influence the Project Committee in any way whatsoever.

Eventually, the project could only succeed from the quality of the resource persons or scholars it could recruit. These have come mainly from the tertiary institutions in Rivers, Bayelsa, and Delta States. The Ijaw Peoples Association of London and its President, Rowland Ekperi, have been very supportive, as

The early British colonial official, Major Arthur Glyn Leonard, in his book, *The Lower Niger and Its Tribes,* (1906), summarizing European knowledge of the Niger Delta coast through the nineteenth century, had this to say:

> "...in the triangle formed by the Nun and Gana-Gana [River Forcados], also outside it, to a small extent, both eastward and westward, dwell the Ijo, the most important tribe in the lower Delta, and indeed, after the Ibo, in the whole of Southern Nigeria" (Leonard 1906/1968, 18).

British colonial officers gave Ịọ the alternative spelling of "Ijaw", both spellings being used interchangeably in official documents and reports. The colonial author, P. Amaury Talbot gave "Ijaw" the stamp of preference in his book, *Tribes of the Niger Delta,* first published in 1932. According to Talbot:

> "...the Ijaw...people inhabit practically the whole coast, some 250 miles in length, stretching between the Ibibio and Yoruba. The Niger Delta, therefore, is, with the exception of a few small tribes, occupied by this strange peopLe—a survival from the dim past, beyond the dawn of history—whose language and customs are distinct from those of their neighbours and without trace of any tradition of a time before they were driven into these regions of sombre mangrove" (Talbot 1932/1967, 5).

The two terms Ịọ and Ijaw were fully established by the end of the colonial period in 1960, and through the period of independence. Formal linguistic studies have clarified the roots of the numerous variations of the names by which the people have been identified. The modern study of the language has been pioneered by the late Professor Kay Williamson, the English lady who made Kaiama in Bayelsa State her home. Professor Williamson referred to the language as Ịọ or Ijoid. In her major contribution to the history of the Niger Delta, "Linguistic evidence for the prehistory of the Niger Delta", published in *The Early History of the Niger*

Delta, (edited by Alagoa *et al* 1988), she subdivided Ijoid into two branches, Ịjọ and Defaka. Ịjọ she identified as the language spoken by the majority of the peoples of Rivers, Bayelsa, Delta, and Ondo states of Nigeria. She agreed with Talbot that Ijo was, indeed, distinct from the languages of its neighbours, its nearest relative being Defaka, the language of the small Afakani community in Nkoro in Opobo-Nkoro local government area in Rivers State. Ijo she classified into four groups, namely:

1. Eastern Ịjọ, comprising Kalabari, Okrika, Ibani (Bonny/Opobo), and Nkoro.
2. Nembe-Akassa, comprising Nembe and Akassa.
3. Ịzọn, comprising South-Eastern Izon dialects, North-Western Ịzọn dialects, and South-Western Ịzọn dialects.
4. Inland Ịjọ, comprising Oruma, Okordia, and Biseni.

Professor Williamson thus brought into focus the central position of the term Ịzọn, the third legitimate term for the nationality itself along with Ịjọ and Ijaw.

Professor Williamson's definitive classification of Ịjọ was probably the one she proposed in her 1990 joint article with J. D. Lee, "A lexicostatistical classification of Ịjọ dialects" in *Research in African Languages and Linguistics* (Vol. 1, No. 1, 1-10). In this detailed classification, she divides Ịjọ/Ijoid into the two primary groups of Kẹnị and Gbọrị, the terms for the numeral 'one' within these two groups.

The Kẹnị group she subdivided into
1. Inland Ịjọ (Biseni, Okordia, and Oruma)
2. Izon, being the most numerous and complex sub-group.

The Gbọrị group she subdivided into
1. Nembe and Akassa
2. Koin (Kalabari, Okrika, Ibani, and Nkoroo).

role of the Ịọ states in the Atlantic slave and palm oil trade from the late fifteenth to the nineteenth centuries, and in recent times, its role as the producer of crude oil and gas that sustain the Nigerian economy.

The subtitles of the three books by Dike, Jones, and Alagoa, indicate the focus of each author. Dike focused on the development of economic and political institutions in the Niger Delta in the context of European commercial activities; Jones on the history of political institutions in a comparative framework; and Alagoa on the internal history, culture and development of the Ịọ people within the Niger Delta.

The Izọn of the Niger Delta begins in the Niger Delta as the home of the Ịọ people, and tells their story from antiquity to the present and proceeds to tell the story of the relations between the Ịọ and other nationalities of Nigeria from antiquity to the present. The strategy is to arrive at an authoritative account of the evolution of the idea of an Ịọ nation through the centuries, in the company of its neighbours in and beyond the Niger Delta. Thus, the Nigerian context is deliberately emphasized: a story that extends beyond the Niger Delta to the northern borders of the Federal Republic of Nigeria. This Nigerian coverage of Ịọ history from antiquity to the present should produce new insights, knowledge, and understanding.

Diaspora

The Ịọ are to be found not only across the length and breadth of Nigeria, but also along the entire length of the Atlantic coast of West and Central Africa; in Europe, North America, South America, and in the Caribbean or West Indies. This wide distribution of Ịọ outside Africa must be studied as a part of the African diaspora resulting from the triangular trade across the Atlantic, in which Europe carried African slaves to the Americas to work in plantations and mines to fuel European development.

The Ịọ have not featured in studies of Africans in this global diaspora because, as the middlemen in the African leg of the trade, they were thought to have been the agents for the collection of other Africans for export at the ports of the Niger Delta, and were not conceived as victims as well. This study should finally put this misconception to rest. We discover that internal conflict between Niger Delta Ịọ communities provided victims for sale, and internal conflicts and customs threw individuals out of communities and families, who were sold into slavery within communities, and out of communities into the diaspora.

The Ịọ entry into the diaspora across the Atlantic would have taken place from the fifteenth through the nineteenth century from locations in the neighbourhood of the Escravos and Benin Rivers, the estuary of the River Forcados in the Western Niger Delta; and the ports of the Nembe, Kalabari, and Bonny kingdoms of the Central and Eastern Niger Delta. The Ịọ city-states of Nembe, Kalabari, Bonny, and Okrika were the principal dealers in the trade, utilizing ports at the estuaries of the Brass and Nun rivers at Twon-Brass and Akassa for Nembe; Elem Kalabari (New Calabar) for Kalabari; and Bonny and locations on the Andoni River for the Ibani kingdom of Bonny, Okrika kingdom and the Obolo (Andoni). The combined estuary of the Bonny River and the New Calabar River was so significant that the Portuguese named it Rio Real (Royal River), and the two major ports on it, Bonny and Elem Kalabari (New Calabar) became the most important ports for the evacuation of slaves, and later, palm oil in the Niger Delta, and for periods, in West Africa.

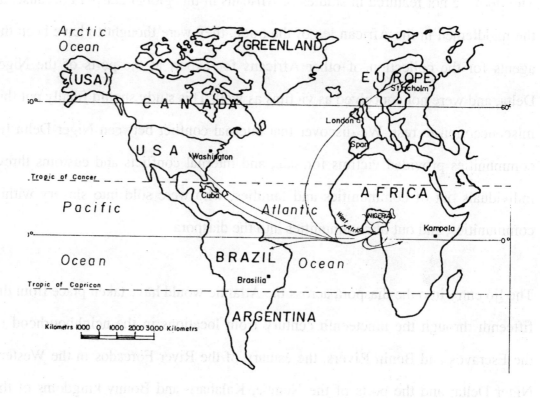

Fig. 1.2: The Ịjọ Diaspora

In the Western Delta, the important centres for the palm oil trade were Forcados and Burutu. Because of the pull of the Benin kingdom, inland ports such as Ughoton on the Benin River had been prominent in the literature.

The chapters on Africa, Europe, North America, and the Caribbean, begin the task of documenting the causes, history, and size of the Ijo diaspora into each of these regions of the world. We have documentary evidence of Ijo in Sierra Leone from Koelle's *Polyglotta Africana,* and, recently, from the Berbice Creole of Guyana in the Caribbean. This must count as one of the most important contributions that this book makes to our knowledge of the African diaspora. Professor Kay Williamson has left studies of both instances of Ịjọ outside Nigeria, and the Berbice Dutch is the subject of a new study by a team in the University of the West Indies at Mona, Kingston, Jamaica reported in this book. Williamson identified Koelle's two informants and dialects as derived from Orupiri in Bonny, a speaker of Ibani in the Eastern Delta, and from the Egbesubiri quarter of Arogbo in the Western Niger

8

Delta fringe. The Ibani informant named the language Ịjọ, and the Arogbo informant gave it as Ujo/Udjo. The Ijo dialects composing Berbice Dutch, were identified by Williamson as Ibani, Okrika, Kalabari, and Nembe.

Scope and Concept

The broad concept of the book is to provide a global history of the Ịjọ people from their homeland in the Niger Delta through their interactions with other nationalities across Nigeria, and their dispersal or migrations, forced and voluntary, through West and Central Africa, and over the Atlantic to Europe, the Americas and the West Indies or the Caribbean.

This book provides chapters that take an overview of issues on the environment of the Niger Delta, an analysis of the Ịjọ population, the language, culture, resources, history and linkage to the rest of Nigeria and the world. In effect these chapters provide a synopsis of the Ịjọ in the past and their situation in the present. It is clear that the notion of being Ịjọ has not been constant, and is a growing concept. The nature and concepts of Ịjọ nationalism are discussed, along with possibilities of developing a language base for it. A concluding summary and future view brings the work to a close.

The concluding chapter should reveal the extent to which the Ịjọ struggle for identity has succeeded or failed to bear fruit. The struggle has changed focus and direction through time, and entered a violent phase in recent times with the youth taking matters into their own hands. It is a phase dictated by the huge sums of money accruing to the Nigerian state and the multinational corporations in the face of continuing poverty of the Niger Delta environment and people. It is a dangerous development which poses a challenge to Ịjọ leaders and elders, scholars, the Nigerian political class, and the international community.

The Ijaw History Project presents the results of its research as a contribution to clarity of thought in the search for solutions to what has been termed the Niger Delta crisis; but, above all, for all Ịjọ people to gain a better sense of who they are, have been, and can be.

CHAPTER 2
ENVIRONMENT

B. L. Nyananyo, I. Daminabo and E. R. Aminigo

Introduction

In biology, environment refers to the entire range of external influences working on an organism, both physical and biological forces of nature surrounding an individual. In the social sciences, however, theories that concern the importance of environmental factors are usually referred to as environmentalism. There are three such theories, namely, the theory of

a. environmental determinism

b. environmental possibilism and

c. environmental probabilism.

The theory of environmental determinism states that the physical milieu of a people, including natural resources, climatic, and geographical accessibility, constitute the major determining factor in the formation of their culture. This theory therefore rejects history and tradition, social and economic factors, and any other aspects of culture as explanations of social development.

The theory of environmental possibilism on the other hand suggests that habitat acts only to create possibilities from which man may choose. In the most extreme form, possibilism rejects the environmental influence on the form that the choice might take. This theory, however, fails to recognize that possibilities are distributed unequally over the world. Although, casual relations are no longer thought to be clear cut as believed by some early environmental determinists, cultural phenomena often cannot be fully understood without consideration of environmental factors.

In the theory of probabilism, modern environmentalists recognize that physical surroundings are only part of a total environment that includes social and reciprocal influences between societies and their environment. This theory is what most contemporary environmentalists recognize and use. In the context of this chapter, we wish to work with the holistic concept of the ecosystem.

Ecosystem

Although the term ecosystem was first proposed in 1935 by a British ecologist, Arthur George Tansley, the concept is much older. Allusions to the idea of the unity of organisms and environment, as well as the oneness of man and nature, can be found far back in written history and often as a basic part of many religions. The word ecosystem is a contraction of ecological system. An anthropocentric, or human centred definition of ecosystem is "Man as a part of not apart from, a life support system composed of the air, water, minerals, soil, plants, animals, and micro-organisms all of which function together and maintain the whole". A more formal definition is "any unit—including all the organisms (biological factors)—interacting with the environment (physical factors) so that a flow of energy within a system leads to a clearly defined trophic (nutrient requiring) structure, to biotic diversity, and to an exchange of materials between living and non-living sectors".

There is no size limit implied in the definition of an ecosystem. It may be a square meter of a pond, desert, city, farm, closed container of small organisms (e.g. an aquarium or a vivarium) or a square kilometer of jungle or forest. The largest ecosystem is the biosphere, the entire world of life, and its associated geosphere, that is, the inanimate earth. This ecosystem, as a result of its magnitude, is often referred to as the ecosphere. Whereas natural ecosystems blend together at overlap areas called ecotones as at the edge of a forest or at the seashore, man-made ecosystems are discrete and the boundaries are clear.

The Ijo Environment

The Ijo home land is situated mainly in the Niger Delta, Africa's largest delta covering some 7,000 square kilometers. About one third of the Niger Delta is made up of wetlands, and it contains the largest mangrove forest in the world ($5,400 - 6,000$ km^2) (Afolabi, 1998; Nyananyo, 2002). It is the most densely inhabited delta in the world. In addition, it contains a number of distinct ecological zones such as coastal ridges, barriers, fresh water swamp forests and lowland rainforests (Nyananyo, 1999, 2002). This is the most physiographic section of Nigeria that protrudes into the Gulf of Guinea and covers about 480 km of the coastline of Nigeria from the Oni River in the west to the Andoni River in the east. It is worthy of note that the point at which Niger water gets distributed has been identified as the Nun-Forcados bifurcation near the villages of Onya and Samabiri. The triangle of territory formed by this apex and the estuaries of the Forcados and Brass (Rio Bento) Rivers is, in fact, the nuclear area of Ijo settlement (Alagoa, 2005). The Ijo in their homeland and in the Diaspora have their settlements/communities closest to the rivers and oceans of the world, e.g. Ijo settlements in Nigeria are found all along the coast and river banks in the Niger Delta and all over the southern part of the country; in the Diaspora from west to central Africa and tropical America bordering on the east and western shores of the Atlantic ocean.

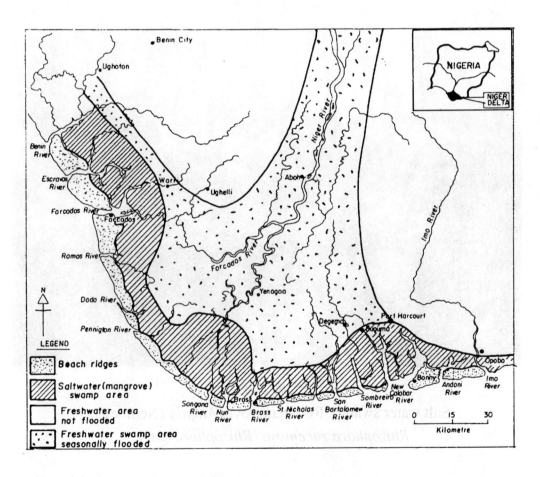

Fig. 2.1: Land forms of the Niger Delta

13

The Niger Delta, the home of the Ijo, has been built up over ten thousand years, from sediment brought down by the rivers Niger and Benue. In the course of these years many complicated factors have changed the extent of the delta, the beds of feeder creeks and rivers, as well as the amount of sediment deposited (Alagoa, 2005). These sediments get trapped in the prop roots of the red mangrove, *Rhizophora* sp., which over time gets stabilized. As these areas got stabilized, the colonizing species of the red mangrove, *Rhizophora racemosa* Meyer, got into new niches. The soil hitherto stabilized is peaty and usually referred to as 'chikoko' now gets occupied by two other species of the red mangrove, *Rhizophora mangle* L. and *R. harrisonii* Leechman (Nyananyo *et al.*, 2004). The water in this mangrove environment is brackish as it is a mixture of salt water from the sea and freshwater from the hinterland.

Plate 2.1:
Salt water swamp. Red mangrove, *Angala* (Nembe),
Rhizophora racemosa (Rhizophoraceae)

The culture and economy of the Ijo is greatly influenced by their environment. Fishing is a major occupation in the region and the communities depend heavily on fish as a source of cheap animal protein. In addition, other sources of relatively cheap animal protein are shell fish including shrimps, oysters and

14

periwinkle. The periwinkle, *Tympanotonus fruscatus* and *T. radula,* popularly called 'Isemi' and oyster popularly called 'Imgba' among the Nembe, Kalabari, Okrika, Bonny and Opobo people in whose brackish water and mangrove ecosystem they occur. Whereas *imgba* occurs attached on to the prop roots of *Rhizophora* sp., *isemi* occurs on the peaty floor of the land stabilized by the *Rhizophora* sp., popularly called 'chikoko' from where it is gathered by mostly women and children at low tide. These sources of protein are an essential source of trade and generates income for the Ijo people. The demand for fish in Nigeria is currently greater than the supply. The situation is such that Nigeria now imports frozen fish from other countries. Some of these countries have less favorable environments for fish than what is in Ijo land. The point to note in all this is that the aquatic resources of the Ijo have been degraded by new external forces, and have not been properly harnessed in such a way as to ensure sustainable development in conformity with the United Nations sustainable development prescriptions (WCED, 1987; Nyananyo, 2002).

Plate 2.2:

Fresh water swamp. Water hyacinth. *Lakwa* (Nembe), *Eichhornia crassipes* Solms (*pontederiacaea*)

Geology

The Niger Delta and its coastal fringes are the youngest of rocks in Nigeria. Their origin is traceable to Quaternary times, over 25 million years ago. This was when the sea retreated, providing shallow offshore water which was very necessary for delta formation. Thereafter, erosion and deposition activities became prominent. Besides the low energy of the waves, the river must be large with tremendous load of river sediments such as gravel, mud, clay, sand and silt. Sedimentation incorporates marine deposits such as shale and sand. The Niger Delta can be considered to consist of three units:

a. the basal unit, primarily composed of marine shale and sand beds.

b. the layer that consists of inter-bedded/sandwiched sand and shale. The sandy parts constitute the main hydrocarbon reservoirs. Oil is produced from this sandstone.

c. the top most unit consists of gravel and sand (Ukphor, 2002).

The accumulation of sediments is over 10 kilometers thick. The sediments being subjected to heat, pressure and tectonic movements produce certain complex features beneath. Such features include shale diapers, slope instability and collapse growth faults.

On the surface, along the coast and delta regions are numerous features of great interest which gradually disappear while new ones are formed. The features are lagoons, islands, sand bars and spit braided rivers and levees. The depositions in the Quaternary have been of great importance. Apart from the rich soil and varied vegetation, the Nigerian nation's economy, for several decades, has been sustained by the oil extracted from the delta of which Ijo land is the major contributor. It has been discovered that the Niger Delta region has one of the highest reserves of natural gas in the world. The region has been termed a gas province laced with oil. Although oil has been the main production since its inception in 1958 when the first hydrocarbon reserves were discovered in Otuogidi, a town near Oloibiri, the district headquarters, the oil industry is gradually metamorphosing into a gas industry.

Climate

The type of climate experienced within the Ijo home land is equatorial. This climate is characterised by heavy rainfall. No month of the year passes without some amount of rainfall. Temperature is high and varies very little. Humidity is high during the wet season and moderate at periods of low rainfall.

There are two dominant air masses in the region:

a. tropical continental and
b. tropical maritime air masses.

The tropical continental air mass is a dry wind that flows from the north across the Sahara desert. The period is associated with relative dryness. It is during this period that a local wind called Harmattan is experienced. Harmattan wind is cold and dry and lasts for a short period of about two months due in part to the southerly position of Ijo land and in part to the regular influence of the Atlantic Ocean.

The tropical maritime air mass on the other hand is a moisture laden wind that flows across the Atlantic Ocean. It is a saturated warm wind and the period when it flows over Ijo land is associated with rainfall. The geographical position of Ijo land is such that much of the moisture is deposited on its land. This accounts for heavy rainfall experienced in Ijo land. Slight variation, however, exists. Although Ijo land records the highest rainfall in Nigeria, the towns of Akassa, Forcados and Twon-Brass have recorded the highest in Ijo land with records of 4000m with a duration of 360 out of the 365/366 days of the year (Walter, 1967). The reasons are that:

a. the southwesterly projection of the land into the sea is greater around the places mentioned above than those of Bonny and Opobo axis and
b. the adjacent position of the land to the moisture-laden wind is an added advantage.

Comparatively, Ijo land towards the Western Delta fringe experiences low rainfall of 2,500 mm annually and a duration of 270 days. This is a mild extension of the effects of the upwelling cold current experienced around the coast of the sovereign state of Ghana in West Africa. Although there is virtually no month without rainfall in Ijo land, the months of March to October are periods of heavy down pour with a break in late July or early August. The break in rainfall is referred to as "August break". This is a sunny period with reduced amount of rainfall. The break implies that Ijo land experiences double periods of heavy rainfall in July and September.

Temperature in Ijo land is relatively high. Bonny, for example records mean annual temperature of 27°C, Warri, 27.6°C and Akassa 25.5°C. The mean monthly temperatures vary very little throughout the year and an annual range of 3°C is common. For instance, Akassa records a maximum temperature of 27°C and a minimum of 24°C in a year. Diurnal temperature is highly moderated by sea breeze. The difference between the day and night temperatures is also low. However, high temperature is recorded in the region whenever the sun is overhead.

Humidity is high with slight variation during the dry season. The coastal position of the region moderates differences that would have existed in dry and wet seasonal records.

The Aquatic Environment

The aquatic ecosystems in Ijo land are composed of seas, rivers, creeks, swamps and lakes. The motion and salinity of water in these water bodies are varied. Based on salinity, the zones in the ecological water system are:

  a. freshwater
  b. brackish and
  c. marine.

Three water types have also been identified in the region

  a. white
  b. clear and
  c. black waters (Dahlin, *et al.*, 1985).

Each of these water types has peculiar characteristics. White water rivers generally contain large quantities of inorganic sediment and have low transparency while clear waters lack sediment and have high transparency (Payne, 1986). Black waters have relatively lower transparency than clear

18

waters and contain very little suspended inorganic material. The swamps in the region are either seasonally or tidally flooded with water.

The aquatic communities are composed of a tremendous diversity of organisms such as finfish, shellfish, phytoplankton, zooplankton, bacteria, and other plants and animals. The phytoplankton are primary producers in aquatic ecosystems. Studies of phytoplankton in the lower Bonny estuary showed the presence of forty (40) species belonging to thirty three (33) genera and the most abundant species belonged to the Class Bacillariophyceae (Aleleye –Wokoma and Hart, 1999). Fish feed on phytoplankton and zooplankton and so the conservation of these organisms is of utmost importance to fisheries.

Fisheries Resources

The aquatic ecosystems in Ijo land and throughout the Niger Delta support a rich diversity of fish and shellfish resources. At least, 150 species of fish inhabit the waters in the Niger Delta which is the largest in Africa and one of the largest in the world (Afolabi, 1998; Nyananyo, 2002; WWF., 2006). The brackish water and marine fish species include marine mullets, catfishes, snappers, grunters and an abundance of penaeid shrimp resources (Amire, 2006). In addition to finfish and shrimps, there are a variety of mollusks including oysters, clams, periwinkles and cockles.

Artisanal (small scale) and industrial (large scale) fishermen play important roles in fish production in the region. The Ijo operate mainly in artisanal fishery which is labour intensive. They use mainly simple fishing gear and dug out canoes built by the Ijo using mainly paddles or motorized canoes by a very marginal proportion of the Ijo fishing population. These fishermen exploit mainly the brackish and coastal waters not the marine. About 80 – 90% of the annual fish production in Nigeria is attributed to the artisanal fisheries (Amire, 2006). The industrial fishermen on the other hand employ modern fishing gear and are equipped to operate in deeper coastal and marine waters. The marine resources available to the industrial fishermen consist of demersal, pelagic and shellfish stocks which are available in commercial quantities. A legal no trawling zone extends to five (5) nautical miles from the shores of Nigeria. This is with a view to restricting the fishing and shrimping activities of industrial fishermen. Be that as it may, trawlers mainly from foreign countries frequently fish in the no trawling zone and this has led to conflicts between artisanal and industrial fishermen (World Bank, 1995). This is also the case in the coastal waters of Nigeria and it is detrimental to the economic activities of the Ijo. The damage caused by the trawlers contributes to excessive fishing in shallow areas, disturbance of the benthic environment and destruction of fishing gear used by the artisanal fishermen.

During flooding periods in the freshwater areas of Ijo land, fish spread into inundated areas in the flood plain swamps. Many of the fish remain in the pools that are formed after the receding flood. These fishes are caught by fishermen using a variety of fishing gear. Fishermen also dig pits in the flood plains to prevent fish from escaping with the receding flood. The resulting small pools are drained in the dry season by bailing out the water to gather the fish. Harvesting fish from small pools involves collective effort which involves even the children, particularly where the pool is owned by more than one individual. Inland waters in the flood plains are the main sources of fish in freshwater areas (Scott, 1962; Otobo, 1986).

Species of Fish of Commercial Importance

The fisheries resources which are most exploited by the Ijo are fish and shrimps. Fish species belonging to the families *Clupeidae, Mormridae, Citharinidae, Claridae* and *Cichlidae* are of commercial importance in the area (Sikoki and Otobotekere, 1999). In the artisanal fisheries of Nigeria, the *Clupeidae* and *Sciaenidae* dominate the coastal inshore pelagic and demersal finfish fisheries, respectively. The fish of commercial importance in the family *Clupeidae* include *Ethmalosa fimbriata* (bonga), *Ilisha africana* (shad) and *Sardinella maderensis* (sardine) while the dominant species of the family *Sciaenidae* (croakers) is *Pseudotolithus elongatus*. Other important fishery species in Ijo land and the Niger Delta include the shrimps (e.g. *Penaeus notialis, Nematopaleamon hastatus)*, oyster (*Crassostrea gastra)*, and the periwinkles (*Tympanotonus fuscatus*) and *Pachymelania* spp. (Otobotekere and Sikoki, 1999; Amire, 2006).

Fishing Gear

Several types of fishing gear are utilized by the Ijo. It is not certain how the traditional gear were developed, but it is obvious that some changes in fishing gear and methods have taken place over the years. At the time when fishing was mainly for subsistence, the use of inefficient traditional gear was sufficient as the target was not large catches. The need to increase the fish supply to meet increasing demands and provide income as well as the availability of better gear has led to the present structure of commercial fishery.

Common fishing gear used in the artisanal fishery included spears, machetes, fences and stakes, traps, lines, hooks and a variety of nets (Sikoki and Otobo, 1999). Spears and machetes are wounding gear used for piercing and transfixing fish. They are used to catch fish at the inter-tidal zone. Fences and stakes are used as barriers to control the movement of fish and thereby aid their capture. They are either used independently or in conjunction with other gear. Traditionally, traps are manufactured from forest materials. They are used in the harvesting of both fish and shrimps. Hooks and lines are used baited or un-baited, and lines may have single or many hooks. Gillnets and several other types of nets are constructed from synthetic netting materials. The industrial fishermen use purse seines, mid-water trawls, bottom trawls and dredges.

Processing and Marketing of Fish and Shrimps

Finfish and shrimps are the most important fishery resources in Ijo land and the Niger Delta. These sea foods are, however, highly prone to spoilage due to their high moisture content and microbial and enzymatic activities. The micro-flora of freshly harvested fish and shrimps reflect the micro-organisms present in the waters from which they are harvested. In order to prevent spoilage of these resources there is a need to apply preservation techniques promptly after harvest. Whereas industrial fishing vessels are designed to meet this need, modern preservation techniques are not available in the dug out canoes and motorized boats used by artisanal Ijo fishermen. Consequently, fish and shrimps are processed after landing and selling to the processors who are mainly women. Thus the men dominate one aspect of fishing while the women are in control of processing and marketing.

The main fish and shrimp processing technique employed by the Ijo is smoke drying. In this process, the raw sea foods are heated at high temperatures using firewood as the energy source. The traditional smoking kilns are simple and constructed with mud or other materials. They are either placed inside or in the vicinity of the home. Large fishes are often cut into chunks prior to smoking. Apart from the reduction in moisture levels and impartation of desirable flavour, the smoking process produces chemical substances which react with food components to inhibit microbial growth. Smoked sea foods are kept in baskets, jute bags or other containers and sold in local markets or transported and marketed in other parts outside Ijo land.

Due to inadequate packaging of smoked sea foods, re-absorption of moisture and post-process contamination are common. The distribution of these products to distant markets is also faced with the problems of poor storage and transportation facilities. In a study of the microbial load of smoked fish and shrimps in Port Harcourt, the microbial counts varied considerably with bacterial counts, ranging from 3.2×10^3 to 1.1×10^7 cfu/g (Aminigo and Okoro, 2002). Variations in fungal counts were lower and ranged from 1.2×10^2 to 9.9×10^3 cfu/g.

Pollution of the Aquatic Environment

Pollutants of various kinds gain access to aquatic ecosystems from many sources. These pollutants include domestic sewage and industrial waste effluents resulting from human activity. Waters polluted by domestic sewage become eutrophic, and cause serious damage to fisheries resources or even eliminate them (Kusemiju, 2004). Some of the micro-organisms present in sewage are pathogenic (disease causing). Examples include *Vibrio cholerae* and *Salmonella typhi,* the causative agents of cholera and typhoid fever, respectively. Water borne diseases constitute a major cause of the disproportionately high fatality rates in Ijo land and the Niger Delta where potable water is available to only 20-24% and 60% of rural and urban communities, respectively.

The increase in industrial activities in Nigeria especially in Ijo land which is the home of the oil industry, over the years, has greatly improved the national economy. In no other aspect has development occurred as in the petroleum industry. Treated and untreated effluents from industries gain access to the ecosystems in Ijo land. Ninety percent of the total quantity of oil which enters the aquatic ecosystems results from activities such as normal operation of oil carrying tankers, merchant and naval vessels, oil production and refinery operations (Kusemiju, 2004). Fishermen and riverine communities in Ijo land and elsewhere in Nigeria have reported about the mortality of fish and shellfish and the destruction of breeding grounds through increased turbidity resulting from dredging, construction, drilling and transport (World Bank, 1995).

Sustainable Development in Ijo Land

The Niger Delta, home of the Ijo, is at once the largest body of freshwater and one of the largest forest areas in Nigeria. It has, since the coming together of the various ethnic groups to form the political group called Nigeria in 1914, been neglected by the Nigerian authorities. This is perhaps due to its remoteness, or its transitional character: seasonally flooded forest, tidal freshwater etc. To a depressing degree, the landowners have no hand or voice in projects which affect their lands and waters – the oil industry; the northern reservoirs which affect the Niger's annual flood pulse on which the Delta's ecology depends; and profit-oriented agro-forestry activities funded by outside interests (Powell, 1993).

The Ijo developed flourishing commerce with the Europeans from the 16th century. The articles of commerce were purely indigenous articles. The trading activities were mostly agricultural products and included such items as the grains of paradise (alligator pepper, from *Aframomum melegueta*), palm oil, palm kernel (from *Elaeis guineensis*), and timber products. Some of these timber products are rare. In fact, one of these is a monotypic (only one species in the genus) species, *Piptadeniastrum africanum*, known as '**sanga**' in the Nembe dialect of the Ijo language.

23

After the middle of the 17th century, however, the demand of the Atlantic trade for slaves was practically insatiable. At its peak during the 18th century, slaves left the West African coasts through Ijo land. These slaves were mostly not of Ijo extraction but people brought down from the hinterland, especially people of Igbo extraction. The Ijo communities of fishermen and salt makers who controlled the waterways to the interior developed city states whose whole fortunes came to be bound up with the Atlantic trade.

It is important to keep in mind the nature of the delta, which dictates an approach different from what may obtain in most parts of the country. Much of the area is floodplain, fertilized yearly by the Niger flood, so shifting cultivation is not a major feature. Most of the area is remote and without roads; little useful work of any kind can be done except through persons based within the area with the support of local communities. What appears on maps as unoccupied land is often the economic base of the landlord communities which depend on wild stocks. Most of these communities have long established local laws for floodplain fisheries and often promulgate, at the village level and as the need arises, new bye-laws on other natural resources.

The presence of many large or common animals in the areas – even the African elephant, *Loxodonta africana,* and common pests –is not recorded in the scientific literature. The gross biodiversity of major freshwater swamp forest zones based on the distribution of large mammals and the fact that two types of estuaries, beach ridge forests, large raphia swamps and floodplain lakes occur in Ijo land is not documented. Even the presence of large conspicuous mammals such as elephants, red colobus monkey and hippos has remained unknown to experts. No forest in the area was among the 30 odd sites counted for the Forestry Department's 1% enumeration, used for forest classification in southern Nigeria (Powell, 1993). Ijo land seems an unrecognized centre of biotic diversity and no one can be sure of how many important species remain to be discovered. At present, the only outsiders with a visible presence within Ijo land, are those exploiting and degrading it – oil companies, loggers and a few immigrant groups. Those government bodies, research institutes and universities whose mandates cover the biodiversity and living natural resources of Ijo land, have failed to give the area due attention. Consequent upon this, previous scientific work done by contract and oriented towards pollution studies and the oil industry, were ineffective in terms of major taxonomic groups of economic and scientific importance.

New and Major Animal Species Recorded for Ijo-land

Ijo land contains an undetermined number of species (e.g. mammals, fish) new to Nigeria or new to science, including a Red Colobus monkey which is probably a new subspecies. It is significant that this discovery was made under the nose of an Environmental Impact Assessment (EIA) study being done by an oil company for a gas plant in Ijo land. The red colobus monkey discovery is one of several such cases which raise questions on the effectiveness of Elias in terms of biodiversity and wildlife issues (Powell, 1993). The basic infrastructure required for the study of Ijo land biota by primary taxonomy specialists, needs to be established. Evidence available shows that 'normal' biologists, without basic taxonomic training and usually experienced only in the fauna and flora in other parts often misidentify or overlook interesting species in Ijo land and other parts of the Niger Delta. Exotic species are often brought into Ijo land by coastal waters. As a result, special attention should be directed to baseline studies around ports.

Major species present in the area include

- a. Chimpanzee (*Pan troglodytes*).
- b. Leopard (*Panthera pardus*)
- c. Forest elephant (*Loxodonta africana cyclotis*)
- d. Manatee (*Trichechus senegalensis*)
- e. Pygmy Hippopotamus (*Choeropsis liberiensis*)
- f. Hippopotamus (*Hippopotamus amphibious*)

There are, however, other species present in the area. Whereas some of these are highly endangered, others are vulnerable and some not in immediate danger. Highly endangered species include:

- a. Chimpanzee
- b. Forest elephant
- c. Leopard
- d. Hippopotamus

Vulnerable species include:

a. Tree Pangolin/Long-tailed Tree Pangolin
b. Pygmy Hippopotamus
c. Water Chevtorain
d. Red Colobus monkey

Common and not in immediate danger

a. African Grey Parrot
b. Angwantibo or Golden Potto
c. Olive Colobus Brush-tailed Porcupine
d. Red-capped Mangebey
e. Sitaatunga
f. Manatee
g. Nile Monitor lizard
h. Royal Python
i. Rock Python
j. Nile Crocodile (in protected lakes)
k. Short-nosed Crocodile.

Plate 2.3:
African Grey Parrot, *Okoko* (Nembe), *Varanus niloticus*

Plate 2.4:
Nile monitor lizard, *Abedi* (Nembe), *Psittachus erithacus*

Recommendations for the Sustainable Development of the Ijo Environment

The United nations (UN) set up a Commission on Sustainable Development (CSD) by UN Resolution 47/191 as a functional commission of the UN Economic and Social Committee (ECOSOC) to ensure the effective follow up of the Rio Conference including, specifically, examination of the progress of the implementation of Agenda 21 at the national, regional and international levels. The concept of sustainable development as provided for by the Brundtland UN Commission in its report 'Our Common Future' (WCED, 1987) defined sustainable development as:

> 'development that meets the needs of the present generation without compromising the ability of future generations to meet their own needs'.

Consequently, parks, reserves and sanctuaries should be established for the sustainable development of the Ijo environment. The following recommendations are presented herewith. The responsible authorities should establish:

a. National Mangrove Parks which will cover the coastal parts of Ijo land in the present Rivers, Bayelsa and Delta States. From the coast inland, the area would include sea turtle beaches around Agge and dense freshwater beach ridge forest for leopards and chimpanzees around Rivers Ramos and Dodo and the adjoining block.

27

b. Wildlife sanctuaries in the beach ridge island between the Rivers Ramos and Dodo estuaries; the land mass straddling Sagbama and Ekeremor Local government Areas especially in the Ogbosuwari-Kunou axis; the forests between Kolo Creek and the lower Orashi River; the Rivers Nun and Forcados bifurcation, specifically the area between Trofani and Odoni; the Andoni Island with its elephants which will include the Bonny Island where there are Hippopotamuses.

c. Crocodile Lakes—there are several large lakes in Ijo land where there is community protection for crocodiles and some other wildlife. These should be given legal status to check future adverse developments.

d. Taylor Creek Forest Reserve (TCFR) – this is a forest reserve that has long been earmarked for conservation by the National Conservation Fund (NCF). Nothing has so far taken place. In fact, logging is continuing at an alarming rate. This project will not only save plant species but the fast shrinking elephant herd, the Asamabiri/Akpede-Biseni hog bush and chimpanzee, and the Odi bush elephant population.

CHAPTER 3

POPULATION

C.O Ikporukpo and Osi S. Akpoghomeh

Introduction

This chapter deals with the population of all Ijaw. From all indications this is a herculean task given the diverse nature of the size and spatial distribution of the people. For effective planning, government and private individuals alike must have a fairly accurate knowledge of the people's population, its rate of growth, distribution and composition. This is with a view to providing adequate educational opportunities, good water, electricity, medical care, sufficient food, housing, transport and communication facilities, employment opportunities as well as ensuring a favourable environment for business. Thus there is the need to know the number of expected beneficiaries. Population has also been identified as the source from which the potential skills acquired are mostly drawn.

The task in this chapter therefore is to examine the migration and settlement of the Ijaw, the size and spatial distribution of their population and an explanatory framework for the spatial pattern, their population structure and composition as well as habitation.

Population Size and Distribution

In this section, the population size and distribution of the Ijaw shall first be examined from the perspective of all the Ijaw and thereafter the analysis shall be based on LGAs. Further discussion on the population size and distribution of the people shall be sub-divided based on the location of the LGA in the Niger Delta Area where they are concentrated. Consequently, the area is divided into the *Central Niger Delta*, the *Eastern Niger Delta* and the *Western Niger Delta*. The Central Niger Delta houses the largest number of Ijaw in the country accounting for over 40 % of all the Ijaw in the country. This pattern is not surprising considering the fact that all the Ijaw in the Niger Delta started their second migratory movement from somewhere in this region. The next most

29

populous area is the Eastern Niger Delta. This region accounts for more than 36% of the population of the whole Ijaw in the country. The Western Delta represents 23.5% of the Ijaw. In spite of this general distribution pattern, it is pertinent to note that within each of these zones there are internal variations. For instance, Tables 3.1 and 3.2 which illustrate the population size and distribution of the Ijaw across the country according to LGA, show that the most populated LGAs among the LGAs occupied by Ijaw in Nigeria are Southern Ijaw, Andoni/Opobo, Okrika/Ogu Bolo and Warri South LGAs. The following section shall examine the internal variations in population distribution within each zone.

ZONE 1: *Central Niger Delta*

The *Central Niger Delta* is made up of Bayelsa State. This region/state is mainly made up of Ijaw unlike its Eastern and Western counterparts where the Ijaw population constitutes only a part of each state's total population. In 1991 the Ijaw in this Central Niger Delta were 1,121,693 in all. Thus going by demographic criteria, this is the greatest single concentration of the Ijaw in any part of the world. Table 3.1 shows the population of Ijaw according to Local Government Areas (LGAs). In terms of concentration, over fifty percent of the Ijaw in the Central Niger Delta (Bayelsa State) are located in three of the eight LGAs viz Southern Ijaw 23.84%, Ogbia 14.2%, and Nembe 13.71%.

ZONE 2: *Eastern Niger Delta*

The Ijaw in the Eastern Niger Delta are found mainly in seven LGAs in Rivers and only one LGA in Akwa Ibom State. In Rivers State the Ijaw are about 1,006,216 where they are known as Kalabari 102,169; Ibani (Bonny) 76,124; Andoni 229,475; Abua/Odual 134,420; Degema 95,887 and Okrika and Ogu 201,351. In Rivers State therefore the Ijaw constituted about 32% of the state population. In Akwa Ibom State the Ijaw are located in Eastern Obolo LGA (from former Ikot Abasi LGA) where their population in 1991 was 14,547.

ZONE 3: *Western Niger Delta*

The Ijaw in the Western Niger Delta Area are found in order of magnitude in Delta, Ondo and Edo states. In Delta State they are found in three LGAs:

Bomadi, Burutu and Warri South. These three LGAs had a total population of 514,157 and constituted 20% of the state's population. They are also found in Warri South West and Warri North where they share predominance with Itsekiri and Urhobo respectively. In Ondo State, the Ijaw are found in Ese Odo LGA (which was carved out of the former Ilaje/Ese Odo LGA) where together their total population was 137,167 in 1991. They constituted less than 5% of the state population. The settlement, Inikorogha, in Ovia North LGA is the home of the Ijaw in Edo State. The population of this settlement and the surrounding fishing villages is about 7,000, thus, constituting the smallest aggregation of the Ijaw in the western axis.

West Africa

The Ijaw outside Nigeria are scattered in parts of the Cameroon, Equatorial Guinea, Republic of Benin, Togo, Ghana, Liberia and Sierra Leone. The discussion on the size and distribution of the Ijaw within and between these countries could not progress beyond mere mentioning due to lack of reliable data. The position is equally bad for the Ijaw in Nigeria outside the Niger Delta, and in the diaspora in Europe, the Americas, and the Caribbean.

Population Density

This is the spatial distribution of the population in relation to the land area occupied by the population. The population densities of the Ijaw predominantly occupied areas are presented in Table 3.1. Data was not available for Ijaw LGAs in the Western Niger Delta. For those in the Central and Eastern Niger Delta, the most densely populated LGA is Asari Toru with over 1300 persons per square kilometer. Next are the LGAs with more than 200 inhabitants per square. These LGAs include Okrika including Ogu-Bolo, Ogbia, Andoni/ Opobo and Yenagoa. An explanatory framework on the concentration of the Ijaw is the fact that some of the high density areas are islands (Okrika, Andoni/Opobo and Asari Toru), while others are located in the Upper Niger Delta where lands are relatively drier. This probably explains the sparse population of the other LGAs which have extensive land areas but with very difficult terrain as almost all of them lie in the Lower Niger Delta which is characteristically flooded all year round. Consequently, for these LGAs, the

31

people will cluster in the dry areas of the LGA. Population densities generally do not inform much about the spatial variation that exists at the level of settlements.

Explanatory Framework for the Spatial Pattern of Distribution

The factors that influence the spatial variation of population are more varied and they include: Topography, Climate and Vegetation; History, Economy, Social, Political and Cultural factors (Udo1979, 1982; Clarke 1979 and Ojo 1979). These factors broadly classified could be grouped into two: natural and human factors. The triple natural factors of topography, climate and vegetation could be said to be common to all Ijaw settlements with marginal differences and so may not have had any significant influence on the spatial variation of Ijaw population.

The Ijaw, by nature, inhabit riverine areas. These are areas that are not only accessible by water alone but whose main economic activities are water dependent. By this definition therefore, the Ijaw are a riverine people. This principally explains the location and spread of the people across the coastal areas of Nigeria and parts of West Africa. Most of these areas, geographically, consist of swamps and creeks with very limited and rather isolated habitable land. Suitable farmland is therefore limited in these areas. The Ijaw settlements are therefore net exporters of population to other parts of the states wherein they are located, and to the country in general.

The human factors, therefore, hold the key to the explanation of the spatial variation of Ijaw population (Akpoghomeh and Okorobia 1999). These are considered under ancient and modern factors of population movements.

Ancient: Occupation

Perhaps the oldest determinant of Ijaw migration beyond several state boundaries is their occupation. Today, the Ijaw are found either as temporary or permanent residents in several states of Nigeria and neighbouring African countries: Lagos, Ondo, Edo, Delta, Rivers, Akwa Ibom and Cross River States; and Benin Republic, Togo, Sierra Leone, Ghana, Liberia, the Cameroon and Equatorial Guinea.

32

Communal Hostilities

Ijaw oral traditions record that disputes within and between communities some times leading to physical clashes, were often terminated by out-migration.

Slave Trade

The Atlantic slave trade was both a boom and a burst to the population of many Ijaw settlements. In other words, while the slave trade led to the increase of the population of certain communities, it also depopulated some other communities. For instance, while the inter-communal raids within the area led to the depopulation of communities like Egwema, Liama, Beletiema in Nembe area, as well as some Ogbia and Izon communities, the same trade led to the growth of Bassambiri, Ogbolomabiri, and other Nembe villages which saw the trade as an opportunity for acquiring able-bodied men and women to build personal followership, chieftaincy houses and to man trading canoes (Akpoghomeh and Okorobia, 1999).

Modern: Government Policies and Programmes

Some policies and programmes of the governments (colonial, federal and state) that presided over of Ijaw areas in history had remarkable impact on the size, structure and composition, distribution and density of the population of the Ijaw. Some of these were of limited duration while others have endured to the present. The taking over of the functions of the sea ports of Bonny, Akassa and Twon-Brass by the modern port of Port Harcourt, and of Forcados, Burutu and others by Warri led to movements out of these areas to Port Harcourt, Warri, and other cities outside the Ijaw area.

State Creation

When the old Rivers state was created in 1967, Port Harcourt emerged as the capital as well as the commercial nerve centre of the State. This move naturally resulted in the concentration of population in what was popularly known as the Garden City. The pull of Port Harcourt caused many to move to other parts of the old Rivers State from the riverine areas. These lost the most virile segment of their population to the city. The Ijaw areas, especially those of the present Bayelsa State, suffered most severely. Many of the infrastructures that would have attracted people to the Ijaw areas were located in Port Harcourt and in the mainland parts of the old Rivers State. This encouraged rural-rural and rural-urban migration. Depopulation of many rural/riverine towns and villages followed. The same situation seems to be playing itself out with the creation of Bayelsa State in 1996, leading to migration to Yenagoa, the state capital.

Population Structure

The structure of a population is the distribution of its age and sex data. Information on age and sex is very important because they influence all other characteristics of that population. Due to lack of adequate information and the difficulty in discussing the population structure of all Ijaw because of their diverse locations, this section shall use the structure of the population of the Central Niger Delta Area (Bayelsa State).

Age and Sex Structure

A graphical representation of the distribution of the population of Bayelsa State by age and sex would appear in the form of a pyramid. This pyramid has a broad based age structure which is typical of most developing countries. This reflects high fertility and high mortality pattern. The age structure of the Ijaw, therefore, is like that of most African countries and most developing societies: 50% of the population are children aged between 0-14 years, the aged (65 years and above) constitute only 4.7%, while the working population (15-64 years) make up 47.3 percent of the population. There is, however, a balance in the sex distribution.

Median Age

The average age in a population is usually measured by the median age, which indicates the age above which one half of the population lies and below which is the other half. The median age of the Ijaw is about 16 years, using Bayelsa as benchmark. The population of the Ijaw can, therefore, be described as "youthful". The consequence is that government will be under pressure to provide education and health facilities.

Sex Ratio

Sex ratio is the number of males per 100 females in a given population. Table 3.2 presents the sex ratio for the LGAs in the Central Niger Delta area. This Table shows that the sex ratio is clearly in favour of males in the Central Niger Delta area, and by extension, in all other Ijaw areas as well. A further examination of the situation in the area shows that Ogbia has the highest sex ratio among the LGAs, with a ratio of 135 males to 100 females. Other LGAs with high sex ratio include Bonny (111), Yenagoa (110), Southern Ijaw (110) and Akuku Toru (110). Of all the Ijaw LGAs, the LGA with the lowest sex ratio is Nembe with 88 males to 100 females, showing a sex ratio in favour of females. The high sex ratios manifest a high level of male in-migration or female out-migration. The reverse (male out-migration) could explain the case for Nembe LGA.

Dependency Ratio

Age dependency ratio is a measure of the relative size of the non-working age population (those under 15 years and those 65 years and above) to that of working age population (those between 15 years and 64 years). It indicates the burden on the working age population in having to support the non-working age population. The higher this ratio, the higher the number of persons each worker has to support as regards education, food, shelter, health etc. The Young Dependency Ratio, Old Dependency Ratio and the Total Dependency Ratio for Bayelsa State are given below:

(1)　　Young Dependency Ratio $= \dfrac{\% \text{ pop. aged } 0-14}{\% \text{ pop. aged } 15-64} \times 100 = 102\%$

(2)　　Old Dependency Ratio $= \dfrac{\% \text{ pop. aged } 65 \text{ and above}}{\% \text{ pop. aged } 15-64} \times 100 = 9.9\%$

(3)　　Total Dependency Ratio $= (1) + (2) = 111.9\%$

The dependency ratio for the state is quite high considering the fact that 100 persons in the productive ages (15-64) have to support about 112 persons. Incidentally, the ratio for the Central Niger Delta area is higher than that of Nigeria. The implication of this for the social and economic development of the Ijaw area is that individuals may have smaller dispensable income when compared to persons in other parts of the country and this will no doubt hamper development initiatives from individuals.

Literacy

Table 3.3 shows the age-specific literacy rates of both males and females. The literacy rate for the area ranged between 52.2 % in age group 6-9 and 95.8 % in age group 15-19. Thereafter this declined steadily with increasing age. The much lower literacy rate among those aged between 6 and 9 can be explained by the fact that the majority of children in this age group are still in the primary stage of education for those who attend school. Moreover, some of these children do not start any formal schooling until they get to the next age group. The steady decline as age increases most probably indicates a progressive improvement in the level of literacy in the state over the years.

Economic Activity Status

Table 3.4 presents the parameters of employment and activity status of the population of the Ijaw using data for the Central and Eastern Niger Delta Areas as surrogate. The area accounted for 5% of the country's labour force. This status no doubt reflects the position of the Ijaw area as an important economic centre in the country in addition to their large immigrant, vibrant and active population.

The employment rate, that is, the ratio of employed persons to the labour force is also shown in Table 3.4. Data show that the Central and Eastern Niger Delta areas had the least employment rates (87.4%) in the country. The national average was 95.3%. The National Population Commission (1991) associated the high employment rate with the loose definition of work and lack of distinction between the nature of work, that is, between full as against disguised and under-employment.

Conversely, the unemployment rate for the area was the highest in the country in that year. The rate was about three times that of the national average. According to the National Population Commission, unemployment rate is the component of the labour force which is seeking for work. The situation with the Central and Eastern Niger Delta areas could be associated with the industrial

36

position of the area and the recent efforts towards further industrialization in the area. This may have encouraged the steady rise in the number of migrants into Port Harcourt, and, now, Yenagoa, with the aim of seeking employment.

Conclusion

In conclusion, the existing pattern of population distribution in the Ijaw areas of settlement is the outcome of the interplay of such factors as physical, economic, social, historical, cultural and political factors. Population, it has been observed, tends to concentrate in Ogbia and Yenagoa LGAs. At the risk of being repetitive, it is also suggested here, as has been done in other contributions, that planners must avoid over-concentration of infrastructural facilities and amenities in Yenagoa, the state capital, in order to avoid mass inflow of people from the surrounding settlements to the state capital. This can be done through a well planned and articulated integrated rural development.

Table 3.1: Regional Grouping, Location and Population of Ijaw

Regional Grouping	Location	Population 1991
Central Niger Delta	All of Bayelsa State	1,121,687
Eastern Niger Delta	Seven LGAs in Rivers State (1,006,216) One LGA in Akwa Ibom State (14,547)	1,020,763
Western Niger Delta	Three LGAs in Delta State (514,157) One LGA in Ondo State (136,169) and settlements in Edo State (about 7,000)	657,326
West Africa	Parts of Republic of Benin, Togo, Ghana, Liberia, Sierra Leone, Cameroon and Equatorial Guinea	n.a.
Total	**All IJAW in Nigeria**	**2,798,275**

Source: The 1991 National Population Census results

Note: Data on the polulation of Ijaw in Cross River State and West Africa were not available.

Table 3.2: Population of Ijaw LGAs of Predominance in 1991

S/No.	LGA	Total	Male	Female	Sex Ratio
Central Niger Delta		**1,121,687** (40.1%)	**584,117**	**537,570**	**108.7**
Bayelsa State					
1	Southern Ijaw	267,371	139,821	127,250	109.6
2	Ogbia	159,369	91,459	67,910	134.7
3	Nembe	153,821	72,227	81,594	88.5
4	Brass	126,912	65,440	61,472	.106.5
5	Ekeremor	124,279	64,637	59,642	108.4
6	Sagbama	119,759	62,163	57,596	107.9
7	Yenagoa	104,061	54,554	49,507	110.2
8	Kolokuma/ Opokuma	66,115	33,816	32,299	104.7
Western Niger Delta		**657,326** (23.5%)	**321,224**	**336,102**	**104.6**
Delta					
9	Bomadi	140,436	70,100	70,336	99.7
10	Burutu	160,445	85,352	75,093	113.7
11	Warri South	213,276	109,818	103,458	106.1
Ondo					
12	Ese Odo	136,169	67,232	68,937	98.3
Edo					
13	Inikorogha & other settlements	7,000	3,600	3,400	105.9
Eastern Niger Delta		**1,020,763** (36.4%)	**530,998**	**489,765**	**109**
Rivers					
14	Abua/Odual	134,420	69,955	64,465	109
15	Akuku Toru	102,169	53,509	48,660	110
16	Andoni/Opobo	229,475	119,047	110,428	109
17	Asari Toru	116,788	86,650	80,138	108
18	Bonny	76,124	40,105	36,019	111
19	Degema	95,889	49,901	45,988	109
20	Okrika + Ogu Bolo	201,351	104,456	96,895	107
Akwa Ibom					
21	Eastern Obolo	14,547	7,375	7,172	103
	Grand Total	**2,798,275**	**1,452,217**	**1,348,558**	**107.4**

Source: Federal Government of Nigeria (1997) The 1991 Population Census of Nigeria: Census '91 Final Results. Abuja.: National Population Commission

Table 3.3: Population Densities of Ijaw LGAs 1991

S/No.	LGA	Land Area of State	Persons/sq. km Population density
Central Niger Delta		100	122
Bayelsa State			
1	Southern Ijaw	32.2%	90
2	Ogbia	6.4%	272
3	Nembe	9.4%	179
4	Brass	10.0%	132
5	Ekeremor	21.4%	63
6	Sagbama	8.0%	163
7	Yenagoa	4.8%	237
8	Kolokuma/Opokuma	7.8%	92
Western Niger Delta			
Delta State			
9	Bomadi		
10	Burutu		
11	Warri South		
Ondo State			
12	Ese Odo		
Easter Niger Delta		5,230 sq. km	333.33
Rivers State			
13	Abua/Odual	1,074 sq. km	125.16
14	Akuku Toru	1410 sq. km	72.46
15	Andoni/Opobo	411 sq. km	268.68
16	Asari Toru	128 sq. km	1,303.03
17	Bonny	781 sq. km	97.47
18	Degema	994 sq. km	96.47
19	Okrika and Ogu Bolo	432 sq. km	466.09

Source: Computed from Federal Government of Nigeria (1997). The Population Census of Nigeria. Abuja: National Population Commission.

'Table 3.4: Age-specific literacy rate: Central and Eastern Niger Delta 1991

Central and Eastern Niger Delta	6-9	10-14	15-19	20-24	25-29	30-34	35-39	40-44	45-49	50+	Total
Population in age group	558,235	638,165	549,980	412,662	371,140	293,757	204,029	174,800	114,612	286,641	3,604,101
Literate Population	293,101	602,465	521,614	371,342	361,221	228,895	151,237	117,402	73,657	138,277	2,814,211
Literacy rate	52.2	94.4	94.8	90.0	85.2	77.4	74.1	67.1	64.3	48.2	78.1
Literacy rate (National)	52.0	77.2	75.0	66.5	61.5	53.9	52.7	44.2	43.9	28.9	56.7

Source: Federal Government of Nigeria (1997) The 1991 Population Census of Nigeria. Abuja: National Population Commission.

Table 3.5: Parameters of employment for Central and Eastern Niger Delta 1991

	Total Population	Total Pop. 10 Years	Labour Force	Employed Labour force	Employment Rate	Unemployed Population	Unemployment Rate
Central & Eastern Niger Delta	4,309,557	3,045,866	1,399,639	1,223,425	87.4	176,214	12.6
Nigeria	88,992,220	60,147,873	27,936,926	26,624,926	95.3	1,311,603	4.7

Source: Extracted from Table 7.9A in the Final Result of the 1991 Population Census of Nigeria

CHAPTER 4
THE SOCIAL CONTEXT[†]
Marida Hollos and Philip Leis

The Web of Relationships

Like a pebble falling into the centre of a pool of water, at birth an Ijo infant enters a proverbial web of kinship that ripples outward in ever-widening circles. Initially the significant linkages are based on residence in the household and village quarter, and on the choices a child's parents have made about strengthening or weakening particular relationships. Later in life the decisions will shift to the individual, as he or she combines individual preferences and historical happenstance with the expectations of how an Ijo should act. Although all societies have such rules, they receive either more or less explicitness in the form of "laws" and rulings by persons in positions of authority.

For the Ijo in Ebiama and Amakiri, two sets of rules coincide or, at times, collide with each other. In one set, rules are largely consensual, based on assumptions acquired during socialization, reaffirmed by living elders as the practice of the past, and enforced by beliefs in a High God who predetermines the course of human and natural events; in the authority and power of deceased elders; and in the spirits *(orumo)*. In the other, the rules are part of the new social order: Nigerian laws enforced by the police, authoritative statements from political officials, from people with wealth and positions of power, and from schoolteachers and other professionals. In this chapter we describe the interweaving of social rules with social practice in social organization, economic relations, and religious convictions to provide the format for viewing the lives of Ijo youth in the 1980s.

---

† This chapter was first published as Chapter 2 of Hollos, Marida, and Philip E. Leis, *Becoming Nigerian In Ijo Society,* pp. 24-34. Copyright 1989 by Rutgers, The State University. Reprinted by permission of Rutgers University Press and the authors. Amakiri in the text refers to Patani where Hollos studied, and Ebiama to Korokorosei, Olodiama *ibe* where Leis carried out his research.

Social Organization

The Ijo in both Ebiama and Amakiri stress that on marrying, a woman should join her husband (a virilocal rule of residence), who should reside in his father's quarter (a patrilocal rule). In Amakiri these rules are consistent with the inheritance of rights and property through agnatic links so that a village quarter can be unambiguously defined as a patrilineal descent group. When a man pays bridewealth to his bride's family (referred to as a "small-dowry" marriage by English speakers in Amakiri), he acquires the right to incorporate the children he procreates with his wife into his descent group.

In Ebiama, bridewealth gives the man the right to have sex with his wife, and, should she commit adultery, he can claim a fine from his wife and her lover. A marriage fee, however, does not always give the husband the right to add the children of his marriage to his descent group. He can do so in one type of marriage, where his wife is acquired through "big dowry" *(fe ere),* which is similar to the "small dowry" *(ekie ere)* in Amakiri. Although the English terminology is confusing, the Ijo terms are parallel when we see that another form of marriage once practiced in Amakiri is recalled as *fei ere,* "big dowry," the same term as in Ebiama.

To contrast the difference in the types of marriages between the two communities, it would be as though Amakiri Ijo dropped the significance between small- and big-dowry marriage in favour of the latter. The Amakiri people reflect that this probably was the case because they realize they are unique among Ijo in stressing patrilineal instead of matrilineal descent and inheritance. How recently this change, or its cause, occurred is impossible to determine. It appears to reflect the interconnected influence of contact with European ideas; marriage with neighbouring peoples, the Isoko and Urhobo, who are patrilineal; and an affluence amply demonstrated in the form of permanent dwellings which give impetus to sons claiming the inheritance of the houses they grow up in. The latter, economic, factor can be seen influencing a similar change to patrilineality in Ebiama (P. Leis 1972, 17).

The small-dowry marriage in Ebiama is by far the most frequent; a smaller amount of bridewealth is paid, and inheritance is matrilineal—between mother's brother and sister's son, and between mother and daughter. When a greater amount is paid, and such marriages only occur with non-Ijo women who are then brought to live in Ebiama, inheritance passes between father and children. Even though the emphasis on residence in both forms of marriage is patrilocal, the opportunities for residing with maternal kinsmen for children of small-dowry marriages are attractive. The residential group, then, is usually interconnected through both agnatic and uterine ties so that the quarters form what may be called ambilineal or nonunilineal descent groups.

The bridewealth in Amakiri is set at fifty naira, the major part of which is paid to the father of the bride. (In 1982 the average exchange rate for the naira was one naira = $1.60.) Smaller amounts are given to her mother, to her mother's father, and to the bride as consent fees. The total amount in Ebiama comes to one hundred naira, with the distribution similar to Amakiri, even though the bride "belongs" to her mother's brother. There is no set amount for a big-dowry wife.

There are seven quarters in Amakiri and five in Ebiama. The quarters in both towns were spatially removed from one another in the past, but as a consequence of population growth, they spread until they became contiguous, except in Ebiama where the river has kept one of the quarters separated. There are no other boundary markers to separate the quarters from one another, but all families within a quarter consider themselves closely related. They recognize a distant kinship to members of all the other quarters, but if genealogical ties cannot be traced, propinquity is the main point of reference for social cohesion or conflict. When referring to social units, we find similar extensions of meaning in the Ijo word *ware* as we do in the English usage of *family*. Literally translated, a *ware* is a house, or those who live in the house, or all those descended from the head of the household, or all those descended from the founder of the quarter or subdivisions of it. The word is understood by its context.

Members of a *ware* have rights to certain plots of land within the quarter. When a man contemplates marriage, he asks permission of the leaders of the *ware*, usually the oldest men, to erect a building close to his father's compound. To this building he brings his wife or wives, and it is here that ideally his children grow up. As we shall see, there are many exceptions to this rule. Without exception in Amakiri, however, spouses are never buried in the same location; every man and woman will be brought to his or her father's place of residence for burial. In this way a person's spirit joins with those of the deceased of the quarter. In Ebiama the place of burial will depend on where the deceased has resided the longest.

The multiple meanings of a *ware*, and especially the variety of choices that enter into the composition of kin groups in Ebiama, make the "household" a complex unit to define, which is not an unusual problem in comparative research on households (Netting, Wilk, and Arnould 1984). Ideally, Ijo households contain a man, his wives, and their unmarried children. Each wife is provided with her own living area, consisting of a room for sleeping and occasionally another to use as a sitting room. All the wives' rooms are adjacent to each other in a common structure and open onto a common porch area. The porch is used for eating, grinding foodstuffs, and washing dishes, and it is here that the wives and older girls spend much of their time tending the younger children. Wives also have separate kitchens, somewhat removed from the main structure. The husband has his own living area within the compound, and his own reception room where he entertains visitors. He alternates sleeping with his wives, either in his own or in the wife's bedroom. Similarly, he alternates eating meals prepared by each of his wives. The children of each mother share her sleeping quarters, moving to vacant rooms or to other compounds as they get older.

In practice there are many exceptions to this household arrangement. If there is no space available in her husband's compound, a woman may live with her parents or in a separate apartment. If she is divorced, a woman leaves her husband's compound and may take up residence with her new husband, her parents, or her relatives. On divorcing, a woman usually leaves the older children with the husband and takes the younger ones with her until they mature, when they also should return to the father's residence. Thus, it is not unusual to find a household occupied by children aged nine and older, whose mothers are absent. The household composition is further complicated by the addition of children of brothers and sisters who live elsewhere but who send their children to the home village for schooling. This mobile, indeterminant character of households is typical of many African societies (Guyer 1981, 98).

A household, then, is a descriptive term that refers to a group of individuals, one of whom is recognized as the head; the others are related to him or her consanguinely or affinally. (The head of the household is most often a male. When a female is the head of household she is usually elderly and divorced or widowed.) They share the proceeds, to some extent, of their labour. They may reside in one or more houses, or two or more households may occupy one large dwelling. A 'compound" refers to the physical arrangement of buildings for one or more households and can also include unrelated visitors or migrants. When there is more than one household in a compound, the heads are usually brothers or a father and son.

The difference between Amakiri's patrilineal and Ebiama's matrilateral emphasis is not as great as it might appear. On the one hand, the value placed on patrilocality in Ebiama gives sons *de facto* rights to the property held by their father's quarter, even though they may choose to join their mother's brothers. On the other, in Amakiri, children of the same mother share matrilateral kin affiliations and common economic interests, and thereby constitute a subgroup among the agnatically related siblings. Full siblings usually give more financial assistance to each other than to half siblings, and after their mother's death, they claim her accumulated wealth or private property, such as money, jewellery, cloth, and even buildings she has erected for her business activities. These inheritance patterns reflect the distinctions—and contradictions—between inheritance rules, marriage types, and the affective relationships formed through common residence. Because of both the high rate of migration and the availability of land, there has been little conflict thus far in either community for building lots. Another distinction in types of marriages that has come to be increasingly recognized in recent years, especially in Amakiri, is one between "customary" and "Christian" marriages. The latter require the additional step of a church ceremony. Christian marriages may be polygynous, with a man marrying his first wife in church and several subsequent ones in "customary" union. Both of these forms are recognized as equally binding and respectable as long as the bridewealth is paid. While the Anglican church tries to discourage polygynous unions, it does not openly object to them, especially in places such as Amakiri where the majority of its staunchest supporters are polygynously married.

Marriage in Ebiama and Amakiri is most frequently polygynous. Even though acquiring additional wives is not considered an expensive proposition, the conflicts engendered by jealousy and the necessity of treating each subhousehold unit equally appear to inhibit the stability of large numbers of multiple marriages. Those husbands with more than two wives are politically astute, at least in their domestic spheres of influence. They are usually considered wealthy too, since women do the farming and provide for the everyday needs of the children. Furthermore, children represent potential wealth, as well as additional labour, because the Ijo perceive of inheritance as flowing from sons to fathers as readily as the reverse. Men believe that having many wives and therefore many children is one way to achieve economic success and social esteem.

Until recently the quarters were exogamous, since individuals felt that potential partners within the same quarter were "too closely related" to marry, even when the kin ties could not be traced. Preferred marriage partners were members of another quarter, of another town in the *ibe*, or of another Ijo *ibe*, in that order of preference. Nevertheless, Amakiri men will marry Isoko and Urhobo women because they too are organized patrilineally. Ebiama men wishing to obtain a big-dowry wife had to marry afar, usually an Igbo, since local Ijo women would not be allowed to enter into this type of marriage. To remove a daughter's

46

children from the matrilineal line of inheritance would be, for those in Ebiama, similar to placing her in the category of slave. Marriages now occur between members of the same quarter when elders find it difficult to trace the specific genealogical connections between the two.

Divorce is relatively easy and frequent. Most often women will initiate the divorce, invariably so if they do not become pregnant and believe it is their husband's fault. Women will also divorce if their husband treats them badly by not sharing his time and gifts equally among them.

Widows are inherited in accordance with the agnatic and uterine principles discussed previously. In Amakiri, widows are supposed to marry one of the deceased's brothers or sons who is older than the woman in question. In Ebiama the same is true in the case of a big-dowry wife; a small-dowry wife would be expected to marry the brother, mother's brother, or sister's son of her spouse. Frequently, however, women prefer to return to their own natal villages and live with a brother or sister or in their father's compound. This is especially true for older women who have no sons and are no longer of childbearing age. Social differentiation has shifted from being primarily based on age, sex, and number of descendants to one also influenced by education and occupation. In Amakiri, distinctions based on wealth and power are more clearly visible than in Ebiama, where an egalitarian ethic remains in effect despite differences that are beginning to appear in types of housing and in other expenditures such as the purchase of speed boats and the expenses of a burial. In Amakiri a number of families have managed to achieve higher status by sending sons to secondary and postsecondary schools, or into business or politics, which resulted in prestigious, high-paying jobs. Among these successful sons are three elected representatives to the state and the federal government, whose display of wealth and power clearly places them into a separate category, along with dentists, lawyers, school principals, and doctors who have built spacious houses in the community where they return for the holidays and for the town festival. The addition of a number of migrant professionals—schoolteachers, nurses, doctors, and engineers—has resulted in the emergence of a small middle class.

Economy

Horticulture is the primary source of subsistence in both Ebiama and Amakiri, an occupation almost exclusively the domain of women. The women also used to provide fish when it was more readily available. In Amakiri, women are also heavily engaged in marketing, whereas the absence of a local market in the Ebiama area eliminates this activity except for the few who travel to distant markets. Men help cut down trees to prepare a new area for planting, but their primary occupations have shifted through time.

Most of the farms lie along the river, and the farming cycle is dependent on the annual flooding of the delta rivers and creeks. The water levels begin to rise in June, reach a crest in late October, and then steadily subside until January. During the flood period, the farms on the low side of the river bends are covered by water, limiting their use but making them especially fertile. Farmland is plentiful, and if a woman finds she needs land, as is often the case with the Isoko and Urhobo in Amakiri, she can rent land from one of the quarters.

The farming cycle begins in late January, when the land is cleared and titled. In early February, pepper, groundnuts, cassava, and sugar-cane are planted at the water's edge. Later in the month, yams, plantain, and cocoyams are planted somewhat farther inland. Yams are tended and weeded throughout the dry season. Harvesting of yams and of most other crops is done before the flooding starts again. Plantains and cassava, however, may be harvested throughout the year since they are planted above the high water level. Ebiama and Amakiri women use most of their crops for their households; the latter usually have a surplus, however, which they sell.

No day's diet is complete without fish. Women used to be able to supply their household needs, but as mentioned previously, frozen fish is now being imported. Fishing is not an everyday activity for most women, and some women do not fish at all. During the dry season, the fishing is done by nets in the river or in the ponds found in the forests. Most of the fishing is day fishing; a woman alone or with one or two others leaves early in the morning and returns in the late afternoon. Shrimping during the rainy season takes longer since several days are required to set up traps and then collect the catch.

In addition to farming and fishing, most Amakiri women as a matter of course are involved in marketing and trading. For the most part, these activities are dependent on the other two occupations and involve the selling of foodstuffs grown by the woman herself. A number of women also buy and sell produce grown by others, or items, such as cloth or pots, made by others. Trading is thus either part time or full time. The latter involves taking wares to markets outside of the town, sometimes as far as Onitsha or Warri. A few women, who are not primarily involved in farming and fishing, work as seamstresses, shopkeepers, or schoolteachers.   In Ebiama, women also find daily wage employment at the nearby oil palm plantation. The plantation, since it has only recently been developed, has had small economic impact on the community, but its implications for the future are far-reaching. The Nigerian government's aim, aside from increasing palm oil production, is to provide an incentive to the rural population to remain at home rather than to migrate to the cities. At the same time, such actions create a precarious economy by inducing women to give up their farming and fishing for home consumption in order to receive an unsteady wage Income from the plantation, when and if the opportunity arises.

The majority of the non-food-producing occupations are filled by males. These men may be divided into two sectors: (1) those who are self-employed, and (2) those who are daily wage earners or are on professional contracts. These sectors represent not only a division of labour but also a shift from the past, when most men worked individually or in cooperative groups as palm oil producers, gin distillers, or canoe carvers, to the present-day emphasis on service occupations and wage-earning tasks. In the first sector we currently find barbers, carpenters, shoemakers, and tailors. Also included in this sector are small-scale business entrepreneurs: bakers, transporters, builders, and owners of hotels, restaurants, beer parlours, or small shops. Jobs in the second sector include block moulders, gravel diggers, and plantation workers. Many individuals are active in both sectors. One may own a shop, but also haul gravel; another may operate a speed boat, work as a labourer in block moulding, and also run a beer parlour, and so on.

While the numbers and types of occupations have increased during the past years, many men still look for employment in the cities. They may do so for a relatively short period of time, save money to set up business or to build a house, and then return. Others stay longer, only returning to the community when they are ready to retire. For the young people of the town there are few employment opportunities. This is especially true for those who have completed the secondary school and do not wish to continue in their fathers' footsteps. Out-migration for females as well as males has begun now that girls are completing their schooling and searching for employment.

Religion

The majority of people in Amakiri and Ebiama think of themselves as Christian, which they see as consistent with the native belief in a single High God. The rest believe in the power of a number of local deities. There are no cult houses or cult groups dedicated to the worship of the High God. Although she is a distant figure, she is the ultimate explanation for all worldly events. Of concern in helping to understand the vagaries of everyday life are beliefs in the local deities, ancestors, and witches (P. Leis 1964a). Cult houses for local water and forest spirits are located along Amakiri's "front" road. In Ebiama all the cult houses had been destroyed or abandoned when we arrived early in 1982, but one was restored during the course of the year.

The Ijo in Amakiri have small shrines for their ancestors in the compounds where they lived during their lifetimes. In Ebiama, appeals to an ancestor are performed in front of the deceased's last dwelling. The dead are asked to protect their descendants from witches and to help the living prosper and bear children. The dead may also cause illness or harm if they are offended by certain kinds of transgressions, such as adultery, or if a menstruating woman touches the food she serves to her husband.

Christianity came to Amakiri in 1906 and to Ebiama at approximately the same time via the Christian Missionary Society of London. In Amakiri, St. Matthew's Anglican ministry is still the largest in the community and the seat of a regional subdivision of the Anglican Archdeaconry, serving a large area in both Rivers and Bendel states. The Anglican church in the past few years has been losing popularity to a revivalist group, the Cherubim and Seraphim. There is also a Catholic, a Seventh-Day Adventist, and a Jehovah's Witnesses church, each with a relatively small following. The Cherubim and Seraphim have also established a small church in Ebiama, and there are other small Christian sects, but the majority of Christians are Anglicans.

Christians and non-Christians alike believe in the power of witches. While there are supposed to be both good and bad witches, they are mostly considered a possible explanation for infertility, for children's illness or death, and for all sorts of misfortunes in adult life. People may become witches without being aware of it and thus do ill to others unwittingly. Diviners, who also form the interpretive link between the living and the spirits and ancestors, help determine whether somebody is a witch, but no cure exists for ridding oneself of this affliction.

It may be said that the religious life of the two communities receives its fullest expression in dramatically similar and different ways. The similarity lies in the extended funerals given to individuals with two or more generations of descendants. It is a time when the extensive and interdependent social ties of the living and the dead are reaffirmed. The difference is found in an annual festival in Amakiri, called *seigbein,* which is absent in Ebiama. The Seigbein is celebrated in March or April, depending on the correspondence between the appearance of the new moon and the next scheduled market day. The spring festival is said to serve the dual purpose of cleansing the town of sins and wrong deeds, and of rededicating it to the ancestors. An important part of the festival is the ceremonial dance held by newly circumcised women, which we describe in chapter 4. Women never receive a clitoridectomy in Ebiama, which may partly account for the absence of the festival there. The patrilineal emphasis in Amakiri also provides an ancestral following that is more clearly coincident with the totality of the town than is the case in Ebiama.

CHAPTER 5

LIFE STAGES[†]

Marida Hollos and Philip Leis

In the early or mid-teens a major physiological event, puberty, occurs in all normal humans. This physiological transition into reproductive maturity is marked by a sudden growth spurt in both males and females and by changes in body shape, in the proportion of muscle and fat, and in a number of physiological functions. Females experience the onset of menarche and the growth of breasts and pubic hair. In males, the growth of testes and penis, the appearance of pubic and facial hair, and a change in voice characterize this period of development. These changes are initiated in males by a large increase in the levels of testosterone and in females by the increase of estrogen levels in the blood. There is also evidence that, during the early phase of this growth period, the human brain undergoes significant physiological reorganization.

One of the persistent questions about this stage of life has been the relationship between physiological change and behaviour. While physiological changes are universal, are there also universal correspondences in what is identified as "adolescent" behaviour? We began with the assumption that adolescence, unlike puberty, is a culturally defined status that varies from society to society. Of course the meaning of puberty also varies with its cultural context and may indeed be affected by it, as illustrated by the significance of diet on the timing of the average menses. Nevertheless, puberty occurs whether or not a population treats it as a significant event; adolescence, on the other hand, is more problematic, and the Ijo are an example of how a population can ignore it, at least until fairly recently..

---

† This chapter was first published as Chapter 4 of Hollos, Marida, and Philip E. Leis, *Becoming Nigerian In Ijo Society,* pp. 64-77. Copyright 1989 by Rutgers, The State University. Reprinted by permission of Rutgers University Press and the authors. Amakiri in the text refers to Patani where Hollos studied, and Ebiama to Korokorosei, Olodiama *ibe* where Leis carried out his research.

The Ijo language specifies a number of life stages, none of which, however, corresponds directly to the English usage of the word *adolescence*. With the introduction of Western-style schooling and an expected delay in the age of marriage, the possibility of a prolonged period between puberty and marriage has come to define an adolescent period in the life stages of the present generation.

This chapter presents a brief set of data on the physiological changes that occur during puberty in the Niger Delta, reviews Ijo life stages, and indicates a new recognition of the adolescent period that has occurred in the Ijo conception of the life cycle. We also describe some of the difficulties we encountered in collecting the data.

To determine the approximate period when puberty occurs we collected physiological data on height and weight. The subjects were weighed and measured a few months after the beginning and very near the end of the 'research periods. The first measurements were taken in Ebiama and Amakiri in March and April 1982, and the second in December 1982 and January 1983, respectively. Since a growth spurt is considered to be a more reliable indicator of puberty than weight gain, we relied on the rate of growth, along with our visual observations and knowledge of a female's menses, to assign individuals to a status of prepuberty, pubescent, or postpuberty. We determined the growth rates, or velocity, by multiplying the difference between the first and second measurements by the number of interval days, divided by 240. The latter number—the average number of days between measurements, was used to arrive at equivalent velocities for subjects who could not all be measured on the same day.

Physiology

We encountered three major problems in obtaining physiological data. The first was the technical difficulty of recording height and weight accurately. Since we used ordinary bathscales and took height measurements by marking off walls with a tape measure, our data offer reliable measures of differences rather than valid numbers per se. The second was the mobility of our subject population. As mentioned earlier in our discussion of the PSUs, a goodly number of those initially present in the PS U were not there at the end. This was especially true of Ebiama, where a third of those weighed and measured at the beginning of our study were not present at the time of the second measurement.

Determining accurate chronological ages was the third and most time-consuming problem. Since only a few Ijo in Ebiama have recorded their birth dates, we had to use several techniques to arrive at an estimated birth date for each subject. These are described in chapter 3. Our confidence in the final age determinations of our general samples ranges from certainty to plus or minus a year.

Although we have data from only two Ijo communities, the differences in height between the two support an observation often heard that Ijo in the southern part of the Niger Delta tend to' be shorter than those in the area nearest the mainland. In Amakiri the height for boys ranged between 127 cm and 175.5 cm; for girls the range was from 130 cm to 170.5 cm. In Ebiama the heights ranged from 126 cm to 172 cm, and from 118 cm to 168 cm, respectively. The maximum height velocity was reached at somewhat different times: for boys, in Amakiri the peak velocity of 3.08 was attained at age twelve; in Ebiama the peak of 3.97 was reached at age fourteen. For girls, in Amakiri the peak velocity of 3.57 occurred at age twelve, in Ebiama the comparable figures were 3.93 at age twelve.

In both communities the age of menarche was estimated to be between thirteen and fifteen years.

Life Stages: Past and Present

The Ijo recognize a number of named stages in the life cycle. These are not well-defined age-grades in the sense conceived of in many other African cultures, where cohorts have specific functions. Rather, the Ijo label individuals as being capable of performing certain tasks appropriate for them. Moving from one stage to another is dependent on physiological and mental development. Setting age limits for a period, as we do below, is somewhat arbitrary;

chronological age was relevant in the past only in the important identification of relative age. "Birthdays" were unknown. The emphasis on comparative age continues in matters of social etiquette in that drinks, for example, should be passed to the eldest first, and in joking relations one is always a *kala tobou* ("small child") to an older person. The emergence of an adolescent period in the life cycle, along with the status gained from schooling, gives absolute age more significance than in the past.

Table 5.1
Ijo Names for Age Periods

Age Period	Male	Either Sex	Female
Birth - 2		ayapede	
2 - 5	kala tobou		kala eruoba
6 -12			
6 - 14	kala awou		eruoba
13 - 19			
15 - 25	kala pesi		ereso
19 - 45			
25 - 45	asiai pesi		erera
45 - 60	okosi-otu palemo		okosi-ere
60 -		okosi-otu	

Table 5.1 is an approximate identification of age and age periods in Amakiri; the age periods have slightly different names in Ebiama but the dialectical variation does not represent major differences in expected behaviours.

The age labels in contemporary usage tend to use schooling as a criterion for defining the boundaries of an age period. *Kala tobou* now refers to preschool boys and those just beginning school and *kala eruoba* to girls of the same age. Then there are primary-school boys or girls, which *kala awo/eruoba* now implies. Secondary-school boys and girls are those called by *kala pesi/ereso,* respectively. The use of this institutional criterion has resulted in prolonging the period between childhood and adulthood and in fact has created a new substage for "older children still schooling," referred to as "big schoolgirls" or "big schoolboys," which we would define as a stage comparable to what is meant by "adolescence." In the past, this period was considered the appropriate time for girls to marry and for boys to participate in communal work.

56

Now, as before, children are very much desired by all adult Ijo. The birth of a child is greeted with happiness by males and females alike. Due to improving health and sanitary measures, infant and child mortality has declined in the past few decades, resulting in an increasing fertility rate for the community since most adult women still desire to become pregnant every two years. Parents in both communities claim to want several children of each sex, but in Amakiri they clearly prefer males and worry if only females are born. Males are important for the future of the patrilineage and for the past as well, since they must propitiate the dead elders. Men often explain that when their first wives were "too weak" to bear males and only gave birth to females, they were induced to seek second wives.

The youngest children (up to age two), referred to as *ayapede*, are considered helpless and in need of constant care and attention. A child in this category spends most of the time in close physical contact with the mother, being carried on her back to the farm or kitchen, or held on her lap while she performs other domestic tasks. At night the infant sleeps with the mother on her bed or sleeping mat. The child is breast fed on demand, and the breast is also used as a pacifier.

Few rituals mark the life cycle, but two occurred in the past within this period. One was held when the child's first tooth erupted. First the child was taken to one of the elders of the village to ensure that the tooth would not disappear. Then the head was shaved, and after three days for a male or four days for a female, the new hair was trimmed. The child's scalp was then decorated with white paint, cowry shells were placed around his or her waist, and the mother walked the child around the village.

The other ritual was a naming party, usually held at the time the first teeth appear, at which friends and relatives gathered to celebrate the occasion. This is done today, if at all, only for a woman's first child, and naming may be done at any time after birth. As in the past, anyone can suggest a name, and not infrequently a person may assume several names, both Ijo and English ones, during the course of childhood.

The native names are usually descriptive and refer to either a behavioural trait in the child or a circumstance surrounding its birth. The Ijo names often have no gender distinctions. Thus, a name such as *Emomotimi* (stay-with-me) may be used for a boy and a girl alike. English names, on the other hand are gender specific. During a lifetime, the individual may use either name, depending on the context. The majority of educated adults prefer to use their English names, but there is currently a growing tendency among young, educated Nigerians to use only native names.

Around two years of age the birth of a new sibling usually signifies the end of the close mother-child relationship. The *ayapede* (babies) become *kala tobou* (little, small, or young boys) or *kala eruoba* (little, small, or young girls) and are now completely weaned.

If they cry or protest, they are simply picked up by the mother and put outside the door. They are entrusted to the care and surveillance of older siblings who either carry them around or tag after them to make sure they do not fall into the river or into a cooking fire, but otherwise the youngsters are free to move around, explore, and play. Neighbours give them food from the cooking pots, and wherever the youngsters go people tease and play with them. They are not thought to be responsible for their actions and are only rarely chastised. When a child reaches about five years of age, especially if the child is the eldest of a mother, he or she is increasingly given simple chores to do. Discipline is still not strict and if the child is unwilling to work or obey, he or she is thought to be "stubborn" and may occasionally be yelled at but not often beaten. Little differentiation is made between boys and girls.

By six years of age, when children enter school and are responsible enough to take care of themselves, they enter the next age period. Girls are referred to as *eruoba* (girl), and boys as *kala awou* (young boy). A major change that has occurred in this generation is that both boys and girls are sent to school, whereas most of the mothers of the schoolchildren have had two or three years of schooling at most, and few of them are literate.

In many respects children are freer now than in the younger period. They no longer require constant supervision by an older sibling, and they are not yet required to participate fully in household tasks. Still, their labour is increasingly relied on in the household. They are given simple chores around the house and on the farm. They accompany the mother fishing and farming, and help in selling at the market or in the family's shop. They carry firewood, water, and supplies; they sweep, wash dishes and clothes, and begin to watch their younger siblings. Before the next age period, however, they will have learned to care for themselves and their wards, and to perform many of the tasks they will need to do as adults. In this stage, gender distinctions in the assignment of chores are not yet evident. Mothers will use whichever gender child is around in the appropriate age group for these menial tasks. There are no recognized girls or boys chores, although if there are six-to-twelve-year-old children of either gender available, girls are more likely to be asked to tend a baby and boys to sweep. Similarly, in social behaviour no distinctions are made between boys and girls in this age range. They are supposed to be responsible, respect their elders, and be available for service when called. Boys, however, seem to get away with more disobedience, and parents tolerate more "rascally" behaviour from them even at this younger age. Responsibility and respectfulness are highly desired by parents of children in this age period, but discipline is not consistent. Disobedience may elicit punishment one day but not another. Children learn that hiding from the parent is often a successful technique for avoiding work and punishment.

Circumcision is prerequisite to male adulthood but it is not a marker of entry into a new life stage. Two generations ago boys were circumcised during this stage, at around seven or eight years of age. It was not an occasion marked by ritual, and it was done either individually or in groups of two or three. Now the operation is usually performed seven days after birth, and in Amakiri it is done by a doctor in the presence of the mother. As in the past, in Ebiama any man can perform the operation, but a few have gained a reputation for doing it.

As children become older, a definite gender distinction is made by their parents in their treatment. Beginning around twelve to fourteen years of age, boys are referred to as *kala pesi* (young person) until they have reached manhood at about the age of twenty-five. Girls are called *ereso* ("nubile" woman) until the age of nineteen. Boys are increasingly allowed to roam, to visit friends, and to play games. Appropriate social behaviour for girls at this age increasingly involves staying around the house, not only because they are expected to work, but also because it is thought inappropriate for girls of this age to "stroll out." Boys of this age are usually found with large groups of same-gender friends, away from the house. Girls also have same-gender friends, but they visit each other in their homes and their group size tends to be much smaller.

Older boys are allowed to delegate most of their household chores to their younger brothers and sisters, but the girls become more and more burdened with work. Even though girls now also attend school full time, parents still expect them to perform all labour that was appropriate to females of their age level in their mothers' time. Although boys of fourteen are relatively free to roam and play after they return from school, girls immediately begin cooking or helping to sell fish or produce the mother has brought in during the day. By the time girls reach their midteens they are capable of running the household, permitting the mother to devote her entire time to trading or farming activities. Older boys are expected to prepare themselves for their future occupation, and in many cases this preparation is limited to studying for exams. Only a very few males in Amakiri, even in the preceding generation, learned their father's trade by accompanying him on hunting, fishing, or palm-berry-collecting trips. In Ebiama the change has been slower in that more males than in Amakiri learned the predominant occupations of the past, even though they may not practice them today. These striking differences in the behaviours of the genders, beginning at around age twelve, emerge from our spot observational data, which show that girls at this age and up worked at domestic chores three times as much as boys and spent half as much time in play. Members of this age-group are the main subjects of our study.

Entry into adulthood varies considerably. In the past, one was either a child or an adult. The latter was determined by the attainment of the adult roles associated with marriage. For females, adulthood could arrive as soon as they were capable of bearing children, because at approximately the same time they had already learned the necessary skills for maintaining a household. Males married later because they required more time to acquire the physical maturity to perform their occupations and to earn sufficient money to support a household.

Traditionally, the stage of *kalapesi/ereso* was considered to be of "young adulthood." For boys, attainment of this stage of being "big enough" was signified by being required to participate in communal rituals and to supply the manpower at communal works. Males at this age, for example, are called on to dig a grave and females to cook for the visitors during a funeral. In Ebiama the ceremony performed when a boy successfully cut down his first bunch of palm fruit was a good indication that he had arrived at this stage. Although the stage did not take place in special schools or initiation camps, nor was entrance or exit from it marked by rituals, it was a period of training, learning, apprenticeship, and preparation for future roles and responsibilities. Boys would also be fully preoccupied in perfecting their skills of hunting, fishing, and palm oil producing, as well as making "gin" from palm wine and constructing houses.

For most women, entry into this stage of life coincided fairly closely with the onset of menarche and with marriage. The beginning of menstruation is not recognized with a ritual, but most girls used to be married either before or immediately after its onset.

Data on the mothers of the current generation of adolescents in Amakiri indicate that the average age at marriage in the 1920s, 1930s, and 1940s was fifteen, approximately the same as the age for the onset of menses or slightly earlier. The average age at the birth of their first child was 16.5 in the 1920s and 17.5 in the 1930s and 1940s. To ensure an appropriate match, marriage was arranged by the parents or by senior members of the couple's lineages, often long before the girl reached puberty. Nevertheless, adults insist that a girl had to agree to the marriage or it could not be consumated.

In Ebiama, where age assessments are problematic for the reasons mentioned earlier, marriage and pregnancy histories are difficult to reconstruct. The practice in the past, as evidenced during our previous study in 1958, was for all females to be married by the time of or shortly after their menses, which we approximated as fourteen years of age. The average age at first birth of women born in the 1950s, for whom we have relatively precise data, was eighteen. The general opinion in Ebiama, as in Amakiri, is that girls cannot be forced to marry a man, regardless of their parents' wishes. Ijo claim that the objectives of arranging a marriage for a young girl were to strengthen the social relationships between the girl's father and her intended husband, or to help the father pay off a debt to another man. Of course, the profound value on having many children was the ostensible reason for marrying as young as possible.

Marriage is a long and elaborate process, whether it is big dowry or small dowry. Both procedures involve several steps over a period of time. Bridewealth includes cash payments to the bride and to her parents. The groom is also expected to give them numerous gifts and to donate his work as well. For example, in Amakiri the mother-in-law may receive a canoe and a yam barn as her share, and the father in-law is entitled to help in building his new house.

Before a bride consents to have sexual relations with her husband, he also gives her special gifts, such as bedding, a mosquito net, and some cloths, as well as paying her a "sleeping fee." Frequently, a young wife remains with her parents, occasionally visiting her husband' until she delivers a child. When she finally moves to his house, the husband gives a specified number of bottles of gin to his in-laws and is supposed to complete the payment of the bride-price. Her arrival at his house is celebrated by his kinsmen, who gather and drink to her health.

Even though a woman is adept at performing household tasks by the time of her marriage, when a young wife moves to her husband's house she is given instructions on how to cook and to farm by her mother-in-law or by an older co-wife. She may live with the older woman, cooking at her fire and helping her on the farm or with trading for a period of time lasting from a few months to a year. This period ends when the bride declares herself *ware anga* (capable of maintaining a household). If he has not already done so, her husband will give her cooking pots, an iron ring for holding a pot over the fire, and cooking utensils.

In Ebiama, five of twenty females between the ages of sixteen and twenty had married, and were not attending school, but one had not yet gone to reside with her husband. Of the remaining 15, 12 were in the primary or secondary school and 3 were not in school. The delayed marriage for a majority of those in the marriageable age range contrasts with the past, when all of them would have married. Only one of the females in our general sample became pregnant during the year. She was not one of the five who had married.

Girls of the present generation are postponing marriage because of schooling, but they are not delaying their sexual activity. Pregnancy is not an uncommon result. While they may produce babies, they are not marrying in the same sense as in the past. Pregnancy and schooling are not perceived as contradictory, although they are not necessarily a desired combination. No girl under twenty was married in the Amakiri PSU, whereas approximately half of the girls in the sample between the ages of sixteen and eighteen gave birth or became pregnant during the research period. In the case of the boys, they are not yet in a financial position to pay the marriage fees. Schoolgirls do not marry because their husbands would not allow them to continue in school, and because schooling may ultimately lead to employment as a teacher or in other, nonmanual jobs. Having a child is not interpreted as a contradiction to this attitude because in most extended households there are several available caretakers, and the girl may resume her schooling. Similarly, a woman' is not prevented from taking a job as a result of having children.

Unmarried girls at this age are required to attend rituals and communal works like adults, since they are "big enough," but in Amakiri they are not allowed to attend the women's association meetings, which are limited to married women only. No similar disadvantage pertains to unmarried males, who are free to attend council meetings.

In this era of free primary education, most people consider that schoolchildren reach adulthood after they finish schooling, an event that usually occurs around eighteen to twenty years of age. The major concern of these young adults is making a decision about their future. Many of them want to continue their schooling and hope that either their father or another relative will pay their school fees. Others want to work and look around for employment either in the community or in nearby towns. The two or three years following graduation from secondary schools is a period of indecision for both males and females. The males take odd jobs, help out in the store, and leave for shorter or longer periods, only to return again. The females stay at home, taking care of their infants or helping their mothers. Some of them move in with the families of their boyfriends for a while, then go home again. Both sexes are involved in community work projects, attend ceremonies and family meetings as adults, and are treated as such to some extent. Most people recognize, however, that these young adults are in transition either to marriage, or to further schooling, or to a job in another town.

There is a striking contrast between what is required of a pregnant woman in Ebiama and Amakiri. In the latter, before a woman's first child is born, her clitoridectomy has to be performed. In Ebiama, individuals say they heard from elders that' the operation was once performed in the village long ago, but no one in memory has done so. According to legend, seven girls died following the surgery, and this was interpreted as a sign from the water spirits that they did not want females to be circumcised.

In Amakiri the clitoridectomy is usually done in the seventh month of pregnancy. The husband (or if not yet married, the boyfriend) is responsible for paying a fee to the midwife, for buying a number of specified presents for his wife (or girlfriend), and for sponsoring a small celebration in her parents' home. If she has previously moved away, she now returns for the operation and for the delivery of her first child. Following the operation, the woman remains in the care of her mother, who dresses her wound with ointment and massages her body with camwood for a period of seven days. In recent times, the payments made during the marriage preliminaries are being replaced by the circumcision fees and gifts to the girl by the father of her child. Furthermore, more and more girls prefer to have their clitoridectomy done prior to becoming pregnant and either pay for the operation themselves or ask their fathers to pay for it. While it is possible to become circumcised without pregnancy, to deliver a child without the mother being circumcised is an abomination. An uncircumcised woman cannot be buried in the village because the fertility of the earth would diminish. If the operation is not performed, it is believed that the child will be devoid of human status and will bring harm to the village.

Women circumcised during the year perform special dances during the town's annual spring festival, the *seigbein,* a twelve-day celebration of the ancestors and a purging of bad spirits from the town. Every woman has to perform the dance before she dies, whether she has had a child or not. If she dies without doing so, her daughter should dance in her place or the community's well-being would be endangered. A woman dances in the seigbein held in her natal quarter, and her expenses are born by her husband. The expenses include a number of special cloths she has to wear during the several days of the festival, coral beads, cowry shells, as well as drinks to her kinsmen and gifts of cash to her. Only non-Christians continue to perform the *ayo,* at the time of the next full moon after the seigbein is completed. This dance is believed to ensure their fertility, and they present gifts at the shrine located at the extreme southern end of the town.

Whereas in Ebiama the steady progression from childhood to womanhood is marked only by pregnancy, in Amakiri the recognized steps are of a different order. Pregnancy and clitoridectomy initiate womanhood; performing in the seigbein completes the process. There has been a growing tendency toward delaying the last step, however, because of the expenses associated with dancing in the seigbein. Consequently, virtually no young woman performs it after the birth of her first child. The most common age at which the ritual is now performed is between thirty and forty years of age. Nevertheless, a married woman, whether she has had children or whether she has performed the seigbein, may participate in the women's association in her husband's village.

No ceremonies marked the attainment of adulthood by the men at the age of around twenty-five. Their age reference, *asiai pesi* (mature person), no longer carried the connotation of "kala" (little, young, or small). Apart from having to shoulder increasing communal and family responsibilities, which come with their increasing age, there is less of a change in the lives of men at this stage than in the lives of women. Men begin to play an active role in community youth associations, which are important political action groups in both Ebiama and Amakiri. Nevertheless, at this age very few men have the resources with which to build a house, so after marrying they continue to live in their father's compound, where a separate room is given to the new couple, or, more usually in modern times, they live away from the community and rent accommodations in a town. Women, on the other hand, are almost invariably married by the age of twenty-two. Referred to as *erera* (mature women), they have come to join their husbands and have to establish new sets of relationships.

Individuals in the next stage of adulthood (between forty-five and sixty years of age) are known as *okusi ere* (older women) and *okosiotu palemo* (older men). This category is made up of mature adults who are responsible for the planning and organization of community projects and for the town's welfare. The town is administered by males, including the *amayanabo,* the headman of the town, and the court and quarter chiefs.

Women also have their own organization in Amakiri. A president is elected for the whole town. There are also a number of helpers from different quarters as well as a spokeswoman, a treasurer, a secretary, and a town crier for the whole town and one for each quarter. These women are responsible for organizing certain aspects of the seigbein, for settling disputes, and for discussing women's aspects of community development with the men. (The importance of these womens' associations was also noted by N. Leis, 1974.)

Individuals in this age period are key participants in leading various community ceremonies, but they are not exempt from communal labor projects. Most of the women are past childbearing age and have become grandmothers many times over. They occupy a central role in the lives of their children, especially in the help they provide as care takers of grandchildren. Most men in this age-group have acquired second or third wives and continue to be both sexually and reproductively active. With the increase in the number of their descendants, they receive a great deal of respect. They have built their own houses and have become the major sources of opinion in the family councils.

The age of elder or *okosi-otu* is reached between sixty to seventy years of age. Men in this stage of life are often the mediators and the judicial officials of the community. In Amakiri, the oldest of them in each quarter are the caretakers of the sacred relics. Elders are exempt from communal labour but act as supervisors on work projects. Older women continue as members of the women's council in Amakiri, but in neither community do they play political roles comparable to the male elders. The majority of old women continue to be economically active, going to farm or to trade.

The accomplishment that brings most prestige to men and women is their ability to produce many children and to live to see the birth of a great-grandchild, or beyond. Their funerals are especially elaborate, including the performance of special dances and ceremonies. Grandparents receive slightly less elaborate funerals. In either case, the death of an old person with generations of descendants is celebrated and honoured more than any other transition point in life.

CHAPTER 6

LANGUAGE:
SOME HISTORICAL IMPLICATIONS

Ozo-mekuri Ndimele, Ethelbert E. Kari
& Jones G.I. Ayuwo

1. Introduction

The Ijaw people of southern Nigeria predominantly occupy the Niger
Delta region of Nigeria. They are scattered in six states of the Nigerian
Federation, namely Rivers, Bayelsa, Delta, Edo, Ondo and Akwa Ibom.

It is an established fact that of all the cultural indices used to determine
the history and origin of a people, language appears to be the most relevant
and most convincing. Other traditions and customs of the people, including
their belief systems, can be altered due to cultural contact; the linguistic
facts are the last to be given up, no matter how overwhelming the contact
may be. In other words, language loss is a gradual process which takes
several centuries to accomplish.

Our purpose in this Chapter is to identify, as much as possible, all the
languages and dialects spoken by the Ijaw people of Nigeria, and to show
the degree of genetic relationship existing among them, and the implications
of all these to the history of the people. We shall also show the pattern of
communication, and how the people communicate among themselves in the
absence of a common indigenous language.

2. Genetic Relationship

Just as it is possible to say that two or more apparently different settlements
can be proved to be related to each other in terms of tracing their origin to
a common ancestral home, two or more speech forms can be argued to be

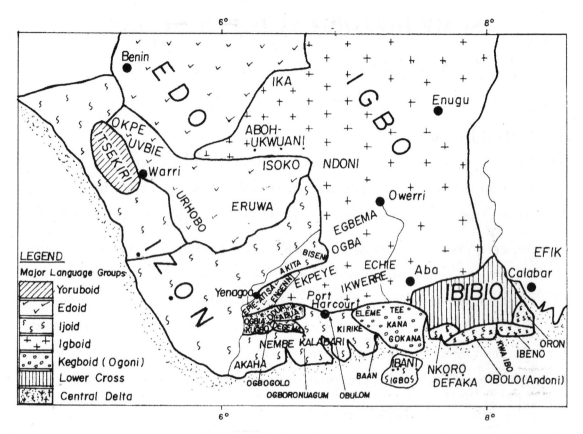

Fig. 6.1: Niger Delta languages

related because they are descendants of a common ancestral language. The ancestral language from which other speech forms originate is called the **proto-language**. Unless there is an accident in history which will compel the speakers of a language to totally abandon it in preference to another, every speech form is capable of growing into a proto-language with two or more evolving speech forms. A proto-language can die due to a normal process of linguistic attrition, while its linguistic characteristics are carried over by the speech forms which originate from it. The degree of resemblance or similarity in the surviving speech forms will depend on the amount of the linguistic features of the proto-language that have been retained by each of the surviving speech forms. In other words, linguistic relationship between speech forms is determined by shared linguistic characteristics (words and other grammatical features) in the speech forms.

If the linguistic features of the parent language are not significantly divergent in the evolving speech forms, the speakers of the different speech forms can easily understand themselves without the help of an interpreter. When this happens, linguists will say that the speech forms in question are **dialects** of one language. Dialects are speech forms which are mutually intelligible, that is, the speakers of dialects of a language will not require an interpreter to understand each other. It is also possible for the linguistic features of the parent language to be so significantly different that speakers of different speech forms (even though they can recognise few words in terms of their pronunciation and individual meanings) do need an interpreter in order to understand each other. In this situation, we say that they speak different, but related languages. Another scenario is a situation where only speakers living next to each other understand themselves, while others living at the extremes of a continuum may not understand themselves. This is what is referred to as a language cluster.

From the foregoing, we can see that the relationship between languages can be close or far apart, depending on commonly shared linguistic features. Languages which are closely related are called sister languages. The degree of sisterhood relationship decreases as we move higher up the genealogical tree. The highest level on the tree of linguistic relationship is known as the phylum. The phylum is the ultimate ancestral language beyond which no linguistic relationship can be traced. Any linguistic resemblance between two different phyla is accidental.

There is strong linguistic evidence to prove that all the people that are culturally or historically regarded as Ijaw have a common origin, even though early migrations and major dispersals that took place in the Niger Delta region may have been responsible for the divergences that we witness in their speech forms. Alagoa (1988:14ff) and Horton (1995) have discussed some of the early major migrations and dispersals within and outside the

Niger Delta region that have altered the course of events. Williamson (1988:65) argued that prehistoric movements of the Ijaw people may have also accounted "for the present-day geographical distribution of the languages", and perhaps the divergences in their speech forms. Changes in speech forms are mainly occasioned by physical separation of a people who previously spoke a homogeneous language. In fact, Williamson (1988:89) has also observed that:

> It is thus possible that it was the arrival of the Central Delta speakers, and even **Delta Edoid speakers** (emphasis ours) pushing a wedge into the previously Ijọ-settled parts of the Central Niger Delta, which caused the major breaks in communication that resulted in the major differentiation between today's Ijọ speakers.

Based purely on the lexicostatistical investigation and extensive reconstruction work embarked upon by Williamson (1988 and 1989). the languages spoken by the Ijaw people can be traced to be descendants of one big language family, which is commonly called **Niger-Congo**. The name 'Niger-Congo' was first used by Greenberg (1955, 1963) to refer to the earliest ancestral language from which a number of languages spoken around the basins of River Niger and River Congo evolved. There are many families and sub-families of languages within the Niger-Congo phylum. All the languages and dialects spoken by the Ijaw people belong only to two of these families. They are **Benue-Congo** and **Ijoid**.

Now, we shall provide a fairly comprehensive list of the languages and dialects spoken by all the Ijaw people in Nigeria. We shall discuss them according to their families.

2.1 The Benue-Congo Family

There are only two branches of Benue-Congo to which some of the languages spoken by the Ijaw people belong. They are Delta Cross and Delta Edoid.

2.1.1 The Delta Cross Group

There are two groups of Delta Cross that some of the languages spoken by the Ijaw people belong. The groups are Lower Cross and Central Delta.

2.1.1.1 The Lower Cross

Obolo (also known as Andoni) is the only language spoken in the Niger Delta which belongs to the Lower Cross group of languages. Obolo is spoken in Andoni Local Government Area of Rivers State and Eastern Obolo Local Government Area of Akwa Ibom State. It has a number of dialects which are grouped under western, central and eastern dialects. The western dialects comprise Ataba and Unyeada. The central dialects comprise Ngo, Ilotombi and Ikuru. The eastern dialects comprise Okoroete, Ibot Obolo, Iko and Ibino.

The Language Committee for Obolo is very active, and the members are working closely with the Nigerian Bible Translation Trust in Jos to produce more literature in the language. The language has Readers for use in schools. There are story books published in different dialects of Obolo. This language has the New Testament Bible, including portions of the Old Testament already published, for instance, the Book of Psalms and Exodus, and other scripture materials, and a grammatical sketch by Nick Faraclas (1984). There is also a full-length PhD dissertation on Obolo written by Dr. Uche Aaron (1994). There are also two M.A. theses on Obolo written by N.E. Enene (1997) and Jones G.I. Ayuwo (1998). Obolo is used in the broadcast media in Rivers and Akwa Ibom States. There is, however, no accepted standard dialect for the language.

2.1.1.2   The Central Delta Group

A number of languages belong to the Central Delta group. Whereas the Central Delta speech forms spoken in Rivers State are treated as separate languages, those spoken in Bayelsa State are treated as "a cluster of closely-related languages, often known under the general name of Ọgbịa" (Efere and Williamson, 1999:103). Below is a family tree showing the nature of genetic relationship within the Central Delta group:

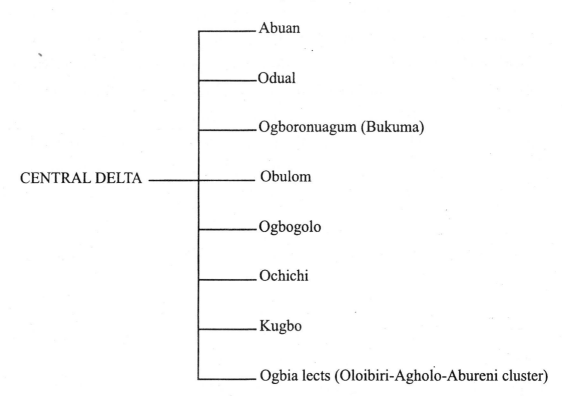

A.   Abuan: Abuan is spoken in Abua/Odual Local Government Area of Rivers State. It has four major mutually intelligible dialects: Central Abuan, Ẹmughan, Okpeden, and Ọtapha (Ọtabha). It has an orthography, Reading and Writing Book, Primers 1 & 2, Post-Primer books, the New Testament Bible, other scripture materials, and an Abuan-English dictionary.

Abuan is related to Oḍual, Obulom, and Ọchịchị (a near extinct lect spoken by the people of Ikwerengwo and Umuebulu in Etche Local Government Area of Rivers State).

B.   Oḍual: Oḍual is spoken in Abua/Odual Local Government Area of Rivers State. It has two mutually intelligible dialects: Aḍibom and Arughunya. Oḍual has an orthography, Reading and Writing Book, Readers 1 & 2, translated portions of the Bible, published folk tales, creation story and Oḍual-English wordlists. The noun class system of Oḍual has been recently described by Kari (2006). Its closest linguistic relative is Abuan.

C. Ogbronụagum: This is also known as Ḅukuma. It is a small language spoken in Degema Local Government Area of Rivers State. It has a published grammatical sketch (Kari 2000).

D.   Obulom: Obulom is a small language spoken in Abuloma town in Okrika Local Government Area of Rivers State. Its closest linguistic relatives are Abuan and Ọchịchị (a near extinct language spoken in Etche Local Government Area of Rivers State). To the best of our knowledge, Obulom has neither an orthography nor any published work on it.

E. Ogbogolo: This is a little known lect of the Central Delta group of languages spoken by only one community in Ahoada West Local Government Area of Rivers State. It has no accepted orthography. Ogbogolo is begging for documentation and in-depth description of its structures, so as to determine the extent of its genetic relationship with its sister lects in the group. To the best of our knowledge, Ogbogolo has just an unpublished wordlist.

F. **Ọchịchị:** This is also a little known lect of the Central Delta group of languages spoken in Etche Local Government Area by two communities: Umuebulu and Ikwerengwo. It is heavily threatened by Echie, an Igboid lect spoken in Etche and Omuma Local Government Areas of Rivers State and some parts of Abia State. In fact, the very few people who can speak it are bilingual in Echie. Politically, the people see themselves now as Etche, and not Ijaw. Apart from a few words collected by Bro Achonwa (1981), Ọchịchị has no written form.

G. Kụgbo: This is spoken in several communities in Abua/Odual Local Government Area of Rivers State and Ogbia Local Government Area of Bayelsa State. There is an unpublished wordlist in Kụgbo.

H. **Oloibiri:** According to Efere and Williamson (1999:103), this lect is spoken in several towns, namely Abobiri, Ạkoloman, 1 & 2, Amakalakala (Emakalakala), Otu-Ạbị (Ewema), Ẹwoi, Itokopiri, Omo-Ẹma, Oloibiri, Otu-Aba, Otu-Abagi, Otu-Abula 1 & 2, Otu-Akeme, Otu-Aka, Otu-Egila, and Otu-Ogidi in Ogbia Local Government Area of Bayelsa State. There is a Reader for Oloibiri produced by the Rivers Readers Project.

I. **Anyama:** This is spoken in several towns in Ogbia Local Government Area of Bayelsa State. The speech forms in the Anyama group are very similar to those of the Oloibiri group. We do not know of any published work in Anyama.

J. **Agholo (Kolo):** This is spoken in several towns in Ogbia Local Government Area of Bayelsa State. Agholo is more developed than either Oloibiri or Anyama in terms of the availability of literature. Agholo has an orthography, a published modernised counting system, and a number of scholarly publications by Mrs. Caroline M. Isukul. There is also Reader 1,

Reading and Writing Book, and the New Testament Bible in Agholo-Ọgbịa. Mrs. Caroline M. Isukul has written a PhD dissertation on some aspects of Agholo morphology.

K.   Abureni: This is also referred to as Mini by the Nembe people, the name by which the speech form was previously known by linguists. It is spoken by several communities in Ogbia Local Government Area of Bayelsa State. We do not know of any published work in Abureni.

2.1.2   The Delta Edoid Group There are three major languages which belong to the Delta Edoid group of languages. They are:

A.   Degema: This is sometimes referred to as Ụdekama (no longer fashionable). Degema comprises two closely related dialects: Atala and Usokun. It is spoken in Degema Local Government Area of Rivers State. Degema has an orthography (Reading and Writing Degema) based on the two varieties, and Reader 1 published by the Rivers Reader Project. Degema has been extensively described by Dr. Ethelbert E. Kari. It has a Reference Grammar (Kari 2004), a published PhD dissertation on the clitic system (Kari 2003). There are other scholarly works by Dr. E. E. Kari, including a Degema-English dictionary which is still in draft form.

B.   Engenni: This is also known as Ẹgene. It is spoken mainly in Ahoada West Local Government of Rivers State and in some communities in Yenagoa Local Government Area of Bayelsa State. There are three dialects of Engenni spoken in Rivers State. They are Inedu, Ogua and Ediro. The dialect of Engenni spoken in Bayelsa State is known as Zarama. Engenni has an orthography, Readers, a grammatical sketch by E. Thomas (1978), published scripture portions, and the New Testament Bible.

C.   Epie-Atisa: This is also written as Epie-Atissa. It is spoken in several communities in Yenagoa Local Government Area of Bayelsa State. It has several dialects which have not been properly studied to determine their boundaries. It has a Reader, Reading and Writing Book. There is a wordlist for Delta Edoid which comprises Epie-Atisa and related languages. Epie-Atisa is used in the broadcast media in Bayelsa State.

The Ijoid Family The Ijoid family is divided into two main branches, which are Defaka and Ịjọ. All the languages in the Ijoid family are spoken by the Ijaw people.

Below is a family tree showing the nature of genetic relationship within Ijoid:

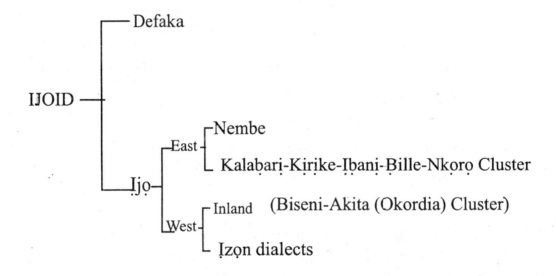

2.2.1 Defaka Defaka is also known as Afakani. It is spoken by a small community in Nkọrọ town and Iwọma Nkoro in Opobo/Nkoro Local Area of Rivers State. Even though Jenewari (1983) has identified Defaka as Ịjọ's closest linguistic relative, it is not mutually intelligible to any known variety of Ịjọ. It is a fast receding language on the endangered languages' list. Its speakers are bilingual in Nkọrọ which is the language of the wider community. To the best of our knowledge, nothing has been written in Defaka, with the exception of an extended wordlist by Dr. Charles Jenewari (1983).

2.2.2 The Ịjọ Group

Ịjọ is a typical example of a language cluster. Mutual intelligibility is possible only between speech forms which are spatially contiguous, while those living far apart or at the extremes of the chain need interpreters in order to understand themselves. Ịjọ is a very large language group whose varieties are spoken along the coastal area of five states of the Federal Republic of Nigeria. They are Rivers, Bayelsa, Delta, Edo and Ondo States. It is often claimed that Ịjọ is the fourth largest language group in Nigeria after Hausa, Yoruba and Igbo in that order.

Based on shared linguistic characteristics, Ịjọ has been divided into two main branches, which are East Ịjọ and West Ịjọ.

2.2.2.1 East Ijo Branch East Ijo comprises Kalabari, Kịrịkẹ (Okrika), Ịbani, Ḅille, and Nkọrọ, all spoken in Rivers State, and Nembe-Akaha (Akassa) cluster, which is spoken in Bayelsa State. The first four speech forms of the East Ịjọ branch are mutually intelligible, and can therefore be argued to be varieties of one language. But unfortunately there is no common name to refer to them. The first three have separate orthographies, and other language engineering processes in them have been pursued separately.

A. Kalabari: Kalabari, as a group, is sometimes referred to as New Calabar (but this name is no longer fashionable). Kalabari is spoken in Asari-Toru and Akuku-Toru Local Government Areas of Rivers State.

Jenewari (1989:105) claims that "Kalaḅarị was, as far as is known, the first Nigerian language recorded by Europeans". Kalaḅarị is officially used in the broadcast media. It has an official orthography, two full-length PhD dissertations, Primers, Readers, Reading and Writing Books, published portions of the scripture, and a number of scholarly publications by Dr. Charles Jenewari and Dr. Otelemate Harry. It has a dictionary which is still in draft form.

B. Kịrịke: This is also referred to as Okrika (the anglicised version). Kịrịke is spoken in Okrika, Ogu-Ḅolo and Port Harcourt Local Government Areas of Rivers State. It has Primers, Readers, Reading and Writing Book, published traditional proverbs, the New Testament Bible and portions of the scripture. It has a dictionary which is still in draft form.

C.   Ịḅanị: Ịḅanị is often referred to as Ụḅanị by their Igbo neighbours. Its anglicised version is Bonny. It is spoken in Bonny Local Government Area of Rivers State, and few old people in Opobo-Nkoro Local Government Area of Rivers State.   Ịḅanị is a fast receding speech form, which is threatened heavily by extinction due to the presence and influence of Igbo in the area. The presence of Igbo in Bonny and Opobo has a historical explanation.   Ibani has Primers, Readers, Reading and Writing Book, published portions of the scripture, and an Ịḅanị-English dictionary is almost ready.

D.   Ḅille: This is also written as Ḅile. Ḅille is spoken in Degema Local Government Area of Rivers State. It is structurally similar to Kalaḅarị. At the moment, it has not got any accepted orthography. There is an unpublished wordlist and counting system in Ḅille. The late Professor Kay Williamson encouraged some local writers to show interest in the development and documentation of Ḅille.

E.   Nkọrọ: Nkọrọ is spoken by a relatively small community in Opobo-Nkoro Local Government Area of Rivers State. Some of its speakers are bilingual in Defaka (a heavily threatened Ijoid language). Nkoro is somewhat different from other speech forms of East Ịjọ in Rivers State with which it forms a cluster. Like Defaka, Nkoro is an Ijoid lect begging for documentation and in-depth description of its structures, so as to determine the extent of its genetic relationship with its sister lects in the cluster.

F. Nembe-Akaha (Akassa) Cluster: Nembe is spoken in Nembe and Brass Local Government Areas of Bayelsa State. There are several published works in Nembe. Nembe has an orthography, Primers that date as far back as 1982, Readers, published traditional folk tales, Nembe-English dictionary, a complete Bible, prayer books and hymnbooks, some translations of classical works (e.g. Plato's Phaedo), book on traditional culture, a collection of oral traditions in volumes with English translation, published scripture portions, etc. Nembe is used in the broadcast media in Bayelsa State.

Akaha, which is sometimes referred to as Akassa, is spoken in Brass Local Government Area of Bayelsa State. Alagoa (1972:131) observes that there is an emerging dialect which combines features of Nembe and Akaha. The dialect is spoken around Egwema town and some other nearby communities in Bayelsa State.

2.2.2.2 The West Ịjọ Branch West Ịjọ is divided into two main sub-branches: Inland Ịjọ and Ịzọn.

(i) Inland Ịjọ All the speech forms that make up Inland Ịjọ are spoken in Bayelsa State. Inland Ịjọ comprises three main speech forms. They are:
A. Biseni: This is sometimes referred to as Amegi. It is spoken in Yenagoa Local Government Area of Bayelsa State. There is no accepted orthography in Biseni. There are, however, a number of undergraduate long essays on Biseni in the Department of Linguistics & Communication Studies, University of Port Harcourt. Speakers of Biseni use Kolokuma for wider communication.

B. Akita: This is sometimes referred to as Okordia. It is spoken in Yenagoa Local Government Area of Bayelsa State. Akita has no orthography, and no existing literature in it. Its speakers also use Kolokuma for wider communication.

C. Oruma: This is spoken in Ogbia Local Government Area of Bayelsa State. Oruma has no orthography, and there is no publication in it.

(ii) Ịzọn

Ịzọn is the largest language of the Ijoid family of languages. It comprises mutually intelligible dialects spoken predominantly in Bayelsa State, and the three other states in the Western Niger Delta region, viz. Delta, Edo, and Ondo. The speakers of Izon are found along the coastal lagoons, spreading from Yenagoa in Bayelsa State through Bomadi, Burutu and Warri Local Government Areas in Delta State to as far west as Okitipupa in Ondo State. There are publications in a number of dialects of Izon. The majority of these are in Kolokuma due mainly to the activities of late Professor Kay Williamson in that area. Izon is officially used in the broadcast media.

Williamson (1965) classified Izon dialects as follows:

(a) South-central dialects (including Bụmọ, East Tarakiri, Oporomọ, East Olodiama, Basan, Apọị, Koluama, Oiyakiri). All these lects are spoken in Southern Ijaw Local Government Area of Bayelsa State. There is a published PhD dissertation in Bụmọ written by Dr. E.E. Efere (2001). Portions of the scripture and Bible stories have been published in Bụmọ and Oporomọ. Poems and a Reader have also been published in Olodiama.

(b) North-central dialects (including Kolokuma, Opokuma, Ogboin, Ikibiri, Gbarain, Ekpetiama). These lects are spoken in Kolokuma-Opokuma Local Government Area of Bayelsa State. Kolokuma is the most developed of all Ịzọn dialects. It has an official orthography, a published PhD dissertation by late Professor Kay Williamson (1965), an Ịzọn-English dictionary, a number of primary school textbooks, prayer book with hymns, and a number of scholarly publications, especially by late Professor Kay Williamson. Kolokuma is also used in the broadcast media.

(c) Northwestern dialects (including Mein, Seimbri and Tuomọ, and other Ịzọn dialects spoken in Edo State). Mein is spoken in some parts of Sagbama Local Government Area of Bayelsa State and in Bomadi, Burutu and Warri

82

Local Government Areas of Delta State. An Ịzọn-English dictionary has been published in Mein.

(d) Southwestern dialects (including Furupagha and Arogbo which are spoken in Edo and Ondo States). J.P. Clark has also published The Ozidi Saga.

3. Major Linguistic Characteristics of Languages Spoken by the Ijaw People.

There are a number of linguistic features which are peculiar to the languages spoken by the Ijaw people. In what follows, we shall highlight some of these peculiar linguistic features:

(i) **Word Order:** Synchronically, the basic (neutral) word order of simple declarative sentences of all the languages spoken by the Ijaw people is Subject-Object-Verb (SOV). Obolo, Delta Edoid, and Central Delta languages, however, have Subject-Verb-Object (SVO) word order. The auxiliary verbs, and other markers of tense and aspect in all the Ijoid lects normally occur postverbally, perhaps stemming also from the fact that all Ijoid lects exhibit an SOV pattern of word order.

(ii) **Voiced Implosives:** There is an overwhelming presence of voiced implosives [ɓ, ɗ] in most of the languages spoken by the Ijaw people, as we see in Delta Edoid, Central Delta, East and West Ịjọ languages. In fact, Jenewari (1989:109) has proposed an interesting phonological phenomenon in Kalabari which he calls "implosive harmony". According to him, a simple word can either contain only the implosive set [ɓ, ɗ] or the plosive set [b, d], but not a mixture of the two.

(iii) **Nasal Vowels:** One other characteristic of the Ijoid lects is the presence of nasal vowels. In fact, some lects have equal number of oral and nasal vowels which are phonemic, that is, they are capable of making a difference in the meaning of words which are otherwise identical.

(iv) **Long vowels:** There is also the presence of phonemically long vowels in the Central Delta languages (cf. Alex 1987, Comson 1987, Kari 2000, Isukul 2006).

(v) **Pitch-Accent System:** All the languages spoken by the Ijaw people, as is the case for almost all Nigerian languages, make use of a variation in the pitch of the voice to bring about a difference in the meaning of linguistic units (e.g. words, phrases and sentences) which exhibit striking structural similarities. This variation in the pitch of the voice is known as 'tone'. Amazingly, however, there is overwhelming evidence that Nembe and many southern dialects, including Bumo and Arogbo have pitch-accent. No other language in any other linguistic group represented in Nigeria has been reported to have pitch-accent. It is possible that pitch-accent system is a linguistic characteristic of the ancestral language of the Ijaw people, i.e. proto-Ijoid, which is still retained by Bumo, Nembe, and many other southern dialects of Ijo.

(vi) Subject Agreement Markers: There is an overwhelming presence of subject agreement clitics/markers, especially in the Delta Edoid and Central Delta languages, which can cause the pronoun in the subject position to be suppressed or dropped in simple declarative sentences. In fact, Obolo has both subject and object agreement clitics/markers which can cause the pronouns in both the subject and object to be dropped, so that their contents can be recovered from the subject or object agreement clitics/markers, as the case may be.

(vii) **Noun Class System:** There is evidence of noun classes, especially in the Delta Edoid and Central Delta languages, a feature which is pervasive in Bantu.

(viii) **Vowel Harmony:** The majority of languages spoken by the Ijaw people, especially those in Delta Edoid and Central Delta groups, with ten vowels, display an interesting symmetry in the manner their vowels combine in simple words. In these languages, the vowels divide into two neat sets (narrow and wide), so that in a simple word, only vowels from one set can co-occur.

(ix) **Gender System:** Another interesting feature of the languages spoken by the Ijaw people, especially those that belong to the Ijoid family is their gender system, which involves both animateness and sex distinctions (Jenewari 1989:114).

4. Historical Implications of Genetic Relationship:

In the foregoing section, we examined the extent of the genetic relationship existing within the languages spoken by all the different groups who see themselves today as culturally, and perhaps historically, integral parts of the Ijaw ethnic nation. Our position here is that linguistic evidence can be used to lend support to whatever other cultural indices that may have been employed to trace the genealogical link that exists among all the peoples of the Ijaw ethnic nation.

We had earlier stated that all the languages spoken by the Ijaw people belong to one big family known as Niger-Congo. The implication of this is that in some remote past, the ancestors of all the present-day Ijaw people spoke one language, and that the divergences we witness today in the different speech forms are normal changes which are bound to occur in all human languages. Since they spoke a common ancestral language, it therefore follows that they have a common origin.

From some preliminary investigations so far, it is obvious that the languages spoken by the Ijaw people fall into groups, and within each group, linguistic relationships are obviously noticeable, while some of the groups are related at a higher level, showing evidence of longer separation from their ancestral root.

Linguists arrive at conclusions of genetic relationships among languages through various methods, including lexicostatistical count of cognates (i.e. look-alikes) in the basic vocabulary. Basic vocabulary items refer to objects or phenomena which are universal and less likely to be borrowed from another language, e.g. names for parts of the body, names for natural phenomena, such as day, night, rain, sun, moon, star, sun shine, etc. When linguists compare basic vocabulary items for two or more speech forms, and discover elements of similarity, they conclude that the speech forms are related, at first-hand impression. The beauty of lexicostatistics and its sister method known as glottochronology is that one can determine not only the percentage of resemblance between speech forms, but also the approximate periods o between them.

The late Professor Kay Williamson and her associates have undertaken a lexicostatistical and glottochronological study of the languages in the Niger-Congo phylum, and have therefore arrived at some preliminary conclusions regarding their degrees of resemblance and the tentative time-depth during which separations within the family occurred. Judging from the degree of cognacy between Ijoid and the other languages in the Niger-Congo phylum, it is obvious that the speech forms in Ijoid are more remotely related to the rest. In fact, Williamson (1988:88) had earlier observed that Ijoid is highly differentiated from all its neighbours. The implication of this observation is that Ijoid separated earlier from the ancestral language than the other languages in the Niger-Congo phylum.

Within Ijoid, the linguistic bond is tighter, and by implication the historical tie, with the exception of Defaka, which is more remotely related to the other speech forms in the family.

There is strong evidence that the languages that belong to the Delta Edoid and Central Delta also have close linguistic ties, and their speakers see themselves as coming from one ancestral home, located precisely within the old Benin Kingdom.

The speakers of Obolo of the Lower Cross branch of languages are the only isolated group within the Ijaw ethnic nation. Their relationship with the rest of the group is at a much higher level.

The conclusion we draw from the foregoing is that similarity in language between people is a strong indicator of a common historical origin, and that any legitimate historical account of the origin(s) of the Ijaw people must be pursued along this line.

5. **Linguistic Contributions of Ịjọ to the World:** There is strong evidence of the presence of Ịjọ in the Caribbean. It has been widely reported that the Ịjọ-speaking people of Nigeria were among the first set

of people in West Africa to come in contact with European missionaries and slave merchants. The consequence of this early contact was that Ịọ were transported through slave routes to the Caribbean. For purposes of breaking the communication barrier which hitherto existed between the Ịọ-speaking slaves and their neighbours in the New World, a "make-shift" means of communication emerged. Today, this make-shift means of communication has grown from pidgin into a full-fledged language. It is called Berbice Dutch creole. Dr. Silvia Kouwenberg (1993) has demonstrated the fact that this Dutch-based creole is heavily lexified by East Ịọ lects, particularly Kalabarị.

6. A Common Language for the Ijaw Nation: The Ijaw nation is linguistically complex, and no one indigenous language is used as a common means of communication in a pan-Ijaw gathering. Although Jenewari (1989:107) has observed that Ịọ "is usually spoken as a single language; its speakers think of themselves as related and like to refer to the differences between various forms of Ịọ as differences between dialects". He notes, however, that "there is neither mutual intelligibility between all the dialects nor an accepted standard variety". Efere (2001:126) also observed that the various dialects are mutually intelligible, but most dialects are not mutually intelligible with dialects from other languages in the Ịọ language cluster.

What is happening at the moment, in the case of the Ijaw nation, is that people tend to learn their neighbours' languages at least enough for everyday communication needs. In few cases, the situation is reciprocal, but in some other cases, it is unidirectional, that is, speakers of smaller languages or dialects tend to learn the languages or dialects of their larger or more domineering immediate neighbours for wider communication. For instance, many speakers of Degema are bilingual in Kalabarị, and speakers of Biseni, Akịta, and Epie-Atisa tend to learn the Kolokuma dialect of Ịzon for wider communication. In the past, speakers of Ọgbịa tended to learn Nembe for the same reason (Efere and Williamson, 1999:105). Efere (2001:126) has also pointed out that "Ḅumo speakers understand Okrika and Kalabarị".

Considering the fact that there is a great deal of mutual intelligibility in all the linguistic groups that make up the Ijaw nation, coupled with the fact that there is an impressive degree of inter-language and inter-dialect learning going on in the Ijaw nation, is it possible, therefore, for a common language to evolve or to be recommended for the people? The answer to the above question is not a simple one. Language, as we know it, is not "culturally neuter" as a new born baby. It is a socio-cultural phenomenon, and a powerful instrument of an empire. People have all sorts of sentimental attachment to their language. As people continue to become more and more aware of their linguistic rights, coupled with inter-group conflicts and sometimes very fatal hostilities, the possibility of promoting any one of the indigenous languages as a common medium of interaction for a group that is linguistically pluralistic becomes more and more remote. The Ijaw situation is no exception.

There are various ways of getting a people that are linguistically diverse to speak a common language for purposes of wider communication. First, one of the speech forms can gradually evolve because of its relevance to the communication needs of the various groups. The speech form in question can be relevant either because its speakers are culturally, historically or economically important. In this way, speakers of other tongues will endeavour to learn it. The other way a common language can evolve is through imposition, so that the speakers of other tongues are coerced to learn the language. The problem with this method is that people can resist it if they have a choice. In the Nigerian Federation, for instance, Hausa, Igbo and Yoruba have been elevated to the status of official languages on the sheer strength of population of speakers, and not because of rich aesthetic cultural values in any of them. People, particularly speakers of other tongues, have continued to oppose this official recognition given to Hausa, Igbo and Yoruba. Some have even described the situation as a malicious dictatorship of numbers, since there was no referendum, and therefore no consensus to accord them this recognition.

If our experience of the Nigerian experiment in nation-building is anything to go by, then caution should be exercised in arriving at a common language for the Ijaw nation. What we recommend is that the people of the Ijaw nation should be encouraged to continue to learn their neighbours' languages, so as to break any barrier to communication that might arise. The small group languages should see the need to learn the languages of the more dominant groups for purposes of wider communication. But if we adopt again the conspiracy of size and spread of speakers, then Iẓọn may be a likely candidate for the common language for the Ijaw nation. It is the only variety of Ịjọ that is spoken in four states of the Federation.

CHAPTER 7

THE WESTERN DELTA AND LIMIT:
Basic Socio-Linguistic Survey

C. Budonyefa Agbegha

Introduction

Izọn is an Ijoid language (Williamson & Timitimi, 1983; Efere and Williamson, 1999) which is spoken in parts of Bayelsa, Delta, Edo and Ondo States. However, within the Izọn *bẹẹlị* (language), there are quite a lot of variations (*fie pọn*) which, in most cases, fall within the precincts of clans or *ibe*. *Fie pọn* which is dialect, however, according to Quirk, *et. al.* (1973:2), "is a well established label both in popular and technical use" for the regional variety of a language. In other words, since the people of Patani speak Izọn differently from those of Sagbama who are their neighbours; and since the difference is distinctive yet mutually intelligible, then they can be said to be speaking dialects of the same language. As it is, Patani speak Kabụ *pọn* while Sagbama speak Kumbọ *pọn*. And at the same time, all communities that speak Kabụ fall within Kabụowei *ibe*, while those who speak Kumbọ fall within Kumbọ *ibe*; each with its own *Pẹrẹ*. As Quirk (1973:2) states, "geographical dispersion is the most classic basis for linguistic variation". In other words, dialects or even languages develop over a period of time when a people separate. For instance, Ogbe-Ijọ and Isaba dispersed from Ekeremọ but they no longer speak Izọn the same way; even Ogbe-Ijọ and Isaba now have noticeable differences. Diẹbiri, on the other hand dispersed from Seimbiri.

Characteristics of a Dialect

The first characteristic of a dialect is phonological: the pronunciation of words. However, we must note that some persons have a manner of pronouncing words that are peculiar to them. However, when the manner of pronouncing words is peculiar to a people in a particular community, it is referred to as dialect. Quirk (1973:2) says "regional dialects seem to be realized predominantly in phonology.

That is, we generally recognize a different dialect from a speaker's pronunciation before we notice that his vocabulary (or lexicon) is also distinctive". Traugott and Pratt (1980:313) agree that the term accent "describes the phonological characteristics of any dialect" but say further that many linguists tend to use lect or variety.

Phonological Variations

The table below is a list of some basic words tested among the speakers of the various Izon lects in Delta, Edo and Ondo States. However, it must be added that words pronounced in isolation may differ when they are used in a phrase or sentence.

Table 1: A **List of Some Basic Words**.

Lect	Head	Nose	Mouth	Eye	Fish	Sun
Kabụ	tịbí	niní	bịbí	tọrú	indí	ụraụ
Kumbọ	tịbí	niní	bịbí	tọrú	indí	ụraụ
Ekeremọ	tịbí	nìní	bịbí	tọrú	èndí	owụra
Tuomọ	tịbí	nìní	bịbí	tọrú	èndí	owụra
Mein	tịbí	nìní	bịbí	tọrú	èndí	owụra
Obotebe	tịbí	nìnì	bịbí	tọrú	èndì	owụra
Ogbe-Ijọ	tịbí	nìnì	bịbí	tọrú	èndì	owụra
Iduwini	tịbí	nìnì	bịbí	tọrú	èndì (ìdì)	agbal
Ogulagha	tịbí	nìnì	bịbí	tọrú	ìdì	agbala
Gbaranmatu	tịbí	nìnì	bịbí	tọrú	ìdì	agbala
Egbema	tịbí	nìnì	bịbí	tọrú	ìdì	ovọrọn
Olodiama	tịbí	nìnì	bịbí	tọrú	ìdì	ovọrọn
Arogbo	tịbí	nìnì	bịbí	tọrú	ìdì	ovọrọn

Using the criteria of similarity of tones and other lexical items, it is possible to tentatively classify lects into four groups. In other words, mutual intelligibility is higher within each group than across the groups.

Group One:

Tụbụru-Kabọ and Kumbọ together with some lects from Bayelsa state are reffered to as Tụbụrụ using the Mein word for East (Eastern).

Group Two:

Bolou Tọrụ is used to describe Ekeremọ and Tuomọ speakers, meaning from within the creek. **Opu Tọrụ** or **Mein** which is used to describe all the communities along the River Forcados, from Bomadi down to Gbẹkẹbọ also fall within this same group.

Group Three:

Tobu comprises Obotebẹ, Ogbe-Ijọ, Isaba and Diẹbiri.

Group Four:

Okun, derived from the word for south (sea), is used to describe Iduwini, Ogulagha, Egbema, Olodiama, Okomu, Fụrụpagha, and Arogbo.

Tone (Pọn)

In Izọn, tone is a major criterion in differentiating lects. The table above shows that even when a basic word remains the same across the lects, there is usually a difference in the rise and fall of the voice (tone) during pronunciaton . We have indicated that variation by the use of tone marks. For example, the word for head remains the same for all the lects tested, yet we can see that *tịbị* has the feature of a low-high tone in *Mein* and a low-low tone in Obotebe (*tịbị*). We can even observe that each lect has a consistent tone pattern. However, according to Wallwork (1985:101), "where pronunciation is concerned, the differences are always reffered to as differences of accent".

Vowel Variation

The difference in Izon lects is not limited to accent (tone); some vowels also change from one lect or group of lects to another. A ready example is *indi* (fish) in the table above. The initial vowell [i] changes as shown in the following variants: *indi, endi, ịndi* and *idi*. In the case of *idi* the nasal [n] has been dropped. Vowel change is not restricted to one word class. For instance, knife is *adẹin/ẹdẹin* (noun), *arẹ/ẹrẹ* (name - noun); *arị/ẹrị* (to see - verb). Changes involving diphthongs include *tei/toi* (play); *dei/doi* (to change); *pei/poi* (to listen). *Dein/duin* (night).

Consonant Variation

In some cases, the change in word may affect consonants. For example, the verb to climb *uwou* is *ugou* in some dialects. While the word road, *owọu*, is *ugọu*. So also *yọu/zọu* and *yọunmọ* and *zọunmọ* are variants of some words found in some of the lects.

Pronouns

Pronoun is another area of major variation among Izọn lects. A simple sentence can show the difference:

English:	I am coming	We are coming
Tụbụrụ:	I boyemi (kumbọ)	Wo boyemi
Bulou Tọrụ/Mein:	I bomini	Wo bomini
Tobu	E bomini	Wo bomịnị
Ogulagha	E bonu	Ba bonu
Okun	E bomịnị	Wọ bornịnị

Posssesive Pronoun

Ist Person: I,me,my,mine	Singular	Plural
Tụbụrụ	i , i , i , inie	wo, wo,wo, woye
Bulou Tọrụ/Mein	ị ,ị , ị , ịnịe	wo, wo, wo, woye
Tobu	ẹ , ẹ , ẹ, ẹnịe	wo, wo, woni, wonie
Okun	ẹ ,ẹ ,ẹ ,ịnie	wọ, wọ, wọ, wọyen

Dialects Spoken

These include Obọtẹbẹ lect spoken in Obọtẹbẹ and its villages of Tẹlẹmọtu, Bilazigha, Labọbulọuseigha, Bulọu Izanma, Ogbogbịnị, Aluma, Asịnịkiri, Falịoweigbịnị Asisaghagbịnị, Bulou Abadigbịnị, Opuapalị, Esanmagbịnị, Etokogbịnị, Obirita, Kẹnịlụgbịnị. All Obọtẹbẹ communities are in Burutu LGA of Delta State. As the name implies, Obọtẹbẹ (he alone) started as a single community but now has a number of villages. The Obọtẹbẹ *pọn* is fast dying away. It is fast being assimilated by Mein *pọn* which is spoken by Gbẹkẹbọ and Ayakoromọ, its neighbouring communities.

Kabụ is spoken partly in Delta and Bayelsa States. Patani, Abarị, Aven and Kọlọwarị are in Patani Local Government Area of Delta State while Trofanị, Adagbabiri, Asamabiri, Elemebiri and Ekpẹriwarị are in Sagbama Local Government Area of Bayelsa State. The Kabụ dialect (its *pọn*) is quite endangered because its speakers are surrounded by the Isoko on one side and Ukuani on the other. Therefore, it is possible for a child to grow up in Patani speaking Isoko and Ukuani in addition to Kabụ which is the mother tongue. There seems to be a conscious effort on the part of parents, particularly, the older ones to teach their children to speak Kabụ. However, this effort has to be sustained if the Kabụ *pọn* must continue to exist because the rate of intermarriage among the neighbours is high.

Kabụ *pọn* has been used in Radio and T.V. Broadcasting. It was first used by late Ambakẹdẹrimọ Tamụkunu in the late 1960s in Radio Nigeria Enugu and in Delta Broadcasting Service (DBS) Radio and T.V. Warri in the 90s. In recent times, Calabar Akpọbomịere continues the use of Kabụ in the Delta Broadcasting Service, Radio and T.V. Warri.

Kumbọ is spoken in Agọlọma, Bulou Angiama, Apẹlẹbiri (Bedeseigha) in Delta State. It is spoken in Sagbama main town (Agbedi) and Owunbiri in Sagbama Local Government Area of Bayelsa State. Apẹlẹbiri is fast becoming Urhobo. The signpost to the town reads Bedeseigha which is the Urhobonised form for

Bịdẹseigha. The situation here is comparable to Kiagbodo of Ngbilebiri Mein where Urhobo becomes the main language while Izon is reserved for sacred occasions of marriages and burials to be spoken by a select few. However, late Professor Egbe Ifie did a number of works using the Kumbọ *pọn*, including *Kemefiere; The Ogress* (1988) and *Deinyi 25 Moon Night rhymes* (1979). Kumbọ is also endangered to the extent that the Apẹlẹbiri community is fast becoming Urhobo.

Mein ranks as the Izọn *pọn* with the widest spread in Delta State, but it is also spoken in parts of Bayelsa State in the towns of Ogobiri which is the traditional home of all Mein, Agoro, Agorogbịnị and Ogboinbiri, all in Sagbama Local Government area. Mein is divided into Akugbịnị, Seimbiri, Ogbolubiri and Ngbilẹbiri, with headquarters at Akugbịnị, Okpokunou, Agbọdọbiri and Kiàgbọdọ, respectively. Although each Mein *ibe* has its *pẹrẹ* (King) but linguistically they speak the same Izọn *pọn* with differences that are not significant.

Akugbịnị Mein consists of Akugbịnị, Kpakiama, Bomadi (Bọmọdi), Ogiriagbịnị, Edegbịnị, Esanma, Ogbein-ama, Okoloba, Ogodobiri and Ezẹbiri.

Seimbiri Mein comprises Okpokunou, Oboro, Enekorogha

Ngbilẹbiri Mein comprises Kiagbọdọ, Bikorogha,Oyangbịnị and Ayakoromo which has over forty communities, including Bụbọụgbịnị, New Town, Akparịmo, Egọligbịnị, Ogborobogbịnị, Azoloba, Agaradama, Sọsịgbịnị, Warịkirigbịnị, Bịbịabịnabogbịnị, Kokodịẹgbịnị. But Kiagbọdọ which is the headquarters of Ngbilebiri Mein is fast being assimilated by the Urhobo language which is the language of their upland neighbours with whom they have maintained intimate marriage ties. Therefore, Urhobo is spoken very freely in Kiagbodo and a number of people now even speak Izon with Urhobo accent; the younger generation speaks little Izon. However, Izon remains sacred, it is used during marriages and burial ceremonies.

Ogbolubiri Mein consists of Agbọdọbiri, Egọdọ, Ofonibẹingha (Okirika) and Gbẹkẹbọ.

Among the Delta Izon, Mein has the highest number of publications, some of which are M. L. Agbegha, *Ezonmị Beke Mọ Ten–eye Fun* (1961), *Izọn Bịbị Teghe Fun* (1968) and most significant of them is the *Izọn- English Dictionary* (1996). T.O. Onduku's publication includes *Izon Gẹ Bramị* (1960). Recent publications in Mein include Clement Oruekpedi's *Izon Bẹẹlị Funbo* (1995, 2000). But Mein *pọn* has been used for broadcasting for sometime now. C.F. Agbegha started broadcasting in Mein with NTA Benin City in the 80s and down to DBS with the creation of Delta State. Mein is currently used by Victor Ayabotu and Asịnịere Egolukumọ in the Delta State Broadcasting House.

Tuomọ is spoken by a group of communities jokingly referred to as T.T. clan. It comprises Tuomọ, the head town, Tọrugbịnị, Tụbụegbe and Tamụegbe (*tọrụ-* outside and *bulou* -inside), all in Burutu Local Government Area of Delta State.

Ekeremọ (Oporomọ) comprises Ojobo (Ozobo), Bulou Ndoro, Egirangbịnị, Orugbịnị, Ekogbịnị, Ekumugbịnị and Abadiama in Burutu Local Government Area of Delta State.

It is also spoken in Ekeremọ, Amabulou, Obirigbịnị, Foutọrugbịnị, Tamọggbịnị, Pẹrẹtorugbịnị and Tọrụ Ndoro in Ekeremọ Local Government Area of Bayelsa State. Although, Efere and Williamson (1999: 101) include Ogbe and Isaba as Ekeremọ, we shall rely on Alagoa (1972: 50) who classifies Ogbe (Ogbe- Ijọ) as a "small *Ibe* of three major settlements (Ogbe, Dịẹbiri/ Dịọbiri, Isaba) on the creeks to the south of the modern town of Warri".

Ogbe-Ijọ comprises, Izansa, Izelezele, Ekeremọ, Takẹmọbogbịnị, Birisibe (Ofiriki) gbịnị, Bankiggbịnị, Alokpagbịnị, Eniebọgbịnị, Ogunkoroye, Dịẹbiri (Batangha), Tekedọụ Kusini-Egwa, Ọdidi, Sụrụghagbẹnẹ, Izanfọun, Afẹrẹsụogbịnị, Mamumamụgbịnị (Zion City), Azuzu community, Toweigbịnị,

Egbegbegbini, Ekeinseibokorogha, Ekidetabuye, Egodogodogbini, Ebiyegbini, Torufa (Tudougbini), Eginagbini and others.

Isaba comprises Peręama, Tubuama, Pamię, Ayama, Orubeke, Peręotugbini, Isegbelegbini, Sibedogbini, Igbaregba, Egbeletibigbini, Amaręnggbini, Ingobozighagbini, Otugbo, Gbonweigbini and Ofigbini.

Ogbe-Ijo and Isaba differ significantly in the use of the first person singular pronoun 'I'. Where Ogbe-Ijo says *amini*, Isaba says *emini*.

Diebiri, on the other hand, has fled its original site near Aladja because of Warri crisis and some of them have settled at Batangha. Dịebiri *pon* has become endangered. It is difficult to find Dịebiri speakers.

Iduwini is spoken partly in Delta State and Bayelsa State. The major Iduwini speaking communities in Delta State are Ọfọugbini (Izon Burutu) and Odimodi in Burutu Local Government Area of Delta State.

Ọgulagha (Ogunlagha) comprises Ogulagha, Obọtọbo I, Obọtọbo II, Youbibi, Sọkębulọu, Youkiri, Abara, Guọgbini, Obuuru, Okuntu and Benibouye. There is need to make a quick reference to the name Ogunlagha. Relying on R.J. Hook's account of the Ogula clan, Alagoa (1972: 81) translates Ogulagha as *ogulagha* "a place of meeting but where there is no council". In other words, "no case", "no case for judgement". However, the name is not Ọgulagha but Ogunlagha. Ogun is the Izon word for slave raid; Ogunlagha means beyond slave raid, not affected by slave raid. This becomes meaningful when we realize that there is a community some how opposite Burutu called Ogunkoroye – a community affected by slave raid.

Gbaran-amatu (Oporoza) include Oporoza, Kunukunuama, Ekeręnkoko, Ikokodiagbini, Benikurukuru, Inekorogha, Ugoba, Pępęama, Opuede, Opuede Bubọu, Tebizọ, Ikpokpo and Azaama.

Egbema speakers are found both in Delta and Edo States. They consist of nine major communities with several sub-communities.

The four major Egbema communities in Delta State are Polo Bụbọụ (Tsekelewu), Opuama, Ogbinbiri and Ogbudugbudu while the sub-communities include: Opia, Ekenyan, Daụgbolo, Edẹkụ, Edebagbịnị, Sọni Zion, Asantụagbịnị, Bobirakui, Kpokugbịnị, Kokoye, Ebiororo, Deinkoru, Fịkọrọmọ, Uyatoi, Itinyan, Arigbagha, Bẹịnkoro. Opuakaba, and Azaama, all in Warri North Local Government Area.

The major Egbema speaking communities in Edo State are Ajakoroama, Ofoniama, Jamagie, Gbulukaka, Gbeoba and Abẹrẹ (Tọrụkubuagbịnị), all in Ovia South West Local Government Area of Edo State.

Egbema tend to be more prominent than the other lects in Tọrụ-*Ibe* (communities within Benin River). The language was used by Efẹrẹsụọa in the 1980s in Bendel Broadcasting Service Radio and Television, Benin City. J. B. Efẹrẹsụọa has also authored a number of books in Izọn, including a dictionary. The people maintain a close tie with their Izọn neighours: Gbaranmatu and Egbema in Delta State and Arogbo in Ondo Srate. This tie is reflected in their vocabulary: *obọn* is used for market in place of *fọụ* and *odọn* is used for year in place of *kụraị* as applicable in Arogbo. Other similarities between Egbema and Arogbo include: *akpakpa* for harmatan, *akpụrụ/bata* for shoe, *udẹn* for basin, and *okoka* which are *okiriyẹn*, *agbụka*, *akpomaku* and *gbe*, respectively. The tie is so close that Egbema spoken in Abẹrẹ is almost like Arogbo.

The language is not being taught in the Primary schools. The school subject time table makes provision for Edo which is not being taught. Therefore , the survival of the language is solely dependent on the efforts of parents. Arogbo and Egbema have the same pronoun system.

Arogbo *pọn* is spoken in a number of communities in Ese-Odo local Government area of Ondo State, South West Nigeria. The people who number a little less one million, according to the 1983 census, are spread well over seventy communities which include, Arogbo township, Ajapa township, Agadagba-Obọn, Opuba, Akpata, Biagbịnị, Bọlọwoghụ.

They are surrounded by the Ilaje and Yoruba people whose language they speak freely. In other words, most Arogbo are bilinguals who speak Ilaje/Yoruba in addidtion to Izọn. As a result of this interaction, the Arogbo *pọn* is replete with borrowed words. For instance, the *do* popular Izọn greeting has its Yoruba equivalent of *ẹlẹ* dominating. *Ẹlẹ* is used as a synonym of the Izọn *do*. The Yoruba *ekabọ* is used for welcome instead of the predominant Izọn I *bodọ/I botẹị*. The list of the Yoruba/ Ilaje words in the Arogbo *pọn* is very extensive: *sibi* for *kuyẹrẹ* or *engasi* (spoon), *agbodo* for *aka* (maize). The Isekiri word for market (*obọn*) is also used in Arogbo in place of the Izon word *fọụ*.

In all, the Yoruba/Ilaje borrowed words are understood by older generation as synonyms to the Izọn words. But the situation is not the same with the younger generation who use more of the foreign words.

The Arogbo are conscious of preserving the language as their heritage. For instance, after the Nigeria Civil War, Yoruba names were changed to Izọn; typical examples include Oluwade Zion which was changed to Tamaraụbotẹị while Agwẹ ẹri was changed to Aseri-ama. The effort of Prince Richard Jologho (an Arogbo son) who was Speaker in the Ondo State House of Assembly during the Michael Ajasin led government {1979-1983} saw the approval of a pirmary school curriculum for Arogbo. However, it is only haphazardly taught in a few schools despite the National Policy on Education (NPE) stipulation of teaching mother tongue in primary schools.

Prince Asuwaye Mesarawọn has published some primers in Arogbo *pọn* yet the patronage is low because the language is not being taught; the excuse is lack of man power. This writer was reliably informed that there is the opportunity of teaching Izon even in Ondo State College of Education, Ikare Ekiti. The Arogbo, and indeed all Izon sons and daughters, should be challenged and come to support the teaching and learning of Izon in Arogbo. The truth is that every subsequent Arogbo generation is being assimilated into Yoruba/Illaje, and it may not take long for them to be completely assimilated.

Olodiama (west) is spoken at Ikoro, Irikorogha, Iboro, Ikusangha (Ekenwan), Gelegelebiri, Igbeleoba, all in Ovia South West Local Government Area of Edo State. The Olodiama peoople have both Edo and Isẹkiri as neighbours. Therefore, a number of them speak Edo and Isẹkiri in addition to Izon. For instance, Isẹkiri is freely spoken in Ikoro. However, the people consciously treasure the Izon language as their heritage and so hold it sacred.

Olodiama lect differs from Egbema, their immedate Izon neighbours, in a few areas. The word for sun in Egbema is *ọvọrịn* which is realised as *ovẹrịn* in Olodiama; salt which is *adaụn/fụ* in other dialects is *umẹrẹn* in Olodiama; canoe which is *arụ* is *ukọ*. In all, Olodiama tends to have more borrowed words than Egbema.

Okomu is a single community clan. It seems to have been assimilated by Olodiama, their immediate Izon neighbours. There is no significant difference now between Okomu and Olodiama.

Fụrụpagha is spoken in the major communities of Zide and Gbelebu. They speak not much differently. from Olodiama. Fụrụpagha has the same pronoun system with Egbema.

Apoị has the traditional nine community structure of Izon *ibe* like Egbema and Gbaranmatu. Significantly too, the nine major communities have Izon names which include Gbẹkẹbọ, Kiribo, Igbobini, Oboro and Igbotu. Living in the midst of the Ikalẹ and Ilajẹ Yoruboid people, the Apoị no longer speak Izon. They have adopted Yoruba and use Izọn songs which are reserved for sacred occasions. The very old ones among them understand some Izọn but majority of them hardly acknowledge any Izọn affiliation.

Izọn as an Endangered Language

IAn endangered language is one that stands the risk of dying. As human beings die so languages die. We have the classic example of Latin which we now refer to as a 'dead language'. In other words, Latin exists more as a written language than as a spoken language. Krauss (1992) says that a language dies somewhere in the world every two weeks. (Emenanjo (1999) says that any language that has less than 100,000 speakers is in danger of dying. By that reckoning, Izọn is not an endangered language. But C.B. Agbegha (2002) states that Izọn is endangered for other reasons. The situation is clearer when we take the various Izọn lects one by one. I have already cited the example of Ngbilebiri Mein where Kiagbọdọ, one of their major communities is fast becoming Urhobo-speaking. Bẹdẹseigha (Bulou Apẹlẹbiri) of Kumbọ is also becoming Urhobo-speaking; Kabụ has Isoko and Ukuani to contend with. Apoị is almost completely lost to Yoruba; Arogbo is highly endangered. Benstowe-Onyeka (2000) has also commented on the Kabụ situation. Even among Izọn lects, smaller ones like Obotebe are being lost to Mein. Okomu has been assimilated by Olodiama.

Above all, Warri which is a melting pot for all Izọn lects poses a threat to the survival of the language because of its multi-lingual setting. In addition to the fact that several languages are spoken, Pidgin has become a predator language devouring Izọn and other languages along its way. It is pertinent to note that Pidgin is spoken freely across all Izọn communities. Pidgin becomes a veritable option when Izọn people from different lects interact; but this option gradually erodes the Izọn language leading to its further endangerment. The most worrisome thing is that Pidgin is spoken not only in the street corners and market places but right into the bedroom even in homes where both parents are Izọn.

Salvaging the Situation

According to Bamgbose (1993:29) "The fate of an endangered language may lie in the hands of the owners of the language themselves and their will to make it survive". It is therefore, the responsibility of every Izǫn son and daughter to rescue the language from extinction. Late Professor Kay Williamson of blessed memory has put in place all it takes to study and develop Ijaw (Izǫn). Her popular slogan should challenge all "use or lose your language". For the Izǫn to be alive we must use it at all times, we must study it and develop it.

Izǫn language (Mein) is studied at the College of Education, Warri, up to the NCE. Level in combination with English, or other teaching subjects. However, the response to studying the language has been very poor. We should encourage our students by offering scholarships or bursaries; encourage writers to publish books or give research grants to teachers of Izǫn language. We must all rise to the challenge; we either use our language or we lose it.

CHAPTER 8

A COMMON LANGUAGE FOR THE IJAW
ETHNIC NATIONALITY?

Lecture for the 1st Pan-Ijaw National Congress
Saturday 1 March 2003

Kay Williamson

When I was asked to speak on "identifying a common language for the Ijaw ethnic nationality', my first impulse was to decline. This is because I do not think it is possible to find such a common language. But upon consideration I decided it was better to explain the conclusions that my studies have led me over the years.

Terms such as 'ethnic nationality' are difficult, for several reasons. First, they are often ill defined. For example, the first time I ever attended a gathering of this type, in the 1950s, the various 'clans' making up Ijaw were called one by one and their representatives, if present, answered. There was no argument over whether Andoni should be called or not. Someone insisted 'Call Andoni', and Andoni was called in a half-hearted way. No one answered. So, was Andoni at that point a part of the Ijaw ethnic nationality or not? Some obviously thought yes, others no. Secondly, some groups may be either considered components of the larger ethnic nationality or as separate entities of their own. Thus the city-states of the Eastern Niger Delta, which in pre-colonial times had quite separate political existences and were in active competition with each other, were and are sometimes considered to be separate entities—Kalabari, Okrika, Ibani, Nembe, and so on—and sometimes part of a larger entity Ijaw. Thirdly, definitions of an ethnic nationality can change over time. For example, Andoni, whose Ijaw status was doubtful in the 1950s, is included as a clan in the Eastern Zone of Ijaw as defined by the Constitution of the INC.

These difficulties have made some social scientists to claim that 'ethnic nationalities' were a colonial invention: that before the arrival of the colonial administrators people were not rigidly assigned to one or other of such entities, and that more fluid and overlapping classifications existed. I do not agree that ethnic nationalities are completely a colonial invention, because in some cases people who are very distinct in culture, political system, and language live side by side, must be regarded as different and certainly regard themselves as different. For example, Okrika and Eleme have long been neighbours, but remain quite distinct. In other cases, however, there are gradual rather than abrupt changes, and here it is more difficult to judge when we should say we are dealing with two ethnic nationalities or one.

As a linguist I usually avoid these problems by talking about languages rather than ethnic nationalities. But similar problems arise when it is necessary to state how many languages are spoken in a particular area. For example, Nembe and Bumo (Boma) do not need interpretation; Bumo and Kolokuma do not need interpretation; but Nembe and Kolokuma do. So, do we regard these as three dialects of one language, or dialects of two different languages? If the latter, where does Bumo, the intermediate form, belong—with Nembe or with Kolokuma? This is a case of a *dialect chain* or a *dialect cluster,* as linguists call them; the extremes need interpretation (or, put technically, are not *mutually intelligible*), but intermediate dialects exist to serve as links. In colonial times, when administrators paid little attention to language, it was usual to group them together and say that there was a single language with three dialects. In more recent times, research has shown that while Bumo is a link, it goes somewhat more closely with Kolokuma than with Nembe; hence, Bumo and Kolokuma have been classified together as Izon, while Nembe and Akassa (Akaha) are classified together.

In addition to the problems of deciding whether or where to draw boundaries within areas where the speech-forms are clearly related, there is a major problem when certain speech-forms are included within the area which quite clearly belong to quite different language groups. For example, among the 'clans' recognized by INC are Andoni, who speak Obolo, a language classified as Lower Cross and thus related to Efik, Ibibio, and Anaang; Opobo, who speak Igbo with some Ibani words incorporated; Abua, Odual, and ?gbia, classified as Central Delta languages; Engenni, Zarama, and Epie/Atisa, classified as Delta Edoid languages; and Apoi in the Western Zone, who speak Yoruba. It is thus quite clear that Ijaw as an ethnic nationality does not correspond with the Ijo language area. For this reason, I shall use the Nigerian spelling Ijo for the language area, and the anglicized spelling Ijaw for the ethnic nationality as defined by the INC. All of Ijo, the linguistic entity, is included within Ijaw, the political entity; but the reverse is not true.

From what I have said so far, it is clear that we are dealing with a very complex linguistic situation. Let me now define a few terms which linguists have found helpful in describing such a situation accurately.

First, the term *dialect*. This is sometimes used in ordinary English to describe a small language, or a language whose speakers have little political influence, or an unwritten language. But linguists use it differently. For a linguist, a dialect is a variety of a particular language. Speakers of another dialect of the same language can generally understand it without interpretation, or at least the two dialects should be connected to each other by a chain of intermediate dialects. A small language (which may have only a few hundred speakers) is not to be called a dialect simply because its speakers are few in number or grouped politically with speakers of a larger language. Provided that speakers of the larger language cannot understand them without having learnt their language, it is a language and a dialect. For example, in one ward of Nkoro Town a quite different language, called Defaka, is spoken. Defaka is a language and not a dialect because it cannot be understood by speakers of any other language without being learnt or without interpretation.

A *language* normally consists of a number of dialects. Speakers of different dialects of the same language can normally converse without interpretation. Sometimes the language has an agreed common name, for example, Abua. Sometimes the language has no agreed common name; for example, speakers of

Bille, Ibani, Kalabari, and Okrika can converse easily, but there is no common name for their language. In such cases we may speak of a *dialect cluster*.

Where we find a number of different dialects or dialect clusters forming a chain or network, such that people can partially understand those nearest to them but not those further away, we call them a *language cluster*. Thus, I would say that Nkoro, the Bille-Ibani-Kalabari-Okrika dialect cluster, the Nembe-Akassa dialect cluster, Izon with its many dialects, Okordia, Biseni, and Oruma, together make up the Ijo language cluster.

Where languages are obviously related but distinct from each other, not in a chain or network relationship, we call them a group of languages. For example, Degema, Engenni with Zarama, and Epie/Atisa form the Delta Edoid group of languages.

Some groups are related at a higher level as *branches* of a *family* of languages, and the highest level of relationship recognized is called *phylum*.

All the languages mentioned are ultimately related; they all belong to the Niger-Congo phylum. Ijo, however, together with Defaka, belongs to one branch known as Ijoid, while all the other groups mentioned belong to a branch known as Benue-Congo, which is itself very large and diverse. Thus their relationship is very remote.

We can now face the question of a common language. How do common languages develop? It sometimes seems to be thought that quite different languages can somehow be combined into one. This is something that rarely happens. It is true that languages whose speakers are regularly in contact do influence each other. Languages often borrow words from each other quite freely. It is less often that they borrow grammatical structures. It is therefore quite common to find languages that share many words, especially names for everyday objects that are bought in the market, but which still retain quite distinct grammatical structures. Occasionally, when speakers of many different languages need a neutral common language for everyday transactions, a pidgin develops in which most of the words come from one language that has achieved some kind of dominance in the area, but the words are put together with a grammar and idiomatic usages that agree with those of the other languages in the area. This is the case with Nigerian Pidgin, where most of the words are from English but the way they are used is based on the grammar and usage of Nigerian languages. Very rarely, a genuine 'mixed language' develops, usually in cases where a great deal of intermarriage has taken place between two communities that speak two different languages.

Designing a mixed language, however, is not practicable. Enthusiasts sometimes do design such languages, but they face a serious problem in persuading other people to learn them. Even trying to combine different dialects within a single language is extremely difficult. People sometimes point to the example of Union Igbo, which was used for the first translation of the Bible into Igbo. Although outsiders generally believe it is a success story, most thoughtful Igbo speakers do not regard it as such. Today, they emphasize that for intercommunication between speakers of different dialects, people usually speak naturally but just drop what they know to be peculiarities of their own dialects. They do not consciously try to use a 'standard' Igbo, although one is gradually evolving naturally as people communicate over dialect boundaries.

The usual way a common language develops is by people learning and using a language other than their own, simply because it is convenient. In an area with many languages, such as we live in, it is natural for people to acquire their neighbours' languages. Generally speaking, the smaller one's own languages, the more one will tend to learn the languages of the communities surrounding one's own for ease of communication. Once any language or dialect has got some advantage over others, by being the first to have a school, by being the language of a political centre, by being the language of a commercial centre, or by being chosen as a vehicle for the mass media, more people will tend to learn it. This will in turn make it more likely that it will be chosen for other purposes, such as being the approved language for educational textbooks. Each new choice reinforces the influence of the chosen language, and increase its chances of being learnt by more people as a useful language in the society.

The languages spoken by the Ijaw ethnic nationality are spoken over a number of states and therefore have no common centre; moreover, they co-exist with other languages in the states. Traditionally, people have managed comfortably by learning their neighbours' languages, mostly quite informally by living with them. It is only when umbrella bodies such as the INC ask if they could make use of an indigenous language rather than English, or the state radio and television services decide in what languages to broadcast the news, or a State Ministry of Education has to make decisions about what language(s) to use in textbooks, that formal choices have to be made. The choices made will be different in the different states. Kalabari is an appropriate choice in Rivers State, but not in Bayelsa State or Delta State, where Izon would be more appropriate. Bayelsa State is the only state where almost all the citizens are defined as members of the Ijaw ethnic nationality, and even there four languages have been accepted as necessary: Epie/Atisa, Izon, Nembe, and Ogbia. I therefore conclude that it is not practicable to try to identify one common language for the Ijaw ethnic nationality.

This may seem a negative conclusion. But there are two very important positive aspects we should consider. First, even if we cannot select one language to be used in all the contexts where an indigenous language should be used, we can try as much as possible to develop a common orthography which can be used for all the languages. This has already been done to quite some extent. Thus, all the languages use dotted letters for the same vowel sounds, use dotted consonants for the implosive sounds *b* and *d* if they have them, use a final **-n** to show nasalization, and so on. This helps us to write and read correctly people's names and other words in a language we may not yet have learnt, and makes it easier to learn to read a new language if children begin schooling in a new area. It should be encouraged.

The last most important consideration is that all the languages should be encouraged. All Nigerian languages except the very largest are threatened, particularly by English. When children are sent to nursery school in English, primary school in English, secondary school in English, University in English, it is not surprising if they grow up as speakers of English only. They will bring speak their own language(s) at home to their children so that the children grow up with the basic knowledge they can build on later. The children are going to learn English at school; let them learn their own languages at home, so that they face the world with more than one language. Recently I was at an Ịzọn event hosted by students. They began formally in English. At a point, one of the invited guests stood up and made a speech in Nembe. The gathering was electrified. A woman rushed up and sprayed him. Thereafter a number of people spoke in Ịzọn and the whole gathering became much more exciting. That way, those who knew little Ịzọn could learn more, naturally and enjoyably. Let me end by repeating what I have said on previous occasions:

USE YOUR LANGUAGE OR LOSE YOUR LANGUAGE!

Appendix 8.1:

Family Tree of the Ijoid Language Cluster

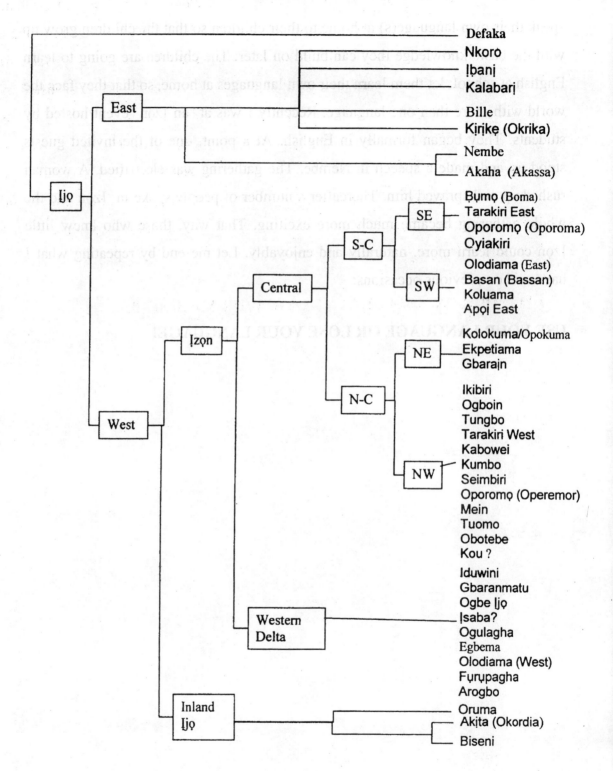

Appendix 8.2:

Family Tree of the Central Delta Group

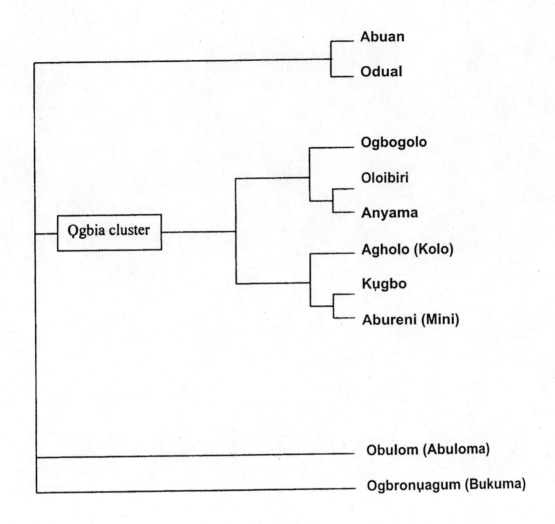

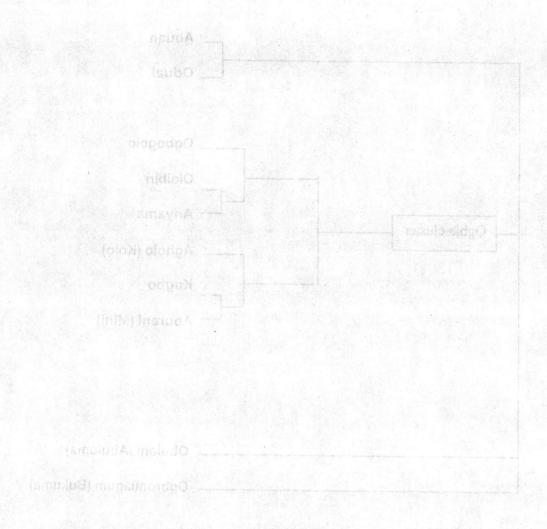

Ayuan

Oguzi

Ogbogolo

Ololibu

Anyama

Agholo (Kolo)

Kugbo

Aduani (Mini)

Oghia-cluster

Obulom (Abuloma)

Ogbronuagum (Bukuma)

CHAPTER 9
VISUAL ARTS[†]
Martha G. Anderson

Residents of Bayelsa State spin fascinating tales about underwater towns celebrate their watery environment by staging regattas, fishing and masquerades that bring fantastic aquatic beings to life. Their art and rituals reflect the Niger Delta's fascinating history as well as its riverine landscape. Reports of warfare and piracy feature prominently in both local histories and the accounts of early European visitors to the region. Images of spirits wearing top hats and wielding weapons recall a time when clan war gods conferred titles on proud warriors; other types of spirit emblems — including bronze bells, tableware, and plastic dolls — recall the region's long involvement with foreign and domestic trade.

Although numerous traditions have been abandoned or altered as the population has become increasingly Christian, Bayelsa State has many vital art forms, as well as a rich artistic heritage. The following account focuses on the arts of the Central Ijo and their immediate Western Ijo neighbours. The Nembe Ijo have similar forms and practices, although their masking societies correspond more closely to those of the Kalabari, an Eastern Ijo group in neighbouring Rivers State. The arts of other peoples living in the region have yet to be documented, but promise to be as richly varied as those of the Ijo.

The Creator

According to traditional Ijo beliefs, human beings originate as disembodied spirits, or *teme* in the realm of the creator, Wonyinghi ('Our Mother'), and return there after dying. While awaiting birth, people often establish relationships with nature spirits *(Oru, or Orumo, 'the spirits')*, who may later wish to join them on earth. Before leaving the spirit world, each person seals an agreement with Wonyinghi that not only determines the course of their lives, but even specifies the way they will die.

---

† This Chapter is reprinted from Chpater 9 in Ebiegberi Joe Alagoa (Ed.): *The Land and People of Bayelsa State: Central Nigeri Delta.* Port Harcourt: Onyoma Research Publications, 1999, pp. 127-148.

Plate 9.1: Shrine of the Creator, Woyingi, "Our Mother", Lubia, Bassan

Wonyinghi has little to do with daily affairs, yet appears to be more responsive to human appeals than other African creator deities. Some communities perform festivals in her honour. In addition, diviners sometimes address problems attributed to an unfortunate destiny by performing a ritual called *zibe bari* in an attempt to revoke the original birth agreement and replace it with a more favourable one. Wonyinghi lives so far off in the sky that no one knows what she looks like, so shrines like the one at Lobia in Bassan *ibe* sometimes represent her with a type of staff & and stool combination that can also serve for other spirits. Songs portray her as an old woman dressed in white, a colour associated with purity, wealth, and the spirit world.

Nature Spirits

Most people lose contact with the spirit world and must consult diviners in order to learn why they are experiencing problems like infertility, ill health, or bad fortune. Diviners, whose nature spirit contacts enable them to 'see' into the spirit world, may attribute problems to other agents, including ancestors and witches, but most rituals focus on nature spirits, most shrines are devoted to them, and virtually all carvings depict them. The Ijo even claim to have acquired masquerades, dances, and funerary rites from these anti-social, but creative beings.

Plate 9.2: Osuwowei, Umbugbene

117

Although people and spirits live together in Wonyinghibou, they have separate domains on earth, where the latter can move about as disembodied spirits or materialise as people, animals, and objects. Some spirits call on human sponsors to acknowledge relationships stemming from Wonyinghibou by providing them with emblems or shrines; those who prove to be exceptionally powerful can command large numbers of followers and demand extensive rites.

The contrasting appearance and behaviour of two types of nature spirits reflect differences in the way the Ijo perceive their respective realms: both can kill people for trespassing on their territory or resisting demands, but water spirits (*bou oru*) who roam the forests. Water spirits who have assumed human form tend to be beautiful, fair skinned beings with long, flowing hair; bush spirits tend to be grotesquely ugly, deformed, or handicapped creatures, with very dark skin and messy hair. The two even specialise in the benefits they offer: people sometimes approach water spirits to ask for children and money; they consult bush spirits to ask for protection and for help, especially in warfare and wrestling competitions.

The types of offerings, songs, rituals, and images the spirits require also reflect their domains. For example, bush spirits, who live on land like people and resemble them more closely, eat local produce; water spirits, who live in a largely foreign environment, have acquired a taste for imported food. Bush spirits wear dark blue or black to signify strength and invincibility; water spirits typically use white to reflect their spirituality and purity. Carvings depict bush spirits as proud, irascible warriors; water spirits tend to forgo figurative images, preferring found objects or trade goods as emblems. A custom observed in Olodiama *ibe,* and perhaps elsewhere, confirms role of sculptures in providing spirits with bodies. A ceremony is held when an infant cuts his first tooth to celebrate his attainment of human status; a comparable rite is performed when a figure's teeth are carved to mark its transformation from a log of wood into a receptacle for a spirit. The prominent mouths on most Ijo carvings reflect the importance of this essential equipment, for a spirit's ability to accept offerings of food and drink makes it receptive to human attentions.

Ijo shrines are not simply static collections of objects and images, but often the focus of ritual performances that can rival masquerades as entertainment. Shrine renewals, which typically occur in the dry season, often involve drumming, singing, dancing, and possession; some include elaborate drama and masquerades Although his shrine is in ruins, residents of' Olugbobiri in Olodiama still talk about the spectacular rites staged for lsobowei, which attracted crowds of onlookers. Simply raising a divination ladder to establish contact with a spirit can have sensational results, for some are said to exert so much force that they can pull their ladders across wide rivers, bearers and all.

Bush Spirits

Because water spirits tend to prefer other types of emblems, most figure carvings represent bush spirits. Though carvings made for spirit companions and secondary shrine spirits often depict females, the central image in most bush spirit shrines portrays an authoritative male. His wives and children often accompany him, for an Ijo male must marry and bear children to be considered a man. He typically holds weapons to announce his readiness to fight, wears wooden replicas of medicine gourds to signify that he is protected by 'bullet-proofing medicines', and displays the body paint and eagle feathers of his clan's *peri* warrior society to show that he has taken human lives. He often sports a top hat, a style of headgear that continued to signify prestige in the Niger Delta long after it had gone out of fashion in Europe.

Although priests usually describe these carvings as photographic likenesses, few show evidence of the deformities widely associated with bush spirits. However, images may be larger than life-size and have multiple heads in keeping with the idea that bush spirits are gigantic, grotesque beings, who command superhuman powers. Figures of this type recall a volatile character named Tebesonoma, or 'Seven heads', who features in the epic tale of Ozidi (or Izutu), which is told throughout the region (see Clark 1977).

119

Plate 9.3:
Man with bush spirit companion which he acquired as a youth when
the spirit announced that it wanted a carving by making him overly
aggressive when he was wrestling, Ikibiri, Ekpetiama

Bush spirit shrines tend to be specific to Ijo communities; Osuwo-owei or 'Rain Man', who has both land and water aspects, may be an exception; a number of shrines throughout the region honour a spirit by that name, though each worships him in a different way. Shrines for Agwanran, a warrior who appears in the Ozidi saga, also turn up from place to place; however, some shrines, like Dirimobou of Ikebiri, honour particular sections of the surrounding forest, including sacred lakes. Perhaps because they offered protection to warriors in the past, many bush spirit shrines are off-limits to women and outsiders. Although bush spirits began advertising other than military benefits following the Pax Britannica, residents of Olugbobiri report that lsobowei offered help to soldiers during the Biafran war.

120

Water Spirit Shrines

Like many of their neighbours, the Ijo associate water spirits with 'imported' manufactured items as well as with things that are bright and shiny. The conception of water spirits as wealthy foreigners may well predate overseas trade, for the ljo envision underwater towns where articles lost in the rivers accumulate, making water spirits immensely wealthy. They believe that these largely benevolent beings can bestow children and ensure financial success, particularly in fishing and trading.

Priests often say that the emblems in their shrines appeared in the water mysteriously. Some claim that water spirits have brought them gems and precious metal objects, but diviners can determine even mundane objects like sticks and keys which mysteriously appear in the river to be sacred. Objects of this type are frequently secreted away behind curtains of white cloth or hidden between two white saucers. In addition, shrines display both equipment associated with the rivers, like miniature canoes, paddles, and fishing spears, and trade goods, like lengths of cloth, plastic dolls, glass tumblers, and china plates.

As already noted, major water spirits seldom designate carved figures as their emblems, though a few choose to materialise as masquerade headpieces. Even prominent spirits like Bini Kurukuru, who is worshipped several locations in the region, may require only a cloth curtain or a divination ladder as shrine furnishings. Adumu (Onumu or Azuma), who is a manifestation of the python, is an exception. Though his shrines depict him as a water spirit, he also has a bush or land aspect, which may his preference for figure carvings. People now describe Adumu as the patron of traders, but his original role seems to have been as patron of fishermen. Images photographed in Apoi, Bassan, and Olodiama in the nineteen-seventies are similar in style to those made for bush spirits, but portray him as a fisherman equipped with a miniature canoe and fishing gear; however, some of the paddles and spears may be water spirits in their own right. Unlike most water spirits, Adumu is described as very dark-skinned, and the carvings in his shrines at Azuzuama and Kemebiama are painted black to emphasis this feature. Figures of Adumu and his wife displayed by a shrine at Diebu in Bomo are painted blue and white, colours associated with pythons in the eastern delta.

Ijo Masking Traditions

The Ijo credit water spirits with introducing masquerades. Spirits may approach people while they fish or travel by canoe, order them to perform masquerades, then return in dreams to teach them songs and dance steps. A story recorded in Olodiama recalls the Kalabari legend of Ekineba, because it includes an abduction:

> A man known as Kperighada, [who] was fishing in the Cameroons, wasn't seen for seven days. When he reappeared, he told the people who had been looking for him that he was taken by water spirits, who taught him how to dance a masquerade. He returned to Ondewari, where he called the elders together to inform them of the water people's ultimatum that he must perform the masquerade or he would die. They carved the masks out of wood and he performed the [Ofurumo or Shark] play, just as we are performing it now.

Alternatively, people claim that their ancestors observed water spirits performing on sand banks, stole their masks and drums, then returned to their villages to stage the plays there.

Plate 9.4:
Mask performing at Egbesu festival, Olobiri, Kolokuma clan

In the Nembe region, it is women, acting under instructions from water spirits, who introduce both dance societies and individual masquerades. In the Central Ijo area, water spirits typically approach men in visions and dreams, but they can also communicate through diviners, and many of these are women. Shrine members trace the origin of the Eleke masquerade of Korokorosei, another Olodiama town, to a female diviner named Bouomini, who probably lived in the early nineteenth century. Bouomini interpreted an object found in a fishing trap as a sign that the community must establish a masquerade shrine; she instructed the original priest on every aspect of the shrine and showed the members how an elaborate, three-day masquerade.

123

Even though spirits may threaten to kill people who do not perform their plays, most masquerades are only mildly religious in nature. The masks themselves may not be considered potent, for the Ijo distinguish between those that incarnate spirits, and those that merely imitate their appearance and behaviour. The former can be invoked to punish criminals or settle disputes; the latter have no real power, although their performances may be considered beneficial. Some mimic the medicines, sacrifices, and possession involved in masquerades staged for powerful spirits simply for dramatic effect.

Even the most potent spirits initiate masquerades largely out of a desire to associate with their human friends. Throughout the Delta, drum calls and songs implore the spirits to come out and play. The Ijo word for play, *tol (or ti),* has much the same connotations as its English equivalent, and applies to the performance itself as well as to games and light hearted banter.

Ijo Masking Traditions

Ijo groups living east of the Nun River have masking societies known as Sekiapu ('Dancing people') or Ekine, in honour of a legendary Kalabari woman, Ekineba, who taught her towns people to perform masquerades. The group's primary function consists of staging an extensive cycle of Masquerades which climaxes with a festival that includes all the masks. The Nembe version, *Owuaya aru* or Canoe of the mother of Masquerades', is similar to the Kalabari's *Owu aru sun* or 'Canoe of the water people'. These spectacular festivals also renew the spiritual element of the masks in preparation for a new one (Horton 1963: 95 Alagoa in Nzewunwa 1982: 268-69).

In addition to placating spirits and calling on them for help, Sekiapu Instils masculine virtues and promotes cultural knowledge. In Nembe, as in the Kalabari region, some masquerades include a sequence known as the pointing ordeal that tests the members' understanding of drum language. The masker must respond to drum calls by indicating the town or the shrine the drummer calls out. Failure to do so brings disgrace on a performer; success proves him to be a fully cultured member of society who possesses extensive knowledge of its history, mythology, and proverbs. Sekiapu also appears to have played an important judicial role in the past by punishing members not only for minor offences like tardiness at group events, but for more serious crimes like rape and theft. (Alagoa 1967a: 145-55).

Plate 9.5:
Ungozu masquerade, Olugbobiri, Olodiama clan, 1992

Central and Western Ijo groups do not have institutions comparable to Sekiapu, nor do they use the term Ekine in reference to masking. In the region west of the Nun, masking traditions not only differ from one group to another, but from one village to another within the same group. Even the types of events at which masks perform—including traditional festivals and modern civic celebrations—tend to take distinctive forms in each village. For instance, because certain wards and villages trace the origin of funeral ceremonies to nature spirits encountered by ancestors, some involve masking while others do not.

Only a few enshrined masks survive in the region, but they suggest a more serious attitude toward masking in the past. Moreover, despite the highly

125

secular nature of many of the masquerades performed in recent times, people still consider them a means of placating spirits and garnering benefits. They credit masquerades with bringing children, preventing infant deaths, averting epidemics, and otherwise assuring prosperity. In addition, masquerades undoubtedly satisfy a need for aesthetic expression, provide a recreational outlet, and promote unity among various factions. At least in the past, they also served as an important means of enculturating youth.

Masquerades and Ijo Culture

Symbolism relating to warfare and violence pervades masquerades. Though most maskers only play at being blood thirsty spirits, they carry weapons and spend a good deal of their time chasing spectators. Headpieces often represent predatory fish, menacing reptiles, and composite 'water monsters'; they have names like *fanu pele* ('fence cutter'), *angala pele* ('mangrove cutter'), *pelekere-biye guru* ('when it cuts it is happy'), and *bighebighepele* ('cut without inquiring'), which reinforce the idea that they are ready to attack anyone who gets in their way. Their drum titles, like the of Ijo warriors communicate qualities like strength, vindictiveness, and invincibility. For example, Eleke, the most powerful mask in the region, is praised as *Toru seighe seighe bite,* 'The cloth that does not fade;' his son is called *Indikoribo siko korighe,* 'You cannot catch a fish by the fin'; the slave bears the title *Omini loloa seibi,* 'A slave's vexation knows no limit'.

Some masquerades make the analogy to warfare or head hunting more explicit by claiming prerogatives war gods once bestowed on men who had taken human lives. Eleke dances to the drum rhythms of the *peri* warrior play with his priest, who wears a distinctive costume to signify the spirit's right to the status. One of his titles, *Waribaba-Kiribaba,* 'The wicked one, killing both family and outsiders', directly alludes to the *peri* title; an Olodiama man who killed

126

someone from another group reported to Egbesu's shrine in Ikebiri, where he sacrificed a slave.

Though highly entertaining, these performances convey messages about socially acceptable behaviour. Boasting about how many lives they have taken helps masks like Eleke establish their credentials as effective judicial agents, but many masquerades suggest an ambivalence about physical violence. Maskers seldom portray warriors as heroes; in fact, many openly mock and ridicule them by taking their behaviour to a cartoonish extreme. Parodying an institution devoted to taking human life may be a way of easing tensions created by the cultural emphasis on masculine aggression.

Masks In order to impersonate water spirits, Ijo dancers wear costumes designed to alter appearance and make them look less human. Most costumes incorporate carved wooden headpieces, though one Nembe masquerade features bronze ones believed to have been made by water spirits (Alagoa 1967a: 151). Cloth and raffia masks are also common.

The oddly juxtaposed features of guitar fish, skates, and other members of the ray family may have suggested the forms of the composite headpieces for which this region is best known.

Typically, anthropomorphic features, including eyes, mouth, and a skull-shaped forehead, project aggressively from a flat base, which may also incorporate an assortment of fins and other forms suggestive of marine animals or reptiles. Secondary heads and figures may be added to represent the spirit's family members or followers. Several small terracotta found at Ke in the Kalabari area and dated to around 1000 AD, contain the seeds of the style and may have served as models for earlier masks (Alagoa 1974/75).

More naturalistic masks also appear throughout the region. The Nembe claim they originally named their dance societies after fish and other animals and made masks to represent them (Alagoa 1967: 145), so zoomorphic masks may even predate the composite type. Anima's associated with water—including fish, crabs, lobsters, hippopotami, and crocodiles—appear most frequently, but dancers can also represent bush cows, leopard, antelopes, monkeys, and other land animals. Anthropomorphic headpieces also appear, and look much like miniature versions of the images found in nature spirit shrines. *Angala pele* or 'Mangrove cutter', a character who appears in numerous villages, including Akede in Qyakiri, often takes the form of a figure, an upright head, or tower of heads. All masks, including those of land animals, represent water spirits.

Virtually all Ijo headpieces rest on top of the head instead of covering the face. Masks of the composite type and some of the zoomorphic variety, like the heads of goats and bush cows, 'face' skyward. Informants usually explain that masks worn in this manner resemble spirits floating on the surface of the water, but fish could also have suggested a horozontal orientation. The costume helps to create the impression of a spirit who has come out of the water to play. It typically includes a *siko,* or fish tail, which is made by mounting a cane framework over the dancer's buttocks. Padding may be added at his waist to accentuate his stomach. Locust bean rattles are strapped around his ankles, and he carries objects like cutlasses, sticks, or switches in his hands.

Performances

Performers draw on a variety of dramatic devices to portray water spirits as unruly beings under the precarious control of drummers, dance demonstrators, and attendants. Each performance incorporates certain songs, dance steps, and tableaux, but allows for a great deal of improvisation. Maskers must not only execute the set dance sequences, but exploit the element of surprise in order to add interest to, or 'sweeten' the event. For instance, although maskers from one

Olodiama town are said to dance so well that they can make their leg rattles speak, people have criticised them for failing at dramatic improvisation. Musicians and others who participate in masquerades by singing, dancing, and playing with the masks, also contribute to the success of a performance.

Performers use a variety of methods to build excitement before a masquerade. In Ondewari, a mullet mask appears early in the day to alert people that Ofurumo is coming out to play; a song sung by his supporters warns little fishes to run and hide. Excitement builds when the giant shark appears on a raft pulled toward town by a canoe loaded with musicians. In Olugbobiri the three masks in the Ungozu group tease the audience by appearing to come out of their shrine, then retreating, before their priest finally pulls them out one at a time. In many cases, the actual performance begins when the masks slash through a palm frond fence *(fanu)* and enter the arena. Fences of this type once kept evil forces from entering Ijo villages, so this device reinforces the idea that wild spirits have invaded the community. Once the masks have come out, they take turns executing the steps indicated by a dance demonstrator and chasing spectators through town Drummers alternatively call on masks to dance, incite them to chase people with machetes, and pet them to cool their tempers. They sometimes deliberately provoke the maskers by insulting them in drum language; in some cases the musicians sit behind a pole fence designed to protect them from attacks, but masks can still slash at them through the openings or dart around to the other side. The Ijo believe fences of this type also act as barriers which prevent possessed maskers from going inside the river to join their water spirit friends.

The possibility of being cut adds excitement to the performance, and some spectators — especially young boys — invite the masks to attack by taunting them, then run away or plunge into the water to avoid being cut. When masquerades incarnate powerful spirits, however, many choose to watch from a

129

safe distance in canoes off shore. In some cases, maskers may be restrained by ropes; in Korokorosei, people explain that a type of mask called Alagba would cut people mercilessly if it were not restrained, because it lacks the wooden headpiece which impedes the movements of other masks.

Egberi The Ijo often embellish masquerades with stories, or *egberi,* which portray events in the lives of water spirits, but simultaneously mirror or mock some aspect of Ijo culture. The plots are quite simple and assume the audience's familiarity with the situations portrayed. Although highly entertaining, they can convey social criticism or instruct people on proper behaviour (Alagoa 1967:155); for example, stories which revolve around the taming of troublesome spirits — a common theme — may comment on society's need to control overly aggressive individuals.

Plots often draw on everyday situations, including domestic dramas. For example, in a masquerade once performed in Korokorosei, a woman prepares to return to her mother after a quarrel with her husband. She loads her canoe, one possession at a time, while compound members try to talk her out of going. She insists on leaving, but is finally persuaded to stay when she comes back to collect a forgotten article.

Stories which feature dramatic encounters between men and animals are also popular, and nearly always involve a taming theme. Oki, or Sawfish, one of the most popular characters in the Delta, stars in a masquerade of this type performed in Akede. The Ijo regard Oki as a great spirit living in the sea, but fishermen are eager to catch sawfish. When struggling with one which has been caught on their line, canoes loaded with supporters may try to convince him to come out by pouring libations, beating drums, blowing horns, and calling, "Oki, come up. Let us play. The tide has already ebbed". When he co-operates, they kill him.

130

The masquerade capitalises on the comic aspects of the situation by staging the hunt on land: Oki's canoe parades along the waterfront while songs and drums repeat the fishermen's invitations to come out to play at ebbtide; when he comes ashore, he alternately chases after spectators with his cutlass and dances in the arena. Finally, a fisherman appears there with his canoe and begins stalking Oki with his net. After many comic mishaps, the masker's headpiece becomes entangled in a fishing line; assistants help haul the captured fish into the canoe, where the fisherman pretends to slit its throat, but Oki stages a triumphant comeback to conclude the performance.

Festivals Bayelsa communities celebrate occasions ranging from traditional funerals to modern holidays like Christmas by staging festivals which feature spectacular masquerades, regattas, dance performances, and various kinds of competitions. Traditional rites like fishing festivals may have lost much of their ritual importance, but continue to express civic pride. Even local wrestling matches may be transformed into artistic events by processions on land and water which involve drumming, dancing, and singing. The Ijo traditionally marked the start of their new year by renewing their shrines and performing purification rites designed to rid the town of pollution left behind by the annual floods. This period generally falls in November, but additional rites may be necessary later in the dry season, for this is the time when epidemics threaten riverine communities. These celebrations often include masquerade performances and other sacrificial rites; for instance, at Ekowe in Bomo, raffia masks travel the length of the main avenue to sweep the town clean.

In other communities, sacrificial canoe effigies know as *ikiyan aru* are loaded with offering, carried through town, then either mounted along the riverbank or floated downstream. Smaller canoes may be deployed secretly in the dead of night, but larger ones, like *Opu Ikiyan* (Great ikiyan) of Olugbobiri, are the centrepieces of dramati c performances. Residents of Azuzuama take another approach by appealing to Wonyinghi whenever epidemics threaten their community. Shrine members communicate with the creator through a divination ladder, renew the medicines in the shrine's medicine pot, and parade through town, using a small broom to sweep away disease. Many communities stage dry season fishing festivals in connection with sacred lakes. Traditionally, these take place at intervals of three or seven years and include offerings at shrines, as well as drum calls to warn spirits living in the lake to leave, so that none will be killed. Although the event no longer seems to involve much ritual importance, residents of Osiama in Oyakiri still perform a festival for Lake Adigbe; it begins with a masquerade that averts evil by harnessing the power of a voracious tiger fish that once devastated the lake.

Traditionally, Ijo clans were united primarily by war gods who required annual festivals. Although most have been abandoned, some groups have continued to maintain shrines. In the late seventies, a festival held at Olobiri in honour of Egbesu, the war god of Kolokuma, featured masquerades and a ceremonial war canoe reminiscent of the immense craft that once plied the Nun. An annual festival held nearby at Odi, which is also in Kolokuma, celebrates a modern battle: the killing of a wild buffalo which threatened the town several decades ago. The *Ogori Ba Uge*, or Buffalo Killing Festival, observed the same year included the deployment of a raffia mask to purify the town, a performance by a group of local maskers, gunpowder salutes, and a dance barge with reggae music provided by a local band. In 1991, notices which appeared in Lagos newspapers to announce that year's festival promised visitors a 'Love Boat-Like' atmosphere.

Beyond Bayelsa

Relatively little sculpture from Bayelsa State has been collected or published because few expatriates have visited there. Nevertheless, the region is noted for producing some of the largest figure carvings and masks in all of sub-Saharan Africa, as well as originating a style which may indirectly have inspired Cubism, a revolutionary movement in Western art. The Sharp-edged geometry that characterises much of the sculpture from the region resembles the projecting forms and voids in the works of the European Cubists, and Piscasso, who 'invented' Cubism, owned two masks in the Ijo-influenced style adopted by the Grebo of Liberia.

Unfortunately, many of the objects that have entered western collections lack proper documentation. The Fowler Museum of Cultural History at UCLA has a number of Ijo figures, but no record of their origins. The Merseyside County Museums in Liverpool house the largest collection of Bayelsa sculpture outside Nigeria, and it is also one of the earliest. A colonial officer named A.A. Whitehouse assembled it in the vicinity of Wilberforce Island during a 1903 punitive expedition which targeted a 'pirate' known locally as Bebeke-ola. Another early group of figures once belonged to King Josiah Constantire Ockiya of Nembe. He commissioned the carvings as portraits of himself and his family, but turned them over to Bishop Crowther of the Church Missionary Society when he converted to Christianity in 1877. Their naturalism contrasts markedly with the prevailing 'Cubist' style, and may have been affected by exposure to the figureheads of European ships (Fagg 1963: plate 111). The figures have been dispersed: one is now in the National Museum of African Art in Washington, D.C.; another in the Manchester Museum in England. Finally, while the traditional art forms continue to develop within the communities through change and continuities, a new breed of artists in direct dialogue with western and international traditions have come into being. These artists, trained in western or western style art schools, are yet inspired and motivated by local culture and traditions. The best known of this generation are the late Jubilee Owei, painter and portrait artist; the late Jackson Waribugo, whose monumental sculptures are to be seen in Port Harcourt and several riverine urban centres; and Pius Waritimi, the experimental sculptor and art teacher. These young artists follow in the footsteps of the veteran literary artist, and winner of the Commonwealth prize for poetry, Gabriel Okara, all of whose work is rooted in the local cultural heritage.

CHAPTER 10

OGBOINBA:
THE IJAW CREATION MYTH[†]

Gabriel Okara

There was a large field, and in the field stood a large Iroko tree with large buttresses. From the sides of the field appeared men and women in pairs. Each woman held a broom, and each man a bag. As the women swept the field the men collected the dirt into their bags. And the dirt was Manillas. Some collected ten or more Manillas, others none, and when the field had been swept clean, they disappeared back into the sides of the field, pair by pair. The sky darkened, and there descended on the field a large table, a large chair and a large 'Creating Stone', and on the table descended a large quantity of earth. Then there was lightening and thunder; and Woyengi (Our Mother) came down and sat on the chair and placed her feet on the 'Creating Stone'. And out of the earth on the table Woyengi molded human beings. But they had no life and were neither man or woman and Woyengi asked them one by one to choose to be man or woman, each according to his choice.

Next Woyengi asked them one by one, what manner of life each would like to lead on earth. Some asked of her riches, children, short lives, and others, long and peaceful ones and all manner of things. And these Woyengi bestowed on them one by one, each according to his or her wish. Then Woyengi asked them one by one, by what manner of death they would return to her. And out of the diseases that afflict the earth, they chose each a disease. To all their wishes Woyengi said, "So be it".

In this group of newly created men and women, were two women. One of them asked of Woyengi rich and famous children, and the other asked for only powers, mystic powers that would have no equal in the world—and this woman was OGBOINBA. Both wished to be born in the same town.

[†] This Chapter was first published in *Black Orpheus*, **2**, 9-17, January 1958.

Woyengi finally led these created men and women to two streams, streams flowing to the habitation of man. One was muddy and the other clean. Into the muddy stream she led those men and women who had asked of her riches, children and all other worldly possessions. Into the clean stream she led the other men and women who had asked of her no material possessions.

And so Ogboinba and other women came to be born in the same town and became inseparable friends. They ate and played together, sharing all their secrets and grew up as children of the same parents. But Ogboinba was an extraordinary child. At that early age she could heal and cure and had second sight. She understood the tongue of birds and beasts, trees, and even of the blades of grasses. She prophesied and performed things strange and wonderful. Her name at that early age became a by-word on every lip.

When Ogboinba and her friend came of age, each took to herself a husband. Soon Ogboinba's friend had her first child. But Ogboinba had no child and was not expecting any. Her power however continued to increase. Her friend became pregnant the second time and soon delivered the second child. Still Ogboinba had no child but her fame went far and wide and she became the most sought after medicine woman of all time. In spite of this, she was worried. She felt her life bare - she wanted a child. She wanted children and yearned for them.

Her friend had more and more children according to what she had asked of Woyengi, and Ogboinba loved them all and took care of them with her mystic powers as if they were her own children. But she had no satisfaction from that. She wanted children of her own to care for. Her mystic powers however continued to increase just as she had asked of Woyengi. But there was no joy in her heart.

After a time, she could not bear it any longer and secretly resolved on a journey, a journey back to Woyengi to recreate herself. So one day, she went into her medicine room, where she also kept her mystic powers, and asked them one by one if they would accompany her on the journey she had resolved to undertake. All of them showed signs of their willingness to accompany her. But out of them all she only picked the most mystic powers and the most powerful medicines and put them into a bag. She then went to her friend and told her she was going on a short journey. When her friend heard this, she became aggrieved. For, since they came to know themselves as friends they had not parted, even for a day. So the prospect of not seeing Ogboinba for a day and more made her very sad. Her children too would then have no more protection. But Ogboinba assured her that even though she would be away the children would still be under her protection and that nothing would harm them. With this, Ogboinba took leave of her and started her journey to Woyengi.

So along a wide road Ogboinba walked with her bag of mystic powers and medicines slung over her shoulder. A wide road that led to a large sea. Between her and the sea was a forest, a mangrove forest where dwelled Isembi, the king of the forest. As she walked along, day and night without food or rest she soon heard the noise of the sea, the waves breaking on the shore. With each forward step the noise came nearer, the kingdom of Isembi.

As she picked her way through the forest she heard a voice, a voice calling from behind. She turned, and it was Isembi. "Are you not Ogboinba I've heard so much about?' he asked raising his voice. Ogboinba replied, "There is only one Ogboinba in the world, and I am the one." "If you are", Isembi said, "You've not treated me well by not calling on me as the king of this place. We've all heard your fame and to find you here like this is an honour. Come with me to my house". So Ogboinba went with Isembi to his house and there was well entertained to a sumptuous meal and palm wine. After the entertainment, Isembi asked Ogboinba where she was bound for. In reply Ogboinba said, "I've not given birth to a child since I was married many years ago. So I 'm going to Woyengi to ask her to recreate me." "Turn back from here," said Isembi "It's impossible to see Woyengi when you are yet alive. Your journey is vain, so turn back from here". But Ogboinba said her mind was made up and though she was yet alive, to see Woyengi she must. With that she left Isembi and his wife to continue her journey to the sea. But she only went a little way and came back to Isembi and asked him if he would try her powers with his. Isembi said he will not fight a woman and asked Ogboinba to go on her journey. Still Ogboinba insisted on the trial of powers, adding that though a woman she was challenging him. This enraged Isembi and he said, "Haven't you heard of my powers? I'm Isembi the king of the forest. How dare you, a woman, challenge me?" With this he went to his medicine hut. There, all his pots of medicine showed negative signs. But he was not to be daunted by such things when a woman was concerned. So, in spite of the warnings, he went out armed with such medicines and mystic powers that he required, to fight it out with Ogboinba.

Outside, he asked Ogboinba to try her powers on him first. But Ogboinba declined. She said that he Isembi, being the elder of the two, should try her first with all he had. Isembi, being anxious to do away with Ogboinba without any further delay, repeated his incantations. Immediately Ogboinba's bag became empty of all her powers. Her mystic powers and the powerful medicines had all gone! She at once repeated her own incantations circling round and round to counteract Isembi's powers. As she did so, her mystic powers and medicines returned to the bag, one by one. And when she came to the end of her incantation they had all returned to the bag and she was once more herself. Then she asked Isembi, to try her with more of his powers. But Isembi had nothing more powerful than the powers he had already used on her, and asked her to try him with her powers if she had any. So Ogboinba started to repeat her incantations circling round and round. As she did so, all the powers and medicines of Isembi entered her bag one by one and Isembi himself fell down dead. Then she slung her bag over her shoulder and proceeded on her journey. But as she was leaving Isembi's wife called her to come back and wake her husband for her. Ogboinba did not want to go back, but Isembi's wife entreated and wept. This touched her heart, she being a woman with a husband herself, and Ogboinba went back and after repeating some of her incantations Isembi woke. Then Isembi's wife further pleaded for the return of her husband's powers and medicines. But that Ogboinba said she would not do and left to continue her journey.

Soon, Ogboinba left the mangrove forest behind her and reached the town of Egbe by the sea shore. And as she passed by somebody hailed her from behind. She looked back, and it was Egbe. "Is that not Ogboinba I've heard so much about?" asked Egbe. In reply, Ogboinba said, "There is only one Ogboinba in the world, and am the one." "Your fame has been here before you," continued Egbe. "Come to my house," he said. "I'm the king of this town and you can't pass like an unheard of person through my town. Come, I 'll entertain you." Ogboinba went with Egbe to his house and there was well entertained with plenty of food and palmwine. After the meal Egbe asked Ogboinba what the object of her journey was. Ogboinba replied, "I've been married many, many years but have not had a child. I've not for once been pregnant; so I'm on my way to meet Woyengi to recreate myself." Egbe was astonished on hearing this and counseled her, "Turn back from here. No person who is alive ever sees Woyengi." But Ogboinba said that she had made up her mind to see Woyengi and there was nothing in the world to stop her. With that she slung the bag of powers over her shoulder and left to continue her journey. But she came back presently to Egbe and asked if he would like to try his powers with hers. Egbe was enraged on hearing this and was choked with anger. When he found his voice again he said with contempt, "Go your way, you are a woman." But Ogboinba would not budge and insisted on their trial of powers, their mystic powers.

Egbe had not been known to have refused a challenge from any living being and this, though from a woman, he would not now overlook since she insisted on it. So he said, "Come on, and let's see who's more powerful, you, a woman, or Egbe, the king of the town and the sea shore." With this he went into his medicine hut and armed himself with the most powerful medicines he had always used in overcoming all those who had come to challenge him. He came out and asked Ogboinba to try him first. But Ogboinba, as usual, refused and asked him to try her first with all he had. And Egbe, not wishing to make this a long argument, at once repeated his long incantations. As he did so Ogboinba's bag became empty of all her powers. All her powers plus those of Isembi she had acquired had been scattered away in all directions by Egbe's mystic powers. On noticing this, she at once repeated her counteracting incantations moving round and round in a circle. And as she did so, her own powers plus those of Isembi returned to the bag. When she found all the powers complete in her bag, she stopped her incantations and asked Egbe to try her once more with more of his powers. But Egbe had nothing more powerful than the powers he had already used and asked Ogboinba to try him with her own powers. So Ogboinba started her incantations and before she had been half way through, all the powers of Egbe had entered her bag and when she stopped, Egbe fell down dead. With Egbe on the ground she left to continue her journey to the sea with the bag containing her powers plus those of Isembi and now those of Egbe, slung over her shoulder. But Ogboinba had taken only a few steps when she heard Egbe's wife weeping and calling her to come back and wake her husband for her. Ogboinba taking pity on her went back and after repeating her incantations brought Egbe back to life. Egbe's wife again pleaded for the return of her husband's powers. But Ogboinba refused this request and resumed her journey to the sea.

And so Ogboinba came to the brink of a mighty sea. A sea that no living person had ever crossed. A sea with high waves breaking thunderously on the shore, a turbulent roaring sea. It struck terror into the heart of Ogboinba. But cross she must; there was no other way.

As she stood regarding the sea, it spoke! "I am the mighty Sea that no one ever crosses." Then Ogboinba with all the audacity at her command said, " I am Ogboinba, the only Ogboinba in the world, and am on my way to Woyengi. I must cross". The Sea replied, "I am the mighty Sea that no one ever crosses. I'll take you into my bowels if you dare." Ogboinba was terrified by what she heard. But she wanted a child and the only way to get it lay in her seeing Woyengi. Nothing would stop her.

Urged on by this resolve, she made for the sea and as her feet touched it, waves rolled towards her and submerging her feet, began to rise. Soon it was up to her ankles and then to the knees. Fear gripped her. Ogboinba could not move herself, she was powerless, hopeless, and just stood there watching herself being swallowed up by the sea. It continued to rise and soon the sea was up to her waist. She raised her bag of powers above her head. Still the sea continued to rise and now it had come up to her chest. Still the sea rose until it came up to Ogboinba chin. Then she cried out in fear. "O Sea, are you really the sea that no one crosses?" and repeated her incantations. As she did so, the sea immediately started to recede. Soon it had come down to her waist, then to her knees and then to her feet. So it continued to recede until the bed of the sea lay bare exposing the gods and spirits of the sea. Then Ogboinba, with her bag of powers, picked her way across. On the other side, she turned to the dry bed of the sea and commanding it back to its place, continued her journey.

The next Kingdom that she came to was that of the Tortoise. Tortoise was the king and lived with his parents Alika and Arita and his wife Opoin. Tortoise saw Ogboinba as she walked along and calling her, wanted to know if she was not the Ogboinba he had heard so much about. Ogboinba gave her usual reply, "There is only one Ogboinba in the world and I am the one." "Come, let's go to my house," Tortoise said, "We've heard so much about you and we all want to know you. Please come." So Ogboinba went with Tortoise to his house and there had food and palm-wine with the family. After the meal Tortoise, always curious, asked Ogboinba, "What has brought you over this side of the sea? No human beings live this side, pray, tell me, what has made you come like this?" Ogboinba replied, "I have had a husband for many years but have not had a child, so am on my way to see Woyengi and ask her to recreate me." "Go back from here," Tortoise advised, "No one who is yet alive sees Woyengi." But Ogboinba said her mind was set on seeing Woyengi and that she would not turn back. Then Tortoise warned her. "Beyond me live the gods Ada and Yisa the great, the most powerful, who possess two small 'creating stones'. Nobody ever goes that way. So end your journey here." But Ogboinba said nothing would stop her shouldering her bag, which had now become quite heavy with the powers she had acquired on the way, left to continue her journey.

After going a little way she came back to Tortoise and confronted him with her usual request for a trial of powers. Tortoise did not take it seriously and asked her to go on the journey she had set her heart on. But Ogboinba insisted on their contest of powers. Then Tortoise began to boast, "Haven't you heard of me?

My name has gone round the world for my mystic powers. If you really mean what you say, I'm ready for you." With this he went into his medicine hut and armed himself with his powerful medicines and mystic powers. When he came out Ogboinba asked him to try her first with his powers. But Tortoise said that could not be, for he was a man and besides he was the Tortoise. Still Ogboinba insisted on his starting the contest and so Tortoise began his incantations. As he repeated them Ogboinba's bag dropped from her hand to the ground and all the powers were dispersed to all the corners of the world. Ogboinba at once repeated her own incantations to counteract the powers of Tortoise. First the bag returned followed by the powers, one by one. When the powers had all returned Ogboinba asked Tortoise to try her with more of his powers. But Tortoise had no more and asked her to do her worst if she could. So Ogboinba began her own incantations and before she had gone half way. Tortoise had fallen down dead and all his powers had entered Ogboinba's bag. With Tortoise lying on the ground Ogboinba shouldered her bag and made to continue her journey. But before she could take a step she was stopped by the weeping voice of Opoin the wife of Tortoise. Opoin begged her to wake Tortoise her husband for her. Ogboinba took pity on her and waking Tortoise with her mystic powers resumed her journey.

On and on she walked day and night, with her bag of powers over her shoulder. Soon she reached the kingdom of the god Ada. Ada, on seeing her asked her if she was not the Ogboinba he heard so much about. Ogboinba gave her usual reply. "There is only one Ogboinba in the world and I am the one." Ada said he would not allow her to pass on like that without entertaining her, she being a famous person. So Ogboinba, as usual, went with Ada to his house and there was well entertained to a meal of yam, plantain and all other choice dishes that befitted a god and king to entertain a famous person. After the meal Ada asked Ogboinba, "What has brought you here where only the gods dwell? This place is virgin to the feet of human beings. No human being has been here before you; tell me, why have you come?" On Ogboinba giving the reason for her journey, Ada said, "Turn from here for no one ever sees Woyengi, not even me." But Ogboinba would not turn, for her heart had been hardened by desire for a child. So she told Ada she would not now turn and would continue her journey to Woyengi wherever she might be. With that Ogboinba shouldered her bag of powers and left to continue her journey. But she came back presently to Ada and asked him if he would try his powers with her own. Ada was surprised – a human being to seek contest of powers with a god! All he said was to ask Ogboinba if she really meant what he had heard her say. Ogboinba replied by repeating her request. Ada went into his medicine hut. But there, there the contents of all his medicine pots had turned to blood! "No" he said, "I wont heed this; she is but a human being". So heedless of the warning his medicines gave him, he came out and asked Ogboinba to try him with her powers. But Ogboinba refused and asked him instead to try her first. Ada, moved with anger, at once directed his powers on Ogboinba. Ogboinba fell down apparently dead. But she regained her consciousness after a while and began her own incantations. As she did so all the powers of Ada left him and entered her bag, and in the end Ada fell down dead. Once more victorious, Ogboinba shouldered her bag of powers and continued her journey.

On and on she walked, a lone figure on a wide road, until she reached the kingdom of Yasi, the great and powerful god. Yasi had seen her and had watched her progress a long way away even before she came within range of human vision. So as she wandered along on his territory Yasi asked her if she was not the Ogboinba he had heard so much about. Ogboinba gave her customary reply. "There is only one Ogboinba in the world and I am the one." Yasi said, "I am the king of this place; come and I'll give you food and drink." So Ogboinba went with Yasi to his house and there again was well entertained to a meal of rare dishes and palm-wine befitting a king to entertain a famous guest. After the meal, Yasi asked Ogboinba why she had come on her journey. Ogboinba told him, "I'm a woman as you see, and have been married many, many years, but I am without a child, I've not even for once been pregnant. I am barren so am on my way to see Woyengi, and ask her to recreate me." Then Yasi said, "No living person ever sees Woyengi, so turn from here". But Ogboinba would not listen and said she would continue her journey. With that she shouldered her bag of powers and set forth. But she came back presently and made her usual request for a contest of powers. Yasi could not believe what he had heard and asked Ogboinba to repeat what she had said. Ogboinba repeated her request. Yasi then replied in anger, "I am the greatest and the most powerful of all gods. How dare you, a human being, a woman, throw a challenge at me for a contest of powers. Go your way, you're no match for me." But Ogboinba insisted on the contest. So Yasi in fury went to his medicine hut. But there the contents of his medicine pots had turned to blood! "This can't be." He whispered in surprise, "She's but a human being. She shall have the contest she wants," and taking the two small 'creating stones' came out and asked Ogboinba to begin. But Ogboinba, as was her wont, refused and asked Yasi to begin. Yasi at once directed the force of his powers on her. Ogboinba's head was immediately severed and went up into the sky while her body remained standing, holding the bag of powers. Soon the head came down from the sky and rejoined the body and Ogboinba was once more whole and alive. Ogboinba then asked Yasi to try her with more of his powers; but Yasi having none more powerful than the ones he had already used asked Ogboinba to try him with her powers. So Ogboinba started to repeat her own incantations, moving round and round in a circle. The force of her powers also severed the head of Yasi from the body and it went up high into the sky. But his body remained standing on the 'creating stones' and Ogboinba noticing this, pushed it down on the ground. When Yasi's head came down from the sky there was no body for it to rejoin and it smashed itself on the ground. So Yasi the god was overcome and Ogboinba was once more victorious. But she would not move on without the 'creating stones' and made for them. She tried to lift them but found that they could not be moved, small as they were. For a moment Ogboinba was at a loss what next to do. Then she repeated some of her incantations and immediately she was able to move them and lifted them on to her shoulder. She then moved on, bent double, with the weight of the 'creating stones', and the bag of powers to the kingdom of Cock.

Cock, on spying Ogboinba from the roof of his house flew down and asked if she was not the Ogboinba every body even the gods had heard so much about. On Ogboinba giving her usual reply Cock said, "If you are the Ogboinba I've heard about, come in to my house and I'll give you food and palm-wine befitting me as king to entertain you." So Ogboinba, never refusing, went to Cock's house and there was well entertained to a meal of choice dishes and palm-wine. After the meal Cock asked Ogboinba the reason for her journey and she said, "I've been married many, many years but am without a child. I possess all the parts of a woman but I am barren. I am barren and so I'm on my way to see Woyengi face to face and ask her to recreate me." "Journey no further," said Cock, "No one ever sees Woyengi alive. Mine is the last kingdom. Beyond me is void; so turn back from here," Cock advised. But Ogboinba said she would journey on, and shouldering her bag of powers and the 'creating stones' took to the road. Presently she came back and asked Cock for a trial of powers. But Cock liked nothing better than a show of powers and at once began to boast. "My fame has gone round the world for my powers. I am the ruler of the first and the last kingdom of things that die. Come, and I'll show you my powers; nothing pleases me more." So boasting, Cock flew to the roof of his medicine hut and crew several times, summoning his powers. Then flying back, stood in front of Ogboinba and asked her to begin. But as was usual with her she refused and asked Cock to begin. Cock, not wishing to prolong matters, began with all he had at once. Immediately Ogboinba became bare of all powers and Cock noticing this, began boasting once more. "Mine's the first and the last kingdom of things that die. How can you stand my powers?" As he boasted thus, Ogboinba had repeated her own incantations and had got all her powers back. She asked Cock to try her with more of his powers. But Cock said he had used all the powers he had and if Ogboinba had any powers to match his, it was now her turn to use them on him. As Ogboinba repeated her incantations, Cock's town suddenly burst into flames and burned down to ashes.

Thus with more powers in her bag, Ogboinba journeyed beyond Cock's town and kingdom, the last kingdom of things that die, to the large field. The large field with the large Iroko tree with the large buttresses. There she hid herself in the buttresses of the Iroko tree and watched.

Soon, men and women appeared in pairs from the sides of the field. The women carried brooms and the men, bags. As the women swept the men collected the dirt into their bags. When the field had been swept clean they disappeared back onto the sides of the field, pair by pair. As she waited, she saw the sky darken and a table descend on the field followed by a chair and a large 'Creating Stone'. Then there was lightning and thunder. And Woyengi went through her usual process of creation and led the men and women to the two streams, the streams that flowed to the habitation of man. Then Woyengi returned to the field and ordered up the table, the chair and then the 'Creating Stone'. These things went up one by one into the sky. And when Woyengi was about to ascend, Ogboinba rushed out from her hiding place and challenged her to a contest of powers. Then Woyengi said:

"I know you were hiding in the buttresses of the Iroko tree, I saw you leave your town on your journey to find me. I saw you overcome all living things and gods on the way with the power that I gave you which were your heart's desire. Now it's children you want, and for that you have come to see me and to challenge me to a contest of powers. You have come to challenge me, the source of your powers, strong hearted Ogboinba. I now command all the powers you acquired on the way back to their owners".

Immediately Woyengi made this pronouncement, Isembi, Egbe, the Sea, Tortoise, the gods Ada and Yasi, and Cock, all had their powers back. And Ogboinba, overcome by fear, turned from the face of Woyengi and fled in panic to hide in the eyes of a pregnant woman she met on the way.

On seeing this Woyengi left Ogboinba alone, for a commandment she had given to men that pregnant women should never be killed —and she would not now violate it because of Ogboinba. So Woyengi turned and went up to her abode. But Ogboinba remained in hiding and is still in hiding not only in the eyes of pregnant women but in the eyes of men and children as well. So the person that looks out at you when you look into somebody's eyes is Ogboinba.

CHAPTER 11

CANOES AND FISH IN ỊJỌ
ART AND RITUAL †

Martha G. Anderson

Paddle, paddle
Oh! Paddle
The carp was paddling
A canoe underwater
But the paddle
Broke in his hand
Paddle, paddle
Oh! Paddle

-Song sung by Ijo women while paddling to and from their farms

The extreme wateriness of the Niger Delta begs questions about the relationship between environment and culture. Though natural surroundings do not predetermine worldviews, art forms, or other cultural phenomena, they clearly limit the choices people make regarding such fundamental matters as modes of production and transportation. To a greater or lesser extent, they also define how people experience the world. Moreover, most peoples do ascribe a sometimes capricious agency to their environment. According to Croll and Parkin, whose study of ecocosmologies explores a paradox:

> people create contrasting categories such as "village" and "bush" to explain their environments, then look for ways to build bridges between them (1992,3).

Numerous studies indicate that work plays a critical role in the construction of social identity and cultural values (See Wallman 1979; Pahl 1988). Canoeing may not be a mode of production, but the canoe - called the "river horse" because of the role it plays in riverain cultures - often functions as a tool in facilitating production (Plate 11.2).

---

† This Chapter was first published in: Anderson, M.G. and P.M. Peek (Eds.) 2002. Ways of the Rivers: Arts and environment of the Niger Delta. Los Angeles: UCLA Fowler Museum of Cultural History. Chapter 4, pp.133-161. It is reprinted courtesy of the Fowler Museum, UCLA, and of the author.

Plate 11.1: *Water spirit headdress. ljo. Wood, brass, and ceramic. L: 71.8 cm. Krannert Art Museum and Kinkead Pavilion, University of Illinois, UrbanaChampaign; Faletti Family Collection. Carved in the clean geometric style of the Central and Western ljo, this composite mask mixes skull-like human features with aquatic references. The element behind the head evokes either a fish tailor the stern of a canoe. The brass inlays on the forehead and the porcelain eyes suggest the bright, reflective surface of the water and the supernatural powers of the spirits who reside within it. Miniature masklike faces, such as adorn this headdress, typically represent the children or followers of the spirit.*

Plate 11.2: *Canoe headdress. Urhobo. Wood, pigment, and fiber. L: 60 cm. FMCH X86.2504; Anonymous Gift. Numerous Delta masquerade headdresses suggest canoe forms or incorporate scaled-down canoes, such as this Urhobo example. The neighboring ltsekiri make a version so large that it requires two maskers to support it. Headdresses representing modern conveyances bicycles, helicopters, and airplanes-have also become popular, and some Kalabari ljo headdresses depict ocean liners.*

Paddling a canoe constitutes a form of work, because it involves the expenditure of energy and fulfills several other criteria of a "folk work" concept (Wallman 1979, 4; Wadel 1979, 370). Notions of work and play, however, vary from culture to culture and need not be well defined or mutually exclusive. As in Wallman's example of jogging (1979, 3), both canoeing and fishing - another activity appropriate to a riverain

148

environment - may be work or recreation, or simultaneously work and recreation, depending on the mental attitude of the fisher or paddler. To complicate matters further, the actions of play can denote combat and other forms of "not play" (Bateson 1972, 177-93), and those of art and ritual often mimic or "play on" work.

The Ijo (or Izon) living near the center of the Delta place a high value on physical labor, particularly on work done outside the village (N. Leis 1964, 34, 79-80, 120). Adults communicate the idea that work is good in itself by encouraging children to practice paddling canoes and fishing, just as they reward them for working on "play farms" (P. Leis 1962, 119, 125, 145, 171). Moreover, one of many Ijo canoe proverbs observes that, "When you are paddling toward good things, the way does not seem long" (*Ebi iye timiyoyou alaghe*). This saying, which can refer to a variety of tasks, not only confirms that the Ijo regard canoeing as labor but also suggests that they perceive varying degrees of work, depending on the destinations or goals that they pursue (Plates. 11.3 - 11.5).

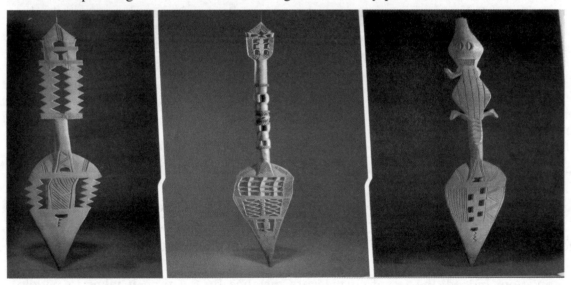

Plate 11.3: *Paddle. Itsekiri. Wood. L:124.5cm. FMCH X63.8; Gift of Mr. and Mrs. Peter Furst*

Plate 11.4: *Paddle. Ijo or Itsekiri. Wood. L: 165.1 cm. FMCH X65.4509; Gift of the Wellcome Trust.*

Plate 11.5: *Paddle. Ijo or ltsekiri. Wood. L: 139.7 cm. FMCH X65.4522; Gift of the Wellcome Trust. Paddles such as these, which are often labeled "Benin River, " seem to have been produced by the Itsekiri. Local carvers probably made them as souvenirs for the traders and colonial officials who visited the region during the late nineteenth and early twentieth centuries. Openwork designs render most of them nonfunctional, and none shows signs of use. Many combine intricate geometric patterning with figurative motifi, including reptiles, aquatic creatures, and occasionally human figures (Kathy Curnow, personal communication, 2001).*

In a cross-cultural analysis of work, Schwimmer uses the Orokaiva of New Guinea, who garden, as an example of the close identification that can occur between work and moral values, and between workers and the environment in which they labor (1979, 294-302). Although Ijo living in freshwater regions of the Delta farm and perform numerous other land-based tasks, they tend to identify more closely with the riverain environment, especially the dugout canoes that enable them to maneuver and the fish that provide a prized part of their diet. They do not have a canoe/fish mythology comparable to the garden mythology of the Orokaiva, nor do they consider canoeing or fishing to be "a religious act like a sacrament," but the many ways they transform both activities into art and ritual suggest that they closely identify with and define themselves through them. Thus canoes and fish prove to be particularly useful vehicles for exploring how the Ijo respond to their watery surroundings.

Canoeing

The canoe operates as a common denominator of Ijo village life. In regions of the Delta where roads are nonexistent and even footpaths limited to seasonal use, canoes still provide the primary, and sometimes the only, means of transportation and intervillage communication. Indeed, the Ijo often measure distance by the time it takes to paddle from one point to another. Canoes seem so fundamental to their riverain lifestyle that some assume the art of canoe making "came from heaven with them" (Alagoa 1970, 323). Nearly every traditional occupation practiced in the freshwater region - including fishing, farming, distilling gin, and trading - necessitates water travel. Canoes also serve other mundane functions that are harder to classify, satisfy social and recreational needs, and figure prominently in performances of various types. Canoe effigies even play a role in shrines and rituals, as will be discussed below.

Learning to paddle seems to be largely a practical matter without religious or mythic significance, but the process plays a critical role in shaping the way people view the environment. As children, the Ijo begin to differentiate between two zones, the rivers and forests, and to associate different levels of danger with each. Though both present physical hazards, beliefs about their supernatural occupants clearly contribute to cultural attitudes expressed toward each realm. Parents teach children to fear not only the dangerous animals that live in the forests but the violent spirits who lurk about there, waiting to shoot people or club them to death. In contrast, despite concerns that adults express about water safety, youngsters learn to regard the rivers as a comparatively safe place to play. Although the Ijo occasionally blame evil spirits who reside in the rivers for killing people, stories about water spirits typically portray them as benevolent beings who live in fantastic underwater towns. Encounters with them, which often take place in canoes, tend to be magical, not fatal, affairs.

The Ijo first experience canoe travel at the age of about two or three months, when mothers begin taking their infants on almost daily trips to their riverside farms. As soon as they develop sufficient motor skills, children imitate adults by using sticks or small paddles - the only toys they own aside from dolls - to propel benches, planks, or verandah rails; they then hone their skills by pretending to help paddle real canoes. As all Ijo are expected to master the skills needed to maneuver a canoe, this type of play serves a practical purpose. Adults correct children who hold their paddles incorrectly or use them awkwardly, and praise those who match the rhythm and motions of adults. After youngsters learn to swim, at the age of about four or five, parents allow them more freedom to practice on their own (P. Leis 1962, 99, 109). By the time they reach eight, they have usually developed sufficient dexterity to manage steering; one seven-year-old boy reported that he had already visited a neighboring town on his own, a trip that takes over an hour each way when traveling at average speed - about five kilometers an hour.

Plate 11.6: *Canoe headdress. Ogoni. Wood, iron, pigment, glass mirror, and incrustation. L: 69.5 cm. Indiana University Art Museum; Rita and John Grunwald Collection. Photograph by Michael Cavanagh and Kevin Montague @ Indiana University Art Museum. This sculpture probably served as a masquerade headdress. The "house," which adds to the impression of domestic harmony, may have been included to shelter the canoe's occupants or cargo from the sun or rain on a long journey. The "wife" sits at the stern, like most Delta women, and acts as her husband's chauffeur.*

Given this emphasis on canoeing, one might expect the Ijo to have developed athletic contests based on ability, but the only competitions staged at present require contestants to paddle across a river while blindfolded, which results in comical meandering and does not test skills used in real life. Nevertheless, people who spend a good part of their lives in dugout canoes acquire excellent balancing skills, and boys and young men sometimes show off their agility by walking the length of a canoe along its edge.

As they grow older, children begin to use canoes for work as determined by gender: boys use them primarily to fish (Plate 11.7) and girls to assist their mothers in farming, fishing, and trading ventures.

Plate 11.7: *Boys fishing from canoes. Photograph by Martha G. Anderson Korokorosei, 1991.*

Although men continue to use canoes, their wives more frequently own them, because they bear primary responsibility for feeding their families. Women do the bulk of the fishing and need canoes on a regular basis to commute to their farms, which may be three or more hours away from the village. In fact, they spend so much time in canoes, they occasionally give birth in them; some families name babies who arrive in this fashion Arukubu, "Inside-bottom of canoe," or Arukeghezi, "Born in a canoe," to recall their origins. In addition, women typically serve as chauffeurs. If a husband and wife travel together, the man may offer to help paddle, but his wife typically takes the stern position and does at least the bulk of the work (Plate 11.6).

Women generally acquire their first canoe soon after they marry; others follow as needed at intervals of about seven years, depending on the type of wood used and the care taken in maintenance. Some men specialize in carving canoes, but a husband who lacks money to buy one for his wife may carve it himself, if sufficiently motivated and physically equipped to accomplish the arduous task (Plate 11.8).

Plate 11.8: *Firing a dugout canoe so it can be bent into shape. Photograph by Martha G. Anderson, Korokorosei, 1991.*

Demand nearly outstrips supply, for carvers often claim to sell canoes faster than they can produce them; however, work is so physically demanding. A canoe of average size sold for about forty and thefts do occur. Remarkably, given the simplicity of the form, the Ijo can recall instances in which people visiting towns in other clans have spotted canoes stolen from friends back home.

A few men specialize in producing paddles, but traders also import them from other parts of the Delta. The decoratively carved paddles women once used can no longer be found in the Central Delta, and most now buy the simpler blank forms stocked by local tradesmen and take them to paddle painters for decoration. They generally choose to have their first names written on one side and their married names on the other, so paddle decoration becomes a statement about social identity as well as a means of marking personal property. Men use either the same type of paddle or a broader one, which requires more physical strength.

154

Canoes from Work and Play to Art and Ritual

The Ijo find innumerable uses for canoes. Besides transporting people, farm produce, fish, building materials, fuel, trade goods, corpses, unfinished canoes, and, until recently, the mail, they can serve as recreational vehicles. The Ijo even have an equivalent of a drive-in theater, for they sometimes watch masquerades from canoes (Plate 11.9).

Plate 11.9: *People watching a masquerade (Ungozu)from canoes on the river to avoid being injured by the masks. Photograph by Martha G. Anderson. Olugbobiri. 1992.*

When moored at the waterside, canoes provide convenient places to play, eat, launder clothes, bathe, and eliminate wastes. A spirit medium drawn to the river when possessed by water spirits collapsed in one during a performance staged at a town in Apoi clan in 1991. On land, canoes can serve as bathtubs for invalids and as containers for separating palm oil.

Thrifty Ijo reuse worn-out canoes by turning them into everything from sacrificial vessels to duck houses. In former times, residents of at least one clan loaded the bodies of women who had died in childbirth into old canoes, then took them into the river and capsized them (Amangala 1939, 12). Taboos enforced by Owei, a war medicine shrine in Ondewari, suggest other, mostly outmoded forms of recycling: Owei forbids any Ondewari man to use fragments of a broken canoe as Plates, firewood, or gutters designed to collect rainwater from roofs. According to his caretaker, he even kills people who eat food from anything used to bail canoes. On the other hand, the Nembe, who believe a particular type of wood brings luck to traders, patch new canoes with bits broken from damaged ones in hopes of transferring the older vessels' good fortune. Their inland neighbors, who provide them with canoes, may well share their beliefs about the magical and medicinal properties of various types of wood used to make them (Alagoa 1995,126-31).

Canoes also perform a variety of esoteric functions. Even those ordinarily employed in domestic duties can become vehicles for communicating with the spirit world. Diviners occasionally work by interpreting the movements of their canoes as messages sent by water spirit contacts, and followers sometimes employ them to carry sacrifices to water spirits, who indicate where offerings should be deposited by causing vessels to falter. A special type of canoe known as *ikiyan aru* functions as a sacrifice to rid communities of pollution, avert disease, and keep evil forces at bay. The Ijo, who describe these scaled-down effigies as "spiritual war boats," sometimes man them with crudely carved warriors armed with guns and cutlasses. They load the vessels with offerings of food and drink, then mount them on forked sticks at the riverbank or set them in the water to float downstream (Plate 11.10).

Plate 11.10: *A small sacrificial canoe (ikiyan aru) mounted along the riverbank to keep evil spirits and diseases from entering the town. Photograph by Martha G. Anderson, Korokorosei, 1992.*

Larger examples can approach the size of real canoes, and bearers often parade them through town - escorted by drummers and supporters singing songs - before deploying them at the waterside.

Several types of canoes can participate in a single ritual. Rites performed to appease a powerful Korokorosei water spirit after it has been invoked to punish an enemy or a criminal include an ordinary canoe, two sacrificial canoes, and a conceptual canoe. When the rite's sponsors arrive at the waterside, shrine members push their canoe back three times before allowing them to land. Before the all-important masquerade can begin, the priest and several followers set off in a canoe to position the *ikiyan aru* above and below the town. These "war boats" supposedly prevent evil spirits and other forces from disturbing the performance. Finally, one of the masks executes a "canoe dance," as described below.

Plate 11.11: *Funeral party returning from the bush with firewood. The wood will be used in cooking food for visitors during the mourning period. Photograph by Martha G. Anderson, Korokosei, 1979.*

Though the Ijo do not ordinarily embellish canoes, they seem well aware of the aesthetic potential of aquatic expeditions, even when such excursions serve ostensibly practical functions, like collecting medicines for curing rituals or fetching firewood for funerals (Plate 11.11). They also take advantage of the river as a performance space by using canoes and other watercraft as moveable stages. Dancers perform on the river as their boats travel to and from funerals or festivals. Wrestling canoes announce their arrival by parading noisily along the waterside to the accompaniment of drums, songs, and vociferous boasting, and spectacular war canoes highlight festivals of various types, recalling the Ijos' warlike past. Manned by dozens of "warriors" sporting war paint, brandishing weapons, and chanting war songs, they assault the senses by incorporating sporadic gunfire and smoking medicines, along with conspicuous arrays of raffia fronds and other "bulletproofing" charms (Plate 11.12).

Plate 11.12: *A war canoe appearing at a festival for Egbesu, the war god of Kolokuma clan. Photograph by Martha G. Anderson, Olobiri, 1978.*

 Because water spirits, like people, navigate the waterways by boat, maskers - who represent them, can also exploit the intrinsic drama of aquatic travel by arriving from the water (Plate 11.13).

Plate 11.13: *A masker representing Oki, or "Sawfish," traveling to the arena in his canoe. Photograph by Martha G. Anderson, Akedei, 1992.*

When drums on shore hurl abuses at them, they threaten onlookers with their machetes. Some express their annoyance and eagerness to attack by cutting their paddlers for failing to move quickly enough.

The irony inherent in the idea of canoeing on dry land obviously appeals to the Ijo. In a dance introduced by bush spirits and copied by numerous villages in the region, young girls make paddling motions with appropriately shaped dance wands, then transform a bench into a canoe (Plate 11.14).

Plate 11.14: *A girl pretending to paddle a bench during a dance called Inamu, which was originated by bush spirits. Photograph by Martha G. Anderson,*

They paddle it, dance on it, drag it around the arena, and eventually tumble onto the ground when they "capsize" it. Masquerades often include similar parodies. Some reenact fishing expeditions, as discussed later in this chapter. A performance formerly staged at Korokorosei in Olodiama clan portrays the aftermath of a domestic quarrel. The wife prepares to leave for her father's house by loading her canoe one article at a time, while onlookers beg her to stay. At first their entreaties only make her more annoyed, but they finally persuade her to remain when she returns home to collect a forgotten machete. In another performance a mask named Eleke (who also figures later in this chapter) simply acts out the lyrics of a song, leading his followers in a dance that carries them forward and back, forward and back, to illustrate the way his canoe moves in the water.

References to canoeing also abound in songs and stories, especially those involving water spirits. Canoes, paddles, and fishing spears feature prominently in shrines, including those of certain bush and water spirits (Plate 11.15).

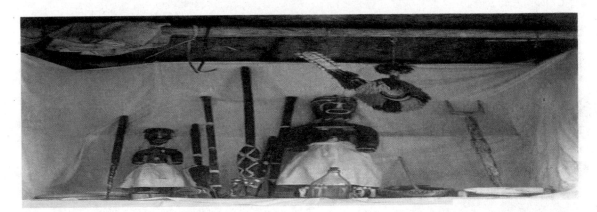

Plate 11.15: *Shrine for a water spirit named Adumu. Photograph by Martha G. Anderson, Keme Mbiama,* 1979.

In some cases, priests explain these articles as the gear their spirits use when traveling or fishing; in others they identify them as spirits or their emblems, noting that some turned up in the water and were subsequently "proved" by diviners to be water spirits. In addition, residents of the area periodically report seeing spirit canoes, which mysteriously appear then vanish, in the rivers. Diviners in Korokorosei pour libations for Bolighe, or "Unfinished canoe," a bush spirit who owns and protects a sacred lake behind the town, "just like a father or guardian cares for his child." People say that another Bolighe - this one a water spirit - resides in an estuary west of Amassoma.

Given the importance of canoes and canoeing to the Ijo, one might expect the canoe itself to have symbolic significance along the lines of the Akan stool, which is closely associated with the soul of its owner (Fraser 1972). A prohibition against sitting in the canoe of a woman whose husband has recently died seems to attest to a similar identification, but it may also refer to the symbolic role the canoe plays in the funerary context. The Ijo conceive of passage to the land of the dead as a trip across a river. Songs sung at burial rites sometimes allude to this journey, and mourners toss sacrificial coins

160

onto the masquerade field to pay Saibo, the ferryman. One song likens death to a voyage and focuses on the reluctance of the living to part with the deceased: the dead person begs "Load the things in the canoe and let me paddle away," as family and friends try to persuade him or her to stay. Women may dramatize the lyrics by using a bench as a canoe.

The canoe obviously serves as a "vehicle for ideas" for the Ijo, as it does for the Fante of the Ghanaian coast (Coronel 1979) and the riverain Bamana of Mali (Ganay 1987), who similarly invest canoes with symbolic meanings or employ them in funerals, festivals, and other contexts divorced from the workaday world (Plates 11.16, 11.17).

Plate 11.16: *Water spirit headdress. Eastern Ijo. Wood and iron nails. L: 39.3 cm. Charles and Kent Davis. The shape of this mask resembles Kalabari headpieces worn by a character called Igbo (see interleaf H), but its knoblike eyes and clean geometric lines may indicate an origin further to the west. It lacks references to reptiles, but, as in Igbo headpieces, its overall form clearly alludes to a canoe, a popular motif in both water spirit shrines and masquerades.*

Plate 11.17: *Water spirit headdress. Eastern Ijo. Wood.L: 35.5 cm. Charles and Kent Davis. Another variant of Igbo (cf Plate 11.16), this highly abstracted headdress exaggerates the canoelike shape of the jaw and transforms the forehead into a rectangular block.*

Nevertheless, the "concept of the canoe" does not appear to permeate "practically every aspect of social life" among the Ijo, as it does among the Fante, nor does it serve as a fundamental metaphor of and for Ijo social life, as it does for the distant Murik of New Guinea (Barlow and Lipset 1997). Though the Ijo have "canoe proverbs," canoe metaphors do not dominate or pervade either social or ritual contexts, nor do canoes play an important role in signifying rank and prestige.

By assigning emblematic meanings to canoes and exploiting their visual drama, the Ijo and other water-oriented people celebrate and reaffirm their aquatic lifestyle; moreover, as new modes of water transportation become available, new "traditions" - and meanings - emerge. An announcement that appeared in a Lagos newspaper in 1991 conjured up pleasant memories of a festival at Odi in Kolokuma clan, which the author attended in 1978. A barge, packed with colorfully garbed revelers and presided over by a "priest" and "priestess" dressed to resemble members of a popular Christian sect, moved up and down the river while a band played a local version of reggae (Plate 11.18).

Plate 11.18: *Barge loaded with dancers at the Ogori ba uge, or "Buffalo killing festival."*
Photograph by Martha G. Anderson, Odi, 1978.

The advertisement endowed the 1991 event with a "Love Boat atmosphere," suggesting that the Ijo identification with water travel guides their taste in American television programs.

The word for canoe, *aru,* now designates a variety of vehicles. Drawings collected informally from Ijo children mix fantasy with reality by including: "engine" boats *(inzini aru)* and launches *(beke aru,* or "European canoes"), a common feature of Delta rivers these days; helicopters *(join* or *fuin aru,* "air" or "flying canoes," also used for airplanes), which are seen carrying oil company employees in and out of the Delta from time to time; and cars *(biye you aru,* or "land canoes"), known to many only from trips to the mainland or videos, which have recently become available in even the most remote of Delta villages. Despite children's fascination with these more technologically advanced modes of travel, canoes and paddles feature prominently in almost every drawing - an indication of the central role they continue to play in village life.

Fishing

As might be expected, most residents of Central Delta villages not only fish but enthusiastically proclaim fish to be their favorite food. This dietary passion even extends to the ancestors and bush spirits, who often request fish as offerings. Indeed, area schoolteachers sometimes complain that they can only induce adults to attend

163

educational programs by promising to teach them how to catch more fish. Women sometimes dance as they carry their fish into the village from the bush, rejoicing in their good fortune.

The Ijo obviously identify with fish on a deeper level, for references to fish and fishing turn up almost as frequently in verbal and visual arts as do those to canoes and canoeing. Fishing implements appear alongside canoes in shrines for water spirits, and wooden fish occasionally join paddles as props for dancing. Like other animals, fish can serve as metaphors for human beings; numerous proverbs hinge on either fish or fishing, including one that some masks have adopted as a praise name: *I inimi indi siko kori indi baagho-unfe*, or "You can't catch a fish by its fin." Moreover, as a form of hunting, fishing can stand for war, as it does in a war song sung for a bush spirit named Benaaghe, enshrined at Azama in Apoi clan. The lyrics employ the metaphor of a fishing expedition to chide him not to be lazy when called to battle:

> Benaaghe my father
> I've prepared my fishing basket
> And taken it to the lake
> Anyone who doesn't fish
> Is afraid of the lake

That fish should play such an important role in the lives of a riverain people is hardly surprising; more so are the results of a survey conducted in the late 1950s. In contrast with the saltwater region, where men and women fish nearly full-time, only one man and a few women living in the freshwater village of Korokorosei considered fishing to be their primary work (P. Leis 1962, 16; N. Leis 1964,83-84). Indeed, Korokorosei men rarely fish while living at home, because, as already noted, their wives are charged with feeding their families. Nevertheless, numerous residents of this area have spent extended periods fishing along the coast, whether by joining fishing expeditions to the adjoining saltwater region or by traveling as far away as Calabar or Duala to reside in fishing camps for several months or years at a time (see Wilcox, forthcoming); thus, neighboring groups tend to think of the Ijo as fishermen.

Ijo men and women employ different methods of catching fish. Women fish using lines, traps, and baskets. The average woman manufactures between sixty and a hundred traps each season, adjusting the spacing of the struts to suit various prey, including prawns, lobsters, tilapias, and various types of swamp fish. The most ambitious may set over eighty traps at each of three locations, checking them daily, or at least every other day. In addition, women sometimes work together in groups, digging ponds to strand fish during the annual floods or driving them to one side of a shallow pond so they can be harvested more easily.

As soon as girls acquire sufficient dexterity, they assist their mothers by weaving traps and paddling their canoes. Young boys fish using the same methods as their mothers but gradually become more proficient at techniques employed by men, such as weaving and throwing nets, setting spring traps, and spearing fish at the waterside (see Plate 11.7). Like their sisters, they turn over any of the larger fish they catch to their mothers; thus, "fishing provides the principal means by which boys can contribute to household needs" (P. Leis 1962, 18, 142).

Women smoke fish for future use and occasionally for sale to traders, but their families' prodigious appetite for fish guarantees that they seldom have a surplus (P. Leis 1962, 18). In fact, many blame current shortages on modern technology. Older residents of the area agree that the Kainji Dam, located far up the Niger at Bussa Rapids, has significantly lowered flood levels in recent decades. Though reliable data is lacking, studies confirm that damming up the river has significantly lowered flood levels and nutrient inputs, and cut sedimentation rates by about 70 percent (Human Rights Watch 1999, 53, 97; Okonta and Douglas 2001). Exploitation of the Delta's rich oil reserves has proved to be far more devastating. Oil producers and government agencies made little attempt to monitor environmental changes before recent protests threatened to disrupt production. They now admit that hundreds of oil spills and ton after ton of industrial sludge dumped into the sensitive environment over nearly four decades have fouled both the coast and the Delta's inland waterways. Other activities involved in oil production - including dredging, operating large craft, constructing roads and canals, and flaring natural gas - have also damaged the environment (see Human Rights Watch 1999, 5, 56-97). One environmental watchdog group warns that constant flaring now causes acid rain to fall in the Delta one day in every ten, in addition to blanketing it with layer after layer of fine particles and reputedly cancer-causing soot (Environmental Research Foundation 1997). Overpopulation undoubtedly contributes to the diminishing returns reported by fishers; although reliable data are lacking, visual evidence alone suggests that area villages have expanded significantly over the past fifty years. In any case, shortages had become so severe by the 1970s that the Ijo began to supplement their diets with "ice fish," frozen cod imported from Northern Europe and purchased from mainland suppliers.

Fish and the Spirit World

In addition to observing taboos against eating specific types of fish as dictated by various shrines, the Ijo associate certain varieties with the spirit world. They freely kill and eat most catfish, which normally have brownish skin, but return rarer white ones (called *pere*) to the water, for they consider them to be manifestations of a water spirit known as Binipere, or "Rich man of the water." They identify cichclids of the genus *Hemichromis* and characins of the genus *Alestes* as tricksters; instead of alerting water spirits that dry season is approaching, these cunning fish sometimes deceive them, causing them to become stranded on land when the floodwaters recede. A spirit medium who used to dive underwater to bring out a live fish while possessed still sings songs about various types of fish, including one that terms *Hemichromis,* "the trickiest man in the world." People also regard certain events involving fish as ominous; for example, if a small saltwater fish travels upriver and lands in a canoe as it leaps homeward, the occupant(s) will consult diviners or herbalists. This occurrence, which is unusual enough to be considered remarkable, may signal the onset of a minor illness.

The Ijo widely believe that anyone who excels at an endeavor has backing from the spirit world. Hunters, wrestlers, and warriors derive support from a variety of bush spirits, but rumor holds that successful fishers and traders have assistance from a prominent water spirit named Adumu, who is considered to be an aspect of the python (see Plate 11.15). A song sung for him conveys his whimsical nature-typical of water spirits in general-by relating a remarkable incident:

> As I was fishing, Adumu
> The owner of a small canoe
> Came straight to my canoe and took a fish
> Oh Adumu, what a wonderful story

A local school teacher invoked the old saw about carrying coals to Newcastle to explain why people would find the idea of the patron of fishing stealing fish to be so amazing. People can visit his shrines and those of other spirits to request help in fishing, or they can consult herbalists for charms to improve their luck.

Conversely, fishers repeatedly disappointed by the size of their catch might suspect sorcerers of burying charms to spoil their fishing. Some claim that witches (*ifoinyou* or *fuinyou,* lit. "the people who fly") - believed to have become active in the area around 1950 - can also pose problems. According to a tale that circulated in the *1970s,* a Nembe man's *foin* mother got him a *foin* wife to help her claim him as one of her victims. One day he returned home from fishing to find his wife mortally wounded. She told him to gather people so she could tell them her secret before she died; once he had done so, she revealed that his mother had instructed her to turn herself into a shark, tear his net, then end his life by pulling him underwater. The plan backfired when the twine broke from his spear as he hurled it into her body. She showed him the wound she had suffered, then told him what to do to free himself from his mother's spell and regain the money he had lost due to her efforts. Like all good tales, this one alludes to eyewitnesses and provides enough details, including a reference to the wife's burial at the coast, to lend credibility.

Confronting large marine animals, such as sawfish and sharks, from canoes, as men do, would seem treacherous enough without the risks posed by witchcraft. Women fishing deep inside the forest swamps are also considered to be exposed to great danger, for bush spirits are notoriously hostile creatures, certain to inflict severe punishment on anyone who defiles their territory, transgresses their laws, or simply annoys them. Even if women assiduously avoid fishing at locations the spirits have claimed for themselves, they risk catching fish that have ventured outside; misfortunes can beset an entire family if someone kills a fish that incarnates a spirit. On the other hand, women can take advantage of the bush spirits' vindictiveness by invoking them to punish people who steal fish from their traps.

In a recent twist on tradition, the Ijo have begun calling on Christian prophets to address problems with evil spirits blamed for spoiling their favorite fishing spots. An Olodiama woman disappointed by the size of her catch once asked a prophet to rid a place in the bush of "juju" but realized this plan had backfired when she and her sister no longer found any fish in traps set there. Fearing more serious repercussions from the spirit world, they turned to the priest of a bush spirit shrine, who determined that the holy oil the prophet dumped on the house of "a very great spirit" had landed directly on its head. After the priest propitiated the irate spirit and others in the vicinity, the women began catching fish again.

Many Ijo villages recognize spirits as the owners of lakes located in the surrounding forests (Plate 11.19).

Plate 11.19: *People displaying a portion of their catch at the fishing festival for Lake Adigbe. Photograph by Martha G. Anderson, Ossiama, 1992.*

The presiding spirits usually permit access during festivals held at periodic intervals (often every seven years, the number considered to be most ritually auspicious). On these occasions, drums alert spirits to leave, so people can fish freely. The festival for the lake known as Dabiyeyinghi (lit., "Mother of kolas") commemorates a local legend about two hunters who witnessed a bush spirit funeral there and returned home to teach their townspeople how to perform the rites. Before fishing begins, Korokorosei residents anoint a cane coffin with chicken blood and set it on poles in the lake. In a festival for Danghanlughu, or "Tall palms," a lake behind the same town, people beg permission to fish from a shrine dedicated to that section of forest, erect two figures along the path to the lake, and leave offerings of fish for them when they return. In both cases, participants sing as many songs as possible and beat drums throughout the entire day. In a third instance, residents of Amassoma in Ogboin clan say that crocodiles once prevented people from fishing in Lake Adigbe, so the community sent a slave inside the lake to deliver a sacrifice; after killing the slave, the crocodiles became calm and allowed people to fish. Nevertheless, each quarter of the town mounts a war canoe before fishing begins, suggesting that people must wage a symbolic battle against the lake's spirit owners over control of fish.

Water Spirits and Aquatic Masks

Most Ijo now consider themselves Christians, but the idea of a different world inside the Delta's rivers and creeks continues to captivate them. Some tell stories about encounters with aquatic spirits or describe marvelous, underwater towns they have visited in person or in dreams. Although these tales usually portray water spirits (*biniyou*, "water people," or *bini orumo*, "the water spirits") as more agreeable than their volatile counterparts in the forests, they live in a very different environment and resemble the Ijo less closely in both appearance and tastes. People often describe them as beautiful, light-skinned beings with long, flowing hair, but they can also materialize as animals, composite creatures, and objects that turn up in the water. In keeping with their image as wealthy "foreigners" with close ties to trade, many prefer offerings of corned beef and Sprite to local produce, such as plantains and palm wine, and designate manufactured goods—including dolls, cloth, and white saucers—to serve as their emblems. Of the major spirits, only Adumu, who is said to be dark-skinned and amphibious, calls for figurative images. Others, including Binipere, choose to remain in the water and do not even have shrines.

The term *owu* (or *ou*, depending on the dialect in question), means mask, masquerader, and masquerade dance. All *owu* represent aquatic beings, although only a few are believed to incarnate them. Interestingly, however, masks neither conform to the stereotype of the beautiful, light skinned mermaid nor capitalize on import symbolism, suggesting that they may represent an older conception, as well as a distinct category, of water spirits. Most maskers wear wooden headpieces (*ou tibi*) that depict water spirits in one of several ways: (1) as composite creatures that mix skeletal human features with aquatic motifs like crocodilian snouts and sharklike fins (much like "bush monster" masks found elsewhere in Africa) combine the horns, tusks, and gaping jaws of land animals; Plate 11.20); (2) as bush cows, goats, and other land animals, as well as reptiles and aquatic animals (Plate 11.21); and (3) as human figures and heads (Plates 11.22, 11.23).

Plate 11.20: *Water spirit headdress. Ijo. Wood and pigment. L:52.1 cm. FMCH X65.9041; Gift of the Wellcome Trust. This headdress would have been worn horizontally, with its skull-like face looking skyward. Like most composite types, it incorporates references to the aquatic world, including fins and a flaring form at the rear that could allude either to a fish tail or a canoe prow.*

Plate 11.21: *Water spirit mask, crocodile. Delta peoples. Wood. L:145.1cm. Iris and B. Gerald Cantor Center for Visual Arts at Stanford University; 1984.225 Gift of Victor and Paula Zurcher. The crocodile is a favourite at performances staged throughout the Delta. It appears alongside sawfish and sharks in Abua and Ekpeye masquerades, but the forms of crocodile masks checkerboard patterns on their skins are quite similar. A generic "Delta" attribution therefore seems advisable resemblance to documented examples.*

Plate 11.22: *Multibeaded water spirit headdress. Ijo. Wood, pigment, and incrustation. H:59.7 cm. Indiana University Art Museum: Gift of Toby and Barry Hecht, 89.24.3. Photograph by Michael Cavanagh and Kevin Montague © Indiana University Art Museum. Ijo headdresses represent hundreds of characters, many confined to single communities. This one probably represents Angala pele, or "Mangrove cutter," who appears in villages throughout the region. Ost masks vigorously chase spectators, but Angala pele—whose name implies his ability to slice through even the toughest wood—is so hostile that he must be restrained by ropes or surrounded by attendants armed with sticks.*

Plate 11.23: *Janus water spirit headdress with feathers. Ijo. Wood and feathers. H:54 cm. Peabody Essex Museum. Photograph by Jeffrey Dykes. Following a pattern seen among neighbouring groups in Southern Nigeria, Central and Western Ijo headdresses that take the form of anthropomorphic heads and figures usually project vertically from the masker's head. This janus-headed example, with its strongly projecting moughs, is reminiscent of aggressive bush spirit figures. It's feather ruff may allude to status in the* peri *warrior society*

Unlike anthropomorphic types, which stand upright, both composite and zoomorphic headpieces face skyward; the Ijo explain this unusual orientation by claiming that they look like spirits floating on the surface of the water. The majority of maskers alter their appearance further by mounting a structure known as a *siko*, or fin, over their buttocks (see Plate 11.32). By manipulating their costumes and assuming peculiar postures, they intensify the impression of beings from another world.

Western scholars have long considered the "cubist" conception of composite headpieces to be quintessentially Ijo, but zoomorphic types may well precede them. The Nembe and Okrika Ijo originally named their dance societies after fish and other animals and made masks to represent them (Alagoa 1967, 145; Ibuluya 1982, 208); moreover, the unusual forms of guitar fish, skates, and other members of the ray family, could have suggested the oddly juxtaposed features of composite headpieces. Finally, although the Kalabari admit to borrowing specific masquerades, including Oki, or "Sawfish," from the Abua (Horton n. d., 65-66, caption no. 13, 103), it seems more likely that they and other coastal Ijo groups, who work as fishermen, originally introduced fish masks.

The contrasting styles of masquerade headpieces may seem antithetical, but abstraction and naturalism coexist in many Ijo villages (Plate 11.24).

Plate 11.24: *Masks of different types appearing together at a festival for Kolokuma Egbesu, the clan war god. Photograph by Martha G. Anderson, Olobiri, 1978.*

Masquerade ensembles not only mix composite and zoomorphic types but often include one anthropomorphic figure (Plate 11.25).

Plate 11.25: *Water spirit headdress with janus figures.Delta peoples. Wood. H: 66 cm. FMCH X78.124; Anonymous Gift. This headpiece with its janus form each figure baring its teeth-and its surmounting animal-apparently a monkey-resembles certain Ijo bush spirit images. On the other hand, the overall softness and delicacy of the features might indicate an origin among neighboring Edo or Igbo peoples on the northeastern fringes of the Delta.*

The term "naturalism" should be qualified, however, for artists typically simplify forms and take great liberties with such details as the number and position of fins, so that the fiercest animals take on a whimsical or even cartoonlike appearance. The Ijo do not consider the relative naturalism of a mask to be an issue, given their belief that water

173

spirits can materialize as anything from fish and mermaids to sticks of wood, iron pots, and sewing machines. When asked to account for differences in appearance, owners invariably explain that headpieces either resemble the spirits they represent or conform to instructions issued by the spirits themselves. Moreover, though maskers representing fish usually imitate their behavior, most depict predatory fish-sharks, barracuda, mackerel, and penfish - and chase spectators like composite and human types do.

Masking

Masking provides the best opportunity for people raised on tales of water spirits to glimpse inside their fascinating underwater universe. Masquerades not only bring these wonderful beings to life but compound the central paradox of masking-masker as man/not man - by bringing them on land (Plate 11.26).

Plate 11.26: *Water spirit headdress, Pipligbo. Kalabari Ijo. Wood. H. 34.3 cm. Krannert Art Museum and Kinkead Pavilion, University of Illinois, Urbana Champaign; Faletti Family Collection. This mask wears a British-style "crown" composed of a tortoise flanked by coiled snakes. The Kalabari believe that water spirits can materialize in the form of animals, and all reptiles are considered to have strong ties to water spirits. Ikaki the tortoise, a notorious trickster features in stories told throughout the Delta. The small heads on the cheeks of the mask allude to the spirit's followers or children.*

The Ijo, who credit water spirits with the invention of masking and particular masquerades, often tell of people who in the past watched water spirits dancing on distant sandbanks, stole or copied their masks, and returned home to stage the masquerades for their townspeople. Some accounts feature abductions by water spirits who teach their captives how to perform masquerades; others tell how spirits approach people as they travel by canoe, then return to them in dreams to offer instruction on songs and dance sequences. Diviners consulted about unusual phenomena can also communicate the instructions of spirits.

Residents of Ondewari tell a typical story about the man who introduced their Ofurumo, or "Shark," masquerade, some years before his death in 1936. A man known as Kperighada was fishing at Kongogbene in the Cameroons, when he vanished for seven days. When he reappeared, he told people that he'd been kidnapped by water spirits, who taught him how to dance a masquerade. He returned to [his hometown] Ondewari, where he called the elders together to inform them of the water spirits' ultimatum that he must perform the masquerade or he would die.

As in this instance, spirits often threaten their human sponsors with death if they do not agree to perform masquerades, but they also offer rewards; people often claim these performances avert evil spirits and disease and bring children and prosperity to their communities. When asked if masks demand sacrifices, an Ijo friend emphatically responded that masks are sacrifices. In addition to providing entertainment on secular occasions, they appear at funerals to accompany the dead into the afterworld; at purification ceremonies to sweep towns clean of pollution; and at performances held to call off enshrined spirits after they have been invoked to punish criminals or settle disputes.

Surprisingly, even though masquerades derive from the spirit world and involve a variety of sanctions and benefits, the spirits who introduce them may not be especially powerful or even particularly concerned about enforcing their edicts. For example, the custodians of a masquerade associated with a sacred lake arbitrarily changed one of the masks from a lake perch to a tilapia, a substitution that would be unthinkable in the rare instances in which masks are believed to be animated by deadly spirits, capable of killing performers for making the least mistake in carrying out their instructions. Because most masks simply imitate, rather than embody spirits, Christians often feel free to wear them, as well as to participate in masquerades as musicians, supporters, and spectators. Masking societies like Ekine or Sekiapu, which control masking among the Eastern Ijo, do not exist west of the Nun. Individuals, families, friends, and shrines can own masks, and anyone who wishes to join in performances can generally do so.

The Ijo call masquerades "plays" and refer to masking as "playing," reflecting their belief that spirits initiate masquerades largely out of a desire to associate with their human friends. Followers claim that even those exceptional masks that manifest deadly spirits delight in playing with their followers. Performances typically begin with drum calls, libations, or songs inviting people and spirits to come play. Spirits - like people - seem to enjoy the artistic aspects of these occasions as well as the camaraderie they provide. An elderly horn blower reminisced that when he was a young virtuoso, the spirits expressed their appreciation for his exquisite music by "entertaining" him with gifts of food, so that fish filled the surface of the river whenever he played for one of the masquerades.

Fish Masquerades

The Ijo may consider water spirits to be more playful and less troublesome than the irritable spirits who roam the forests, but neither variety is bound by society's constraints. Although masks representing aquatic creatures rarely appear outside the Niger Delta region, they belong to a broader tradition that embraces both the fearsome "bush monsters" seen in other parts of Mrica, including the Poro region of Liberia (Anderson and Kreamer 1989,47-49), and the "wild beasts" that appear in other parts of the world, including Europe (Poppi 1994,211). Like them, the aquatic creatures display threatening features, behave unpredictably, and aggressively attack people. Many enter the arena by slashing through palm frond fences (*fanu*) of the type that formerly shielded villages from evil spirits and other invaders. Armed with weapons, they spend much of their time chasing spectators.

Instead of taking the threatening demeanor of their aquatic monsters seriously, however, the Ijo tend to spoof it, finding humor in the way masks interact with other performers and members of the audience. The violence in Ijo masquerades tends to be of the cartoonish variety - exaggerated and mixed with liberal doses of slapstick. Though they can wound anyone who does not remain vigilant or run for cover when they approach, most maskers only play at being murderous. Nevertheless, the hostile, transgressive behavior they exhibit amounts to more than comic relief. Masquerades operate on the same principle as a type of ritual called *seimo* (to spoil), which attempts to beat back hostile spirits and neutralize their power. Indeed, maskers play much the same role as the spirit warriors who man *ikiyan aru,* the sacrificial canoes mentioned earlier.

The risk of injury keeps performances lively. The audience judges the success of a masquerade not only by the maskers' skill at impersonating wild spirits and executing complicated dance steps but by their ability to "sweeten" the performance by exploiting the element of surprise. Both drummers (who instruct maskers to dance or chase spectators in drum language) and dance demonstrators (who show maskers which steps to perform by executing abbreviated versions of each sequence) control a masker's movements to a certain extent, but he can interrupt a dance sequence to dive at the drummers through the pole fence provided for their protection or dart around it to attack them. He might go crazy, slashing wildly at his own supporters until others join forces to restrain him, only to follow this by locking one of his human friends in an affectionate embrace. He relentlessly pursues spectators but periodically returns to the sidelines, where he patiently awaits his turn at dancing.

The Ijo often embellish these performances with stories, or *egberi,* which ostensibly portray events in the lives of water spirits but simultaneously mirror, mock, or pay tribute to some aspect of Ijo culture: The plots, often conveyed through songs that summarize the action, frequently assume the audience's familiarity with the situations being portrayed. They tend to be quite simple, for the Ijo believe that an elaborate plot might spoil the drama (Nzekwu 1960, 140-41). Maskers can also act out a series of vignettes or simply pantomime characteristic behaviors, like a sawfish that responds to a drummer's instructions to "chase mullets" by executing a sequence of mincing steps. Most performances, however, package social criticism and messages about proper behavior in the guise of entertainment (Alagoa 1967, 155). In any case, the audience finds the masks' antics hilarious.

The drama of the hunt - which can conclude with killing, or capturing, or taming a wild beast - makes it a crowd favorite. Elsewhere, it usually involves subduing bush spirits, as in the Bie masquerade performed by the Dan of Cote d'Ivoire (Fischer and Himmelheber 1984, 89-94), or stalking land animals, as in the bear hunt masquerades mounted by Alpine villages in Europe (Pappi 1994, 211). Though composite masks can play this role in the Niger Delta, the Ijo and others often add a paradoxical twist by bringing aquatic animals on land (Plate 11.27).

Plate 11.27: *Water spirit headdress. Ijo. Wood, basketry, nails, and pigment. L: 97.5 cm. Seattle Art Museum; Gift of Katherine White and the Boeing Company, 81.17.530. Photograph by Paul Macapia. All composite headdresses represent aggressive-looking monsters, but the toothsome, crocodilian snout of this example suggests that it represents a particularly voracious spirit. The Ijo generally explain the mix of features on headpieces of this type by saying that they look just like spirits do as they appear when floating on the surface of the water.*

Masks representing freshwater fish are fairly common in the Central and Western Delta, but the formidable size, intimidating appearance, and rapacious behavior of large, predatory sea animals - which, according to the Ijo, sometimes become water spirits - make them particularly popular as masquerade characters. Perched atop the maskers' heads, they manage to look both preposterous and menacing; the acquisition of human limbs allows them to wield machetes and give chase on land.

Although introduced by spirits, fish masquerades, like other Ijo performances, often draw inspiration from real-life situations: after braving the shark-infested waters off the coast in their canoes, generations of fishermen have undoubtedly returned home to tell spellbinding tales of their heroic exploits. By reenacting expeditions of this sort, performers transform the work of fishing into theater, but instead of glorifying it, they parody the dangers involved in capturing fearsome marine animals and mock tales about the big fish that almost got away. Instead of contrasting idealized humans with monstrous animals, as masquerades sometimes do (Poppi 1994, 196), these performances typically expose human follies.

The Ofurumo masquerade Kperighada introduced to Ondewari (see above) irreverently models itself on a shark hunt. The young men who recently revived Ofurumo credit it with driving evil spirits from the village. It begins when Izeghe, a masker wearing a mullet headpiece, runs through town to the accompaniment of a song warning, "Sharks are coming so little fishes should run and hide." Excitement builds as spectators anticipate his arrival; they rush to the riverbank to watch a canoe tow him upriver on a raft, as crew members and assorted supporters sing and drum his praises (Plate 11.28).

Plate 11.28: *A caged Ofurumo, or "Shark," being hauled upriver while a fisherman and his wife circle his raft in their canoe. Photograph by Martha G. Anderson, Ondewari, 1992.*

As he and his retinue move slowly toward town, Ofurumo alternately dances and uses his machete to slash at the raffia-covered cage that contains him. Meanwhile, a fisherman and his wife repeatedly circle the raft in their canoe, as if stalking their prey. Each time the man throws his spear, the canoe capsizes, and the pair ends up in the water, acting out the lyrics of another song: "Anyone who spears this fish will upset his canoe."

After many dunkings, the performers come ashore, where Ofurumo's son and wife join him in dancing and chasing spectators. Their drum titles *Poupou-fi pou-fi*, "Force someone to give food," and *Fulo-opitei-ke-yei-pirifi*, "To remove all the fish and give fishless soup to one's husband" - suggest their antisocial dispositions and mischievous behavior, traits that typify nature spirits. The masquerade concludes with a pantomime in which the fishing couple reappears, dragging their canoe around the arena in pursuit of their prey. Even on dry land, they periodically capsize. Finally, after many misses, the man spears Ofurumo and hauls him into the canoe; remaining in character, he hawks his catch to members of the audience.

In the Central Delta, masks representing sawfish, dolphins, and sharks often only hint at the size larger marine animals can attain, partly because life-size headdresses would impede maskers when chasing spectators through crowded villages, as anyone who has ever attempted to maneuver a step ladder through a house can easily imagine. Ofurumo's supporters claim that he always wears a huge, cane-supported headdress on the raft but ordinarily exchanges it for a smaller, wooden one when he comes ashore. In the performance described above, Ofurumo and his son wore the larger versions on land because the wooden headpieces had deteriorated. Because of their increased width, the maskers kept getting trapped in rafters, narrow passageways, and the fence that protects the drummers. One suspects that the enormous masks found to the east of the Nun among the Abua, Ekpeye, and their closest Ijo neighbors perform somewhat less athletically than the smaller versions commonly used further to the west (Plate 11.29).

Plate 11.29: *Shark masquerade headdress. Delta peoples. Wood and pigment. L: 155.9 cm. Indianapolis Museum of Art; Gift of Mr. and Mrs. Harrison Eiteljorg, 1989. 893a-g. Delta residents consider sharks to be terrifying and awesome. Headdresses can depict generic sharks or specific varieties, including hammerheads, barracudas, and tiger sharks. Many masquerades reenact shark hunts, which simultaneously capitalize on peoples 'fear of these mammoth marine creatures and celebrate the courage and skill required in capturing or "taming" them.*

Another colossal marine animal, Oki, or "Sawfish," stars in masquerades performed throughout the Delta (see Plate 11.13). Named for its distinctive rostrum - a long, rigid blade with fourteen to thirty-four pairs of enlarged toothlike scales mounted along its edges - this sharklike creature is classed as a ray within the order that includes both types of elasmobranchs. Though sawfish have not been well studied, scientists recognize six species: some prefer the shallow, brackish water of lagoons, mud flats, and estuaries, and rarely ascend rivers to visit freshwater areas; others frequent freshwater systems and only occasionally visit the coast (Bigelow and Schroeder 1953, 15-42). Two species - one primarily saltwater *(Pristis pectinata)* and the other primarily freshwater *(Pristis perotteti)-inhabit* Delta waters, but artists take such liberties in portraying Oki that it is impossible to determine which variety a particular mask represents.

Though full-grown sawfish range from ten to twenty feet in length - a size that makes them menacing enough to coastal fishermen - their wicked looking snouts account for the extensive mythology that surrounds them in cultures scattered all over the globe, as well as for the tremendous popularity Oki enjoys in the Niger Delta. Despite rumors to the contrary, sawfish do not attack large animals and are incapable of "sawing" chunks out of their prey. Nevertheless, people have long associated them with warfare: several Oceanic groups once fashioned their "saws" into weapons, and a number of German and American vessels sported sawfish as insignia during World War II (McDavitt 1996).

Numerous Africans, including the Bidjogo, Akan, and Yoruba, revere sawfish or assign them supernatural powers. The Kalabari Ijo display their rostra in shrines as trophies, alongside crocodile and bush pig skulls (Matthew McDavitt, personal communication, 1998; Tasie 1977, pl. 3). Ijo living to the west of the Nun River regard Oki as a great spirit but are nonetheless eager to catch sawfish. When struggling to capture one caught on their line, fishermen sometimes bring canoes loaded with supporters, including women possessed by Oki, and attempt to lure the reluctant fish out of the water by pouring libations, beating his praises on drums, beckoning him with horns, and calling, "Oki, come up. Let's play. The tide has already ebbed." When he cooperates, they kill him.

As in the previous instance, the masquerade performed at the Western Ijo town of Akedei in Oiyakiri clan capitalizes on the comic aspects of the situation by transferring the action to dry land. Oki appears in a canoe, which parades along the waterfront while songs and drums repeat the fishermen's invitation to come out and play on the sandbanks. He taxes the audience's ability to suspend disbelief even further when he comes ashore (Plate 11.30).

Plate 11.30: *Oki, or "Sawfish," appearing in a masquerade sponsored by the author. Photograph by Martha G. Anderson, Akedei, 1992.*

There he chases after spectators with his cutlass and takes turns dancing with another mask that comes out to play with him.

The performance climaxes with a segment that reenacts the struggle described above: assistants help a fisherman drag his canoe into the arena, where he chases Oki around with his net. After many clumsy misses and mishaps, he nets the sawfish after the masker's headpiece becomes entangled in a fishing line. Assistants help haul the captured fish into the canoe, where the fisherman pretends to slit his throat (Plate 11.31).

Plate 11.31: *Having netted Oki, a fisherman cuts his throat. Photograph by Martha G. Anderson, Akedei,* 1992.

They carry Oki off, but he makes a dramatic comeback, triumphantly returning to the arena to play his part in the next segment. The mood now shifts from the humorous nonsense of the hunt to the serious business of preventive medicine: Oki grabs a baby, who awaits him in the center of the arena, then chops at it with his machete until someone comes to its rescue. A succession of mothers brings their babies to him, believing the ordeal will ward off illness and other dangers that account for a high rate of infant mortality in the region. The sequence confirms that the hunters, as inept as they may be, have succeeded in harnessing Oki's power for the good of the community. Spectators who participate in other masquerades might derive similar benefits, though most simply consider dodging the masks' blows to be an exhilarating form of play.

A masquerade associated with a sacred lake near Ossiama, another Oiyakiri town, represents one of the most sought after game fish in the world, the African tiger fish. These swift, rapacious, salmon-shaped characins whose knifelike teeth show even when their mouths are closed - have earned a reputation as the freshwater counterparts of the great white shark (McEwan 1997). Though not nearly as large as the aptly named "goliath," which can exceed four feet and a hundred-and-fifty pounds, *Hydrocynus vittatus,* the species found in the Niger Delta, can measure more than two feet and attack prey nearly the same size. Tiger fish sometimes hunt in packs, much like their South American cousin, the piranha.

This masquerade differs from Oki and Ofurumo in several respects. According to legend, a tiger fish and a crocodile took up residence in Lake Adigbe, which was formed by an earthquake, and frustrated the ancestors by devouring most of the fish. When local fishermen eventually caught Kabi, the voracious tiger fish, townspeople decided they should harness his exceptional hostility by carving him as a mask. They added headpieces representing *Uku*, or "Golden perch," and *Apedeu*, or "Lake perch" - which descendants later replaced with *Tabala*, or "Tilapia" -to complete a set of three, the number the Ijo regard as the most auspicious after the number seven.

Unlike the previous examples, the Adigbe masquerade does not tell a story; the secondary masks come out first to warm up the crowd, then Kabi, the vicious carnivore, enters the arena in a portable cage. After slashing through it with his machete, he takes turns dancing in the arena and vigorously chasing spectators (Plate 11.32).

Plate 11.32: *Kabi, or 'Tiger fish"* during *a performance of his masquerade sponsored by the author.*
Photograph by Martha G. Anderson, Ossiama, 1992..

The other masks also behave in typical *owu* fashion, abruptly switching from carefully controlled dance steps to wild rampages (Plate 11.33).

Plate 11.33: *Apedeu, or "Lake perch," during a performance of the Kabi masquerade.*
Photograph by Martha G. Anderson, Ossiama, 1992.

Christians now predominate in Ossiama, and the festival lacks the type of public fanfare formerly associated with events of this type, but some rites may still be performed privately at the shrine for Lake Adigbe. Though people still consider the spirit owner of the lake to be very powerful, the masks' ties with the shrine appear to be rather loose. Their caretakers simply store them in the rafters of their houses. They pour libations before dancing the masks but claim to do so only to make the performance interesting. The masquerade probably had more significance in the past; townspeople say, "We dance it New Year's Day," or "when the water is down [the floods recede], we set a date for the Adigbe fishing festival and dance it then. When we dance we say, 'You are a very hostile fish, drive away all evils from the town.'" This explanation confirms masquerade's role as sacrifice and establishes its ties to the ritual calendar, which coincides with the rise and fall of the Niger's branches. The new year begins a lunar month after the floodwaters crest. Elsewhere in Africa, masking and ritual mark critical stages in the agricultural cycle; people living in the freshwater regions of the Delta farm, as well as fish, and rites must be staged to clear away pollution left behind by the floods before planting can begin. Sacrifices, including masquerades, may be necessary at other points in the dry season as well, because this is when villages are most vulnerable to epidemics.

If even comical performances like Oki and Ofurumo can avert misfortune and bestow other benefits, those at the other end of the spectrum, which actually incarnate deadly spirits, draw on their perceived power to protect their followers and enforce the law. Masks of this type ordinarily remain hidden inside shrines that are off-limits to most local women, as well as to outsiders. When people invoke them to punish criminals, they respond by killing off relatives of the guilty party until the affected family agrees to make reparations and sponsor the costly performance required to nullify most invocations. The cowry-covered medicine bands (*egbe* or *gbinye)* that encircle the maskers' headpieces on these occasions not only empower them but visibly manifest their potency. Because possession and other ritual elements make their performances particularly compelling, other masquerades often mimic them by including "priests" and employing "medicines" to cool the masks' hearts when they become overheated from chasing spectators.

Eleke, the Korokorosei *owu* whose dance mimics canoe motions, has a reputation for being so lethal that people living in far-off clans speak of him with awe. His name refers to a type of dolphin that reportedly appears in every pond; the Ijo, who consider dolphins dangerous prey, regard the white finned Eleke as the most wicked. Unlike the masks discussed above, Eleke's headpiece not only represents a water-dwelling mammal, instead of a true fish, but belongs to the composite type; it superimposes human features on a body that resembles that of a dolphin (Plate 11.34).

Plate 11.34: *Eleke embracing his priest. Photograph by Martha G. Anderson, Korokorosei, 1991*

His son, Kunokorogheowei, has a similar headpiece, but his slave, Ikirikawei, who completes the set, takes the form of an upright human figure.

The Eleke masquerade spans a three-day period and incorporates two sets of cloth masks in addition to the wooden ones. The most dramatic segment reenacts *peri toi*, the play performed by titled warriors who have killed human beings or certain animals, for Eleke, the notorious crime fighter, earned the title by killing people when invoked to do so. His priest wears the red jacket and cap reserved for titleholders in Olodiama clan, and all three masks display eagle feathers to denote his *peri* status. Despite his lethal tendencies, supporters claim that Eleke not only protects the community but that he promotes its welfare by bringing children and prosperity.

The Ijo have abandoned most of their mask shrines. Many seem to have called on powerful fish like Oki. The neighboring community of Ikebiri performed a masquerade known as Uguberi, or "Hammerhead shark," before abandoning his shrine about fifty years ago. The ensemble included four masks: Uguberi, the father; Noi-noi-ere (untranslatable), his wife; and their two sons, the furtive Miye-miye-gudu, or "Whatever he does he keeps in his mind," and the voracious Aka-karaghe-karaghe-buru-fi, or "He eats yam without carving his teeth." Residents recall that the male headpieces looked exactly like the intimidating sharks but say that the wife's took the form of a beautiful woman with plaited hair, a slender body, and a "very nice figure." Uguberi - described as so murderous that he held the *peri* title from birth - reportedly cut his victims' stomachs, causing them to urinate or defecate blood. He is rumored to have killed numerous followers for abandoning his shrine, yet people say he formerly protected Ikebiri from harm. They maintain that his priest could avert epidemics when he became possessed, simply by moving through town as he waved his sword and shouted, "Sickness is coming and I am driving it away."

Masking as Serious Play and Playful Work

Like masquerades everywhere, Ijo performances function on many levels and yield multiple layers of meaning. In addition to their stated aims of ensuring prosperity, averting misfortune, and enforcing the law, they provide an opportunity for youths, including a few daring girls, to display their physical prowess and courage - qualities the Ijo have historically prized - by daring masks to attack, then narrowly dodging their blows. The most audacious spectators taunt even enshrined masks like Eleke, whose tendency to become possessed makes them so dangerous that more cautious observers watch their performances from canoes anchored a safe distance from shore. By turning combat into play, masquerades must have once provided a training ground for warriors; thus, performances like Oki and Ofurumo might feature the fishing methods men employ, not only because they are more dramatic but also because they provide a clearer metaphor for warfare.

On the other hand, Ijo masquerades mock the same behaviors they reinforce. Even the most lighthearted examples, like Ofurumo, illustrate the negative consequences of antisocial behavior and comment on society's need to control overly contentious individuals. Though the Ijo valorize physical bravado, they realize that combativeness can exceed socially acceptable limits and turn people into wild, uncontrollable "beasts," like the domineering bully whose townsmen killed him, then "tamed" his spirit by providing it with a figure carving. As Horton (1967, 236-39) observes in his analysis of a Kalabari Ijo masquerade, masking provides a similar means of concretizing the fears of sociopaths that can surface in any community, then symbolically addressing them.

If catching unruly fish and taming wild spirits metaphorically harnesses their powers for the good of society, playing with masks can also mitigate people's fears of the vicious spirits and ferocious beasts that inhabit the natural environment. It is important to note, however, that the Ijo express a profound respect for nature rather than a desire to dominate it. For example, they mount a rite called *bou gbee* (pay the bush) to compensate the forest whenever someone kills a bush spirit, just as they compensate the families of humans who die as a result of murder, war, or accident. As sacrifices performed at the behest of nature spirits, masquerades likewise provide a means of repaying the environment for its gifts, including fish and the raw material used in manufacturing canoes.

Finally, Horton (1963) has described Kalabari Ijo masquerades as approaching art for art's sake because they have more to do with aesthetic display than ritual. Despite their ritual significance, most masquerades performed by Ijo groups living to the west of the Nun River could easily be mistaken for secular performances. This may well be appropriate, for water spirits stage their own masquerades, as two Ijo friends reminded me. One recalled that anyone who ventured into the water during Uguberi risked being cut by water spirits, who not only mounted their own version inside the river but periodically sent pieces of dead fish to the surface to show how they dealt with spectators: The other - a diviner, whose numerous contacts keep her abreast of events in the spirit world - confided one morning that water spirits would be dancing Oki inside the water that afternoon and that she would be going to see it. Apparently these creative but often wayward spirits feel no need to justify their own performances as anything more than a day's entertainment.

Conclusion

Canoes and fish have transcended their roles as transportation and food to become emblematic of Delta cultures. War canoes and fishing tableaux adorn festival T-shirts, like one produced to celebrate a secular festival in Bumo clan in 1992 (Plate 11.35).

Plate 11.35: *Fishing motif on T-shirt designed for a civic festival.*
Photograph by Martha G. Anderson, Opuama, 1992.

Indeed, a close identification with a riverain lifestyle has figured in the development of at least a tentative regional identity. Despite ongoing ethnic bickering among groups living at its fringes, Delta residents have exhibited a surprising degree of political solidarity based partly on their shared environment; feelings of difference from mainland peoples helped fuel the movement to create Rivers, then Delta States. The paddle proudly displayed beneath the Nigerian coat-of-arms on a school notebook for Rivers State, *circa* 1978, signifies this identity, as does the dazzling, if anatomically incorrect, Ofurumo who appears in the first calendar issued by Bayelsa State (created out of Rivers State in 1997). Befringed, befeathered, and gleaming with metallic paint, he serves as the sole example of the region's "cultural displays."

The use of canoes and fish in shrines and rituals has dwindled as Christianity has come to dominate the region and as increasing poverty limits the number of masquerades villages can support. The Ijo frequently complain that the lack of roads in the Delta has hampered their progress. If wishful thinking could overcome the many obstacles involved in engineering and paying for roadways in a swampy region traversed by rivers, beset by floods, and deluged by intense rainstorms, their relationship to the environment would change radically. For the foreseeable future, however, water still rules the Delta, and canoes and fish continue to hold a secure place, not only in the economic lives of its inhabitants but in their hearts.

CHAPTER 12
LITERATURE OF THE ỊZỌN

Eldred Ibibiem Green and Seiyifa Koroye

Oral Literature

A survey of this nature necessarily starts from Oral Literature. As that aspect of literature, the composition and transmission of which is oral, it predates any other form currently in existence and depends on performance for a full appreciation of its attributes. Performance takes place at such events as moonlight and other story-telling sessions, births, deaths, marriages, and the installation of chiefs and monarchs. Items performed include tales, songs, panegyrics, dirges and elegies.

Deserving of special mention, amongst the modes of performance, are masquerading, stampedes and fishing festivals. Masquerading is, literally speaking, second nature to the Ijo and among the Eastern Ijo for example, the combination of costuming, music and dance has developed into high art as expressed in such masquerades as *Otobo* (hippopotamus), *Siki/Seki* (crocodile), and *Ófúrúmá/Ófírímá* (shark). A lot of masquerades are common to the major Eastern Ijo groups—Ibani, Wakirike, Kalabari and Nembe. Over time, however, some groups seem to have focused attention more on some than on others—*Ódúm, Piorú* and *Peri Angála* by the Wakirike, *Otobo, Ókóbá, Abaji-Opóro* and the various forms of *Agidi Owúu* by the Ibani; *Okí, Okolokúrúkúrú* and *Owúáma* by the Kalabari, and *Ófírímá* and *Angaláyai* by the Nembe. Common to these performances are the use of drum language and evocative chants both of which employ a lot of proverbs and symbols to create rich imagery.

Stampedes—*Átá nwángí* (Ibani), *Igira sara* (Kalabari), *Egele gbán* (Nembe), and *Ogéle* (Kolokuma and many Central and Western Ijo groups)—take place at times of important celebrations or political agitation and serve as times for praise poetry or abusive chants as the occasions demand. Fishing festivals are more common among the Central and Western Ijo and may be related to the fact that the freshwater environment of those areas and the serious flooding that takes place in the rainy season, make full-scale fishing a predominantly dry season affair. This seasonal characteristic thus makes for celebration and the performance of various forms of oral literature. One of the best known of these festivals is the Sabagreia Fishing Festival.

Outside those aspects of performance that can be described as communal, there is that in which individual composers/performers feature. In this category the individual composer/performer is usually backed by a group he or she has formed. In order to reach a wider audience and to, also, preserve their works, several such performers have made use of records, audio and video tapes and compact discs. According to Elechi Amadi and Eldred Green,

> "One very important area through which modernity has impacted on the performance and transmission of oral literature has been through the use of records, audio and video cassettes and, of course, the electronic media." (189–190).

Some of those 'who have performed in this mode' are the late Cardinal Jim Rex Lawson and Erasmus Jenewari. Alive and still performing are, for example, Prince David Bull, King Sunny Brown, Robert Ebizimo and Asu Ekiye. For these, highlife has been the medium of performance. Asu Ekiye, specifically, belongs to the gospel end of the highlife spectrum. Some others are essentially traditional artists but have availed themselves of modern recording facilities. Examples are John Halliday (Ibani), Íkúléle and Sasoróbia (Kalabari), and Biscuit (Wakirike) (Amadi and Green 190).

There are yet others who have performed through the avenue of choral music. Some examples are the late Ikoli Harcourt Whyte and Oyibosiya Eberewariye. Among those living, and performing in this mode are the duo of Enitoun Iyalla and Barasua Brown. As Amadi and Green have stated, even though all these have performed as musicians, '... it is important to add that a lot of what is performed in song – proverbs, aphorisms, riddles, tales and so on – is literary material (190). For example Barasua Brown sings,

194

Bomá nā Túminí finí wá nyánábó píríi	Blessing and Praise be unto our God (Owner)
Fíáfíá álábo ibi mie mie Támuno	Holy king, God that does good
Kuro nyanabóo, bomá finí Íyé ére píríi	Powerful One blessed be your name
Omieibíi finí gbámásó	His good deeds endure forever

or Bébióke states in song that,

Kímítóbóu ńdú bíā bouigbá ko tímíghā
If man's life were like a rope/vine in the bush.

Né dióko ówéíbé wéní bó búó tímíghā kwí pélé dóú
An enemy will pass by and cut it off

Wó yé ngí ki Kímí ńdú kókóú ní lá péléghā ó
Because God keeps/preserves life your enemy cannot cut it off.

Támáráú mie mí Ayíbáráu wó Í kúlé mī
God has done well, God we thank you.

(Lambert Ototo and Kofi Odiowei, Interviews, 4 November and 2 December, 2006).

As can be seen from these exampes, they are performing religious praise poetry. When Robert Ebizimo states that

E dey saki me something like kai kai	It intoxicates me like native gin
E dey saki me something like Ogogoro	It intoxicates me like native gin

he is alluding to the seductive power of a woman as being akin to the intoxicating power of native gin – an Ijo staple, a drink that has been described as 'push me, I push you' – in a use of simile that is most apt. Similarly David Bull's,

Iné é e	Mother
Buru biatéē	(Yam) Food is ready
Fíyé sakí láāté	Meal time has come
Anī Í sóari	That is when you are leaving

sung at the funeral of his mother, is clearly a dirge.

Sagas, epic accounts of generations of families, exist among the Western and Central Ijo. The most common of these is the Ozidi collected and translated as *The Ozidi Saga* by the poet and playwright J. P. Clark, who has also used it as the basis for his play *Ozidi*. Less popular than the Ozidi, is Krakaowei, another saga that emanates from the Western Ijo, and Fimaseri from the Central Delta.

It is important to note that at the centre of a lot of the performances mentioned in this section, is folk drama. Whether it is in masquerading, fishing festivals or sagas, enactment of a plot, usually unwritten but known to the populace, exists. For example in the *Ófírímá* (shark) masquerade of the Nembe, there is apart from spectacle, music and dance, an enactment of the process involved in the stalking and eventual capture of the shark. This is usually done in the *tiri* (playground) complete, with a fisherman, a net and a canoe. Once stalking of the ever elusive shark is through and the fisherman casts his net and captures the object of the hunt, there is applause in the audience followed by general dancing. In Bonny the performance of the *Otobo* (hippopotamus) masquerade cannot be done without an enactment of the animal's social life and the effects of man's predatory activities. The sagas are even more elaborate in their literariness as beyond plot and characterisation, they make use of elaborate dialogue. Among the Tarakiri – Ijo, the performance of the *Ozidi* saga, takes place over several days and nights.

Creative Writing

Gabriel Okara

The first Ijo to do major creative writing was Gabriel Imomotimí Gbaíŋgbaíŋ Okara. His poem 'The Call of the River Nun' was victorious at the Nigerian Festival of the Arts in 1953 and 'The Iconoclasts' won the first prize in a short story competition of the British Council in 1954. He can rightly be described as one of the pioneers of modern Nigerian poetry. According to the *Encyclopaedia Britannica* Premium Service, he is,

> ... the first significant English–language black African poet, the first African poet to write in a modern style and the first Nigerian writer to publish in and join the editorial staff of the influential journal *Black Orpheus* (started in 1957).

Plate 12.1: Gabriel Okara (Courtesy: Andrea Scaringella)

Okara's collection of poems titled *The Fisherman's Invocation* was published in 1978 and was joint winner of the 1979 Commonwealth Prize for Poetry. His second volume titled *The Dreamer, His Vision*, was published in 2005 and was the entry which won him, jointly with Ezenwa-Ohaeto, the same year, the Nigeria Prize for Literature, sponsored by Nigeria LNG Limited.

Culture conflict between African and Western values has been identified by Beier, Moore, Vincent, Dathorne (1976:175) and Nkosi (1981:152–3) as a major concern in Okara's early poetry, especially in such poems as 'Spirit of the Wind', 'Once Upon a time' and 'Piano and Drums'. Outside culture conflict, Okara also treats the problems of an already independent Nigeria in both his early and more recent poetry. Some of these from *The Fisherman's*

Invocation are 'Cancerous Growth' 'Rain Lullaby', 'Freedom Day' and 'The Glowering Rat'. In *The Dreamer, His Vision*, some of these are 'The Dreamer', 'Self Preservation' 'Mass Transit Buses' and 'Civil Servants'. In addition to poems of a public nature, Okara has written private poems which appear in the two collections. Some of those in the earlier volume are 'The Call of the River Nun', 'New Year's Eve Midnight' and 'One Night at Victoria Beach'. In the latter volume, some of them are 'The Passing of a Year', 'Spark In The Sky' and 'Waiting For Her Son'. (Green, 2006:3–5).

On technique, Okara's ability to create apt imagery and use symbolism to convey profound meaning has been highlighted by Dathorne (1976:175) and Nkosi (1981:153). In addition to these, Green in 'Nostalgia in Selected Poems of Gabriel Okara' identifies the ability to evoke nostalgia as one of Okara's strengths. Added to all these is the outstanding lyricism of Okara's poetry and as Dathorne observes, Okara, 'reorganizes language by rendering it lyrical, and it is the ease of a songster that makes him such a satisfying poet' (174–175).

Even though it is in poetry that he has acquired his reputation, Okara has also written fiction and children's literature. His novel, *The Voice* was published in 1964 and deals with an individual, Okolo, who is on a quest for moral rectitude and is, as such, a threat to a corrupt society and its rotten leadership. Even though Okolo is eventually set adrift to die we are confident that his ideas will live. The novel is unique because it is the first known attempt in fiction by any African writer to compose in an African language and then transliterate into English. Even though the language is uneven in some areas, it successfully retains elements of Ijo sentence structure. Okara by virtue of this experimentation in *The Voice* becomes the literary ancestor of the Ngugi wa Thiong'o of *Devil On The Cross* and the Ken Saro-Wiwa of *Sozaboy*. (Green, 2006: 7–8).

Okara's works of children's literature are *Little Snake and Little Frog, An Adventure to Juju Island* and *Tonye and Kingfish*. Creative writing apart, Okara's manifesto of sorts for his experimentation in *The Voice*, an interview titled 'African Speech . . . English words', was published in 1963. Okara has articles in academic journals, chapters in books and a book of essays titled *As I See It*, published in 2006. Okara holds the national honour of Officer of the Order of the Niger (O.O.N.). The citation was entirely based on his poetry and the fact that he had become a role model for younger writers (Okara, Interview: 22/1/2007). He was also one of the first three persons awarded honorary doctorate degrees by the University of Port Harcourt in 1979.

John Pepper Clark–Bekederemo

J. P. Clark's work, writes Professor Abiola Irele, "can be said to have assumed a specific historical significance in the evolution of Nigerian, and indeed, African poetry in English, for it is indisputable that his early efforts were central to both the thematic re-orientation and profound transformation of idiom that led to the decisive advance that the new poetry came to represent ... Clark helped to inaugurate a new kind of Nigerian poetry in English."

Plate 12.2: John Pepper Clark (Courtesy: Andrea Scaringella)

Clark As Scholar, Critic and Essayist

The first African writer to be appointed to a Chair of English, Clark has done incisive work as a scholar, critic and essayist. Some of his best known works in this area are *The Example of Shakespeare* (1970), *The Hero As A Villain* (1978), *A Peculiar Faculty* (2000) and *The Burden Not Lifted* (2001). In *The Example of Shakespeare* he examines the issue of the language of African characters in literature, the 'themes of African poetry of English Expression', communication between the poet and his audience, the various facets of African drama and what he considers a lapse in Shakespeare's *Othello*. As Clark puts it, his role in this collection of essays 'is that of a workman seeking solutions to a number of problems ... [arising] on the job. In *The Hero As A Villain*, his inaugural lecture, he highlights the paradox that emanates from a situation in which the typical hero in traditional societies attains that status by shedding blood, thus becoming in a way, a villain himself, and therefore is required by society to make propitiation a *sine qua non* for re-integration into society. In *A Peculiar Faculty*, Clark's concern is with the devastation that slavery and the slave trade across the Atlantic as well as the Sahara and the Indian Ocean brought upon Africa. It also highlights the opprobrium these have cast on the African at home in the eyes of his cousin in the diaspora and challenges the Nigerian Academy of Letters 'to research and find ... answers [to the uncomfortable questions from our past] for the good of our people ... ' In *The Burden Not Lifted*, his Award Winner's Lecture for the Nigerian National Order of Merit, Clark returns to the theme dealt with, earlier on, in *The Hero As A Villain*. He states, however, that unlike the accepted practice in traditional societies, Nigeria has re-integrated her soldiers without propitiation. In his own words 'our crisis remains the burden that has not been lifted all these years after our Civil War. If anything the burden has grown heavier' (10). He therefore encourages Nigeria to lift the burden.

> Let us therefore have a better understanding of ourselves as a society and some sympathy for the soldier. He swore to serve his country to the best of his ability and to lay down his life when called on to do so (48).

But the *Ozidi Saga* which Clark collected and translated from the Izon oral tradition is his major work of research and scholarship. He also produced a film, *Tides of the Delta* (jointly with Frank Speed), from the seven day performance at Orua in Tarakiri *ibe*. According to Isidore Okpewho:

"... we celebrate *The Ozide Saga*, as a landmark in the study of African oral literature and, in many respects, oral literature generally; it has made it possible to discuss this literature in a way we never did before, by showing us what it is really like in the only context in which it makes any sense, that is, in the warm interactive atmosphere of an audience ... I am delighted at the opportunity to bring to my job as usher a long-standing admiration of the genius of John Pepper Clark-Bekederimo ... ."

On retirement from the University of Lagos in 1980, he set up, with his wife, Ebun, PEC Repertory Theatre. Clark is one of the seven elected foundation fellows of the Nigerian Academy of Letters and received the Nigerian National Order of Merit in 1991 (*The Poems* : iii).

Clark's Poetry

His collections of poems are *Poems* (1961), *A Reed in the Tide* (1965), *Casualties : Poems 1966 – 68* (1970); *A Decade of Tongues* (1981); *State of the Union* (1981) and *Mandela and Other Poems* (1988). *Casualties* deals with the Nigerian crisis and, later, civil war, of the mid 60's up to 1970. Apart from "Epilogue", poems in *A Decade of Tongues* had been published previously, as the title indicates. *State of the Union* voices the poet's misgivings about the Nigerian state, while *Mandela and Other Poems* concerns itself with man's movement from the cradle to the grave.

Clark describes *The Poems 1958–1998* (2002) as 'a selection of my poems by myself at this stage of my life'. Its contents come from his previous titles. A few emendations have been made but in his words, 'no faith has been broken and no expectations lowered' (*The Poems ...* ix). *Of Sleep and Old Age* (2003) reflects wholly on life and mortality. Two poems that aptly illustrate this are, 'The Collection' and the title poem, 'Of Sleep and Old Age'. In the companion collection, *Once Again A Child* (2004), Clark does a poetic autobiography, presenting to his readers, a window into his early life. Significantly, within the collection is provided, a profile of the poet, covering his first ten years, and a 'Prologue'—'For Granny (from Hospital)—one of Clark's earliest, a fitting pointer to the subject matter, that is, parents, grandparents, siblings, and all the other subjects that make up early childhood.

Some of his most popular poems are 'Ivbie', 'For Granny (from Hospital)', 'Night Rain', 'Agbor Dancer', 'Fulani cattle' and 'Abiku'. Clark is well known for his ability to use the imagery of the tides, creeks and rivers of his Niger Delta environment. According to S. O. Asein:

> The most important features of Clark's poetry typified by such early poems as "Fulani Cattle," "The Cry of Birth," "The Imprisonment of Obatala," "Olokun," "Agbor Dancer," "Night Rain", "Abiku," and his celebrated long poem, "Ivbie," consisted in: his strong sense of locale; an attachment to his homeland, and in particular, the riverine landscape of his native Ijawland; and atavistic interest in lost moments of childhood innocence and strong emotional attachments to his loved ones; and a nostalgic celebration of his ancestral origins (1988:69).

Clark, also, aptly conveys meaning through the use of description to evoke visual imagery. Two typical examples are 'Ibadan' and 'Ibadan Dawn' (after *Pied Beauty*)'. The former, for instance, states,

> Ibadan,
>
> running splash of rust
>
> and gold—flung and scattered
>
> among seven hills like broken
>
> china in the sun. (*A Reed in The Tide*, 12).

Clark's Drama

J. P. Clark is a dramatist whose plays exhibit an underlying poetic sensibility. For example, *Song of a Goat* opens with Masseur speaking to Ebiere,

> Your womb
>
> Is open and warm as a room:
>
> It ought to accommodate many.

He continues,

> An empty house, my daughter, is a thing
>
> Of danger. If men will not live in it
>
> Bats or grass will, and that is enough
>
> Signal for worse things to come in.

In these lines there is a gradual build-up of the imagery of the womb as an organ that has a specific function and, of an argument on the need to keep it occupied. In this argument, an open, warm and inviting room is contrasted with an empty, cold, unoccupied and perhaps abandoned, house. Syllabic length plays a role, as the speech with its lyricism builds up a sense of doom. This drama, with its language of poetry which Clark adopts not only in *Song of a Goat* but also in *The Masquerade* and *The Raft*, all published together, in his *Three Plays* (1964), has been favourably compared by critics to classics of the Greek, Elizabethan and Irish theatres: *Song of a Goat*, had, however, been published, earlier, in 1961 by Mbari.

Song of a Goat centres on a family some of whose members are labouring under curses. The impotence of the protagonist, Zifa, is at the root of the incest between his wife Ebiere and his brother Tonye. Tonye hangs himself and Zifa walks into the sea. *The Masquerade* is sequel to *Song of a Goat* and traces further, the fortunes of a section of the family of the latter play. Tufa, it turns out, is the product of the incest between Tonye and Ebiere. As implied in the title of the play, Tufa is a man whose real identity is unknown and Diribi's opposition to marriage between his daughter, Titi, and Tufa results in tragedy. Tufa's death is in a way the completion of a tragic sequence that begins in *Song of a Goat*. *The Raft*, shows four lumber men adrift, in circumstances that look like those of Nigeria in the early 1960's on a raft that disintegrates on its passage to port under poor pilots.

Other plays by Clark include *Ozidi* (1966), *The Bikoroa Plays* (1985) and *All For Oil*. The play *Ozidi* is revenge tragedy based on the saga, of the same name, performed by the Tarakiri-Ijo at Orua in the Western Delta. *The Bikoroa Plays* draw attention to aspects of the history of the Ngbilebiri people of the Mein Clan of the Western Delta. *The Boat*, the best known of these plays, concerns itself with the concept of justice in a situation in which a man has killed his brother. *The Wives' Revolt* (1991), described at the time of publication as 'Clark's first comedy in twenty-five years of playwriting' (Blurb), deals with the conflict that arises in a community over the sharing, between men and women, of compensation paid by an oil company, and the attendant anti-women legislation enacted in the land. At the end the men not only swallow their pride and plead with the wives to return home after abandonment en-masse but, also, pay reparation.

In *All For Oil*, Clark recalls the exploitation and oppression experienced in the 19th century by the peoples of the area known as the Oil Rivers Protectorate, at the hands of the Royal Niger Company and its local collaborators. The poignancy of the play is heightened by the fact that over a hundred years later, the region (now known largely as the Niger Delta) and its people are still abused and exploited by a combination of foreigners and their local collaborators. Whereas previously the foreign component of wickedness, theft and general inhumanity was an agent of the British Colonial administration, today, it is made up of several transnational companies originating from virtually everywhere in the Western World, actively backed by their home governments. The 'local collaborator' component has also undergone some transformation, from Judas-like Chief Dore Numa to a combination of the Nigerian State, wicked and corrupt politicians pretending to represent the victims, and various other Non-Niger Delta Nigerian Birds of Carrion, keeping their fortunes in safe nests while boldly and voraciously eating up the patrimony of the Niger Delta.

Incidentally, Clark's concern in *All For Oil*, has also been dealt with by Ola Rotimi in *Ovonramwen Nogbaisi* (1971), and more fully in *Akassa You Mi*, (acted in January 1977 but published posthumously in 2001). It is obvious from the way things are going, that many more of such plays will be written in the future. In 1991 the poems and plays already listed, *Collected Plays and Poems: 1958-1988,* was published in the United States by Howard University Press.

Extensive studies, beyond what can be listed in this survey, have been done on Clark. Some of these are Robert Wren's *J.P. Clark* (1984); *J.P. Clark-Bekederemo Festschrift* edited by Adelugba, Ashaolu and Asein (1986); and J. Egbe Ifiè's *A Cultural Background to the Plays of J. P. Clark-Bekederemo* (1994). There are also the authoritative contributions by Abiola Irele's introduction to Clark's *Collected Plays and Poems (1991)* and Isidore Okpewho's 'Critical Introduction' to the Howard University Press edition of *The Ozidi Saga* (1991).

The Association of Nigerian Authors awards the J.P. Clark Prize for Drama annually and the University of Lagos Department of English has the J.P. Clark Distinguished Lecture series, the first of which was delivered by the playwright and poet, Professor Osofisan.

Ola Rotimi

Born to a Yoruba father and a Nembe Ijo mother, Ola Rotimi has, in some of his writing, identified with his mother's people. The particular ones are *If: A Tragedy of the Ruled* (1983), *Hopes of the Living Dead* (1985), and *Akassa You Mi* (2001). *If ...* is set in Diobu outside the fringe, to the East of Ijoland, *Hopes ...* is set in that section of Port Harcourt that was acquired from the Wakirike–Ijo, while the setting of *Akassa You Mi*, is Nembe in the Eastern Ijo area. In terms of characterization in *If ...*, Professor Dokubo is clearly Ijo while Fisherman and his sister are also Ijo (Kalabari). In *Hopes of the Living Dead,* the hero, Ikoli Harcourt Whyte, is Kalabari–Ijo, while Alibo, one of the patients, is Wakirike–Ijo.

Plate 12.3: Ola Rotimi (Courtesy: Marshall Enenajor)

Thematically, two of the works—*If ...* and *Akassa You Mi* raise issues that have been central to the Ijo struggle—the despoliation of the environment and subsequent threat to the people's livelihood and the struggle for resource control, respectively. In *If ...*, Fisherman, speaking in Kalabari, protests vehemently to the lawyer about the activities of oil companies, the degradation of the environment and the fact that these have impacted negatively on his occupation. *Akassa You Mi*, set in 1895, and a few years before, deals with British imperialism and its effects on Nembe, a hitherto prosperous city-state, and the action carried out by the people, to break the yoke. The Nembe case is one in a long line of actions against the Ijo and some other Niger Delta peoples by the British. It began with the deportation of King William Dappa Pepple I of Bonny—a man E. J, Alagoa has described as the Father of Resource Control—in 1854.

Hopes of the Living Dead deals with the callous attitude of the British colonial government towards the disabled. Even though the human environment of the play is Pan-Nigerian, it can be argued that successive Nigerian governments have, like the colonialists, maintained a callous coldness towards the Ijo and the rest of the Niger Delta. It can even be argued, further, that the situation is worse now, that whereas the British did not cause the disability of the lepers in the play, the Nigerian state and several other Nigerians are active culprits in the actions and circumstances that are actively disabling the Niger Delta— environmentally, economically, in terms of its human resources—and expropriating its oil. In concluding, it can be said that Rotimi is 'acknowledging, in these plays, the influence of his mother's geo-political region on his life and work' (Green: 2004:400).

Simon Meshu Ambakederemo
Simon Meshu Ambakederemo is the author of a play, *Isaac Boro* (1968), and a collection of poems, *Justicia* (2004). *Isaac Boro* is in the nature of an epic drama and is a case for resource control. It is the first known, published work of literature on the Boro phenomenon. The poems in *Justicia* deal with such societal issues as governance, injustice, inequity, marginalization, greed and corruption. A third book titled, '*Dancing Around the Boro Epic*'—a material described as a saga of experiences of patriarchs—is in press.

Tekena Tamuno

Tekena Tamuno, man of letters, first principal of the University College Ilorin and a former Vice Chancellor of Nigeria's premier University, the University of Ibadan, has published three collections of poems. They are: *Songs of an Egg-Head* (1982), *Festival of Songs and Drums* (1999) and *Lamentations of Yeske* (2005). With the exception, perhaps, of poem number XL 'An Ode to EGBE IFIE', in *Lamentations of Yeske*, a lament or tribute to a friend, mentioned by name, the poems in the three collections are generally about man, life and society. In each collection, Tamuno uses a fictional environment – Labuja in *Songs ...,* Kolok in *Festival ...* and Yeske and Samabad in *Lamentations ...* . Similarly, the *persona* in the first collection is Afari, in the second it is Kolok and in the third it is Yeske. While it may amount to guess work and an exercise in futility to attempt to decipher the meanings of all these terms, there exist, for some of them, internal pointers to meaning. For example in 'Knight of the Banter, Scourge of Nightmares', Afari's full name is revealed as 'Afarikorodo Oko Iya Alamala (Afarikorodo, husband of the lady/or mother who sells *amala*)'. Broken down further, *Afarikorodo* (Yoruba) means, firstly, a man with a clean-shaven head and secondly, a man who eats on credit/one who is maintained by his wife. This makes sense within the context of 'Oko Iya Alamala'. There is, however, another angle to this. Within the Eastern Ijo environment of the poet, there is a kind of fish (*ilishia Africana/ethmalosa fimbriata*) called *afari*. It is very playful and moves in large numbers. (Hart, Otobotekere, Iyoyo, Interviews: 18/10/2006). Mention is made in the poem of several *afaris* and of *amala* being eaten / ... on credit until the next pay-day/. The feeling is that some 'punning' is being done here, that Afari the persona is part of a group of *afaris*, light-hearted/unserious/playful men that eat on credit and gather to grandstand on one pretentious intellectual cause or another. In the same vein, Labuja reminds one of Lagos and Abuja, early and later capital cities of Nigeria.

Beyond these, it is important to note that Tekena Tamuno's style in these poems is unusual. Sometimes the lines are plainly lyrical and convey a touching poetic sensibility. For example,

> Unlimited is their choice of substance
> Unlimited is their choice of style
> Unlimited is the accident or choice of circumstances:
> Yours and mine (lines 32 – 35, *Songs* ... p.2)

Also in the opening lines of 'Waiting for Coconuts to Fall?',

> Eh, are coconuts not meant to fall?
> Won't they, too, like many plants,
> The Law of Gravity obey?
> But how many laymen that force know? (lines 1–4,
> *Lamentations* . . . p32)

In the former, particularly, it is obvious that repetition has done a lot for the attainment of lyricism.

Sometimes the lines sound chatty and prosaic as in 'B – Complex'

> Blest are they of B–complex
> Be not their complex:
> Not the magic tablet
> Of their affable drug expert
> But that complex
> For the masses, no matter their sex. (lines 1 – 6, *Songs* ...
> p.70)

Here, it is obvious that the attempt to attain end-rhyme has not helped matters. Sometimes, also, Tamuno's lines are dense and suffused with imagery, symbolism and references from the classics, and from Nigerian languages. This occurs particularly in the narrative and descriptive poems. Most of these are long. Some of these examples are 'Knight of the Banter, Scourge of Nightmares' in *Songs of an Egg–Head*) and 'Kolok's Last Beat' in *Festival of Songs and Drums*. For example, the poem 'Knight of the Banter . . .' is long (18 pages) and is structured in such a way that it calls to mind some of the descriptive scenes in Homer's *Iliad*.

Owing to the vast differences existing in the execution of the poetic exercise, from one poem to the other, an unevenness of style shows in a consideration of Tamuno's poems. The poet seems to be aware of the 'unusualness' of his work and so in the manner of the oral performer who in his overture not only stakes his claims as a performer, but actually sets the parameters for the performance, the statement is made, in 'Choices Unlimited', the first poem of *Songs . . .,* that love and hate exist together and it is a matter of choice, whichever of them anyone identifies with.

> So, people love what you hate
>
> And hate what you love.   (lines 23 – 24)

Afari has, therefore, chosen simplicity instead of complexity as the mode for the rendering of his songs:

> We love verse
>
> we love prose
>
> we also love to promote the marriage
>
> of prose and verse . . . .   (lines 60 – 64)
>
> verse de-mystified makes sense –
>
> Sound, but rare, commonsense –
>
> Not otherwise.   (lines 77 – 79)

and concludes by stating,

> We surely love whatever shrinks language
>
> Further for easier-word-digestion
>
> As in all Afari's songs.   (lines 100 – 102)

Tekena Tamuno's poetry deserves more critical *cum* scholarly attention. With the exception of the slight commentary by Elechi Amadi and Eldred Green in *The Land and People of Rivers State* (Alagoa and Derefaka, 2002 : 196) and Dapo Adelugba's Foreword to *Lamentations of Yeske*, it is difficult to find published material on his poetry. The fact that he has written in an 'unusual' Nigerian style should rather than constitute an obstacle, be seen as an alternative style, suggestive of what Gabriel Okara (in *The Voice*), Ngugi wa Thiong'o (in *Devil On The Cross*) and Ken Saro-Wiwa (in *Sozaboy*), have done to African fiction.

Alaboigoni Inko-Dokubo

Before he died, Alaboigoni Inko-Dokubo had, as at 1982, published *Before I Sleep*, *Go to the Ants* and *Songs of the Eagle*. Most of the poems are occasional. Some are tributes to people like Claude Ake, the Ellahs, Haig and Betanova David-West, Wilfred Feuser, Charles Jenewari, Zeeky Rukari, Kay Williamson and Harold Dappa-Biriye. Two poems he dedicated to Tekena Tamuno have appeared in Tamuno's own collection/anthology—*Festival of Songs and Drums*. They are titled 'Songs of an Egg-Head Revisited' and 'Incarnation'.

Some of Inko-Dokubo's poems like 'Memories' and 'Green Revolution' (*Songs of the Eagle*) also deal with the Nigerian state and its affairs. As Elechi Amadi and Eldred Green have remarked in Alagoa and Derefaka (2002:196),

> In spite of the ordinariness of several of the poems, Inko-Dokubo's ability to create effective imagery out of such natural objects as the sun, moon, stars, the vegetation and particularly the rivers and riverine phenomena of Rivers State, creates empathy between the reader and the material before him.

Dagbo Alazigha

Dagbo Alazigha's *Akiroro: Thought Currents in Poetry* (1986) calls to mind the verses of the Ghanaian, R.E.G. Armattoe and his Nigerian counterpart, Dennis Osadebay and deals with such subjects as 'Nature', 'Destiny', 'Education', 'Celibacy', 'Anxiety of Youth' and 'The Living God', each of these, the title of a poem. Put together, they are an expression of the author's philosophy of life, put in verse form between 1947 and 1985. Even though the contents of *Akiroro* might not sound familiar to a lot of contemporary readers, *Akiroro* deserves attention for the interest it shows in the use of words. According to Kay Williamson in the Foreword,

> Poetry begins as playing with words and arranging them in patterns. It is clear that Dagbo Alazigha began by enjoying words and playing with them till they fell into patterns.

Before his death in 1989 he had completed a manuscript for a novel in Izon and several others for poetry. Dagbo Alazigha was the father of the award-winning writer, Bina Nengi-Ilagha.

Henry Leopold Bell-Gam

Henry Bell-Gam is the author of several plays. Some of these are, *Orukoro*, *Adamma*, *Jehovah*, *Mrs. Edwin*, *Love Abuse*, *Restoration Story*, *Cash Parade*, *King Jaja*, *Igbuduogu*, *No Sacrifice No Marriage*, *Enemies of Destiny*, *Erebie*, *The Royal Burial*, *The Hidden Treasure* and *Ube Republic*. Of these, the most popular have been *Orukoro* and *King Jaja*. Orukoro is a play of culture conflict between Africa and Europe and was performed in 1991 at Sheffield, England, at the World Universities Games and Cultural Festival. *King Jaja* deals with Jubo Jubo Fem the slave boy who became King, and the oppression he experienced before his elevation. Of the others the two most topical in the light of contemporary experience are *The Hidden Treasure* and *Ube Republic*. *The Hidden Treasure* focuses attention on the centrifugal forces that come into play once oil money flows into the average impoverished community in the Niger Delta; while *Ube Republic* highlights the 'thief-thief'/'chop-chop' politics that has become the hallmark of Nigeria's post-military governance.

Miesoinuma Minima

Miesoinuma Minima has three plays - *King Jaja or The Tragedy of a Nationalist* (1997), *Odum* Egege (1997) and *The Referendum* (2006). In *King Jaja ...,* Minima deals with the founding of Opobo (Opuboama) and the pressures external and internal that culminate in Jaja's deportation by the agents of British imperialism. Jaja's portrait, here, is that of a nationalist.

Odum Egege still deals with King Jaja of Opobo, albeit a different Jaja from the one in his other play and that celebrated by Bell-Gam. The Jaja of *Odum Egege* is one who, now oblivious of the slavery and oppression he had experienced in Bonny, becomes a tyrant over his Ndoki and Ibibio neighbours. He even orders the Ndoki chieftain, Odum Egege, to be skinned alive. Even though the two plays were published the same year, and the historical setting of *King Jaja ...* is earlier, there is evidence that *Odum Egege* was the first, written. This is because of reference to the curse put on Jaja for killing the man, Odum Egege.

In *The Referendum*, set in the fictional Democratic Republic of Monzonia, Minima examines governance according to the whims and caprices of rulers—a situation that leads to the murder, by the king, of his daughter and son-in-law. It is this personalizing of the state and its rulership that perhaps explains the illogicality of Monzonia being a republic and having a King, and the fact that government policies result in tragic consequences for the land and its people.

Odum Egege was the Rivers State Silver Jubilee Play (1992) and the Nigerian International Bank (now CitiBank) play of the year (1997), while *King Jaja or The Tragedy of a Nationalist* was the convocation play at the University of Port Harcourt in 2002.

Barclays Ayakoroma

Barclays Ayakoroma has published *Dance On His Grave* (1997), *A Matter of Honour* (1999), *A chance to Survive and Other Plays* (2002), *Castles in the Air* (2004), *A Scar For Life* (2006) and *Once Upon A Dream* (2006). He has also written jointly with A. Arikpo, *All For A Canoe and Other Plays* (2000) and with Arikpo and Betiang, *Our Forests, Our Future and Other Plays* (2000). Of these, two, *Dance On His Grave* and *A Matter of Honour* seem to be the most popular. Reminiscent of J. P. Clark's *The Wives' Revolt*, *Dance On His Grave* centres on the struggle by women in a Niger Delta community—Toru Ama—for their rights. The men react forcefully but this only ends in tragedy for King Olotu. Like *Dance ...*, *A Matter of Honour* is set in a Niger Delta community and deals with the senseless struggle, caused by misunderstood concepts of honour, over places of burial. In the play, two communities almost go to war on this matter. Fortunately, however, reason prevails and the matter is resolved amicably without any loss of life. *A Matter of Honour* was the convocation play at the University of Port Harcourt in 1996.

Adiyi Martin Bestman

Adiyi Martin Bestman has three published collections of poems. They are, *Textures of Dawn* (1998), *Une Calebasse d'aubes* (1999) and *Longing for Another Dawn* (2004). The first of these explores landscapes of pain as an individual and collective experience and focuses on the devastation of the Niger Delta and man's ultimate return to dust. The second, written in French, examines a world in which pain, decay, confusion, war, injustice and oppression reign – a world in which, however, there is a profound sense of hope. In the third collection, the poet relates with the cosmos through a range of feelings—love, sympathy, the hurt of history and the haunting desolation, violence and wounds inflicted on the Niger Delta. There is also a painful awareness of the widespread nature of man's inhumanity to man. Professor Bestman's poetry is cerebral, deep and thought-provoking.

Ibiwari Ikiriko

Ikiriko's *Oily Tears of the Delta* was published in 2000. Most of the poems in it lament the colonisation and despoliation of the Niger Delta by the rest of Nigeria. In 'Them and Us', the *persona* states,

> As jaki the ass
> Said to its Sahelian Drover:
> "Allah alone it is
> Who will judge the case
> Between you and me"
> So be it between
> Us and them—
> These lease-louts
> Thieves of our everything

Before his death in 2002, Ikiriko had been several things to the literary community, among them, teacher, critic, radio commentator and organizer of creative writing workshops.

G. Ebinyo Ogbowei

Ogbowei has been writing since 1978 and has had poems published in *Idoto, Matatu, PRISM International, Black American Literature Forum, Ariel, Okike* and *Liwuram*. However, his first collection of poems, *Let the Honey Run and Other Poems* was published in 2001. His other collections are *The Town Crier's Song* (2003) and *The Heedless Ballot Box* (2006). There are in these collections, poems on public as well as private themes. Some of the public ones are 'june 12, 1993' and 'hero's day' in *Let the Honey Run*; 'letter to the minister', 'woodpeckers and saviours' in *The Town Crier's Song;* and 'april 19' and 'may 29, 1999: for chief a. k. dikibo' in *The Heedless Ballot Box*. A number of the private poems are 'desire' and 'lament for uncle sam's mother' in *Let the Honey Run* and 'tears for florence efebo' in *The Heedless Ballot Box*. Ebinyo Ogbowei's *Let the Honey Run and Other Poems* made the shortlist for the Nigerian Prize for Literature, sponsored by Nigeria LNG, in 2005, and has been described by Remi Raji as,

> a confident reproduction of metaphor, in imagination, feeling and message ... the work of a mature craftsman whose recognition ... [on] the national literary canvas is long overdue (7).

Eldred Ibibiem Green

Eldred Green started writing poetry in the 1970's and has published some of his poems in *Kiabara, The Nigerian Tide, Expo Magazine, New Sokoti* and *Working Papers*. His collection of 54 poems, *Ogolo,* was published in 2005 and contains poems on the art of poetic composition, for example 'The Poet as a Bat' and 'The Anxiety of Influence'; private poems like 'To the Memory of a Grandmother' and 'Mother and Daughter' and public poems like 'Mala-Aria' and 'Let it Flow'. According to Chidi Ikonne,

> Positively adorned with local colour and spiced with biblical allusions, ... Green's style is, certainly down-to-earth. Yet its simplicity does not preclude the presence of thought-provoking images and symbols (viii–ix).

Emmanuel Opigo

Before the publication of *Frothy Facades*, his collection of poems, in 1979, Emmanuel Opigo had published in *Bits of Greenery*, the literary magazine of the Federal Government College, Port Harcourt, and written specific poems for some competitions. One such, needs special mention. Poem number 13 of Opigo's collection, titled 'Anthem', written in 1976, was submitted (Entry No. 394) for the New National Anthem Competition, from which to choose a replacement for 'Nigeria we Hail Thee', the Independence National Anthem. According to Opigo,

> The final choice of anthem was a mix of bits and pieces from
> five winning entries. The five entries were published on the
> front page of *Daily Times* sometime in 1977. The sixth number
> was 394 (Interview. 6 November, 2006).

Emmanuel Opigo is a good hand at the writing of acrostic poems and his collection has three of them—'Apartheid, A Crime Against Humanity', 'Who Killed Dele Giwa' and 'Christmas'. His poems, for example, 'Ease, Muse, Thy Reins', 'And Into Seedlings, Too' and 'Apartheid ...', display a reasonable level of lyricism. Opigo is one of the very few poets that have written in Izon. The poem Okokodiya,

Ayiba Pabu Sisei	God I beseech thee
Eri toru kpo fa wei	I am one who cannot see
Okokodiya	Show me but
Aki idiya	A coconut!

was based on an experience the poet and his siblings had as children, searching for coconuts that had fallen into the undergrowth behind their house.

Vincent Egbuson

Vincent Egbuson is a writer of fiction and his first published work was *Moniseks Country* (2000). Since then he has published *A Poet Is A Man* (2001), *Love Is Not Dead* (2002) and *Womandela* (2006). *Moniseks Country* deals with the theme of political corruption even as the name Moniseks suggests that money and sex are the main ingredients that fuel it. Love becomes the common denominator in the rest of the works. It combines with political corruption in *A Poet Is A Man,* exists alone in *Love Is Not Dead* and together with Freedom, becomes the subject of the quest in *Womandela*. Egbuson's *Love Is Not Dead,* made the shortlist for the Nigeria Prize For Literature in 2004 and *Womandela* won the ANA/NDDC Ken Saro-Wiwa Prize for Prose in 2006.

Nengi Josef Ilagha

Nengi Ilagha's first collection of poems, *Mantids* (1999), won the ANA Poetry Prize in 1995 as a manuscript. *Apples and Serpents*, a collection of poems, (1998), received honourable mention as the first Runner-up for the All Africa Christopher Okigbo Prize for Poetry, in 1998. Some of the poems in these collections have appeared in newspapers, journals and anthologies, in and outside the country, including *The Guardian, Post Express, For Ken for Nigeria, ANA Review, Ofirima, Voices from the Fringe* and *Junge Nigerianische Lyrik*. According to the judges for the 1995 prize, Nengi Ilagha's "poems are carefully sculpted, yet possess an irresistible lyrical grace. His poetry is located within our contemporary times, treating our travails and· dilemmas not only from a personal point of view, but with a poet's deft, elliptical and richly metaphorical touch." (*Mantids*: Blurb).

Ilagha's collection of stories, *A Birthday Delight* (2007) deals with down-to-earth issues like drunkenness, abuse of power, irresponsibility, family life and survival, and love together with the demands they make on, and the consequences they have for, society.

Bina Nengi-Ilagha

Bina Nengi-Ilagha's *Condolences,* (2002) won the ANA Prose Prize in 2001 as a manuscript, and honourable mention, placing first of three in the controversial maiden Nigeria Prize for Literature, sponsored by NLNG, in 2004. According to the judges for that competition, 'Bina's strength in this novel lies in her ability to explore the atmosphere of mourning to unravel the complex patterns of human behaviour. The story is very well focussed, and there is skilful use of narrative devices. The author's language is lucid, and there is an admirable vividness in the way she describes events and characters.' (*Condolences*: Blurb).

Crossroads (2003), a collection of 11 stories received honourable mention, placing third in the prose category of ANA's 2002 awards as a manuscript. *Crossroads* is strong in characterisation and in its overall ability to present to the reader a realistic portrait of human life.

New Writing

Classification, here, is not cast in stone. The term 'New Writing' is here used to represent the works of those who have found creative voice fairly recently. It is for that reason; that people who had started writing earlier in journals and literary magazines have been mentioned earlier even when publications in book form had come much later.

Christian Otobotekere

Christian Otobotekere is the author of *Across the Bridge*: *Diadems Forever* (2002), *Around and About Book 1* (2005), *Around and About Book 2* (2005) and *Poetry World–An Introduction* (n.d.). These are basically works of children's literature. *Across the Bridge* ... has a particularly Christian flavour and can be described as Christian poetry. Even though *Poetry World—An Introduction* has an adult ring to it, it is still, at heart, a celebration of innocence, and the simplicity of rural life. It even has two poems—'A Backdrop of Nature' and 'Life', contributed by Adeyemi Oyenekan (aged 18) and Soso Nimi Walson–Jack (aged 14), respectively, two of Otobotekere's grandchildren. Otobotekere stands out as one of the very few writers composing in Izon (in some segments of some of the poems in *Around and About Book 2* and in *Poetry World* ...). In the latter, a full poem (a funeral song) in Izon titled 'Face Upwards [Adidi-ama]', is rendered.

Igoni Barrett

Barrett's short fiction has been published in the print magazines *Nigeria Monthly* and *Farafina*, and in several online magazines, amongst which are *The Stickman Review*, *Fictionville*, *The Laura Hird Showcase* and *Barfing Frog*. His short story, 'The Phoenix' was a winner of the 2005 BBC World Service Short Story Competition, and was broadcast on the 2nd of January, 2006 on the BBC World Service Programme 'Off the Shelf'. He was featured in 2006 on the Raintiger Networks Artists platform as their spotlight artist for the month of May. He is the fiction editor for the online literary magazine *Black Biro*. His first book, a collection of short stories titled *From Caves of Rotten Teeth*, was published in 2005.

Igoni Barret was selected in March 2006 as one of 14 young writers from 11 countries of the Commonwealth whose short stories were collected and published in book map form by the Australian publisher Express Media. The book map *Incommunicado* was launched in Melbourne during the 2006 Commonwealth Games.

Some other new writers are Lambert Ototo, Ebi Yeibo, Sophia Obi, Leonard Emuren, Tonyo Birabebe and Apei Porbeni. Lambert Ototo has published

Ebiakpo The Orphan (2003) and *Ovie and The Housefly* (2006); Ebi Yeibo, *A Song for Tomorrow and Other Poems* (2003), *Maiden Lines* (2004); Apei Porbeni, *Wise Mother Hen and Other Stories* (2005); Sophia Obi, *Tears in a Basket* (2006); Leonard Emuren *Scenes of the Sinful Dancers* (2006); and Tonyo Birabebe, *Undercurrents* (2006). Lambert Ototo's major concern so far is children's literature, Apei Porbeni is a teenager.

This presentation of writers and writing in spite of all the effort, may not be all-inclusive and is the kind of work that would require periodic reviews, to capture yet newer writing and to update the works of already published ones.

Observed Characteristics of Ijo Literature

The concerns of Ijo Oral Literature—of the communal or individually composed and recorded types—are either mythological (explaining the origins of man, places or things) as in Oyibosiya Eberewariye's, *'Ori Teme Ama Sese'* and '... *Pirí ná buu ná, buu ná piri ná, So ké wá pírím'*; philosophical as in Rex Lawson's,

Owu ná derí nā, ini ṅgba muna apú	Weeping and mirth, they are both related
J'ápú ówúari j'ápú deríarí	Some are weeping, others are laughing
Owu ná, owu ná derí nā	Weeping, weeping and mirth

or are plain statements of determination as in Adam Fiberesima's 'We shall win the Championship, We shall bring home a great Prize'. There are, in addition some that are topical because they are used for specific occasions, for example, the Ibani–Ijo dirge,

Kaá sómá, kaá sómáám	Completely torn, completely torn
I sibíi gbé mbiláari kaá sómám	The umbrella that covered my head is completely torn.

To this group of specific topics for specific occasions, belong panegyrics, all other praise poetry and various kinds of religious poetry.

Creative writing, too, has its own set of characteristics and a lot of these cut across genres. Since people are born, grow-up and otherwise interact with specific locales, it might be necessary to state an intense awareness of the environment, as the first of these characteristics. The habitat of the Ijo is predominantly swampland—either mangrove or freshwater swamp. While this environment has largely determined the traditional occupations of the Ijo—fishing, salt-making, canoe-carving, long distance river trade, seamanship and the piloting of ships, and a little farming; the harshness of this environment and its effect on the citizenry seem to be beyond the ability of most Nigerians to comprehend. It has in fact been used as the reason for not focusing any meaningful attention, since the days of the colonial administration, on any meaningful development. Indeed one of the most stupid reasons for this malfeasance by government was the one given in 1991 by the Babangida administration, through its Chief of General Staff, Admiral Augustus Aikhomu. He had said, after the states' creation exercise in 1991, (that saw Jigawa created out of Kano State and the number of local government areas in each of those two virtually doubled), that the reason why the old Rivers State was not split was because most of it was water. This, coming from a sailor, in an administration that purported to believe that creation of states was a means of political development, was a tragedy of immense proportions.

Ijo literature, as stated earlier, expresses an intense awareness of the environment and the harshness that the people have to cope with. For example, Gabriel Okara describes an aspect of Okolo's journey to Sologa,

> The engine canoe against the strong water pushed ... Soon, the day's eye became bad. It became so bad and black and closed that it could not be looked at ... and the thunder sounded like the sound of one hundred cannons going off near your ears... . Then the sky suddenly broke and when the rain from above poured, it passed telling. The rain drops were like six-inch cannon balls. It did not rain like rain. It rained more than raining (*The Voice*, 61–62).

The passenger' reaction was, of course, one of petrifaction,

> 'Ee, Woyengi, sorry for us!'
> 'Things of the soil of the town, for today only save us!'
> 'How is it! How is it! Amadasu will you see us die?
> 'Blow it away, blow it open!'
> 'Things that follow me! This about – to – happening
> big thing take away!'
> 'Kolokumo Egbesu! How?'
> 'O God deliver us! O, Christ, sorry for us O.'   (61–62).

Another concern is the despoliation of the environment which, in spite of its harshness, has sustained the Ijo – validated by history as one of the oldest ethnic entities in Nigeria – for several millennia. This despoliation is largely done by companies backed by government and, exploiting for oil and gas. The despoliation is such that it makes the rivers unfit for anything. According to Ibiwari Ikiriko,

> I am of
> the Oil Rivers
> where rivers are
> oily
> and can
> neither,
> quench my thirst
> nor
> anoint my head (*Oily Tears of the Delta* 20)

The struggle for resource control is another concern of the writing of the Ijo. It is one of the oldest, politically. Started politically in the 19th century, the struggle by the Ijo to exercise suzerainty over their terrain and to control their natural resources and the proceeds deriving therefrom, had culminated in the deposition and deportation of King William Dappa Pepple of Bonny in 1854, the Nembe War against the Royal Niger Company at Akassa in 1895, the declaration of a Niger Delta Republic by Isaac Boro in 1966, the Kaiama Declaration of 1998 and the spate of agitations in Ijoland and most of the Niger Delta, since the 1990's. A situation in which oil and gas are derived from

Ijoland and other parts of the Niger Delta but the proceeds are used to develop other places especially Abuja which has become the beauty of Nigeria, is seen not only as annoying, but evil. The evil and wickedness are specially underscored by the fact that Ijoland is still the most underdeveloped part of Nigeria today and the average person lives below the poverty line in spite of several so-called interventionist programmes which successive Federal Governments claim to have put in place over the years. In drama, Ola Rotimi captures it in *If: A Tragedy of the Ruled* and *Akassa You Mi* and J. P. Clark in *All For Oil*. In poetry, it is a continuing concern and Ibiwari Ikiriko, Nengi Ilagha, G. Ebinyo Ogbowei, Adiyi Martin Bestman and several others have treated it. As Eldred Ibibiem Green states it in 'Let it Flow',

> Those who Fight against us
> who claim to have made us
> Forget that for their pyramids
> and chocolates, We Gave:
> the oil palm, rubber, timber
> copra and others.
>
> Today Crude has become
> the Whitlow which allows its owner
> No sleep, no rest, no food;
> and Gas the unending day
> that Denies All of creation
> Nature's True Cycle;
>
> So let it Flow
> from Chad's waters
> and Nguru's dunes
> to Osun's groves
> and Ekiti's forests,
> from the Rima
> to the Benue,

That All may partake

> of its Curses;
>
> let it flow
>
> Everywhere
>
> That Envy may Die
>
> the Death of Shame (*Ogolo* 88 – 89)

A particular quality for which Ijo literature, particularly poetry, has become known is lyricism. Writing about Gabriel Okara, O. R. Dathorne (1976), states that,

> Okara ... reorganizes language by rendering it lyrical, and it is the ease of a songster that makes him such a satisfying poet. He adopts the techniques of song-writing by repeating whole phrases, each time with a slightly different emphasis, by beginning with dependent clauses, and by making the poem grow into a long main statement which gathers momentum as it develops   (174–175).

Commenting on J. P. Clark's use of alliteration, N. J. Udoeyop states that 'it would seem then that for Clark, the most significant possibility of the alliterative style is musical.' (86).

This lyricism is not limited to the two 'senior citizens' but is manifest, also, in the works of younger poets like Ibiwari Ikiriko, G. Ebinyo Ogbowei, Emmanuel Opigo and Nengi Ilagha. In 'Lissia', for example, Nengi Ilagha combines parallelism and antithesis to attain a reasonable level of lyricism:

> I have stoked the fires of all my desires
>   cannot find an oasis to conquer your thirst
>
> I have captured contraband across borders
>   cannot match the largess of your heart
>
> I have riffled through cabinet gazettes
>   cannot trace top secrets
>   to top the security of your calm . . . .

I have strummed the harpstrings of my soul
cannot strike the chords to twang aright
 your name

So hush, Lissia, hush
 this bereft song of gratitude
 must never find a tune!
                              (*Mantids* 38, lines 5 – 21)

Gabriel Okara believes that the lyricism that exists in his and Clark's poetry, derives from their concern with the Niger Delta environment—its rivers, birds, forests and other natural sounds. (Interview, 9 Sept, 2006). Since a concern with the environment is a major characterstics of Ijo literature, it is not surprising that the younger poets are lyrical. Nor is it surprising that this is the same ethnic environment that has produced great popular musicians like Rex Lawson, Erasmus Jenewari, David Bull, Robert Ebizimo and Asu Ekiye; a father of contemporary choral music like Ikoli Harcourt Whyte and the duet of Bara Brown and Enitoun Iyalla, and great composers like Adam Fiberesima and Oyibosiya Eberewariye.

Prospects

Oral Literature at the communal level is still on and still stands its ground; the modernist group, members of which compose individually and record and disseminate electronically is still thriving and one of its members—Asu Ekiye, nicknamed 'Prince of the Niger Delta'—has won awards across Africa.

In the area of writing in Izon, apart from Emmanuel Opigo's 'Okokodiya' and sections of Christian Otobotekere's *Around and About Book Two* especially 'Nama Olotu' and 'Grum Grum Kpoa' which are written in Izon; there is not much, in the twenty six or so components of the Izon language cluster, done in the indigenous language. This is one area where positive results can be achieved if the various state and local governments, and cultural associations provide encouragement in the form of literacy programmes and literary competitions, with accompanying prizes.

An indication of a bright future is the amount of literary activity that is going on among people of Ijo extraction. For example since 2000, nothing less than twenty five works of creative writing cutting across genres (including Children's Literature) have been published by writers from Bayelsa State, alone including *Yellow Yellow*, by the promising lady of letters, Kaine Agary, winner of the 2008 NLNG Literature Award for Fiction. Bayelsa also produced the first West African Idol, the new songster, Timi Dakolo. This portends well for the future.

CHAPTER 13

Night One of *The Ozidi Saga:*[1]
Collected and translated from the Ijõ of Õkabou Ojobolo

J. P. Clark

Caller: O STORY!

Group: YES!

So it happened. There lay the forest of Orua, the forest of Tarakiri. Long ago in this forest of Tarakiri, there was indeed a great city, deep there in the forest of Orua.

An enormous city it was.

Seven districts there were to it.

In this city of seven wards, there were more than enough warlords, but the man called Ozidi was the hero of all the town.

Behind him were lieutenants.

Although he had deputies, Ozidi being the foremost champion in town was the most alert of men.

As the city flourished, its citizens enthroned one king after another.

From each ward, a king.

Now each time they installed a king in a ward, it was always Ozidi holding the front of the fight until a man was captured and brought back for the magnification of their king.

After taking a man to glorify the king, came the showering of money over him, then they would cook and offer him a variety of dishes. That was how they fared.

But while they feasted like that, the kings did not live and reign long.

Some of the kings died in the first month.

Others died in two months.

---

[1]   For the full Ijo/English text of the Seven Night Saga, see The Ozidi Saga: The Ijõ/Izõn text of the performance by Õkabou Ojobolo. Collected and Translated by J. P. Clark. First published in 1977 by Ibadan University Press, Ibadan, Nigeria. Published in 1991 by Howard University Press, Washington D.C. Published in 2006 by Pec Repertory Theatre, Lagos and Funama, Kiagbodo, with a grant from the Government of Bayelsa State, Nigeria.

And so in this state they installed king after king, until having crowned all their seven kings, only Ozidi's district was left.

Now in Ozidi's district there were no people.

All the people there were dead.

He and his brother alone were left.

With them like that, the townspeople after looking steadily at this matter, spoke out:

"Yes, with the matter as it is, if we do not go to install a king in that district, we would have insulted them.

Therefore, let us go there, and install in Ozidi's district a king."

Now the brother of Ozidi, Temugedege was his name.

He was the elder of the two.

Arriving there, [they called out]:

"Oh, Ozidi!"

"Yes, what is it?"

"Well, in your district the position is now like this; to crown is yours now to wear, others have all been through it; and they all are dead.

Since it's now your turn at the throne, will you please tell your brother so they can crown him king?"

As they finished, Ozidi replied:

"Yes, greetings to you all.

Citizens, you have done very well.

This crown does not fit us in this district.

I and Temugedege, that is all the district.

If there is any other person around, that person around, that person cannot be found.

So take the crown and place it on whoever you please."

"Well, this is not proper!" the people were saying when Temugedege himself rose there in rage.

How he fumed!

"You Ozidi, your silly-evil head - so it is the food I eat that now hurts your eyes?

So the meal I eat hurts your eyes so much that you have come out to say you disapprove of the office I should fill?

I certainly shall sit on the throne."

After Temugedege had spoken in this tone, Ozidi said he well understood:

"Go and sit on your throne."

Thus the city took the crown and placed it on Temugedege.

Next all rose as a body.

On rising like that, as soon as day broke, how Temugedege watched out for royal tributes, with a chewing-stick this long, far out it stretched, and aloud, loud, and loud he chopped away at it, and every now and again he would peer this way, crane his neck that way, then peer back again.

Ozidi's bowel became bile.

Believe me, he paced past the man, stared at him, and pacing past him again, took another look at the man.

"Oh, Temugedege, what folly!

Day has grown this big, right now it is ten o'clock, and is it not time the people of this town came and greeted us?

Is it not time they brought drinks for us to take?

Now you're chewing your big stick, if you chew away long enough you will soon tire."

The other paid no heed. So it went on until such a time, it came to eleven o'clock.

"No, I'm tired of this!"

Next he jumped into his house, and brought out a bottle of gin:

"Temugedege, take this and rinse your mouth of chewing-stick.

If it is state ones you are expecting, you will wait for so long, you may as well be dead."

Temugedege now laughed:

"Hi hi, hi, hi, oh, Ozidi, thanks!

You too have done well."

"Is that so? Is it now I have done well?"

"Oh, yes"

So with the gin he rinsed his mouth of chewing-stick.

When day broke a second time, waiting again was time wasted.

Another day, and waiting was time again ill-spent.

So it went on for seven days. When it came to the seventh day, yes, by my word, Ozidi's bowels turned bad.

Said Ozidi:

"Oh, was this what you people agreed on? Now I 've heard."

Even as he spoke, Ozidi's rage mounted against the city, and he cut the town down with abuse:

" Look, this state of Orua, this territory of Tarakiri, so you have made a slave of me; I who have gone and killed men for you to grace your kings; so you, now that my brother is king, I being the man of the small ward, have indeed refused to come by my house up till this day, may your heads all be laid down and chopped up piecemeal.

May you perish to a man.

Let not one of you be left standing.

Indeed are you men?"

He abused them to that end, he abused them to this end.

Then he retired to his compound.

Once he entered his house, the townspeople met in council:

"Is it this fellow without family has cut up the town from one end to the other; is it because he is the strong man?

The way he has cut the state to shreds, let's go and show him something.

Tomorrow we shall go to war; when we have told him that, let's all take cudgels and only cudgels; let none take a sword.

Ozidi, if cut with a matchet is not dented; if shot with a gun suffers no bullet-hole; if struck with a spear cannot be pierced: that's the kind of man he is.

You all know him well.

Therefore, when everybody has taken stick and only stick, let us lay an ambush in the forest and when he comes let us hit at him all together, and since he has no magic charm against cudgels, we shall fell him down. Once he falls down, we'll decapitate him, and carry off his head to Temugedege for him to be king!"

"Hear hear! It's agreed!"
So they held consultations through the night, then at dawn, they all entered the forest, took to the road.

They took up positions all around the route.

They prepared for the fight and not being goats, they kept to the front.

In no time, the rest of the raiders, all of them leading warriors, filled the front.

Then they sent a messenger:
"Go and tell Ozidi, tell Ozidi to hurry up, tell Ozidi to come here at once."
As soon as this was said, a man ran to summon Ozidi:

"Oh, Ozidi, right now Agbogidi and his group Ōgueren and his gang,Ōfe and his followers. Azezabife and his fighters, indeed everybody has moved in.

Therefore you are to come at once and join them—so they said."

At this, leaping at a bound and rearing on the floor of his house, he asked:

"Is it the true Ijõ thing?"
"Oh yes."

"Why didn't they as much as say so?

Say I've heard and will come."

Having said so, he rushed into his shrine.

As he came out, a male lizard ran towards his head - with short hurried steps, it leapt out and fell on his path. His wife now clung to him. ?r?a, she who was called so, now cling to him:

"Ah, my husband, don't go!"

Caller: O STORY
Group: YES!

"My husband, you must not go.
Don't go to them.
Stay, it's right even if they go alone to bring your brother honour.

You yourself must not go."
Then he asked, whether it was he the hero of all the state that should not go?
Of course he had to go.
His wife pleaded:
"Do not go!"
But although she implored, he did not agree.
There, straight he stood, and once he leapt out, and snatched his sword, he raced out.

The woman raised a lament:

>Oh Ozidi my man, my man, my man, my man!
>
>Oh leader of the vanguard, my man, my man, my man, my man!
>
>Oh my leader of men, my man, my man, my man, my man!
>
>Oh Ozidi my man, my man, my man, my man!"

By now, he could not tell whether anyone was wailing or not.

Heedless he rushed in

As he charged on like that, the moment he burst upon the forward troops, everybody there fell down rolling, one over the other they rolled.

They fell rolling, trampling down all the grass blades.

He halted.

"What, by what thing are you scared of me?

Look, don't be afraid of me.

I am Ozidi - or aren't I?

How! Will you not stay with me,

Are you so scared of me you flee?"

Caller:

O STORY

Group: YES!

As he spoke, he stood like this looking at them, and since they merely stared at him, he plunged onwards.

So he sped onward, and as he came upon the group of commanders, each of them had a cudgel; and sweeping in like that, many at the mere sight of him, on seeing his eyes and body alone, fell down milling on the ground.

Next, almost at once, they fell upon him from behind, blow after blow.

When he raised his sword like this, the ground became one rolling mass.

Yes, soon, they hit him again blow upon blow.

He tried to lift his hand but cramp seized it.

So it went on, because these were his own people, because he had no thought of killing them, he let his sword drop, and his hand went limp.

And so they pummeled him, pummeled him until he tumbled.

When they had struck him down, they hacked at his head but could not cut through.

Though they sawed at it with matchet till they wearied, it was all drudgery.

They tried it this way but the same strain.

Thoroughly tired out, they sent a man in a hurry with this message to Ozidi's wife:

"Right now your husband has slain a great warrior, but to cut his neck has been impossible.

Therefore be swift and send at once that secret for cutting up captive heads."

So briefed, the man ran off to tell Ōrea.

The moment he delivered his message to Ōrea, she said:

"Yes, I know.

My husband it is they have murdered.

Look, go and carve him up, and bring me his head.

When you have gone and plucked leaves of the coco-yam and covered up his face, cut him up, and only then can you cut through."

As she spoke, the messenger sped off. The messenger on that take-off ran without stop, and upon meeting them [burst out]:

"Here, here, it's coco-yam leaves!

Gather in coco-yam leaves.

Fetch them here to cover up his head, then cut away and you can cut through."

And truly, when they cut down coco-yam leaves and covered up his face, and cut again, like fish, they cut with ease and it took.

Having cut him up to carry, Azeza said:

"Bring it here, let me carry it.

I'm Azeza.

It was I with my staff hit the man first."

And so once they left it to Azeza, and Azeza snatched up the head, the moment he placed it there, he could not move.

He walked up this way, there was no way; he walked up this way, there was no way; he walked up this way, there was no way; there was no longer road anywhere.

232

Caller :   O STORY
Group :   YES

Now, as soon as Azeza turned full on the road, to press on was impossible.

Now he took up song:
                    SONG
Solo :   Look, I am Azezabife
Chorus :   Azeza Azezabife!
(*Repeated seven times*)

Upon my word, Azeza did not know again where to go.

He went this way, there was no road; he went this way, there was no road.

Said Õfe:
"Halt! halt!

Now, bring it round to me."

And so as he pulled to a stop, Õfe stepped straight into the place.
The man called Õfe no higher than this, a downright dwarf was he, an out and out midget of a man.

As he snatched up Ozidi's head to place on his own head, the man's wife, Ozidi's wife, Õrea, this woman at home now spoke:

"If that road stays blocked like this, I shall not see my husband's head to weep over.

Oh, my husband, please open up the way for them so that they can bring your head to me."

She offered in this way sacrifice at home.

As she worshipped at the shrine, Õfe lifted the head swiftly to his shoulder, but to go forward, to move on, came a blackout, so that moving this way, all was dark.

SONG

Solo :   Õfe me gbudumano

Chorus: Kpainzama, kpainzazama e

                 Kpainzama, kpainzama e

        (Repeated four times)

Caller :   O STORY!

Group :   YES!

Now when Õfe rushed in with the head, the road opened out—into one straight stretch of land.

As Õfe marched off with the head, the rest milled behind him.

Song rose aloud, it rose aloud, went on and on, until they emerged from the forest of Orua into town.

Emerging, they made straight for the house of Temugedege.

On to Temugedege's place they marched, and arriving three, upon my word, straightway, they hurled the head down on the grounds of Temugedege.

Having dumped it, [they said]:

"Temugedege, here is for your coronation.

Take it as your royal skull.

That's it, take it!"

When Temugedege looked closely at the head, it was his brother's face.

"Oh, Ozidi, my brother, my brother, my brother, my brother, brother!

Ah, what is this, people of Ado have done hard by me, my brother, oh my brother, brother!

Ah, Ozidi, oh my brother, my brother.

My own general, my brother, oh my brother, my brother!"

While he wailed, Õrea, the wife came out; quickly, she carried off the head.

As she did so, all fled out of sight.

234

Each fled straight for home.

And so she carried off the head, and setting it upon her lap, broke down weeping:

"Ah, Ozidi, my man, my man!

The man who was warned but would not listen, my man, oh my man!

He who held the front and rear of all fights, my man, oh my man!

The general is gone, oh my husband, my husband!

Oh Õreame, come over and see my man, my man, oh my man.

Oh, Ozidi, my man, oh my man, my man!"

So she carried on, then came a time, and Õreame saw all from far off:

"What, is it my son-inlaw they have gone and killed in that sad manner?

Well, I'm dead!"

Directly, she struck out with her magic fan and lifted, she flew far from sight,

Her wings rushing as the wind.

On, on she flew, then alighted weightlessly on the scene, and touching down there like that, and rushing straight in to the house, there was her daughter wailing over the head of her husband upon her lap.

Caller :   O STORY!

Group :   YES!

"Don't cry, don't cry, don't cry.

You girl, be quiet.

Is it not your husband they've killed?

Don't cry, do not cry!

Don't you see you are with child?"

Caller :   O STORY!

Group :   YES!

Believe me, Õreame summarily took over the head of her son-in-law. Having collected it, she carried the corpse head, had a grave dug outside and there buried it.

After she had it buried, she struck her daughter with her magic fan, and that instant both became air-borne for home–town.

You see, they came from another land.

They were not of that city.

On their arrival home, this woman that seemed not pregnant before, had in fact received her dead husband into her womb, so that the woman indeed became pregnant.

And so his wife was heavy with child until by the ninth month, when she fell into labour, and a great storm appeared. Once the storm rose, it blew till nightfall, then it blew till dawn; blew till dusk, and on till dawn and so to fall of night and then to break of day.

So it raged, and as it became a seven-day storm, the woman delivered.

And when she delivered, it was a baby boy, big and upright.

Once you saw the father, you saw the son.

The moment he was born and on the ground, believe me, Ōreame snatched up the boy and threw him into a cauldron. She took the new-born baby and threw it inside.

Steeped in there, the child remained under for seven nights, before she fetched him out.

The boy was just as he was when born – bouncing and brawny.

Only then did she take the child and wash him.

With her water of herbs and water of herbs alone she washed the child, until the child grew up.

And the boy lived with them.

Caller: O STORY!
Group: YES!

Came a time, and the boy took so much to playing that he could not be held back for anything.

The spirit of play was strong in him, it really was strong.

So he went on playing and if he but ran into any little child, swiftly he would pick it up, toss it, and dash it to the ground.

And parents would come in crying:

"You Ōreame! has that son of yours come for our children, is it our children your son will beat to death!"

"What, this child I bore only a couple of days ago? Your children are older by far.

Have you come again? Do let me down gently, you that are left of this town!"

As from that time, Ōreame became engaged with them in constant quarrels.

So it went on, even where they played top, it was this Ozidi, who won all the tops.

They had as yet not given him a name.

They just called him child.

His mother too had not given him a name.

So they all lived with him in secrecy, and he too when he called his mother,

"Oh mummy" was all he called.

And whether this was Ōreame he also did not call.

So it went on—believe me, come night come day, come night come day, come night, and the youth in a short time became a sturdy man.

So he grew up, until one day, by my word, his grandmother sent him on an errand:

"My boy, come here!"

Sent for like that, he went.

"What is it, mother?"

"Come, let's go and fetch some wood."

Next he followed her behind.

They went and on coming to the bush:

"My son, stand there while I go to stool."

"All right."

He stood in the middle of the road like this.

While he stood, she went in there. Adroitly, and turning up round the corner, she went to the middle of the road and changed into a hillock; taking over the whole place.

And the hill now blocked up the whole road from the front, [she said]:

"Now, my boy, you may come."

When she said this, yes, thinking his mother was in front and calling him, he tried to move, but there rose the hill.

To pass this way, he found nowhere to enter.

The hill in fact began to pursue him.

Help!

When he bolted, it was for town.

He did not even wait for his mother.

On running and arriving in town, his little mother asked him:

"Where's mother?"

"Oh, one huge hill it was chasing me, so I fled home."

"So you couldn't wait for mother before fleeing home?"

"Well, that thing, was it not to kill me it did all that?

What it did was so threatening, I got scared."

"It was enough to scare one."

After she spoke, not quite long, their mother came in carrying some wood:

"Ah, the shame bearing a lazy child:

Oh, the pity, what a lazy child!

Now, you boy, where was it you went?"

"Oh, well, when you called I was coming,

But a huge hillock so pursued me I had to return home."

Next:

"Oh, so this child is a child with no sense, a child lazy to the extreme, oh the shame!'

Then she grew calm and left off.

On the next day, having bathed the boy with as much magic herbs as she could, she asked him:

"Come and let's go out again."

And so again he set out wither.

Setting out, on getting to that same road, again she told him:

"I'm going now to stool. The last time you ran away. Now you just stand here quietly."

"Yes, I will."

Again after disappearing mysteriously in to the place, she changed into a leopard in front, a leopard blazing all over.

Indeed into a leopard she turned, believe me, with a mane spotted all over, all very bright, dazzling and full of fire.

Having done that, she called him again from the front:

"Now, you child, come up here. I have finished stooling. I'm this way."
"True?"
Before he could move up, there was no place to enter.
Sparks and spots everywhere:
"Oh, isn't this dog huge?
Can a dog be this huge, what teeth the dog has!
The eyes blaze forth!
You fellow, please keep to one side so I can pass."
The beast itself stood still.

Caller: O STORY!
Group :   YES!

"Help, why, you male dog, if you dare bite me, I won't take it.
You better leave here.
I'm begging you – my mother is there anxiously waiting for me.
Last time I didn't go, she scolded me severely.
You dog, move to one side!"
The leopard merely flicked its head, and he bolted.
Running off like that with short light steps, he ran and burst into town.
As he showed up in town, his mother again asked him:
"Look, you child, have you come again?
Now where is mother?"
"Oh, this time there was a dog in the middle of the road almost mauled me to death. That's why I have run home."

Caller: O STORY
Group: YES!

"Is it a dog chased you this time?
Is there no day you alone can go and find wood to fetch home, so that you aren't scolded do you hear? Have you come again?"

"Do not as much as say it, there is none would see that dog and not be scared.

The dog was too big."

After he spoke, not quite long, his grandmother came in quietly.

"Yes, what shame bearing a cowardly child.

Oh, the shame I have eaten!

Yes, today again I alone have had to bring home a little bunch.

Oh, oh, oh, this boy, what shall I do to this child?"

So saying, she swiftly disappeared into the forest.

Indeed she disappeared into the forest.

She disappeared into the forest, and gathered there magic herbs, believe me, things for scrubbing a man, for scrubbing her son, his mother squeezed some of these into his eyes, so that he had all with which to fear nothing, all these she took, worked over, and then came a time, a certain day, once that day came, as goes the story, Ozidi grew hot in body like a man.

As the children of the town were out playing at archery, he said he would go too and shoot, but when he appeared because whenever they played at tops, it was he that always trounced the lot, they refused to play with him.

As he stood forward [they all said]:

"You, this time we shall not admit you.

In this arrow game, we won't have you shoot with us."

"Why won't you enter me in the shooting?"

After he spoke:

"Well, you, whenever there is shooting, always break the rules.

But we won't mind including you in the shooting today.

We have, however, put up an entry fee for everybody.

Have you up to twenty cowries?

Now loosen your loin-cloth and see,

So we too can see."

On loosening his cloth there was none.

"Well, since you have brought nothing we'll not admit you.

We won't as much as register you."

"In that case I'll go to my mother and bring it."

And he ran off to his mother.

Caller :	O STORY!
Group :	YES!

On getting there, he reported to his mother:
"Right now, they are playing here at archery, but they say admission by money and money only.
Without that fee, they won't have me play, so they said."
"Go there and look at the altar, and count yourself the coins you want."

Rising, she poured him money.

"Now, go."
She also made for him a special bow.

"When you go, this bow, when you get there, don't aim it direct at any target before shooting.
Just shoot it at the sky."
Then, having dipped the arrows for the bow into her pot of herbs, she gave them to him.
Immediately she handed them to him, he ran with them back to the place, and there the rest stood.
"Have you come? Where is your money?
Where is your money?"
He replied:

"This is my money, these are my coins.
Here they are."
"Well, in that case, you may stand and shoot."
By my word, when the others shot, when they shot aiming straight at one point, hard luck! It was into empty air.

None hit target.
Now it came to him.
"Now you too shoot.

That's the target we are shooting at, you better know that.

If you shoot wide, you win nothing as well."

"All right."

No sooner said than he aimed his bow like this at the sky.

"You, you, that's the target there!"

He well understood, he said, he could see it quite well.

He shot as they had and off it sprang! The arrow sped whizzing way, it went on and on, zoomed on into the sky, and while all there searched and strained for it, the arrow swung back and hit the plantain leaf, standing there rattling.

"Do you see?"

All turned their thoughts gazing on the ground.

"Why did you shoot at the sky?

Yes, if it's like that, we won't pay you."

"If you don't pay me, then you won't as much as move. Just take a step..."

Because they were all afraid of him, it was "Oh take, oh take, take it. Oh take, take it," and so all counted down their money to give him.

Caller :   O STORY!

Group :   YES!

After they totted up and paid him, loaded with this money, he ran home:

"Oh mama! oh mother! I have brought those things home. I ate up all.

 I polished off the whole place."

"Is that so, then pour the money inside."

He poured it out like water.

After it was poured out, when day again broke, the woman said:

"Now, get yourself ready.

Do prepare yourself. We must go into the grove."

Next, [he said]:

"Is that so? Are we going into the forest again? Are we setting out once more?"

"Oh, yes."

Believe me, soon, they went once more to where firewood is found.

Once again setting out to find firewood, they pressed on.

They went as far as a place of swamp, and again the woman disappeared.

"I want to stool."

And again she retired.

As she went in again, so the hill of old sprang into place.

Now she had given him a huge matchet.

Made to hew wood, it was a tall cutlass.

As she stepped in, in no time she was out in front.

"My son, I have got here. Now, you come along."

"Yes."

Even as he moved, the hill comes again?

Has this huge hill come again and blocked the road?

Today, this is how I shall dig at this hill, and not until my mother appears shall I leave off."

Leaping at the hillock, he struck at it stroke after stroke.

Down crumbled the hill.

White ants littered the place.

"You boy, have you come again? Oh!"

Another blow.

Next, with his cutlass, he hacked through.

Believe me, soon, the woman cried.

"Oh, this boy will pound me to death if he goes on."

So saying, swiftly she withdrew, and the hill vanished from the place.

And so he walked through.

As he showed up [she asked]:

"Now where have you been all this time?"

"That huge hill of the other day was on the way again for me to dig, that's why I stayed long".

"All right, go and find some wood to carry, and come."

His mother, all of them, tying up wood that was dry, returned home.

On arrival home, not quite two days it was:

"Come and let's set out again."

"You want to go out again? Let's go then."

Again he followed her.

He followed her and after a time, as usual she wanted to stool.

Again she stepped aside.

She stayed on for a time, then suddenly.

"My son, come, I have got here."

"Is that so?"

That same dog—the leopard—was in the middle of the road, right in front crouching and growling.

"What, has this dog come again? Oh, ah, look at it! Today what a feast! Oh, we've gorged ourselves today!

There, come, oh, come here.

Oh, please, perhaps its best I lured him."

So saying, stealthily he approached the dog, while very warily it moved its body to one side.

"You fellow, are you running, are you?

Please, come.

Come so that, when I have done with you here as it should be done, I can take you to a huge pot and cook it full of food, after which we shall eat for two, three days running."

Even as he baited it, it leapt up and crouched outside.

"Now, this dog, if I don't get round to kill it, I really will be disappointed."

So saying, stealthily he bore upon it, but oh, the dog suddenly sped away.

"Oh," he cried, "what an animal to escape me! How sad! How shall I tell my mother that she will listen to me? Oh, oh what shame!"

So he moaned.

Moaning still, he got to his mother.

Then his mother said:

"How long you were!"

"Woman, that dog of the other day came again, it was that dog I was chasing made me stay long.

This time the dog ran for it.

And maul it almost mauled me to death."

She replied:

"The child's a little strong now in the eye."

    Caller: HERE'S STORY!

    Group: YES!

"The child's a little strong now in the eye. He's improved."

Carrying the wood, again she turned back.

Back in town, another two days, his mother again was crying for wood.

"Oh, this house runs out of wood far too fast."

"All right," he said, "my mother, you wait, and I'll go and fetch you some."

"Yes, this time you'd better go alone." Again he went in. As he went deeper, a huge iroko tree lay across the road.

Walking up to it, he could just circle it round.

The iroko was all dead, and it rose this high in size.

Making for it, with his cutlass he felt upon the tree, one stroke, two strokes, three strokes, and he cut it loose at one end.

Then cutting down the other end, at one dip, he lifted it to his shoulder.

He carried it all the long way, right to his mother's doorstep and heaved it down.

No place was left to pass.

The mother said:

"Now, what's all this? You child, how is it you've gone and brought that thing to hurl at our doorstep?

"Didn't you say I should go and fetch wood?

Now are you asking? It's what you sent a man he has done!

245

You said go fetch me firewood, and now I have found firewood, must there be trouble?"

"Is this how you see people find and fetch firewood? This wood, if you were asked to split it, can you split it?"

"Well, wait, and I'll break it for you, I'll break it for you, I'll break it for you."

Swiftly, reaching out with one hand, he heeled it to one side.

Then snatching an axe, oh, like fish, stroke after stroke he split it, split it, all wide open, the place filling with firewood.

Caller :   O STORY!

Group :   YES!

Wood filled up the place.

"Today I said the child is stronger and you wouldn't believe. Now push the wood to one side."

"All right."

He gathered them up, all into one place in a great heap.

They became all silent.

"This boy, if left as he is, will come to no good.

What if he takes off for the city of Orua - the strong in that city are teeming, so they are in that site of Orua. The strong simply teem there.

For that reason, if I don't walk out with him a little before then, not to do so will indeed be wrong."

So saying, she, one day, after counting out money for herself, called him:

"Now, come here. Come and let's go out to play."

No sooner said than they sauntered out.

So they tripped on, until they arrived at the house of a wizard.

SONG

Solo: Oh yes, kill and be off!

Chorous: O, Tebekawene, kill and be off!

              (*Repeated six times)*

246

Caller:	O STORY!
Group:	YES!

By my word, as they arrived at Tebekawene's, there was Tebekawene reeling round for all the world to see, railing in circles.

"Where comes that thing?

Yes, from where?

Yes, is it a town in this grove?

Where indeed?"

So he stormed as Õreame and son walked in.

As they appeared, he vaulted to his feet:

"O, Õreame, wrong gnaws you!

You have reason to be.

That way they of Orua murdered Ozidi was terrible.

The story really is dreadful.

It's good to take the boy out.

Yes, but you still must go on.

I am not up to the task.

Since a man stronger than me lives in front, go straight to him."

So he spoke.

Caller:	O STORY!
Group:	YES!

As directed, so they journeyed on.

Caller:	O STORY!
Group:	YES!

Believe me, they pressed on.

On, on they went, and in front as they listened, song was talking, in front song was talking.

Said Õreame:

"There, where in front a song is coming we cannot pass."

Solo: Karakarabiri it is!

Chorous: O grove, O hero!

           (*Repeated eleven times*)

Caller: O STORY!

Group: YES!

Believe me, Karakarabiri, somersaulting and standing like this declared:

"I am Bou-Karakarabiri! I am Bou-Karakarabiri! Now who is it?

Oh, Ōreame! Have you too walked this way? Look, what have I more than you?

Yes, is there anything not in your hands that is in mine own?

You Ōreame, what is it?"

Then Ōreame replied:

"Not so. Even though I may have the thing, what is of another is better by far than that in my hands.

And though you may say so, I really am not your equal, don't you see? You are so powerful you are the limits of the grove, while I merely perch upon a cliff on the beach."

Next [he said]:

"O, it is as well. You come and sit down."

They went and sat down.

After they were seated, Karakarabiri cavorted about the place possessed:

"I am Karakarabiri!

I am Grove's End!

Where is there that person?

Yes, the way this boy's father was killed, should the child not seek restitution but leave off? He must seek reparation."

After he shook up the whole place, he moved to Ōreame :

"O Ōreame, Ōreame Oh ! Here Ōreame!"

"Yes!"

"Now, can you endure? Yes, can you bear it?"

She replied:

"I am Ōreame, what I cannot endure does not exist in this world.

What is it? What is there will befall to pluck my eyes that I cannot endure?

Of course, I can bear it."

"Well, that you can endure, I've now heard."

Next, almost at once, he gathered a number of bags, and headed straight in to the forest.

> *Caller:*   O STORY!
> *Group:*   YES!

Ōreame and her son sat there waiting.

They sat down, they did, for a long time.

So they remained, until in a little while, he swept in loaded.

As he swept up, his bags of herbs filled out, trailing the ground.

And getting there, after emptying the bags on the ground, he vaulted right round into this shrine, and after snatching his magic fan, and lashing out once, twice, thrice! Now lashing out here, now lashing out there, and then having lashed at seven spots, seven pots sprang out of the ground.

Next he twirled his hand, and fire blazed out, twirled it, and fire blazed out, and still he twirled.

In no time he had put fire to all of them. Soon, their inside filled with water. Out came the herbs, straight inside; out they came, straight inside; out and straight inside.

And so when he had primed these seven pots with magic herbs, oh, how they boiled over, like hail upon a place of stone.

As they raged like that, next he moved to a huge mortar, and having stood up, he took out a pestle, one well worn and stout.

Then he summoned the boy.

"You boy, come out here. Boy, you are Ozidi. You are indeed Ozidi! You in your true self can take no other name. Ozidi is your name."

So he spoke.

The boy did not open his mouth.

Soon after, he handed the boy the pestle.

"Take it. Take this pestle, and watch over here. Keep watch over here and whatever tries to alight on the edge of this mortar smash it right inside, and pound away."

"All right."

He too took up guard.

And he gathered fresh leaves and poured them in.

"You go on pounding the herbs."

The boy had begun pounding the medicine, with heavy thuds.

He had not pounded the herbs for too long, when Karakarabiri turned his mouth to the sky:

"Oh monkey, I beg of you! Okpe!

Oh monkey, I pray you!

I pray you, pray you! Pray you!

O male monkey, I pray you, pray you, pray you, pray you, pray you!

O male monkey come, o come, come, come, come, come!"

Our man here went on pounding.

From the distance came the monkey:

"I am! I am!"

"Oh male monkey, come, come, oh come, oh come!

Oh come, oh come, oh come, oh come, oh come!

Oh male monkey, I pray you, come, oh come, oh come!

I pray you, I pray you, I pray you!"

"I am! I am! I am Kpingikpin!

　　　I am!"

He glanced down only to withdraw.

After peering down here, he withdrew.

"I pray you, oh come, oh come!

Oh come, oh come, oh come, oh come, oh come, oh come!"

Long he called, then came a time, when briefly the male monkey alighted on the mortars edge, but before he could strike, it was off! And back on a treetop, yelling "I am!" here and "I am!" there.

Our man kept calling, kept calling. And when Bou- Karakarabiri himself was called, he no longer had time [to listen]. With time for nothing else, next, he could not contain himself again.

Oh, back it came.

With short hurried steps it climbed down, leapt forward, landed at last upon the edge of the mortar, and at once! Oh, the blow, and so with stroke after stroke, he pounded it.

So he pounded at the male monkey, until he pulverized the monkey.

Caller: O STORY!
Group: YES!

After he had pounded the monkey to bits, the man began again to call.

He said:

"Just pound on.

Whatever stands on the mortar, just pound it to bits."

"Oh yes."

And so our man pounded on.

For long he pounded, then once more:

"Oh come, oh come, oh come, oh come,

     oh come, oh come, oh come, oh come,

Oh come, oh come! Oh come! Oh come!

O kingfisher, come, kingfisher come, kingfisher come!

Kingfisher, come, kingfisher, oh come!

Kingfisher come, come, come, oh come!

Kingfisher, oh come, oh come, oh come, oh come, oh come!"

Sharp, sharp, the shriek of the bird!

It rose, hopped and hopped, then sharp its shrill cry.

How the bird played there as a dragon fly:

The roll, roll, and roll of it.

251

But on approaching the mortar's edge, it would veer back, on approaching the mortar's edge, it would veer off.

So it performed, until at long last as it alighted on the mortar, down came the blow crushing it.

Bashed it was already.

Next, he called for a lizard.

Now he called the lizard.

"O male lizard, come, come, come, come!"

Light the footsteps.

"O male lizard, come, come, come, come, come!

Akparakpo, do come, do come, do come, do come!"

As the male lizard came so he was caught.

He pounded it also to shred and powder.

Caller: O STORY!
Group: YES!

Soon after:

"Hornbill, oh come, oh come, oh hornbill!

Yes, hornbill, oh come, oh come, oh come!

Breaker of tree front, oh come, oh come, oh come, oh come!"

And the hornbill from far off screamed and screamed and screamed and screamed!

It hopped and perched here, but found no foothold; it hopped and perched here, and still no foothold.

Through the forest it went flapping and fluttering, wondering, who was it calling him?

So it rushed around the place, and then suddenly falling, falling, falling, falling, it plummeted on the mortar's edge.

Caller: O STORY!
Group: YES!

It too he pounded to bits.

He kept pounding at it, all the herbs in there he served them alike.

When he looked, oh [he said]:

"Now it is good."

Then snatching the mortar, and placing it out there, he spread a large piece of cloth on the ground; next with what is used for sewing medicines he wrapped up all the herbs.

Then he fell to stitching.

He went on stitching, and when he had stitched all across, cowries lined here, lined there, lined everywhere.

Into seven lots he sewed the cowries, and having stitched all, he said:

"Now it is good. Here, ?r?am?!"

"Oh yes!"

"Now ask the boy to stand forward."

As ordered, promptly, he stood forward. And stepping out like this, upright he was, a most strapping youth.

Now, this man Bou-Karakarabiri took him by the jaws, opened out his palm, and slapped him, sharply.

With that sharp slap, his mouth opened out this wide.

His mouth became - ah! And his eyes shot blood.

Caller: O STORY!

Group: YES!

Next, suddenly grabbing one pot like this, he hurled it therein. Again, he seized the second and served it the same way. Into his mouth he tossed them; all the pots he threw them into his mouth. All the cauldrons he hurled them down. Then throwing that stitched up charm also down his throat, he slapped him sharply once, twice; and mouth became as it was before, all pursed.

Belly too became as it was before, flat as a plane.

Caller: O STORY!

Group: YES!

By my word, he now stood out there, his body breaking into sweat.

His body grew hot.

So his body gathered heat, and then he said:

"Now you may find yourself a place to sit down."

Only then did the boy seat himself down.

Seated now merely to look down, he had no kind eyes again for the earth.

Eyes rolling, he glared here.

Still rolling, he scowled there.

And the way his bowels growled, there was no other outlet.

To fight, to begin battle, to cause a fight was all that he now set himself.

Right hot he was now.

"Now you may go."

To which Ōreame replied:

"O, you Karakarabiri! Isn't one thing left, you man, you man?"

Caller:	O STORY!
Group:	YES!

"What is this you are doing? Have I on my own come all this way to you, so that when you have acted like this, the very next day, should the child you initiated meet with ill, would you like it?"

"Well, yes, Ōreame, are they things not in your hands? All along, er, they have been things well within your reach, not so?"

"Yes, don't as much as say it.

Unless that thing is done, all is dud,"

Back Bou-Karakarabiri rushed into the forest.

He went in a long time, and when he emerged, what he brought with him turned out to be the wrong thing.

Ōreame merely laughed:

"You Karakarabiri, of course this is not it, it is the other one."

As she spoke, so he retorted:

"E! er , Ōreame, you weary me!"

So saying, again he dived into the bush.

254

He dived in there a long time, and emerging, finally brought the right ingredient.

No medicine by another, no sword by another, could now kill him.

This charm was left out before.

Now he inoculated this into his body.

Into his belly it disappeared completely.

"There! it's finished.

At last we can leave."

So saying, they left.

Now on setting out, before they got anywhere, by my word, once Ōreame lashed at her son with her fan, both landed in the middle of their compound.

Caller:	O STORY!
Group:	YES!

And they entered their house.

Indeed they went into Ōreame's chambers.

Having entered, Ōreame said:

"My son, go and find a place to sit. Don't go out again. I'm tired. So be calm. Whether those who killed your father are not in this town, we shall go round the wide world a little."

After she told him this, Ozidi himself kept silent and did not open his mouth, and so it was, night fell and day broke; dusk fell and broke, and then he started.

"Hush, it looks as if people murdered my father; that's what it seems grandmother was saying."

He went to his other mother, to his small mother he went.

On getting to her, he asked:

"Now, Ōrea, where is my father—yes my father?"

Caller:	O STORY!
Group:	YES!

After he shot this question, his mother said:

"Oh, your father is there in Orua land.

He is there right in front of the god of Tarakiri.

Very great that. Nothing like this little town. That city is a large one. Seven districts there are to that town. In that town he is."

He did not open his mouth again, but waited a while, and then suddenly, oh, his bowels turned bile.

Again he went to her.

"Woman, my father, how is it since I was born I have not set eyes on my father? Look, how my body feels is not at all good. How about my father?"

"Well, he is there."

Next, he went to his grandmother.

"Oh, Ōreame, though I have asked my mother, your father lives, your father lives is all she says. Now where is my father's town?"

She replied:

"Now, your father's town, from the left here if you set out for it, it won't be long before you are there."

"Well, I want to go to my father's town.

That I do not see my father is not at all to my liking."

Said Ōreame:

"Your father is in the land of Orua.

It's a big town.

It is not like this small town.

He's in that town."

"Indeed, is he?"

"Oh yes."

"In that case, what day shall we go?"

"Oh, we shall soon go."

After this was said, and the matter was settled like this, and he stayed on with them for a time, one day he spoke thus:

"Oh, my grandmother, isn't it terrible the way I alone am settled here! The thing is unnatural.

So I haven't even one relation?

That I should be without relation is terrible."

When he said this, oh, she replied:

"You have lots and lots of relatives."

"And where are they?"

"Oh, right now, they are all gathered underground."

"Oh, my relatives, so those that are my relatives are now under the earth, when everybody is above, is that how it is?"

"Oh, they are many."

"All right, in that case call them out so I can see them."

Caller: O STORY!
Group: YES!

By my word, with him that way, now, she said:

"Your father is in the land of Orua."

After she said this, he asked:

"If so, what day are we going?"

So he dragged it with them until came a time, came a day, and she began to break palm kernels before the doorway of his house.

With okra varnish she had polished her whole floor, polished it so high it slipped, and now she sat in front of the house.

"Here, my son, come quickly, quickly.

Go over there to that rack against the wall and fetch me my pipe.

Go quickly and get me my pipe."

"Is your pipe there?"

"Oh yes."

And so having walked past her, just to put his foot down—mine, was daring-do.

To put it down was impossible.

"Is it that I may not fetch the pipe or what!"

He staggered through the place trying to clutch at the pipe, and the stampede there from.

He paused, then stepped cautiously, so he flew through the loft, and tearing out of the house alighted outside.

"I am Ozidi! I am Ozidi! I am Ozidi! I am Ozidi."

So by himself he named himself.

That was how, there and then, he took a name for himself.

He proclaimed himself Ozidi.

That his father's name was his name.

After he had taken this name, in a short while Ōreame said:

"O my son! O my son! O my son! O my son! Act as you please!"

So urged, oh, he became possessed. His bowels turned cauldron, boiling, boiling, boiling, boiling.

"It isn't that day yet!"

Thus Ōreame from this end:

"It isn't that day yet! It isn't that day yet!"

By my word, how he rampaged through that plane, leaping across the house; at one bound he was there, at another he was here.

All cried:

"Help! Help!"

Those ululating ululated.

After a while, she took out a magic gourd, squashed it underfoot; and his eyes relaxed.

Then he found himself a place to sit. After sitting down, the next moment, he dragged his mother so much with his father's name that his mother said:

"Ōrea, it's time we went."

As soon as that day came round,

       Caller: O STORY!
       Group: YES!

as the day came, Ōreame braced herself.

After bracing herself, having seen to all that should be done right, she spoke to Ōrea:

Ōrea, you too pack all your things at once.

Now it is time we took the child to his father's home."

Accordingly, both Ōreame and Ōrea prepared their kit.

They carried their luggage, carried and had them tied in one piece.

After fastening it, Ōreame with her fan in hand, and all her charms decking her body, [said]:

"Now, there, tie your cloth each to each."

And immediately they tied one cloth to the other and she lashed out with her magic fan, striking them both like this, yes, all of them, she flew with all in full tow, wings beating the wind.

They flew for a long time, straight to the city of Ozidi, straight down on Ozidi's homestead they landed.

And so all of them touched down.

Grass overgrew the place.

Indeed the place had become bush.

Temugedege, he who would be king, before a silk cotton tree, among grass was hidden.

Lost he was inside the grass.

He had packed some grass out there, and heaping it all over the place, lived there in the open, and when night fell, he would pick left-over food to eat.

| *Caller:* | O STORY! |
| *Group:* | YES! |

Yes, rubbish food was what he picked to eat.

Next, after they touched down there, Ozidi fell silent; he looked this way, he looked the other.

Ozidi fell silent; he looked this way, he looked the other.

"Now all this forest, how will this bush be cleared? Is that not the town over there?"

"Well, this is your father's homestead."

"Really, this heap my father's house?

"Oh yes."

"Well, what shall we do?

We can't even find people to weed the grass."

"Why, labour is not hard to find. You boy, don't you know anything?

Now didn't you see the people who came to welcome you?"

"Yes, I saw them."

"Wasn't it you who said: turn back, turn back? Wasn't it you said so?"

"Oh yes."

"I see."

"Even now, right now, at one word, all the youths would come and work for us."

"Well, then say it and let them come and work."

Yes, with a wave of her fan, a way opened wide, and so opening, oh, a crowd of people poured in – in one big melee.

"Ōreame, I kneel to you.

Ozidi, greeting! Ōreame, I kneel to you!

Ozidi greetings! Ozidi greetings!"

Each had a matchet in hand.

Next:

"Now start working," and at that word yes, one group cleared the plot right to the end.

They cleared it to the end, right to the ground.

Ordering in tree-fellers - oh, the bush became all men, woodcutters filled it round.

Then entered the thatch-cutters, in fact thatch-cutters had gone in a long time. My word, the milling there.

All in one day, houses sprang up at one end, sprang up at the other, and sprang up here.

They erected them all over the place.

Where Temugedege squatted under a silk cotton tree was all mowed to the ground.

Temugedege now sidled up:

"Now, what's all this? What is all this?

Who are all these people?

Please, this has been my place of hiding. Now, what type of people are these?"

Temugedege stood there trembling.

If you saw him, all moulting he was. "Look, I'm so scared.

Who are these, these people, oh pity, have they come to kill me?"

He stood there shaking in fear.

Caller:	O STORY!
Group:	YES!

So it went on, and when at last they cleared up the whole place, Temugedege cried:

"Please, isn't this too wilting, please! And I have no cover-cloth on!"

Caller:	O STORY!
Group:	YES!

"Only yesterday I left my body all open!

Alone I have holed myself up here.

Has it turned out like this?"

So Temugedege bewailed himself there.

He moaned on like that until one day, on my word, Temugedege came out at night to pick himself some food, and coming to the place, look, yam peeling left over on the ground was what he picked up to eat and take home.

Because Ozidi had at first forgotten, when Ozidi now suddenly appeared, he wondered:

"Where is my father's brother that you spoke of? Is he dead?"

"Oh, that man under the silk cotton tree, that's him."

"Yes, really?"

Both Ōreame and Ōrea went over and greeted him.

When they went to greet him, he recognized Ōreame, he also knew Ōrea.

"Oh, my mother-in-law, why, since they killed your son-in-law and you took away your daughter. I haven't set eyes on you again.

Is it today you have come over to greet me?

Well, greetings, greetings!"

"Oh, yes." "Oh, so it's you cleared this ground?

Yes, it must be you who cut it all."

Really, well, then, that's good.

Mm, as for Ozidi, he's a man dead.

Oh, that you brought her back, you've indeed done something."

"Look, right now, over there, your son too has come."

"My son too has come?"

"Yes."

"Now who exactly is my son?"

He had himself no child, like a thing dropped was his life.

He had no wife.

That was how he was.

As for Temugedege, he had no wife, he had no child.

That was all his life.

> *Caller:*   O STORY!
> *Group:*   YES!

When they returned home, she said to Ozidi:

"Ozidi, that's your father.

Look, that fellow there under the silk cotton tree, that is your father's brother by one mother.

You go and greet him first."

"Yes, yes, I understand."

He directly walked across, and came to him:

"Father, I kneel to you."

"Yes, rise, rise, my son, greetings.

Now, whose son are you?"

" I am your son."

"Oh, you people of Orua, have you come again to laugh at me? Since I grew up, I have fathered no child.

That's how I am.

I've found no woman to sleep with.

That is how I have lived till this day. Now you say: 'I am your son,' that's what you said.

Now whose son are you?"

"Oh, I am your brother's son.

Ozidi gave me birth."

He looked at him closely like this.

"Ooh, he really looks like Ozidi!

Oh, Ozidi my brother, my brother, my brother!

O Ozidi, my brother, my brother, my brother, my brother, my brother!

Well, so he had a child like this? O Ozidi, my hero brother.

Ah, my hero brother.

Are you indeed Ozidi's son?"

"Yes, I am Ozidi's son."

"A child Ozidi had with whom?"

"Oh, with Ōrea, of course."

"Ōrea?"

"Oh, yes."

"Well, well, and all this time you were born, I didn't know at all.

Yes, I didn't know at all."

"There, my father—my mother was in fact pregnant when they killed my father, so they said."

"Well, yes, it is good.

Greetings, greetings, greetings."

So he welcomed him, and then he walked back.

When he walked back, and got home,

Ōreame asked him:

"Your father, how did you find him?"

He reported to her all his father said.

"Oh, that's all right then,"

Ōreame looked at him fixedly:

"It's not right this child walks the world alone.

263

For him to walk the world alone will not be right."

Next [she called]:

"Ozidi."

"Yes."

"It's not safe for you to walk by yourself. I shall now give you bodyguards.

As it is, you have no sword to seek battle.

You don't even have a knife.

With things like this, I'd better call in men to forge you a sword, to fashion you a knife.

When all the little things have been done for you, then you may go out to play, and all will be well."

"All along, it is you I have looked up to. Let anyone but set upon me now, and I stand helpless.

Have those who killed my father ever had any good thought for me? Since, since, they don't mean well by me, you can as well act."

In a flash, once her fan hit the earth, the earth split open.

Next, conjuring a blacksmith to come out quickly, in great haste a blacksmith scrambled out.

With quick, hurried steps he ran in - and lo, there, yes, his blower of bellows, was there too…

"Quick, quick, forge for my son a sword – quick, oh, quick!"

"Yes, whatever you direct I mould.

Is it drag we shall drag?

Whatever it is you say I will mould for you."

"Hurry!" she said and there and then a smithery was up and ready.

And look, impregnable steel stretched out straight.

He struck at it, blow after blow.

So he forged, all that day he forged it into shape.

> *Caller*:   O STORY!
>
> *Group*:   YES!

That steel was true steel, real true steel; all gleaming it was, oh, he burnished it, had all its head fitted beautifully.

The fitting finished, oh, he called him (ah, is it the mother?) the blacksmith called the mother.

"Oh, Ōreame!"

"Yes!"

"Please speak to your son, that he should come and see steel.

There, the steel, I have moulded it.

So call your son, let the boy please come out, let him come and look at steel, let him come here and see the sword!

Oh, the sword is beautiful."

To which [she replied]:

"Here, Ozidi, you go and look at the sword, and if it's good, bring it over."

When Ozidi got there [he asked]:

"Have you in infact moulded it well? Is it good - is it?"

"Oh, very good, whatever you say, I will mould it for you."

"Then bring what you've moulded and let me see."

And when firmly he grabbed the sword, hand and handle fitted into each other.

Then stepping out into the open, he wielded the sword this way, in great circles, and with much fury, brandished it until, oh, the front of the sword broke with a snap.

Caller:	O STORY!
Group:	YES!

As the sword front snapped, the sword front ululated:

"Ōfe, I am falling you way!"

"Ōfe, beware yourself!"

(*Repeated seven times*)

Caller:	O STORY!
Group:	YES!

Truly, the sword-front began to ululate, woe, woe, woe, woe, woe, woe, woe, woe, woe.

Ōfe and others, all of them, were at this time in a hall, drinking, roistering, making a great commotion.

The generals were all there drinking and bellowing.

With that ululation, a child of his, his eldest, all dressed up and ready to go out to play, holding erect his figure, before he could step out of the compound, the flying sword piece at one blow plunged into his head.

Caller:	O STORY!
Group:	YES!

Down he dropped, twitching and threshing.

"What happened to him What fell on him Hold him, hold him! Oh, hold him!"

They held him, but although they lifted him, he slumped back to the ground.

When they looked at his head, it fell wide open.

The sword head lodged deep inside the head.

"What is it has fallen from above" peering hard, they tried in vain, not knowing a broken sword-front was buried there.

"Oh," Ōfe cried, "Oh, from where comes the misfortune, oh this misfortune Yes, this town, when Ozidi himself lived quietly, still with sticks and staffs we beat him to death, so we'd have peace, now is there any other thing I have done wrong - yes, what has caused this accident

And has it come, and killed my eldest child Oh what terrible task! Who are so envious of this one sovereign task! Who are so envious of this one sovereign I have"

And so Ōfe thrashed about this place.

Those holding Ōfe held him down there.

Long they struggled, and now the child was stone dead.

And so they bore him off to bury without ceremony.

Now, our man, as if he would beat the blacksmith to death, hit at him with the sword stump.

"Please, please, please, don't beat.

266

I'll forge for you.

Just be patient, I'll make you another.

Do you hear

 Softly, touch nothing.

Whatever you order, I will mould for you."

As he begged, Ozidi angrily flung down the sword like this.

"You can't even mould a thing, yet you say you know how to mould a lot.

Is it that you are a mad person"

"I beg you, don't be angry, please, please."

Oh, the other picked up a piece, and holding it, struck it till it folded over.

Bringing in new steel, again he struck at it.

Loud rang the anvil.

He too turned frantic.

"At this rate this man will kill me!"

Fear so gripped him, he struck hard.

The bellows man too did not rest his hands, puff, puff, puff, he puffed at his tools.

Caller: O STORY!

Group: YES!

So he blew at them; kept blowing until all glowed, with blow after blow.

He blew at it, then stroked it in, and again hit at it.

After withdrawing indoors for a while, he called him again.

"Now come again and see."

"All right."

So on that same day he returned there.

"Fellow, last time you played false with me.

This time, if I swing the sword and it breaks again, you'll end up in two halves, after which another will make me my sword."

"Please, do it gently, do it gently.

Whatever you say I do for you, don't you see Don't kill.

Don't kill, hear me."

"All right, I have heard."

So saying, once more he snatched the thing.

Again how he wielded the sword, with all the fury of a whirlwind, on and on he whirled it, and just as he was coming out of his vision, the sword front snapped again out of sight.

Once the sword broke again in its front, so did ululation a second time, into the sky it rang first like a bell, then like wind.

"Now, what thing is yelling like this"

Ululating it sped off, and upon reaching the compound of Azeza, began to circle the place, revolving in wide arcs.

Caller: O CITY!

Group: YES!

The blacksmith truly became scared this time.

His body shivered in fear.

His body felt awful.

"Will this man not kill me another time

Yes, certainly next time the fellow will kill me."

He went on:

"If again I forge this sword and it breaks again, this time I certainly will not survive."

So saying, on this day, he took a length of steel that never never never could be cut, and hurled it on the ground, then he thrust it into the furnace, bending it over at once into two.

And then how he hammered at it!

As each melted into the other, he forged them, forged all till it became one, forged it straight.

Next at its crest he placed seven prongs.

All the seven prongs he polished white. They all began to blaze.

The handle fitted perfectly to hand, taking up the whole hand.

Believe me, this was the sword of seven prongs he forged for him and when he swung it, the sword lapped his hand round, and when the sword opened out again, at this point, when he unfurled it, after he hurtled it open, opening, oh urged to brandish it again, there, things entered Ozidi.

He is Ozidi! He is Ozidi! He is Ozidi! He is Ozidi! He is Ozidi! And so proclaiming he hurtled on, hurtled on till he pounced upon the silk cotton tree under which Temugedege lived, attacking it so roundly from all sides that it crashed down rolling around Temugedege on the ground.

Cried Temugedege:

"Murder! I'm this way!

I am here! Yes, who is this crazy boy they have gone and brought

Oh, what a world! Oh, oh, I'm dead. All along I have been a man quietly picking grubs to eat.

Now, Ozidi, have you brought back your troubles To live in a house I may not. Now to live in the open too I may not.

If you'll agree, child, isn't it better, boy, you killed me instead This one seems worse than the first, this one seems worse than the first."

So he moaned.

So it went on, and again once the mother trod a magic gourd underfoot, his eyes came down.

He became calm.

Later she took away his sword.

Immediately his mother snatched the sword from him and stowed it away deep inside his stomach, is body grew limp.

And so he remained there quiet.

Caller: O STORY!
Group: YES!

until his mother struck open the earth wide open a second time, and out came a guitar-drum player together with a horn-blower.

As they issued forth, and came up to him, [she said]:

"Ozidi, these are your attendants.

They will walk behind you ."

When she told him this, he replied:

"Really, that's good."

269

Now this was Ozidi's house.

If Ozidi but sneezed, if he but whispered, they heard all.

And if they too whispers, Ozidi could also hear them.

If anyone came to Ozidi's house to spy on him, their job was to watch him.

Night and day they did not sleep a wink.

So it went on, then came one day, yes and Azeza said:

"Oh, what disgrace! So Ozidi, so he had a son who has now come and killed my eldest child."

He immediately walked over to Õfe:

"Look, Õfe, that the son of Ozidi has been in town and killed both our children - do you hear"

"Oh yes, is it so The way that boy died was cold–blooded.

So it's Ozidi's son Oh, was it Ozidi's son, wielding and breaking his sword, came and killed both our sons Now what shall we do to kill swiftly"

So saying, when the day came—

Caller:	O STORY!
Group:	YES!

by my word, it was not long:

"Yes, how shall we do it"

They called a meeting,

Again they called a meeting.

They consulted there for a long time, for a long time they deliberated, then came a time:

"Oh this very day, let us send one man to fight him—that seems the best thing.

Now, in all this city, when leaders are called, yes, when heroes are called, Õfe it is, since Ozidi died.

And I am the next man."

Caller:	O STORY!
Group:	YES!

Meanwhile, a day came round for Ozidi, and Ozidi spoke to his mother:

"My mother, I'd like to go to market."

That day was market tide in Orua land.

Ozidi said he would like to go to market, he would like to go and know the market.

Ōreame replied:

"Yes, you go and look.

Your men, take them both, and you go and see the market."

Since Ōreame saw at home everything abroad, she did not worry.

And straightaway Ozidi set out, both hornblower and drummer close behind him.

Ozidi found a proper dress, and standing to his full height, was well worthy of youth. Out he sauntered, and whoever saw him [wondered aloud]:

"Oh, doesn't this young man look like the hero who once lived and died in this town?"

As this was said, he behaved as if none had spoken, instead he walked on undistracted down the road, until, in the middle of the market road, a tree stood by, gigantic and tall.

On getting there, he paused like this for a time, then he addressed his drummer and hornblower:

"Now, you two go in there.

Step in there and hide yourselves.

Hides yourselves, stay quiet there, and don't open your mouths."

"All right."

And deftly they went in.

Immediately they moved in, Ozidi stretched himself right across the road.

> Caller: O STORY!
> Group: YES!

As he lay straddled across the road of the women who came by, of all of them, of the whole lot he knew just which of them were wives of prominent people.

They stepped to one side, and took a good look at him.

271

"Why should a handsome boy like this come here, how is it, why is he sitting like this here? Yes, why is he sitting here like this?"

After a while, Õfe's wife together with Azeza's wife, two of them, these were the two leading ladies now approaching.

They skirted him round like this.

"Oh!" cried the woman in front, "Azeza my husband! Indeed, my man is great; it is great to be wife to a strong man, oh yes!"

So she flaunted herself and wiggled in. The other woman too began from her end: "O Õfe my husband! Yes, great is my husband! It's market I'm going. There, let me have good shopping."

"Oh yes."

They went on—there was where Ozidi lay straddled, and here they were.

Next Azeza's wife:

"A stump! Yes, how? What stump is this will trip me up? What, let no evil stump knock my toe like this another time, or else trouble!

Caller: O STORY!

Group: YES!

Yes, I am Azeza's wife.

I'm going straight on to market, and dare some evil stump trip me?

The way this bad stump struck me is not to my liking.

Is there any person in this market that does not know I am Azeza's wife and will dare shoot his mouth my way?"

Azeza's wife said all these words in front.

While she spoke, Õfe's wife was behind.

"What happened to you?"

"Well, one bad stump struck me just now, very hard it was, terribly hard."

"Is that so? Now, is there an evil stump or person can trip you on this earth? We only have to appear in open market, and everybody knows immediately.

Whatever we bid, they get so scared of us, they shower us with wares."

Caller: O STORY!

Group: YES!

"This is Azeza's wife; and this is Õfe's wife; what they say holds as price. Once we say 'won't you give it to us?' they get afraid of us, is that not so?"

"Yes, yes!"

Walking further and pulling up again, yes, Õfe's wife began boasting again: "O, Õfe my husband! What's this? See, wife of Azeza, that evil thing that tripped you would knock me over too! Now what's all this? Shopping must surely be good for us today.

Yes, we shall have plenty to pack home today.

Today we don't have to buy anything with money.

It's us two have come to market today, yes, today we really shall do things." So saying, she swept on, but there was Ozidi stretched right across the road.

Caller: O STORY!

Group: YES!

By my word—

"Look, you , you boy, we who are wives of strong men, we who have married important men are the ones approaching. Get up, get out there quickly.

We don't want any trouble.

Since our men do not brook any nonsense leave the place quietly for us to pass."

All this time, on that day, Ozidi did not even open his mouth.

Whether it was human beings talking to him or beasts or fish, he refused to say.

He remained silent, just lay there straddled, like a man asleep he lay sprawled right across the place.

They walked on, and coming near him:

"You, this little boy, how handsome a boy! Oh, oh, doesn't the boy were a nice face! Do rise.

You child of some people, don't get killed by strangers.

Do get up, please get up.

273

Get up, get up so that we can pass. I, I here am Azeza's wife.

Do you hear? Of course, you know who Azeza is.

Azeza is no good.

One false step taken, and it's another matter, so get up.

You handsome boy of a stranger, rise, please rise."

Are you man, are you beast!

"You boy, it's with you I'm talking - you, get up there, boy.

Didn't you hear what I said?"

Are you man, are you beast?

Now Õfe's wife too began:

"You—you boy, don't you hear what you're told? I am Õfe's wife.

Do you hear? Rise, rise, rise so we may pass."

Whether it was man speaking with him, or beasts speaking with him, he did not respond.

"Hey!" cried Õfe's wife, " Come, come, come!

Even Ozidi who was strongest in the city did not lie across highways.

Yes, do you hear?

Caller: O STORY!

Group: YES!

Ozidi for all his strength never slept across a street.

How is it you small child will lie across the road?

Perhaps, you have not heard of Õfe, have you? Now what town are you boy from? Indeed, what town are you from? You haven't heard of Õfe? That man Ozidi - with sticks and staffs they beat him to death.

When with sticks and staffs they beat him dead, on that day, yes, it was Azeza first carried his head.

On that day, because Azeza could not carry his head, Õfe took over the head to present to Temugedege the idiot.

That fellow fast asleep at the root of that silk cotton tree.

Caller: O STORY!

Group: YES!

And Ozidi was his name, boy.

Even that man, though a great general, they beat him to death, and dare you a little child stay on the public way, and when we wives of very important persons come along, do you indeed refuse to rise?

Now we're going to push you to one side, right out of the way.

Well, you child of strangers, because you are handsome, we asked you to rise, but since you refuse to, now get up, boy!" As they spoke, his belly began to turn. That they carried his father, trundled off with his head, his belly began to turn, his belly began to turn.

As his belly whirled him like that, out broke the hornbill screaming, similarly the kingfisher, all shouting Ozidi the grove—O Ozidi!—and the woods darkened, and the monkey king himself boomed his cry,

"I am! I am! I am!" and out spiraled the sword-

SONG

Solo:	In ata mani
Chorus:	E!
Caller:	Oh, Ijō
Group:	Yes!
Caller:	Hip hip hip!
Group:	Hurrah!!!
Caller:	Oh, Ijō
Group:	Yes!
Caller:	Oh, Ijō
Group:	Yes!

He cut the two women into pieces, both of them at one blow, slicing them from end to end upon the ground.

After dropping them, he told Azeza's wife:

"You woman, you said you're Azeza's wife.

Go then and tell Azeza:

Ozidi right now has a son.

That son of Ozidi having come and slashed us into mess-chop, says you should brace yourself, and come and do battle with him.

Deliver that message to Azeza and then tumble down to a shattering fall - fall wide apart."

Oh, Azeza's wife rushed out there, all pieces cutting through the air.

So she was swept out.

Next he spoke to Õfe's wife:

"You woman, you said you are Õfe's wife, so you said.

It was your husband who carried off my father's head and hurled it down, you said.

When you go, be quick to tell him:

Ozidi whose head you bore off has a certain son.

That son now has slaughtered and sent us to tell you to brace yourself, and then come and fight him.

He is waiting just beyond that bend.

He is down at Ozidi's homestead.

After saying come and do battle with him, then I may fall down splintered."

Yes, when Azeza's wife fled off and got into town, there was Azeza with others deep in drink, laughing aloud, and making a great noise.

On she came in pieces, so she came.

"Now what manner of thing is that?

What are these?"

Dripping and running she came with just a hand, just a foot, she clung to each, then fell down, barely speaking to him, and as soon as she told him, dribbling, she fell down in two.

Said Azeza:

"Oh, please, take that thing there to one side - it dribbles so, oh goodness!

Yes, it's so wet and messy!

What did she say befell her?"

"Oh, Ozidi's child it is has chopped her into the mess, ordering her to tell you that son born of Ozidi has killed her; and having told you that she should fall down dead, and that's why she has fallen down in pieces."

"Now, did Ozidi ever bear a child?

How! That Ozidi, what child could he have had? Take her out to bury."

And off they bore that thing.

Caller:	O STORY!
Group:	YES!

When Õfe's wife ran off to her own people, when Õfe's wife also arrived there after some time, Õfe?s too with his group was carousing and bawling.

Now, in came that apparition, all pieces and halves, with one eye, half a nose, with all the parts in halves.

Getting to Õfe:

"Oh Õfe, oh Õfe, yes, I'm directed to tell you, Ozidi's son right there on the highway has slashed me and Azeza's wife in pieces, ordering us to come and tell you so, after which we should fall down splintered, fall in two and die, so he decreed.

You must therefore prepare yourselves and come and fight him.

You should come and fight him.

He is at his father's homestead, so he said.

You come and fight with him, so he said. And fall down broken before dying, so he told me".

Then crash!

Said Õfe:

"Goodness, what's this? What manner of wicked wet things are these? Yes, all wet and sickening."

Even as he spoke, everybody broke into commotion:

"What, so Ozidi had a son! Has Ozidi's son actually arrived, and done all this- for a child like that, a boy we didn't know was there- well, well, what news, indeed, oh how!"

Soon—

Caller:	O STORY!
Group:	YES!

the man-who-owned-the –town, that's Ewiri Mr Tortoise himself, known also as Abam?lakpa, because in all the town he was the fabulist, now he spoke:

"I have long told you this story.

A man wronged will often bear a strong son, didn't I tell you so?

Now trouble has come again.

Indeed the thing has come."

"Look here, have you come with your cunning, that knack of yours for telling scare-stories.

All along none of us has heard this kind of story.

You just leave things alone.

There, well, it's all child's talk, well he cannot do a thing."

"Really? I have told you and it's finished."

And so he took off himself and went home quietly.

> *Narrator:* Now the story, this is where we'll end it.

It's tomorrow we'll take it forward.

I am not telling again, the story is ended.

Group: YES!

> *SONG*

Solo: Oh fly out and come

Chorus: Fly and come

          (*Repeat nine times*)

(END OF NIGHT ONE)

CHAPTER 14
RESOURCES
Adaye Orugbani

Introduction

While there is no generally accepted definition of what constitutes resources, we shall for our purpose define resources as everything that serves as a source of supply or sustenance to a people or a community. So defined, resources can be divided into several kinds. For instance, we have renewable and non-renewable resources. Renewable resources include land resources, forest resources and water resources. Each of these divisions can be further subdivided. Land resources can be subdivided into agricultural and mineral resources. There are also non-renewable resources such as crude oil and gas. Resources can also be divided into human and non-human resources. Human resources are synonymous with labour- that factor of production without which all the other factors of production cannot be utilized. By this classification, all the other types of resources are non-human.

Ijawland is primarily in a deltaic environment. This environment is generally regarded as inhospitable. Yet it is this environment that has sustained the Ijaw people from their cradle to the present day. As the inhabitants of the Niger Delta and the lands surrounding the Delta, the Ijaw people have been able to master their environment by utilizing the resources available in their environment for sustenance. What are the resources that have sustained the Ijaw people over time; how have these resources contributed to the development of Ijawland; how has the incorporation of Ijawland into the Nigerian state affected the control and management of these resources? A substantial fraction of Nigeria's oil resources is in Ijawland. How has the discovery and exploration of crude oil affected the lives and economy of Ijawland? In this regard, how has Nigeria's petroleum law, and revenue allocation formula affected the Ijaw people? The Ijaw people are now clamouring for resources control. What has been the response of the Nigerian state to this demand, these and related matters will be the focus of this Chapter.

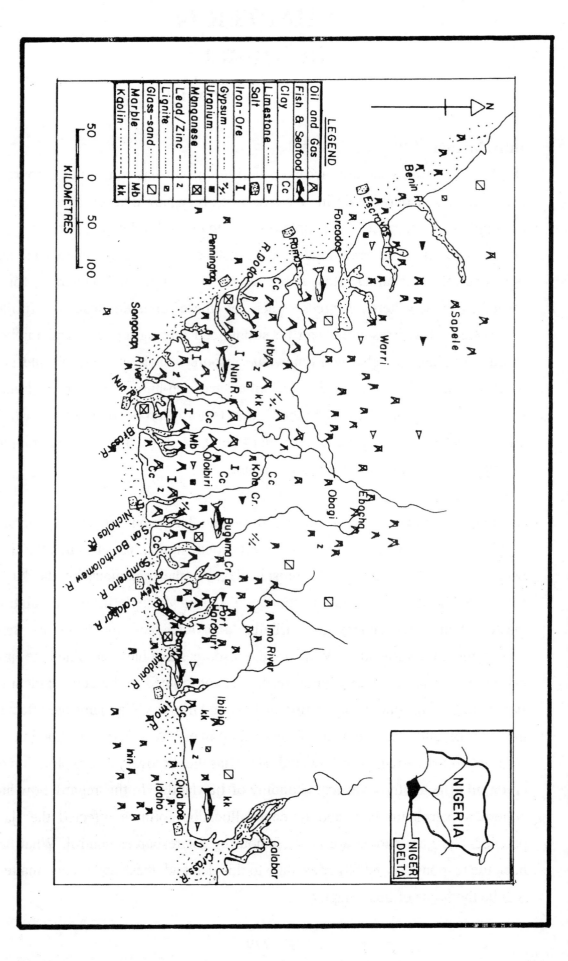

Fig. 14.1: Natural resources of the Niger Delta Region

280

The Resources of Ijawland

The Ijaw people whose home is in the Niger Delta are blessed with a variety of resources. In this chapter we are going to discuss the resources of Ijawland under three main headings. These are

(1)   Forest resources

(2)   Marine resources and

(3)   Crude oil and gas resources

Forest Resources

The forest resources of Ijawland include the woodlands, wetlands as well as the plants and animals that are found therein. Ijawland has three main types of forest. These are brackish water swamp forest which is made up of mangrove forests and coastal vegetation; freshwater swamp forests; and riparian forests. Each of these forests has different characteristics and habitats. These forests provide plants and animals that have sustained the Ijaw people throughout the ages. Some of these plants are used for food. Some of the plants that serve as food include plantain (*Musa paradisiaca*) for which Ijawland is a major producer; coco yam (*Xanthosoma saggitifolia*); another crop produced in abundance in Ijawland is cassava (*Manihot esculentum*); yam (*Dioscorea* sp) which is produced in limited quantities in Ijawland; banana (*Musa paradisiaca*-var, *sapientum*); this crop also yields well in the soils of Ijawland, and the wild mango (*Irvingia gabonensis*). Others are the bitter leaf (*Vernonia amygdalyna*); grains of paradise (*Afarmonum melegueta*); the small pepper (*Capsicum frutiscans*) and the African black pepper (*Piper guineensis*); (Nynanayo in Alagoa, 1999: 47-50); the pepper fruit (*Dennetia tripelata*). The plants listed above are the major but not the only food plants in Ijawland.

Besides plants that serve as food, there are plants that serve as medicine. These plants are so numerous that it will be difficult to mention all of them. Besides the functions of the different curative plants is a well guarded secret among traditional medicine practitioners. Needless to say that the efficacy of these plants are not in doubt as it is on them that the health needs of the Ijaw depended before the introduction of European manufactured drugs.

281

Timber is another forest resource that abounds in Ijawland. Ijawland is home to different types of timber, prominent among which are the mahogany (*Khaya* sp), the tree (*Newbouldia laevis*) and the iroko (*Milicia excelsa*). Others are abura, (*Macrophyla ciliata*); silk cotton tree, (*Ceiba pentandra*); the star apple, (*Cambeya africana sun*); kuru (*Lophira alata*); and the palm tree, (*Elaeis guineensis*).

Besides food plants, the forests of Ijawland is home to different kinds of animals which have been a source of protein to the people. These animals include but are not limited to the monkey, the bush big, antelope, elephants, leopard and porcupine. The forest of Ijawland is home to different kinds of birds of which the cuckoo and the parrot were commercially significant during the Atlantic trade, (more about this later). From the above, it is clear that the forest of Ijawland is the source of several resources.

Marine Resources

As riverine dwellers, the rivers and waterways are, arguably, the most important resources of the Ijaw people. It is the means of communication among themselves and with their neighbours far and near. It was also through their waterways that they came in contact with European seafarers from the fifteenth century onwards with all the consequences this had on their economy and society.

Within the creeks and rivers of Ijawland are different types of fish species. Indeed fishing is the single most important occupation of the Ijaw as a people. Given the variety and abundance of the fish types in Ijawland, space precludes us from naming any but a sample of the available species. Some of the species in the rivers include croaker, the shiny nose, sardine, catfish, mullet, bonga fish, spanners, sharks and the barracuda. Others are a variety of shellfish comprising shrimps, periwinkles, cockles, oysters, lobsters and crabs. Some of these species are in the brackish waters, some are in the fresh water, while some migrate seasonally from the brackish to the fresh water, and *vice versa*.

Besides serving as food items, sea foods, as we shall show later, were an important item of trade between the Ijaw and their hinterland neighbours. The marine resources of Ijawland include mammals and reptiles such as dolphins, the turtle and the hippopotamus. Over time, Ijaw fishermen have developed different types of gear that are specific to the different species. The most common ones are nets, hooks and traps. In this regard, there are cast nets, set nets and drift nets. There are also set hooks and line hooks. The traps are usually in different shapes of basketry. It is with these gears that the Ijaw people harvested the sea. Until recently their catch was impressive.

Oil and Gas Resources

Based on ethnic nationality, the Ijaw nation produces by far the greatest percentage of Nigeria's crude oil. It is also the greatest reservoir of Nigeria's gas deposits. Though oil was first discovered in Epe in what was then the Colony of Lagos, the oil was thick and was abandoned as not commercially viable at the time. Oil was first discovered in commercial quantity at Oloibiri in Ijawland in 1957.

Plate 14.1: Gas Flare (Courtesy: Tam Fiofori)

Since then, exploration has indicated more extensive finds in the forests and swamps of Ijawland. The oil resources of Ijawland include the deposits found off the shores of Ijawland.

What is true of crude oil is also true of gas deposits. Ijawland is also the greatest repository of natural gas in Nigeria. It is thus not surprising that Ijawland is the center of Nigeria's oil and gas resources. The extent to which the Ijaw people have benefited from the oil and gas resources in their land will be discussed under a separate heading.

Writing on the economic resources of Ijawland, Alagoa (1972) has pointed out that in physical terms there are three belts in the Niger Delta, the home of the Ijaw people: these are, the sand beach ridges, the salt water swamp area and fresh water swamp area. According to Alagoa, these are also "belts along which the lives of the communities change, population densities differ, and occupations suitable to the particular environment are carried on." (Alagoa, 1972:12).

On the crops that grow in Ijawland, Alagoa listed the coconut, plantain, oil palm and "the useful rafia tree" for the fresh water area. According to Alagoa, though:

> The lower delta people never produced more than a few plantains and coconuts in backyard gardens. The groups of the upper delta, on the other hand, farmed their river banks after the floods receded each year, depositing rich silt. They farmed water yam (dioscorea alata lynn), plantain, banana, cassava (manioc), coco yam (taro) and more recently swamp rice; as well as peppers, okro, sugar cane, maize and other crops in smaller quantities. ...There are traditions of species of banana and plantain that were indigenous to the delta...(Alagoa, 1972:13-14).

Of the salt water swamp mangrove tree, Alagoa tells us that;

> Its wood is bad for making canoes or other utensils, except for building and cooking. But its aerial roots and other parts were used in the making of a peculiar type of local salt. The making of this mangrove salt and of

284

other salt distilled from seawater were some of the most ancient pursuits of the inhabitants of this belt. Fishing, however, has remained the occupation of the majority (Alagoa,1972:13).

Resources and Economic Development

The economic development of any people is influenced or conditioned among other things by the resources available in their environment. Ijawland is no exception to this rule. The creeks, rivers, and coastline of the Ijaw people constitute their most valuable resources. The Ijaw people "inhabit practically the whole coast, some 250 miles in length stretching between the Ibibio and Yoruba" (Talbot, London, 1932:5). It is thus not surprising that fishing is the primary economic activity of the Ijaw people. Indeed, practically the whole life and thought of the Ijaw man center on water.

The different types of fishing gear, lines, traps and baskets are all produced from the forest resources of Ijawland. The Ijaw people do not only fish. They harvest the creeks and rivers in their environment thus producing the different types of seafood in their marine environment.

Another important economic activity of the Ijaw people is carving. The forest of Ijawland abounds with timber which is used by the Ijaw for carving. By far the most important product of this industry is the canoe and the paddle. The Ijaw are the best canoe carvers in Nigeria. The canoes vary in size. As Dapper tells us during the seventeenth century some of these canoes were "fifty to seventy feet long with twenty 'rowers' (paddlers) on each side" (Jones, 1963:38). The canoe is the most important means of transportation of the Ijaw people, and in years gone by the canoe was a status symbol. Talbot captured the importance of the canoe of the Ijawman when he said "Perhaps, it is not wonderful when one considers how large a part canoes play in the lives of waterside peoples that all such crafts are thought to have souls living in the bow" (Talbot, 1932:270).

Besides fishing and carving, some farming is also done in Ijawland. Farming is done mainly in the northern dry part of Ijawland. But even the extensive region

285

of mangrove swamp is "interspersed with unsuspected stretches of dry land" (Talbot, 1932:1) where farming is carried out. The most important foods crops produced in Ijawland are different types of cocoyam, plantain, cassava, banana and coconut. Others are palm fruits and assorted vegetables.

Other economic activities of the Ijaw include pottery and salt manufacture. Writing on pottery making among the Ijaw, Talbot had this to say "The Okrika town of Ogu is a center of pottery making - especially of Juju jars (Oru Bele) of varying size from a few inches to three and four feet." (Talbot, 1932:276). Talbot also tells us how the Ijaw manufactured salt. According to him;

Native salt is made from the leaves, roots and young shoots of the mangrove. This is more valued than that imported from Europe, and its manufacture forms a side industry of some importance. Among the central and eastern Ijaw the salt was often made in large brass pans (Talbot, 1932:281).

The rivers and creeks of Ijawland are not only a resource that provided food to the people. It is also through the waterways that the Ijaw trade among themselves and with their neighbours in the hinterland. Professor. E.J, Alagoa (1970) has pointed out that this internal long distance trade was the basis of state formation in the Niger Delta long before the appearance of the Europeans on the scene. When Europeans first came to this part of the world they were attracted to Ijawland because of the "large number of navigable creeks, (which) make the country almost unsurpassed for facilities of water transport and is therefore natural that it should form one of the most important centers of trade in Africa". By the nineteenth century, Ijawland was the center of the trans-Atlantic trade in this part of the world.

So far we have examined how the resources of Ijawland contributed to the economic development of the land and its people. It now remains for us to see how the inclusion of Ijaw people in the Nigerian state has affected Ijawland and its people.

The Nigerian State and Ijawland

The Ijaw people were among those who first lost their sovereignty to the British as the latter gradually imposed their rule over the territory that eventually became Nigeria. Their territory was part of the consular administration which started with Consul Beecroft in 1849. When the Oil Rivers Protectorate was created in 1885, Ijawland was at the heart of the new protectorate. In 1891 they became part of the Niger Coast Protectorate and in 1900 part of the Protectorate of Southern Nigerian (Tamuno, 1978). Finally on 1st January, 1914 the Ijaw people and their territory became part of the Colony and Protectorate of Nigeria. (Orugbani, 2005).

It is important to note that the Ijaw people were not consulted before their land was included in what is today known as Nigeria. In the same vein, as the Akassa War and the Jaja Episode demonstrate, the Ijaw people did not submit to British rule without a fight.

Due to constitutional changes introduced in the 1940s and 1950s, Nigeria became a federation with three regions - namely east, west, and north (Orugbani 2005). The government in each of these regions was controlled by a political party which derived its core support from the major ethnic group in that region. Thus in each region, there was an ethnic group which was in the majority, and others which were minorities. In the north, the Hausa-Fulani were the majority, while the Yoruba and the Igbo were the majority in the west and the east respectively. The Ijaw were split between the eastern and western regions and in each of these regions they constituted a minority (Orugbani, 2005). In 1963, the Mid-west region was carved out of the Western region and the Ijaw thus became a minority in three regions.

From the beginning of regional administration in the 1950s, the Ijaw people were deprived in each of the regions where they found themselves. This deprivation took the form of discrimination in employment, award of scholarships and the provision of social amenities (Okorobia, 1999 and Ake-Okah, 2002).

287

This neglect of Ijawland by the regional governments where they lived was confirmed by the Commission appointed by the colonial government to inquire into the fears of minorities in all the regions. In its Report in 1958, the Henry Willink Commission described the Ijaw people as "poor, backward and neglected". The report also noted that "If... in the course of our report we imply that the Regional Governments are more to be feared by minorities than the Federal Government, these proceed from the fact that in each of the Regions there is at present an assured majority with one main interest..."

The advent of political independence did not improve the lot of the Ijaw people. If anything, their condition worsened. What was most appalling in the early post-colonial period was the economic neglect of Ijawland. In the Eastern Region, the only fishery industry was not located in Ijawland but at Aba in Igboland. The deplorable neglect of Ijawland by the regional governments is captured by Isaac Boro in his book, the *Twelve-day Revolution*, in which he said:

> First, we may run our eyes through the health services for the area concerned, covering a territory of 10,000 square miles and about two million inhabitants, there are just a few hospitals of ordinary health centre status. One is at Degema, the second at Yenagoa and the other at Okirika. It takes two days to travel by canoe from most of the remote villages to any of the hospitals....

> There are few dispensaries not better than first aid boxes scattered about in some of the villages. There are no maternity homes. How do people in such an environment survive? No wonder the high death rate. The survivors of these horrid conditions live paramountly on herbs. (Boro, 1982:64).

Of all parts of the country, the Niger Delta is the richest in water and so the government has not found it necessary to give the inhabitants pipe-borne water, be it in the salt water washed creeks or in the muddy fresh water rivers. People drink from the most squalid wells and so dysentery and worm diseases are rife (Boro 1982:6).

Due to the neglect and marginalization of Ijawland by the colonial and post-colonial governments, Isaac Boro and his compatriots, Captain Owonaro, Nottingham Dick and others organized the Niger Delta Volunteer Service (NDVS) and declared the Niger Delta Peoples' Republic. Under the leadership of Boro the NDVS closed down the Niger Delta Development Board agricultural station at Peremabiri, the Eastern Nigeria Agricultural Station at Abobiri, blew up the Oloibiri Oil pipeline transmitting oil to Port Harcourt and destroyed the Ughelli-Port Harcourt pipeline. The NDVS closed courts and schools at different parts of Ijawland including Abari, Odi, Patani, and Ipidiama. This was not wanton destruction but a war to liberate Ijawland from the regional and federal governments that were insensitive to the plight of the Ijaw people.

Federal forces were eventually called in on February 25 and though Boro and his men fought gallantly, they eventually succumbed to the superior fire power of the federal government. Thus ended the twelve day revolution to liberate Ijawland. Boro and his two compatriots Sam Owonaro and Nottingham Dick were condemned to death but were later granted state pardon by Major General Yakubu Gowon, the then Head of state. Later day agitators to free Ijawland from the clutches of the Nigerian state would appear to have taken their cue from Isaac Boro.

If Isaac Boro and the NDVS represented the violent approach to improve the lot of the Ijaw people, the demand for state creation represented the constitutional approach. The history of state agitation in Ijawland has been adequately covered in Alagoa and Tamuno (1989) and Alagoa (1999).

Though the agitation for an Ijaw state started in the 1950s, it was under the military government of General Gowon that the Rivers State was created in 1967. Isaac Boro made the supreme sacrifice fighting for the liberation of this state from the clutches of the secessionists.

While the creation of Rivers State was a dream come true for the Ijaw people, it did not solve all their problems. First, within the Rivers State the provision of infrastructure and other social amenities was concentrated in and around Port Harcourt. Second, not all Ijaw people were included in the River State. This state of affairs led to the demand for the creation of another state for the Ijaw people especially as other ethnic groups were being split into more and more states. This demand was fulfilled when the Abacha administration created Bayelsa State on October 1, 1996 (Okoko and Lazarus, in Alagoa, 1999).

With the creation of Bayelsa State, the Ijaw people now have two states in which they are in the majority or constitute a formidable force; namely Bayelsa and Rivers. They appear as minorities in Delta, Edo and Ondo states. As the Federal Government controls the nation's resources and distributes this to the component units, the Ijaw people are at the mercy of the revenue allocation formula. Revenue allocation is the name given to the statutory distribution of revenue from the Federation Account among the different levels of government. In the early post-colonial period, the revenue-sharing formula was tilted in favour of derivation. For instance, during the first republic, 50 percent of the revenue went to the states from where the resources came. By the Fourth Republic this had been reduced to 13 percent. (Ake-Okah, 2002:124-131).

The drastic reduction of the percentage accruing from derivation has not been matched by a commensurate increase in the amenities provided by the Federal Government whose share of the revenue has increased considerably. It is this neglect of Ijawland by the Federal Government that is the root cause of the on-going agitation for resource control in Ijawland.

Resource Control
Though there is no generally acceptable definition of the term resources control, we are going to adopt the definition of the Southern Governors after their meeting in Benin, on Tuesday, March 27, 2001. According to the Governors, resources control is:

The practice of true federalism and natural law in which the federating units express their rights to primarily control of the natural resources within their borders and make agreed contribution towards the maintenance of common services of the sovereign nation state to which they belong. In the case of Nigeria, the federating units are the 36 states and the sovereign nation is the Federal Republic of Nigeria. (The *Guardian*, April, 2001:17).

The agitation for resource control in Ijawland is carried on at two levels. There is at one level the constitutional approach represented by the Ijaw National Congress (INC). The INC is an umbrella organization of all Ijaw people irrespective of the state where they are domiciled. The INC keeps within the public purview the lack of development in Ijawland characterized by lack of provision of amenities, unemployement as well as the adverse effects of oil exploration. These adverse effects include oil leakages which in the absence of pipe-borne water, pollute the creeks and rivers from which the people obtain water to drink. Gas flaring and destruction of aquatic life are other adverse consequences of oil exploration. Thus the Ijaw people not only do not get a fair share of their oil resources, they also suffer environmental degradation. As Human Rights Watch pointed out in their book *The Price of Oil,* (1999), "at the heart of the discontent among the oil producing communities is an acute sense that wealth derived from their land is siphoned off by the federal government and never returned...the seemingly dry debates on revenue allocation are central to the cycle of protest and repression" (Human Rights Watch 1999).

There is no consensus among Ijaw people regarding the degree to which the INC has succeeded in its campaign for resource control. Some have criticized the INC for its inability to mobilize and sensitize the people to the same degree as the Movement for the Survival of the Ogoni People (MOSOP) did for the Ogoni people. In addition, the INC is weakened by periodic leadership tussle. Nevertheless the INC still remains the chief spokes-organ of the Ijaw people. The emergence of various associations geared toward the struggle for resource control is some indication that not everybody in Ijaw land is satisfied with the operational tactics of the INC. The youths of Ijawland influenced perhaps by the legacy of Isaac Boro and the Niger Delta Volunteer Service (NDVS), are impatient with the constitutional approach of the INC, especially since it has failed to yield any dividends. The frustration of the youths and their extra constitutional approach to the struggle for resource control first came to the open in the Egbesu affair and the Kaiama Declaration (Dangana, 2002). It was at Odi that the youths resolved to establish an Ijaw Youth Council (IYC) to coordinate the struggle of the Ijaw people for self determination and justice. Though Ijaw elders brokered a peace which ended the Kaiama confrontation, Ijaw youths continued to press home their demands through closure of oil flow stations and the occasional kidnapping of oil workers, and demand for ransom for their release. To date, the destruction of Odi due to militant youth activity remains the high water mark for the stream of demands for resource control in Ijawland (Dangana, 2002).

In conclusion, Ijaw culture and society has developed through the ages based on their resources. With the creation of the Nigerian State, these resources passed into the hands of the Nigerian Government. Successive Nigerian Governments have been insensitive to the plight of the Ijaw people in spite of their oil wealth. On their part, the Ijaw people want to control their resources.

CHAPTER 15
PREHISTORY

Abi A. Derefaka and Stanley Okoroafor

Introduction

The common understanding of the word prehistory is that it is concerned with the period before man could record his experiences on earth in writing. The time frame prehistory covers starts from more than two million years ago when our human ancestors first appeared on earth and ends with the beginnings of written history. For African societies, this time frame includes the period for which oral tradition can be considered a valid source of history. Prehistory is anonymous while much of conventional history is about identifiable people. Prehistory is more concerned with trends than with events, and embraces the whole range of human activities. It deals with social groups and societies.

The prehistoric aspect of this project is basically based on the archaeology of the Niger Delta. There is yet the Western area (and even the fringe) of the Niger Delta, where the Ijaw are also found, to be explored. In these areas, no archaeological work has been done to support the reconstruction of the history of the Ijo based on oral traditions and written sources. The chronology that emerges from archaeological research in the Niger Delta should help strengthen and extend the existing chronological framework for the prehistory of the Ijaw of the Niger Delta.

The other point of interest in the prehistory/history of the Ijaw is the slave trade. This was one significant event that occurred in the Niger Delta. It is significant in the sense that it occurred for about three hundred years in the second half of the last millennium, and because it was through it that we now have the other part of the title of this volume, that is, the Ijaw in diaspora (the Americas, especially in the Caribbean; and Europe).

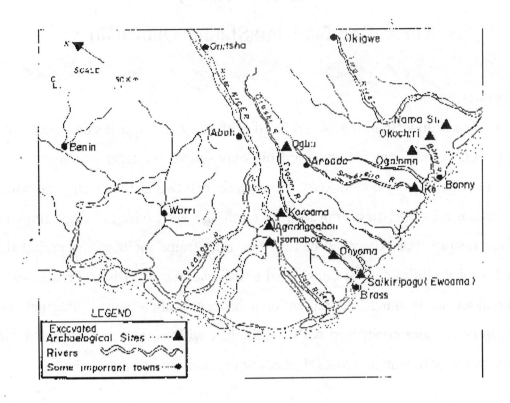

Fig. 15.1: Map of the Niger Delta showing excavated archaeological sites

Consequently, a hypothesis can be formulated with a deliberate policy to search for and locate the localities where the inhuman transaction took place, with the objects associated with the trade such as the chains etc. in archaeological context. Where they were embedded and discovered through excavation in situ (undisturbed), they can be used to enhance awareness among the Ijaw, both at home and abroad. Of all the excavations carried out so far, none has yielded any such items. Should we uncover such items, there would be more physical evidence for this period of the past about which the Ijaw, like other Nigerian participants in the infamous trade, have chosen to have collective amnesia.

Following from the pioneering work of E. J. Alagoa (which was the first properly and systematically conducted historical research based on Ijo oral traditions) in the Niger Delta, it became evident that the resultant reconstructions needed to be assessed for accuracy against archaeological evidence. Again, it was E. J. Alagoa who invited and has sustained archaeological interest in the Niger Delta. Between 1973 and 1976 he was actively involved in the excavation of five sites in the salt water eastern Delta directed mostly by F. N. Anozie with the last excavation there directed by N. Nzewunwa. The five sites are Onyoma, 4Â° 32Â´ N, 6Â° 24Â´ E excavated in 1973; Ke, 4Â° 27Â´ N, 6Â° 24Â´ E excavated in 1973; Ogoloma, 4Â° 44Â´ N, 7Â° 05Â´ E excavated in June 1974; Saikiripogu (Ewoama), 4Â° 21Â´ N, 6Â° 15Â´ E excavated December 1975; and Okochiri (Okopiri), 4Â° 42Â´ N, 7Â° 08Â´ E excavated in December 1976. Alagoa's division (Alagoa, 1972:12) of the Niger Delta into Eastern, Central, and Western is adopted in this contribution. This is because this division allows the application of physiographic, linguistic, and ethnic criteria for a subdivision to largely coincide. In this division of the Delta, the Pennington River to the West and the River Nun to the east delineate the Central Delta. East of the River Nun is the Eastern Delta and west of the Pennington is the Western Delta. Alagoa also says:

> The Ijo have lived in the lower Niger for a long time. They have lived there so long that their life has become fully integrated with the unique environment of the Delta, and their oral traditions can no longer remember a place of origin outside the Delta. The Ijo may indeed have separated from their mainland neighbours, the Igbo, Edo and Yoruba, as long as five thousand years ago. Such brothers, and such a length of physical separation from her bigger brothers, and such length of sojourn in the Delta can be contemplated since the geological age of the Delta itself may be in excess of ten thousand years.

We may put the information in the foregoing statement into the form of a simplified time-chart as follows:

4000 B.C. - A.D. 0	Ijo settlement of the Central Delta.
A.D. 0 - A.D. 1000	Migrations to the Easter and Western Delta.
A.D. 1000 - 1200	Development of the fishing village type institutions of the Eastern Delta.
A.D. 1400 - 1600	Development of all the major institutions of the Eastern Delta city-states.

A.D. 1600 - 1900   Full impact of the Atlantic trade leading to various

changes and modifications, secondary migrations

to the Delta peripheries (Alagoa, 1975:19).

Concerning migrations, Alagoa has concluded that the major direction of migration was from the Central Delta to the Eastern Delta although there is a cautious rider to this conclusion as he says:

> The traditions of the Eastern Delta states clearly derive the peoples from the Central Delta although there are suggestions of original proto-Ijo populations in parts of the area. The four states (Nembe, Okrika, Elem Kalabari and Bonny) tell traditions of origin, which put them into two simple categories. Nembe and Okrika routes of migrations lie completely within the Delta West to East. Elem Kalabari and Bonny traditions tell of periods in the hinterland followed by a return into the Delta. These two states also seem to refer to the same dispersal centre in the Central Delta, namely, the Ogobiri-Igbedi Creek region. (Alagoa, 1972:158)

This concern with the ethnographic dimension in Niger Delta studies predates the efforts of Professor E. J. Alagoa. As Anozie (1976:89) rightly points out, anthropological work on peoples and institutions in the Niger Delta had been carried out by Leonard (1906), Thomas (1910), Talbot (1926, 1932), among others, before academic historians started work in the Niger Delta. Although Jones (1963) had doubted the usefulness of oral traditions as a source for reconstructing the past in the Niger Delta (describing such traditions in the area as either a mass of uncoordinated and often contradictory material or authorized version(s) for external consumption), it is now evident that oral traditions have led to the shedding of more light on what he has referred to as the prehistoric and protohistoric stages of the Niger Delta's past. Less sceptical of the potentialities of oral traditions, Anene (1963) admits that the oral traditions are clearly inconclusive evidence, but makes the important suggestion that eventually the disciplines of comparative linguistics and archaeology may throw considerable light on what is now very obscure.

Now to archaeology and how it has been used in the reconstruction of the past of the Niger Delta. Indeed, there is no gainsaying the fact that archaeological research in the Niger Delta began at the instance of an oral historian, Professor E. J. Alagoa. As he has explained (Alagoa, 1976b: 3-4):

> Because of the difficulties and limitations already apparent in the use of oral traditions and anthropology, it was decided to resort to archaeology in the study of Niger Delta history. The expectation is, that archaeology would add concreteness and a more secure chronological base to cultural reconstructions that would be considered mere fabrication if derived from oral traditions alone, or as merely hypothetical if derived from anthropology. The plan is, that excavations should eventually be carried out at old sites indicated by the oral traditions. Thus, each individual excavation not only tells the story of developments [but also increases] understanding of inter-relationships, contacts, migrations, trade, and diffusion of goods and ideas throughout the Niger Delta and with the Nigerian hinterland.

To this list of expectations from archaeological research in the Niger Delta, we need to add the objectives stated by Anozie and Nzewunwa for the research they subsequently undertook in the Eastern Niger Delta with the active participation of Alagoa. But perhaps before examining their objectives, which indicate how archaeology has been used in the Eastern Delta research, it would be useful to summarize the history of archaeological research in the Niger Delta.

It is interesting to note that of the 400 sites produced by the reconnaissance of Eastern Nigeria by Hartle between 1963 and 1967, none appears to have been in the Niger Delta. None of the fourteen sites excavated by him (Hartle, 1967) was in the Niger Delta (Anozie, Nzewunwa and Derefaka 1987:122). As Anozie (1978:3) has rightly chronicled, the first organized archaeological fieldwork in the Niger Delta was undertaken in December 1972 by a research team from the University of Ibadan made up of Professor Thurstan Shaw, Professor E. J. Alagoa and F. N. Anozie, then a junior research fellow in

Archaeology. The team carried out reconnaissance at Onyoma, Nembe, Oruokolo, Kaiko (Okpoama), Ke, Brass and Ogbolomabiri and spent a few days studying these sites, which were previously recorded by Alagoa while studying the oral tradition(s) of the area. This statement agrees with Anozie's earlier information (Anozie, 1976:90) that:

> Alagoa, while recording the oral traditions, noted many ancient settlement sites, which were regarded as dispersal centres of the Ijo people. It was therefore, decided to start by investigating some of these sites.

When the team returned to Ibadan about the end of December 1972, the data obtained was analyzed and so it was decided that test pits should be excavated at Onyoma, Ke, and Oruokolo to study the cultural materials they contain and date them. The excavations at Onyoma and Ke were done in May, April and December 1973. Transport, among other difficulties, made it impossible for excavations to be carried out at Oruokolo. Apart from Alagoa and Anozie, Dr. (Mrs.) M. A. Sowunmi, a palynologist participated in the excavations, and her main concern was to study the present and past vegetations of the area (Anozie, 1978:6).

It was in June 1974 that the Ogoloma site was excavated. Alagoa had drawn attention to the site and reconnaissance was carried out in December 1973. In December 1975, the Saikiripogu site was excavated (Anozie, 1978:8). A new dimension to the research came in December 1976. Nwanna Nzewunwa, a junior research fellow at the University of Nigeria, Nsukka, arrived from Cambridge to undertake the excavation at Okochiri. The explanation for this assertion will become evident when the research objectives before and after his introduction to Niger Delta archaeological work are examined. Perhaps one should state here that there are now accounts that have brought this summary of the history of archaeological research in the Niger Delta up to date except for the most recent excavations at Finima excavated near Bonny (see Anozie, Nzewunwa and Derefaka, 1987 and Nzewunwa and Derefaka, 1989).

Anozie has stated that one of the aims of the excavations in the Eastern Niger Delta was to date the sites (Anozie, 1976:97). Nzewunwa has, therefore quoted him rightly when he reports him as having said the aims (of Niger Delta archaeological research) included an attempt to establish the nature and age of the earliest settlements in the Delta and to compare with estimates based on oral traditions and linguistics (Anozie, 1976a:1). This guided Anozie's excavation of nine shell middens at four sites, which have produced a series of radiocarbon dates providing a chronological framework within which the material culture of the Eastern Delta could begin to be analyzed. Professor Thurstan Shaw, the father of Nigerian Archaeology, who could be considered the pioneer archaeologist in Niger Delta Archaeology, has made a challenging remark in his book on Nigerian Archaeology and Early History. Shaw (1978:51) says:

> Just when the Niger Delta was first colonized and a way of life
>
> evolved to exploit its highly specialized type of environment,
>
> is one of the problems awaiting Nigerian Archaeology.

In the light of the objectives of the pioneering efforts in Niger Delta archaeological research, it stands to reason that Nzewunwa should state for his aims and objectives in his PhD thesis for the University of Cambridge as follows:

Derefaka's archaeological investigation in the Central Niger Delta was primarily oriented towards answering three related questions:

- What are the ecological and archaeological manifestations of the Delta way of life in terms of their basic subsistence economy?
- What are the material cultural manifestations of the Delta way of life?
- For how long has this way of life been in operation?

This is clearly a logical development from a situation in which excavations had already been carried out at four sites in the Eastern Niger Delta and radiometric dates obtained for them. When Nzewunwa excavated at Okochiri with the aid of Dr. Anozie, the picture of prehistoric developments in the Eastern Delta was beginning to be defined in broad outlines based on excavation already carried out. This is why it was necessary that he should examine the available data using an explanatory framework that could synthesize the information on this relatively new and unique region of Nigerian Archaeology. This is how his arrival on the scene introduced a new dimension to Niger Delta Archaeology.

For Thurstan Shaw and Anozie, moving into a unique environmental zone in Nigeria to do archaeological research, it was useful and indeed necessary, for them to concentrate on building up a reliable chronological framework (based on radiometric dates) for the Niger Delta. However, given the physiographic delineation of the Niger Delta, all the sites excavated being in the salt water mangrove swamps sub-zone has made the chronological framework not applicable to the entire Delta. Following NEDECO (1961) and Udo (1978:227), Nzewunwa (1979:4) has described the Niger Delta as being made up of four ecological sub-zones, namely:

- The freshwater swamps and forests on both sides of the Niger;
- The coastal plains on the west and east of the freshwater swamps;
- The salt water mangrove swamps, south plains sub-zones, made up of mud and silt covering about 10,360 square kilometres;
- The sandy beach ridges just at the front of the outer Delta.

This is a fair summary of the physiography of the Niger Delta and so it should be accurate to indicate that until a majority or all four sub-zones have been systematically sampled, it would be inadequate to apply chronological data from only one sub-zone to the entire Delta.

Lastly, another use to which Nzewunwa has put archaeology in Niger Delta research is a concentration on economic prehistory in which he has attempted to reconstruct the subsistence economy aspect of the people's life. His use of a combination of techniques and concepts from various disciplines (Nzewunwa, 1979:10) has greatly illuminated his analysis. However, it is only valid, to a large extent, to his data universe.

Both Anozie and Nzewunwa are interested in a contextual analysis of material culture and so have classified and discussed the artefacts recovered from the excavations in the Eastern Niger Delta. It is also useful to note that the focus of archaeological research has been on the Ijo who constitute a majority of the occupants of the area.

The Central Delta, as earlier indicated, is part of the Niger Delta and it is on the northern portion of the Central Delta, specifically, Wilberforce Island and environs, on which Derefaka's work has concentrated (see Derefaka, A.A., 2003:30 [fig. 1.2]). The Island itself (circumscribed by the Nun River, Igbedi Creek and Ogobiri River) is about 19 kilometres long (that is, from the extreme northern to the extreme southern points) and about 21.5 kilometres wide (taking the extreme western and eastern points). Of the three sites that have been archaeologically investigated by Derefaka, two, namely, Agadagbabou and Isomobou, are located on this Island. The third site, Koroama, is located on the southern bank of Taylor Creek (so christened in 1854) which is a tributary of the Nun River, which is, itself, one of the two major bifurcations of the Niger near Aboh as it enters the floodplain (the other being the Forcados River). The three sites therefore lie in the freshwater floodplain of the Niger Delta covering an area of about 25 square kilometres.

The Niger Delta is part of the sedimentary basin of southern Nigeria whose origins go back to cretaceous times. What is said to have emerged in the late cretaceous was what has been referred to as proto-Niger Delta (see, for example, Sowunmi, M. A., 1981:726). The growth of the Niger Delta as it exists now has been traced to early tertiary times. Since then, the Delta is said to have continued to move in a cumulatively seaward direction (see Allen, 1964; Hospers, 1965; Stoneley, 1966; Short and Stauble, 1967; Allen, 1976). Within this general seaward expansion of the Delta, there have been local regressions and transgressions (Short and Stauble, 1967). The seaward expansion of the Delta is said to have reached its maximum limit (so far) during the Plio/Pleistocene period. Eustatic rise in sea levels are said to have caused a transgression in the submerged area that forms the present estuaries in the Niger Delta (Short and Stauble, 1967).

For the Central Delta, the main source is the Niger-Benue drainage basin. However, the significance of this lies in the fact that fossil pollen from the continental environment (alluvial/upper deltaic plains) in which the excavated sites in this study are located, would include evidence from the major vegetation types in all the zones traversed by the rivers draining into the Niger Delta.

According to Asseez (1976:263), from sedimentological and faunal evidence, it appears that the geological character of the present Niger Delta is not different from what it was in the past. He notes that Short and Stauble (1967) identified three subsurface stratigraphic units in the modern Niger Delta-Benin, Agbada, and Akata formations. It is the upper part of the Benin formation, which is about 5,000 feet deep (maximum), that is encountered in the archaeological excavations carried out in the Central Niger Delta. This formation is described as:

> over 90% sandstone with shale intercalations. It is coarse grained,
> poorly sorted, sub-angular to well rounded and bears lignite streaks
> and wood fragments. It is a continental deposit of probable upper
> deltaic depositional environment.

Its surface structural units (the point bars, cut-off channels, levees etc.) have already been discussed. This formation is said to be of Oligocene age in the subsurface in the north becoming progressively younger southward. In general, it ranges from Miocene to Recent. The other observation of Asseez (1976:264-5) that is of some significance for this study is that every little hydrocarbon accumulation has been associated with the formation. Indeed, although according to Hospers (1965), the maximum thickness of the total detrital sediments of the Niger Delta to date is about 8,000 metres, it is instructive that archaeological investigations in this study have only examined a very small fraction (about 2 metres on the average) of this pile of sediments. In this connection, Sowunmi's finding that there was a sudden and substantial upsurge of the pollen of *Elaeis guineensis* (4.3% at 5.90 metres dated to c. 2800 B. P.); having been absent as from 20.35 metres and occurring feebly only thrice earlier i.e. 0.5% at 35.46 metres; 0.6% at 32.40 and 1.0% at 23.20 metres (Sowunmi, 1981a:136), is significant since she says:

> Its presence in appreciable quantities in a rain forest community is indicative of a previous opening up of such a forest (by man). Its sudden and notable increase c. 2800 B. P. as recorded here is thus taken to be an indication of the destruction of high canopy forest trees by man for farming purposes resulting in gaps within the forest floor. (Sowunmi, 1981c: 468).

The core from which these results have emanated was obtained from a spot about 100 kilometres south of Wilberforce Island with a gradient of the deltaic plain seaward of about 8cm/km (Allen, 1970:139). Then the two archaeological sites on Wilberforce Island are about 800cm or 80 metres or 0.8km higher than Shell B.P. boring 22 which produced the core. Allowing for this difference in elevation, one could project that a comparable layer to that which yielded the date of about 2800 B. P. in the mangrove swamp of the Delta could be obtained at about 5 metres below surface on Wilberforce Island. There is, thus, indirect evidence that agricultural practice could date at least as far back as about 800 B. C. in the Central Delta especially if one goes by ethnographic data on the practice of farming in the Delta. It should, therefore, be plausible to suggest that the evidence under discussion could have originated further inland than where it was found. Indeed, contemporary economic practices indicate that crop farming is a more prominent subsistence strategy in the freshwater swamps of the lower floodplain than in the saltwater mangrove swamps of the Niger Delta, where it is a marginal (almost insignificant) component of the subsistence strategies of the inhabitants and where exploitation of aquatic resources is predominant.

Another significance of the evidence obtained from the sudden substantial occurrence of *Elaeis guinneensis* pollen is that both G.I. Jones and K.O. Dike's implication or suggestion that the Delta environment has been a hostile one and so its inhabitants needed to have been forced into living there needs rethinking. This is particularly so because there is no record of forced movement of peoples from the hinterland coast wards about 800 B.C. And appreciation of the diversity in faunal, floral and mineral resources available in the Delta would suggest that people who have been accustomed to relating to a riverine environment both from their economic and religious practices (perhaps in the immediate hinterland of and from around the eastern and western extremities of the Niger Delta) could have recognized the abundance and diversity in resources as well as the attendant economic opportunities beyond their immediate environments and so decided to move. Although the movement to occupy parts of the Delta may have been brought about by different historical circumstances for the different groups, the preferred settlement zone of the groups in the Delta would have been influenced by both the kind of subsistence strategy they were used to and the attendant technological package available to them.

For the Central Delta, both terrestrial and aquatic resources were available and there was ample land for crop cultivation as well as forest for hunting and gathering. It does seem as if, having moved into the ecological transitional or buffer zone (which the area covered by this study represents), the Ijo were able to increasingly depend on fishing as their occupation of the Delta continued to expand towards the sea. Thus, for example, even if their distant kin were farmers in the freshwater Delta, the Nembe (in the saltwater mangrove eastern Delta) were able to concentrate on fishing and later, trading combined with fishing, as their major means of livelihood. Indeed, the staple food of the Nembe, like that of their Izon kin has remained plantain. Moreover, that all Ijo groups of the Eastern Delta, that is, Okrika, Kalabari, Ibani, etc. have, at some point in their long history, shared in this common farming origin is attested to by the way they express the sensation known as hunger. Almost all of them say what amounts to I need to have yam. For example, in Okrika it is, *buru I tari a be*. Linguistic evidence amplifies this for all Ijo groups such that it is noteworthy that yam (*Dioscorea spp.*) is referred to as *buru* by the Kalabari, Okrika, Nkoroo, Ibani, Nembe, Kolokuma, Amegi, Okordia, Boma, Olodiama, Oporoma, Kabo, Mein, Arogbo, and the Iduwini (Williamson 1970:167).

This corroborates the suggestion being made here and underscores the antiquity of yam in this region.

The Archaeological Site in the Niger Delta

A working definition adopted in this contribution is that an archaeological site in this area of study is a location in which one can find material remains that are evidence of human activity or habitation in the past. It is perhaps important to indicate that the main emphasis has been to locate abandoned open human habitation sites in the Central Niger Delta with a view to discovering both original habitation sites of the Niger Delta Ijo or the people's centre or centres of dispersal (primary or secondary) as had been indicated by the oral traditions.

Excavations

The Central Niger Delta

The excavations at Agadagbabou, which began on 15th February, were concluded on 1st March, 1980. Given the main aim of this research, and the limitations of time and resources available, it was decided to use the test pitting, which is a variant of the trenching method of excavation which derives from the concept of vertical excavation. As Fagan (1972:85) points out, this technique involves the excavation of limited areas for specific information. On a limited scale, vertical excavation does, indeed, aim at uncovering information about stratigraphy or the sequence of occupation layers. Also, since this was the first site in the Central Niger Delta to be excavated, it was decided to use the unit-level technique in excavating at Agadagbabou. This technique was also adopted (using the arbitrary unit-level variant) because it is, as Hester, Heizer, and Graham (1975:79) state, best employed in projects emphasizing chronology or culture history.

Finds

Pottery

It is reported that most (about 67%) of the potsherds recovered from the Agadagbabou site are not decorated. In contrast, only about 13% of the potsherds are decorated. Similarly, whereas most (about 82%) of the potsherds are body sherds, rim sherds are only about 18% of the total number of sherds recovered from the site. The ratio of decorated to plain rim sherds is 179:270 or 1:2 while the ratio of decorated to plain body sherds is 155:1914 or 1:12.

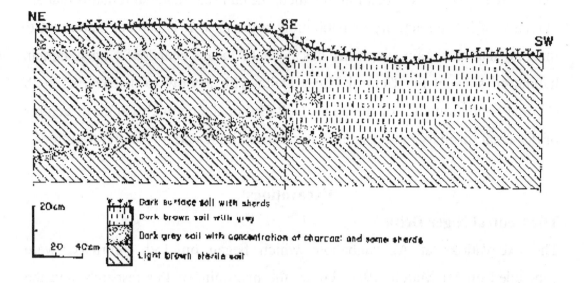

NE SE SW

20cm

20   40±cm

Dark surface soil with sherds
Dark brown soil with grey
Dark grey soil with concentration of charcoal and some sherds
Light brown sterile soil

Plate 15.1: Agadagbabou Pit II, 1980

Stratigraphy

For the Agadagbabou site, stratigraphic sections were drawn for all the excavated units. However, a discussion of the stratigraphy of Test Pits II and IV will be quite adequate as it would reflect the nature of the depositional history of the site. The profile to be discussed for Test Pit II is the East wall defined by the North east peg and the south east peg of the test Pit. The stratification seems straight-forward consisting of four bands or lenses of Dark grey soil each containing a high concentration of charcoal and potsherds. The first three of the four bands are almost regularly interspersed with an average distance of about 20cm between the bands. The distance between the last two however, is much smaller (about 15cm on the average). These four bands of cultural debris have an average thickness of about 15cm each. They are separated by a light or yellowish brown sterile soil from the top of the stratigraphic section or profile to the bottom.

The fact that the second (from the top) of these four cultural layers is discontinuous along the east wall and the third (from the top) is also discontinuous towards the north-east peg, without a pit profile suggests that the materials have been periodically washed down from the site located east of Test Pit II. This conclusion is supported by the location of the Test Pit in the dry bed (during the dry season) of Opuba creeklet and the relatively worn nature of the pottery recovered from Pit II as compared with the pottery from Pit IV. Moreover, if the East wall of Pit II were a continuation of the depositional sequence in Test Pit IV located to its immediate east on the open habitation site itself, the stratification would have been similar to that on the west wall of Test Pit IV with an average thickness for a single midden deposit of about 30cm. The soil is clayey in all the layers except the four midden deposits that have a silty texture where there are no pieces of charcoal. The depth of the profile for the east wall of Pit II is about 80cm.

Test Pit IV also has a fairly straight-forward stratification. There are three distinct layers delineated on the basis of colour and inclusions. The topmost layer consists of a light brown silty top-soil with relatively few sherds. This is followed by a layer made up of black silty soil with a large concentration of charcoal, potsherds and burnt clay. This is the midden deposit which has a maximum thickness of about 30cm and an average of 20cm along the east wall of 2 metres length and 15cm along the south wall of 4 metres length. It is interesting to note that the midden deposit terminates near the North-west peg along the west wall and also just after the north east peg along the north wall of Pit IV. The deepest portion of the midden deposit is near the south east peg of Pit IV. The third layer is the compact, yellowish brown and sterile sub-soil. This is a natural deposit that is clayey in texture. The depth of the profile exposed by the excavation in pit IV is about 1 metre. The yellowish brown loamy alluvium of the freshwater Delta is what constitutes the matrix of the strata and the subsoil in the stratigraphy discussed above. These soils belong to soil derived from recently (in the geological sense) deposited materials.

Dates and Site Interpretation

Three samples were sent to A.E.R.E Harwell, Oxford, for Radiocarbonn dating. The earliest date obtained was 1640 A.D. The details are as follows:

S/No.	Sample Ref. Number	Lab. Ref. Number	Provenance	Type of Sample	Radiocarbon	Radio-carbon Age A.D.
1	UPH 009	HAR 4398	AG IV, 25cm	Charred	310Â± 70	1640
2	UPH 010	HAR 4396	AG IV, 40cm	Kernel	220Â±	1730
3	UPH 011	HAR 4395	AG IV, 77cm	Charcoal	220Â± 90	1730

From the above, it would appear that the oldest date obtained comes from a point nearer the surface of the Test Pit IV than the provenance of the younger two dates which come from as far below the surface as 40cm and 77cm respectively. This apparent inversion can be explained using the effects of ethnographic refuse management practices observed in Sabagreia and Kaiama, which are Kolokuma settlements located along the River Nun and at Igbedi on the Igbedi Creek which flows into the River Nun. At these extant settlements, the inhabitants use pits dug to obtain mud (lateritic soil) to build houses for refuse disposal. When these pits are full and a mound begins to appear, the material at mound top is shovelled to lower ground after burning and new refuse material thrown on top. The result of such actions is a mixing of younger and older refuse materials which, with time, gets compressed to form a midden deposit in the stratification of the site.

As Nzewunwa, (1979:135) also noted, this practice is common in the Niger Delta, and indeed, all over Eastern Nigeria. He says, (1979:135-136).

> In collecting datable samples such as charred wood there is the possibility that the turning of midden refuse before and after firing may bring about a distortion in the age of organic matter being collected. What is more, there is equal possibility that fresh wood burnt at the time of midden firing and thrown into lower stratigraphic levels of the midden may turn out dates that are younger than those from levels above it.

What is important to note, however, is that absolute radiometric dates obtained so far from samples from the Agadagbabou site place the age of the site between 1640 and 1730 A.D. This is a period after the beginning of contact between the Eastern Niger Delta and Europeans. It is, therefore, striking that apart from beads there is no material evidence at this site of European trade goods. The other two dates tally at 1730 A.D. and are consistent with the homogenous nature of the midden deposit recorded for Test Pit IV.

In discussing further the interpretation of this site, one needs to comment on the information from oral traditions that led one to the site. It would also be useful to examine the possibility that the portion of the site excavated might not represent an accurate identification of the ancient settlement site of Agadagbabou, given the fact that the name refers to the entire back swamp forest between the edge of Wilberforce Island adjacent to Sabagreia, to just before Igbedi on the same Island and extending several kilometres inland on the Island (oral information from both late Uncle Precut and Udisi, the hunter 1979). Indeed, what led one to the Agadagbabou site was the history of the Central Niger Delta as reconstructed by Alagoa (1979:103), as well as the oral traditions of the Kolokuma and some of their neighbours, which indicated Agadagbabou as a dispersal point and an ancient settlement site in this part of the Delta. Moreover, the priests of Kolokuma Egbesu are said to be buried at Agadagbabou, but that location is kept secret and should hold the key to the ancient site referred to in the oral traditions.

It will be recalled that in the area of research focus for the Central Delta (See Derefaka, A.A.2003), the Ijo occupants are the Kolokuma, Opokuma, Gbaran, Mein, Ogboin and Ekpetiama. The oral histories of the Kolokuma Ibe and the Opokuma Ibe (see Alagoa, 1972:207) suggest close relationship between the two. Essentially, their movement seems to have been eastwards on the Igbedi creek to Agadagbabou and then a dispersal that led, first to settlement on the western bank of Oruamatoru (opposite present-day Igbedi), Barasouba (north of Agadagbabou on Wilberforce Island) and later the twin settlements of Okoloba and Seibokorogha, now jointly called Sabagreia, as well as the other settlements on the River Nun north of Sabagreia. This pattern of movement suggests movement into back swamp freshwater environment exemplified by the site of Agadagbabou and later, movement back to the banks of major creeks and the River Nun.

Also, having noted a number of fish ponds (artificial lakes) created by fish farmers from Sabagreia and Igbedi on Wilberforce Island and given the secondary forest vegetation in the area around the excavated area at Agadagbabou, which suggests clearing for farming (confirmed orally by Uncle Perekumo and the local labour employed), one is inclined to believe that our guide took us to an abandoned settlement area discovered during farming activities on a piece of land belonging to his family. It was therefore, recognized from the onset ˈ kαɔ ˌadagbabou site eventually excavated, is not likely to be the exact location for the Agadagbabou referr kαɔ in the oral traditions. If the burial practices of the contemporary Kolokuma are used as guide, it would appear that there would be one or more settlements in the vicinity of the area where the priests of Kolokuma Egbesu are buried in the revered forest of Agadagbabou (which the etymology of Agadagbabou suggests).

In interpreting economic activities at the Agadagbabou site, reference was made, first to economic practices observed and recorded in the oral traditions of the Kolokuma and other freshwater Delta Ibe. The major economic activities are based on the exploitation and management of the resources of the environment. For example, *Afantan* (corkwood tree) can float and *Bolo* (*Ochrocarous africanus* olive) is used for constructing canoes. Another important forest tree is the oil palm (*Elaeis guineensis*) from which palm oil, palm kernel oil; palm fronds for brooms and roof thatch; and the trunk for fuel are obtained. Each of these has given rise to a source of income.

Apart from the natural bounties of the forest, the rich silty soil resulting from the annual flooding associated with the waters of the River makes farming profitable. Like other Ijo Ibe, the Kolokuma have plantain (*Paradisiaca* Linn) as staple food which they prefer to eat unripe. Other staple crops include cassava, yam, cocoyam and bananas. The bulk of the agricultural (farming) work is done by the women, although the men clear the new farms. Also, although farming is primarily aimed at satisfying the family's subsistence needs, the effects of a money-based economy has necessitated the production of excess for the purpose of purchasing other items of subsistence needs such as

310

meat and fish as well as cloth and other ornamental ware and basic necessities such as canoes, paddles and equipment for the construction of shelter. Indeed, most of the movement of the Kolokuma is by canoe even to reach their farms. The canoes are locally made and construction is usually during the flood season. Today in most settlements, outboard engines are fitted to locally made canoes by those who can afford it or those in the transport business.

Apart from participating in farming, the men engage in fishing, canoe-carving, gin-making (from the sap of *Raphia vinifera* and *Raphia hookeri*, Leis 1962:13), thatch-making, hunting, and trading. Artisanal fishing is practiced mostly during the flood season in the rivers, creeks and creeklets. In the dry season, lakes and individually or communally owned fish ponds are harvested. So aquaculture is important. There are also some full-time hunters operating in the vast forest of Wilberforce Island and adjacent Islands with plentiful tropical rainforest fauna including medium-sized and large mammals. Examples of the game brought home by hunters are the range of animals killed by the excavation crew's resident hunter (Udisi of Igbedi) during the period that the excavation lasted. These ranged from the alligator through the duiker to the bush pig. The construction of canoes is undertaken mainly during the flood season. The fronds and other parts of the bamboo or raphia palm provide materials for the weaving of mats, baskets and cordage, for example. Gin-making has been an important occupation in this area. The gin is distilled in the raphia palm (koro) *Raphia hookeri* bushes in the back swamp microenvironment. Palm wine (*Izon-uru*) is tapped from the koro, fermented and distilled into gin (*Koun-uru*). One such gin industry is located at Ozunbou behind Igbedi (see Gbaranbiri, 1976). It is the women who manufacture mats, baskets, and cordage. Pottery is also a female occupation.

From the foregoing summary of the range of economic activities of extant Central Delta Ijo communities, especially the Kolokuma, who trace their dispersal point to Agadagbabou, it is possible to interpret the finds from the archaeological excavation in terms of their socio-econmic significance. Starting with the most numerous class of artefacts recovered, namely pottery, one can say that although there is no evidence of a firing mound or other direct evidence

311

of manufacture, the rather remote location of the site as well as the number and diversity of vessels as well as smoking pipes suggest that it is likely that some, if not all the ceramic objects were manufactured at or quite close to the site excavated.

This view is supported by the fact that even the smoking pipes have incision as the main decorative technique. In this regard, specimen Nos. 1, 2, 4, 7 and 9 are noteworthy and will be discussed in some detail. Specimen number 1 is the stem and pedestal of a locally made smoking pipe with a vertically oriented, incised, inverted V groove pattern (the inverted V are increasingly larger from near the pedestal). The fabric is sand tempered and of brown clay. The bowl is broken off. It has a stem with a width of 1.7cm and a length of 4.2cm. The hollow inside the stem is 5mm wide. It has an undifferentiated pedestal 1.7cm long and 1.5cm thick. The provenance is surface find from North of Test Pit II. Probably eroded and washed down by flood water or surface run-off water. Specimen 2 is a bowl and a small part of the stem. It has a sand tempered fabric of brown clay. Its average thickness is 2mm and the bowl diameter is 2cm. The bowl is undifferentiated as it curves to form the short stem which like specimen 1, would require a longer (perhaps wooden stem) for the pipe to be used for smoking. Two grooves are incised to form a large X on each side of the bowl to decorate the pipe. The hollow is 1.7cm wide at the rim of the bowl and 3.5cm at the stem. The provenance is surface level find in Test Pit II. It is likely to have been eroded from the vicinity of Pit IV end, washed down to the Opuba creeklet bed where it was recovered. It is of a finer finish than specimen I.

Specimen 3 is a smoking pipe pedestal fragment recovered from spit level 2 of Test Pit IV. Specimen 4 is the larger portion of a smoking pipe bowl fragment with an average thickness of 2mm and a diameter of 2cm at the rim. Unlike specimen 2, there is a sharp angle at the point of connection between the bowl and the little bit of the stem attached. This specimen was also recovered from level 2 of Test Pit IV. Specimens 5 and 6 are smoking pipe bowl fragments, but whereas 5 is a finely made pipe specimen with a thickness of 2mm at the rim of the bowl and 6mm toward the base of the bowl, specimen 6 is more coarse and has a fairly uniform thickness of 7mm. Specimen 7 and 9 were recovered from the surface just south and just north of Test Pit I respectively. Specimen 7 is a stem fragment showing the pipe end of the stem. Again incision is the predominant decorative technique at the collar of the smoking pipe stem. Alternate grooves round the collar have produced raised portions on the collar which are then further decorated with short pairs of horizontally incised lines. Specimen 9, on the other hand, is the complete bowl of a smoking pipe although the bowl has broken off at the point of its attachment to a stem. It has a thickness of 3mm and a rim diameter of 2.6cm. The other specimen is specimen 8. It is a short cylindrical and hollow clay object identified in the field as *Kara* worn with a string on the neck by women during the circumcision ritual.

Extra site information indicates that the leaves of the bush mango (*Irvinga gabonensis*) could have been smoked.

It is also important to note the low level of occurrence or absence of European-made goods (especially smoking pipes) in the sequence at the Agadagbabou site. The J.J.W. Peters gin bottles were recovered along Somoun Creek near the excavated site and helped this writer date the site to 1640 A.D. even before the radiocarbon dates arrived.

From the finds discussed above and earlier, there is evidence of a number of economic activity options open to inhabitants of the Agadagbabou site excavated. Perhaps the most obvious is pottery manufacture given the large number of sherds recovered and the variety of pipes and other ceramic objects recovered. From ethnographic analogy in the area of study, it is known that pottery manufacture was undertaken by women. Also, the wavy line and herring bone decorative motifs and the presence of fish bones indicates the importance of fishing in the subsistence pattern of the occupants of Agadagbabou.

The animal bones recovered, some of which have been identified as duicker bones, and the presence of snail tip impressed pottery, also indicate the importance of hunting and gathering. Men did the hunting while women and children the gathering of fruits (for their flesh and the seeds dried and used as condiment *ogbono*, for preparing soup).

Again, the presence of palm kernels indicates that the oil palm (*Elaeis guineensis*) was being exploited. Also, that most of the palm kernels encountered were charred shows a high level of exploitation as the kernels were used as a source of fuel for cooking and other purposes. Other uses of the palm would include palm oil production, thatch making, broom making and palm kernel oil production. The preponderance of pots among the pottery recovered also suggests that apart from water potterage and storage, other liquids for which pots were used, would have been palm wine and perhaps locally distilled gin. Surely, by the 17th century, palm-gin was locally distilled. Surely, by the 17th century palm wine tapping would have been an important male occupation, and smoking appears to have been an important pastime.

Related to smoking is the significant indication that the short stems of the locally manufactured smoking pipes required an additional hollow wooden stem to facilitate the use of the pipes. This indicates another craft, namely, carving. Carvers would work on wood and the range of products (from ethnographic analogy) would include the production of walking sticks, masquerades, and most importantly, canoes. Another craft inferred from the pottery decoration is basketry, cordage, and possibly, fabric manufacture. The range of cane and other raphia products would have included different kinds and sizes of baskets, mats, fish-drying rafters and fish traps. Being of wooden materials, these have not survived in the archaeological record at this site.

Similarly, no evidence of the farming activities of the occupants of this site has been uncovered mainly because both the indigenous and introduced food and cash crops that ought to have been grown at this site were root crops such as yams (especially the water yam), cocoyams, and cassava; and it is almost impossible to have direct evidence of their cultivation. Although soil samples were submitted for pollen analysis there have been no results received yet. The glass beads are perhaps the major indication of external contact at this site and their presence also suggests trade.

Also, the absence of materials, known from ethnography and oral traditions to have been used as money in trading transactions is striking. If one did not find cowries, one expected to find manilas or metal bars. There are at least two possible explanations for the absence of this class of artefacts that are known to be common in the Eastern Niger Delta sites earlier excavated (see Anozie, 1987:151-153; and Nzewunwa, 1979:272-273). One possible explanation would be that money was quite scarce and therefore very valuable in these relatively remote parts of the Niger Delta and so it would be unlikely to find it in the midden or rubbish deposits which were encountered during the excavation of the Agadagbabou site. If money is to be found, it is probably more like to be recovered from living shelter (house) spots and specifically in the sleeping areas. The other possible explanation is that the economy of the occupants of this site had not become monetized by 1640 A.D. The second explanation appears less likely to be valid than the first, especially when one takes into account the evidence provided by the beads and the J.J.W. Peters gin bottles that the occupants of this site had had contact with the Atlantic trade to the Americas and Europe.

Another aspect to be considered is whether or not what has been encountered at this site is a temporary or seasonal habitation site such as a fishing camp or a relatively permanent open habitation site. In taking a stand on this important issue, one is guided by both the stratigraphy of the site as exemplified by that of Test Pit IV and the range and nature of artefacts recovered from the site especially during the excavation. The stratification as earlier described is one in which there is a humic topsoil with cultural inclusions followed by a black midden deposit with high concentration of charcoal, ash and pottery. This main cultural layer has a natural deposit, the subsoil, underlying it. It is important to note that the midden deposit appears undifferentiated suggesting continuous rather than intermittent deposition of household waste materials. If the deposition of the waste materials had been seasonal, then sandy or silty flood deposits or other time markers would have differentiated the deposits into smaller layers that would have been observed by visual inspection.

Moreover, the presence of quite a number of broken smoking pipes and the wide range (both in terms of vessel form and decorative motifs) of pottery receptacles as well as the relatively expensive (now empty) bottles of gin and the beads recovered, indicate the presence of both men and women at this site, and suggest social and economic activities akin to those in progress at extant

Kolokuma settlements. Further proof of this is the *Kara* recovered which is worn by women during circumcision which is a very important aspect of the customs of the Ijo of the Central Niger Delta. Such an important cultural practice takes place at the home base, not at a temporary or seasonal settlement. Also from the presence of *Kara* one could infer that new offspring are likely to have been produced at this site since the circumcision rites are usually performed during the first pregnancy.

Koroama

Located on the west bank of Taylor (Gbaran) Creek, which is a tributary of the Nun, Koroama (5002 N, 6018 E) was the second site investigated in this project. It was chosen for investigation mainly because oral traditions indicated and the reconnaissance visit showed, that this was one of the pottery manufacturing centres along Taylor Creek that supplied the Ijo of the Central Delta with ceramic products. It was also decided that it was necessary to determine what measures needed to be taken to make excavation in the Delta during the rainy season both possible and successful. However, the month of August, when there is usually a lull period in the usually very heavy rains of this tropical rain forest zone, was chosen for excavation at Koroama.

First, two Mounds were identified for excavation. Mound A was a pottery firing mound on which the number, concentration, and nature of potsherds suggested that pots and perhaps other ceramic objects were fired in bonfires. To the south of Mound A was another mound near the Opuada shrine and Mr. Martin Orumokumo's mud house with zinc roof. This second mound is referred to in this work as Mound B.

Finds

The artefacts recovered from the excavations at Mound A were mostly potsherds. The excavated material from the northern half of Test Pit I, at spit level I of Mound A was sieved and all the pottery recovered and counted. The method used was to write serially the numbers I to 300 on sheets of paper and let each one represent 100 sherds. Once a hundred sherds were counted, the number 1 on the serial list of numbers is neatly crossed. The next one hundred sherds were counted and the figure 2 neatly cancelled and so on until the last of the sherds was counted. The total number of sherd thus recovered was 25,400 sherds. Sherds 1 to 8,200 were large while sherds 8,202, 25,400 or 17,200 sherds in all were small. This is an indication of the overwhelming number and weight of pot sherds encountered during the excavation of the two test pits on Mound A which was a pottery firing Mound. Some of the sherds had evidence of insufficient oxidation during firing while others were properly fired but appeared to have been casualties of the open air pottery firing technique common in the Niger Delta. Pot sherds were also recovered from Mound B.

The pottery recovered from the excavations at Koroama are understandably numerous. The study of all of them would take a long time to complete, and is still continuing. However, the main characteristics have been identified from a study of over 3,600 sherds from Mounds A and B. To start with, a study of the fabric by using a hand lens was first undertaken. This was done by studying a representative sample. The study was done by Dr. Samiyu Wandiba of the National Museums of Kenya in Nairobi.

The Koroama pottery falls into two fabric types. The first is characterised by specimens that have a generally compact texture, with abundant inclusions of quartz grains. Other inclusions (in this fabric type) include iron ore and occasional specks of white mica. This was the result of the microscopic study using a hand-lens (x10). The thin-sectioning and examination under the petrological microscope revealed that the fabric appears as an anisotropic mass of baked clay containing abundant inclusions of sub-rounded and rounded, ill-sorted quartz grains. The quartz grains are fairly evenly distributed in the matrix. The matrix also contains iron ore, pyroxenes, feldspars, clay pellets, white mica and a grain of zircon. The fieldspars are represented by both potash and plagioclass example, according to Wandiba.

On the second type of fabric to which Koroama pottery specimen has been assigned, Wandiba says it is generally less compact than the first fabric type. It is characterised by abundant inclusions of quartz grains that appear to be slightly larger than those of fabric 1. Other inclusions include iron ore and occasional specks of white mica. The thin-sectioning and examination under

317

petrological microscope revealed that this second fabric type appears as an anisotropic mass of baked clay, containing abundant inclusions of fairly well sorted, mainly sub-rounded quartz grains, evenly distributed in the matrix. The matrix also contains some quartzites, iron ore (including one very large one) and a few pyroxenes. The size and shape of the quartz grains distinguish this fabric from fabric 1.

For the Koroama pottery, all the specimens examined macroscopically and microscopically belong to these two fabric types of the five types identified in the study. It is also important to note Wandibba's conclusion that:

> The nature and composition of the inclusions of the two fabrics are such as to suggest that the two fabrics probably originate from the same source. This would mean that the observed differences are a reflection of different potting skills practiced at the same centre. On the whole, the pottery seems to have been manufactured locally on the (site) where it was found.

These conclusions accord with the nature of Mound A and extra site information gathered from Late Madam Salome Tuosenda, the last known potter in Koroama, who confirmed that the material for making pots was obtained from near Koroama. Not only did I talk to her, she showed me a sample of her work and some implements she used for making pots. One was a paddle and the other a small sharp-edged piece of bamboo. Essentially, therefore, the variety of pottery forms and decorative patterns described for the pottery from Agadagbabou and Isomabou is similar to that recovered from Koroama. For example, as earlier stated, there are more pots than bowls. Also there are more necked pots than globular pots. The thickness of the necked pots ranges between 5.5 milimetres through 6.5mm to 7.5mm with most specimens falling on or near the highest value. The globular pots are thicker with measurements of up to 9 millimetres. The bowls (especially carinated ones) have a thickness of 8.5cm. The rim diameter measurement for the necked pots ranges between 6cm (for a pot suspected to have functioned as a palmwine pouring receptacle) through 16 centimetres, to 20cm with the majority of the specimens falling between 16cm and 20cm. The rim diameter of the carinated bowls are between 12cm and 16cm.

The gun flints recovered from Mound B, Pit II are all of the platform type and not the wedge type as differentiated in the Diagram on page 91 of the Chelsea Speleological Society Newsletter, Vol. 20, No. 7 of April 1978 and Plate XIV accompanying the article by De Lotbiniere, S. (1977). Plate XVI of the same article illustrates the stages in the manufacture of the platform type of gun-flint. Also, comparison of the excavated gunflints with Plate XVIII A of Lotbirniere's article under reference shows that they are double edged flints with reverse trim on both firing edges. This detailed comparison is made because without recovering the flints in association with portions of the gun itself (although at this site portions of the gun were recovered) it is possible to interpret the flints to be scrapers. The significance, especially chronological, of these finds will be discussed when the site is interpreted later. However, for now it needs to be noted that the platform type was introduced from France and is believed to have reached Kent in about 1785, and Brandon only a few years later (De Lotbiniere, S. 1978:89). Elsewhere (De Lotbiniere, S. 1977:41), he states that it reached Brandon around 1790. Also, significant are the metal hoe from level 3 of Pit I, Mound B and the fish hook from level 2 of the same test Pit on Mound B.

Another class of artefacts recovered from Koroama comprised smoking pipes. They are categorized separately from the pottery here because there was only one locally made smoking pipe recovered from Mound A, Pit II, Level 3 whereas up to twenty-four (24) European factory-made pipe pieces were recovered from Mound B, Pit II from spit Levels 1 and 2 as well as levels 4 and 5. From level 1 there were sixteen (16) pieces two (2) of which were partially broken pipe bowls; eight (8) are pipe stem fragments; and six (6) are pipe bowl fragments. From level 2, six (6) pieces were recovered and whereas only one (1) was a partially broken pipe bowl; four (4) were pipe stem fragments; and only one (1) was a pipe bowl fragment. From spit level 4 there is only one stem fragment and from level 5 there is a complete smoking pipe bowl. In interpreting the site comparisons with published European factory made pipes will be a guide to chronology. There were also some pieces of Chinaware of porcelain (mostly plates) that were recovered. Blue glass beads were also recovered. All these further confirm external (especially European) trade. Cowrie shells were also recovered. Another significant find was the fragments of J.J.W. Peters gin bottles from Pit II on Mound B.

The next category of finds are food debris. These include shells of the giant African snail (*Helix Pomatia*), fish and animal bones and palm nuts. Most of the terrestrial snail shells were recovered from Test Pit II on Mound B although some came from Pit I and Mound B. The fish bones were identified in the field as those of *Burau* (Cat fish, *Glarotes laticepts*). Other fishes represented were Torii; (cat fish, *Clarias anguilaris*); Umah, (Electric fish, *Malapterus electricus*); Uluma (cat fish, *Clarias lazera*); Akama-Itoun (Perch, *Tilapia* species) and Ikpoki (cat fish, *Synodontis* species). The animal bones have been identified by comparison to zoological laboratory reference specimens at the University of Ibadan as belonging to the local goat (*Capra* sp.).

Fishing methods could be inferred from the species of fish identified so that other aspects of the economy can be linked to the fish remains when this site is interpreted later. However, before one leaves the discussion of fish bones, it is important to note that the fish bones identified from any site only represent a small percentage of the fish actually consumed at the site (Shackley, M. 1981:181). Also, most, if not all the fish from the Koroama site is freshwater fish. Finally, it needs to be noted that all the bones recovered at the Koroama site represent animals and fish killed by man for meat, that is, as a protein source.

The other category of food debris recovered comprised oil palm (*Elaeis guineensis*) nuts recovered from Test Pit I of Mound B. What is interesting about the nuts is that they were discarded after the extraction of palm oil from the flesh of the fruits. The next stage of cracking the nuts to obtain the kernel was not undertaken. It needs to be noted that apart from the kernel serving as hunger breaker, the oil from the kernel has medicinal as well as beautification uses. It serves as pomade. Discarding this group of palm nuts, the way they were done in this instance, therefore, appears to be an economic waste.

Stratigraphy, Dating and Interpretation

The stratification of the site as seen from the excavations at the two mounds is one in which there are five layers of cultural deposits interspersed with layers of natural deposits. The south and west walls show that there is a light grey topsoil followed by a dark grey cultural layer with charcoal and a lot of potsherd inclusions. Along the eastern half of the south wall there is a lens of palm nuts of variable thickness at the bottom of the second layer described above. This is followed by a natural deposit devoid of artefacts that is yellowish in colour. However, to the west of the southern wall, the lower portion of this culturally sterile layer (as can be extrapolated from its reappearance near the north west corner of the west wall) is occupied by a layer of palm nuts.

The impression one gets, therefore, is that the palm nuts form one layer in the stratigraphy which appears to have been broken on the south western part of the south wall during the phase of deposition of the natural soil deposit. This view is borne out by the fact that the layer of palm nuts could not have been part of the succeeding layer of very dark soil with evidence of firing and lots of potsherd inclusions. An interesting feature of this midden deposit is the fact that there is a lens of compact reddish soil with some sherds towards the bottom of the midden deposit. The reddish soil is of an average thickness of 10cm and appears to have been house floor material. Not having encountered post holes or post molds at that level during the excavation of the test pit, one cannot interpret this to be a living floor. It is likely to have been discarded house floor material. Below the major layer of very dark firing soil is a layer of light brown soil with some potsherd inclusions. Below that is the sub-soil which is a natural deposit and culturally sterile.

Mound A was chosen for excavation because of the evidence that it was a pottery firing mound. The correspondence of the stratification sequence on all the walls of the two test pits excavated on this mound is striking with five distinct layers. At the top is the light grey topsoil with a very high concentration of sherds and very little soil material. The second layer is also characterised by a very high concentration of potsherds but the little soil material is much darker than in the top layer. The third layer which also contains some potsherds, consists of a light brown soil with a lot of potsherds. The fourth layer is the reddish soil which is perhaps discarded house floor material or oxidized clayey soil with strands containing ferric substance.

The fifth layer is the subsoil, which consists of a yellowish brown soil that is compact and silty with small grain size. It, therefore, appears that the stratigraphy reflected in Mound A, Pit II, is more representative of the generalized stratigraphy for the Koroama site except that the extent of the humic topsoil in terms of thickness appears to have increased as a result of the pottery firing activities on the Mound. On Mound B, Pit I, the excavation was to a depth of 140cm and for Mound B, Pit II it was to a depth of 160cm whereas in the test pits on Mound A, excavations were to a depth of 120cm in Pit II and more than that in Pit I.

With regard to dating of the site, relative dating based on the European trade goods recovered from Mound B has been possible. Two categories of artefacts, namely, smoking pipes and the flint musket parts have been used. As earlier indicated, the gun flints are of the Platform type which is said to have been introduced into Britain from France about 1785 to 1790. It is, therefore, reasonable to estimate that the flint musket could have reached Koroama before the mid nineteenth century. Indeed, it needs to be recalled that it was on July 18, 1854 that Baikie named Gbarain Toru, Taylor Creek after one member of his crew. That the gun flints were recovered from levels 1, 2 and 6 of Test Pitt II of Mound B is significant because spit level 6 refers to a depth of about 120cm. This suggests that if the deposition sequence of the strata encountered in the Test Pit had not been disturbed, then the entire sequence represents the period of European contact. Although one did not encounter any pit profiles or other evidence of disturbance, the rubbish dump management practice earlier described in discussing the Agadagbabou site could have resulted in the mixing of European trade goods with older locally produced artefacts.

However, before coming to a conclusion on this issue, it would be useful to also consider the contribution of the European smoking pipes recovered from Test Pit II on Mound B to the chronology of the Koroama site. This is because the European smoking pipe typology has been fairly well worked out in terms of chronological significance (especially for British pipes). Adrian Oswald (1975) has produced a useful guide. Apart from indicating that both *Nicotiana tabacum* and *Nicotiana rustica* (varieties of tobacco) were in use in Europe (France, Portugal, Spain, Italy and England) in the 16th century, Oswald (1975:15) also shows photographs of tools used for the manufacture of European smoking pipes. But the most significant contributions of Oswald's monograph is in Part II titled the Archaeology of the Pipe.

Since the pipe fragments recovered at Koroama did not have dates written on them, one has found the drawings of pipe types very useful in the process of determining dates for the few complete or near complete pipe bowls recovered. From Figure 3, G: simplified General Typology, it was noted that one of the excavated pipe bowls was similar to number 12 described as Bowls with fairly wide mouths, medium to tall with walls and stems becoming markedly thinner with time. Bases becoming smaller and squarer. C. 1730-1780. (Oswald, 1975:37). Again, taking the upper limit of the dating of this type of pipe, it is important to note that the smoking pipe fragments were recovered from spit levels 1, 2, 4 and 5 of Test Pit II on Mound B. The pattern of distribution in terms of provenance is similar to that for the gun flints earlier discussed. Also, among earlier works consulted in the process of analyzing the smoking pipes are the reports of Ozanne (1969); Shinnie and Ozanne (1962); Shaw. (1960 and 1961; Walker (1975); Galvocoressi (1975); Hill (1976) and York (1973). These were all quite useful guides.

Finally, apart from using the European Trade goods to date the Koroama site, charcoal samples were taken from Test Pits I and II of Mound A. This was done because unlike Mound B, there were no European Trade goods recovered from Mound A. However, the results from the Radiocarbon Laboratory in Oxford confirm the conclusion on chronology tentatively arrived at based on relative dating. The radiometric dating procedure returned a Radiocarbon Age (BP) determination of Modern for the two samples sent as shown in the Table below:

Table 15.1: Radio carbon dates for Koroama

Material	Laboratory Reference	Measurement Reference	Submitters Reference	Radio-carbon Age (BP)	Provenance
Charcoal	RCD-30	LSO 13/3/90 LS2 27/5/90	UI 7224	Modern	40cm depth at 76cm West on South wall, Pit I Mound A, Koroama
Charcoal	RCD-31	LSO 13/3/90 LS2 27/5/90	UI 7225	Modern	Level 3(40-60cm) Pit II, Mound A, Koroama

The result of Modern means that the Radiocarbon result lies in the period of uncertainty for the technique, i.e. in the last 300 to 400 years during which period it is impossible to carry out Radiocarbon dating. This occurs because the level of C-14 in the atmosphere fluctuated considerably in this period with the same level repeating at different times. (Radiocarbon Measurement Report, 14th June, 1990; RCD-30 and RCD-31).

Thus, one can say that evidence from the two mounds excavated at the extant habitation site of Koroama indicates that settlement at this site cannot be older than 400 years ago (that is about the 16th century A.D.). Indeed, the settlement appears to have been established about the same time as European contact with the Niger Delta began to affect Delta fringes. However, this is not to suggest that the establishment of the settlement was a response to the coming of Europeans to the Niger Delta coast. Evidence of a potting industry from Mound A, for example, suggests a sedentary population whose economy was already diversified and in which trade was important such that the range and variety of European trade goods noted from the excavations could be acquired and the damaged ones discarded.

The results of the Archaeological investigations at Koroama have justified the choice of the site for excavation. First, it has enabled one have an insight into the nature of the pottery industry among the Gbaran of Taylor Creek who have been identified by other Central Delta Ijo groups as the manufacturers of the ceramic ware used in various settlements. Secondly, it has shown that it is possible to excavate part of a site in the Central Delta and find no European Trade goods whereas at another part of the same site, such goods can be recovered. At least the later phase of the sequence on Mound A must have been contemporaneous with the phase of European contact represented by the associated artefacts in the sequence at Mound B.

Another significance of the excavations at Koroama is the illustration of the importance of activity loci on a site. Mound A, had little or no evidence of daily subsistence activities especially food debris and domestic waste material such as damaged tools and utensils. Mound B, on the other hand was a rubbish dump and so had distinct midden deposits in the stratigraphic sequence. Moreover, located on a creek that is smaller than the River Nun, but bigger than the Opuba creeklet, Koroama represents a settlement category higher than that of Agadagbabou. The oral traditions of Koroama, which is part of Gbaran Ibe, indicate that the people last moved from a settlement opposite present-day Kaiama on the River Nun, to occupy the portion of Taylor Creek near its junction with River Nun as a result of the discovery by the ancestor of the Gbaran, who was a hunter, that the creek had a lot of fishes.

The presence of the flint gun parts and the rusted matchet confirms that hunting is likely to have been an important part of the economy of the people of Koroama. In fact, extra site information collected during the excavations indicates that hunting is still important. The guns and matchets could also have been used for defence. Although the general Gbaran market is at Ogboloma, each settlement has its own daily market in the evenings. Apart from fish which is obtained mostly by men during the flood season of June to August, agricultural produce are obtained locally through farming, which is the major occupation between January and May. Canoe carving is undertaken between October and December. It is the adult men who carve for themselves and their wives. The men also engage in the cutting of palm fruits when they are ripe. The palm trees exploited are mostly wild, although improved varieties are now being cultivated in some parts of the Central Delta.

Although women are involved in farming and fishing, they alone practice the crafts of basketry, mat-making, hair plaiting, and the now virtually extinct manufacture of pottery. Women and children also collect from the forest items

325

such as the fruits of the bush mango (*Irvinga gabonensis*) for the making of ogbono for soup and larvae from the trunk of the raffia palm (*Raphia hookeri*) as a protein source. They also collect firewood from the forest.

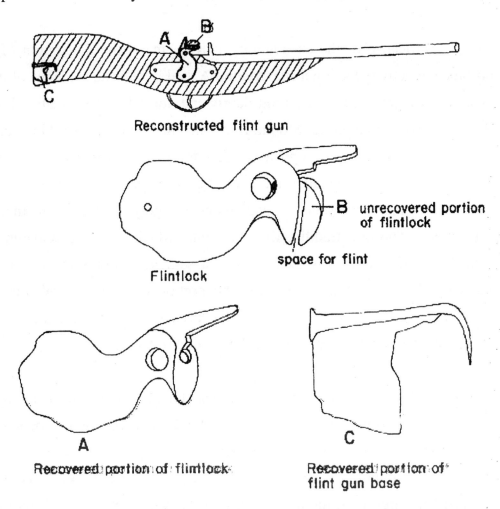

Plate 15.2: Gun parts found at Koroama, Mound II, Pit 2, Level 2

All told, the Koroama site shows a link between the excavated materials and the pattern of material culture of the present occupants of the site. For one thing, the once vibrant pottery industry is now dead with the last of the potters having died. Moreover, plastic and aluminium receptacles have now virtually replaced the ceramic receptacles used in house-holds of the past. There are similarities between the pottery of Koroama and the pottery recovered at Agadagbabou. In the first place, as at Agadagbabou, most of the ceramic vessels represented by the potsherds from Mound A at Koroama, for example, are pots while a smaller percentage are bowls. Secondly, as at Agadagbabou, the major decorative technique is incision.

Also, the first guns are said to have been invented in the 14th century A.D. during the Edwardian period in England. Little wonder then, that no evidence of the use of guns was found at the Isomabou site. It is also useful to note that if only Mound A at Koroama had been investigated, there would have been no European goods found but the radiocarbon date determinations would have indicated the recent age of the site. It is therefore, important to combine both relative dating using trade goods, and radiometric dating methods to determine chronology. Again, identification of activity loci at archaeological sites in the Central Niger Delta is important if the researcher is not to make misleading conclusions. This is particularly relevant to industrial activity locations.

From extra site information (oral) gathered at Koroama and Obunagha on Taylor Creek, the practice of pottery firing was to locate firing spots behind, rather than in front (that is, by the shore), of the settlement. What this suggests, if it is true, is that where a pottery firing mound is, at present, located in front (by the shore) of the settlement, it means that river or creek erosion has continually advanced into the settlement forcing the inhabitants to continually move their houses further inland in response. Thus, Mound A at Koroama could represent a former inland end of the settlement. Therefore, it is quite possible that the older portions of the settlement may have been lost to the Taylor Creek through flood water erosion of the shoreline over the years. The fact that Mound A showed evidence of on-going erosional effects during the excavations supports this suggested reconstruction of the dynamics of site formation and destruction in the Central Niger Delta.

Finally, the subsistence situation at both Koroama and Agadagbabou is similar for the periods represented in the sequences examined. Also, a generalized stratigraphic section for both sites would show the stratigraphy to be compatible. In terms of material culture, therefore, the two sites present similar packages and the environmental conditions are similar, although not identical.

Isomobou
Although Isomobou is about 5.5 kilometres, as the crow flies, from Ikibiri, it is about 9 kilometres following the winding footpath through the forest. Ayala

Lake is nearer the site than the present inhabited Ikibiri settlement. Isomobou is an abandoned open habitation site located at 4055N, 6010E on the south bank of Torukubu creek, which is between 16 and 20 metres wide. The extent of the area of the site investigated during the 1983 excavations was about 85 from east to west and about 36 metres from north to south. It was decided that Test Pits of 2 metres square be used to sample the site. Five Test Pits were excavated. Of these only Test Pit III was culturally sterile.

1.   Finds

By far the largest class of finds was pottery. All told, some 4,500 sherds were recovered from which 4,389 were not too fragmentary for meaningful analysis. Decorated potsherds from the Isomabou site examined are 18% while plain or undecorated sherds are 82% of the total number of sherds examined. Of the decorated potsherds 27% are rim sherds while 73% are body sherds. Of the plain potsherds examined, on the other hand, 13% are rim sherds while 87% are body sherds. To avoid wrong identification during the sorting, all sherds that were from below the neck of the vessel were put together as body sherds. There were no fragments from lids or handles noticed in the pottery from this site.

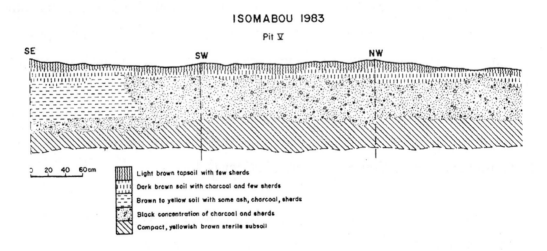

Plate 15.3: Isomabou Pit V, 1983

Isomabou Pottery Statistics Summary

Percentages:

Decorated sherds at Isomabou site = 17.94%

Plain sherds at Isomabou site = 82.06%

Of the Decorated potsherds at the site, 26.91% are rim sherds while 73.09% are body sherds.

Of the Plain potsherds at the site, 13.17% are rim sherds while 86.83% are body sherds.

Finally, it is useful to comment at some length on the fabric of the pottery from Isomabou. Wandiba's analysis (see Derefaka 2003, Appendix C) has assigned the pottery from Isomabou to two fabric types. The first is characterised by abundant inclusions of quartz grains that appear to be slightly larger than those of fabric 1, and has occasional specks of white mica. Under the microscope, the fabric appears as an anisotropic mass of baked clay containing abundant inclusions of fairly well sorted, mainly sub-rounded quartz grains. The quartz grains are evenly distributed in the matrix also, one very large and a few pyroxenes. The size and shape of the quartz grains distinguish this fabric from fabric 2.

The second type of fabric to which Isomabou pottery has been assigned is Wandiba's Fabric 5 described as:

> Characterized by abundant inclusions of quartz grains together with many inclusions of what appear to be meta-sediments. The matrix also contains large inclusions of iron ore, some of which are 7mm long. Thin sectioning reveals an anisotropic groundmass of baked clay containing inclusions of ill-assorted grains of quartz, which are mainly sub-rounded and rounded. The matrix also contains fairly common inclusions of shale and a pyroxene. The presence of shale distinguishes this fabric from the other four already described.

The second fabric type is unique and as Wandiba observes in his conclusion, since shale offers good resistance to both expansion and shrinkage, it is most probable that it was purposely added to the clay body as a temper. Potters rarely travel far for tempering materials; as a matter of fact, they normally employ whatever material is available on the site. This is, therefore, evidence that some of the pottery was manufactured on the Isomabou site.

329

Beyond what has been said about Isomabou pottery, not much more can be said in terms of moving from the material to the non-material.

Other Finds, Features and Interpretation

Apart from pottery, the other find at the Isomabou site which was recovered from Pits I, II, IV and V was charcoal. It occurred in association with other cultural materials in the stratigraphic sequence of each Test Pit and has been used for radiometric dating of the site. The only pit in which post holes, and indeed, fragments of house posts, were encountered was Pit I. One of the two post fragments was near the south wall and the other in the north west corner. From the buildings still standing in the fishing camp, it can be suggested that the post fragments represent part of the wooden framework for the walls of a house built with lateritic soil on the wall and floor and thatch on the roof which is also of a wooden framework.

There is also an iron object identified in the field as a fishing spear tip. It was recovered from level 2 (20-40cm) of Test Pit IV in the north west corner near the north wall. This would have been fixed to a long wooden handle to make it a spear. Apart from fishing, it could also have been useful as a hunting implement. The other important category of finds consisted of animal bones. From Level 1 of Pit V some calcified bones were recovered. Also, from Level 2 (20-40cm) of Pit I very fragile (almost powdery) bones were recovered mixed with soil matrix. Most of the bones were fish bones while some of the limb bones have been identified as antelope (duiker) bones. There is, therefore, confirmation of the practice of fishing and hunting among the inhabitants of the Isomabou site at the time of the cultural deposits at this site. The secondary rain forest vegetation at and near the site also suggest that farming would have been practised and the cutting of palm fruits as well as exploitation of other products of the oil palm undertaken. Moreover, the carving of canoes would also need to have been undertaken to ensure effective exploitation of the fauna and flora of this secondary creek (fresh water) environment. There is also evidence, from the shore of the Torukubu Creek next to the site, that flooding has been a factor in the provision of silty soil and the degradation of some areas of the site. Two shorelines of the Torukubu Creek were discernible. One was the dry season flow tide shoreline and the other was the flood-water level shoreline.

Also, important to note is the presence of hearths or fire places at this site. At Level 3 (40-60cm) in Pit IV near the south-east corner a hearth was encountered that produced mainly ash and charcoal. Also at the same level of the same Pit another fireplace was encountered near the north west corner. This hearth produced some burnt clay which might have been used to construct a simple firewood stove. This is a circular thick-walled clay structure open at the top and with provision of space for stoking the fire with firewood. The clay cooking pot can then be placed on the stove. The other hearth encountered at this site was near the middle of the south wall of Pit II at level 2 (20-40cm) and it produced charcoal, ash and relatively fewer potsherds than the rest of that spit level.

Perhaps the most significant aspect of the finds at the Isomabou site is the fact that all the artefacts recovered are locally made. There were no European or other external trade goods recovered from the four test pits that were fully investigated. The significance of this is that the interpretation of the artefacts from this site can be restricted to independent invention and not diffusion. Also important is the relationship between the nature of the artefacts and their stratigraphic distribution on the one hand and the chronology of the site on the other.

Stratigraphy and Dating

For each of the four test pits fully investigated at the Isomabou site, stratigraphic sections have been drawn. For Pit I the section drawings of the north wall and the east wall show that excavation reached a depth of about 120cm. The sequence of stratification of the north wall shows a succession of three distinct layers to the west namely, a dark brown soil with some sherds and relatively little charcoal on top; followed by a very dark or black soil with high concentration of charcoal and numerous potsherds; the last layer (unlike the first two) is a natural deposit consisting of a compact, clayey yellowish brown subsoil.

The eastern half of the sequence of stratification of the north wall is a little more complex. First, there is on top, a pit profile about 65cm deep. Within this, the first layer is a compact yellowish brown soil (part of the subsoil) containing some potsherds. About the middle of this layer is an ash lens followed by the rest of the top layer. The next layer is the midden deposit with high level of charcoal concentration and numerous potsherds. Below that is the compact, yellowish brown and naturally deposited subsoil. It is also interesting to note the extent of vertical transport of the midden deposit into the subsoil (almost to the final floor of the Pit). Roots and burrowing animals such as worms have contributed to producing that effect in the stratigraphy. On the eastern wall where the elevation of the ground surface level is generally higher, the humic topsoil with rootlets and a few potsherds is evident. This is followed by a compact yellowish brown soil with few sherds followed by an ash lens which is followed by the rest of compact yellowish brown soil with few sherds.

The next layer is the core midden deposit and presence of some of the ash lens in this layer as well as the fact that the midden deposit is broken by the second layer about midway on the east wall suggests some disturbance. It does seem, therefore, that there was a pit dug in the location of Test Pit I into which midden materials were thrown, but this deposit was later disturbed in some places by the digging of smaller holes or pits by man.

Dating

By a letter dated 12th September, 1990, Radiocarbon Dating in Oxford forwarded certificates on the seven samples which had been dated using the carbon-14 method. For the Isomabou samples the results as stated in the Radiocarbon Measurement Report are as follows:

Table 15.2: Radiocarbon Dates for Isomabou

Laboratory Reference	Measurement Reference	Submitters Reference	Radio-carbon age (BP) half life 5370	Calibra-ted age range 20 Cal.	Provenance
RCD 26	LSO 13/3/90	UI7218	660Â±90	AD. 1220-1430	Isomabou T.P.I., Level 5 (80-100cm)
RCD 27	LSO 13/3/90 LS2 27/5/90	UI7220	680Â±60	AD. 1240-1400	Isomabou T.P.IV; Level 2 (20-40cm)
RCD 28	LSO 13/3/90 LS2 27/5/90	UI7221	560Â±90	AD. 1270-1480	Isomabou, T.P. V, Level 1 (20cm) S.W. corner
RCD 29	LSO 13/3/90 LS2 27/5/90	UI7223	810Â±70	AD. 1030-1290	Isomabou, T.P. V, Level 3 (40-80cm)
RCD 31	LSO 13/3/90 LS2 27/5/90	UI7219	650Â±140	AD. 1045-1480	Isomabou, T.P. II (100cm) at 75cm south from N.E. peg along east wall

In discussing the above dates, we found the condensed information in Richard Gillespie's (1986) *Radiocarbon User's Handbook* quite useful. Gillespie's summary of what a radiocarbon date is (1986:1), can bear reproduction here as it is quite apt:

> When a living organism dies or when a carbon-containing compound is no longer able to exchange carbon freely with the atmosphere, the initial concentration of radiocarbon begins to decrease by the process of radioactive decay. Knowing the initial concentration of radiocarbon and the half-life, and what the concentration is now, it is possible to calculate how much time has passed since the sample was last in equilibrium with the atmosphere. Thus a radiocarbon date relates to the time elapsed since the carbon isotope ratios were fixed at the natural levels in the sample. For most laboratories, the range of application is from about 200 to 40,000 years before present (B.P.).

For the laboratory that processed the samples that produced the above dates for Isomabou, the period of uncertainty for the technique used lies in the period of the last 300 to 400 years, and this is indicated for the two Koroama samples earlier discussed. On a more positive note, however, Gillespi's (1981:25) remark that a radiocarbon age relates to the time elapsed since the carbon in the sample was last in equilibrium with the atmosphere, reinforces ones confidence in the calibrated dates for Isomabou. Moreover, the laboratory's explanation that,

> The calibrated age ranges given are calculated using the program provided by Washington University (Stuiver & Reimer, 1986) which uses the recommended calibration data of Stuiver & Pearson (1986), Pearson & Stuiver (1986) and Pearson, et al (1986), makes the calibrated age ranges provided at both one sigma and two sigma standard deviation quite reliable.

The pattern of chronology both horizontally and vertically at the Isomabou site is quite interesting. For example, it seems that the portion of the site where Test Pit I is located is relatively younger than the portion where Test Pits IV and V are located as evidenced by the age range of 1220-1430 A.D. as deep down as 80-100cm in Pit I as compared with the range of 1030-1290 A.D. from Test Pit V (40-60cm). Similarly, the age ranges of 1270-1480 A.D. at level I (20cm) and 1030-1290 A.D. at level 3 (40-60cm) of Test Pit V are indicative of an undisturbed stratification at the Isomabou site as the lower portion of the stratigraphy has produced an older age range as expected.

Furthermore, what the dates from the Isomabou site indicate is that the site had been occupied between about 1030 A.D. and 1480 A.D. Isomabou is said to have been the original settlement of what is now known as Ogbo Clan (Central Delta) and the Ogoloma of the Eastern Niger Delta. The Pit referred to in the oral traditions in which Ogbo, son of the apical ancestor of the clan was buried during the raid on Isomabou was not found during this phase of archaeological research. He is said to have been lowered in the Pit along with all his possessions and he is presumed to have died of starvation. If it is true that the defeat and sack of Isomabou was a result of the use of firearms by their enemies, Oweikorogha, then that would have been during the sixteenth century at the earliest.

What is noteworthy, however, is that there is now evidence of the occupation of the Central Niger Delta by the Ijo from early in the 11th century A.D. The absence of European trade goods among the artefacts recovered from Isomabou also confirms the age range of 1030 to 1480 A.D. for the occupation of this site. Perhaps if charcoal samples from the top levels of Test Pit I had been processed, the upper limit for the occupation of the site would have been later than 1480 A.D. It is also significant that the iron spear point recovered from level 2 (40cm) of Test Pit IV can be dated by association to between 1240 and 1400 A.D. Although there is no evidence from the excavations of iron working, it is known that metal working was well-known in south-eastern Nigeria by the 10th century A.D. The presence of an iron spear point before the 15th century at Isomabou is, therefore, not surprising. Finally, confidence in the lower limit of the dates is provided by the results indicated for samples RCD-29 and RCD-32 in which the lower limits are A.D. 1030 and A.D. 1045 respectively. Given the distance between the location of Test Pit IV and Test Pit II at the Isomabou site and the relative elevation of the present land surface at both Pits, the vertical location of the samples that provided dates with almost identical lower limits makes sense.

Relating the Central to the Eastern Delta

Perhaps in comparing the archaeology and aspects of culture history of the Central Delta with that of the Eastern Delta, one should start by stating that the macro-environmental conditions for the two areas are different. Whereas the Central Delta has freshwater swamp with raffia palms dominating the vegetation except in the thick forest, the Eastern Delta has salt water with mangrove dominating the vegetation. This difference has implications for what subsistence strategy is dominant in the two zones. Whereas farming is quite important and fishing is practiced in the Central Delta, fishing is very important and farming is virtually non-existent in most of the Eastern Delta.

Even in the area of language and ethnic sub-grouping, although most inhabitants of both the Central and Eastern Niger Delta are Ijo, the languages of all of the sub-groups in the Central Delta are more mutually intelligible than they are with any of those of the Eastern Niger Delta. Similarly, the languages of most of the sub-groups in the Eastern Niger Delta are mutually intelligible. Also, although the common foodstuff among both Central and Eastern Delta are largely similar, the methods of preparation and especially the method of presentation are different. For example, whereas plantain is preferred unripe by virtually all Ijo of the Central Niger Delta, most Ijo of the Eastern Delta use ripe plantain either alone or pounded with yam in their diet. Similarly, the common practice in the Central Delta of eating starch or garri and soup plus plantains and pepper soup at a meal is uncommon in the Eastern Delta.

As for musical instruments, the animal skin drums and metal gongs are common to both the Central and Eastern Delta but the set of musical or talking pots common among the Eastern Delta Ijo is a recent introduction from there into the Central Delta. Eastern Delta Ijo have also tended to pass on dress patterns developed primarily as a result of early contact with Europeans but raffia cloth was known and used quite early among the Ijo as evidenced by its role in the big bride-wealth type of marriage.

Also, in both the Central and Eastern Delta, the Ijo lived in rectangular house structures constructed with wooden frames and plastered with mud and having raffia palm-leaves thatched roofs. Their settlements were different in outline with those in the Central Delta sprawling lengthwise along the creek or river bank while those in the Eastern Delta are mostly on islands, although even their settlements appear to have begun from the water fronts and gradually spread to the centre of the island with time. However, the concept of town squares for market, recreational, political and ritual purposes is common to both Central and Eastern Niger Delta Ijo. But in the Eastern Delta, the periodic markets are generally located on the mainland to facilitate trade with non-riverine trading partners. Division of the settlement into wards or quarters is common among all Ijo.

There has also been a long-standing exchange of economic products between the Ijo of the Central Delta and those of the Eastern Delta. For example, farm products, palm oil, *Ogboli*, canoes, basketry, mats and gin from the Central Delta were traded for salt, fish and shell-fish from the Eastern Delta. There have also been intermarriages especially between the Nembe and the Kolokuma for example. Even in religion there are relationships. For example, there is a deity known as *Ogula* in Ikibiri which is said to have been the origin of the name Ogoloma in the Eastern Niger Delta. Moreover, the concepts of *Amatemeso* and *Amakiri* are common to both the Ijo of the Central Delta and those of the Eastern Delta. The former refers to the soul of the settlement and the latter the physical essence of the settlement.

Now, one can examine the archaeological record for the Eastern Niger Delta in order to compare it with what has been presented here for the Central Niger Delta. Thereafter, comments can be made on possibilities with regard to origins and migrations of the Ijo in the Niger Delta. The culture history of the Eastern Delta has been reconstructed from the artefacts recovered from archaeological excavations and it begins from prehistoric times (See for example, Anozie, 1987:141-185; Nzewunwa, 1979; and Nzewunwa, 1987:187-229). While Anozie's synthesis deals with culture history, that of Nzewunwa deals with the economic aspect. Reviewing the information from excavations at Onyoma, Ke, Ogoloma, Saikiripogu, Okochiri, Agadagbabou, and Koroama, Anozie (1987:157) came to the following conclusion with regard to the finds from these sites:

> In terms of cultural array there are points of similarity. These are in the use of smoking pipes locally-made and imported. While we can identify a smoking habit in the area, there is still no clue as to what was smoked, and none even for what chronological gap exists between the two main types. The numerous snail shells from Mound II of Koroama recall the ubiquitous shells from a variety of shellfish species. The numerous mammalian and fish bones emphasize the availability and exploitation of mammals and fish within a reasonable economic distance from the settlements, as in the saltwater zone. However, we are yet to identify the actual species

represented and to evaluate their caloric value and also their carrying capacity within the freshwater zone. So far there is reason to believe that the recovered data will go a long way towards our understanding of man, his environment and development within the freshwater area and also suggest further areas of research.

The basis for this comparison between the Eastern and Central Delta with regard to the latter is Anozie, Nzewunwa and Derefaka, (1987:121-140). To start with, it is possible now to take a closer look at the smoking pipes recovered from the excavations at Niger Delta sites. One could use Ogoloma in the Eastern Delta and Koroama in the Central Delta as case studies for this discussion. Table 6.4 (Anozie, 1987:150) shows the stratigraphic distribution of smoking pipes from Ogoloma and it is reproduced below.

Table 15.3: Smoking Pipes from Ogoloma by Provenance

S/No.	Level	IA	IB	IC	ID
1	0.20cm	0			0
2	20-40cm	+	+++	0	0
3	40-60cm		+		
4	60-80cm	0	+000	0	0
5	80-100cm	0	0	+000000	+0
6	100-120cm			0	
7	120-140cm		0	+	
8	140-160cm		+		
9	160-180cm	+	++	+	+
10	180-200cm	+++		++	
11	200-220cm	+		+	
12	220-240cm	+++	+		
13	240-260cm	+	+++++	+++++	
14	260-280cm	+		+++++++++++++	
15	280-300cm		+++++	++	
16	300-320cm			+++++	
17	320-340cm	+	++		
18	340-360cm				
19	360-380cm				
20	380-400cm				

S/No.	Level	IA	IB	IC	ID
21	400-420cm				
22	420-440cm				
23	440-460cm				
24	460-480cm				

Legend:
0 = European Factory-made smoking pipe
+ = Locally-made smoking pipe.

The above table shows clearly that from spit level 8 (140-160cm) in the stratigraphy of the Ogoloma site down to spit level 17 (320-340cm) no European factory-made smoking pipes were recovered and only locally-made clay smoking pipes were recovered. Using his Table 6.8 (1987:168) showing Eastern Niger Delta radiocarbon dates, and his statement (1987:162) that sample N-2052 whose date ranges between A.D. 1255 and 1410 was collected at a depth of 360cm which is 20cm below the earliest deposited clay smoking pipe found during the excavation, it is reasonable to conclude that the making of smoking pipes (since there is evidence of pottery manufacture at the site) began sometime between 1255 and 1410 A.D. at Ogoloma.

It is also clear that the manufacture/use of locally made smoking pipes at Ogoloma continued beyond 1840 A.D. Table 6.1 above also indicates popularity trends for both locally-made and European factory-made smoking pipes. The locally-made smoking pipes make their first appearance at spit level 17 (320-340cm), become quite popular between levels 16 (300-320cm) and 13 (240-260cm) representing an age range with the upper limit at about the beginning of the 19th century. The same table also suggests that with the arrival of imported European factory-made smoking pipes from spit level 7 (120-140cm), the locally-made pipes seem to have become less popular than they were before the introduction of the European factory-made pipes. As Table VIII.4 (Nzewunwa, 1979:292) shows, of the 96 smoking pipes recovered from excavations at the Ogoloma site, 69 were locally-made and 26 were imported. Overall, imported smoking pipes account for 28.2% and locally-made smoking pipes 71.2% of the total number of pipes recovered from the Eastern Delta.

As for Koroama, all but one of the smoking pipes recovered from the site are fragments of European factory-made pipes and as earlier discussed in this Chapter these smoking pipes would have arrived at Koroama in the 19th century A.D. Even the locally-made pipe fragment recovered from Mound A at Koroama dates to about two hundred years ago at the earliest. Thus, the guide provided by the distribution of smoking pipes at Ogoloma is still the most informative for the Niger Delta. However, if the *Nicotiana tabacum* and *Nicotiana rustica* varieties of tobacco were in use in Europe in the 16th century, then the invention of the smoking pipe in the Niger Delta could not have been dependent on the introduction of tobacco or the European smoking pipe into the Niger Delta. Indeed, the first appearance of the locally-made clay smoking pipe as has been shown clearly ante-dates the introduction of tobacco into the Niger Delta. From extra site information in the Central Delta, the *ogboin* (bush mango) leaves have been suggested as a possibility of what was smoked in the Delta before the introduction of tobacco; and given the connection between Ogoloma and Isomabou, one is inclined to suggest that such knowledge of this or/and other leaves might account for the early invention of the smoking pipe at Ogoloma. As Nzewunwa (1979:304) observed, it is interesting that no European styles before the 18th century seem to have influenced the pipes at Ogoloma.

It is useful to note that, at all the sites in the Niger Delta, pottery is the most numerous class of artefacts; and a detailed comparative study that would examine the evolution of vessel forms, decorative techniques, manufacturing processes and distribution patterns needs to be done on a regional basis. This can only be done when attribute analysis parameters and classificatory systems used to present the information on pottery in the Eastern and Central Delta have been harmonized. Nzewunwa's analysis of Eastern Delta Ijo pottery (1979:366) provides some basis for comparison. To this we shall soon return.

Apart from pottery and smoking pipes, the other clay objects found in both the Eastern and Central Delta sites are clay beads (from Ogoloma and Agadagbabou). There are clay pots and bowls from all the Niger Delta sites. However, clay cups and oil lamps have been recovered from Ke and

Ogoloma and Onyoma. Artefacts found in the Eastern Delta excavations that are absent from the Central Delta sites include manilas, cowrie shells, brassware, copperware, ivory ornaments, saltwater shells, terra cotta figurines, crucibles, tuyeres, iron slag and human bones. However, fish and animal bones as well as snails have been recovered from both the Eastern and Central Delta sites. The absence of the manilas and other artefacts from the Central Delta shows the relative isolation of the sites of the Central Delta, particularly Isomabou and Agadagbabou, from the outside world. In the case of Isomabou, the absence of such trade goods is understandable given the period of occupation of the site and its location. In the case of Agadagbabou which appears to have been occupied up to the 18th century A.D., perhaps it is the remoteness and relative inaccessibility that can explain the absence of European or other trade goods in the inventory of artefacts recovered in primary and stratigraphic context at the site. As for the food debris, which features prominently at all the Niger Delta sites, they provide a clue to the subsistence strategies employed by the Ijo in the different Delta environments. However Nzewunwa (1987:221) rightly points out:

> For the freshwater delta, the food wastes are in the form of fish and animal bones and freshwater snails. These do not submit to shell midden analysis. This is why a comparative analysis of the quantitative and qualitative implications of the food debris from Eastern Delta sites and Central Delta sites is not feasible: Indeed, the overwhelming preponderance of shell fish in the Eastern Delta Ijo diet is not replicated or approximated at any of the Central Delta sites where extra site information indicates that there are freshwater shell fish (even if not as numerous or varied as those of the saltwater) that feature in the diet of extant Central Ijo peoples. Instead of shells of such shell fish, what was found to be numerous at the Koroama excavations, for example, were land snail shells. There is also ample evidence of a high level of exploitation of the land snail protein resource among extant Ijo groups in the Central Niger Delta. In none of the excavations in the Central Delta were human bones encountered and this correlates with the mortuary practices earlier discussed.

To return to the comparison between pottery of the Eastern and Central Delta, a common feature is that in the latter, as in the former, the manufacture of ceramic vessels is the work of women. In his classification of Eastern Delta pottery, Nzewunwa (1979) has identified thirty two classes of ceramic vessels based on shape. His class 33 (1979:328) which he calls miscellaneous fragments, discusses Handles, Bosses and Bases. The thirty two classes (1979:315-328) are: large wide-mouthed carinated hemispherical bowls; small shallow wide- mouthed bowls; large flanged-rimmed bowls; small shallow flange- rimmed bowls; small hemispherical bowls; heavy thick-walled wide-mouthed bowl; very small bowls; large wide-mouthed shallow dishes; long narrow-necked jars; large, long wide-necked jars; large, wide-mouthed funnel-necked jars; large, wide mouthed, very short necked vessels; grooved short-necked vessels; short-necked large globular vessels; small, shouldered jars; medium sized shouldered jars; large wide-mouthed, shouldered jars; small globular, shouldered jars; necklace jars; small cylindrical-shaped vessels; small oval-shaped vessels; small, shallow baggy vessels; plain ovoid vessels; crucibles; perforated pots; pot stands; lids; heavy thick-walled trough-shaped vessels; tuyeres-like nozzles; large egg-shaped vessels; vessels; mortars; and well-made glazed plates. According to Nzewunwa (1979:311):

> Of the 13,306 potsherds examined during the analysis, 10,633 were used for this study. They were distributed in this order: Onyoma 151; Okochiri 2,173; Ogoloma 2,591, Ke 2,746 and Saikiripogu 22,970.

As he also noted, only simple descriptive methods were employed in the classification although he was aware of the possibility of sophisticated statistical and computer analysis (Spaulding 1971, Cowgill 1971, Shepard 1976, Clarke 1962).

What is certain is that, dates are now available for Isomabou and Koroama. As expected, the inhabited site of Koroama was established no earlier than four hundred years ago. The occupation history of the abandoned open habitation site of Isomabou, on the other hand, began about the eleventh century A.D. If this represents the oldest date for that site, then the dates from Ke and Okochiri are older, and the expectation of archaeology contributing to the resolution of problems of origins and migrations of the Ijo in the Niger Delta would appear to remain unmet. However, the date from Isomabou raises hopes that further archaeological research in the Central Delta might yet reveal the existence of sites there that are contemporaneous with or older than Ke and Okochiri in the Eastern Delta. Moreover, the possibility of more than one dispersal centre for the Ijo located in the Eastern, Central and Western Niger Delta needs to be considered.

It seems plausible to expect that while some Eastern Delta Ijo might find their roots in the Central Delta, others might find their ancestral home located within the Eastern Niger Delta. One makes this proposition on the extra site evidence obtained from the Central Delta, that some wards of a particular settlement could trace their origins to other than the one to which their settlement belongs. This situation is also known to exist in some Eastern Delta Ijo settlements although for political and social reasons many members of such wards or *Polo* would not admit this readily. That this is possible is further suggested by the transhumance life style which a mostly fishing subsistence strategy requires. If one then extrapolates this phenomenon into the past, population movements would not need to have always been dramatic or massive. A scenario of gradual movements resulting in the gradual change of the composition of the dominant group in a given settlement and ultimately of a linguistically, religiously, and politically related group of settlements is possible. It is hoped that more extensive and intensive archaeological excavation strategies would in future expose the critical stages. More importantly, the reason for the very late arrival of radiometric dates for Koroama and Isomabou was lack of funding for the processing of samples sent since 1983. This fundamental issue needs to be properly addressed and solutions found if archaeology is to contribute to the resolution of the problem of settlement history of the Niger Delta of such developments at individual sites.

In concluding the section on settlement history in his synthesis, Alagoa (1987:236) says:

> It is in the area of cultural and economic history that Archaeology has made substantial contributions to our understanding of the history of the Niger Delta.

But even in the area of reconstructing culture history, he rightly draws attention to the issue discussed earlier in this Chapter, namely, the need for a systematic study of pots and potsherds from excavations in the Delta and ethnographically. He puts it succinctly (1987:237) thus,

> A comprehensive record of types, methods, and the economy and culture of pot-making over the Niger Delta basin is necessary to provide information for the proper interpretation of the prehistoric data.

The other issue which needs some comment in that section of Alagoa's analysis is the reference to the speculation of the significance of the absence of stone objects among the artefacts recovered from the excavations in the Eastern Delta (see for example, Anozie 1987:165). This speculation stems from the fact that the traditional division of prehistoric time in Africa into a Stone Age as distinct from a Metal age has not been found to be represented in the archaeological record of the Niger Delta. Indeed the only stone implements recovered from the excavations in the Central Delta were the flint pieces for the flint gun recovered at Koroama and which were imports from Europe. It needs to be recalled here that there was so much continuity and change even during the Stone Age that it is sub-divided into Early, Middle and Late.

However, even from Early Stone Age times, materials other than stone were used to make tools. Indeed, wood is a softer material to work with generally. Wood or even bone would not have the same potentials for surviving in the archaeological record as stone. This helps explain why continuity and change in stone tool traditions in Africa have been documented from about two and half million years ago to Late Stone Age times characterised, for the most part, by microlithic tools and polished stone tools as well as grinding stones in the Neolithic. Stone has not been a very common raw material in the Niger

Delta environment whereas wood has been common. However, even if wood-working stone tools were used very early in the History of Man in the Delta, they are likely to have been treated as heirlooms and would be rare to find in midden deposits. They are more likely to be found, if they exist, when horizontal excavations devoted to exposing building structures and settlement layouts in the past are carried out in the Niger Delta. Moreover, the dates so far obtained from all the Niger Delta sites are well within the Metal Age segment of the Prehistory of Nigeria; and even in Eastern Nigeria, by the tenth century A.D., as evidence from Igbo Ukwu shows, metal working was quite established. It is quite possible that the Metal Age in South-eastern Nigeria had begun before the canoe could be made in large numbers and the effective occupation of the Delta, particularly the part adjacent to the sea proceeded in earnest.

The observation about the conspicuous absence of stone tools is significant only to the extent that it draws attention to the role of stone tools in hunting which has continued to be important in the subsistence activities even in the Niger Delta. However, the example of use of nets to hunt among the Bambuti (Mbuti pygmies) of the Ituri forest in the Congo basin, indicates that hunting can be done successfully without using stone tools. Indeed, apart from nets, other traps made from wood are known to be effective in the forest environment. If snares have been effective, projectile points made from stone may not have been as important in the forest environment as they would have been in the derived savannah and cleared forest environments that result from the forest being continuously cleared for farming and fire-wood-need induced over exploited forest environments in the areas bordering the Niger Delta. However, it is noteworthy that there is a site, Oruokolo, which is said to be the home of a stone cult, *Ogidifariye*, (meaning whetstone). Alagoa (1987:240) says, the stones were identified as grinding stones and assigned to the Iron Age during the reconnaissance trip in 1972. This site deserves excavation especially as it is likely to throw some light on the use of stone tools in the Niger Delta before and/or during the Metal Age.

In the area of economic prehistory, the evidence from the excavations in the Central Delta indicates that fishing was a more reliable and better developed source of protein than hunting in the traditional economies of the Central Delta Ijo. Although farming appears equally, if not more important than fishing, the nature of the food plants grown foreclose the recovery of direct evidence of their cultivation from the sites excavated. However, the linguistic and ethnographic evidence show that there were wild species of yam and most oil palm trees grew in the wild as did the raffia palm. The yam was domesticated and other root crops such as the water yam (*Dioscorea alata)* and later, cassava, were introduced. Plantain (*Musa paradisiaca*) and banana (*Musa sapienta*) were also introduced, according to evidence from linguistics, by Austronesian sea-voyagers. See Appendix D (Derefaka 2003) for the nutritional content of these and other food sources in the Central Delta.

As summarised by Alagoa (1987:243), bones of goats, cows, antelopes, leopards, dogs, elephants, manatees, hippopotamus as well as cat and waterbuck were recovered from Okochiri and Ogoloma. Since there were bigger animal bones at Ogoloma, it was inferred that it had improved hunting methods and possibly the introduction of guns. Also, as a result of the evidence from the results of the excavations in the Eastern Niger Delta, Alagoa said:

> Both for fishing and hunting, archaeology has not recovered any gear or weapons. As for nets, one does not expect them to survive easily in the archaeological record in the Niger Delta, but hooks and spear points as well as some gun parts ought to survive. That none was recovered in the Eastern Delta excavations is striking but not totally surprising. These are durable and valuable economic assets in the Delta environment and so are likely to be very well taken care of and constitute part of the inheritance to be passed on to descendants.

In the Central Delta excavations, however, a spear point was recovered from Isomabou and flint gun parts were recovered from the excavations on Mound B at Koroama which date to modern times and so some metal parts of the gun for hunting have survived. So archaeology has now recovered some implements for fishing and hunting in addition to fish and animal bones.

An artefact class that was not recovered in the Central Delta excavations was currency. Very few cowry shells (*Cypraea moneta* or *Cypraea annulus*) and no manilas of any kind were recovered from the three sites excavated in the Central Niger Delta. However, from Koroama and Agadagbabou, there is ample evidence of external trade as indicated by the beads, imported smoking pipes, J.J.W. Peters gin bottles, flint gun parts and Chinaware. This is an indication that perhaps like along the Brass River, manilas were not quite so important on the Nun River and its tributary creeks and creek lets. Also, the absence of cowries confirms Alagoa's conclusion (1987:244) that the cowry shell was, apparently, not used to a great extent in the Niger Delta.

In the area of chronology, whereas the evidence from palynology indicates positive evidence in the vegetation for human occupation of the Delta from about 3,000 years ago, linguistic evidence indicate that the Ijoid language group had become separate and moved into the Niger Delta about 7,000 years ago. Archaeological evidence, on the other hand, has provided radiometric dates of about 1,000 years ago on the average for some early settlement of the Niger Delta. The dates from Isomabou in the Central Delta conform to the age range obtained from the Eastern Delta sites. What this means is that contrary to the impression that the first radiocarbon dates from Agadagbabou suggested, there appears to be some truth in the oral tradition claims of the freshwater Central Delta being an area of Ijo dispersal. However, the chronological framework now available is as follows:

Ke, A.D. 770-1270; Okochiri, A.D. 850-1500; Saikiripogu, A.D. 1010-1640; Ogoloma, A.D. 1030-1480; Onyoma, A.D. 1275-1690; Isomabou, A.D.

1030-1480; Agadagbabou, A.D. 1640-1730; Koroama, last 400 years. Its seems as if more than one centre of dispersal for the Ijo in the Niger Delta is a possibility.

As an example of how culture traits among the Ijo in the Delta have been similar but not identical, one could now briefly discuss mortuary practices in a comparative manner. The categorization of corpses on the basis of age and cause of death is common to the Ijo of the Central Delta and those of the Eastern Delta. Although the maximal grouping of Ijo in the Central Delta is called *Ibe* whereas in many Eastern Delta Ijo communities, it is called *Se*, the adoption of identical mortuary practices is one line of evidence of a settlement belonging to a given maximal group. Also common to both Central and Eastern Delta Ijo is the provision of different burial sites for different categories of corpses. In this regard the idea of bad death is common as is that of bad bush, but whereas there is burial at sandbanks in the Central Delta it is not done among the *Wakirike Se* for example, in the Eastern Delta to which the Ogoloma belong. However, the idea of bringing back home the soul of a deceased who died outside the home base is considered of great importance among the Ijo of the Central and Eastern Delta. Among the Wakirike, for example, it is referred to as *Fonguma*. The influence of Christianity on mortuary practices among the Ijo is the same with the distinction between *chochi duein* and *amakububie duein*, that is, church corpse and traditional corpse, has been made among the Wakirike for example, since they embraced Christianity. The most remarkable difference in mortuary practices is the presence among the Central Delta Ijo and the absence among the Eastern Delta Ijo of the corpse interrogation process. As was confirmed at Amassoma in the course of the research for this Chapter, the *Ozigo* mat is used for the corpse to determine the cause of death, and the question whether or not the deceased was a wizard or witch was done by a ladder and pole divination. Alagoa (1972) has discussed this phenomenon and its distribution among the Ijo.

Conclusion

With regard to the chronological framework for the Central Niger Delta, the present evidence is that there has been continuous occupation and exploitation of resources in the Central Niger Delta by the Ijo from about 1030 A.D. to the present. Whereas some sites like Isomabou were occupied between the 11th and 15th centuries A.D. and abandoned, others like Agadagbabou were occupied until the early 18th century and abandoned, while yet others like Koroama were established not more than about three hundred years ago and are still inhabited. It would be useful for future archaeological investigations in this part of the Niger Delta to accumulate more evidence for consolidating or if necessary, modifying this initial reconstruction of a chronological framework for the establishment of open habitation sites in the Central Niger Delta, particularly by the Ijo. It is also interesting to note what late Chief N.I. Okoko of Obunagha, who was 58 years old (in 1979), a retired Local Government staff said, that a major reason why Gbarain moved with his people to Taylor Creek was that he noticed it was full of fish. The large, even if mostly fragmented, fish remains recovered in the Koroama excavations have borne out this aspect of the oral traditions. Perhaps security considerations and easy access to aquatic and terrestrial resources of the Central Delta environment were responsible for the initial location of habitation sites in back-swamp micro-environments, as such resources were more abundant and easily accessible there. It also seems that with greater interaction with and influence from external sources and increase in population, the Central Delta Ijo began to move out of the interior into more accessible locations, perhaps for the purposes of trade in such items as fish, plantains, yams and gin which they produced.

Finally, for all three sites excavated, sub-soil which was culturally sterile was yellowish brown loamy alluvium of the fresh water Delta, which is compact and its grains size is small. This is confirmation that the three sites are in the same environmental zone. The details of the stratigraphy of each site have been presented and discussed, but a common feature is that at all three sites, we are dealing with midden deposits of relatively limited vertical extent. This is unlike the situation in the Eastern Delta where the shell middens are of extensive vertical and horizontal distribution.

Also, unlike in the Eastern Niger Delta, the water table was not high enough for ground water to be struck during the excavations of the three Central Delta sites thereby causing the abandonment of the excavation of any of the Test Pits. It needs to be emphasized, however, that the excavations at the three sites were exploratory in nature and given the major aim of providing a chronological framework for Central Delta archaeology, we had to use test pits for this initial archaeological investigation.

After the above discussion of settlement hierarchy and chronology for the Central Niger Delta, we can now proffer some conclusions, indicating in some cases, theoretical underpinnings or implications of such conclusions. Thereafter, this Chapter concludes with a discussion of suggested future directions for research in the Central Niger Delta in particular, and the entire Delta and its fringes in general. Apart from the specific conclusions provided at the end of the discussion of the observations for each of the excavated sites, there are general conclusions which will now be presented.

First, from extrapolations from Sowunmi's (1981c:468) palynological analysis of Shell B.P. Boring 22 core, one has suggested that there is a strong possibility that by 800 B.C. the practice of agriculture was going on in the Central Niger Delta. Apart from the details provided earlier of how Ijo as a language group has been subdivided, Kay Williamson's comments (1989:10, 13, 16, 18, 20 and 21) concerning the place of the language group in the classification of the Niger-Congo language family is useful as they show how far removed Ijoid is from the languages it is said to have separated from some 7,000 years ago, namely, Yoruba and Igbo.

Also, from the list of rulers collected at Sabagreia, and the dates obtained for Agadagbabou, an interesting correlation has emerged. By extrapolation it was calculated that Kala I reigned from about 1778 A.D. This appears to be in consonance with the 1640-1730 dates from the Agadagbabou site confirming that Sabagreia, one of the Kolokuma settlements, was founded after Agadagbabou was abandoned.

350

The predominance of pottery from the surface collections at Agadagbabou and information from oral traditions, raised the question of whether ceramic wares were locally produced or acquired through trade from outside the Central Niger Delta. Reconnaissance of Taylor Creek settlements showed a similar predominance of pottery in the surface scatter of artefacts. Moreover, oral traditions at Sabagreia and other Kolokuma settlements indicated that the Gbarain were primarily responsible for producing pottery for the inhabitants (mostly Ijo) of the Central Delta. The conclusion from Dr. Wandiba's examinations of the pottery from all the sites in the Central Delta to the effect that the pottery was largely produced at the same source, further bears out this assertion.

Also, the imported goods such as the flint gun and flints, as well as the European factory-made smoking pipes and porcelain wares recovered from the Koroama excavations, indicate contact with the outside world through trade. Indeed the radiocarbon dates from the Koroama site confirm that the European trade goods could have been relied upon to accurately date the site. Consequently, the Koroama site can be described as a historic site.

As Hume (1975:9) rightly points out, it is very important that we realize that the techniques of archaeology can be usefully applied to any period, no matter how recent, if by digging something up we can learn more than is to be found in written records. Historical archaeology is therefore as viable as pre-historic archaeology.

Also, the location of the Isomabou site, and to some extent the Agadagbabou site, show that the oldest sites in the Central Delta are more likely to be found in the back swamp micro-environmental areas of the Central Delta and near smaller creeks and creeklets than along the banks of the major creeks and rivers. From the Isomabou excavations, a number of conclusions need to be reiterated.

First, the presence of a fishing camp and evidence of on-going farming activities at an abandoned open habitation site is a good example of the nature of site use and reuse in the Central Niger Delta. While the oral traditions preserve the historical importance of the abandoned site, the present activities at the site indicate the economic reasons which appear to have influenced the initial choice of the site for habitation.

Secondly, Isomabou is the only one of the three sites excavated in the Central Delta from which no European trade goods were found. The artefacts recovered were locally made or obtained. Related to this and reinforcing it were the range of radiocarbon dates obtained for the Isomabou site, which show it to be the oldest of the sites excavated in the Central Niger Delta. The founding of the site predates the coming of Europeans and the abandonment of the site appears to coincide with the period marking the beginning of European commercial interest in the Niger Delta.

Furthermore, it is the Isomabou site that provides some evidence of links between the Central Niger Delta and the Eastern Niger Delta. Specifically, the oral traditions indicate relationships between Isomabou and Ogoloma in the Eastern Delta. The lower limit of the radiocarbon age range for Ogoloma and some of the dates for Isomabou show an overlap that makes it possible that founders of Ogoloma may have originated from Isomabou.

Another important conclusion from the archaeological investigations in the Central Niger Delta is that the consistent absence of certain artefacts and features at the three sites is significant. For example, at none of the three sites was any manila found. The absence at the sites, of this important class of artefacts which is known to have been used as currency in trade is noteworthy, not only because of its economic use, but also because of its role in religious rituals. Their absence at the excavated sites can be explained in either of two ways. First, the manilas may have been considered too valuable to have been thrown away to form part of the midden deposit which was, essentially, the nature of the sites excavated. Perhaps, if living floors (possibly bedrooms), in houses had been encountered, some manilas might have been found. Secondly, the manilas in circulation in the Central Delta might have been relatively few as

352

a result of a lower volume of external trade, given the apparent emphasis on food rather than cash crops in the farming practiced in the Central Delta, and the limited role of fishing in the cash economy of the people. However, that manilas have been noticed in shrines in the Central Delta suggest that they were known and used in the past and so their absence at the excavated sites in the Central Delta deserves mention, especially because they are an important class of artefacts among the finds from sites excavated in the Eastern Niger Delta.

Similarly, the absence of human burials is noteworthy because in extant Central Delta Ijo settlements, it was observed that the dead are not usually buried within the settlement. The dead are buried away from the living. From the evidence obtained during this study, it can be said that even by the 12th century A.D., the practice of not burying the dead in the settlement of the living had been going on among the Central Delta Ijo.

From the available evidence, the mainland was occupied earlier than the rest of the Delta. In short we are saying that the site of Obrikom in Ogba, a mainland site, was occupied or settled at an earlier date than the site of Ke, a saltwater site situated close to the coastal fringes, which is the oldest of the saltwater sites. Thus, there is a separation in space and time between them.

These conclusions and a number of speculations about the phases in the settlement of the Niger Delta are based on dates obtained from a dating method that was still being developed (see Oduwole *et al*, 1983). Nzewunwa was aware of the tentative nature of the dates obtained from this method (1988:44).

As regards cultural relationships between the Ijo of the Central Niger Delta and those of the Eastern Niger Delta, perhaps the most striking is the similarity of the locally made smoking pipes from Ogoloma and other Eastern Delta sites and those recovered from the archaeological investigations at Agadagbabou and Koroama, for example.

It is now necessary to indicate some directions in which archaeological investigations in the Niger Delta should be guided in order to increase our knowledge of the sequence of developments in human occupation and use of the Niger Delta environments. Firstly, it is important that the prehistoric developments on the northern fringes of the Delta be investigated. The efforts of the late Professor Nzewunwa in the Ogba area have produced dates in the second millennium B.C. but have not demonstrated the link between the developments there and the Delta proper. Similarly, it is expected that the research initiated by Professor E. J. Alagoa in the Ogoni area will produce useful chronological information, and since there is ample ethnographic evidence of socio-economic relationship between the Ogoni and some of their Ijo neighbours; this line of evidence should throw much light on mainland/riverine, interaction in the Niger Delta through time.

However, a more comprehensive location of all abandoned or/and occupied ancient settlement in the Eastern and Central Delta needs to be done as this would be a good starting point. Thereafter, a systematic categorization of the sites on the basis of perceived potentials for contribution to pressing questions in the reconstruction of the Niger Delta people's past should be done. A priority list for systematic archaeological investigation of the sites would then emerge. However, in the future, the multi-disciplinary approach that has guided Niger Delta research to date needs to be sustained with equal emphasis extended to ethnographic research. Also, future archaeological research would need to be extended southwards to include the *Ibe* referred to as Southern Ijo. This would bring settlements such as Korokorosei, where Leis and Martha Anderson have done ethnographic and Art Historical research, and other settlements, where the fishing festival in lakes have been investigated and documented, into the purview of Archaeological research.

An important direction for future archaeological research in the Niger Delta is Rescue or Salvage Archaeology. Given the importance of petrochemicals in the Nigerian economy, economic considerations are likely to continue to override considerations for protecting cultural heritage. This type of archaeological research is vital in the Niger Delta where crude oil and gas are produced. The recent situation in Finima and the excavations there by Nzewunwa and Derefaka (thanks to sponsorship from the University of Port Harcourt) is a case-in-point. More work needs to be done in Finima if the Federal agencies involved on the Liquefied Gas Project there can appreciate the urgent need for such work to be done as indicated in the proposals already sent to them. There are likely to be more of such construction situations that would require emergency action to salvage important portions of the cultural heritage of Niger Delta peoples.

Finally, for the Central Niger Delta, the areas of obvious gap in our knowledge of its Archaeology have been indicated. The most glaring is the fact that we do not yet appear to have obtained the final picture of the chronology of the settlement history of the Central Delta. This is because although the earliest date of A.D. 1255 from Ogoloma is younger than the oldest date of A.D. 1030 from Isomabou, and tends to confirm the tradition that the people of Ogoloma originated from Isomabou, the ultimate proof of the oldest date coming from the Central Delta in the settlement history of the Niger Delta has not yet been obtained. Also, there is need to extend systematic archaeological investigations to the Western Niger Delta.

CHAPTER 16
HISTORY

Atei Mark Okorobia

Introduction

This chapter takes a brief look at the experiences of the Ijo in historical times; beginning with the traditions of origin through to the twenty first century. It also tries to identify the forces of continuity and change, including external forces such as the Trans-Atlantic Trade. It further explores the origins of the Ijo Diaspora; the Ijo under European rule; their experiences in independent Nigeria; and a prognosis for the Ijo in the twenty-first century.

In terms of scholarly attention, the Ijo cannot be justifiably described as disadvantaged. Indeed, compared to most of their neighbours, particularly, the Ijo of the Eastern Delta and Limit could not escape notice. Due to their early contact with the Europeans, and their own active involvement in maintaining close commercial, political and social intercourse with them, the Ijo have had many aspects of their history and culture documented. Ijo history has attracted the attention of many scholars of great repute, including Talbot, Dike, Jones, Horton, Ikime, Williamson, Ejituwu and Derefaka. However, in matters of Ijo origins, migrations, settlement, and culture, the contributions of Professor Alagoa remain dominant, because of their quantity, analytical rigour and general acceptability. It is for this reason that we have felt free to tap deeply into his time-tested conclusions on Ijo history and culture in this chapter.

The Ijo have made virtually the entire Nigerian coastline their home, while their area of greatest concentration remains the Niger Delta. Bayelsa State or the Central Niger Delta is the base region, but many Ijo sub-groups have their communities in the littoral parts of Ondo, Edo, Delta, Rivers and Akwa Ibom States. Using geographical and ethno-linguistic parameters, scholars (Alagoa

1972; E. E Efere and Williamson 1989) have classified the Ijo into five main groups, namely:

(a) **The Ijo of the Western Delta Fringe:** composed of the Apoi, Arogbo, Furupagha, Olodiama, Gbaranmatu (or Oproza), Egbema and Ogbe. They are found in the present Ondo, Edo and Delta states.

(b) **The Ijo of the Western Delta:** composed of the Obotebe, Mein, Seinbiri, Tuomo, Tarakiri, Kabowei, Kumbowei, Operemo, Oyakiri (or Beni), Ogulagha, Iduwini and Kou of Delta State.

(c) **The Ijo of the Central Delta**: composed of the Apoi, Bassan, Olodiama, Oporoma, Ogboin, Tungbo, Kolokuma, Opokuma, Gbarain, Okordia (Akita), Biseni, Oruma (Tugbene), Ekpetiama, Tarakiri, Bumo, Akassa (Akaha) and Nembe (Brass) of Bayelsa State.

(d) **The Ijo of the Eastern Delta**: composed of the Kalabari (New Calabar), Okrika (Wakirike), Ibani (Bonny) in Rivers States.

(e) **The Ijo of the Eastern Delta Fringe:** composed of the Nkoro (Kala Kirika), Defaka and Ibani (Opobo) in Rivers State.

Although the Ijo are the dominant indigenous ethnic nationality along the Nigerian coastline, they are clearly not the sole occupants of this sub-region. They share the area with other ethnic groups. In the Western Delta Fringe, for instance, they have the Yoruba and Edo as their neighbours; the Western Delta Ijo have the Itsekiri, Urhobo, Isoko and Igbo as neighbours; the Central Delta Ijo have the Epie-Atissa, Engenni, Odual, Ogbia and Mini (Abureni) as neighbours; the Eastern Delta Ijo have the Igbo, Engenni, Abua, Odual, Ikwerre, Obolo (Andoni) and Ogoni as neighbours; while the Ijo of the Eastern Delta Fringe have as their neighbours the Obolo (Andoni), Ogoni, Ibibio and the Igbo.

Similarly, it needs to be noted that while the delta environment tends to isolate the Ijo from their hinterland neighbours to some extent, the river network provided by the delta also constitutes communication links and highways for the exchange of goods and ideas. It is clear then, that the delta environment provided the isolation over several millennia in which the Ijo group itself, differentiated into the several communities which spread over most of the littoral region of Nigeria

Conceptual Clarifications

The different Ijo groups are referred to generally as *'ibe'* or *'se'*, and they usually share a sense of belonging together. This term *ibe* is used mainly among the Ijo in the Central and Western Delta. The Nembe who occupy a transitional cultural zone between the Central and Eastern Ijo tend to use both terms, *Ibe* and *se,* sometimes interchangeably, while at other times applying se in a wider sense to mean a 'nation'. For the Eastern Ijo, especially the Kalabari, Okrika, and Ibani, the preferred term is *'se'*. These groups are recognized by their neighbours as forming a unit for various reasons. The usual reasons are, first, that the members of the *ibe* speak a common Ijo dialect; and second, that they believe in a common ancestor or place of origin; and third, that they worship a common tutelary deity. The Nembe, Kalabari, Ibani and Okrika who use the term *'se'*, developed city-states in the past which brought under their influence neighbours who belonged to different ethno-linguistic backgrounds. These protected neighbouring communities were members of the city-states or *'ibe'* only in a political sense, although they tended ultimately to learn the language and culture of the metropolitan city.

Ijo Antiquity

Over the years, there has evolved a high degree of consensus among scholars in the historical sciences such as anthropology, (Talbot 1926, Jones 1963, Horton 1969), history (Dike 1956; Alagoa 1972), palynology (Sowunmi 1975) and linguistics (Williamson 1988), that the present speakers of the various Ijo dialects are the descendants of the earliest settlers of the coastal Niger Delta region of Nigeria.

Ijo Origins

One fact about the Ijo traditions of origin is that they do not tell the exact time the people came into being. Rather, they merely tell of migrations, movements and the formation of breakaway groups in more recent times. The very ancient times during which they entered and occupied the Niger Delta is too remote for them to remember in their oral traditions. Modern geological and linguistic studies suggest that these events occurred some ten thousand years ago. Definitely, no oral traditionalist will be able to remember things that happened that long ago. We can confirm this suspicion from the cases in which the custodians of the traditions say that their ancestors 'came down from the sky' or 'came from the depths of the creeks or sea'. We think what they are trying to say here is that they 'do not know!' They are not alone in this predicament. Oral informants among the Hausa, Yoruba, Igbo, Edo, Ibibio, Efik, and others are similarly ignorant of how they came to be or from where they had come. They had generally attempted therefore, to explain the beginning of their world in their creation myths.

Historians, both local and foreign, have tried to explain the origin of the Ijo people. We will try to understand some of these theories first, and see how much of them may be taken as historical. We will then consider the traditions of the various groups themselves, to identify the migrations and inter-relations between them across the length and breadth of the Niger Delta in early times.

(a)   Theories of Ijo Origin

While there exists a high degree of consensus on the pioneering role of the Ijo in the occupation of the Niger Delta, scholars do not readily agree on the roots of the Ijo. At present, there are three schools of thought on Ijo origins. The first school of thought, upheld mainly by those who had come under some Judo-Christian influences holds that the ancestors of the Ijo peoples migrated from Palestine. This argument is based on the similarity between the name 'Ijo' of Nigeria's Niger Delta and one of the ancient cities of Palestine known as 'Ijon' (I Kings 15:20; 2 Kings 15:29: and 2 Chronicles 16:4). Members of this

360

school attempt to show the similarities in the cultural practices of the Ijo and the Jews, such as male circumcision, ritual laws and abstinence from sex during menstruation, which are similar to the Levitical rituals listed in the Mosaic Law. This school, though popular mainly amongst cultural nationalists, is difficult to prove. Apart from the reference to the city of Ijon, there is no direct evidence to lead us to conclude that the Ijo of the Niger Delta had their roots in the Middle East. The so-called ritual laws such as male circumcision, abstinence from sex during the female monthly cycle, amongst others, are not the sole cultural attributes of the Jewish people. In fact, pre-historians have established that they, the Jews learnt most of these customs from the Ancient Egyptians (Diop 1974).

Talbot (1932:5), in the 1920's and 30's speculated on the origin of the Ijo and stated that the Ijo language was the oldest language in Nigeria. Since Talbot considered the Niger Delta where they now live inhospitable, he concluded that the Ijo must have originally lived in more northern parts of Nigeria, but as later and larger groups of Nigerians entered the country, they were forced to move into the inhospitable Niger Delta. Again, this explanation has been queried for several reasons. First, it is difficult to determine the oldest language in Nigeria. Therefore, his conclusion, that the Ijo language and the Ijo people are the oldest Nigerian group, is open to question. Second, there is no known evidence among the Ijo or among other Nigerian groups, of a time when the Ijo were forced southwards into the Niger Delta. The only case Talbot mentions concerns the migration of the Kalabari from Amafa to Elem Kalabari. Talbot speculated that the Kalabari were driven southwards into the delta by the Ikwerre. This suggestion however lacks any supporting evidence, as neither Kalabari nor Ikwerre traditions record any clashes between the two friendly neighbours. Rather, the Kalabari state that they went to Elem Kalabari because they were better used to the deltaic environment, having moved from original homelands in the Central Delta. They were therefore like "fish out of water", living on the mainland at Amafa, and chose voluntarily to re-enter the Niger Delta

The Kalabari example, therefore, does not support the theory of an original northern homeland and Igbo pressure for the Ijo occupation of the Niger Delta. Rather, it supports the view that the Ijo have been in the Niger Delta as long as any traditions can remember, and that the traditions of origin only refer to migrations from one part of the Niger Delta to another.

The second theory may be credited to Dike (1956:24), who stated that the Niger Delta was settled by "three waves of migration from the tribal hinterland. The first wave came from the Benin, the second from "all the tribes to the Delta hinterland", and the third was a wave of slaves brought into the delta against their will, in the course of the slave trade.

Alagoa has commented rigorously on this to the effect that Dike's third 'wave' or the introduction of slaves was, in fact, important in the city-states of Nembe, Kalabari, Okrika, and Bonny, but definitely, not as significant among other Ijo groups, particularly those of the Central and Western Delta. These city-states developed the institution of the house (*wari*) for absorbing the slave population into their lineage system. The first or Benin 'wave' also occurs in the traditions of some Ijo groups and so we wish to deliberate on it extensively. It is the second "wave" of migration from the hinterland that does not occur in any Ijo traditions. It is this theory on which views of an Ibo origin of the peoples of the Niger Delta generally are sometimes expressed.

This movement from the Delta hinterland is described as 'the most important', and to have occurred 'between 1450 and 1800'. According to Dike, it was connected with the Atlantic slave trade, and all the tribes of the hinterland moved into the delta, the largest tribe of the hinterland, the Igbo, being in the majority. Since the migrants were moving south to take advantage of the Atlantic slave trade, they seized control of points suitable for use as harbours for the European ships. The large number of new migrants resulted in the conversion of the small Ijo fishing villages into city-states. The traditions of origin of the city-state of Bonny are cited as confirmation of this wave of migration from the hinterland: 'A famous chief and hunter, Alagbariye, ... came upon the site on which Bonny now stands, and aware of its potentialities for directing the new trade, brought his people to found the town'.

Only a few brief comments are required on the hypothesis of a mass movement of peoples into the delta. First, Dike does not see the delta as the unattractive place Talbot would make it. According to Dike, the earlier "Benin" settlers became fishermen, and also made salt—a product in great demand in the hinterland—and the second wave of migrants were apparently attracted by the slave trade. On the other hand, Talbot's observations concerning the antiquity and distinctiveness of the Ijo language clearly refutes the suggestion that the Ijo population has been made up as recently as 1450-1800 of Igbo and 'all the tribes to the Delta hinterland' in numbers large enough to convert 'fishing villages' into 'city-states'. And in this case, modern linguists agree with Talbot that Ijo is distinct from all other Nigerian languages, and may be as many as 7,000 years distant from Edo (the language of Benin) and Igbo (Williamson 1968). Furthermore, Yoruba, Edo and Igbo are more closely related to each other than any of them is to Ijo – confirming the long separation of Ijo from all of these languages.

The traditions of the particular case cited as an example, Bonny, also do not support an Igbo origin or wave of migration into the delta. Alagbariye is said by Ibani traditions, to have been, not an Igbo chief, but the descendant of Ijo migrants who had left an original home in the Central Delta and taken a route through the Igbo hinterland. And further, on arrival in the area, he chose a site not at the port of Bonny, but some two miles inside a creek at Orupiri. His choice of Orupiri is stated to have been influenced by its suitability for hunting and fishing. Bonny traditions assign the period of the Atlantic slave trade to a date subsequent to Alagbariye and the foundation of the city-state (Alagoa and Fombo 2001:3-5).

Happily, there is independent documentary evidence in support of the view that it was the earlier Ijo fishing and salt-making villagers who became the slave traders and builders of the Ijo city-states by integrating slaves into their communities; and that therefore, there was no intermediate 'wave' of voluntary migration from the hinterland. The Portuguese sea-captain, Pereira described an Ijo village that may be identified as Bonny as it was known around 1500. It was a very large village of some 2,000 inhabitants. The people made salt which they traded with the peoples of the hinterland for 'slaves, cows, goats and sheep'. Pereira was impressed by the considerable size of their trading canoes, which, according to him, were the largest on the Guinea Coast, carved out of a single trunk (the same type of canoes made and used by Ijo today) which he observed all along the delta from the Benin River to the River Bonny (Kimble 1937:128).

The claims to Benin origin deserve greater respect since they are based on the traditions of Ijo groups, except that some of the claimants go beyond the conclusions justified by the evidence. It is sometimes claimed for instance, that Benin exercised control over the entire delta 'from Lagos in the West, to Bonny River in the East' (Dike 1956:24). This is against the fact that only two Ijo groups, the Nembe and Mein, tell traditions of ties with Benin, that are historically defendable (Alagoa 1972). In the Nembe case, it is clear that a number of early Ijo migrants were established before the arrival of refugees from the Itsekiri Kingdom of Warri (Iselema) and, in time, seized first religious, and later, political control of the city-state. The connection with Benin is, therefore, derived from the Itsekiri traditions of Benin origin. The Benin claim of the Mein is even more questionable. After the Mein had left Ogobiri in the Central Delta for the Western Delta, they broke into three sections, the Akugbene, Ngbilebiri and Ogbolubiri Mein. It was to gain precedence among the leaders of these sections that Kalanama, head of the Akugbene-Mein, travelled to Benin to obtain emblems of authority and took the title of *pere*. He was followed by the leaders of the other two groups, all of whom still have bronzes of Benin type as symbols of their position (Alagoa 1977:335-337).

None of these instances would justify the conclusion that Benin exercised political control over, or provided large numbers of settlers for the Ijo in the Niger Delta. Even the Mein application to Benin followed an already familiar pattern in the area. The Urhobo neighbours of the Mein sent their rulers to Benin for insignia of office. Rupert East (1965) also reports that the Tiv sent their chiefs to learn the ceremonial practices and obtain royal insignia from the Wukari and Katsina Ala courts of the Jukun for a fee without considering themselves subject to these rulers. This would appear to have been the case in the ties between the Mein and Benin. There are other elements in the many Ijo claims to Benin origins which suggest that the influence of Benin in Ijoland was clearly external and marginal.

In the first place, we note that the distribution of Ijo groups claiming Benin origin diminishes from the Central Delta westwards, and in the Central Delta, the number has increased with time to such an extent that it is now no more than a cliché. Thus, when Major Leonard suggested Benin origin for all the Ijo of the Central and Western Delta in 1906, he did so 'on the slenderest of evidence', but in 1938, out of ten *ibe* investigated by Newington (1938:9) in the Central Delta, six namely, Kolokuma, Opokuma, Ogboin, Ekpetiama, Okordia-Zarama and Oporoma mentioned Benin in their story. At least, one, Oporoma *ibe*, was even then noted to have changed its position. An earlier investigator, Porter (1931) had been told that the Oporoma were autochthonous. Again, the Okordia-Zarama mention of Benin was made on the basis of the alleged Benin origins of Nembe, since both Okordia-Zarama and Nembe traditions derive these peoples from Nembe. In the Western Delta closer to Benin, out of fourteen groups for which reports were compiled by the British in the 1930s only five, namely Beni, Tarakiri, Kabowei, Kumbowei and Mein mentioned Benin as a place of origin. It should be noted however, that some of the claimants have since dissociated themselves from these claims.

But then the question has often been asked, as to why the Ijo should claim Benin as a place of origin. Two explanations can be given. First, there is prejudice in the Niger Delta generally, and Ijoland in particular, against individuals and groups who are ignorant of their origin or origins. Where a community no longer remembered its place of origin, it is likely to choose one that is expected to bring honour and glory to it, yet sufficiently distant to pose any threat to its independence. From every indication, Benin satisfied these conditions. That Benin was known more by reputation than by actual contact is revealed by the fact that nothing more than the name is mentioned in the oral traditions, and Benin (popularly referred as *Oba-ama*; or the city of the *Oba*), features more prominently in folktales. It is against this backdrop of deliberately choosing a prestigious place of origin that the few recent claims to Ile-Ife, Egypt and Israel should be understood.

The claims to Ile-Ife origin were made by Owonaro (1949). It is apparent that he was familiar with Samuel Johnson's *History of the Yoruba*. Owonaro had become familiar with the fact that even Benin had traditions tracing its kingship institutions and arts to Ile-Ife. This informs his choice of Ile-Ife. Here, it should be noted that no Ijo group had previously been known to claim Ife as their place of origin. The ancestor, 'Ijo', became, by Owonaro's account, the first son of Oduduwa, the father of the Yoruba, senior to the son who is known to have founded the Benin kingdom.

The Ikibiri are for now the only known Ijo community claiming Egypt as their place of origin. They claim, that their ancestor moved from Egypt (*Igipiti*) to their present location in the Central Delta through Benin. This is clearly a claim in the tradition of the claims of the Yoruba, Hausa and other Nigerian peoples to eastern connections. It is obvious that the motive behind this claim is to share in the glory of the ancient Egyptian civilisation and the desire for autonomy.

What conclusions can we then draw from all that has been said above? The best we can do is to adopt the positions of Talbot and Alagoa (1966:279-288; 1967:47-55 and 1972) that the Ijo have lost all remembrance of a time before they entered the Niger Delta. This does not necessarily mean that the Ijo are autochthonous to the Niger Delta. It rather means that the time span for which the Ijo have been in the Niger Delta has exceeded that for which it is possible to mentally retain the details in the traditions. The evidence of historical linguistics suggests that the distance between Ijo and neighbouring languages is such that no oral traditions or intellectual speculations attempting to derive the Ijo from any of their neighbours can be sustained. Is it then the case, that the Ijo have no traditions of origin and migration from which earnest seekers of knowledge may derive some facts of their authentic origin? Definitely, such traditions of origins and migrations exist. The point must however be made, that such traditions of migration as we know them, generally tell us about movements within the delta and outwards to the delta fringes, and not usually from the hinterland into the Niger Delta.

The details of the traditions of origin, migrations and settlements of the various Ijo groups fall within the mandate of other contributors. On our part, we simply present a synoptic view, defining three categories of traditions of migration:

(i)   Migrations within the Niger Delta from one Ijo area, (mainly the Central Niger Delta) to another;

(ii)   Migrations from one part of the Ijo delta to another, but first passing through the non-Ijo hinterland; and

(iii)   Migrations from the delta northwards to the Western and Eastern Delta fringe areas.

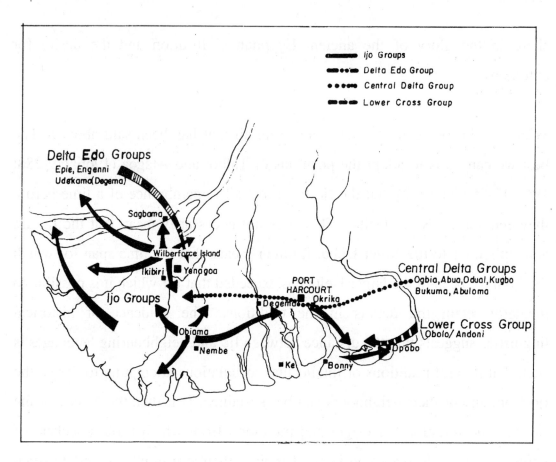

Fig. 16.1: Ijo migration routes

Category 1: The traditions of migrations within the delta give us a number of primary dispersion centres, prominent among which are Obiama, Ikibiri, Oporoma and Ogobiri in the Igbedi-Sagbama Creek area. The Apoi Creek, Nembe, Ke and Okrika in the Eastern Delta and Oproza in the Western Delta have been identified as secondary centres, since their populations have traditions of earlier movements from one of the primary centres, or account for only a small number of migrations. A brief survey of the traditions of migrations mentioning these places justifies the basis for these categorisations.

Obiama, the ancestral settlement of many Ijo groups in the Central and Eastern Delta, has been abandoned for an unknown length of time. The entire Bumo and Tarakiri *ibe* are said to have been established by migrants from Obiama. The traditions of all Nembe-speaking communities at the Atlantic coast, especially Liama, Egwema, Twon, Okpoama and Odioma claim Obiama as their ancestral home. Similarly, some of these coastal traditions suggest that the city of Nembe also received some of its pioneer settlers from Obiama, and although traditions at Nembe itself are contradictory, they, at least, show evidence of early ties with Obiama. Traditions of origin at Ogoloma in Okrika also name Obiama as a major transit place for its early settlers.

There are varying accounts on the fall and dispersion of Obiama. According to Bumo traditions, Obiama itself was founded by one Obi whose roots are unknown. The community grew to become a large city with many quarters (*polo*). Each year, a quarter was mandated to hunt for a *wan* (togo hare or duiker) for a ritual feast. The soup was believed to give fertility. In the course of one of these feasts, a quarter took more than its fair share of the soup. The consequence of this dishonest act was a civil war in which the people were forced to disperse. Two 'sons' of their leader, Obi, is said to have thereafter established Bumo and Tarakiri. Other traditions claim different reasons for the dispersion, while some traditions blame external invasion. The Okrika versions, however, claim that the founder of Obiama came from Ikibiri, the other major centre of dispersion, located to the north-west of Obiama.

Ikibiri situated on Wilberforce Island in the Central Delta is the ancestral home of Seinbiri *ibe* of the Western Delta. The actual site of the ancient city of Isomabou is stated to be six miles west of Ikibiri, and is the place named as the original home of Ogulaya, the founder of the Ogoloma community in Okrika. Isomabou or places close to it, and named variously as Opuanbou and Opuanbiri, also supplied the founders of many towns of Ekpetiama *ibe* and Onopa in Epie-Atissa. Other traditions mention places in Kolokuma, Opokuma and Aboh as also settled from Ikibiri. Ikibiri traditions assign the destruction of Isomabou to attacks from the Tarakiri (migrants from Obiama) to the south. Alagoa suggests that this southern origin of the cause for dispersal probably accounts for the migrations north, east and westwards, but not southwards.

About twenty miles southwest of Ikibiri is the town of Oporoma, which is one of the few places in the Central Delta whose inhabitants have claimed to be autochthonous, since they believe their founder 'dropped from a cloud'.

Ekeremo, founder of Operemo *ibe* in the Western Delta is stated to have migrated from Oporoma by connecting Olodiama *ibe* in the Central Delta to the immediate south of Oporoma with the same migration. Aguo, the founder of Yenagoa in Epie-Atissa to the north is also derived from Aguobiri in Oporoma *ibe*, while the town of Oporoma in the Kalabari area of Rivers State, far to the east, was originally a part of Oporoma of the Central Delta.

Another area that shows evidence of being an important dispersion centre is the Sagbama-Igbedi creek around Ogobiri also on Wilberforce Island. The traditions of Tarakiri and Mein *ibe* in the Western Delta, and those of Kolokuma and Opokuma *ibe* in the Central Delta, claim locations in this area as their homelands.

The complicating traditions concerning the dispersion centre of Oproza near the north of the Escravos River in Delta State need to be resolved. The traditions of Arogbo *ibe* in Ondo State, Gbarain *ibe* and the town of Gbaran in Apoi *ibe* in Bayelsa State (Central Delta); all refer to Oproza. The Apoi *ibe* of Ondo State is also clearly to be associated with this network of migrations. The problem is to determine the sequence, directions and starting points of the migrations relating all of theses widely separated Ijo *ibe*. One interpretation of these inter-related traditions suggests migrations of the following pattern: Oproza itself would seem to have been founded by migrants from Gbaran town in the Apoi creek in Bayelsa State. Later groups of migrants fanned out from Oproza, some to Arogbo in the Western Delta fringe, and some on a rebound eastwards to Kabowei and Kumbowei in the Western Delta, and a few ultimately to Gbaran *ibe* in the Central Delta.

By contrast with these primary centres of migration, the Nembe and Okrika themselves have strong claims to external places of origin for their founding fathers. They are, however, centres of migration because the destruction of the ancient Nembe settlement of Oboloma is said to have released migrants who founded Biseni, Okordia and Oruma. Nkoro is believed by its people to have been founded from Okrika, although some Nembe traditions derive it from Oboloma and Fantuo. Ke, in the Degema Local Government Area of Rivers State on the contrary, has a reputation in the Eastern Delta for being the oldest settlement. The people of Ke also claim to be autochthonous, that their founder 'dropped from the sky'. When Talbot visited Ke in 1932, he observed a number of things tending to confirm Ke's claim to be of great antiquity, including the unusually large number of sixty-one rulers cited on her king list. It is this reputation that would appear to have attracted the use of Ke's name as a place of origin by the people of Liama and Idema (Mini) in Nembe and Ogbia *ibe* and Ekeni in Bassan *ibe*.

Category II:

These are migrations involving passage through the Igbo hinterland. The traditions of both the Ibani (Bonny) and Kalabari (New Calabar) tell of ancestral homes in the Central Delta. Both sub-groups moved up the Engenni creek and then cut across country eastwards. The Kalabari turned south towards the delta and lived for a while at Amafa on the delta fringe before finally choosing the site now known as Elem Kalabari or Elem Ama. The Ibani appear to have wandered farther east and longer in the hinterland, before finally turning southwards again through the Ndoki country down the Imo River to Bonny.

The Bille Community in the Degema Local Government Area of Rivers State which has sometimes been grouped along with the Kalabari, insists on their separate origins from the Kalabari. According to Bille traditions, they were among a group that migrated from the Tarakiri *ibe,* first to the Seinbiri area of Central Delta, and from there to the present Ekpeye area in Rivers State, where they settled briefly around Ihuowo, before moving southwards to a place called Okolo-Bille (also referred to as Akpata-Bille), meaning, 'Bille Creek'. As a result of a serious dispute over the sharing of tilapia pepper-soup at Akpata-Bille, however, they were forced to move under the leadership of Queen Ikpakiaba, first to a place known as Ikpakiaba Daba, and later, to the present Bille town. They claim that all these happened long before their Kalabari neighbours joined them in the area. (Dappa 2006; Bromabo Adokiye Komboinmi, personal communication 2006)

Category III

This involves movements northwards to the fringes of the Western and Eastern Delta. In the Western Delta, the groups which are, at present, no longer Ijo-speaking, include the Apoi, Efurun and Ughele. The Apoi still retain their Ijo identity particularly in their religious rituals, but speak Yoruba for the most part. They recount traditions of migration from the Apoi Creek, Central Delta, on special occasions. Traditions in Tuomo, at Gbaran town (of the Central Delta Apoi), and Oproza, claim the Urhobo-speaking town of Efurun to have been founded by migrants from these places. There are, however, other traditions claiming Efurun to have been founded by Erohwa from the vicinity of Patani in Kabo *ibe*. The Urhobo groups of Owha and Ughele also retain traditions of their connection with Tarakiri *ibe*.

Similarly, in the Central Delta, some of the non-Ijo speaking Epie-Atissa, Ogbia and Mini (Abureni) have traditions of migrations from the Ijo delta to the south.

A clearly different scenario is presented by the Igbo-speaking Ndoki of the Eastern Delta hinterland whose traditions do not claim a direct movement from the delta. Instead, they claim that they and the Ibani (Bonny) are brothers, and that they had both left a common Ijo homeland in the Central Delta, except that while the Ibani moved south, back into the delta, they the Ndoki preferred to remain upland (Ennals 1934). The claimed location of Ndoki origins may, thus, be placed in the Sagbama-Igbedi creek area of the Central Delta as for the Ibani and Kalabari.

The traditions of Ijo migration northwards into the northern peripheries of the delta, as well as the ethnic composition of this region of the Eastern Delta

372

suggest a number of historical conclusions. The ethnic geography of this part of the delta is such that at very few points indeed do the Ijo of the delta directly border on the Igbo of the hinterland. Rather, these two major ethnic nationalities are separated by groups of smaller and distinct linguistic affiliation, such as the Epie, Atissa, and Engenni classified as Delta Edo; the Abua, Ogbia, Odual, Ogoni and Andoni, classified as Benue Congo (Efere and Williamson 1989:42-51). This situation suggests that there was a time when a wide territory of unsettled land separated the Igbo and the Ijo, into which both groups were gradually expanding southwards and northwards. But further, that this stretch of territory was, in fact, filled by migrants from east and west. That is, it was settled by the Benue Congo speaking groups moving in from the east, and by Edo-related groups coming in from the west.

(b)   Chronology

Scholars have not been able to give a precise date to the first settlements of the Ijo peoples in the Central Delta. It would not however, be unreasonable to suggest that they have been separated from the main groups like the Igbo, Edo and Yoruba on the mainland for at least some five to seven thousand years. This estimate is based on the glotto-chronological date of separation between the Ijo language and the Igbo, Edo and Yoruba languages. However, using the genealogies and kinglists of the Nembe and the Eastern Delta states of Elem Kalabari, Okrika, and Bonny, it would appear that the migrations from the Central into the Eastern Delta occurred only about a thousand years ago. The Nembe Kingdom for example, would appear, by these indications, to have been founded around 1400 A.D. The earliest radiocarbon dates excavated from ancient sites in the Eastern Delta at Ke in the Degema Local Government Area of Rivers State and Onyoma in the Nembe Local government Area of Bayelsa State tend to confirm the dates from the oral traditions, that is, that the Eastern Delta was settled about a thousand years ago. The known dates for Ke are the ninth and tenth centuries, while that of Onyoma in eastern Nembe is the early sixteenth century.

However, we have to consider the dates from kinglists as dating the institution of kingship, rather than the age of settlement, since the traditions suggest a time before the arrival of the ruling dynasties.

It can therefore be argued that the institution of monarchy is quite old in the Eastern Ijo states. The lineage institution, House (*wari*) was, however, of a more recent origin. Among the Nembe for example, the oldest known House is that of King Peresuo, which has been dated to about 1660 A.D. Most of the other surviving Houses in Nembe appear to have come into existence between the eighteenth and early nineteenth centuries. It is for this reason that we consider the period from 1600 to 1800 as a significant one during which Ijo states developed their traditional socio-political institutions. Independently documented evidence particularly by the early European visitors supports this conclusion. For example, the Portuguese captain, Pereira, summarising his countrymen's knowledge of the West African coast at the beginning of the sixteenth century, saw all the coast from the Forcados River to the Bonny River (Rio Real) occupied by the Ijo whom he referred to as 'Jos" (Kimble, 1937:128-132). It will not be wrong therefore to suggest that by 1500 the Ijo had already expanded to cover all of the Niger Delta between at least the Rivers Forcados and Bonny.

Also identified by Pereira was a 'large village of some 2,000 inhabitants' engaging in trade. This has been reliably identified as Bonny and some of its customers as Kalabari from their hinterland settlement at Amafa, Okrika, or Andoni (Jones 1963:34). Clearly, this settlement described by Pereira was not a new one, and could have been over a hundred years old.

The direct descriptions given of Bonny and Elem Kalabari in the seventeenth century show that they were already advanced in terms of their institutional development. Dapper in the first half of the century described Bonny, Elem Kalabari and Okrika as established kingdoms. Barbot (1732:459) went further to identify by name kings and trading chiefs (who must have been House Heads) at Bonny and Elem Kalabari in 1699.

Ijo Political History

The history of the Ijo in the fresh water and salt water swamp ecological zones of the Niger Delta has created three principal forms of political culture:

(i)   the farming/fishing village political culture in the fresh water swamp of the Western Delta Fringe, Western and Central Niger Delta,

(ii)   the fishing village political culture in the salt water swamp of the Eastern Delta and Fringe

(iii) the city or trading state political culture in the salt water swamp of the Eastern Delta and Fringe.

The farming/fishing village form of political organization was based principally on the lineage, with the village as the highest point of political affiliation for the individual, and a minimal affiliation only subsisting with the clan, *ibe*. Affiliation to the *ibe* was based on the use of a common dialect of Ijo, claim to a common ancestor, and the worship of a common clan (*ibe*) deity. Membership of the village was also based on descent from a common ancestor. It was the lineage that distributed farmland and fishing ponds or fishing grounds to its members. Political offices were either not established on a formal basis, or non-existent, since leadership was exercised in each case through the acceptance of persons with proven abilities to carry out specific tasks and to persuade people towards achieving set objectives. On the whole then, the only instrument of central control embracing all member settlements of the Central and Western delta *ibe* was the cult of the *ibe* deity, whose high priest, *pere* was accordingly, the only person exercising authority over the entire *ibe*. He determined the date of the annual festival of the deity and presided at its performance. This religious office of *pere* has been changed into a political one in recent times. Perhaps the only exception to this general situation in the Central and Western delta Ijo communities are the cases of the Mein who recognised the eldest son of their founding ancestor as the *Mein Okosowei*

(Mein Elder); as well as the Apoi and Arogbo whose political titles of *Kalashuwe* and *Agadagba* may have been comparatively ancient (Alagoa 1977:340).

The fishing village developed institutions that are slight modifications from those of the farming/fishing village for operation in the circumstance of a fishing economy. The lineage became less important, but the leader of the village became established as ruler, *amanyanabo,* from the lineage of the founder; and a number of cultural and other associations such as cult of the settled earth, *amakiri;* cult of the corporate spirit of the village, *amatemesuo;* cult of the village deity, *amayana-oru;* the social club of mask dancers, *Ekine/Sekiapu*; as well as club of the warriors *peri-ogbo* came into being outside the lineage institutions (Alagoa 1977:343-344).

The city-states or trading states of the Eastern Delta and Fringe expanded and extended the scope of the institutions of the fishing villages. The ruler, *amanyanabo,* became richer and more powerful from control of the pre-European internal long distance and the Trans-Atlantic slave and palm produce trade. The heads of lineages, *wari dabo*, also became richer and more powerful from participation in trade. These states, namely Nembe, Elem Kalabari, Bonny, Okrika, and later Opobo, exercised influence over neighbouring villages of similar culture, and others of different culture, (the Ogbia, Abua, Odual, Abuloma, Engenni, Mini, Okoroma) in the Niger Delta, as well as trading posts in the mainland, especially among the Igbo, Ikwerre, Ogoni, Etche, Ekpeye, Ogbah, Ndoni, Oguta and beyond. The resulting political culture was a diversified and sophisticated system including institutions for the integration of diverse elements and interests. Most of these institutions were actually more advanced versions of those developed in the fishing village political culture era such as the *amanyanabo, amakiri, amatemesuo, amayana-oru* and *Ekine/Sekiapu.*

Inspite of the great ingenuity demonstrated by the Ijo city-states in creating devices and institutions for the resolution of conflicts, the centrifugal forces operating within some of the city-states were too powerful for them to enjoy sustainable peace and stability. In the nineteenth century, therefore, conflicts within Bonny resulted in the creation of the new state of Opobo in 1869. Problems within the state of Elem Kalabari also gave rise to the birth of three independent cities namely, Bakana 1881; Abonnema 1882 and Buguma 1884. Only the city-states of Nembe and Okrika escaped similar disruptions in the nineteenth century, having established relative balance of forces in their political system as a result of earlier conflicts in the eighteenth century.

The Ijo City-States and the Atlantic Trade

As we stated earlier, by the time of the arrival of the European adventurers and supercargoes in the late fifteenth century, there were already state formations in parts of the Niger Delta, especially among the eastern Ijo groups of Nembe, Kalabari, Okrika and Ibani, and organized village democratic formations in all parts of the Niger Delta. Fishing, farming, salt manufacture, and trading within and beyond the region were already established. The supercargoes established trading posts mainly in the centres of population like the Nembe, Kalabari, Bonny and Okrika, with growing central political control. The new patterns of trade strengthened dealing first in slaves, then palm produce, and a variety of other merchandise. The Ijo people in the centralised polities defended their interests through formal treaties, while most of the Ijo communities in the mini-states, resorted to piracy to earn some marginal benefits from the trade. Thus, according to Ejituwu (1999:198), the Ijo pirates were operating in the tradition of national heroes like Sirs John Hopkins, Walter Raleigh, and Francis Drake of Britain, and were accordingly revered and remembered in the local traditions as patriots and defenders of their communities' interests.

The period of the Atlantic trade was, therefore, one in which the Ijo people played a pivotal role in the history of Nigeria, serving as the middlemen in the contact process between the Nigerian hinterland and the Europeans. It was a period during which the Ijo dealt with outsiders, including the Europeans, as sovereign peoples on the basis of partnership, signing treaties on negotiated terms. Ijoland became a clearing house of Nigerian foreign trade.

They established trading posts in the hinterland. Soon these trading posts became established markets with market governments which were for the most part, presided over by powerful Ijo middlemen trading chiefs. To maintain peaceful social and commercial relationships, the Ijo merchants gave credit facilities to the hinterland producers. Each of the Ijo city-states tried in this way, to establish special relationships with particular hinterland communities. The Kalabari, for example, were identified with the Ikwerre communities of Iwofe, Choba, Isiokpo, Ibaa, Ogbakiri, Emohua and Ndele; the Ekpeye; with Abua and the Ogba communities of Omoku and Kreigene, and up the Orashi to Oguta. Bonny was identified with communities on the Imo River and especially, with the Ndoki communities of Ohambele and Akwete. Okrika established close and intimate social and economic links with the Ikwerre communities of Umukoroshe and Diobu. Okrika also participated in the Mboli (Eleme) markets which were attended by producers from the Ogoni area. In a similar way, the Nembe sustained socio-commercial ties with communities on the Orashi River up to Oguta, and further up the Niger to Aboh and the Igala country (Wariboko 1989:125-128).

It was through such means that the number of Ijo middlemen and their boys increased in the hinterland and eventually began to take interest in the internal affairs of the hinterland communities. Elem Kalabari, for example, got involved in the local affairs of Ogbakiri and their role was significant in the deposition and death of King Nnyevunwo. A similar situation arose between King Jaja of Opobo and the people of Ndoki whose king was burnt alive for flouting King Jaja's orders. It was activities of this nature by the Ijo city-states in the hinterland that led the explorers of the river Niger, Richard and John Lander, to write that "the hinterland was ruled by the coastal states". However, most of the Ijo interventions in the local affairs of the hinterland communities were usually for the purpose of debt collection.

The colonial period reversed these domineering attitudes of the Ijo. But this was preceded by successive steps of unilateral actions, the use of gun boats, the imposition of consular posts, and eventually trade monopoly and political control. The British used their navy to enforce the anti-slave trade treaties with a mixture of diplomacy and force, or what came to be known as "gun-boat diplomacy". Thus, from the period 1800-1850 began the gradual erosion of the autonomy of the Ijo people and rulers. The presence of the British navy encouraged the establishment of European communities at the delta ports. Similarly, British business in the Niger Delta increased in value from £23,000 in the 1830s to £492,000 in the 1840s. This increase, coupled with the growth in the population of Europeans led the British government to appoint John Beecroft in 1849 as the first British Consul to the coast of the Eastern Niger Delta.

Almost immediately, Beecroft gave consular recognition to the existing "General Council" dealing with problems between Europeans and local peoples, but renamed it the "Court of Equity". It was supposed to be an administrative institution designed to resolve trade disputes. In reality and practice however, the "Court of Equity" became the machinery for reducing the political power of local leaders. It was established at Bonny, Nembe and Elem Kalabari. Ijo leaders were put up for trials in these courts for various offences and fined. The principle and sprit of these fines were quite damaging to the image and the reputation of the royal institution.

The period between 1850 and 1885 was significant for the socio-cultural development of Ijoland. It was during this period that they negotiated for European Christian missions because of the apparent material benefits that were expected. The missionaries introduced Christianity and western education at Bonny in 1864; Nembe in 1867; Elem Kalabari in 1874; and Okrika in 1880. The material benefits expected included increases in trade, and education of the Ijo children. But the missionaries, collaborating with the European administrators destroyed, violated, and undermined the Ijo institutions and the values they stood for. Traditional burial rites for rulers, the persons of priests, and sacred places were desecrated.. Some of these acts generated social disturbances in different parts of Ijoland (Wariboko 1989: 128).

Around 1862, some unfavourable price fluctuations in the oil palm business affected the fortunes of the Ijo city-states. This led them into competition for more markets with a view to increasing their fortunes. In many cases this led to wars between the city-states. For example, from 1863 to 1871 Bonny fought Kalabari; Bonny and Okrika fought against Kalabari, and Kalabari fought Nembe (Wariboko 1989:128).These struggles for markets and spheres of influence provided excuses for the British to intervene in ways that further reduced the powers of the Ijo leaders while at the same time bringing them under British domination.

Meanwhile, the British on their part continued to take advantage of their growing powers and influence in and around Ijoland. In 1884, they declared the area part of the Niger Coast Protectorate. Thereafter a consulate, treasury, customs house, hospital and prison were established. The consulate administration started to collect export duties. The administration also abolished payments such as comey (trade duties), which was replaced with subsidies. Native Councils later renamed Native Courts, were created to dispense justice on terms defined by the British authorities. The Ijo rulers that contested these steps were sent away on exile, or replaced. Prominent among them were King William Dappa Pepple of Bonny (deposed in 1854); King Jaja of Opobo (deported in 1887); King Koko of Nembe (deposed in 1895); and King Ibanichuka of Okrika (deported in 1896).

The Ijo Diaspora

Two categories of the Ijo Diaspora can be identified: the intra-African and the extra-African Diaspora. The intra-African Diaspora covers those Ijo who have voluntarily migrated to communities and countries in the Central and West coasts of Africa, primarily in response to the demands of their traditional fishing occupation. Though few, it is known that some Ijo were also motivated to venture beyond their traditional homelands in the Niger Delta by colonial labour policies. Of course there were also those who were in the intra-African Diaspora as a result of the demands of sundry private business concerns. The Chapter on the African diaspora in this book suggests that most of the Ijo in the Diaspora are to be found in the Republic of Cameroon, Central African Republic, Equatorial Guinea, Gabon and the Congo states in the Central Africa Region; as well as Ghana, Sierra Leone, Cote d'Ivoire, Liberia and the Gambia along the West Coast of Africa.

A notable feature of the Ijo presence in the Central Africa is the fact that they were, in addition to living side by side with their hosts, also able to establish communities in which they were either the dominant group or the sole occupants. They were also involved in occupations such as fishing for which they were the dominant participants, making it difficult for their hosts to do without them, particularly in Cameroon and Gabon. As a consequence of rigid anti-foreigners policies however, the Ijo presence and impact on the land and people of Equatorial Guinea has remained marginal.

Ijo contributions to their host communities in the Central Africa Region span all spheres of life: religious, cultural and social. However, the area for which their impact is most felt is in the economy, where they have distinguished themselves in the areas of fishing and to some extent, in the distillation of native gin and canoe carving.

The situation in the West Coast of Africa is slightly different. Here, we find a picture in which the Ijo Diaspora appears to have jettisoned to a large extent, their traditional fishing and gin distillation occupations for more modern and general vocations in the private and public sectors including positions in the government ministries and parastatals of their host countries. This was possible largely because many of the Ijo migrants to the West African countries were not only skilled persons, but their hosts were also more liberal.

The second category of Diaspora is that to the Americas and Europe. Oral traditions among the Ijo report internal conflicts and local raids which suggest that small numbers of people from the area were sold across the Atlantic along with slaves from the hinterland. By implication, this would mean that the Ijo Diaspora in the Americas may be sub-divided into two groups: those whose ancestors were exported to that part of the world during the Atlantic Slave trade and those who are voluntary migrants to the area in recent times.

A recent study of Berbice Dutch, the Creole pidgin, spoken along the tributaries of the Berbice River in Guiana (Guyana), shows an unusually large vocabulary derived from the eastern Ijo dialects of Kalabari, Ibani, and Nembe (Smith, Robertson and Williamson 1987; Alagoa 1986:33). Berbice Dutch Creole developed in the mid-17th century. Berbice Dutch was shown to be composed of 60.7-66.5 percent Dutch, 22.5-25 percent Ijo, and smaller contributions from English, Amerindian, Portuguese, and other languages, in spite of the fact that the majority of the present speakers of Berbice Dutch are of Amerindian (Arawak) origin or of mixed race. The explanation would seem to be that the pidgin came into being at a time when a slave population of predominantly Eastern Delta Ijo origin interacted with Dutch slave owners and plantation supervisors. Furthermore, in Surinam, reference was made to the "Calabaris" a possible allusion to, or derivation from the Kalabari of the Eastern Delta; just as a maroon community in Guiana is said to go by the name "Boni", possibly having some links with the Bonny or Ibani of the Eastern Delta. Similarly another community in Guiana has been identified as "Brosi", a name we think is a corruption of Brass, the appellation given to Nembe Town by the early Europeans, which today, is associated more with Twon, where the colonial administrators sited their consulate.

In Europe, Ijo presence can be explained in terms similar to the situation in the West Coast of Africa, where most of them appeared to have settled decades ago as a result of economic attractions. Most of them are gainfully employed both in the public and private sectors while some have also intermarried with their hosts and produced mulatoes. In recent times however, some of them, particularly those in the United Kingdom of Great Britain and Ireland, have seen the need to come together under the banner of The Ijaw People's Association of Great Britain. This association was founded in the 1940s by a group of Ijo sailors with the primary objectives of preserving Ijo culture and ethics; provision of welfare services to its members in need and the organisation of social events with a view to fostering the unity of Ijo people.

The Ijo Under British Colonial Rule

The ousting of the Ijo leadership by the British at the close of the nineteenth century did not lead to a direct destruction of the institutions for internal government of the Ijo communities. The policy of "Indirect Rule" they instituted was a self-serving device for keeping things as much as possible as they were, so that the British would save money and effort. A minimum number of new institutions only was set; such as the Native Courts, systems for the collection of taxes, utilising the local leaders that they found amenable, and creating new leadership positions such as Warrant Chiefs where the existing chiefs did not cooperate or no chiefs were found suitable.

A House Rule Ordinance of 1901 changed the relations within the *wari*, giving greater freedom to the ordinary members against the authority of the House Head (*wari dabo*). By this means and through military operation, the Ijo states and hinterland communities under their influence were brought under colonial rule. Once the colonial administration was established, the people were placed on forced labour. In Ijoland, they were forced to clear the water-ways and creeks of snags. Under the terms of a Forced Labour Proclamation, both men and women between fifteen to fifty years of age were expected to work for twenty days every year. Local chiefs and their people who failed to comply were fined or punished in other more dehumanising ways. In 1903 and 1905 Public Lands Acquisition Ordinances were passed. These compelled the head chief of any community to sell any part of community land not withstanding "any law or custom to the contrary". This was the legal instrument for acquiring some Okrika fishing ports as wells as the Diobu community in Ikwerreland to form the city of Port Harcourt in 1912. Similar actions were taken in respect of Warri, Burutu and Forcados in the Western Delta.

The slide of Ijoland into the political periphery of Nigerian history, therefore, began in the colonial era. The centres of political power and sometimes major economic activities moved into the mainland, as the British shifted their bases of operation out of the Niger Delta to its peripheries at Warri, Port Harcourt and Egwanga; and placed their major administrative capitals at Calabar, Enugu, Ibadan, Lagos, and Kaduna. The visible marginalisation of the land and people of the Ijo had begun. The movement of business and politics out of Ijoland, and the appropriation of its resources for the development of centres outside it became established practice in the period of Nigerian independence from 1960.

It is important to note that in each period the Ijo people have presented leaders who have fought in ways appropriate to their circumstances. In the colonial period, leading to the period of independence, Chief Harold Dappa Biriye tried to combine various community activists to work within the new party political system seeking Nigerian independence to present the case of the Ijo and other Niger Delta peoples to the British. This effort resulted in the Willink Commission leading to the establishment of the Niger Delta Development Board, intended to "allay the fears of minorities". The Ijo activists also tried to forge an alliance with the politicians of Northern Nigeria under the Niger Delta Congress/Northern Peoples Congress alliance. Indeed, it was the fear that the murder of Tafawa Balewa in the 1965 military *coup* had destroyed the final hope of the Ijo people that drove Isaac Jasper Adaka Boro to launch his "Twelve Day Revolution".

The first civilian administration of Nigeria under the Prime Ministership of Alhaji Tafawa Balewa attempted to work through a Niger Delta Development Board established by the departing British, to channel some resources towards the development in the Niger Delta generally, but did not always receive the support of the regional governments. This was however stopped short by the military *coup* of 1966. Thereafter, one military dictatorship after another perfected ways of taking out the oil and gas in Ijoland to serve the interests of other areas and peoples of Nigeria.

Biriye's effort resulted in the Willink Commission, leading to the declaration of the Niger Delta as a 'Special Area', and the establishment of a Niger Delta Development Board, intended to "allay the fears of the minorities". In practice, however, this proved no more than an ineffective palliative. The fear that the murder of Alhaji Tafawa Balewa in the 1966 military *coup* destroyed the final hope of the Ijo people drove Major Isaac Jasper Adaka Boro to launch his "Twelve Day Revolution". In fairness, it should be noted also that it was after a northern military leader, General Yakubu Gowon, took over the leadership of the nation that the Ijo revolutionary, Isaac Boro, was released from prison to lead his final battle to liberate the newly created Rivers State from the Igbo-dominated secessionist state of Biafra under Odumegwu Ojukwu.

The Ijo in Independent Nigeria.

The period of entry into national independence proved an anxious one for the Ijo people like many other minority ethnic groups in the country. The nationalist political parties had generally represented the interests of three major ethnic groups of Hausa-Fulani, Yoruba and Igbo. At the national level, the Ijo and other Niger Delta communities have had no reason to believe that their original fears at the pre-independence constitutional conferences had been allayed There were, accordingly, attempts to reorganize at the level of communities, and also at the level of the Niger Delta, collectively. Various pan-Ijo associations came into being to protect the interests of the Ijo as it was also being done by their neighbours, crystallizing in a series of minority State Movements, of which the Rivers State Movement became predominant for the Niger Delta. After 1967, state creation came to be hijacked by the majority ethnic groups to serve their interest, resulting in fresh fears and grievances for

385

the Ijo communities. These continuing fears and concerns led the Ijo to support the Federal Government during the Nigerian civil war. The same worries led to the formation in 1991 of an Ijaw National Congress for the protection of the rights of Ijo communities. Some of these grievances had arisen out of the exploitation of the new petroleum oil resources of Ijoland, the conditions for the operations of the multi-national oil and gas corporations, rules and regulations made by the Federal government for the use of the income from these operations, as well as the impact of these operations on the environment and on the lives of the Ijo communities.

The Ijo and other Niger Delta communities have been fighting political battles for redress within the national system with very little to show for it, leading to clear frustration on the part of most Ijo people. One consequence of all these is the radicalization of the youths even in traditionally gerontocratic societies. This radicalization reached its peak in the agitation of the Ogoni and the Kaiama Declaration by the Ijo as well as the general clamour for resource control across the length and breadth of the Niger Delta. The struggle has also been internationalised. It is, indeed, in this internationalisation, and in the call for community autonomy and nationality rights through mass action that the recent struggles by the Ijo and other minorities exceed previous reactions by Niger Delta communities to their marginalisation by the Nigerian state and the oil companies.

Perhaps, the only cheering news, as far as the recent history of the Ijo is concerned, is the creation of Bayelsa State out of the old Rivers State in 1996 by a controversial dictator, General Sanni Abacha, who, by that singular act, has become a hero among the Ijo.

The disabilities suffered by the Ijo and other Niger Delta communities in the course of their struggle due to their internal disputes, rivalries and self-inflicted wounds, must be taken into account in explaining the slow pace of progress they have recorded so far. Indeed, organisations such as the Ijaw National Congress (INC) and the Ijaw Youth Council (IYC), give hope of such awareness of cross-cutting ties. The political elite have also begun meetings with even groups outside the Niger Delta in caucuses of 'southern minorities' or the South-South Peoples Association (SSPA). Similarly, groups from the Eastern and Western Delta which were unaware of each other's common heritage only a few decades ago are now holding discussions in their common interest. The maze of waterways in the Niger Delta has always served as highways of contacts. But peaceful ties sometimes led to conflicts, both in pre- and post-colonial times. The recent conflicts between these communities are mainly the result of boundaries set between the communities from colonial times, which have become current causes of war due to the discovery of oil in disputed territories. In the Western Delta, historical rivalries have become concentrated in a tripartite contest over the ownership of the oil city of Warri by the Ijo and their Itsekiri and Urhobo neighbours.

Leadership positions have drastically increased such as would accommodate various categories of aspirants to titles. This proliferation of titles and offices has recruited some progressive persons into the traditional system, but also others whose incorporation has been a liability.

Again, due to the difficult national economic condition, many chiefs no longer possess independent means of livelihood and therefore, serve as contractors to government agencies and to oil companies, thereby further eroding their credibility and autonomy. The masses in Ijoland face anxieties and perceive many gaps in leadership and performance. The level of consultation by governments, their agencies, and even by the chiefs is often inadequate. New associations have, accordingly, come into being in many communities to bridge the gaps in performance by the existing organs. Most of these new associations take care of specific economic, cultural or social interests, but others are created for multiple purposes, including political action. The gangs of unemployed youth which harass oil companies for jobs and favours fall into this category.

Conclusion.

We have carefully evaluated the history of Ijo contacts with other Nigerians and with people from other lands going back many centuries. In the course of our discussion, we have come to realize the gradual process of growth through which the very idea of an Ijo nation came to be, and the chances of its further growth into maturity. National consciousness among the Ijo is still being nurtured from among the forty sub-groups that have been evolving within the Niger Delta environment. Indeed, we may say, 'that the Ijo peoples have grown up, not only within the Niger Delta, but *with* the Niger Delta' (Alagoa 1999:3). The antiquity of the Ijo in the Niger Delta has been firmly established by linguistic studies, to which studies in archaeology and related sciences of palynology and ethnography have provided supporting evidence. The oral traditions of the Ijo tell of the creation of political formations from grassroots democratic patterns at the village level to the more complex centralized units which executed trade across the delta and engaged in many forms of relationships with other Nigerian communities on the mainland. The supercargoes from Western Europe who visited the Niger Delta at the end of the fifteenth century were attracted to trading centres at the ports of the centralized Ijo city-states, whose merchant princes supplied them produce from their hinterland neighbours. The Ijo city-states and their leaders, therefore, played a decisive role in the triangular slave and legitimate trade between the European supercargoes to Africa and the New World, to generate the wealth that made Europe an industrial power. In this intercontinental business, the Ijo merchant princes traded with the European supercargoes as 'sovereign partners, demanding mandatory fees and other levies, as well as negotiating prices, and enforcing other trade regulations at the ports' (Alagoa 1999:5). The Ijo merchants also negotiated prices and conditions of trade in the hinterland markets, in which they determined the codes of commercial conduct. They also contracted marriage alliances with their hinterland customers most of whom came to adopt the Ijo cultural practices as status symbols. In the Central, Western and Western Delta Fringe where many Ijo groups did not benefit directly from the opportunities of the Trans Atlantic trade, these groups took matters into their own hands, preying on the trade.

From the dawn of the nineteenth century, the European merchants and their rulers had accumulated so much from the slave trade and had also industrialised their national economies to a point where they no longer needed the slave trade. They therefore began to sign abolition treaties with the Ijo potentates, while at the same time persuading them to change over to the legitimate trade in oil palm produce. Again, from the 1880s, they began the process of eroding the powers of the Ijo monarchs. First, they introduced the Courts of Equity, which served as a subterfuge to increase their interference in the administration of justice in Ijoland in ways that belittled the local leaders and gave unfair advantage to the European merchants in commercial disputes. Next they began to reduce the trade duties (comey) paid to the Ijo rulers, which they ultimately changed to mere subsidies. It was also during this time that they encouraged the evangelisation of the Ijo people using the Christian missions. But the most dangerous action the Europeans took, however, was under cover of the 'protection' treaties they persuaded the Ijo monarchs to sign. These treaties became the instrument for the subversion of the sovereignty of the Ijo city-states and communities. Those Ijo rulers who resisted these overtures were treated as enemies of the Queen of England and made to suffer deportation, deposition or the destruction of their communities. Ultimately, the entire Ijoland fell into the hands of Britain with the institution of colonial governance at the close of the nineteenth, and the beginning of the twentieth century. In 1960 the British handed over power over Ijoland, not to the Ijo potentates, but to their ethnic majority neighbours, the Igbo, Yoruba, and Hausa/Fulani in an arrangement that has been best described as 'internal colonialism'. Under this new dispensation, Ijoland came to be characterised by environmental degradation arising from the activities of multi-national oil prospecting companies which have created poverty in the midst of plenty; leadership failure both in the traditional and modern sectors; and social disarray both in the urban and rural areas. Perhaps the only good thing that has happened to the Ijo nation in post independence Nigeria is the creation of Bayelsa State by the military government of General Sanni Abacha.

The Ijo nation is, therefore, one which is engrossed in seeming endless struggle over the several millennia of its existence in the inclement Niger Delta environment that has transformed the people into 'a hardy race' (Alagoa 1999:8).

CHAPTER 17

LINKAGES

E. J. Alagoa

The Ijo are a distinct and significant ethnic nationality in the Nigerian nation. Our present need is to search for the linkages that bind the Ijo to their neighbours in and out of the Niger Delta region. Other chapters specify the distinct historiography of the Ijo, and others detail Ijo relationships with other Nigerian groups in language, culture, economy, and politics. Here we outline the manner in which the Ijo have been connected to other Nigerian ethnic nationalities through the centuries to the present.

We have to seek the roots of the distinctions and unities between groups in the fields of historical linguistics and culture, geography, history, economics, and politics. Our definition of the Ijo, as a group, was already based on language, but has to reach back to culture and history as well to be complete. In the Westen Delta Limit, for example, the Apoi now speak Yoruba, but maintain their Ijo identity because of their history of migration from the Apoi of the Central Delta, and because of their Ijo cultural base (Alagoa 1968a; 1968b). Our discussion of the linkages which the Ijo have with other Nigerian groups must, therefore, be set in the framework of more than one criterion or discipline. For the present discussion, historical linguistics and culture, geography, history, economics, and politics will suffice.

Language

According to Professor Williamson, "all the languages of the Niger Delta belong to Greenberg's Niger-Congo family" (Williamson 1988:65). This provides evidence of a relationship between the Ijo and all groups living within the Niger Delta region, going back several millennia. Thus, the Ilaje, Ikale and Itsekiri of the Western Delta and Limit are classified Yoruboid members of the Kwa branch of Niger-Congo. The Urhobo and Isoko of the northern limit of the Western Delta are classified South-West Edoid, and the Epie-Atissa and

Engenni of the northern Central Delta limit are classified Delta Edoid members of the Kwa branch. The Lower Niger Igbo, and the Ogbah, Echie, Ekpeye, and Ikwerre, of the northern Eastern delta limit are classified Igboid members of the Kwa branch. However, the Ogoni languages (Khana, Gokana, Eleme), Lower Cross (Obolo/Andoni) and the Central Delta languages (Abua, Odual, Ogbia, Kugbo) are classified as members of the Benue-Congo branch of the Niger-Congo family.

Williamson departed from Greenberg's classification and concluded that "all languages of the Niger Delta are New Benue-Congo languages, with the exception of Ijo and Defaka [Afakani], which are much more remotely related to the rest" (Williamson 1988:68). Ijo and Defaka she classified as Ijoid from its neighbours in the Niger Delta as follows:

1.   The Ijo have been in the Niger Delta for seven thousand years or more.

2.   Speakers of the Central Delta languages arrived from an easterly direction over two thousand years ago with the South-east Asian plants such as the plantain.

3.   The ancestors of the Ogoni also reached the eastern edge of the Niger Delta before two thousand years.

4.   The Delta Edoid peoples also entered the delta from a westerly direction prior to two thousand years after the Central Delta people.

5.   The South-Western Edoid have also been in parts of their present location over two thousand years ago.

6.   The Lower Igbo speakers possibly reached the apex of the Niger Delta about two thousand years ago.

7.   The Itsekiri, however, entered the Niger Delta from a westerly direction 'less than 1500 years ago'.

8.   The Obolo/Andoni, arrived 'from the east somewhat less than 1500 years ago' (Williamson 1988:95).

These linguistic classifications distinguish communities, but also establish linkages over millennia to the present. Other historical factors link even communities of widely divergent languages.

Geography, Environment, and Culture

The comparatively wide gap separating the Ijo from their neighbouring language communities is narrowed significantly by the linkages created by geographical proximity, and the common Niger Delta environment. Geography determines frequency of intercourse, the borrowing of language items and exchange of cultural traits and ideas. Any innovations achieved by one group are quickly adopted and adapted by its neighbours, and the linkages are strengthened. Some cultural elements result from such adaptation to the environment. Thus, the western Apoi who migrated originally from the Central Delta, have adopted the Yoruba type of housing in their new environment, along with the Yoruba language and dress pattern. However, in religion and the masquerade tradition, they have kept the Ijo of their original home. Indeed, in their divination, **ikpatagha/ikpataka**, the Apoi have retained the more ancient forms that have been lost in parts of the Central and Eastern Delta. They also observe the ancient Ijo ritual of **ikiyan** in their **Boabo/Bouabu** festival at Igbobini, as well as the ritual for dead heroes in the **ju** ritual, equivalent to **peri** among the Eastern Delta Ijo. The drum and dance patterns are similar to those in the Kalabari and Nembe **iju** and **idu** drum and dance sequences.

The masquerading culture is one area in which the Ijo appear to have given much to their neighbours. The lagoon Yoruba, in particular, the Ijebu, may have adopted their Ekine from Ijo, possibly, from as far as the Kalabari region of the Eastern Delta. The Itsekiri of the Western Delta, as well as the Urhobo and Isoko, have exchanged a considerable amount of cultural items with the Ijo because of linkage by geography and environment. Several Kabo, Tarakiri, and Mein communities speak and dress like Urhobo or Isoko, or have become bilingual in their Ijo dialects and Urhobo and/or Isoko.

In the Central Delta, the Atissa in particular, share a common environment with Ijo groups. Similarly, the Ogbia are close neighbours with many Ijo groups, especially the Nembe. Indeed, the Oruma Ijo are completely surrounded by Ogbia communities, and have developed close linkages as a result. The Ijo

393

communities inside Taylor Creek share a common environment and strong links with the Epie and Engenni. Similarly, the Orashi River binds the Engenni, Abua and Odual, to the Kalabari, the Nembe, and other groups. In these and other cases, rivers forged powerful links between communities.

In the Eastern Delta, the Ibani related closely to the Andoni (Obolo) and the Ogoni through proximity, commerce, and history. The Ijo Nkoro people are surrounded by the Andoni. The history of the Afakani, speakers of the Defaka language, now a minority within the Nkoro community, is yet to be fully studied and reported upon. Other cases of small groups encircled by comparatively larger neighbours include the Abuloma in Okrika, Bukuma, Ido, Obonoma, and Udekama/Degema in Kalabari. Some of these have adopted the language of their larger neighbours, or become bilingual.

The power of the environment shows in the culture and history of the Ijo people. Their long sojourn in the Niger Delta over millennia has turned them into a people attuned to water, a water or aquatic people. They developed an affinity to aquatic environments. In the Niger Delta they have naturally bonded with other peoples living through the length and breadth of the region. They also established deep historical contacts through the lagoons to Lagos and beyond, along the coastal regions of West Africa, through the Cross River basin into Bakassi and beyond. Ijo fishing settlements in these distant locations replicate life patterns in their home Niger Delta environment. Along the River Congo, fishing gear and techniques are reported to have been introduced by migrant Ijo fishermen. The Niger River artery, the speculated route of Ijo entry into the Niger Delta (Horton 1998), was the major linkage of the Ijo to the diverse peoples of Central and Northern Nigeria. In the Sokoto region, excavations at Ulaira (Nzewunwa, 1982/83) have revealed potsherds similar to artefacts found in Niger Delta excavations. The terracotta found in the Niger Delta, for example, reveal features similar to the Nok figurines of Central Nigeria.

The Niger Delta environment has, therefore, made the 'Ijo creatures of water with a natural affinity to all peoples living along rivers, waterways, coastlands and lakesides. Our researchers have, for example, located Ijo fishermen at home on the shores of Lake Chad. And it cannot be a fortuitous coincidence that the environment in which the Ijo language has surfaced across the seas in the Caribbean is the aquatic environment of the Berbice River region of Guyana.

Geography, then, may not determine history, but, along with others, constitutes a causative historical factor.

History
There are communities living in the same geographical environment with the Ijo, and have therefore shared historical experiences. Some of these communities may be widely separated from the Ijo in terms of language classification, but can become very closely related to their neighbouring Ijo groups because of history and proximity. Indeed, there are some historical experiences which the Ijo have shared with all Nigerian communities in the Niger Delta and beyond. The phenomenon of colonialism was one such experience that has brought us into the Nigerian nation state. We take the cases of the Epie-Atissa and Ogbia as examples of nationalities with clear linguistic separation from the Ijo, but with converging historical experiences and environmental proximity.

The post-colonial period of independence has produced pressures for ethnic linkages. Pan-ethnic formations came into being, sometimes, with explicit political agenda, such as the Arewa of the north, Oduduwa of the west, and the recent Ohaneze of the Igbo. These nationality interests formed the base for the foundation of political parties such as the Northern Peoples Congress (NPC), the Action Group (AG), and the National Congress of Nigeria and the Cameroons (NCNC). A plethora of Ijaw unity movements came into being, culminating in the Ijaw National Congress (INC). In the agitation for equity in the Nigerian nation, the Ijo have found it expedient to form wider and wider alliances, including membership of the South South Peoples Association, embracing the varied nationalities of Cross River, Akwa Ibom, Rivers, Bayelsa, Delta, and Edo States.

In like manner, the smaller neighbours of the Ijo, such as the Epie-Atissa, Ogbia, Engenni, Abua, Odual, and others, have begun to forge closer links with the Ijo. Some of their elite have even become members of the Ijaw National Congress. These linkages derive in part from common environmental interests, but also from historical factors.

The Ogbia, for example, have had very close historical links with the Nembe Ijo from ancient times, so that the Okoroma and Olei (Oloibiri) Ogbia recount traditions of migration linked to ancient sites in Nembe territory. Only the Opume and neighbouring Ogbia communities tell traditions coinciding with the linguistic evidence of Ogbia migration from the east. Even in this area, the historical links to Nembe Ijo are very strong. Similarly, several Ogbia communities share traditions of common origin from the dispersal centre of Obiama with several Ijo communities.

According to Newns (1935), the Epie-Atissa whose language is classified Delta Edo, told tradtions of origin deriving 15 of their villages from Engenni, 5 from Ijo, 6 from Ogbia, and 1 from Odual. The villages derived from Ijo origins were listed as Onopa, Swali, Ikolo, Ekenfa, and Yenagoa.

We have similar histories of linkages between the Ijo of the Western Delta with their neighbours, such as the Urhobo, Isoko, and others.

Economy
Economic factors are among the most potent for forging linkages between peoples and regions. Within the Niger Delta, for example, its different ecological zones were united by exchange of goods. The salt water mangrove swamp zone specialized in fishing and salt manufacture. It had to buy agricultural produce (plantain, cocoyams, cassava products, etc) from the fresh

water delta ecological zone, inhabited by communities which combined fishing and farming. It was these differing skills and specialisations that led to the development of internal trade within the Niger Delta from the centres of population which became trading states in the Eastern Niger Delta. These trading states (Nembe, Elem Kalabari, Bonny, and Okrika) had already established networks across the Niger Delta and into its immediate hinterland before the arrival of the Europeans on the coast in the fifteenth century.

The arrival of the European traders created new opportunities for expansion, since the demands of the new slave trade required deeper penetration into the hinterland, and up the River Niger. The slave trade became a great agent for linking peoples. The slaves that arrived at the ports in the Niger Delta came from all parts of Nigeria, and not all of them were exported to the Americas, the Caribbean, and Europe. A substantial number were retained in the Niger Delta city states and incorporated and acculturated as full citizens. Our research in the Americas and the Caribbean has also established that some Ijo of the Niger Delta were also exported to these distant lands in the process.

Prior to the Atlantic trade, slave routes ran from the Hausa states of Kano, Katsina, and others and from Borno across the Sahara to North Africa, Egypt and the Middle East from Nigeria. We have no evidence that slaves from as far south as the Niger Delta were sold through this trans-Saharan slave route. In the trans-Atlantic slave trade, the Niger Delta states became the centres of export to the Americas and Europe. The slave routes ran down the Niger, Benue, and several land routes down into the Niger Delta and other coastal ports from all parts of Nigeria. The vast majority of slaves were exported, but a small minority were retained in the Niger Delta states and absorbed into the states and communities.

In the Eastern Delta city-state of Bonny, the Igbo element became very prominent, posing a threat to the Ibani dialect of the indigenous Ijo population. In the Elem Kalabari environment, the process of acculturation of the migrant slave population was assisted by the Koronogbo (the society of the strong) and proved effective in enforcing the supremacy of the Ijo dialect of Kalabari. In Nembe and other communities in the Central Delta, systems such as foster mothers and the lineage system proved adequate to absorb the relatively small proportion of slaves from outside into the local culture and society.

The Twon community of Brass Local Government in Bayelsa State provides an example of the successful integration of immigrants from different places within Ijo communities of the Niger Delta. The names of major lineages and recent searches for roots have revealed that migrants had come from as far north as the Hausa country, and as far west as Akure in Yorubaland.

When the Nigerian component of the African Slave Routes project bears fruit, the full extent of the linkages across the nation and into the Niger Delta will become manifest.

The trans-Atlantic slave trade came to an end when the leading industrial nation, Britain, decided to give up human power in the nineteenth century. They persuaded their European partners and the Niger Delta states through treaties, cash rewards, and force, to join the crusade to abolish the trade. They stationed naval forces at Fernanda Poo, Equatorial Guinea, to seize slave ships and liberate the slaves at Freetown, Sierra Leone. The same ships were used for gun boat diplomacy in the Niger Delta to enforce the abolition treaties and protect British traders in palm produce, the new 'legitimate' trade.

The trade in palm oil and kernel provided new opportunities for linkages between the people of the Niger Delta and their neighbours, and also forged closer contacts between the states and the visiting European traders or supercargoes. The supercargoes began to make bigger investments in on-shore structures and establishments, and the Niger Delta states also began to establish closer peaceful relations with the states and communities of the hinterland. The trading chiefs of the Niger Delta states made marriage alliances along their trade routes deep into the hinterland. It was in this period that some voluntary migration of Awka smiths and a few traders into the Niger Delta apparently took place. Niger Delta clients also consulted Igbo oracles, and did business with the Ndoki cloth weavers in the Eastern Niger Delta.

Similar linkages took place between the Ijo of the Central and Western Delta, the Itsekiri, and the Igbo, Urhobo, Isoko, Edo and Yoruba. We note traditions of links with the Igala and other peoples of the upper Niger and Benue Rivers at Nembe in the Central Niger Delta. The commercial and cultural links between the Nembe, Kalabari, and the people around Oguta Lake, the Abua-Odual, the Engenni, and the Ekpeye were quite substantial. There were also linkages between the Kalabari, Okrika, Bonny and Opobo with the Ikwerre, the Ogoni, Eleme, and Ndoki.

Politics

Politics became a significant factor linking peoples from the period of British colonialism. Communities were forcibly put together in new political /administrative units, and pre-colonial polities were redefined and new boundaries established. New unities and divisions were created in the process. The 'tribes' of the colonial period, the current ethnic nationalities or nations, were redefined, and each sought to identify itself, and establish its fullest geographical and political limits.

In the case of the Ijo, the communities in the Eastern Delta which had established their individual identities as city-states (Nembe, Kalabari, Bonny, Opobo, Okrika), took some time to reintegrate under the emerging Ijo identity. The exigencies of colonial, and post-colonial politics, forced even these groups to adopt the Ijo label of identity. The result is that a great many of the burgeoning Ijo/Ijaw political movements of the colonial and post-colonial periods were run by leaders from the Eastern Niger Delta. Currently, the Ijaw National Congress has had presidents only from the Western and Central Niger Delta. A new zoning formula is likely to produce an Eastern Delta president at the next election.

Conclusion

In sum, therefore, Ijo identity does not separate the people from its neighbours in the Niger Delta, Nigeria, and the rest of the world. The multiple factors of language, environment, history, economics, and politics will continue to forge linkages spreading across the world. This study is only the beginning of the agenda to explore the multiple ways in which the Ijo are, and can be, linked to their neighbours in Nigeria and the global village.

CHAPTER 18

THE WESTERN DELTA LIMIT

E. J. Alagoa, E. A. Kowei, B. J. Owei and J. B. Dunu

Introduction

The Apoi, Arogbo, Furupagha, Olodiama, Egbema, Gbaramatu, Ogbe, Isaba and Diebiri are settled in a part of the Delta where other Nigerian groups are dominant. The Apoi and Arogbo in Ondo State live among the Ilaje and Ikale sub-groups of Yoruba. The Apoi have accordingly adopted Yoruba as their common language, but still use Ijo (which they no longer understand) in their religious ritual, funeral songs and masquerade plays. The Arogbo have retained their Ijo speech, but use Yoruba as a second language.

Furupagha lies astride the boundary between Ondo and Edo states and the people have been influenced both by Yoruba and Edo. Most of their historical associations have, however, been with the other Ijo to the South and East of them, but under the shadow of the Benin Empire. Similarly, Olodiama and Egbema have received varying degrees of Benin influence. Gbaramatu, Ogbe, Isaba and Diebiri to the east of the Benin River have been neighbours of the Urhobo and the Itsekiri Kingdom. There have been commercial and other contacts through time, but no political or other dominion of one group over the other, in spite of the varying degrees of bilingualism in Ijo, Urhobo and Itsekiri among the Gbaramatu, Ogbe, Isaba and Diebiri.

The influences between these Ijo subgroups and their neighbours have been mutual, but some have tended to be overshadowed and obscured to the extent that the Furupagha and Olodiama in Edo State were not counted as distinct groups in the 1963 census, but a few alone of their towns listed under 'Siluko' and 'Oduna' respectively. Early European traders came into contact with some of these Ijo *ibe* through the Mahin, Benin, Escravos and Forcados rivers, as well as from the west, through the Lagos lagoon.

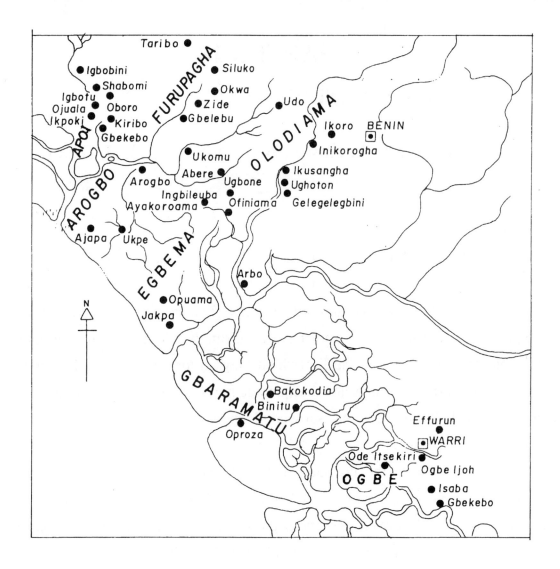

Fig. 18.1: The Ijo of the Western Delta Limit

1. Apoi

The Apoi of Ese-Odo Local Government Area in Okitipupa Division of Ondo State live in the nine towns of Igbobini, Ojuala, Ikpoki, Inikorogha, Oboro, Sabomi, Igbotu, Kiribo and Igbekebo. They are one of the most land-bound Ijo sub-groups. All towns, except Gbekebo, are sited on minor creeks, and are as much main land as delta towns. For these environmental and cultural reasons, some Apoi refer to themselves, by the local name of upland peoples, *Perekiri*. The Apoi are bordered to the north and north-west by the Ikale (Irele and Okitipupa Local Government Council Areas), in the west by Ilaje Local Government Area, to the east by Irele Local Government Area (Ikale) and to the south by the Arogbo-Ijo, their neighbours in Ese-Odo Local Government

402

Area. In spite of their Yoruba speech, the Apoi have not completely lost their Ijo culture. Each town still observes an annual festival at which Ijo rituals and Ijo masquerades are performed. Apoi history, then, has been affected by their *Perekiri* environment and neighbours, but their traditions of origin and migration firmly relate them to other Ijo sub-groups in the Central Delta and Western Delta fringe (Alagoa 1972: 27).

Origin and Migration

The earliest recorded account of Apoi traditions gave their place of origin as Brass, meaning the Brass Division of the Rivers state, an expression covering the entire Central Delta. Two sub-groups in this area, Kolokuma and Apoi, have traditions deriving the western Apoi from their territory. The most recent recorded western Apoi traditions specifically named Kolokuma as the place of origin, presumably from the published Kolokuma account.

According to the Kolokuma account, Opoi, one of the seven sons of Kala-Okun (ancestor of Kolokuma, and founder of the Opoidani lineage of the Kolokuma), "left with his grand father Ijo (Kalasuo) to Apoi creek and founded the Apoi clan in western Ijo". Internal textual evidence points to the conclusion that Kolokuma tradition really refers to a migration to the Apoi of the Central Delta, and that a secondary migration from that area is the subject of the western Apoi traditions of origin. This conclusion is supported by the many points at which the traditions of both Apoi meet.

The central Apoi name Kalasuo as the founder of their sub-group, arriving from an unknown home, in a group of nine. The western Apoi give the name Kalasuo as a title taken by their leader, named by them Apoi, but also migrating with nine "sons". The central Apoi name Oborowei as the war god of their ancestor Kalasuo, the western Apoi still worship Oborowe as their national god and ascribe its ownership to their ancestor Apoi.

The central Apoi have preserved as a sacred spot the site of Okotoaza just south of the village of Apoi on the Kalasuo creek (Apoi creek in the Kolokuma account) from which the western Apoi are believed to have migrated. The Central Delta Apoi worship Oborowe at the water front of this sacred forest site.

Tradition now current among the western Apoi relate their migration to the migration of other sub-groups of the Western Delta limit.

B.O. Duyile (1984) agrees with Alagoa on the origin of the Apoi, that they migrated from the Central Delta. He also confirms that the Ife legend of origin is not supported by any written evidence, and is not popular among the Apoi themselves. According to him, the Ife legend of origin was an attempt by the Apoi of slave origin to trace their origin outside the Niger Delta, in order to exploit the political situation prevalent in pre-independent western Nigeria.

Alagoa (1972) stated that the first stopping place on which all accounts agree is Okomu in the Furupagha area. The Apoi stopped at Okomu for "a long time". Out of the nine lineages, one remained at Okomu, while eight settled at Akpaka (Apaka) about a mile from the present town of Kiribo.

After five Kalashuwe (rulers) at Akpaka, a gradual process of dispersion set in during a long interregnum. The eight lineages from Ukomu were relocated in the new settlements of Igbobini, Igbotu, Oboro, Inikorogha, Ojuala, Gbekebo, Kiribo and Shabomi. But the original number of nine lineages from the Central Delta was made up by elevating Ikpoki (originally an off shoot of Kiribo) to the status of ninth in the new polity.

The Nine Towns
Since the migration from Akpaka occurred during an interregnum, there was the problem of political control of the nine towns. It seems that the former ruling lineages moved out to found a settlement, Toru Abukuba. A *Kalashuwe* was then appointed from this settlement for all the Apoi. Later Toru Abukuba

404

became the two towns of Oboro and Shabomi. Since no *Kalashuwe* was again appointed until Jubo of Oboro in 1914, it is clear that the Apoi had lived for long periods of their history without a central political authority.

Accordingly, there have been disputes in this century as to whether it was Oboro or Shabomi which should provide a ruler.

The blurring of the historical out line in the matter of a central authority is further complicated by the claim at Igbobini that a third branch of the royal family settled at that town.

The order of coronation, however, reveals something of the sense of unity and of precedence among the nine towns. All elders meet at the town of the "most senior man" of the clan to elect a *Kalashuwe*. They take the *Kalashuwe* to his own town and invest him with a white gown, chanting "Shuwe, shuwe". He is then taken to Akpaka and kept for three months unseen in a place called Iselu. The ceremonies of public coronation are performed at Gbekebo which contributes a cow, as against the goats offered by each of the other towns, to the new Kalashuwe. Three months later, the crowned *Kalashuwe* goes on a tour of all nine towns before he settles down at his headquarters at Oboro or Shabomi.

The remembrance of traditions of common origin, of the presence of the last common settlement site at Akpaka within the present territory, and of the common worship of Oborowe at Igbobini, have preserved a sense of unity among the Apoi. In other respects, each of the nine towns seems to have gone its own way after the dispersion from Akpaka. After the migration from Akpaka, there seems to have arisen no occasion for concerted action against an external threat (Alagoa 1972: 29).

Contacts

The traditions refer to contacts with Benin Empire at the settlements of Okomu and Akpaka. One source suggests a Benin attempt when they were at Ukomu, to place them under the direct control of the Oba. Other traditions recorded that the Oba used the Apoi at Akpaka as paddlers on errands to Ugbo. Later some of the slaves of the Oba's mother settled at Iyakeje "on the Akpaka side of the Siluko River".

According to a third informant, the Apoi at Akpaka "started to deal with the Oba of Ado and Oba of Ondo". The Edo of Benin and the Yoruba of Ondo sold slaves to the Apoi (Alagoa 1972).

Apoi traditions recorded cordial relations with their immediate neighbours, the Benin related groups to the east, Ilaje settlers from Ugbo and with the Ikale; all these stated to be comparatively recent settlers on Apoi land. They relied on the Apoi for water transport and gave their daughters in marriage to Apoi men, paid dues, although Apoi never gave their women in marriage to any of these peoples (Alagoa 1972: 30 – 32). According to Duyile (1984), relations between the Apoi and the Ilaje was not limited to the economic level, it extended to political matters as well. A colonial Traveling Commissioner first visited Igbobini in the Apoi area and established a court there. This court was attended by Ikale and Apoi from their various settlements. In 1899 the court was moved to Ondo.

According to Duyile (1984), the Ikale were strictly farmers while the Apoi and Ilaje were fishermen. The Ilaje being sea fishermen while the Apoi were fresh water fishermen. The Apoi, Ikale and Ilaje were thus economically interdependent. The Apoi exchanged fish with the Ikale who supplied garri, pepper and other food items. The Apoi also engaged in towing logs or timber and local gin to Epe and Lagos.

2.   Arogbo

Location

The Arogbo Ijo are located between longitudes 40 and 50E and between latitudes 60 and 70N, in southeastern part of Ondo state in Ese-Odo Local Government Area. They are bounded in the east by the Egbema Ijo, in the north west by the Ikale, north east by the Apoi, and in the west and south by the Ilaje.

The Arogbo Ijo occupy a riverine environment like all other Ijo in the Niger Delta region. They form a minority in Ondo State where the major ethnic group is Yoruba, made up of the Ilaje, Ikale, Ondo, Akure, Owo, the Akoko and Ekiti; and some Edo sub-groups (Magi 2003).

Arogbo lies in the middle of trade routes traversing this part of the Niger Delta. Accordingly, it is the only Ijo sub-group for which direct references can be found or inferred in the European records. It also had contacts with the Ijebu traders to the west, and with Itsekiri on the Benin River to the east. This history of varied contacts is shown now in the bilingualism of the Arogbo (in Ijo and Yoruba). They have retained their Ijo dialect and culture intact because of their Delta location south of the Apoi, and because of their Egbema Ijo neighbours to the southeast. In addition, Arogbo traditions are in the mainstream of Ijo traditions of origin and migration from the Central to the Western Delta (Alagoa 1972: 32).

Migration

Opinion is unanimous on the migration history of the Arogbo Ijo. All available Arogbo traditions derive their ancestors from Gbaraun in Apoi in the Central Niger Delta. Traditions among the Gbaramatu of Oporoza point to the same Gbaraun as the ancestral home of that group and of the sub-groups that broke away from it including the Arogbo, Kabowe, and Effurun (Alagoa 1972: 32-31).

The nine lineages of Agwobiri, Egbesubiri, Erubiri, Akpoghobiri, Ekanabiri, Kakabiri, Laghabiri, Angalabiri, and Ekeinbiri first settled at Oporoza in the Western Delta. According to oral tradition, when the Arogbo Ijo migrated from Oporoza, they left with the founder of the Effurun. The Effurun decided to settle at the present Effurun in Delta state, near Warri. Some oral traditions state that the Arogbo people settled at Siluko, Akotogbo, Ijosun, Gbaraungbini before they finally settled at Ekpetorun the present Ukparama area of Arogbo. Other traditions suggest that they migrated right from Oporoza to Ekpetorun, the centre of dispersion.

During the period of migration the national god, Egbesu, was carried along with them. Other deities including Diapele, Binikuru, Kpokpotin were taken along right from Gbaraun. Perebiyenmo, the son of Ogbonu was chosen as the chief priest of Egbesu, from Erubiri quarters, while other priests were selected from the other quarters. Perebiyenmo, who was the first chief priest, became the first *Pere*, king of Arogbo–*ibe*.

While at Ekpetorun there were internal crises on fishing grounds (Dino) that led to internal migrations of people to settle at Ajapa, Opuba, Akpata, Ukpe Biagbin, Adoloseimo and to Bilebu–Aru–Ugbo. It was at Bilebu–Arogbo that Pa Okpo pioneered the move to settle in the island of Arogbo. Prominent among the people that followed Okpo were Eduwei and Puu from Egbesubiri.

The other group that moved to Arogbo island were the people of Erubiri led by Ikeli the father of Odigbala, who settled at Tebubeleu. Another group from Erubiri led by Benitei, Umiyen Sikoli also settled at the Arogb island at the western part of Egbesubiri people. The last group of people to settle at Arogbo island were the people of Agwobiri assisted by Benitei, Umiyen, Sikoli and others.

Economic Activities

The Arogbo Ijo of the Niger Delta subsist on fishing, lumbering, tapping of raffia palm, canoe carving and marine transportation.

Women are mainly noted for both creek and forest fishing, distillation of the local gin and trading; while the men-folk engage in tapping the raffia palms, lumbering, fishing and carving. The women brew the local gin. The Arogbo man is talented in carving just like the Egbema Ijo, their neighbours. The Arogbo Ijo carve big and small canoes, design paddles of different sizes, walking sticks, and create works of art representing different animals like the eagle, parrots, and horses.

Trade and External Contacts

Arogbo traditions claim a trading market covering the areas from Lagos and Port-Novo westwards, to the Itsekiri kingdom eastwards in the past.

The articles of trade included slaves, carvings, ivory, birds such as parrots, fishes of high value (*eba, iyoro*), and meat such as deer, bush pigs, alligator, crocodile and more.

Alagoa (1972: 34-36) confirms Arogbo Ijo participation in the slave trade. According to Alagoa, Arogbo participation in the trade of this region was supported by early nineteenth century accounts; such as the account of Osifekunde, an Ijebu slave captured by some Ijo who could have been Arogbo.

One of Koelle's slave informants at Freetown on African languages was Okoro who supplied a word list of Edso (clearly Ijo). This Ijo dialect has been identified as Arogbo, and Okoro belonged to the Egbesubiri ward of Arogbo. He had known Ijebu and had been sold into slavery at the Itsekiri port of Bobou on the Benin River.

There are still in Arogbo several relics of the trans-Atlantic trade, including old cannons, and collections of porcelain and china-ornaments. When in 1885, the British came to erect a post of sanctuary for slaves in this part of the Delta; Arogbo was one of the places chosen. The Arogbo date the planting of this *Okpo* or freedom post in the reign of Aaga.

3.   Egbema

The ancient Kingdom of Egbema is politically split into the present day Edo and Delta States of Nigeria. Egbema Kingdom is bounded on the north by the Olodiama of Edo State and the Itsekiri of Delta State, west by the Arogbo Kingdom of Ondo State, east by Gbaramatu Kingdom and the Itsekiri of Delta State and south by the Ilaje of Ondo State and the Atlantic Ocean.

The Egbema people are the most likely Ijo sub-group to which the allegation of Ijo piracy on the Benin River could have been made. The only other sub-group with access to the Benin River are the Gbaramatu.

Egbema traditions, in fact, give indirect evidence of their predatory activities in the region of the Benin River. While they refer to the Oba of Benin as *Ugbo Pere* (Lord of the Lands), the priest king of Egbema was *Bini Pere* (Lord of the Waters). Apart from cultural and other relations with other Ijo groups, therefore, Egbema history was affected by relations with the Benin Empire to the north, and with the Itsekiri to the south and with white traders in slaves on the Benin river and its estuaries.

The dual relationship with the Edo and the Itsekiri is now reflected in the demarcation of the Egbema into the administrative areas of the Benin Division and Warri Division.

Origin and Settlement

According to G. O. Tiemo (2006), there are nine traditional towns in Egbema known as Egbema Isenabiri, namely - Ofiniama, Ajakurama, Abere, Gbeuba, Jamagie/Abadigbene, Opuama/Polobubo, Ogbinbiri, Ogbudu-Gbudu and Jamagie. In addition there are over one hundred and fifty villages and hamlets. The people are fishermen, hunters, canoe builders, distillers of local gin and farmers.

Alagoa (1972) states that the earliest settlement of Ofiniama was founded by two traders Alopomini and Opiti from the Mein town of Gbekebo in the Western Delta. They used to stop at the site to shoot birds (*Ofini*) for food on their way to Ukuroama, Iko, Eko or Lagos.

The founders of Ajakurama, Gbeoba, Abere and Polobubo first lived at Ofiniama for some time before they settled in their present site. The fifth settlement, Gbolukangan, was founded by settlers from Gbeoba. A new group of immigrants came from Operemo in the Western Delta and founded the settlement of Jamagie. The founders of Opuama, Ogbudugbudu and Ogbinbiri

410

were also migrants from the Western Delta – apparently from Amatu in Iduwini *ibe*. The only unifying force in Egbema tradition was the common worship of Egbesu (Alagoa 1972:42-46).

Internal Structure

Egbesu was the symbol of the unity of all Egbema and the *Pere* served as the human embodiment of that unity. But the very importance of Egbesu resulted in disputes over the control of the shrine and over the priesthood. Such disputes were avoided among sub-groups with traditions of common origin, where there was a recognized seniority among the towns, and within the town founded by the common ancestor, the lineage of that ancestor would be accorded right to the priesthood.

In Egbema, Ofiniama acquired *de facto* primacy as the most ancient settlement. But the founders of Ofiniama (Alopomini and Opiti) were never priests of Egbesu. Even the shrine, said to have been originally sited at Ofiniama, is now at Ajakoroama.

According to the Pere Obula, the original location of Egbesu in Egbema was Beleu-Jamagie from where it was removed, first to Ogun-Ode at Ofiniama and finally to Ajakuroma. It was never "stolen" but carried to these places by agreement of all Egbema because of threats by first Olomu of the Itsekiri and later of his son Nana, to steal Egbesu and wage war against the Egbema.

The Egbema collaborated in the installation of a *Pere*. Ofiniama put the sacred chalk on the new *Pere* (*tori pu*), the chief of Ogboinbiri served the wine (*wuru tua*) and was next in status to the *Pere*. This need for a wide consensus must have helped to produce long periods without a *Pere*. It may be noted that the national god of the Mein (from whose territory Ofiniama was founded) is Mein Dirimegbeya, and not Egbesu, and that it is at Ekeremo of the Operemo from where Jamagie migrated that an Egbesu is to be found. These facts suggest that the Egbema may represent a case where political power and ritual authority were separated. That is, that although the temporal rulers of Ofiniama and of its

411

related settlements held political power, the source of ritual authority appears to have come originally from elsewhere; although the ritual centre was eventually moved to Ajakoroma, an offshoot of Ofiniama (Alagoa 1972).

Trade and External Relations

Egbema traditions give prominence to trade and contact with neighbouring groups and even the traditions of origin characterize the founders of Ofiniama as traders to Ukuroama or Iko. Ofiniama, like Arogbo, is situated on the modern route from the Western and Eastern Delta to Lagos. The traditions name two commodities used by the Ofiniama in this trade, namely camwood (*Isele*) and big canoes. Egbema traditions recorded at Ofiniama speak of early contact with Benin. Inabiri, son of Opiti, one of the founding fathers, was already a rich slave owner when contact was established with Benin. It was slaves of Inabiri's slave, Okitia, who met some men from Udo. Inabiri's men made friends with the men of Udo, and soon Inabiri himself went by way of Udo to Benin where the reigning Oba gave him medicine that helped him get his first child. The road through Udo was closed, for some unknown reason, but a second route to Benin was opened in the life time of Inabiri. A third road through Ikusanghan in Olodiama became the normal route until the colonial period. This third route is to be identified with the road referred to by the records of European visitors.

Unlike the relationships between the *Pere* of Olodiama at Ikoro and the Oba of Benin, the rulers of Egbema were apparently, not required to pay special respects in services or presents to the Oba of Benin. The Egbema claim to have dealt directly with the white traders on the coast and to have supplied Edo traders with foreign goods (cannons, guns, matchets, coral beads). Egbema traditions refer to sailing ships bringing goods to them on the coast, but refer the crew men as dark white men (*Dirimo Bekewei*), thus implying mulattoes or people of mixed white and black ancestry, but apparently Sierra Leonians or Liberians.

412

Egbema claims to pre-eminence on the coast and on the Benin River support Itsekiri (and European) reference to Ijo interference with their trade in this area. Traditions of the Egbema in the Benin River area do, in fact, contain accounts of wars and treaties with Itsekiri settlements such as Jakpa, Itebu and others.

Chronology

Egbema king lists and genealogies do not take their traditions beyond the early eighteenth century, but elements in their traditions refer to earlier times.

The official accounts recorded by Alagoa (1972), for example, gave the name of the Oba who administered medicine to Inabiri as Kaladiren, the son of Ogiso. Benin traditions give the name of the son of the last Ogiso ruler of Benin variously as Ekaladerhen and Kaladerhan. These Benin traditions say Ekeladerhan never became Oba, but was exiled south to found the town of Ughoton or Gwato. In any case, the date of about 1170 at which the Ogiso dynasty gave place to the current dynasty is rather early for the Ijo migrations to this corner of the Niger Delta. Other Egbema privately give the name of the Oba who made medicine for Inabiri as Ewai. If this name could be identified as Oba Ewuare the Great, who was also a maker of charms and magic according to Benin tradition, it would give us a date for Egbema migrations in the late fifteenth century. It may be noted in addition, that the route to Benin through Ughoton (Kadaderhan's town) was the last known to the Egbema, and since the Egbema claim to have supplied European goods to the Edo, this must refer to a period after the European factories at Ughoton were removed to locations in the Delta in the mid-seventeenth century. Accordingly, we may date Egbema settlement of the Western Delta limit between the end of the fifteenth and middle of the seventeenth century (Alagoa 1972).

Accounts of early European (Portuguese) trade with some Egbema villages like Arbo, Uloli and Boededoe (Benidodogha, or Beninidodoa) provide a basis for claims to Egbema settlement prior to the seventeenth century.

4. Furupagha

The Furupagha people are surrounded to the north, west and east by Edo-related groups, but the Taribo area in the west is bound by Odigbo Local Government Area of Ondo State. The only direct contact the Furupagha have with other Ijo sub-groups is to the south-west and east through the creeks with the Arogbo and Egbema. The Ikale of the Bini Confederation separate them from the Apoi to the west and from the Olodiama to the east.

Traditions of Origin

Furupagha traditional historians gave their original home variously as "Ijo", that is, some place in the Western or Central Delta, Mein Toru (Forcados River), or "Ijo Furupagha" that is, Furupagha town of the Bassan of the Central Delta.

According to Alagoa (1972) the identity of name would incline one to the last tradition, but there is no other contact besides the names with traditions at Furupagha of the Central Delta. Furupagha traditions do not mention any stopping places on the route of migration outside the Western limit of the Delta. The first place mentioned was Ologbo, the second, Ofiniama (the Egbema Amatu or centre of dispersion), the third, Ukomu (the Apoi penultimate dispersion centre) and then two other unidentified sites in their present area (Pubilobu and Ikiwekiwe) before the present cultural headquarters of Zide.

The first ancestral settlers included Dauyomo, Daa, Ikpokpo or Ikpowei and Opaghanlakumo. Dauyomo was the founder of Zide, but it was Opaghanlakumo who became the first *Pere* or Priest of Furupagha Suwo. Once the Furupagha spread out to found their individual settlements in the basin of the Siluko River, no central political authority was exercised. The priest of Furupagha Suwo has continued to serve no more than ritual purposes and is referred to by the purely religious titles of *Sibewei* (bearer of the priestly burden) or *Koniwei* (the servant) of Amasuwo, rather than by the title of *Pere* which has come to carry political connotations among so many other Ijo groups.

414

As the Furupagha came up the Siluko, there was apparently little initial clash with other groups. Daa, for example, met and made instant friendship with the leader of, apparently, the only Edo settlement in the immediate neibourhood, Okwa. Dauyomo's town of Zide on the east bank of the Siluko was however, occasionally menaced by slave raiders from the Benin Empire. The Furupagha escaped capture by simply pushing off into Siluko in their canoes. But it was sometimes more difficult to deal with raiders by river from the south, like the Egbema, who also came in canoes.

The Furupagha then, did not completely elude the attention of stronger neighbours by choosing a remote river environment, but the environment permitted them to combine small scale fishing with the exploitation of forest products. Like the Arogbo and Olodiama, the Furupagha made canoes from the rich timber resources of the fresh water delta and the regions bordering the mainland.

The king list is not adequate for proper estimate of dates, but it may be inferred from the references to Ofiniama (Egbema) and Okomu (Apoi) as earlier homes that the Furupagha arrived in the area after the Egbema and Apoi. Still, there is evidence that Zide had been a town of some size and antiquity. There is an extensive area of mounds and broken potsherd behind the town indicative of old settlement (Alagoa 1972: 37-38).

5. Olodiama

The Olodiama, settled along the River Osse and on various smaller creeks branching off it, is the Ijo sub-group living closest to Benin. The Olodiama capital of Ikoro lying on the mainland east of the River Osse is actually less than twenty miles from Benin City by road. Two of the other three principal Olodiama towns, Ikusangha (Ekenwhan) and Gelegelegbini, flank the old Benin port of Ughoton (Gwato) to the north-west and south-west. Because of this proximity to the centre of the Benin Empire, the Olodiama have probably come into more direct contact with that Empire than any other Ijo sub-group. In spite of the obvious Benin influences, however, Olodiama traditions relate them

415

directly to other Ijo groups in the Central and Western Delta. They have retained their Ijo dialect and culture, merely speaking Edo as a second language (Alagoa 1972).

Traditions of Origin

Olodiama traditions start off from the Ife origin of the Ijo eponymous ancestor made popular by Owonaro. According to this account, two of the sons of Ojo, son of Oduduwa, were Ikoro and Neiama. After the family migrated from Ife to Benin, Ikoro stayed behind at the town of that name near Benin. Neiama, apparently, went on to the Central Delta from which place his son, Perezigha returned later to Ikoro to found Olodiama *ibe* (Owonaro 1949).

The rationale of this tradition is, clearly, to legitimize Olodiama claim to the town of Ikoro and to place Perezigha on the same lineal pedestal with the Oba of Benin, himself, traditionally descended from Oduduwa. The town of Ikebiri (the home of Olodiama Egbesu of the Central Delta) is mentioned as Perezigha's original home as also the related town of Ekeremo (in Operemo *Ibe*, Western Delta), presumably a stopping place (Alagoa 1972).

Perezigha is stated to have come to Ikoro because it had been his uncle Ikoro's town, but the founder was dead and it was occupied by Edo who tried to impose crushing rules of conduct on him. He returned to Olodiama, Central Niger Delta, or Ekeremo, to bring Egbesu, and reinforcements. His son Perewei came with him, together with Ogbonkoto, Atu of Ikebiri, Bitedon, and Kurokeaki. He was then able to subdue the Edo and take over the town of Ikoro by force. This breach of the peace was, naturally, reported to the Oba of Benin, and Perezigha was summoned to Benin. The Oba accepted him as his 'brother'. They then swore a covenant: no Edo would kill an Ijo and the Olodiama would similarly refrain from assaulting Edo. Perezigha was, however, to bring offerings to Benin at the annual festival in honour of the royal ancestors – consisting of a case of gin and a case of gunpowder. The Oba gave Perezigha dominion over a wide area (Alagoa 1972).

416

Internal Structure

Olodiama traditions base the primacy which Perezigha acquired over other settlers in the territory on his possession of Egbesu. He had brought the war god from the Central Delta and became its priest. Later, Ikusanghawei came from Ondewari (in Olodiama *ibe*, Central Delta), Egbeene from Itokobiri (not identified), and Ikpiti from Olugbobiri (Olodiama, Central Delta). They acceded to the worship of Perezigha's Egbesu, and their settlements, Ikusangha, Gelegelegbini, and Iboro became part of the new Olodiama *ibe*. The town of Iboro sent off men who founded Inikorogha, and Ikoro expanded with the foundation from it of Ingbileuba. According to the informant, the one thing in which all these towns recognize a common concern is Egbesu, and the priest or *Pere* of Egbesu was the single common authority.

It may be inferred from the traditions, however, that part of Perezigha's political ascendancy derived from two other factors. First the fact of prior occupancy; and second, the legitimacy conferred by his treaty with the Oba of Benin. These practical circumstances probably gave Perezigha and his successors an authority in addition to the ritual authority of Egbesu *Pere*.

This aspect of the relationship between the towns is emphasized by the tradition concerning a gift of two slaves (male and female) made by an Oba of Benin to Perezigha or some later *Pere* of Olodiama Egbesu. The man slave became an economic asset to the whole *ibe*. He lived for monthly periods at each of the towns, Ikoro, Iboro, Ikusangha, and Gelegelegbini, tapping palm-wine for the entire community. The woman became the mother of all subsequent *Pere*. It was ruled that only persons descended from her could be chosen Egbesu *Pere*. Thus, out of the political relationship between the leaders of Ikoro and Benin developed a leadership lineage for all of Olodiama.

External Relations

Proximity made the Benin relationship the most potent in Olodiama history. The non-aggression covenant must have been most useful to Olodiama survival against their colossal neighbour. The annual present at the Oba's ritual was a small price to pay for the rights of internal self-government and dominion over the riverine areas west of Benin. Olodiama traditions suggest that the Oba also found the military competence of the Olodiama and of their war god Egbesu useful. The gifts of a male and female slave were made to the *Pere* of Ikoro after he had assisted the Oba in a war against a rebel group - probably in the neighbourhood of Ikoro.

The Olodiama also took part in the slave trade. The centres in this area were Ugbo, Ikusangha and Igodo (Ughoton or Gwato). The white men came to the Benin port of Ughoton, but the Olodiama did not, apparently, deal directly with them, but instead sold their slaves to the Edo. On the other hand, they sold large trade canoes directly to traders from the Eastern Delta state of Nembe, and to other delta buyers.

Chronology

The genealogy of the informant going back to the founding ancestor, Perezigha, offers some basis for an estimate of Olodiama settlement in their present location. Calculating at thirty years to a generation, it would appear that Perezigha and his group arrived in the area late in the seventeenth century.

Benin traditions suggest, however, that Ikoro had been founded in or before the sixteenth century. It is related how Oba Orhogbua (c.1550-78) had stopped at Ikoro, on his way home from a campaign in Lagos, to enquire about rumours of a revolt in Benin while he was away (Egharevba 1960:30). There had been no revolt! Such an incident could be the basis of the Olodiama tradition in which the Oba of Benin had sought the assistance of the *Pere* of Olodiama, and in which the problem had been mysteriously solved by Egbesu even before the *Pere* arrived in Benin City from Ikoro.

Olodiama participation in the slave trade from Ughoton may also be noted as a factor in support of a foundation date early in or before the seventeenth century, since the European factories are reported to have been removed from that port around 1644 (Ryder, 1965:199).

6. Gbaramatu

The Gbaramatu live close to the coast between the Forcados and Benin Rivers, with most of their settlements lying along the Escravos River and adjoining creeks. Their immediate neighbours are the Gborodo Itsekiri, and the Ogulagha Ijo to the south and east. By their location, therefore, they are the only other sub-group likely to have shared with the Egbema the reputation of Ijo piracy on the Benin River and its environs.

Traditions of Origin

Gbaramatu traditions of origin raise important issues for the settlement history of many other groups in the Delta. Oproza (Oporoza), the mother settlement of the Gbaramatu is mentioned in the traditions of origin of the Arogbo in the Western limit; of the Kabo and Kumbowei of the Western Delta; of the Gbaran of the Central Delta; and of the Urhobo-speaking Effurun (Evhro) on the Northern limit of the Delta. Traditions at most of these places conflict in detail while asserting some point at which they had been one or close neighbours.

According to traditions recorded at Oproza, the ancestors of the Gbaramatu, Arogbo, Kabo, Kumbowei, Gbaran and Effurun all migrated together from the town named Gbaran (Gbaraun) in Apoi *ibe* of the Central Delta. After they had left Gbaraun, the ancestors of the Kabo, Kumbo and Gbaran dropped off at points in the Western Delta. Only Usaku, ancestor of the Gbaramatu, and the ancestors of the Effurun and Arogbo arrived at Obodo in the present territory of the Gbaramatu. After Usaku had died at this site, Fiyewei, son of Usaku led the Gbaramatu and Arogbo to a second site at Opugbini. It was here that the Arogbo left and migrated farther west into their present location. Kenibira, son of Fiyewei led the Gbaramatu to Opuba, the present site of Oproza.

The conflicts in the recorded traditions centre around two main points: first, the kinship relationship between the various ancestors; and second, the direction of migration.

419

A 1930 account gave Gbara, founder of Gbaraun (Apoi) as the father of Effurun, Labiri, Akpobiri and Ogbeyama (father of Osako, ancestor of the Gbaramatu). It was stated only in a postscript that the ancestors of the Kabo and Kumbo had also been "full brothers" of Gbara. No mention was made of Gbaran *ibe* of the Central Delta, and the relationship of Arogbowei to the others was not stated. What is clear from the conflicting genealogies is that the exact kinship ties have been forgotten. What is known is that the early ancestors of all these groups had once lived at Gbaraun (Apoi) in the Central Delta.

The traditions recorded at Arogbo agree with recent Oproza (Gbaramatu) traditions that migration was from the Central Delta westwards. The 1930 Gbaramatu traditions suggest that the Effurun migrated out of Gbaraun first and on their own, the Gbaramatu and Arogbo leaving together in a second wave of migration. Traditions recorded among the Kabo, Kumbo and Gbaran imply migrations tending from west to east from Oproza.

These traditions may be reconciled by viewing the Gbaramatu, Arogbo, Effurun migrations as a first wave westwards from Gbaraun (Apoi) in the Central Delta to Oproza in the Western limit, followed by a rebound of the Kabo and Kumbo to the Western Delta and Gbaran *ibe* back into the Central Delta.

Internal Structure

The Gbaramatu are a classic example of a group without formal integrative institutions but yet have a strongly developed sense of unity. This sense is based mainly on the claim that all Gbaramatu settlements were derived from Oproza. The founders of Kunu-kunuama (Kunukunuba), Okirika (Ogebe?), Binitu (Okerenghigho) and Binikurukuru moved directly from Oproza. Kunukunuama gave birth to Ikokodiagbini (Bakokodia) and Ikantu; while Binikurukuru was the parent to Ajama (Ajatiton). In the midst of the dominating Itsekiri neighbours, this strong sense of common origin must be most useful, but there is no evidence that there were corresponding common political or even religious institutions built up.

After the leaders of the earlier migrations from Gbaraun town through Obodo, Opugbini, to Oproza (namely Usaku, Fiyewei, and Kenibira), the entire history of the Gbaramatu at Oproza seems to be the story of Ekiretimi. Ekiretimi won the position of leader 'because he was very rich' and a man of courage. The leaders cited as successors to Ekiretimi, namely Ogelegbanwei and Sebaba, were both quite recent. They were appointed, apparently, "to worship the father Ekiretimi".

After the population had been dispersed into several settlements, there was still no formal integrating institution developed. The *amaokosuwei* of each town controlled its affairs through the *amagula*, and the oldest *amaokosuwei* in the area was informally regarded as the senior man among the Gbaramatu. He exercised no formal authority (Alagoa 1972).

There was a great deal of resistance to colonial rule. In order to stamp their authority the British appointed Warrant Chiefs over the Gbaramatu. When Nigeria gained her independence in 1960, and later republican status in 1963, the power and authority of the Warrant Chiefs gradually diminished and *Pere* were installed. Thus, Zai Teimo was installed as Gbaraun II in 1976, and ruled for twenty four years from 1976–2000.

Trade and External Contacts

The Gbaramatu internal structure is that of the basic Ijo *ibe* and does not in itself suggest any particular relationship to other particular Ijo sub-groups. Not even with the groups, such as Arogbo, to which its traditions relate it. Arogbo, indeed, has closer affinity with distant Gbaraun in religious institutions than with the Gbaramatu. These differences may be explained by rejecting the close kinship relationship and genealogies offered in the traditions. It would then be possible to view the various migrants from Gbaraun as belonging to different lineages and even belonging to different wards (*idimu*), three of which are cited in Gbaramatu traditions. In such a situation, the Arogbo containing migrants from the Gbaraun ward that worshipped Egbesu would develop that religious institution in their new home.

One concrete evidence of contact with other parts of the delta and/or with the Nigerian hinterland is a set of six little bronzes to be found in a forest location at Oproza. The presence of these bronzes (just as in other delta locations), provides evidence of trade or other contacts with bronze cultures in other parts of Nigeria, because either the finished bronzes, or at least the raw materials, must have been traded from elsewhere. The pieces at Oproza are now used mainly as models for masquerade headpieces.

The presence of a huge cannon and a big ship's anchor at the old site of Oproza provides further concrete evidence of Gbaramatu participation in the overseas trade. Like the Egbema, the Gbaramatu describe "dark white men" (*Dirimo Bekewei*) with whom they traded. They similarly refer to these men as coming to the Escravos in sailing ships. The Gbaramatu exchanged salt (from seawater and mangrove roots) and fish for slaves whom they offered to the foreigners for cannon, tobacco and other manufactured goods. Since the Escravos bar was dangerous to ships and the river was not much frequented, the Gbaramatu had to go west to the Benin or east to the Forcados River to obtain a fair share of overseas trade. Gbaramatu traditions state that Ekiretimi obtained the ship's anchor while campaigning on the Forcados River. This would imply Gbaramatu activity (of a piratical nature, possibly) on the Forcados. But since Gbaramatu population was small, and only the leader (Ekiretimi, specifically) engaged in the trade, Gbaramatu share of the overseas trade in this part of the delta must have been small.

Gbaramatu traditions concerning their economic history, actually give greater prominence to their internal trade with the Itsekiri. The masses of the Gbaramatu were fishermen, but the women made salt. This was valuable to the Itsekiri, who called Oproza, Salt Town. The Gbaramatu also needed Itsekiri services, since they supplied the clay pots used by the Gbaramatu women to grind tobacco and, more important, for the salt industry.

Chronology
It is not possible to provide dates for Gbaramatu history. The material objects - the cannon, anchor, and bronzes - may, in time, provide the evidence for a

chronology. The traditions do not provide lists of any description, and no genealogies. The only chronology applicable would be the comparative one. Since the Arogbo migrated from Oproza, and since the Arogbo 'king-list' suggests foundation in the early eighteenth century, it would be reasonable to conclude that the Gbaramatu settled in the Escravos area before the eighteenth century.

7. Ogbe-Ijo

The Ogbe are a clan of about thirty settlements on the creeks south of the modern town of Warri. The Ogbe people claim to be the aboriginal inhabitants of Warri. The town of Ogbe moved from a site on the waterfront of Warri Township only in recent times. The Ogbe have retained their identity and culture in the midst of the Itsekiri of Warri Division and the Urhobo of Western Urhobo Division. Ogbe-Ijo is the administrative Headquarters of Warri South West Local Government Area of Delta State.

Traditions of Origin

The first settlement, Ogbe, states that their founding father Ewein, came from Ekeremo, the *Amatu* of Operemo *ibe* of the Western Delta in Bayelsa State. Operemo traditions derive their ancestors from Oporoma in the Central Delta, and the Ogbe also state that Ipoli, Ewein's father had come from Oporoma.

The Ogbe claim to have arrived at the site of Warri before the Itsekiri, and that Ewein's settlement was there when the Oba of Benin sent men after the Itsekiri migrants from Benin. They were unable to get into the creeks, and settled on the mainland at Okoro, originally called Maiekoro. The only settlers they met at the site were the Agbasa Urhobo in the immediate hinterland.

Ewein's settlement grew into six compounds (*Edumu*), namely, Aruteingha, Perebiri, Ikiyanbiri, Oturubiri, Lotiebiri and Tamebiri. When a British consulate was established at Warri, life became too complicated for the Ogbe. They were required to carry mails in the creeks, to carry the consul in a hammock to Sapele and other places in the hinterland, and they found township regulations irksome. The Ogbe therefore moved to their present site in the creeks (Alagoa 1972:50-51).

Internal Structure and External relations.

Administratively, there are two separate governing bodies in Ogbe, namely, the Ogbe-Ijo Traditional Council, and the Ogbe-Ijo Governing Council. The Traditional Council is headed by the *Pere* who handles traditional matters. The Governing Council is headed by an elected chairman. The chairman of the Governing Council handles political, social and economic matters. Ogbe towns were autonomous, but operated common institutions. Ogbe traditions record cordial relations with the Agbasa on the Warri mainland. They exchanged fish for cassava meal or farina.

Cultural and Economic Activities

Ogbe traditions give prominence to three festivals, namely: *Ofoniokine*, *Owouziowu* and *Amakoro-Ogbo Owu* (masquerade) festivals. The three festivals are celebrated annually. The *ofoniokine* festival is usually celebrated every December. *Ofoniokine* masquerade dances on water. *Owouziowu* festival is celebrated every January. As the name implies, it is the belief of the Ogbe that with the celebration of the *Owouziowu*, there will be increase in child birth. The *Amakoro-Ogbo* festival is also celebrated in December every year. *Amakoro-Ogbo Owu* festival is celebrated to appease the gods of the land.

8. Isaba

Isaba comprises about twenty 20 settlements on the Isaba creeks to the east of the modern town of Warri and Ogbe-Ijo, headquarters of Warri South West Local Government Area. Their immediate neighbours are the Urhobo in Udu Local Government, the Ogbe, and Gbekebo (Mein) in Burutu Local Government Area. Despite their proximity to the Urhobo, the Isaba were able to maintain their cultural identity.

Traditions of Origin

According to Isaba tradition, the founder of Isaba *ibe)* was Isoun. The founder's ancestor was Ekere who migrated from Oporoma and founded Ekeremo in Bayelsa State. Ekere, the ancestor of Isoun, gave birth to Bumoun. Bumoun gave birth to two children, Isaba and Ndoro. Thus, both Isaba and Ogbe trace their origin to a common ancestor, Oporoma, in Bayelsa State.

Internal and External Relations

There are two types of leadership in Isaba; namely, the Traditional Rulers Council and the Town Council. The Traditional Council exercises sole authority over traditional matters, while the town council oversee other matters. Isaba traditions record early cordial relations with the Aladja and Owhawha Urhobo in Udu and Ughelli South Local Government Areas. They exchanged fish for cassava meal and palm oil. Isaba also had close contacts with the Ogbe and Itsekiri.

Traditional Institutions

Isaba had a well organized kingship institution. In order to legitimize his position, *Pere* Isoun left Isaba for Benin, with his royal contemporary *Pere* Kalanama I of Akugbene Mein. Both received the title of *Pere Ogieame,* meaning, king of the rivers. Some of the senior chiefs of Isaba kingdom still bear Benin traditional titles. The present *Pere* of Isaba is *Pere* Donokumo II (JP).

Cultural and Economic Activities

There are cultural activities celebrated at specific periods in Isaba kingdom. Prominent among them are *Oki, Kornowei, Amakiri-Ogbo, Deinowu* and *Agula* festivals. Festivals are usually celebrated every three years; while the *Amakiri-Ogbe* and *Dein-Owu* festivals are celebrated every year. The *Dein-Owu* (night masquerade) festival is celebrated every December. The *Dein-Owu* is believed to be a benevolent spirit which drives away evil spirits from the land.

Some of the major economic activities of the people include; fishing, farming, lumbering and palm wine tapping. The products are usually traded with the Urhobo, Itsekiri and other Ijo groups in the Niger Delta .

9. Diebiri

The Diebiri live close to Warri, Ogbe and Aladja, with most of their settlements lying along the Warri River and adjoining creeks and creeklets. Their immediate neighbours are the Aladja Urhobo, Ogbe and Ode Itsekiri.

Traditions of Origin

The Diebiri are an offshoot of Seimbiri clan in the Western Delta. Diebiri was founded by Dio. According to Diebiri traditions, the founders moved from Oboro to the present place of settlement near Warri.   Diebiri consisted of three original quarters Etwaedumu, Egadedumu and Fiyewaredumu. Since 1995, Diebiri has moved from the site founded by Dio to a new site at Diebiri-Batan (Ubateinghan) because of attack by the Aladja Urhobo.

Internal and External Relations

All Diebiri villages are autonomous units. The eldest *Amaseseokusukeme,* or Town Elder, was and is accepted as leader of the group. The Diebiri are related to the Ogbe, Aladja, and Itsekiri. The Diebiri were part of the 1893 treaty signed by most groups in the Warri area with the British. They were identified by the Urhobo name Turbo. Diebiri is ruled by an *Ebenanaowei* as well as an elected Governing Council. The current *Ebenanaowei* of Diebiri is Chief J.G. Orubu.

Cultural and Economic Activities

In Diebiri, there are some prominent festivals which the people celebrate. The festivals include *Aziza-Ikiyan, Dien owu, Okoroko* masquerade, *Amakiri, Ogbo owu, Opufene* and *Asaramo–Orou. Aziza–Ikiyan* is performed before a Diebiri person tastes new corn. *Asaramo–Orou* is celebrated for good catch of fish as well as for good yield of food crops. Most of the festivals were performed to appease deities.

The major economic activities of Diebiri include fishing, lumbering, farming and petty trading. The people trade with the Urhobo, Itsekiri and neighbouring Ijo *ibe*.

Conclusion

The general sense of the individual group traditions is that migration was generally from the Central Delta outwards to the Western limit. In some cases, stops in the Western Delta can be inferred, or are definitely stated. Egbema, Ogbe, Isaba and Diebiri migrations started from the Western Delta, from groups which had originally come from the Central Delta.

In contrast with the Central and Eastern Delta, we note the absence or weakness of traditions claiming Ife or Benin origin. This area of the delta closest to these kingdoms should logically be the starting point for any migrations from Benin or Ife into the delta. The Apoi tradition recorded at Igbobini claiming Ife origin was clearly a recent minority variant, and the Olodiama tradition stating Ife (and even Mecca) origin and migration through Benin can be similarly explained (Owonaro 1949).

In the Olodiama case, prior Benin origin is one way to establish rights of ownership over land. Practically, it was the new arrangements entered into with the Oba of Benin which conferred legitimacy.

The traditions indicate that, while migrations out of the area of Benin influence are better known, there were also migrations into the neighborhood of Benin. The Olodiama migrated right into the river closest to Benin, siting their capital less than twenty miles from Benin City. On the other hand, the Apoi moved farther west, to avoid direct contact, while the Furupagha stayed in the vicinity of Benin, in spite of slave raids.

On the basis of the local traditions, a number of different types of relations may be seen. First, the direct contact established by Olodiama *Pere* with the Oba of Benin. Here annual "presents" were stipulated during a specific ancestral

427

festival at Benin, and the *Pere* is stated to have assisted Benin in at least one war. There was, in addition, a blood covenant of mutual protection. Second, the case of Egbema, where the leader of Ofiniama went on a visit to Benin for purposes of divination, and later engaged in direct commercial exchange with the Benin kingdom. Third, the traditions of Apoi which state that members of the group had been used by the Oba of Benin to go on missions within the delta, and finally, the case of Furupagha raided for slaves.

The groups farther back in the delta—the Arogbo, Gbaramatu, Ogbe, Isaba (and to some extent the Egbema), were apparently free of direct Benin influence. Their relations were more intimate with the Itsekiri and other ethnic groups active inside the delta. The majority of the Itsekiri on the Benin River seem to have come from Ode Itsekiri in the eighteenth century (although some Itsekiri groups had been settled on the Escravos earlier), and these Ijo subgroups found open spaces to settle and seek a livelihood.

Relations between the groups were largely commercial exchange of Ijo salt and fish for Itsekiri pottery. The Apoi and Egbema carried out similar dealings with the Yoruba to the west and north west, while the Ogbe, Isaba and Diebiri exchanged with the Urhobo.

In the area of economic activity, the particular variant of delta environment dictated the specialization of groups. Thus the Arogbo, Olodiama, and to a lesser extent, the Egbema and Furupagha became canoe-makers to other delta peoples. They live in the fresh water delta in an area of abundant timber supply. And we note that from Pereira in the sixteenth century on, the large trade and war canoes of the delta were remarked upon from Benin River to the Bonny River. The Gbaramatu in the salt water delta, close to the coast, were salt boilers and fisher-folk, while the Ogbe, Isaba and Diebiri are also fisher-folk and farmers.

The internal trade between groups within the delta and with those on the northern periphery was basic to the life of the peoples. But the piracy, much advertised in the European literature, was probably a result of the overseas trade in slaves, palm-oil and manufactures. Ijo piracy was an attempt to participate in the distribution of goods resulting from the overseas trade. Since this trade was organized around state systems the stateless groups were placed on the outside. Thus the earlier Portuguese trade was directed to Benin through the Port of Gwato (Ughoton), until the Dutch moved to Arbo on the Benin River from 1644, and it later came to Itsekiri hands from the eighteenth century. Farther east on the Forcados River, the Itsekiri capital, Ode-Itsekiri, was the focus. Accordingly, Arogbo, Egbema, and Gbaramatu traditions of participation must have been on a secondary basis, and sometimes through forcible entry by way of the piracy so widely reported.

Finally, on a tentative chronology of Ijo history on the Western Delta limit, the king lists and genealogies are all of comparative length and point to seventeenth and eighteenth century dates of migration into the region. But other indirect evidence, for example, for Olodiama and Isaba in comparison with the Benin incidents cited, would suggest much earlier dates even in the sixteenth century. One may postulate the shallow time depth of oral tradition in stateless societies from the short genealogies and "King-Lists". And in internal organization, several of the groups developed the segmentary institutions brought over from the Central Delta into a region of centralizing political systems. The *Pere* of Olodiama, Arogbo, and Egbema are examples of such adaptations. The *Kalashuwe* (*Kalasuo*) of Apoi and the *Pere* of Isaba use Benin-type *ada* or swords of office, suggesting Benin as a model for some of these adaptations.

CHAPTER 19
THE WESTERN DELTA
E. J. Alagoa and Ebiegberi A. Femowei

Introduction

The Western Delta has been settled by its Ijo population for a longer time than the Western Limit. There is, first, the written evidence of the early Portuguese visitors. Pereira, reporting at the close of the fifteenth century, observed all the territory east of the Forcados River occupied by "Jos" i.e., Ijo. He identified the subgroup occupying the lower Forcados as "Huela", a name that may be identified with the Ogula (or Ogulagha) who live there now. The trade centre five leagues up a left branch of the Forcados has, however, been thought to have been an early site of the Itsekiri, which was moved to the present capital of Ode Itsekiri or Big Warri by the mid-sixteenth century. This trade centre up the left branch of the Forcados River sold the Portuguese "slaves and cotton cloths, with some panther skins, palm-oil and some blue shells with red stripes which they call 'coris". The Portuguese gave brass and copper bracelets in exchange. To the east on the Ramos River in territory now occupied by the Iduwini, Pereira also reported "Jos" (Ijo). The area was "densely populated" and the people used "canoes made of a single trunk". And since timber was reported plentiful in the locality, these canoes may be presumed made by the inhabitants, although canoes now used in the Western Delta are mostly made in the Western Limit or Central Delta.

A further evidence of longer Ijo settlement of the Western Delta in comparison with the area to the west is the uninterrupted spread of Ijo groups over the area. We find other Nigerian ethnic groups impinging on the area only on its Northern Limit where the Mein and the Kabo Ijo have mainly Urhobo, Isoko, Aboh and Kwale-Ibo neighbours and the Itsekiri to the north-west. These contacts have been important, involving significant cultural exchange, migration, and marriage, usually, of Ijo men to women from these neighbouring groups.

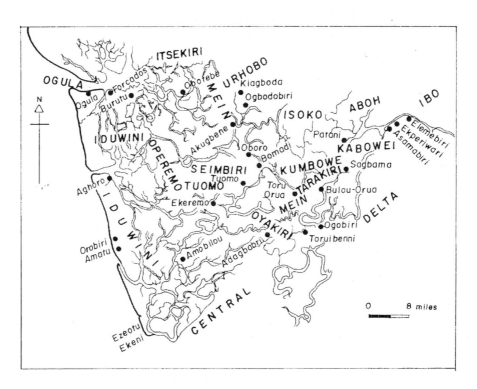

Fig. 19.1: The Ijo of the Western Delta

Finally, the oral traditions of the Western Delta Limit themselves have indicated migrations from the Central and Western Delta. The evidence of the oral traditions of the Western Delta detailed in the following sections would suggest also prior migrations mainly from the Central Delta.

The development of institutions in the Western Delta then may be assumed to depend on the factors of Central Delta origin and of contacts with neighbouring groups. Here, however, the Benin Empire was more remote than in the Western Limit, and the only direct traditions of Benin influence occur among the Mein. The influence of environment was largely uniform since only two subgroups, the coastal Iduwini and Ogulagha are in the salt-water swamp and sandy beach ridge area and all other groups occupy the freshwater swamp zone. In spite of this apparent uniformity of environment and contiguity of the Ijo of the Western Delta, there was great movement and varieties of historical experience and of internal development.

432

1.   Obotebe

The small Obotebe *ibe* lies on the borderland between the Western Delta and the Western Limit. It is bordered on the west by the Ogbe and Itsekiri, and surrounded to the east by Mein settlements. Since they seem to have been threatened with Mein domination in the past, Obotebe traditions relate of wars against the Mein. One account even claims ownership of the land on which the nearest large Mein settlement, Gbekebo, stands—that it was the spot on which their founding ancestor dried his fishing equipment. Wars against the Itsekiri were terminated by two covenants, while the Ogbe are said to have received migrants from Obotebe. Trading relations were early established with the Urhobo on the mainland where a market was set up by mutual agreement.

Obotebe traditions of origin indicate relations with other delta groups and Ijo *ibe*. The ultimate ancestor is stated to be Jock, father of Onido, father of Oro, father of Obotebe, father of Ogini who founded the mother settlement named Obotebe. The man Obotebe had lived originally at Ikibiri (or Ikebiri) where he worshipped Egbesu. A quarrel over duiker (*wan*) meat led to dispersal. He moved up to the Niger confluence town of Onya (Anyan at Obotebe). Obotebe, and his son Ogini came down to Ibeni (Oyakiri) from where Ogini came to found Obotebe town and *ibe*.

This narrative already relates the Obotebe to several Ijo *ibe*. The town of Ikibiri in the Ekpetiama area of the Central Delta is also the place of origin of the Seimbiri of the Western Delta. Traditions at both Ikibiri and among the Seimbiri name Oro or Oromo as an ancestor. But the mention of Egbesu worship suggests that the place of origin could have been Ikebiri of Olodiama *ibe* of the Central Delta where Egbesu is, in fact, worshipped. The relationship implied by the sojourn at Ibeni is strengthened by the further statement that Obotebe's father, Oro, had other sons including Oyakiriowei, Tarakiriowei, Egbemo, and Toru-Agorowei. Oyakiri, of course, is another name for Ibeni, where traditions do, indeed, mention an ancestor named Orumo (Oromo ?).

Tarakiri and Tuomo (Toru-Agoro) traditions contain no indication of kinship with the Obotebe, but some at least of the Egbema of the Western Limit may have come from Obotebe rather than the neighbouring Gbekebo mentioned at Ofiniama (Egbema). The Mein town of Gbekebo stands at the mouth of the river leading to Obotebe, and is much better known.

The bare statements of the traditions are all there is in the way of historical data for the Obotebe. There is little help from ethnography or institutions. There has been no dynastic tradition or central authority over all Obotebe. And in spite of the mention of Egbesu for the place of origin, the Obotebe do not have a national god or annual or other festival to impose religious sanctions of unity. The only institution tending to identify all Obotebe would be the cult of Ogini, the founding ancestor. Being such a small group in the midst of other and often hostile groups, the Obotebe probably required few or no institutional superstructure to unify them.

The genealogy supplied by Giofie Beke, appointed to the new improvised position of *Ibenanawe* (head of *ibe*) in 1956 provides the only indicator of chronology. Since Giofie was born in 1908, six generations from Ogini, that ancestor and the foundation of Obotebe may be dated in the first quarter of the eighteenth century.

2.   Mein

Mein history is among the most complicated in the Western Delta since the group broke into four parts centuries ago and is now widely dispersed. An early account from the dispersal centre at Ogobiri gives a version against which other sectional versions may be interpreted.

According to this account, Mein, the ancestor of the whole subgroup lived at Benin with his wife Obolu. He left because of internal wars and settled at Aboh at the head of the Niger Delta. He had a large number of children here, including, Kor. He fled Aboh with his family after killing a woman caught stealing or violating his god, Dirimegbeya (Dirimoagbiya), represented by an elephant's tusk. He lost the original tusk in his flight but received a fresh one from God. Mein then established at Ogobiri on the Sagbama-Igbedi Creek. Ogobiri soon became too crowded for Mein's descendants.

Kor had succeeded his father Mein as *Mein Okosuwei* (Mein elder), and was himself succeeded by his son, Ogo. Other sons of Kor left Ogobiri in lineage groups as a result of over-population and a quarrel over the division of the meat killed in a hunt. They moved westwards to different sites along the Forcados River. Kalanama became founder of the Akugbene Mein; Ngbele/Ngbile, another son of Kor founded Kiagbodo and became head of the Ngbilebiri Mein; Ogbolu founded the town of Ogbodobiri, and led the Ogbolubiri Mein.

Oral traditions, collected recently at Kiagbodo among the Ngbile Mein, do not challenge the earlier accounts on events prior to the settlement around the Forcados River, but differ in their account of events after the dispersal from Ogobiri. In fact, the Ngbilebiri genealogies made their ancestor, Ngbile, a direct son of Mein, and actually leave out Kor. These recent Ngbilebiri traditions thus conflict with the earlier Mein traditions recorded in 1930.

One major point of variance is the manner in which new political authority was established among the Mein on the Forcados River. The 1930 account states that Kalanama as the senior of the three migrating brothers was accorded due deference by Ngbile and Ogbolu. But since Ogo still retained the title of *Mein Okosuwei* at Ogobiri, Kalanama considered it necessary to obtain a new title, or at least fresh symbols of legitimacy. He decided to go to the Oba of Benin. He was required to sacrifice an unspecified number of slaves at the Oba's shrines on the way, and returned with a collection of bronze artifacts, the title of *pere*, and permission to hold the lands along the Forcados River. According to Benin practice, the kingship title thus conferred should have passed to Kalanama's eldest son. But he quarrelled with his family, and at his death, handed over both the bronzes, and the titles of *pere* and *Mein Okosuwei* to his brother, Ngbile.

The Ngbilebiri account of these incidents differs in several ways. It states that Ngbile went on an independent trip to Benin, and that the bronzes now at Kiagbodo were given directly to Ngbile by the Oba of Benin. The Ogbolubiri Mein are said to have a similar claim of a trip to Benin and the award of bronzes and the title of *pere* to their ancestor.

These accounts raise a number of questions. First, the relationship between the titles of *pere* and of *Mein Okosuwei*. The title of *pere* was clearly not a Benin political title, and refers to the High Priest of the national god of most Central and Western Delta *ibe*. Accordingly, it may be assumed that the title belonged among the Mein to the High Priest of Dirimoagbiya. The second question is whether the High Priest of Dirimoagbiya (or *pere*) and *Mein Okosuwei* were originally the same person among the Mein. This seems likely during the period of migration and settlement at Ogobiri. The leaders Mein, Kor, and Ogo seem to have been custodians of the national god as well as being *Mein Okosowei*. Problems of legitimacy and authority only rose after the migration to the Forcados River. Since Ogo was still *Mein Okosowei* and, apparently, also *pere*, at Ogobiri, Kalanama needed the trip to Benin to obtain a political title distinct from the original religious office of *pere*.

It would appear then that the Mein on the Forcados River developed a system in which the office of *pere* was divorced from the original religious title. This had to be the position if all three sections eventually enthroned independent *pere* at Kiagbodo (for the descendants of Ngbile), Akugbene (for the descendants of Kalanama) and at Ogbodobiri (for the descendants of Ogbolu). This conclusion is inescapable since all Mein, whether at the Forcados River or at Ogobiri, have continued to worship the same national god, Mein Dirimoagbiya; and it would be impracticable for each *pere* of the sections to claim to be High Priest of Dirimoagbiya.

At Kiagbodo the *pere* was distinct from the man appointed to worship at the local shrine of Dirimoagbiya. The *pere* too still exercised some spiritual authority, but only as the priest or representative of the founding ancestor, Ngbile. The office of *Mein Okosuwei* seems to have disappeared after the time of Kalanama and Ngbile. The basis of the transfer of bronzes in the first account was that Kalanama, having become Mein Okosuwei at the death of Ogo at Ogobiri, passed this title on to Ngbile at his own death, together with the bronzes. [Such a transfer would have been an unlikely confusion between the new political office of *pere* to which the bronzes belonged, and the ancient office of *Mein Okosowei*]. Once three *pere* were established over the sections on the Forcados River alone, it was politically impracticable to appoint or recognize an authority over them such as the *Mein Okosuwei* represented.

Benin Influence

The bronze insignia of office now known to be at Kiagbodo and Akugbene also raise problems of historical interpretation. First, we shall consider the idea of going to Benin. There is evidence of wide knowledge of the Oba's great power current in the delta, but no evidence of actual exercise of authority by the Oba outside the Western Limit. The Mein, of course, have the tradition of prior migration from Benin through Aboh to Ogobiri, but the practical incentive for the trip is likely to have come from the example of the neighbouring Urhobo and Isoko on the immediate hinterland. At Ughelli, for example, the sons of Ogele (originally from Tarakiri Ijo) had to decide the issue of leadership by making a trip to Benin. The successful candidate returned with the title of *Ovie* and a brass sword. Similarly, all the first nine *Ovie* of Iyede had to obtain the approval of the Oba of Benin, and by this means acquired ascendancy over the other Isoko groups. The example of these neighbouring peoples must have urged the necessity and possibilities of the particular solution offered by a visit to the court of Benin.

The nature and variety of the artifacts stated to have been brought from Benin, however, raise other problems. They are not all likely to have been brought in one trip or to have been "given" as insignia of office. The 1930 report listed the following material found at Kiagbodo:

(a)   1 brass indented tray with uneven lifted edge
(b)   1 "Right Hand": a hollow short cylindrical vessel of brass, with grooved circles around the outside, and an ornamented bar of brass across the base.

(c)   2 hollow cow tusks, called charms, to be held in each hand.

(d)   1 ivory tusk, brown and polished with age, with a carved alligator on its length, and a carved lion attached to its top.

(e)   1 "Death Mask", a plaque of unknown substance carved with the image of a face, and said to have been given by the Oba of Benin as a picture of Mein.

(f)   1 concave brass plaque with image of a negroid face on the concave side. The chin merges into the image of a bird's claw. Supposed to represent the Oba.

(g)   4 brass bracelets each 6 inches in length, 2 worked in basket tracing, and 2 of ornamented but solid design.

(h)   Many brass bracelets and armlets for wives.

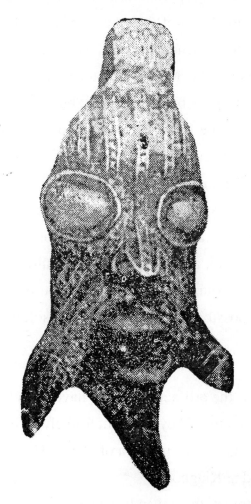

Plate 19.1:

A bronze human face from Kiagbodo, claimed to represent the Oba of Benin

Plate 19.2:

Bronze from Kiagbodo, claimed to be a gift from "the Oba of Benin
as a picture of Mein"

The *pere* of Akugbene also had a "right hand" symbol, stated by the Mein to have been "the most important of them". This item clearly represented the Benin "cult object known as *ikega* or *ikenga*" associated with "the prowess, strength and enterprise of the individual worshiper". This object was identified to Robin Horton as "*bra kon*—a brass version of a personal cult-object common in the area but generally made of wood". A hand cult, *Amabra* occurs in other parts of the upper Delta as well, and the Mein need not have introduced the cult from Benin. But the suggestion is that during and after the first political trip, the Mein rulers ordered bronze objects from Benin for a variety of uses—ornaments, cult objects, royal regalia.

Apart from this traffic in cultural objects and voluntary trade in political insignia, the Western Delta, and even the Urhobo-Isoko mainland, seem to have remained outside the direct control of Benin. No armies came to collect tribute or to enforce the Oba's will.

Other Relationships

Mein traditions do not claim relationship with any other Ijo groups, although at Ogobiri they were neighbours of the Tarakiri to the west and the Kolokuma to the east of the creek. A relationship has, however, been recorded between the Mein and the Olomu and Ewu-Urhobo.

Traditions recorded recently at Kiagbodo claim Ngbile to have left his brother Oghoro with the Olomu on his way to Benin. Oghoro decided to live permanently with the Olomu. According to Hubbard, 'Ngbile and Oghoro had originally come to Kiagbodo from Benin.' Other traditions among the Ewu claim their ancestor to have come from Ogobiri.

The Ngbilebiri traditions recorded at Kiagbodo contain accounts of several wars against the neighbouring Isoko and Urhobo. But the longer periods of peaceful trade and marriage (Ijo men to Isoko-Urhobo women) have left their mark in the interchange of cultural traits; and most Kiagbodo men are bilingual in Ijo and Urhobo. The Mein were obviously influential over all of the Western Delta. The Forcados River (and often all of the Western Delta) was known to Ijo of other parts of the Delta as Mein Toru (Mein River). Ngbilebiri traditions, in fact, claim control of the slave and other trade along the entire length of the river from its junction with the Niger and Nun down to the sea—a claim that was accepted by the Niger Company in the late nineteenth century. And within the Western Delta, it may not be fanciful to see a recognition of some traditional place of honour for the Mein in the ritual of *tutiin*, observed for one lost in the water. The names of three ancestors are called at such a ritual among all Western Delta Ijo: Ikere (Ekeremo) (of Operemo *ibe*), Orobiri (of Iduwini) and Mein.

440

In addition, the Ngbilebiri of Kiagbodo have produced men from time to time who have exercised influence beyond their home areas. In the nineteenth century one Odjede Ivbiadoma (also rendered Ogiede, and Ekede) became a peacemaker over most of the Western Delta. His traditional title was that of spokesman *Ogulasowei* or *Onuombra?* and *pere buo soruowei* (assistant to the *pere*) at Kiagbodo, but he came to be accepted as mediator in disputes between towns and communities along most of the Forcados River. At the beginning of the twentieth century another Kiagbodo citizen, Bekederemo (Ambakederimo) became preeminent as a middleman trader with the Royal Niger Company.

Chronology

The genealogies from Ogobiri (1930) and Kiagbodo (1967) provide some basis for a tentative chronology of Mein history. Main used his 1930 genealogy to date the birth of Mein in Benin to "some time in the late sixteenth century". The recent Kiagbodo genealogy would date Ngbile at about the middle of the seventeenth century. On present evidence then, Mein migrations within the delta and the contacts with Benin probably occurred between the end of the sixteenth and the middle of the seventeenth century.

3.   Seimbiri

The ancestral home of the Seimbiri lies near the town of Ikibiri in the Central Delta, within the territory of Ekpetiama *ibe*. Traditions at Ikibiri and among the Seimbiri agree on the nature of their relationship but differ on points of detail.

The two accounts differ on the genealogy of the ancestors. According to the Ikibiri, the eponymous ancestor was Ogbo who had three sons, Oromo, Ikibiriowei, and Temezebai (Temezibe). The Seimbiri named Oromo the first ancestor, with Seimbiri, Ogbo and Ikibiriowei as his three sons and Temezebai as a grandson of Seimbiri. Accordingly, while the Ikibiri referred to themselves as Ogbo *ibe*, the western section used Seimbiri, rather than Oromo, who was no more than "a dim figure" in their memory.

The migration to the west occurred in the time of Ogbo in the Central Delta when the people were settled at Isomobou, some six miles to the west of Ikibiri town. The Isomobou community had killed and eaten a man of Oweikorogha,

Tarakiri *ibe*. A man passed over in the division of the spoils reported the matter to the Tarakiri of Oweikorogha. The Oweikorogha called other Tarakiri towns to their aid and obtained firearms from the states of Kalabari and Nembe in the Eastern Delta. The firearms were then unknown to the Isomobou, and the number of the allies was overwhelming. They dispersed after hiding the old man, Ogbo, and his family, in a pit.

The dispersion from Isomobou, and later migrations from Ikibiri, are cited in the traditions of origin of the Ogoloma (Okrika), Onopa (Epie-Atissa), several towns in Ekpetiama *ibe*, Akaranbiri (Opokuma) and Akiri in Aboh. The Seimbiri, the main group of migrants moving westwards first settled at Oboro, which later sent off-shoots to Inikorogha and Okpokunu.

Traditions at Ikibiri and Oboro were ignorant of a time before the dispersal. An Ikibiri account stated, however, that an unknown ancestor before Ogbo had lived in Egypt and Benin. This constitutes the only recorded tradition before the 1950s of an Ijo tradition of origin that refers to any place beyond Benin outside the Niger Delta as a place of origin. Even then, the Seimbiri did not subscribe to the tradition, sticking to Isomobou near lkibiri in the Central Delta as their ancestral home.

The Seimbiri have no direct tradition of blood relationship to other Ijo. But the ancestral name of Oromo is the same as that recorded for the Oyakiri or lbeni. Furthermore, traditions collected recently state that some at least of the migrants from the Central Delta stayed among the Mein in the Igbedi Creek (apparently at Ogobiri), and may have brought from there the bronzes to be found at Inikorogha.

The Inikorogha bronzes raise the problem of centralized authority among the Seimbiri. There is no tradition of any such authority—secular or religious—developing among the Seimbiri. The 1931 report states categorically that "no clan head, spiritual or temporal, has ever been recognized", although the oldest *amaokosowei* of the component settlements was regarded informally as *primus inter pares*, as among the Gbaramatu. The presence of the bronzes at

Inikorogha rather than at the traditional centre of Oboro seems to support the suggestion that the bronzes were the personal heirloom of some ancestor taken away from Ogobiri to Oboro and thence to Inikorogha by descendants, and not the emblems of supreme office among all Seimbiri.

4.   Tuomo
Origins
Hook was given conflicting accounts of Tuomo history on two visits in 1929 and 1930. According to one version, the eponymous ancestor came from "up river" and lived in the Aboh area for a while. Tuomo then moved south for fear of slave raiders. He first settled at the site of Isampo (Tarakiri), but finally moved to the present site of Tuomo town, then called Toru-Aghoro (Aghoro-on-the-river) after Okun-Aghoro (Aghoro-on-the-sea) of the Iduwini. The second version stated that Tuomo had been born at the Urhobo town of Afene or Efurun. He left Efurun because of trouble with the Urhobo, and died at the settlement on the site of Isampo, the present settlement of Tuomo being founded by his son Osuku. This earlier account was discounted on the second occasion by the explanation that the founder of Efurun, Afene, was the second son of Tuomo, born at the Isampo site with an Urhobo slave wife. The mother took him away to her home on Tuomo's death, and Afene then founded Efurun.

Both versions retain the connection with Efurun, and the "up river" of one version probably meant Efurun. A recent version also states that Esuku (Osuku), father of both Tuomo and Efurun, lived at the town of Efurun, and that Esuku and Tuomo left for the delta site. These traditions are clearly related to the migrations from the Central Delta, related by the Gbaramatu of the Western Delta Limit, the Esuku/Osuku of the Tuomo being the Usaku of the Gbaramatu. According to the Gbaramatu, Usaku and the ancestor of the Efurun had both come from Gbaraun in the Central Delta.

Summary and Chronology
The Tuomo are a small compact *ibe* all of whose towns are situated close together on the Bomadi Creek. The town of Tuomo is recognized as the senior settlement, with the shrine of the national god standing taller than all other houses in the town.

The traditions of origin indicate relationship with both Efurun and the Gbaramatu, and Tuomo migrations seem to have brought them into contact with many other peoples in the Western Delta and the immediate hinterland. The passage through Tarakiri (Isampo) is said to have been accomplished before the Tarakiri arrived on the scene. But the name Toru-Aghoro (Aghoro-on-the river), originally applied to Tuomo town implies the prior existence of Aghoro of the Iduwini (known as Okun-Aghoro, Aghoro by the sea), since the founders had to qualify the name in order to distinguish it.

The genealogy obtained by Hook in 1930 traced the ancestry of the *Amaokosowei* of Torugbene town through seven generations to Tuomo, and the rulers of Tubegbe and Tamiegbe five generations. These figures suggest a date in the mid-eighteenth century for the earliest events remembered in Tuomo tradition.

5.   Tarakiri

The Tarakiri of the Western Delta are one of the most widely dispersed *ibe* in the Niger Delta, and the traditions assign wars with the Mein and between families as the cause.

According to Tarakiri traditions, their ancestor, Tara or Tarakiriowei, was a brother of the ancestors of the Kolokuma and the Opokuma of the Central Delta. Ondo, their father, lived at Benin, but left with his three sons because the Oba seized private lands and levied heavy taxes. He settled for a while at Aboh. Aboh was unsuitable and he migrated to the site of Amatolo (Ogboin *ibe*) in the Sagbama-Igbedi Creek, where he died. The Kolokuma and Opokuma went east to the Igbedi end of the creek and the Tarakiri stayed behind. The Mein were also at the same creek at Ogobiri.

The first movement of the Tarakiri into the Western Delta from the vicinity of Amatolo was caused by war with the Mein. The Tarakiri left either immediately after or soon after this war to Oruassa a site in the neighbourhood of Angalabiri. Here civil strife caused by the unfair division of *wan* (duiker) meat resulted in a further dispersal. The parent settlement of the Tarakiri was then

444

established at Orua at whose waterside settlement, Toru-Orua, is to be found Sene "the ancestral spirit of the Tarakiri". The founders of the Urhobo groups of Owha, Ogo, Ogele (Ughelli), Agbarha and Orogu are also stated to have moved as part of this dispersal from Oruassa.

A final set of migrations occurred from the various locations to which the Tarakiri moved. The Agbere at the junction of the Niger and Nun say they first moved to a site near the Mein settlement of Kpakiama. War broke out between the Agbere and Kpakiama. Nine leaders and a woman, Ona, fled eastwards first to Odi (Kolokuma) and finally to Odoni (Oyakiri). The Odoni first offered to absorb them, but later agreed to give them land for settlement. The nine leaders were given a male and female lizard—the signs of a permanent settlement—and Agbere was founded.

Summary and Chronology

A series of wars and consequent migrations have led to the scattered settlement of the Tarakiri, but also to contacts with many peoples. Some settlements still counted as Tarakiri are Urhobo-speaking (Ofoni, Uduovhori, Odorobo) while the Urhobo of Owha and Ughelli still retain traditions of Tarakiri origin.

The dispersed nature of Tarakiri settlements ensures that there can be no central political authority although Fellows reported that in 1932 the Chief Priest or *Orukarowei* could summon meetings of the whole *ibe* at Orua.

The Agbere genealogy gives a date in the early nineteenth century to Diagha, one of the founding nine. He was also identified with the "Chief Diarha" on an 1884 treaty. Agbere was in existence by the mid-nineteenth century since both Baikie and Crowther visited it in 1854, naming it the first Oru (Ijo) village south of Aboh.

Accordingly, the last set of migrations occurred in the first half of the nineteenth century and the movements between Amatolo, Oruassa and Orua occurred before the nineteenth century. The Mein chronology suggests that their own migrations from Ogobiri occurred early in the seventeenth

445

century—migrations which were conceivably connected with the wars between the Mein and the Tarakiri. The Tarakiri migrations therefore, could have taken place between the mid-seventeenth and early nineteenth centuries.

6.   Kabowei

The earlier history of the Kabowei is concerned with the little Kabobulou Creek which branches off the Forcados River a little way from the Kabo head town of Patani. The majority of Kabo towns now lie along the Forcados and Niger, but the history of the Kabo and of the related Kumbowei and Gbaran *ibe* (Central Delta) apparently started in the Kabobulou Creek. Now only the Kabo settlements of Kolowari and Aven, and the Kumbowei town of Bolou-Angiama remain in Kabobulou Creek. Kabo history is largely their gradual withdrawal from Kabobulou and spread eastwards to the Niger.

The original settlement in Kabobulou was apparently founded by Okita, son of Oproza (founder of Gbaramatu *ibe* of the Escravos River). Okita lived there with his wife, Mboara, and his three sons, Kabo, Kumbo, and Gbaran. Okita died while his father, Oproza, was still alive; and his son, Kabo, became leader of the community after Oproza.

Kabo persecuted his brothers by enslaving them and giving their daughters in marriage without their consent. Gbaran moved out first eastwards through the Sagbama Creek to the mouth of the Taylor Creek in the Central Delta. Kumbo moved out later, but only a short way off to the mouth of the Sagbama Creek and thus kept in touch with his brother. This left Kabo and his lineage in the Kabobulou Creek. Kabo was succeeded in the leadership by his son, Obodangha, and Obodangha by his son Eleme. The Kabowei are reported to have carried out a stupendous piece of work which dramatically changed their fortunes and history.

Diversion of the Forcados River

The Kabobulou Creek was then the main Forcados River, and the Kabo the principal beneficiaries of the slave trade with the Portuguese at its estuary, the present course past Patani through Mein territory being then a minor branch creek. Then the Kabo heard a rumour that European ships would come up the river during the following flood season and capture any persons they saw. The Kabowei met, and decided to block up the river at its lowest level in the dry season. The Kumbowei came to their aid:

> 'They felled trees all the way along the banks of the river from where it left the Sagbama Creek to the village of Aven and toppled them all into the river. Meanwhile others were at work with branches, brushwood, grass, twigs and anything of that nature, filling up the interstices; finally the whole was filled with sand and earth, and made as secure as possible. The river was blocked over a distance of at least three miles.'

The Forcados River was thus permanently diverted from its original course, becoming the current small Kabobulou Creek. As a result, the Kabowei lost their position in the overseas trade to the Mein. Soon they saw the folly of remaining cooped up in the little creek and began to break out.

Expansion

Eleme's lineage, Elemebiri, was the first to leave Kabobulou. They fought the Mein in a pitched battle and settled on the new main river close to its junction with the Kabobulou. Other lineages followed. The result was the town of Patani, so called from their rallying cry when they went slave-hunting: *paa tein*, let us push adrift.

Baikie and Crowther's statement that the Tarakiri town of Agbere was the highest Ijo town on the Niger in 1854 suggests that the Kabowei towns of Elemebiri (Ofonibeingha), Asamabiri, and Ekperiwari north of Agbere arrived on the Niger after 1854. They were, in fact, the last to leave the new home of the Kabo at Patani. The Elemebiri are said to have moved so far north of all Ijo settlements (to a point on the Niger too wide for even the birds to cross) because their leader, Kurokemefa, as head of Kabo, handed out an unpopular decision. He was rejected by all the other lineages.

447

Internal Organization and External Contacts

The traditions suggest that leadership among the Kabowei passed through the paternal line of the founder, Kabo. That practice was continued at Patani, but the dispersed settlements naturally won autonomy from the *pere* at Patani.

It seems that thenceforward, the position of High Priest of Kabo Ziba became more significant in matters of overall Kabowei politics. The Tawari lineage which came to produce the priests gained prestige, and one Sedeye is credited with applying the office to enforce political control in the late nineteenth century. No raids could be conducted without his authority, and the *olotu* (warriors) could not embark without his leadership.

The Kabowei did not migrate far afield, but contributed settlers to towns in Ogo (originally Owha-Urhobo), Odoni (Tarakiri), and Okparabe (Urhobo). The Kabowei are now often bilingual in Kabo and Urhobo/Isoko because of close contact and intermarriage.

The town of Aven in Kabobulou Creek claims to be Kabowei, but informants at Patani told Hubbard and Rutherfoord that its founder was from "the Epio clan on the eastern side of the delta", or that he was a man named Pio. These remarks clearly point to Epie-Atissa origin on the Northern Limit of the Central Delta.

Kabo contacts would seem to have been largely with the Mein on the Forcados River and with the related Kumbowei. Relations with other peoples may have been mainly in slave-raids. It was such raids that drove the Erohwa inland from their original home on the Forcados River close to the site of Patani.

7. Kumbowei

When Kumbowei withdrew from his brother Kabowei, he settled only a short distance away on the Forcados River. His own sons, Agolo, Sagba, Apelei, and Angia left the new settlement after his death to found the towns of Agoloma, Sagbama, Apeleibiri (Toru and Bolou) and Angiama.

The *pere* of Kumbowei *ibe* now resides at Sagbama, and all Kumbowei worship Kumbowei Ziba, parallel to Kabo Ziba, and Gbaran Ziba. The additional fact that all Kumbowei towns are closely sited on the Forcados River should have encouraged unity and the growth of central authority. On the contrary, Kumbo settlements seem to have attained a position of equilibrium and autonomy, so that each could pursue its own course without reference to its neighbours. This is the obvious explanation of the situation when in 1884, the British consul, Alexander Bedford had to sign protection treaties in turn with Agoloma, Angiama, and Sagbama whereas he needed to sign but a single treaty at Patani with the Kabowei. The other possible explanation is that no *pere* existed in 1884 to provide overall leadership of the Kumbowei.

Sagbama Bronzes

There are few recorded traditions of the Kumbowei, and the historical significance of the bronzes found at Sagbama has not yet been fully explained. Horton, reporting on the Sagbama bronzes, among others, implies that they, along with the bronzes from Akugbene, Kiagbodo and Inikorogha, had a "Benin charter of origin", and were connected with the title of *pere*.

The fact of apparent parity between the Kumbowei settlements, all founded by sons of the common ancestor, present similarities with the Mein case where bronzes from Benin were sought as emblems of authority. But it may be noted that recent tradition claims the Inikorogha bronzes of the Seimbiri to have come from the Sagbama-Igbedi Creek from which the Mein had originally come to the Forcados River. This suggestion does not simplify the problems of interpreting the origin and significance of the Sagbama and other delta bronzes. It shows that no easy explanation can be produced before further work is done on all delta bronzes.

8. Operemo

Operemo traditions claim origin from Oporoma in the Central Delta, and are confirmed in essentials by traditions among the Oporoma and Olodiama *ibe* of the Central Delta, and by traditions of the Olodiama of the Western Limit. The traditions show a relationship between the Oporoma, Operemo, and the two Olodiama (of the Central Delta and Western Limit) as well as with the Ogbe Ijo.

According to Operemo traditions, the ancestor, Ekeremo, came from the Central Delta town of Oporoma. There was a fight between the section in which Ekeremo was leader and another section named Angiama. Ekeremo people lost and fled the town. They settled first at Oru-Ekeremo.

From Oru-Ekeremo were founded the present settlements of Amabilo, Ndoro, Ekeremo, and Ogbe-Ijo: a result, apparently, of a quarrel over the division of meat (*wan*). The large Operemo town of Ojobo was an offshoot of Amabilo.

After the dispersion from Oru-Ekeremo, the dominant lineage would seem to have settled at Amabilo, for that is where the shrine of Ekeremo Egbesu is to be found. To this shrine came representatives of all member villages (including Ogbe-Ijo) to an annual festival at which the head of Operemo *ibe* served as priest.

The worship of Ekeremo Egbesu by a priest-ruler presents the classical model of Ijo *ibe* government through the sanctions of religion. The worship of Egbesu serves to buttress the traditions of relationship among the Operemo, the two Olodiama, and Ogbe Ijo. The Oporoma of the Central Delta do not now have Egbesu as the name of their national god, but Boupere of the Oporoma was also a war god, and its priest presided at all *ibe* annual festivals.

9. Oyakiri (Beni)

Oyakiri relations were close with their immediate neighbours, Ogboin and Apoi of the Central Delta. They also had contact with the Aboh and other Ibo-related peoples at the head of the delta. The Oyakiri town of Odoni is, in fact, believed to contain Ibo elements. Oyakiri traditions of origin contain reference to this contact with the delta confluence.

The earliest recorded Oyakiri traditions named a man, Ijaw (Ijo), as the original ancestor. Ijo lived at Benin but left because of incessant wars there. He came down to Aboh on the Niger. Ijo died at Aboh, and his son Orumo was driven out. He came to Toru-Ibeni. Orumo's son, Oyakiri, moved into the Kunu Creek and founded Ayama-Ibeni. The people, accordingly, derive their name from Oyakiri, whose sons founded the component towns, but the alternative name of Beni or Ibeni, apparently belonged to Oyakiri's wife, and mother of the sub-group.

This Oyakiri account makes three main points that recur in the traditions of other Ijo *ibe* in the Western and Central Delta: a place of origin outside the delta in Benin, descent from a man named Ijo, and a route of migration through Aboh. The Oyakiri tradition differs from the others by making the founder, Oyakiri, a grandson rather than a direct son of Ijo, and by stating that Ijo died at Aboh. But like the other accounts, the ancestors of Ijo himself are not named, neither are his other sons besides the ancestors of the Oyakiri.

The expansion of the Oyakiri from Ibeni town is explained by the stereotype of division of the meat of an animal (*wan*, duiker) killed in a hunt. The lineages of Oyakiri's sons separated to found the member settlements.

The migrations from the parent settlement appear to have ended any co-operative action or central organization. Fellows reported that the town of Adagbabiri used to produce the priest of Ibeni Egbesu before its destruction by a British punitive expedition in 1911, and that for twenty years prior to 1930, no priests had been appointed. He implies that annual festivals of the Oyakiri used to be observed prior to 1911, and that even then some of the member villages never returned to attend after their migration from Ibeni.

Our Oyakiri informants knew nothing of Ibeni Egbesu or of any other national god. The member settlements seem largely to have been governed through their village organizations, being held together solely by the traditions of common origin and a common dialect.

451

10. Ogulagha

The Ogulagha live around the estuary of the Forcados River, an area which was a centre of Portuguese trade from at least 1485 when a royal privilege was issued for trade on the five slave rivers (i.e., the Mahin, Benin, Escravos, Forcados and Ramos). The early sixteenth century document (1522) reproduced by Ryder mentions Warri as Oeyre, and implies the activity of Benin traders, and the sale on the Forcados of produce from the Urhobo and even Yoruba country (Ijebu and Ondo?). The best known early reference to Ijo on the Nigerian coast between the Forcados and Bonny rivers occurs in Pereira who wrote of the Forcados, "the inhabitants along this river are called Huela". It would be fair to consider this a reference to the Ogula who would thus be early dwellers of the Forcados estuary, and probable participants in the overseas trade in slaves, blue shells, pepper, panther skins, and cotton cloths.

Some two centuries after Pereira, Barbot named a village, Poloma, "on a little river which is lost in the Forcados", which was "inhabited mostly by fishermen". No town named Poloma now exists in the area, but both the name and the description of its people are clearly identifiable as Ijo.

Ogula traditions of origin, or the absence of them, may, in fact, be a reflection of the antiquity of their settlement in the region of the Forcados River. The earliest record of their traditions state that the common ancestor, Ogula, "dropped out of a cloud" at Okibo on the west bank of the River Ramos at the site of the fishing village of Idumukpamu. Ogula came with a wife named Ereara. He later left the Ramos and died at the new settlement of Ogula or Ogulagha on the Forcados estuary. He had four sons, Sabagoni, Ikiriaba, Orugboabala, and Akiri. Orugboabala migrated into the Itsekiri area and founded the town of Orugbo near Ode Itsekiri or Big Warri (i.e., Oere or Iwere).

This migration of Orugboabala to the region of the Itsekiri kingdom is the only mention of contact with the Itsekiri. But the traditions of the neighbouring Iduwini, as of the Itsekiri, refer to migrations of the ruling dynasty under Ginuwa (originally of Benin) from a point east of the Ramos (at Amatu) north-westwards to Warri through the Forcados River.

452

The possibility of early Itsekiri movement through this area together with the activity of Benin merchants implied by the Portuguese records may account for the points at which Ogula institutions differ from those of other Ijo *ibe* of the Western Delta. It has been noted, for example, that the name, Olokumieyin, of the national god stated to have been brought by the ancestor, Ogula, is not Ijo and its meaning unknown to the Ogulagha Ijo. Second, unlike other *ibe*, the priest of the national god, Olokumieyin, was not considered head of Ogula *ibe*, the position of informal head being assumed by the elder, *Amaokosowei*, of Ogula town. Third, the very name, Ogulagha, meant "a place of meeting but where there is no council", implying that the Ogula did not originally have the village councils or *Amagula* characteristic of Ijo village organization. In 1930 there were *Amagula*, but "no meeting house or fixed time for meeting."

These divergent traits were almost certainly the source of local speculation which gave birth to the traditions reported by Hook among the Iduwini and other neighbouring Ijo that the Ogula were of foreign Kru origin (i.e., Kru of Liberia transported to the delta as European ships' crew and marooned on the coast).

11. Iduwini

The Iduwini occupy the bulk of the coast of the Western Delta from the Forcados River to the Central Delta. The traditions of the freshwater Ijo to the hinterland ascribe great age to the Iduwini (e.g., Tuomo reference to Aghoro). This is partially confirmed by the earliest European accounts of the Nigerian coast. Pereira (1508?) stated that there were Ijo all the way eastwards of the Forcados River, and reported as follows on the people of the Ramos River:

> 'The inhabitants of this country are called Jos (Ijo)... . There has been no trade here so far, nor do we know if there is any possibility of trade. All this country is densely populated and thickly wooded; the interior is intersected by other rivers... the inhabitants communicating by canoes made of a single trunk.'

453

It is clear then that the Ramos was overshadowed by the trade on the Forcados River in the sixteenth century. But traditions in the area suggest that the slave trade came to be plied on a moderate scale from the port of Aghoro on the Ramos as well.

Iduwini traditions too confirm the reputation of antiquity since they do not mention a place of origin outside their present location. The available traditions name the Iduwini town of Amatu (meaning, the origin of towns) as the place from which all other towns of the sub-group sprang, the migrations moving westwards to the Forcados River from Amatu. The Orobiri and related settlements, also known as Kou are, however, not derived from Amatu.

Although the Iduwini arc now relatively isolated from other peoples of the Western Delta, the presence of bronzes at Amatu indicates contact, possibly of a commercial nature, with the hinterland. All available evidence relate the bronzes to purely religious uses. Horton saw the four bronze bells "in the shrine of Suogbosu" (Suo Egbesu) i.e., Sky God (cf. Suwo Eru of the Furupagha), national god of the Iduwini, and within the shrine they hung round the neck of a wooden figure of Suo Egbesu. Furthermore, recent accounts of the position of *pere* or priest of the Iduwini national god at Amatu rule out any political or Benin relationship. The *pere* of Iduwini was "appointed" by the god directly and merely honoured by all the member settlements afterwards. Once invested, the *pere* stayed at Amatu to carry out purely priestly functions. He was not permitted to go outside his domains—at least not northwards into the freshwater delta. This last taboo confirms the view that the Iduwini *pere* institution was the original Ijo religious office and had nothing to do with a Benin-derived political institution. The bronze bells were clearly imported for purely ritual purposes from Benin or elsewhere.

The Ginuwa tradition of the Itsekiri repeated by the Iduwini could have been taken over directly from published Itsekiri accounts or would refer to early contact between the founders of the Itsekiri state and the Iduwini. This is especially likely as some Iduwini also migrated from Amatu to the Forcados River, settling in the neighbourhood of Burutu. This movement could possibly

454

have followed in the wake of Itsekiri migration in the same direction. In any case, the Iduwini in the Forcados River area were well placed to trade for Benin bronzes or other articles from the international commercial activity on that river—including Benin, Itsekiri, and apparently also Yoruba and, of course, the Portuguese.

Conclusion

A number of broad conclusions emerge from this survey of Western Ijo oral traditions of origin and migration, relations with neighbouring peoples, and of internal developments.

The greater number of Western Delta *ibe* cite Central Delta homes of origin. The Obotebe, Seimbiri and Operemo are unambiguous on this point. This follows the pattern of migration observed for the Western Delta Limit. But the Kabowei and Kumbowei refer to migrations from the Western Limit at Oproza (Gbaramatu) into the Western Delta, and of the Gbaran *ibe* back into the Central Delta. This indicates a rebound, since the Gbaramatu themselves tell of their original migration from Gbaran town (Apoi) in the Central Delta. The Tuomo, too seem to have emerged from the same Gbaramatu series of migrations. There is a third group of Western Delta *ibe* which mention Benin as the original home of a remote ancestor who then moved to Aboh and finally into the Central area of the Delta from where a final migration westwards brought them into the Western Delta. The Mein, Tarakiri, and Oyakiri have such traditions. These traditions seem to indicate the remote influence and prestige of the two most powerful inland kingdoms of Benin and Aboh bordering on the Western Delta. It may be noted that in the Western Delta Limit where the influence of Benin was more direct, no traditions of Benin origin were told. The Olodiama account rather attempted to claim parity of an ancestor with the Oba by deriving both from Ife.

Finally, the Ogulagha, and Iduwini seem to have always been there on the coastal belt, having no traditions of origin from elsewhere.

455

The traditions indicate commercial, cultural, and political contacts with the three centralized polities of this part of Nigeria, namely, the Benin empire, the Itsekiri kingdom, and the Aboh kingdom. Traders from the Western Delta Limit and beyond (e.g., the Yoruba from the far west) were also active. But the most intimate relations were established with the Urhobo and Isoko to the immediate Northern Limit. The Mein sent their political aspirants to Benin to obtain titles and regalia, but it was Urhobo and Isoko women they married. And it was to the Urhobo/Isoko country their adventurers migrated to found related settlements and communities. The exchange of foodstuffs and fish is not specifically mentioned in many traditions but the few direct references obviously indicate diverse points of contact between the Ijo and Urhobo/Isoko.

The bronzes found at various locations in the Western Delta confirm the crossing of various influences over even remote areas of the delta. A political connection with Benin seems confirmed for the Mein bronzes, but not for all other finds. In other cases the bronzes are related completely to traditional religious institutions. The variations in styles too may reveal differences in provenance.

In internal developments we find all stages of adaptation of the characteristic Ijo village political and religious institutions to various circumstances. There were those where the village assembly and its age-based organization was all, and no formal links were forged between member villages of the *ibe*. In others the religious organ of the national god and High Priest provided the only central focus for common action. The Mein, Kabowei, and Iduwini provide interesting variations.

Among the Iduwini, religious sanctions were supreme. The High Priest or *pere* was produced by no human agency and was, apparently, the property of no single lineage or settlement—the only proviso being that he must be the son of a large dowry wife of an Iduwini husband. Once appointed, he performed purely ritual functions over the entire *ibe* and was confined to the home base.

When a representative of Iduwini was required to perform political functions outside the area in modern Nigeria, therefore, the *pere* and people had to elect a new leader, the "clan head", *Ibenanawe*, *ibe*-owner.

Both Mein and Kabo traditions suggest a transmission of authority from the founding ancestor through his lineage on the basis of seniority in age among his surviving descendants. The Mein on the Forcados River modified the idea of *Mein Okosuwei*, substituting a political title combining hereditary succession with the principle of individual achievement. The trips to Benin and accumulation of bronze regalia added the new element. Here, the priest and the ruler became different individuals, but the ruler still had to be invested with some mystical powers—as the representative and priest of the founding ancestor.

The Kabo, too, derived their leaders from the direct descendant of the founding ancestor and developed an organization strong enough to carry out the stupendous job of damming the Forcados River. The political system was adequate to achieve such team work and organization but, apparently, not on a continuous basis, and not after the dispersal from Kabobulou Creek and Patani.

It may be noted that it was these two sub-groups, the Mein and Kabowei, which were most active in the internal trade of the Western Delta—although the ports were in Ogulagha and Iduwini territory.

A complete chronology for the early history of the Western Delta still eludes us. Obotebe and Mein genealogies suggest dates in the eighteenth and seventeenth centuries for the earliest events related in their traditions, but the Portuguese documents show that the Ogulagha and Iduwini, or other Ijo peoples, occupied all of the coastal region long before the sixteenth century.

CHAPTER 20
THE CENTRAL DELTA
Atei Mark Okorobia

Introduction

The Ijo of the Central Niger Delta are significant for our understanding of the history and culture of the Ijo world in more than one way. First, they occupy the geographical centre of the Niger Delta. Secondly, *over* 90% of all Ijo groups in the Niger Delta claim this region as the homeland of their ancestors. Thirdly, the Ijo of the Central Niger Delta have not attracted as much scholarly attention as the Eastern Delta Ijo. The best the area has got till date is, perhaps, *The Land and People of Bayelsa State: Central Niger Delta*, a multi-disciplinary compendium on the Ijo and their neighbours in the Central Niger Delta edited by Alagoa. Finally, the history of the oil and gas industry cannot be written without giving due attention to the Central Delta, particularly, of Otokopiri, near Oloibiri, from where the first oil exported by Nigeria was extracted in 1956.

In this chapter then, we state the role of the Central Delta Ijo people in the history and culture of the Ijo ethnic nationality, paying special attention to their origins, bearing in mind the fact that a clear comprehension of their roots will help our understanding of the roots of other Ijo people who have traced their ancestry to the Central Delta. Other issues emphasized are, their role in the Atlantic Trade; their experiences under British colonialism; the struggle for the creation of Bayelsa State, and efforts at achieving sustainable development.

The Ijo People of the Central Niger Delta

In this chapter, we modify Alagoa (1972, 2005) to include the following groups as the Ijo of the Central Niger Delta:

1. Apoi, 2. Basan 3. Olodiama, 4. Oporoma, 5. Ogboin, 6. Tungbo, 7. Kolokuma, 8. Opokuma, 9. Gbaran, 10. Zarama, 11. Okordia, 12. Buseni 13. Ekpetiama, 14. Tarakiri, 15. Boma/Bumo, 16. Akasa/Akaha/Akassa, 17.Okoroma, and 18.Nembe.

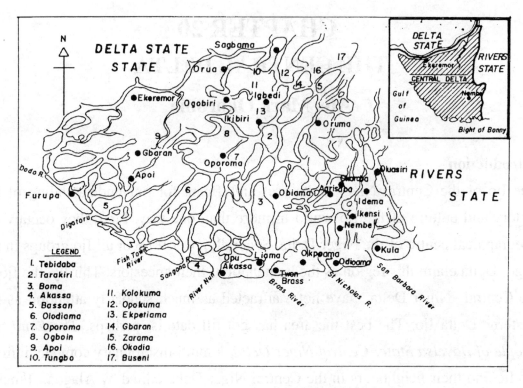

Fig. 20.1: The Ijo of the Central Delta

LEGEND
1. Tebidaba
2. Tarakiri
3. Boma
4. Akassa
5. Bassan
6. Olodiama
7. Oporoma
8. Ogboin
9. Apoi
10. Tungbo
11. Kolokuma
12. Opokuma
13. Ekpetiama
14. Gbaran
15. Zarama
16. Okodia
17. Buseni

Community Traditions.

We trace the historical origins of each community as they have been recorded in their own oral traditions. Thereafter, we have attempted to interpret and evaluate them in the light of supporting evidence from historical linguistics, archaeology, ethnography and palynology. The accounts have been derived mainly from Alagoa (1972 and 1999), with a few updates.

1.   Kolokuma

The Kolokuma share the same ancestral roots with the people of Tarakiri (West) and Opokuma. Their common ancestor has been variously named Ndo or Indo, and he is said to have originated from the ancient Benin Kingdom by Newington (1938) and Ile-Ife by Owonaro (1949). He is said to have eventually settled within the Igbedi Creek. The ancient site of Agadagbabou on Wilberforce Island is named as one of their early places of settlement. Another old site was Orubou or Oruamatoru. The 'sons' of the eponymous ancestor of the Kolokuma, named in versions of traditions as Kolokumaowei, Kala-Okun and Aluku, eventually led the people out of the Igbedi Creek into the Nun River.

460

Plate 20.1: Oloibiri oil well and signboard (Courtesy of Tam Fiofori)

Of the identified nine lineages or *dani* that came to be established on the Nun River, five have been named as founded by sons of Kolokumaowei without variant accounts of origin, namely, Egbebiridani, Isedani, Ofodani, Oloudani, and Opoidani. The other four lineages have variant versions naming outside places of origin. Thus Egbedani is stated to have been founded by Egbe, 'son of Uge and the grandson of Mein, the founder of Mein clan', Osumadani by 'Eweli, an immigrant from Awka in Ibo land', Abadani from Anyama in Tarakiri (East); and Burudani from Awka.

The use of the term *dani* is peculiar to the Kolokuma in the Niger Delta. But more significant is the ordering of the lineages in a prescribed order of precedence or seniority at the *yengidie* ceremony as follows: Burudani, Egbedani, Abadani, Isedani, Osumadani, Opoidani and Egbebiridani. It is stated that Ofodani is an imaginary *dani* created in memory of the last son of Kolokumaowei who had died young. Opoidani is also no longer in existence, having migrated to Apoi (East); and Egbebiridani is also believed to have disappeared in a catastrophe or absorbed into other *dani*. The pre-eminent position accorded Burudani apparently derives from

461

the fact that priests of the Kolokuma Egbesu were chosen form this lineage from the time of settlement at Orubou. In recent times priests have come from the settlements of Oloubiri and Foubiri. Similarly, according to Owonaro (1949: 20, 23), Egbedani owed its second place ranking to the fact that priests of the god, Okpotu, 'one of the principal (if not the chief) idols' of the Kolokuma was chosen from the lineage. There are indications that the worship of Okpotu, indeed, preceded the ascendancy of Kolokuma Egbesu.

2.   Opokuma

Opokuma traditions run parallel to those of Kolokuma, Opokumaowei or Opu-Okun, being the senior brother of Kolokumaowei or Kala-Okun. Indeed, Opokumaowei moved out of Agadagbabou and the Igbedi Creek into the Nun ahead of the Kolokuma. Opokumaowei first settled at Ofonitoru, but later founded the principal town of the group, which eventually took the name of his giant son, Oko, as Okowari. Variant traditions credit the foundation of Okowari to another son of Opokumaowei, named Ise.

In the course of time, the Opokuma are said to have been joined on the Nun by immigrants from Ikibiri in Ekpetiama to establish Akaranbiri, and others from Oyakiri (Ibeni) to found Gbanranbiri. Other immigrants from Ogobiri Mein are said to be responsible for the establishment of Oyobu. Going by Newington (1938), it would appear that the first god worshipped by the Opokuma was Egbelekwe, which they eventually abandoned for Opokuma Egbesu.

3.   Gbaran (Gbarain)

According to Gbaran traditions, each of Gbaranowei's sons founded the towns of Okotiama, Ogboloma, Agbia, Okolobiri, Koroama, Obinagha, Nedugo, and Polaku. Polaku at the mouth of the Taylor Creek was probably settled only after July 18, 1854, when Baikie (1856:39-40) named the Creek after a member of his crew, Taylor who mistook it for the River Nun, and directed the ship into it. As at then they did not report a village at the site where Polaku now stands.

The worship of Gbaran Ziba serves as a unifying force in Gbaran. In every July they gather at Okotiama to celebrate the first fruits festival, *uziye*, and a fishing festival at the pond, Odoidi.

462

4. Zarama

The Zarama community in the Yenagoa Local government Area occupy the interior part of the Taylor Creek along with the Okordia, and Buseni, possibly prior to the arrival of the Gbaran who occupy the rest of the creek outwards to its mouth. The Zarama dialect is related to Engenni, and is classified Delta Edoid along with Epie–Atissa and Degema/Udekama.

5. Okordia (Akita)

This small community along the Taylor Creek in the Yenagoa Local Government Area of Bayelsa State is classified as Inland Ijo along with Buseni and Oruma. According to Newington (1938), Akida, the founder of Okordia, migrated from Ado (Benin) to Nembe, to Oruma, and eventually to 'Aguobiri the senior quarter of Okordia'. Nembe traditions specify the site from which the migration took place as Oboloma, an early settlement site in Nembe history (Alagoa 1999).

The opinions from the Okodia, largely agree with the external testimonies of their origin. According to Idobozi (2000:13), an Okodia-born historian, Akida, the founder of Okodia came from Ado (Benin) and settled at Oboloma (Ogbolomabiri, Nembe). A disagreement arising form the sharing of the duiker pepper soup made Akida to move to the Taylor Creek and settled at the present site of Agbobiri. Here, Akida had four sons, namely Akumoni, Anyamabele and Ikarama. These sons founded the four settlements of Okodia named after them. The name Okodia itself, is believed to be an adulteration of Akida.

According to a variant tradition by the Inogula group in Okodia, it was when settlements had already been established for many years that a second group of people came from Oboloma, Nembe to join the first settlers. The new comers settled at separate quarters near Agbobiri which they called Tein. After some years the population of Tein started to dwindle very rapidly, compelling the remaining people to desert the area for the four earlier settlements.

6. Buseni (Biseni)

Newington (1938:11) recorded traditions claiming the founder of Buseni to be brother 'of the same father' with Akida, the founder of Okodia. Nembe and Oruma traditions similarly assign both Okodia and Buseni to the same migrations from Oboloma through Oruma to the Taylor Creek (Alagoa 1999). In a recent study by Okorobia (forthcoming), the Buseni traced their ancestry to an eponymous ancestor, Biseni, who migrated from the ancient Benin kingdom. Biseni had ten sons, each of whom established a village of his own. Ultimately, they fused into three major settlements, namely Tuburu, (established by Biseni's first son), Egbebiri (established by Biseni's second son), and Tein.

Presently, the Biseni people occupy some seven villages: Akpide, Tuburu, Egbebiri 1 and II, Akodonu (Akionu), Uturuama, Otein I and II, and Kilama. Tuburu is the traditional headquarters of the group.

7. Ekpetiama

Traditions at Ekpetiama in the Yenagoa Local Government Area begin with the cliché of Ado/Benin origin, but it was itself the location of a major dispersal centre named in various versions as Opuanbou, Opuanbiri, Isomabou/Isomobou, or by the name of one of its offshoots, Ikibiri. Pressure from Tarakiri (East), in particular, of Oweikorogha, apparently triggered some of the migrations out of the area. According to some traditions, sons of the founder, Ekpetiamaowei, moved out of Opuanbou to establish Tombia, Bumodi, Agudama, Akabiri and Gbarantoru.

Other migrants of Ekpetiama are claimed to have founded Seinbiri *ibe* in Delta State, Tombia (in the Kalabari area of Rivers State), Swali and Onopa in Epie-Atissa, Assay (in Isoko), and Okiri/Umoru (in Aboh), Delta State.

The Ekpetiama group is held together by these inter-locking traditions of origin, and by their common worship of Amadosu with shrines at Tombia and Bumodi.

8.   Boma (Bumo)

The popular Obiama dispersion centre is claimed by the Bumo of Southern Ijaw local Government Area as their place of origin. The founders of Bumo and Tarakiri (East), believed to be sons of Obi, migrated from Obiama in the neighbouring Okoroma area of the Nembe Local Government Area, to establish their separate communities.

Bumo had twelve sons who are credited with the establishment of the twelve component towns of Bumo. However, in the course of time, new immigrants were incorporated into the group. For example, Peremabiri is said to have been established by a son of Okoroma in the Nembe Local Government Area, while Ikianbiri is also claimed to have been founded by an immigrant from Ogboin *ibe*.

The Oruokolo (Kolobie) community in Brass Local Government Area, are said to be migrants from Bumo. From Igbematoru, migrants also went to Kamatoru/Sangana, while from Ekowe/Ekeu in Bumo; migrants went to establish Ekowe (in Isoko, Delta State).

Bumo towns developed individual religious contacts with neighbouring communities such as the cult of Ekine at Seibiri (now Opuama) related to Ogidiga the national god of Nembe.

9.   Bassan (Basan)

The Basan of Southern Ijaw Local Government Area is a group with disparate traditions of origin, evidenced also by the diversities of dialect. Thus, 'Gbaraun and Koluama speak somewhat differently from the rest and from each other'.

Traditions gathered at Furupa claimed origin from 'Arogbo-Furupa', which is in clear conflict with the claim of the Furupagha of Edo State that they originated from 'Ijo Furupagha', that is, Bassan Furupa. The conclusion we can draw from this is that the people of Bassan Furupa have forgotten a prior place of origin. Ezetu claimed Oporoma migrants; while Koluama received Ossiama

465

(Oyakiri/Beni) migrants; and Ukubie claimed Iselema (Itsekiri) migrants through Lobia/Lubia. On the other hand, Lobia/Lubia received migrants from Okpoama in the Brass Local Government Area of Bayelsa State, and Lobia itself established the offshoot settlements of Azuzuama and Akparatubo. On the other hand, Ekeni claims kinship ties with Ke in the Degema Local Government Area of Rivers State, and possibly with Beletiema, Egwema and Oruokolo (Kolobie) in Brass Local Government Area of Bayelsa State.

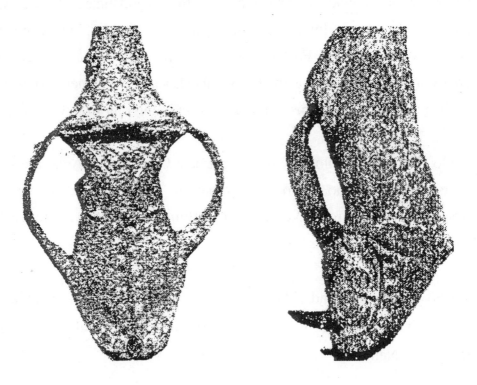

Plate 20.2: Bronze canine skulls from Okpoama

The Bassan have been generally reported to be particularly proficient as middlemen in the internal trade across the Niger Delta between the Itsekiri of the Western Delta and the Nembe and Kalabari of the Eastern Delta. They distributed in the Eastern Delta, Itsekiri pots and cassava meal, farina/*ifenia,* in the seventeenth century. The Bassan were also expert at the manufacture of salt, *Ijo* or *Bassan fu,* (the Ijo or Bassan salt) manufactured from the aerial roots of the red mangrove, a variety of salt in great demand in the internal long distance trade across the length and breadth of the Niger Delta.

10.   Apoi (East)

The Apoi/Kalasuo Creek area in Southern Ijaw Local Government Area was a major dispersal centre. Each of the Apoi settlements has a different tradition of origin. The settlement identified as Apoi was originally composed of nine wards, including Ogboinbou, Apoi, Okotoaza, Umgboluama, and Inikorogha. Apoi was established by Kalasuo, whose sons are also credited with the foundation of Kemebiama, Kokologbene, Ogboinbiri, Sampou and Azama.

Gbaraun, the largest settlement in the group, and which is composed of Egbesubiri, Kapabiri, and Aguobiri, claims origin from Oporoma, and eventually absorbed the remnants of the old settlements of Igwebiri, Umgboluama, and Inikorogha.

The Apoi area has come to gain great reputation as a centre of dispersion because of the many communities that claim origins from the area. For instance, Aguobiri (Tarakiri-East) was established by migrants from Aguobiri (Gbaraun, Apoi); just as Opu-Akassa was founded by migrants from Kassama (Apoi). Similarly, the people of Apoi (West) in Ondo State claim that their ancestors came from Okotoaza and Umgboluama wards of Apoi town (Apoi East). Again, the Arogbo of Ondo State and the Gbaranmatu of Delta State claim origins from Gbaraun town in Apoi (East). In the process of these outward migrations from Apoi, they also gave their Egbesu cult to Arogbo as wells as their Oborowe cult to the Apoi (West).

Like the Bassan, the Apoi served as middlemen in the trans-Niger Delta trade. For canoes in the Western Delta Fringe (Kolomotoru) in Delta and Ondo States, they exchanged local salt and fish, and had similar commercial intercourse with communities eastwards as far as Bonny in Rivers State.

11.   Oporoma (Oporomo)

The headquarters of Southern Ijaw Local Government Area, Oporoma, was a major dispersal centre in the Central Delta. Both Ekeremo (Operemo, Oporoma) in Ekeremor Local Government Area, and Olodiama (East) in Southern Ijaw Local Area, claim to have originated from Oporoma. Porter (1931:7) a colonial administrator who was the earliest to document Oporoma traditions, records a tradition that the founder of Oporoma had 'dropped from a cloud''. Recent traditions claim that the founder came from Ado (Benin). Both traditions are indications that the Oporoma do not remember a prior place of origin. The different wards or constituents of Oporoma were believed to have been established by the sons of Oporoma, the eponymous ancestor. Recent accounts from Angiama claim that its founder was the father of Oporoma. They cite their drum praise name, 'Agi Oporoma' as evidence.

The shrine of the war god of Oporoma, Boupere, is located at Osokoma, which is also the home of the first priest, Osoko, son of Oporoma.

12.   Tarakiri (East)

Eastern Tarakiri has been described as 'a comparatively hard-to-reach group' in Southern Ijaw Local Government Area by Alagoa (1999:86). Going by traditions at Tarakiri, they originated from the Obiama dispersion centre, together with the Boma, many settlements in Brass, Nembe and Ogbia, Local Government Areas. Oweikorogha, an ancient Tarakiri town is also said to have attacked the dispersal centre of Isomabou (Ikibiri, Ekpetiama) with firearms supplied by either Nembe and/or Kalabari middlemen. All the settlements making up the group are said to have been established by sons of Tarakiriowei; with Obelele (Obololi) being the 'senior village', hosting the shrine of Ayama Ziba their group cult (Newington 1938:9-12). Ayama (or Anyama) is the only reported case of outward migration from the Tarakiri (East) group to Abadani in the Kolokuma area.

13.   Ogboin

Ogboin, the founder of the Ogboin clan in Southern Ijaw Local Government Area, is said to have originated from Ado (Benin). Recent accounts named his place of origin to be Orubiribaubolou, inside a creek north of Otuan. His sons are said to have come out of the creek to establish Otuan, Amassoma and Ogbono in (Delta State). It was from Amassoma that Amatolo was established by someone described as the grandson of Ogboin.

External pressures from the Kolokuma, Tungbo, Yenaka (in Epie-Atissa), Akede (in Oyakiri/Beni), and Nembe, in form of wars, helped to unite the competing towns of Ogboin together. The national deity of Ogboin, symbolized by the *Ogboin* (mango) tree had 'moved from Otuan to Amassoma' (Newington 1938:12). The Ogboin have given birth to a number of other communities now located both within and outside Bayelsa State. Oko, son of Alumu, son of Oboro (founder of Amassoma), son of Ogboin, is reported to have migrated to Okrika mainland where he established one of the most ancient settlements in the Okrika kingdoms in Rivers State, named after him as Okopiri (or Okochiri). Other migrants also went from Otuan to Ikianbiri, Boma.

14. Tungbo

The founder, Tungboowei, is stated to have come from the Ogbia town of Otuokpoti. His neighbours were the Mein, but he sought an isolated place. He was unable to escape kidnappers even in his creek location, but managed to establish a community. The protective deity, Akpolokia, was apparently found in the bush behind the settlement. The Tungbo speak a distinctive Ijo dialect.

15. Olodiama (East)

According to Porter (1931:9) and Alagoa (1999:87) the traditions of Olodiama of Southern Ijaw Local Government Area derived the founder, Olode/Olodi from Oporoma. His sons founded Ondewari, Olugbobiri, and Ikeinghabiri; and his grandson founded Ikebiri. Ekpa, founder of Korokorosei, was, however, said to have come from Patani (Kabo). Olodiama (West) in Edo State also derived their founders from Ikebiri, Ondewari, and Olugbobiri.

One institution that confirms the link between the two Olodiama groups east and west is the cult of Egbesu. This cult also links them with Ekeremo (Operemo), another group with traditions of migration from Oporoma. Again, traditions among the Olodiama (East) have it that the priests of Boupere in Oporoma used to pay annual pilgrimage to the shrine of Olodiama Egbesu at Ikebiri, the place at which the founder of Obotebe in Delta State also learnt to worship Egbesu (Alagoa 1999:88).

16. Nembe

The Nembe developed city state institutions of the type identified in Bonny, Elem Kalabari and Okrika in the Eastern Delta. These centralized institutions made them the centres of attraction for the visiting European traders in slaves and later palm produce.

Early migrants came from the dispersal centre of Obiama led by Olodi, believed to be the senior (Alagoa 1964: 126). Others were Obolo and Onyo. These three established Olodiama, Oboloma and Onyoma, the most important of the six or seven wards, which ultimately became part of the Nembe metropolis. Outside the metropolis, the towns of Twon, Okpoama, Odioma, Egwema, Beletiema and Liama, among others (in the Brass Local Government Area) also have traditions of early settlement by Ijo-speaking people from the dispersal centre of Obiama.

In its second period of development, a group of Itsekiri migrants, (described in the oral traditions as immigrants from Benin) arrived with Ogidiga, a war god, and a sacred sword, *ada*. The new arrivals were settled at the Oromabiri quarter of the metropolis. Their Ogidiga cult eventually provided the means of unifying all the component communities of the city-state through religious ties and sanctions.

A third group of migrants came from the Abureni (Mini) area to the immediate north- east of Nembe metropolis. They are credited with the establishment of the united Nembe kingdom through the instrumentality of Kala Ekule, who is sometimes described as 'son' or descendant of Olodi, the founder of Olodiama. From thenceforth a single line of kings ruled the metropolis until about the 17th century, when as a result of an un-reconciled succession dispute, the kingdom was split into two. While King Ogbodo, the last Amanyanabo of the united Nembe kingdom crossed over to the Bassambiri moiety of the metropolis and established his rule over the eastern half of the kingdom, his cousin, Mingi, took over the western half with his headquarters at Ogbolomabiri. This marked the dawn of the dual monarchical system in Nembe political history. In spite of the split, however, the Nembe are known in the course of their long history, to have acted in unity, especially when their collective interest or destiny was threatened.

Plate 20.3:
A terracota figurine from Onyoma, Nembe,
possibly representing a priest king, *Onyoma pere*:

The Nembe accumulated wealth and power in the period of the trans-Atlantic trade during which its contacts with its neighbours in the Niger Delta, especially in the Ogbia and Ijo communities along the River Nun and Ekole Creek, and up the River Niger were expanded. Its influence within the present Nembe, Brass and to some extent, Ogbia Local Government Areas was also considerably increased. The demand and challenges of the Trans-Atlantic trade also brought Nembe into commercial, diplomatic and cultural relations with her Eastern Ijo neighbours, the Bille, Kalabari, Ibani (Bonny), and Okrika, as well as into competition for trading areas along the Orashi, and up the River Niger to Aboh, Onitsha and Idah.

17. Okoroma

The Okoroma *ibe* in Nembe Local Government Area represents a group of communities with traditions of origin relating them to Ogbia, but with very intimate historical relations with Nembe. This explains why most Okoroma people now speak Nembe as their first language and only speak Ogbia as a second language. According to traditions recorded at Ologoama (Otokoroma), the founder of the group was a son of Ogbia, who migrated with his father from Benin through Iselema (Warri), to *Ogbia n'Otokolo* (Ogbia island) on the Brass River. And that it was from there that he eventually moved northwards and established Otokoroma, re-named Ologoama by Nembe traders after Ologo, son of Okoroma.

The Okoroma affiliations to Ogbia are with the Ayama and Oloibiri groups and not to the Kolo group. In addition, most of the settlements now listed as Okoroma were founded in the nineteenth century by Nembe merchant princes such as the Tereke settlements and Dogu-Ewoama (Alagoa 1999:90).

18. Akassa (Akaha)

Going by oral traditions gathered from the Akassa (in the Brass Local Government Area), their ancestor, La, migrated from Kassama in Apoi (East). La is said to have settled at Opu-Akassa on the east bank of the Nun River estuary. However, by the next generation, the Opu-Akassa migrants decided to cross to the west bank which became the centre of Akassa expansion. The descendants of La from Apoi were later joined by fresh migrants from the neighbouring Boma community of Igbematoru. This latter group eventually settled at Kamatoru, popularly known as Sangana.

The Akassa-Ijo dialect is similar to Nembe. That is why linguists (Efere and Williamson 1999) have often labelled the two dialects together as 'Nembe-Akassa' dialect of Ijo. Nevertheless, the Akassa maintain many strong cultural links with their places of origin in the Southern Ijaw Local Government Area and their distinct identity and autonomy.

472

An Evaluation of the Traditions

We base our analysis on Alagoa's (1972) systematic investigation, documentation and publication of the views of the Ijo people themselves.

A number of conclusions can be drawn. First the only places outside the Niger Delta cited by the local traditions as places of Ijo origins are Benin, Aboh, Awka and Ile-Ife. For groups in the Central Niger Delta, we have the single case of the Oporoma, whose people claim that they are autochthonous, that is, that their founding ancestors 'came down from heaven'.

As for the widespread claims to Benin as a place of origin by some Ijo groups in the Central Delta, we can only conclude that such claims are merely a reflection of the desire of the claimants to share in the enormous prestige of the Benin kingdom, and its influence over some of the mainland parts of the Niger Delta. As for Owonaro, who popularised the claim that Ile-Ife was the place of Ijo origin, we can only state that he was persuaded to do so on realising that even Benin had claimed Ile-Ife as a place of origin for their kings. Eboreime (1992) and Banigo (2006) have described the origin of this hypothesis as the crystallization of Ijo cultural nationalism by some Lagos-based Ijo elites who had come in contact with the pan-Yoruba cultural organisation, *Egbe Omo Oduduwa* (which metamorphosed into the Action Group), as a strategy to forge an alliance with a powerful political group against the Igbo domination in the Eastern Region. Outside Benin and Ife, Aboh was another place of prestige within parts of the Central Niger Delta. In this case, there is some credible evidence of actual historical contacts, but these contacts did not reach the level of providing founding populations, beyond supplying small numbers of immigrants. This was the most likely role also for the itinerant Awka blacksmiths (Alagoa 1999:92).

The oral traditions of the Ijo groups in the Central Delta suggest that because they have been in the area for so long it is no longer possible for them to remember the exact places they had come from, or when they came to be where they are. They can only recall aspects of their sojourn that indicate migrations within the delta from one point to another. And here the following places have been identified as

473

primary and secondary centres out of which migrations took place in the Central Delta:

(i)   The Wilberforce Island on which Ogobiri (Mein), Amassoma (Ogboin) and Agudama, Bumodi and Ikibiri (Ekpetiama) stand. This island is the location of the ancient abandoned sites of Agadagbabou of the Kolokuma and Opokuma, and Isomabou and Opuanbiri of the Ekpetiama and other groups

(ii)   Oporoma and its environs.

(iii)   The Apoi Creek region in Southern Ijaw Local Government Area close to the coast.

(iv)   The site of Obiama in the Okoroma area of Nembe Local Government Area bordering both Southern Ijaw and Ogbia Local Government Areas.

Other locations that may be classified as secondary dispersal centres are Oboloma in Nembe metropolis as well as Oruma and Ebala in the Ogbia Local Government Area.

The unrivalled historical linguistic studies of Williamson (1988:95), have provided support for the above conclusions. Her studies have shown that Ijo is a distinct language and developed within the Niger Delta over a period of not less than 7,000 years.

Other disciplines allied to history such as palynology and archaeology have also provided concrete evidence which indicate that the Ijo of the Central Delta have been in continued occupation and exploitation of their present environment for a long time. For example, palynological evidence of farming obtained from cores taken from Ofuabo Creek in Nembe by Sowunmi (1988:46) has shown that the Nembe area was probably occupied by about 2,800 Years Before Present. Similarly, the archaeological investigations in the Central Delta have also provided early dates. For instance, Onyoma in Nembe, produced dates ranging from AD 1275-AD 1845; Saikiripogu at Okpoama/Ewoama, gave dates ranging from AD 1000-AD 1600; while Agadagbabou on Wilberforce Island, has produced evidence dated to the period AD 1640-AD 1730. Koroama in Gbaran provided artifacts dating back to the 17th century AD.

Socio-Political Organisation

The Ijo of the Central Delta evolved three forms of socio-political organisation dictated mainly by environmental and historical forces. The three forms of socio-political organisations were the fishing-cum-farming village system, the fishing village political system and the trading state political system (Alagoa 1970 and 1972).

The Fishing-cum-Farming Village System

The farming/fishing village system is prevalent among the Central Delta communities in the freshwater zone, while those in the saltwater zone developed the fishing village political system. The lineage, *wari* or *polo*, was the primary social and political unit within the farming/fishing village political system of the freshwater delta, since it was through the lineage that a man derived access to farmland and fish ponds. All adult males met in the village assembly, *amagula*, to take decisions on political issues. The oldest member of the village, *amaokosowei*, presided. There was, however, a younger man appointed largely on the basis of merit, for his persuasiveness and gift of oratory, to act in an executive capacity, as spokesman, *ogulasowei*. In ritual matters the village priest, *orukarowei*, took precedence. Unity among member villages of an *ibe* was built on the ideological foundations of culture, history and religion. The unity of the *ibe* was conceived in the areas of culture through the use of a common dialect of Ijo; history through the belief in a common *ibe* ancestor; and religion through the worship of a common tutelary deity, whose priest, the *pere*, presided at the *ibe* festivals. The *pere* also resolved inter-village disputes and protected fugitives from local injustice at his shrine. At the bottom line, the village, and within the village, the lineage, *wari/polo*, remained the basic institutions of the political culture of the communities of the freshwater area of the Central Delta Ijo.

The Fishing Village Political System

The change to the salt water swamp environment, and consequently, to a fishing and salt-making economy by the Nembe resulted in decisive changes in their socio–political organisation, although the same did not happen in every instance.

475

The fishing villages of the Nembe area still had its village assembly, *ama-kobiri*, but it was no longer presided over by its oldest member. The president was re-named *amanyanabo*, meaning 'the owner of the town', and he had to be chosen from the lineage that established the village. The offices of the spokesman and priesthood of the community deity were retained, although the lineage no longer exercised as great an authority on the individual since the fishing grounds on which his livelihood depended came to him through his membership of the village, rather than of a particular lineage. Nevertheless, the bond of common ancestry was weaker than in the farming/fishing village. Accordingly, the fishing village in the Nembe area developed additional institutions for cementing solidarity among its members.

The cultural criteria for belonging to the villages as for the wider Nembe community were strengthened. The scarcity of settlement land in its saltwater environment gave the founding lineage monopoly over the office of *amanyanabo*. Supporting ideology was created in the cult of the settled earth, *amakiri*. The corporate spirit of the village embodying its history, character and destiny was also celebrated in *amatemesuo*. These spiritual entities did not, however, take precedence over the village deity, *amanyana-oru*. They only reinforced the sense of mystical solidarity within the village in its struggles of survival in an inclement environment and against unfriendly neighbours. There were other social institutions like the association of mask dancers, *Ekine/Sekiapu*, and the warriors' club, *peri ogbo*, which provided fora for the achievement of social status based on merit without reference to lineage or birth.

Although the fishing village was autonomous in all its internal affairs and in relations with neighbouring villages within the *ibe*, it was expected to cooperate with others within the *ibe* in relations with external neighbours. It was the opening for leadership of the *ibe* that the city-state rose to fill. It was, apparently, their pre-existing qualities for leadership that drove them to make the choices to develop the institutions of the city state.

476

The City-State Socio-Political Organisation

Many of the elements of the fishing village socio-political organisation characterised the city states. As their success in the internal and external long distance trade made them richer, bigger, and more powerful, the fishing village institutions were radically transformed and additional ones created as the need arose. First, the internal trade, and even more, the trans-Atlantic trade, greatly increased the field of external policy, and therefore, the competence of the *amanyanabo* as the official spokesman in external affairs. This transformed the office of *amanyanabo* into an effective executive authority in the city-state. Second, the *wari* (house) became more or less a trading corporation in addition to other functions appropriate to its continued operation as a lineage institution. The criteria for the selection of a new-head, *wari-dabo*, were focussed on the ability of the candidate to increase the wealth and power of the *wari*. Since the lineage head was now leader of a commercial organisation, he also became the head recruiting agent, recruiting new members to increase the labour and fighting force to protect trading canoes and trading posts in the hinterland markets, and to contribute forces in defence of the city-state. The new House system, which at this stage had become a 'war canoe house,' *omungu-aru wari*, gave the head greater control over the lives of members than the lineage head of the fishing village even though the ordinary member also had a say in the affairs of the house, and indirectly, in the state, through his right to vote a head in a general meeting of the house for that purpose. Here, then, we find that while the individual had direct participation in affairs of his house, the village assembly of all adult males was no longer operative on a routine basis. In its place, the *amanyanabo* was advised directly only by a council of chiefs (house heads). In other ways, the function of institutions such as the *Ekine/Sekiapu* and *Peri Ogbo* which cut across the entire community acquired an even greater significance in the city-state in the context of inter-house rivalries. They now served to hold the community together, and to acculturate the growing number of newcomers recruited by purchase, capture, or otherwise from other communities within and outside the Niger Delta.

The Ijo city-states of the Niger Delta evolved from about 1200 AD. The establishment of the houses as trading corporations would date to a time after the monarchy. The evidence left behind by early European visitors from around 1500 already shows all the ingredients of the house trading system. Among the Nembe, the Peresuo House, which is considered the oldest surviving house is dated to only about 1600, although the period of the full development of the house as a trading corporation came in the nineteenth century, shortly before British colonialism.

The Atlantic Trade

The Atlantic Trade era is one of the best remembered in the popular history of the Ijo, particularly among the Nembe and the Eastern Delta Ijo groups of Kalabari, Okrika and Ibani. This is based on the fact that most of the social and political institutions for which the Nembe and the other eastern Ijo groups have come to be identified were developed to their highest level in the heydays of the trans-Atlantic trade in slaves, and later, oil palm produce. This was also a period in which these states enjoyed a measure of comparative advantage as middlemen between the overseas visitors and the people of the Nigerian hinterland.

Discussions bordering on the role of the Ijo of the Central Delta and their role in the Atlantic Trade have often emphasized the fact that, outside of Nembe land the rest were involved, only as pirates. Recent studies indicate, however, that the role of the Central Delta Ijo in the overseas trade was more than piracy. That the Ijo of the Niger Delta played some role beyond piracy has been documented by a number of local writers. Frank-Opigo (1980:159) has, for example, established, that even though much of the trading and missionary activities that were carried out at the time were confined to the coastal towns of Bonny, Elem-Kalabari and Twon-Brass, some Central Delta Ijo communities like Angiama also participated in both the slave and legitimate trade, especially in the 19th century. The Mein group of communities have also been identified as being among those which played some role in the Atlantic trade, particularly in the slave trade. Alagoa (1986:31) records a tradition among the Kabo which suggest that they lost their control of the slave trade on the Forcados River to the Mein group as a result of a rumour, that some

478

European slave raiders were planning to sail up the river to capture whoever they saw. There are strong reasons to believe that other Central Delta Ijo groups like the Bassan, Olodiama and Apoi also participated in the trade. Indeed, there are Nembe traditions which indicate that the Bassan in particular, established strong ties with the Nembe city-state. The Bassan also formed what may be termed a confederation of communities to enhance their participation in the Atlantic trade. They were among the key suppliers or distributors of goods produced by themselves, and those they had purchased from their Western Delta trading associates. Some of the large canoes used by the Nembe merchants were also bought from this area. Agedah (1984: 45-47) states that 'palm oil from the Kolokuma area was exported to the coastal ports of Brass (Nembe) and Akassa, where it was sold to the European merchants'. He adds, however, that the principal carriers of the Kolokuma palm produce were not the Kolokuma themselves, but traders from Nembe. The works of Forcados (1984), Agedah (1984), and Ekiyor (1984), among some Izon groups, indicate that there was virtually no group in the Central Niger Delta that was not affected by the Atlantic trade, or did not participate in it, directly or indirectly. Some of these groups were among the major suppliers of the palm produce, and to some extent slaves, which the Nembe middlemen sold to the European supercargoes.

Taking all Central Delta Ijo communities into account, then, it is possible to categorise them into three groups. First, there were those which acted as agents, supplying either slaves or palm produce which the coastal middlemen sold to the European super-cargoes. The majority of Central Delta Ijo communities fall into this category, including the Kolokuma, the Opokuma, the Ogboin, the Mein, the Bumo, etc; and lastly, we have the Nembe (Ogbolomabiri, Bassambiri, Okpoama and Twon) which acted as the middlemen, and were the most deeply involved in the Atlantic trade. In the Central Delta, it is possible to isolate communities falling in-between these categories, and those which produced the much misunderstood 'pirates' that disturbed the direct beneficiaries of the Atlantic trade.

In chronological terms, the Central Delta Ijo started having contacts with the Europeans from the late 15th century (Kimble, 1937:132). The Portuguese were the first to come. The English became dominant from about the second half of the 18th century. Most Central Delta Ijo outside of Nembe served mainly as suppliers of slaves and other items, either through Nembe or Itsekiri merchants. Some of the slaves are reported to have come from as far as Idah and Nupe in Northern Nigeria; usually transported through Aboh and Onitsha down the Niger to the Forcados, Nun and Brass Rivers.

The assumption that all slaves exported through the ports of the Central Delta namely, Twon and Akassa, had come from the hinterlands has, however, been proved wrong. Recent findings (Alagoa 1986; Okorobia 1999) have revealed that some of the slaves and other legitimate items of trade marketed by the Ijo had actually come from within Ijoland itself. The evidence for this has been found in different parts of the Central Delta. The traditions of some of the communities as well as their locations away from the major river courses, particularly on the Cape Formosa Island between the Brass and Nun Rivers tell a lot of the story. Here, the Beletiema, Egwema and Liama communities which now stand on the Formosa Creek, linking the Brass and Nun Rivers, according to popular traditions, were occupied only recently. The people still keep their main shrines and other religio-cultural artefacts in the original settlements, namely, Beletiema-Amaogbo, Egwema-Amaogbo and Liama-Amaogbo, situated in the heart of the island. It is apparent, that the rationale for the earlier location of the communities away from the main river was to escape the attention of slave traders, particularly from Nembe.

There is evidence from the Americas of the presence of Ijo slaves. Maroon communities like Boni and Brosi in Guiana, as well as the Calabaris in Surinam suggest Niger Delta connections: Bonny/Ibani, Brass/Nembe, Kalabari (Smith, Robertson and Williamson 1987). Similarly, the high number of Ijo words in the Berbice Dutch language of Guiana in South America, confirms that some Ijo people were sold and transported to the West Indies. It was not every slave bought by the Nembe that was exported. Some of the slaves were retained as part of the society, thereby making the area a 'melting pot' of cultures.

The slave trade went on from about 1500 to 1807 when it was officially outlawed, mainly for economic reasons by the British, although, in practice, it remained active until the 1850s (Dike 1956:52). At this time, the British had established a consulate at Fernando Po, with John Beecroft as consul. His mandate included among other duties, to intervene in the affairs of the Niger Delta in ways that would protect and promote British interests. It also marked the dawn of the era of 'gun-boat' diplomacy in the relationship between the Ijo middlemen and the European supercargoes.

Soon, a consulate was also established at Twon and treaties were signed with the chiefs of Nembe and other Central Delta Ijo communities. The Brass and Nun Rivers began to attract many 'legitimate' traders who wanted to share in the new opportunities available there. Again by 1870, a court of equity was established at Twon. The court was initially meant to be an instrument for resolving trade disputes between the Central Delta merchants and the European supercargoes. In the course of time however, the court became an instrument for eroding and undermining the powers and dignity of the local monarchs. By this time also, the Europeans were making headway in their effort at breaking the monopoly of Ijo middlemen by shifting their interest from the coast to the interior. This move had actually begun with the 'discovery' by the Lander brothers, John and Richard Lander, that the River Niger empties its waters into the Atlantic Ocean through the Nun, Brass and its other channels in the Central Delta.

The eventual destruction of the monopoly of the Ijo, particularly Nembe middlemen, was sealed, when in 1854, Dr. William B. Baikie, a naval doctor, Captain of the *'Plaide'*, using quinine as prophylactic against malarial parasites, successfully explored the Niger up to Lokoja on the Benue River and this threw the trade open to European trade (Ejituwu 1999:201).Although this event was a drawback to the Nembe middlemen, it was a great gain to some Central Delta communities like Kaiama on the Nun River and Patani on the Forcados River . Kaiama came into the picture when, in 1832, King Amaran rescued Richard Lander, who was captured by some men of Odi (Owonaro 1949:27). King Amaran paid the ransom money demanded and was duly rewarded by the British with an allowance of 20 cases of gin, which were later changed to an annual subsidy of £12

(Owonaro 1949:28; Ejituwu 1999:202). Again, according to Owonaro (1949: 28), in about 1859, King Amaran similarly rescued the *'Rainbow'* from the people of Kaiama who had seized it and its cargoes, and eventually sent it to the Europeans at Akassa. Kaiama also attracted local Aboh traders. For instance, in 1854, some men of Sampou captured and enslaved two women from Aboh and King Osai reported it to King Amaran who succeeded in getting one of the women released (Owonaro 1949: 28). By this unique ability to host foreign merchants and provide link between the Central Delta and hinterland, Kaiama gained prominence, playing a positive role beyond the general characterization of the Ijo as 'pirates' (Ejituwu 1999:202). With time, Kaiama expanded rapidly and became important as an entrepot between Nembe and the hinterland.

With their success in bypassing the Nembe middlemen, there followed a period of unhealthy competition among the European traders themselves until 1879, when the companies were amalgamated by Taubman Goldie, into a conglomerate, the National African Company, (NAC).The company opened trading centres at Yenagoa and Sabagreia (Sorgwe 1990), with their headquarters at Bekekiri, Akassa. They also imposed the conditions of trade. However, Goldie was not interested in trade alone, he also wanted to administer the territory, and so secured a charter from the British Government to ensure his control over the area. This he got in 1886, changing the company's name to Royal Niger Company (RNC).

The RNC built some 20 'gun-boats' of light shaft to enable them navigate the shallow waters of the Niger all year round with a view to silencing any opposition. This policy could not, however, silence opposition from the Ijo people. In 1882, for instance, the company's factories at Twon, Akassa and Patani were attacked (Dike, 1956: 212). Earlier in 1832, Richard Lander had died from a gun-shot wound he sustained from some Angiama people, and was buried in Fernando Po. In 1895, frustrations from the company's trade monopoly led the Nembe people to invade the RNC station at Akassa. For their attack on the RNC, the colonial forces struck back at the Nembe in reprisal. The Akassa War exposed the injustice of the company and led to the withdrawal of the charter of the RNC in 1900; and the withdrawal of the charter led to the effective British take-over of the area which they had since 1885 declared a protectorate.

On the whole then, we may conclude that the Atlantic Trade in particular was a great catalyst in its impact on the land and people of the Central Delta, economically. According to Alagoa (1964:76), Kings Kulo of Ogbolomabiri and Mein of Bassambiri were the first on the Brass River to receive comey, an official duty which every European firm or trader had to pay before being granted the permission to do business. The wealth accumulated by some of the merchant chiefs was sometimes large enough to build prefabricated mansions. Some persons of servile background were able to acquire new chieftaincy titles and build up their own houses (*wari*); while some who were already chiefs, used such wealth to buy-over or capture other less progressive chieftaincy houses. In the Izon communities where some of the leading Nembe middlemen had local agents to help-out in their ventures, similar developments took place.

The Atlantic trade has also left its imprint on the socio-cultural life of the people of the Central Delta. To protect their interest in the producing communities some Nembe merchants established marriage alliances with families in these communities. While most Bassambiri merchants established such links with the Abureni communities of Okoroba, Idema and Agrisaba, as well as with a few Ogbia and Odual communities; the Ogbolomabiri, according to Ebiwari (1988), were more active in the Ogbia towns of Opume, Akipelai, Emakalakala, Oloibiri and up the Kolo Creek and Ekole Creek.

A fall-out of the Atlantic trade with a negative social consequence was its acceleration of the pace of moral decadence in the trading communities. This manifested in different forms. In one way, there was an increase in the desire to cheat one's trading partner, as the profit-motive gradually overwhelmed ethical considerations. This was a problem, not just between the Europeans and Ijo traders but also between the Ijo themselves. Some Ijo demanded and received double 'trusts'. Others experimented with adulteration of produce and the use of false measures.

In the area of communication, the Nembe-Ijo dialect was raised from being a local dialect to become a commercial lingua-franca in the Central Delta. Later in the late 19th and early 20th centuries, following the introduction of Christianity and western education, and the leading role some Nembe sons and daughters played in the spread of the gospel and Western education in the Central Delta, the Nembe-Ijo dialect also came to be used in the churches and schools.

The foreign trade era also witnessed in the Central Delta the creation of new fashion styles for different categories of people particularly in the Nembe area. The new styles were initially designed to identify the class or social category to which the wearer belonged. The categories included those of *asawo* (young men) who wore *opu seti*; the *opu-asawo* (gentlemen), who wore *angapu*; the *alapu* (chiefs), who wore *doni*; and lastly the *amanyanaongu* (kings), who wore *ebu* (Okorobia 1999:212).

The Atlantic trade era, especially the period of the slave trade, was characterised by an atmosphere of social insecurity. This was largely the result of the intra-Delta slave raiding activities aimed at securing victims for export. In Ogboin *ibe*, Preye Okosi (1980:71) has suggested that the state of anarchy which ushered in the reign of King Okosi as *Agbedi II* of Amassoma may have been due to the increase in the importation of machetes, gin, canoes and guns by the supercargoes. The possession of these weapons greatly disrupted the peace of the community since they were freely used.

The atmosphere of social instability that characterised the foreign trade era in some Central Delta communities, it has been found, was sometimes the result of the failure of the 'trust' system, the basis on which the trade was conducted. The Nembe merchants in many cases resorted to the use of brute force to enforce their monopolistic regulations or, to punish individuals and communities that abused the 'trust' system. The Ogbia town of Anyama was invaded by an Ogbolomabiri ruler, King Boy Amain in 1846, because the community abused the 'trust' regulation. In 1870, another ruler from Ogbolomabiri, King Ockiya took a punitive expedition against Okiki, an Ogbia village on the Ekole Creek for abusing the 'trust' system, and for killing 'a son of Kulo' named Akpana, who had gone to collect a debt. In 1869, Okpoama launched a similar attack on Otuaganagu; while in 1873, Bassambiri invaded Otuedu for taking 'double trust' from other middlemen (Ebiwari, 1988). Bassambiri also raided the Abureni villages of Idema, Okoroba and Agrisaba, as well as the Odual communities, for similar reasons during the Atlantic trade.

A unique and significant development arising from trade was its impact on the political status of women. While it is true that because of the generally matrilineal orientation of most Central Delta Ijo societies, women were socially influential, none had openly aspired to occupy a politically important position until the time of the legitimate trade. Madam Ṣaifigha from Bassambiri aspired and moved quite close to becoming a chief, a house founder. Saifigha acquired sufficient wealth and slaves to launch a war canoe. But the chiefs (of Bassambiri-Nembe) rejected her application for recognition as an *omungu-aru-alabo*, a war canoe chief. They could only permit her to establish a war canoe house in the name of her maternal brothers, Iga and Opuene. This had qualified her for the honour of having an *okpu*, mausoleum, in the joint names of herself and her brothers (Alagoa 2000).

External and Internal Colonialism

As a colonised people, the Central Delta Ijo were exposed to a number of challenges. One of the early political challenges they faced was the introduction of the Native House Rule Proclamation of November 21, 1901. In the Nembe area, this led to the modification of the House System into Native House Rule causing a reduction in the powers of the *Amanyanabo* and chiefs over their people. The proclamation, among other things, provided that the colonial authorities could handle disputes in the house, and where necessary, transfer cases from the houses to Native Courts of their choice. The proclamation also regulated the punishment for offences committed by erring house members. The communities were reorganised into Native Councils which represented a system of indirect rule through the traditional authorities. Under colonialism, the gerontocratic system in pre-colonial times was radically modified. The British authorities now chose

485

leaders by criteria other than age, such as literacy and the willingness of such persons to cooperate with them. Some of the Native Courts exercised jurisdiction across several villages and ethnic sub-groups. For example, the Sabagreia Native Court served Kolokuma, Opokuma, Ekpetiama, Gbaraun, Epie-Atissa and other sub-groups. There were also the provinces, the districts and sub-districts which did not necessarily follow ethnic lines. According to Ejituwu and Sorgwe (1999: 220-221), the inter-ethnic groupings in some cases created conflicts. In 1927, for instance, the Epie-Atissa people complained to the Resident at Warri that they were at a disadvantage in the Sabagreia Native Court due to the long distance they were compelled to cover to receive justice and their inability to understand the language spoken by the bench.

Economically, the British emphasised the need for the people to supply raw-materials such as palm-oil, and later, palm kernels, as well as provide a market for the products of British industries, creating a dependent consumer culture and economy at the expense of the productive sectors of the traditional economy, which generally emphasised the production of food crops. Taxation and monetary economy were also introduced to replace the traditional system of revenue mobilisation and the trade by barter system. The British also showed interest in the exploration of crude oil which came to fruition when oil was struck at the Oloibiri fields in the Ogbia area in 1956, and by 1958, oil was already being extracted. In the area of ports development no new ports were developed in the Central Delta during the colonial period, outside those of Twon and Akassa that had existed since pre-colonial times. In short, the development of Port Harcourt in particular, caused the speedy decline and ultimate abandonment of the Central Delta ports. A number of inland riverine communities however grew as trading centres within the Central Delta, including Yenagoa.

Christianity and Western Education spread rapidly during the colonial period, introducing a new world view among the people, challenging and alienating them from their traditional heritage. Ejituwu and Sorgwe (1999) observed rightly that the

486

principle of bringing different ethnic groups together, adopted as a basic colonial administrative technique served integrative social functions. The Ijo-speaking people of Nembe, Akassa, Southern and Northern Ijo, the Epie-Atissa, the Ogbia and Zarama for instance, came to see themselves as one people, having found themselves together first in the Brass Division, and later the Yenagoa Province.

Resistance against colonialism did not really stop even after British 'pacification' of people and territories. They continued to attack the British and their local agents over issues like insults against local traditions, and against taxation and other impositions. Instances of these were the attack on the Brass District Resident at Igbedi in 1901; the clash with the Agbere people in 1906 and the Epie women's attack on government establishments in and around Yenagoa in 1956.

The period of resistance passed into that of struggle for self government and independence from colonial rule. The initial basis of the anti – colonial struggle was the collective urge to drive away a common foe, the British imperialists. Unfortunately however, the political parties that emerged, namely the National Council of Nigeria and the Cameroon, (NCNC), the Action Group (AG) and the Northern Peoples Congress (NPC), came to be associated mainly with the three dominant ethnic nationalities in the country, Igbo, Yoruba, and Hausa/Fulani. It is, therefore, not surprising that the 1954 Lyttelton Constitution, which was produced with the active participation of these parties, resulted in the introduction of a distorted federal system in which the leaders were mainly interested in seizing control over their respective regions. The driving force of nationalism in Nigeria was, therefore, not principally loyalty to Nigeria.

Administrative arrangements became a bone of contention between the majority Igbo and the numerous ethnic minorities such as the Ijo, Efik, Ibibio, Ogoni, Ikwerre, Etche, Abua, Odual, and others who felt marginalised and exploited. The people of the Niger Delta in particular, argued that the Yoruba-dominated Western and the Igbo-dominated Eastern Regional Governments at Ibadan and Enugu were too distant from them. They therefore called for a separate province whose capital would be located within the Niger Delta itself.

In 1942 the Ijaw (Ijo) Peoples League was formed under the leadership of Chief Harold Dappa Biriye, to fight for the creation of a Rivers Province which they hoped, would not only bring governmental apparatus closer to them, but would empower them to reddress the decades of marginalisation they had suffered under the Igbo. This dream crystallized in 1947 when the Rivers Province was carved out from the Owerri and Calabar Provinces of the Eastern Region. This geo-political formation was composed of the Degema, Brass, Port-Harcourt, Ahoada, and Ogoni Divisions. This was a significant victory as it became a prelude to the creation of the Rivers State in 1967. After this achievement, many sectional and ill-organised pressure groups surfaced to clamour for greater political autonomy, including an Ijaw Tribe Union (1948); Ijaw Federal Union (1949); Ijaw State Union (1950); Council of Rivers Chiefs (1953) and Rivers State Movement (1954). Most of these groups did not live to see their first or second anniversary. However, an all-embracing organisation, Rivers Chiefs and Peoples Conference (RCPC) emerged to lead the people in the demand for a Rivers State.

It was the RCPC, under Chief Dappa Biriye, that led the people to the 1957 London Constitutional Conference to submit a memorandum for the creation of Rivers State. The chiefs made many significant points in their memorandum.

First, they argued that the people of this area shared a way of life dictated by the geographical circumstances of the territory in which they lived, and that they were united by fear of neglect at the hands of a government which did not understand their needs, and in any case, put the needs of the interior first.

Second, when the British first came in contact with their ancestors, they made treaties of trade and protection with them, and that these treaties were of a special nature, and differed from the treaties made with the hinterland chiefs. They insisted that, in the treaties, the British undertook to provide protection, and to deal with foreign powers, not that the Ijo chiefs should surrender to the British Government a sovereignty which could be transferred to any other authority. And that, if the British Government considered it necessary to end the treaties, the Ijo communities should be allowed to revert to their original status as independent city-states.

The aftermath of this conference was the setting up of the Henry Willink Commission to enquire into the fears of the minorities and the means of allaying them. At the end of its assignment, the Commission could not recommend the creation of a new state for the people. Convinced however, that the area was actually poor, backward and neglected, the Commission recommended the establishment of a Niger Delta Special Area with a Niger Delta Development Board (NDDB), without executive powers.

And so, by October 1, 1960 when Nigeria gained political independence from Britain, the event was received with mixed feelings. While the privileged ethnic majorities who had acquired the state apparatus and treasury from the departing British saw it as a thing of joy and hope, to many minority groups such as the Ijo, it was the dawn of *internal colonialism*.

In spite of the many obstacles on their way, the Niger Delta leaders remained committed to the idea of a state of their own. Realising that the RCPC, as a non-partisan body, could not field candidates for electoral purposes, they decided to form a political party, the Niger Delta Congress (NDC.). And to have a powerful ally with a view to having access to the national government, the leaders went to Kaduna in August 1959 and contracted an alliance with the Northern Peoples Congress (NPC). In the 1959 Federal Election that preceded Nigeria's independence, Chief Melford O. Okilo was elected as the NDC candidate for Brass Division. Okilo was eventually appointed Parliamentary Secretary to the Prime Minister, Alhaji Tafawa Balewa (Opu-Ogulaya 1973).

Throughout the period of the First Republic, nothing substantial was achieved by the NDDB, and nothing came out of the struggle for a Rivers State. The revolutionary movement launched by Isaac Boro in 1966 indicated the level at which the youths of the Central Delta were frustrated by the system. The Isaac Boro declaration of a Niger Delta Republic on 14th February 1966, at the time of the first military seizure of power, was therefore aimed at emancipating the Ijo from internal colonialism (Dappa-Biriye, 1995:52).

The Central Delta Ijo as part of the defunct Eastern Region, experienced many far-reaching consequences of the Civil War 1967-70, which caused the disruption of normal social and economic activities, loss of personal effects and lives, as well as general deprivation. They were psychologically upset because whereas, physically they were in Biafra their hearts were emotionally for Nigeria, where they had looked forward to the day they would enjoy the benefits of their newly declared Rivers State.

Boro, Owonaro and Nottingham Dick, found guilty and sentenced to death were granted amnesty by Gowon and recruited into the Nigerian Army along with Amangala, Nyananyo and others. As Nigerian soldiers, Boro, Amangala, and Nyananyo gave their lives to keep Nigeria united.

For the Ijo people, the creation of Rivers State was clearly the most important fallout of the Nigerian Civil War. Bayelsa State which came out of the Rivers State to meet the peculiar needs of the Central Delta Ijo was a longer term consequence of the war.

The struggle for the actualization of Bayelsa State for the Central Delta Ijo people was a long and tortuous one, passing through several generations and phases - the struggle for Rivers State, the Niger Delta State, the Abayelsa State, and finally Bayelsa State.

At creation, Bayelsa was found to be the least developed state in the Federal Republic of Nigeria. In each of the Rivers State development plans and programmes, from 1970 to 1st October 1996, a number of development projects were earmarked for implementation in the area constituting Bayelsa State, some of which were fully implemented while others were at different levels of implementation (Ibomo, Allison-Oguru and Lazarus 1999: 259-272).

Conclusion

On the whole, we find that the Ijo of the Central Delta have remained largely a 'poor, backward and neglected' people even in recent times, and remain the victims of changing forms of colonialism. The explanation for this reality is not far to seek. First, until lately; the Ijo of this area had not built sufficient historical and political consciousness to guide their efforts at sustainable self-development. Second, many Central Delta Ijo sons and daughters in positions of authority have failed, or even forgotten their communities in the developmental plans and programmes over which they presided, be it at the local, state, national or international levels. Third, the brazen acts of indiscipline and corruption exhibited by the political class and their intellectual and commercial collaborators, who wasted even the scarce resources that were available for the development of the area; and finally, the lack of adequately designed grassroots and people-oriented policies and programmes for the sustainable development of the sub-region.

CHAPTER 21
THE EASTERN DELTA
Abi A. Derefaka and Adaye Orugbani

For the purposes of this contribution, the discussion will focus on the Okrika, Kalabari, and Ibani. For each of these peoples, a reconstruction of their history, beginning with origins and migration routes through the pre-colonial, colonial, and post-colonial periods will be presented. Also economic, socio-cultural, political, religious and other institutions utilized through time will be discussed. In all this, the vectors and processes of change as well as the role of traditions in the development of each society will be discussed.

Origins and Migrations

There is ample linguistic and other cultural evidence that Okrika, Ibani, and Kalabari share considerable affinity. Kay Williamson's 1988 essay (Alagoa *et al* 1988) on the relationship between Ijoid languages became the focal point of Horton's contribution on Eastern Ijo origins, expansion and migration in 1997 (Ejituwu 1997). He has modified Kay Williamson's Table 4.8 titled Relationships in the Ijoid branch (Alagoa *et al* 1988:84) to produce what he calls a Genetic Relationship within Ijoid, with special attention to Eastern Ijo (1997:203). The origin and migration history of the Kalabari, Okrika, and Ibani has a number of versions. Horton (1997:195-255) has reviewed the reconstructions about the origins and migration routes of the Okrika, Kalabari and Ibani. Essentially, he presents what he calls the Alagoa Thesis (1997:197-200) and then uses linguistic and archaeological evidence as well as a fresh look at the oral traditions themselves to re-evaluate the accuracy of the Alagoa thesis. He concludes that on the basis of current data, two scenarios for Ijoid origins, expansions and migrations are possible. In this regard his second figure on page 203 referred to earlier and the diagrams on pages 236 and 238 respectively (showing each of the scenarios), have to be taken together and compared with his first figure on page 199 titled Eastern Ijo origins according to Alagoa. In order that Horton's (1997:235-237) proposed schemes are not distorted; we reproduce below the two scenarios he has proposed:

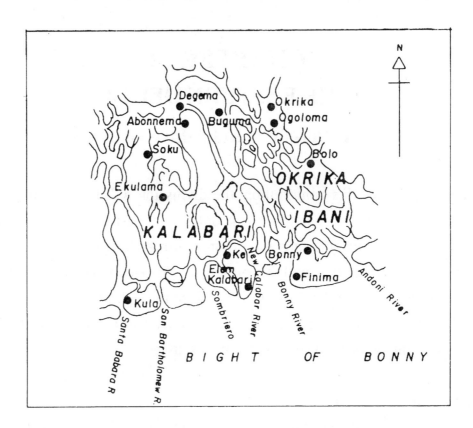

Fig. 21.1: The Ijo of the Eastern Delta

In Scenario One, we have the Proto-Ijoid-speakers coming down the Niger and entering the Delta through its apex. An initial separation of population and consequent language differentiation take place soon after, with Proto-Ijaw-speakers remaining near the point of entry, and Proto- Defakoid-speakers moving south-eastward toward the coast. Before long, a wave of Proto-Central-Delta (Delta Cross) speakers enters the Proto-Ijaw homeland from the east. Some Proto-Ijaw groups stay put, and get assimilated into Central Delta language, culture and polity. Other groups move away from the area in various directions. In the course of the latter process, one group goes back toward the apex of the Delta and develops Proto-Inland Ijaw speech; one moves south-westwards and develops Proto-Ijaw speech.

Concentrating our attention at this juncture on the Eastern Delta, we now see the Proto-Defakoid-speakers occupying the coastal area between the mouths of the Rio San Bartolomew and the Rio Real, with some linguistic differentiation probably developing between the various sub-populations. Next, some of the Proto-Eastern-Ijaw-speakers move to the west of the Proto-Defakoid bloc, to form the nucleus of the Proto-Nembaka-speakers, whilst the others move to the

494

east of this bloc, to form the nucleus of the Proto-Nikio-speakers. To the east at this juncture, another wave of Delta-Cross-speakers, that of the Andoni (Obolo), comes into the Proto-Nikio homeland from the creeks east of the Imo River. Some Proto-Nikio groups stay put and are linguistically, culturally and politically Andonized. Others move west, to form the Proto-Kio-speakers, increasingly frustrated by the confinement of the far eastern creeks, fan out into the main Eastern Delta. The resulting population separation leads to the emergence of distinct Kalabari, Ibani and Okrika dialects. Finally, with the advent of the Atlantic Slave Trade, the Kalabari-speaking town of Bile systematically raids the villages of the Defakoid-speaking bloc to the west, removing large numbers of people for sale into slavery, and provoking the few survivors into flight eastwards, where they come under Nkoro protection.

In Scenario Two, we have the Proto-Ijoid-speakers coming into the Delta through the far eastern creeks. The first round of population separation and linguistic differentiation takes place in this area, with some elements moving north into dry-land territory to form the nucleus of the Proto-Defakoid-speakers, and others remaining in the coastal creeks to form the nucleus of the Proto-Ijaw-speakers. A little later, arrival of the Proto-Ogoni (Delta Cross) speakers results in the linguistic, cultural and political assimilation of most of the Proto-Defakoid speakers, leaving only a small rump in the far south of their former territory. As congestion develops among the Proto-Ijaw-speaking groups of the far eastern creeks, some fan out into the main Eastern Delta. Some of those who fan out quickly reach the Central and North-Central areas of the Delta. Before long, however, another wave of Delta-Cross speakers, the Proto-Central-Delta linguistic group, comes in from the eastern hinterland to drive a wedge, not only between those Proto-Ijaw who have moved toward the Central Delta and those who have moved further north, but also between both of the latter and those who have stayed nearer the eastern homeland. The result is a linguistic differentiation into Proto-Ijaw, Proto-Inland-Ijaw, and Proto-Eastern-Ijaw.

Concentrating our attention on the East, we see next a further separation, between those Proto-Eastern-Ijaw-speakers who move further west along the coast and those who remain nearer the homeland, the result being a differentiation into Proto-Nembaka and Proto-Nikio-speaking populations. Later, a further separation in the west leads to differentiation into Nembe and Akassa-speakers.

In the far eastern homeland, the arrival of the Delta-Cross speaking Andoni (Obolo) has the same sequels for the Proto-Nikio-speakers as we outlined in Scenario One, the only difference being that the villages sacked or dispersed by the slave-raiding Bile are not Defakoid-speakers but Kalabari-speakers.

The two scenarios are reconstructions proposed on the basis of our present state of knowledge derived mainly from linguistics, oral traditions, and archaeology. Horton (1997:239) is, however, flexible enough in his formulations to say; if a third pattern emerges, we may have to reject both scenarios and propose a third. He rightly identifies the crucial role Archaeology is to play in reconstructing settlement chronology in the Niger Delta. It is clearly too soon for any migration scenario in the Niger Delta to be presented as the pattern of movements and settlement of the Ijaw in the Niger Delta. More work still needs to be done by all the relevant disciplines before we can gain absolute clarity on this matter.

The Pre-Colonial Period

So far we have presented migration patterns in the Eastern Niger Delta. We are now going to analyze its history during the pre-colonial period—that is, the period before the imposition of formal colonial rule late in the nineteenth century. It was during the pre-colonial period that the Eastern Delta kingdoms evolved to represent the high water mark in the development of the basic Ijaw institutions to be found in the Central and Western Delta. For clarity of analysis, we shall examine why and how the kingdoms in the Eastern Niger Delta adapted the basic Ijaw institutions developed in the Central and Western Delta to meet the challenges of their environment in the Eastern Delta.

Plate 21.1: A terra-cotta mask from near excavation site Ke II

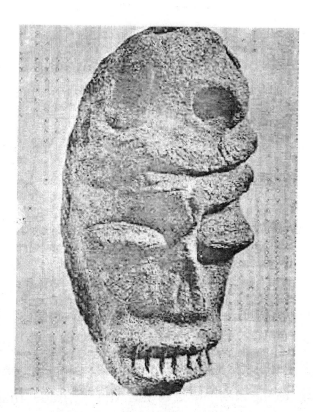

Plate 21.2: A second terra-cotta mask from near excavation site Ke II

Plate 21.3: A terra-cotta mask from excavation site Ke III

Political Developments

Politically, one of the most striking developments was a change in the structure of the state. It was in the Eastern Delta, that the Ibani, Kalabari and Okrika peoples developed a state, territorially based on a central city headed by a king (*amanyanabo*) with authority radiating to hinterland trading stations. Impressed by this territorial organization, Professor Dike called them "city states" (Dike, 1956:30-31). Another scholar, G. I. Jones, called them "trading states", because of their participation in the Atlantic trade (Jones, 1963:34). As to why the Eastern Delta kingdoms developed a complex state structure, Dike and Jones differ in their explanations. For Dike, the critical factor was a change in the criteria for citizenship which came "increasingly to depend not on decent but on residence"—that is, a shift from a state based on kinship to a more open society. For Jones the Delta kingdoms developed their complex state structures in response to the challenges of the Atlantic trade, first in slaves and later palm oil.

498

Professor E. J. Alagoa has established the internal nature of the stimuli to change in the Eastern Delta kingdoms. He pointed out that the most important factor determining full citizenship was culture – "the acquisition of the variety of Ijaw culture developed in these states." On the role of the Atlantic trade, Alagoa conceded that many of the peculiar features of these states were developed in response to the Atlantic trade in slaves, "but others had been developed in response to internal long distance trade and to other local factors such as environmental change". According to Alagoa (1972: 192-193):

> The institutions carried by the migrants from the Central Delta dispersal centres to the different parts of the Delta were modified by circumstance and the pressures of the environment. The most far-reaching changes were effected among the groups migrating to the Eastern Delta.
>
> Here, the indication is that the environmental change from the fresh water delta to the salt water delta was one factor which induced changes. First, these communities changed from a fishing and farming economy to a fishing and salt- boiling economy. The needs of such a situation produced the fishing village institutions from the village community structures of the Central and Western Delta type. Not all the communities in the Eastern Delta achieved the further development from fishing village to city-state. The deciding factor in this second level of change appears to have been, first, the level of participation in the internal long distance trade of the Niger Delta, and finally the position of the community in the over-seas trade. Where one community combined the internal and external trade, a decisive difference was made. Wealth and power were concentrated in one city which attained a position of paramountcy, and became a city-state.

Political Structure

The Eastern Delta States retained the basic Ijaw ethnic unit called the *ibe*—clan. Like in the Central and Western Delta, there was also the feeling of belonging together based on their common tongue and cultural institutions. Unlike those in the Central and Western Delta, however, the tradition of common descent and a common founding ancestor was absent or very tenuous among the Eastern Delta states. As the Eastern Delta states developed central state institutions and the areas over which these states exercised influence increased, even the cultural and linguistic unity tended to disappear. As the territorial influence of these states expanded they came to include peoples speaking different languages and having different cultures. Within the Kalabari territory for instance, there are the Udekama—a people with a different language and culture while in the Okrika territory there are the Abuloma people whose language and culture differ from that of the Okrika people. The existence of such small minority groups within the Eastern Delta States differentiates them from the *Ibe* in the Central and Western Delta.

The cult of a national god is another feature of the political structure of the Eastern Delta states. But since all the communities in the Eastern Delta do not have traditions of common descent, the power of the national god as an instrument of national control is weaker in the Eastern Delta States than in the *ibe* of the Central and Western Delta. Given their diversity, the authority of the national god is often founded on the spiritual kinship of the village gods (*Ama-oru*) to the national god—whose shrine would be sited at the metropolitan city.

In addition to the national god, the states of the Eastern Delta also developed other religious institutions to strengthen the corporate unity of the metropolitan cities on which states were based. One such religious institution was the idea of the *Amakiri*, god of the settled Earth; the other was the idea of the *Amatemesuo,* the spirit of the city as a historical and corporate entity. According to Alagoa, "…the drum priest of *Amatemesuo* served as the national anthem of the state, just as the totem or symbol of the national god served in the nature of the national flag or coat of arms of a modern state". (Alagoa, in Ajayi and Crowder, eds, 1971:341).

The Eastern Delta states retained the basic village organization of the Central and Western Delta. The metropolitan city comprise a number of descent groups called *wari* - a number of *wari* make up a larger segment called *polo*. Each of these deliberated on matters pertaining to the segment while the political authority of the city assembly remained supreme. Unlike the system of government in the Central and Western Delta, the Eastern Delta states abandoned age as a qualification for office. The city assembly was not headed by the oldest man (*amaokosowei*), but the *amanyanabo* who was appointed because he descended from the *polo* or *wari*, whose ancestors founded or discovered the site of the metropolitan city. The only concession made to age in the Eastern Delta states was the separation of elders from the youths in the sitting arrangements at the assembly meetings and the greater respect paid to the elders.

Another significant political development among the Eastern Delta States was the institutions of the monarchy. Before they became city-states, the office of *amanyanabo* was like the ritual heads exemplified by the *pere* of the Western Delta. They were the heads of the village assembly, who performed rituals to the village or national gods, and directed external wars. The beginning of the Atlantic Trade increased not only the economic orientation of the Eastern Delta states but also increased their population. These changes increased the power of the *amanyanabo*. He negotiated with European merchants on behalf of the community and was paid comey and other duties for the protection he gave them. His position as community representative with the European traders enhanced his authority in relation to the other leaders of the community – the House heads. It was the *amanyanabo* who introduced the House heads to the European traders and it was also through him that they obtained credit (trusts) from the European traders. The enhanced prestige and wealth of the monarchy occasioned dynastic changes and succession disputes in all the Eastern Delta states.

The House system was the most revolutionary change in the political history of the Eastern Delta states occasioned by the Atlantic trade. The House system was the adaptation of the old Ijaw *wari* or House to meet the challenges of the Atlantic trade.

To meet the labour demands of the Atlantic trade, enterprising traders began to build up their personal households. They did this by various means. First, a successful trader who had sufficient funds, paid large dowries to the heads of the Houses of the women he married so that the children of such unions would belong to his House rather than theirs. Second, he could become protector or patron of persons in trouble. The third and surest method was for him to purchase slaves from the hinterland. By these means such a trader increased his labour force and therefore his wealth. When such a trader considered himself wealthy and powerful enough he presented himself to the *amanyanabo* and community as a political leader. When accepted by the *amanyanabo* and community, he became a chief and House head.

To be accepted as a House head meant that such a man had a following within the city large enough to provide a fighting contingent or war canoe manned by thirty able-bodied men in defence of the state. He also, had enough money to provide guns and ammunition for the fighting contingent. Hence, the House founded by such a man was called a war canoe house. By virtue of his position as a chief and House head, he became a member of the King's Council which decided on internal and external affairs.

Members of the War Canoe House retained the kinship terminology of original *wari* lineage, not withstanding the different ways by which they were recruited. They all were members of the head's trading corporation or depended on him for recommendation to the European super-cargos. Succession to the position of House head within the city state was very competitive, and was determined not by heredity, but by ability to trade and capacity for leadership, as well as the votes of all adult members of the House.

The "open" criterion for upward social mobility in-built in the institution of the War Canoe House was thus an important step in the development of the Eastern Delta states. But since large numbers of slaves were imported to build the new Houses, there was a need for an institution to integrate these men and women into the society. The house system had an in-built system of turning a slave into a member of the community and kin to all other members of the House. The hair of a slave was ceremoniously shaved by one of the elderly women in the House - usually one of the wives of the House head. After this he was given a new name symbolizing his or her rebirth into the society. The slave was then handed over to a senior woman in the House - sometimes the one who had ceremonially shaved his hair - who became his "mother". From then on, the other children of his "mother" were expected to treat the slave as a sibling and other members of the house were expected to treat him as one of themselves.

Apart from the acculturative method within the House, there were other economic and social forces which also induced slaves to acculturate quickly and completely. First, complete acculturation and enterprise were rewarded. For instance, a completely acculturated slave who acquired wealth of his own or successfully conducted the trade of his House head, could be elected House head. Second, there were societies membership of which encouraged acculturation. One of these was the prestigious masquerade playing society called *ekine* or *sekiapu*, (Horton, 1966). By reason of their ability to dance, members of *ekine* considered themselves particularly well-endowed citizens, because of their mastery of the drum language embodying the historical lore of their community and their ancestors. Mastery of the *sekiapu* drum rhythm and the accompanying dance steps was proof of a thorough understanding of the local language and hence evidence of complete acculturation. Writing on the *Ekine* society in the Eastern Delta states, Professor Alagoa has pointed out (in Ajayi and Crowder, eds, 1971: 344):

> *Ekine* or *Sekiapu,* then, was one institution that enshrined the open society traditions of the delta states where careers were determined by talent. Rise within the society was based solely on artistic ability--to sing, dance, drum, or understand the drum language. Success within *sekiapu*, moreover, was publicly displayed and became the seal of full citizenship, acceptance within the community, and passport to political office. In other ways too, membership of *sekiapu* introduced a man to a measure of political action since the society came to assist the rulers of the states in the administration of justice. *Sekiapu* enforced a code of conduct on all its members, and also collected debts and punished pilferers and offenders against public morality.

Another association which encouraged quick and complete acculturation was the *periogbo*, an association of successful warriors present in all the delta states. *Periogbo* members were courageous men who had performed such feats of valour like slaying an enemy or taking a captive in war, or killed an elephant or a leopard. As a mark of distinction, they put eagle feathers on their hats, drank with their left hands and performed the special war dance *peri* at the close of a war, the death of a king or a member. *Periogbo* was thus another institution which demonstrated the open criterion for socio-political advancement in the Eastern Delta states.

The *Periogbo* was not only an association for the defence of the state. There were aspects of *peri* activities which induced slaves to acculturate quickly. Among the Kalabari for instance, there was an inner group of *Periogbo* called *Koronogbo* (the club of the strong) which performed such a function. On certain nights, members of *Koronogbo* went into the streets and challenged those they met. If the individual was not fluent in the local language or worse still, replied in a foreign accent, he was seized and severely punished or dispatched. Other delta states had vigilante groups that performed similar functions.

In sum, the war canoe Houses in the Eastern Delta states performed several functions. They served as units of assimilating slaves and other stranger elements into full citizens. They did this better in some states than in others. In the state of Bonny for instance, Igbo, the language of the slaves, superseded the *Ibani* language to some extent. They were also units of external defence. However, given the tendency of Houses to fragment, they were also sources of conflict within the states. The ups and downs of the Atlantic trade led to the fission and fusion of Houses – especially in the nineteenth century. These conflicts led to the split of some of the city states into two.

Economic History

The earliest economic activity of the Eastern Delta states was subsistence fishing. The methods used were poisons (such as the mashed endocarp of the fruit of *Raphia vinifera* or *oxytenanthera abyssinica*), basket traps and harpoons. Another economic activity of these states was subsistence hunting, especially in the form of communal hunting. There exists among these states a wide distribution of traditions, using the stereotype of a·quarrel over the division of the soup of an animal caught in communal hunting.

The beach ridge and salt water swamp of the Eastern Delta states is not suitable for agriculture, consequently they produce very little vegetables. However, there are traditions of collecting and gathering palm nuts, certain species of banana and other plants that grew wild. The soil in the fresh water swamp is more conducive to agriculture; and bananas, plantains (*musa paradisiaca*), cocoyam (*taro*), and the water yam (*diascorea alata*) have been cultivated for a long time. The earliest forms of exchange of the Eastern Delta states, was therefore, one between them and the fishing and farming communities of the fresh water swamp region.

Long Distance Trade

The people of the Eastern Delta traded not only with their neighbours in the adjacent fresh water swamp, but also with people farther a field in the Ibo hinterland. The Portuguese who arrived the Delta at the beginning of the sixteenth century, reported such activity between the Delta states and their hinterland neighbouring. In 1506, Pereira reported trade at a delta port on the Rio Real with those in the hinterland as far as "a hundred leagues or more." The traders used large trading canoes made out of a single trunk and brought yams, slaves, cows, goats, and sheep from the hinterland.

In the seventeenth century, Barbot described trading canoes at Elem Kalabari which were very similar to these described by Pereira. Barbot listed bananas, chickens, hogs, palm wine and palm oil as items the delta traders brought from the hinterland. In exchange for these products the delta peoples supplied salt to those in the hinterland. According to John Adams who reported early in the nineteenth century, the Eastern Delta states manufactured this salt by boiling sea water in "neptunes, or large brass pans, taken from Europe to Bonny". A north-south trade developed since food was in short supply in the delta and salt was in great demand in the hinterland. There was also an east-west trade between the Eastern Delta states with the Itsekiri kingdom in the Western Delta, and through them, with regions much further afield. The most important produce the Itsekiri supplied to the Eastern Delta was a cassava meal which the Portuguese called *Farinha (mandioca)*. It is known throughout the Delta by variations of its original Portuguese name. For instance, the Kalabari people refer to it as *ifenica* or *afenia*. According to Alagoa, "The cassava (manioc) apparently spread to other parts of the Delta from Warri." (Alagoa, in Ajayi and Crowder, 1971:357). Barbot described 'a large number of manioc bushes, which they call *mandi-hoka* in their language; of which they make the cassaba or *farinha de pao*, that is in Portuguese, wood meal, which is the bread they commonly feed on'. (Barbot in Alagoa, 1971:357).

The Atlantic Trade

The Portuguese arrived in the Eastern Delta in their quest for a sea route to India. They gradually developed trade with the region by exporting local produce and importing merchandise from other parts of West Africa and beyond. It was the Portuguese who brought manilas from the Congo and distributed same in the Niger Delta. Other European traders later joined the Portuguese to trade in the Niger Delta.

The arrival of the Portuguese, and later of other Europeans, affected the organization of the local long distance trade. By establishing trading posts at various points along the coast, the Portuguese took over the distribution of goods from one point to the other along the coast.

In response to this development, the Eastern Delta states developed trade with communities in their immediate hinterland. Thus Kalabari traders operated the Obia markets, while Bonny traders opened market in the Ndoki country at Ohambele. Okrika traders opened markets in the Ogoni and Ikwerre areas in their immediate neighbourhood .

The arrival of the Europeans also led to the decline of some traditional economic pursuits. The English for instance, imported salt which competed with locally manufactured salt. According to Alagoa (1971), by the end of the eighteenth century each English vessel trading to Bonny carried up to fifty tons of salt. But by far the greatest economic impact of the arrival of the European was the introduction of the trade in slaves,

The Slave Trade

The overseas trade in slaves was conducted on the basis of European demand and African supply. While it lasted the Eastern Delta states were one of the core areas of supply of slaves to destinations in the Americas. Elem Kalabari, Bonny and Okrika traders obtained the slaves from markets in their hinterland, but since participation in the trade required a huge capital outlay only those with the required capital could participate in the trade.

Capital was required to provide canoes large enough to carry a sufficient stock of goods to the hinterland markets, and to bring back enough slaves to make a profit. Capital was also required to provide the large number of paddlers required to operate the canoes. In addition, the canoes had to be armed to provide security against pirates and trade rivals. Barbot tells us that the trading canoes used at Elem Kalabari in the seventeenth century were armed with javelins and shields.

The Eastern Delta states obtained the slaves from the hinterland markets to their north. The people of the hinterland markets, obtained the slaves from other groups farther inland. For instance, the majority of the slaves sold to the Europeans at the Eastern Delta ports came from Iboland. Ibani, Kalabari and Okrika traders did not engage in slave raids in the hinterland. Kalabari tradition mention raids by Agbaniye Ejike, King of Bille, who sold his captives, taken from neighbouring communities within the Eastern Delta, to European slave traders. To maintain a free flow of trade, the Eastern Delta rulers maintained good relations with the peoples in the hinterland markets.

The Introduction of Staple Trade

In the nineteenth century, European Governments abolished the trade in slaves and in its place introduced trade in forest products—the so-called legitimate commerce. Eric Williams has pointed out the economic arguments for the abolition in his book *Capitalism and Slavery* while the case for the trade in forest products was put forward in a book by Thomas Fowell Buxton called *The African Slave Trade and Its Remedy*.

Despite the formal abolition of the slave trade by European Governments, their citizens continued the trade illegally. To effectively stop the slave trade, the British Government resorted to diplomacy. The two were complementary. With regards to diplomacy, the British Government negotiated banning the slave trade with those countries which had not done so. Britain also stationed a detachment of the Royal Navy (the West African or Preventive Squadron) permanently in West Africa to seize ships engaged in the slave trade.

Initial British efforts at abolition concentrated on the demand side, and so the Delta rulers continued to trade with those European countries who were willing to trade with them. Besides, the Delta rulers questioned why Britain should have to dictate to them. As sovereign states they argued that they could engage in any trade of their choice. How, they wondered, did Britain expect them to stop a trade in which they had invested so much? Moreover, while Britain opposed the slave-trade, Spain, Portugal, Brazil and other countries still continued to trade in slaves. This led the Delta rulers to suspect that perhaps Britain was at war with these other countries. Moreover, the Preventive Squadron could not stop this trade as the Delta states shifted their trade to other ports when theirs were blockaded. For instance, when the Squadron blockaded Bonny, Bonny traders transferred their slave-trading activities to Brass.

In an attempt to overcome African opposition, Britain extended her treaty making activity, to the Delta rulers. The Delta rulers were persuaded to sign anti-slave trade treaties in return for the payment of small subsidies if they promise to stop the slave trade in their territories. King Dappa Pepple of Bonny signed such a treaty as did other Delta rulers.

The second arm of the British effort to abolish the slave trade was to substitute it with trade in forest products, such as palm oil and ivory. This was the so-called legitimate commerce. The combined effect of British pressure and gunboat politics compelled the Delta states to switch their economics from slaves to palm oil. By the 1840s, the palm oil, trade had completely replaced the slave trade. We are told by a British naval officer in 1842 that "the slave trade at Bonny and at Calabar has been done up these three years; it is not carried on at all" (Burns, 1972:108). A witness before the House of Common Select Committee on the West Coast of Africa declared that the Africans "scarcely take the trouble of buying slaves in Bonny now, they get so well remunerated by palm oil" (Burns, 1972:108). In 1839 for instance, 13,600 tons of palm oil were imported into Liverpool from the Oil Rivers (Niger Delta). As the Oil Rivers were those between the Benin River and the Cameroons a greater part of the oil to Liverpool in 1839 would have come from the ports of Bonny and Elem Kalabari.

The Staple (Legitimate) Trade

The case for legitimate commerce was put forward in a book by Thomas Fowell Buxton called *The African Slave-Trade and Its Remedy*. The author suggested commerce, Christianity and civilization as a means to end the slave-trade. Eric Williams also pointed out the economic arguments for the abolition in his book, *Capitalism and Slavery*. Briefly, the economic argument for the abolition states that by the 19th century, Britain, and gradually other European countries, had industrialised; and so needed tropical raw materials, markets and outlet to invest surplus capital. Africans were now more useful in Africa to produce the raw materials and provide the market for European goods. This explains why Britain was willing to pay subsidies to the Delta rulers to convert their economies from slaves to palm oil. The combined effect of British pressure and gunboat politics compelled the Delta states to switch their economies from slaves to palm oil.

During the 19th century, palm oil had a number of industrial uses. It was used in the manufacture of soap and candles. It was also used for lubricating the axles of railway carriages. In South Wales and the United States, it was also employed in the preparation of tin plates. The plates, when white hot, were dipped in palm oil, which gave them their smooth and glassy surface.

The switch from slaves to palm oil had several attendant difficulties. First there was the problem of transportation. Unlike slaves who were marched to the coast, palm oil had to be transported from the hinterland to the coast. Palm oil trade thus required huge capital outlay in the form of large canoes to transport the oil and operate the canoes. Secondly, during the slave trade, slaves were brought to the coast. But palm oil was produced by numerous small scale producers in the hinterland. To collect the oil and transport same to the coast required several months of residence in the hinterland during the buying season. It was for this purpose that the Delta rulers acquired domestic slaves from the hinterland as labour to conduct the trade.

Legitimate trade was conducted on the basis of credit. The European traders advanced goods on credit to the Delta rulers who in turn advanced a portion of what they had received to their trading agents in the hinterland. This credit system was known as the trust system.

James Barbot has given us a good description of trade condition in the Delta during the 19th century. According to him (Crowder, 1966: 84-86):

> On the first of July, the King sent for us to come ashore, we staid there till four in the afternoon, and concluded the trade on the terms offered them the day before; the King promising to come the next day aboard to regulate it, and we paid his duties... The second, heavy rain all this morning. At 2 o'clock, we fetch'd the king from shore attended by all his Caboceiras and officers, in three large canoes, and entering the ship was saluted with seven guns. The King had on an old-fashioned scarlet coat, laced with gold and silver, very rusty, and a fine hat on his head, but barefooted; all his attendants showing great respect to him and since our coming

hither, none of the natives have dared to come aboard of us, or sell the least thing, till the king had adjusted trade with us.

We had again a long discourse with the King and Pepprell his brother, concerning the rates of our goods and his customs. This Pepprell being a sharp blade and a mighty talking Black, perpetually making objections against something or the other and teasing us for this or that Dassy or present, as well as for drams, etc,…it were to be wished that such a one as he were not of the way, to facilitate trade…

Thus, with much patience, all our matters were adjusted indifferently, after their way who are not very scrupulous to find excuses or objections, for not keeping literally to any verbal contract, for they have not the art of reading and writing, and therefore, we are forced to stand to their agreement which often is no longer than they think fit to hold it themselves….

We gave the usual presents to the King, etc…. To Captain Forty, the King's general, Captain Pepprell, Captain Boileau, Alderman Bougsby, my lord Willyby, Duke of Monmouth, drunken Henry and some others two firelocks, eight hats, nine narrow Guinea stuffs. We adjusted with them the reduction of our merchandise into bars of iron as the standard coin, viz one bunch of beads, one bar….

The price of provisions and wood was also regulated. Sixty king's yams, one bar; one hundred and sixty slaves' yams, one bar; for fifty thousand yams to be delivered to us. A butt of water, two rings. For the length of wood, seven bars, which is dear; but they were to deliver it ready cut into our boat. For a goat, one bar. A cow, ten or eight bars, according to its bigness. A hog two bars. A calf, eight bars. A jar of palm oil, one bar and a quarter.

We paid also the King's duties in goods; five hundred slaves, to be purchased at two copper rings a head.

We also advanced to the King by way of loan, the value of a hundred and fifty bars of iron, in sundry goods; and to his principal men, and others as much again each in proportion to his quality and ability…

It is generally believed that only European traders advanced credit to the Delta middlemen. But this was not the case; Delta chiefs and middlemen also advanced credit to European traders. Commenting on the trust system, E.D. Morel has pointed out (Morel, 1968: 78):

> Giving out trust is not invariably confined to the Europeans. Native chiefs have been known to give trust to Europeans up to 1000 cases of palm oil, in days too when palm oil was worth 15 per puncheon. This would represent a credit of 15,000.

The trust system was a source of conflict between the European and the Nigerian traders. The European traders never wanted the Delta rulers to fully repay their trust so that they would not trade with other Europeans.

To break this trade monopoly, newly arrived European traders offered higher prices for oil. When a Delta trader broke his trust, the affected European trader would seize the former's goods. Conversely, when a Delta trader felt he had discharged his obligation and the European trader thought to the contrary, the King declared a trade boycott. It was this lawlessness on the part of both European and Delta traders that made Prof. K. O. Dike to describe the traders as "palm oil ruffians".

It was the urge to maintain law and order in the palm oil trade that led to the establishment of the Court of Equity. Writing about these courts in 1854, Baikie reported the existence of "a commercial or mercantile association" organised by some of the merchants at Bonny (Burns, 1972: 140-141).

> The members being the chief white and black traders in the place, and the chair occupied by the white supercargoes in monthly rotation. All disputes were brought before this Court.... and with the consent of the Kings fines are levelled on defaulters. If anyone refuses to submit to the decision of the Court, or ignores its jurisdiction, he is tabooed, and no one trades with him. The natives stand in much awe of it, and readily pay their debts when threatened with it (Burns. 1972:140-141).

The Court of Equity was later given legal backing as it was incorporated into the Order in Council of 1872. By 1870 such courts had been established at Calabar, Bonny, Brass, Akassa, New Calabar, the Benin River and Opobo.

Legitimate trade also affected the House system which was the basis of the political organisation of the Delta states. Houses which were originally kinship institutions, were transformed by the demands of the palm oil trade into trading corporations. As kinship institutions, blood ties were the basis of house membership. But with the palm oil trade, domestic slaves from the Igbo hinterland were absorbed into the Houses to make them effective labour and fighting men. To cope with the challenges of the palm oil trade, Houses had to maintain war canoes manned by thirty to fifty paddlers and capable of carrying eighty to over one hundred soldiers. Hence, in the 19th century the Houses became war canoe houses.

Legitimate trade also brought a social revolution in the Delta states. By the custom of the Delta states only persons of royal birth could become kings, chiefs or house-heads. But in the course of the 19th century some of the domestic slaves from the Igbo hinterland acquired wealth and aspired to political leadership. These were the "new men" of whom King Jaja of Opobo was one of the most prominent. Some of the new men became chiefs and even house-heads. For instance, after the death of King Opubo the Great of Bonny in 1830, the headship of the Anna Pepple House passed to Alali who was an assimilated slave, as Opubo's son, Prince Willian Dappa Pepple, was still a minor. Indeed, in 1833, Alali was appointed regent of Bonny.

Bonny and Elem Kalabari, the foremost trading states of the Delta, typified more than any other Delta states, the social upheaval due to the palm oil trade. After the death of Alali, the headship of the Anna Pepple House passed to another new man, Jaja, who was a purchased Igbo slave. That the new men were now in the ascendancy in Bonny could be seen in the fact that the headship of the Manilla Pepple House at this time was vested in Oko Jumbo, another man of servile origin.

It was the clash between the Manilla Pepple House under Oko Jumbo and the Anna Pepple House under Jaja that led to the civil war which split Bonny. Supporters of Jaja moved to Opobo and founded a new city-state where Jaja became King. In Elem Kalabari, the new men also challenged the traditional nobility and the resultant strife led to the split of the city-state into three, namely Bakana, Abonnema and Buguma.

Legitimate trade led to commercial rivalry and ultimately war among the city-states. The principal cause of the commercial rivalry was falling prices due to increased supply. The increased supply was due to new entrants into the palm oil trade. Calabar, Bonny and Elem Kalabari, the main suppliers were, by the mid 19th century, joined by Itsekiri, Brass/Nembe and Lagos. To maintain their income levels, the Delta states extended their trading activities into the hinterland markets, so as to increase their exports. This increased their costs at a time when prices were falling.

After the second half of the 19th century, the commercial rivalry turned into commercial war as the city-states encroached on each other's market. Kalabari and Brass/Nembe clashed over the markets along the Engenni River which led to Oguta. Bonny, having been displaced by Opobo in her Imo River markets, moved into Kalabari markets along the Sombreiro River, thus forcing Kalabari into the Engenni markets. These wars considerably weakened the Delta states.

Encroachment on Sovereignty

In an effort to stop the slave-trade and ensure conversion to legitimate commerce, British agents encroached on the sovereignty of the Delta states. First, by blockading the Delta ports so that the Delta states would not engage in the slave-trade, Britain violated the sovereignty of these states to trade with whom they liked, as they were not consulted before Britain banned the trade. It was thus not surprising that when in 1836, the Anti-Slave Trade Squadron seized a Spanish ship trading in slaves in Bonny, Alali who was then regent in Bonny retaliated by imprisoning the British merchants in Bonny. When the British Navy threatened to destroy Bonny unless the merchants were released, Prince Dappa Pepple, anxious to get rid of Alali and secure the throne, offered to co-operate with the British. Prince Dappa Pepple had an understanding with the British whereby he agreed never to arrest British subjects again; the British in return agreed to force Alali to accept his own deportation. British subjects thus obtained extra-territorial jurisdiction and lived outside the laws of Bonny. Alali became the symbol of all those who were opposed to British encroachment on the sovereignty of Bonny.

Prince Dappa Pepple's romance with the British did not last long. The Prince soon found that the British were in Bonny to further their own interests, not his own. With the promise of a subsidy for four years to enable him to switch from slaves to oil, Prince Dappa had signed an anti-slave trade treaty with the British. In 1854, Prince Dappa seized a British merchant ship in place of the monies the British were owing him under the treaty. The British had signed the anti-slave trade treaty four times with Prince Dappa Pepple and four times refused to ratify it. This time it was Alali who cooperated with the British. With the assistance of the British Navy and support of the British merchants in Bonny, Alali and his supporters signed a proclamation for the king's deportation and the British deported the king.

However, Alali and the new men could not hold Bonny together. They lacked the divine attribute which was part of Prince Dappa's authority. Consequently, chaos and confusion reigned in Bonny until the British traders called for the reinstatement of the deposed king. Prince Dappa Pepple was allowed to return in 1861 but only on the terms of the British. For instance, the British insisted that he should not engage in trade. He was also forced to rely on comey, that is, the customs duties paid by foreign traders. What the British wanted was a king who would maintain law and order while they controlled trade which was the source of wealth. As G. I. Jones has said, "the consul was convinced that the king should be concerned with government and not with trade, and that King William Dappa Pepple's downfall was due to his neglect of this principle" (Jones, 1963:119-120). King William Dappa Pepple is now celebrated as an early proponent of resource control in the Niger Delta.

The Colonial Period

By the nineteenth century, the Ibani, Kalabari and Okrika had been in contact with the maritime states of Europe for over three hundred years. Throughout this period, the Eastern Delta states retained their sovereignty and maintained a landlord–tenant relationship with visiting European traders. Though the appointment of Mr. John Beecroft as the first Consul for the Bights of Benin and Biafra (now Bonny) marked the beginning of direct British administration in Nigeria, the Consular period was a phase of British interference in the politics of the Eastern Delta states and not one of loss of sovereignty. It was the establishment of colonial rule that ended the sovereignty of these states and converted them into components of the Nigerian state.

Though the Oil Rivers Protectorate had been established in 1885, no steps were taken to make it effective. It was in 1891, six years after the establishment of the Protectorate, that a system of government was adopted for it. The system consisted of Consuls and Vice-Consuls being appointed to the various rivers under a Commissioner and a Consul-General resident at Old Calabar. By an Order in Council, the Protectorate was extended over the hinterland and renamed Niger Coast Protectorate in 1893.

As we have indicated earlier, the Consular era was one of interference in the politics of the Delta states and for the Ibani, Kalabari and Okrika, the establishment of the Protectorate of Southern Nigeria on 1st January, 1900 was the beginning of formal colonial rule as they were inexorably drawn into the orbit of the evolving Nigerian state.

The colonial period was one of economic decline for the peoples of the Eastern Delta. The middleman position which they land lost in the nineteenth century was consolidated during the colonial period. A few centres like Abonema became thriving commercial centres, but the Delta peoples became factors to the European traders and no longer independent traders.

The colonial administration introduced measures designed to consolidate their hold over the territory and to develop the area. To keep the vast complex of creeks and rivers open all the year round, the government of Southern Nigeria required the chiefs and people to provide compulsory labour to clear the waterways under the provisions of the Roads and Creeks Proclamation, 1903.

In spite of the imperial acts of 1807 and 1833 which forbade the slave trade and slavery in British territories, the trade continued in the Eastern Delta states. For instance, in 1836 the Anti-Slave Trade Squadron seized a Spanish ship trading in slaves in Bonny and Alali who was then regent considered it a violation of Bonny sovereignty and retaliated by imprisoning the British merchants in Bonny. In the Eastern Delta states the legal status of slavery was only abolished by the Slave Dealing Proclamation, 1901, issued by the government of the Protectorate of Southern Nigeria.

Before the emergence of a free labour market, the government of the Southern Nigeria Protectorate met its labour needs through forced labour. Several enactments gave legal backing to these arrangements, including the Roads and Creeks Proclamation, 1903. This proclamation empowered the chiefs, on the orders of the District Commissioner, to ask able-bodied men and women to clear roads on such days as the government required but "not exceeding six days in each quarter of a year". The government did not exempt women from forced labour.

Other laws designed to achieve the same end were the Native House Rule Proclamation of 1901, and the Master and Servant Proclamation of 1901. The Master and Servant Proclamation was amended in 1903 to cover government contracts and to enable the chiefs to obtain "apprentices" in place of "bought" domestic slaves. By this amendment, the government also extended the term for which children under 16 years old could be apprenticed to learn a trade from five to twelve years in order to give the chiefs some security of tenure in their services. To safeguard the interests of such apprentices, the 1901 proclamation

517

stipulated that a contract service should be confirmed before a British High Commissioner to whom the apprentice must be brought four times every year (Tamuno, 1972:324-325).

Before he enacted the Native House Proclamation, Moor claimed to have canvassed the wishes of "representative chiefs" at Bonny, Degema, Okrika and other coastal communities.

The Native House Rule Proclamation, 1901 which came into operation on January 1, 1902, was a compromise between slavery and free labour. It ratified the reciprocal duties and obligations the House head and members owed each other under native law and custom. It also tried to meet the cracks which had appeared in the pre-colonial system through the evasions made by both parties to a solemn, though unwritten contract of service. The House head or member who evaded his obligations was, on conviction, liable to a fine not exceeding £50, or to a term of imprisonment not over one year, or both. Where the House head convincingly ill-treated any member, "the Court" had power to free such a member from all further obligations (Tamuno, 1972: 326).

The proclamation also regulated transactions between European and African employers in their business with members of Houses. Employers had to obtain the prior consent of House heads before members of their Houses were engaged. The proclamation also served as a vagrancy and poor law. Any person caught wandering or having no apparent means of subsistence, could be arrested, questioned and punished "unless he proves that he has sufficient means of subsistence, or that his want of such means is not the result of his own fault...." (Tamuno, 1972:326-327). Due to public criticism by various interest groups, the Native House Rule Proclamation (Ordinance) was amended in 1912 and eventually repealed in 1915. By 1915 the government had established firm administrative control and free individual enterprise was accepted by the people.

Another significant development during the colonial period was the introduction of coin currency to oust the old commodity currency. Various items including "trade gin", crystal beads, brass pans, cowrie shells, copper wires called "cheethams" or "citims", brass rods and small alloy horse shoes, called "manilas", were in use as commodity currencies in the Eastern Delta states. In 1903, the government began to import bronze coinage but the people showed little interest in it. In March, 1908, the government introduced pennies and tenths of a penny. In the 1920s international trade collapsed and with it the fortunes of the indigenous traders of the Eastern Delta.

The most obvious political consequence of colonial rule for the Ibani, Kalabari and Okrika was the loss of their sovereignty. Throughout the colonial period the chiefs were subordinates of colonial officials. The earliest form of local government established in the Eastern Delta by the colonial government consisted of Native Councils and Native Courts. Through these councils and courts, the colonial government utilised the indigenous customs and laws of the people in local administration. This was genuine indirect rule distinct from the much publicised Lugardian version in the North.

One of the ten stages in the process of "opening up" Southern Nigeria laid down by Sir Ralph Moor was what he called "Native Council of Chiefs in friendly towns" (Nicolson, 1969:88-89). Great importance was attached by Moor's administration to the native courts and native councils. They were intended to be the main instrument of progress employed directly by the government supplementing the civilizing influences of commence and education. These courts and councils were held to be of great value, not only in the administration of justice, but also in "providing the means of instructing the people in the proper methods of government".

After the amalgamation of Lagos and Southern Nigeria, the Ibani, Kalabari and Okrika people became part of the Eastern Provinces. After the amalgamation in 1914, Lugard extended his northern version of indirect rule to these areas, and gave certificates, called warrants, to the coastal chiefs. It was these warrants which qualified them to sit in the Native Courts.

As commerce followed the flag so did the church and western education. Christian missionary enterprise in the Niger Delta started in the nineteenth century, but it was in the twentieth century during the colonial period that their efforts were consolidated.

Bonny is the home of Christianity in the Eastern Niger Delta. In 1863, King William Dappa Pepple of Bonny instructed his son George Pepple to formally write to the Lord Bishop of London for the establishment of a Church at Bonny. The request was forwarded to Crowther in 1864, and led to the eventual commencement of Church Missionary Society (CMS) activities in Bonny. King William Pepple had been converted while in exile, and baptized at Christ Church, Middlesex, on 3 October, 1856 (Wariboko, 1998:52). Convinced that Britain owed its greatness to Christianity, King William Pepple used some of the money paid to him as "damages for wrongful exile" to recruit missionaries to begin missionary work in Bonny. It was, when those recruited directly by him failed, that he turned to the CMS.

It was from Bonny that Christianity spread to Kalabari and Okrika (Tasie, 1978). Bonny is also remarkable because it produced the first Christian martyr, Joshua Hart, while Garrick Braide of Kalabari became the first Christian charismatic evangelist. Joshua Hart, a young Christian convert of the Chief Captain Hart House suffered martyrdom rather than eat food sacrificed to the gods. On his part, Garrick Sokari Idaketima Braide was a communicant and warden of St. Andrew's Church in Bakana his home town. He left the Anglican Church and became a famous healer through prayer. His rallies attracted large crowds who proclaimed their conversion to Christianity. He was called the second Elijah. Other Christian denominations including the African Church, the Baptists and the Roman Catholics, followed the Anglicans into the Eastern Delta.

Western education in Bonny, Kalabari and Okrika was started by the missionaries. Western education began in Bonny in 1864, Elem Kalabari in 1874 and 1850 in Okrika respectively. By the beginning of the twentieth century, Christian mission schools were to be found in all corners of the Eastern

Delta. As the people came to appreciate the value of Western education, communities built schools. In 1938, the Kalabari people established the Kalabari National College, Buguma, as the first community secondary school.

In those communities, where the missions had not established schools, schools were run directly by the government. Moor as High Commissioner of the Protectorate of Southern Nigeria, had as the declared object of his administration "the education and improvement of the native" and his "elevation". Moor's Administration was more directly involved in the provision of education. During one leave in England, Moor raised £5,000 to help build new premises for the Bonny school (Orugbani, 2005 102-104).

Missionary enterprise and Western education had far reaching consequences on the Delta societies. Delta rulers appreciated western education as providing skills which will make their children more efficient in the palm oil trade, in addition to providing employment with the missions (as catechists and school masters), the mercantile houses and the government. They were apprehensive of the effect of Christian teaching on their indigenous cultural and religious practices. Their worries, in this regard, can be summarized by the views of Chief Bob Manuel, Amanyanabo of Abonema, when he told the missionary Garrick to "teach my people to read and write English book, but leave God palaver alone", because "this God palaver is a trouble" (Wariboko, 1998: 214).

The Post-Colonial Period

The immediate post-colonial period was a period of decline for the people of the Eastern Delta. Abonema which became a commercial emporium during the colonial period collapsed in the early 1960s as the mercantile houses closed down and moved to Port Harcourt.

The creation of the Rivers State arrested this decline for the Ibani, Kalabari, and Okrika people. The creation of the Rivers State redressed the neglect they suffered during the colonial period and the immediate post-colonial period under the Eastern Regional Government. The first Government of the State, the

Diete-Spiff Administration, responded to the aspirations of the people by providing employment, education and social services. The pace set by that administration has been maintained in various degrees by successive governments in the State.

The hub of economic activity in the Eastern Delta shifted to Bonny. The oil industry which started on a small scale in Bonny before the war, is now the mainstay of the economy of the kingdom, and indeed, of the Eastern Delta region. Young men and women from all over the region now flock to Bonny in search of greener pastures. The establishment of the LNG plant at Bonny is another boost to the economy of the region.

Politically, too, the immediate post-colonial period was not favourable to the people. Generally speaking, they supported the Action Group, the Opposition party at the Federal level. This support earned them the displeasure of the NCNC which controlled the regional government at Enugu. The displeasure of the Enugu government was expressed in the form of discrimination in employment for sons and daughters of the area and the provision of social amenities for the people. This was the situation until the creation of States.

In conclusion, the people of the Eastern Delta have had a long history in their present location. Though they migrated mainly from the Central Delta, it was in the Eastern Delta that they developed centralized polities headed by a king (*amanyanabo*), and the peculiar and unique institution known as the war canoe house. During the colonial period they lost their sovereignty as they were incorporated into the Nigerian State without their consent. Political independence, especially, since the creation of the Rivers State, has improved their lot.

CHAPTER 22
THE EASTERN DELTA LIMIT

Nkparom C. Ejituwu, Jones M. Jaja
and John H. Enemugwem

Introduction

The Eastern Niger Delta Limit is the home of three distinct groups, namely, the Obolo (Andoni), Opobo and Nkoro.

Obolo (Andoni):

The Obolo (Andoni) in the Eastern Niger Delta Limit are found in eight local government areas: the Andoni Local Government Area in Rivers State; in Eastern Obolo, Ibeno and five local government areas in Akwa Ibom State.

Andoni oral tradition categorize the Obolo (Andoni) as an Ijo ethnic nationality. This view was taught in schools in Eastern Nigeria down to the period of the First Republic. Their strong Ijo and Cameroonian connections remain in their traditions of origin and external relations.

Traditions of Origin, Migration and Settlement

Three waves of Obolo migrations from their homelands led them to their present location between the Rio Real and the Cross River estuary. Ejituwu (1991:34-37) postulated that the first wave of migrants came from the Cameroons. Two brothers, Obolo and Oro, left the Rio del Rey (Ramby) area, through the Cross River estuary, for the Niger Delta in search of good fishing grounds. Finally, they settled in the Eastern Delta Limit and built the Obolo primary settlements, Unyangala, Egwede and Agana. Uya (1984:10-31) added that there were rifts between the children of these two brothers which made Oro and his group depart from the Obolo for the Cross River estuary and found the Oron group of settlements. Linguistic evidence tends to support this tradition. Williamson (1988:65-119) states that the basic vocabularies of Obolo and Oron are 45% cognate, and classifies both as part of the Delta-Cross language family.

The Ijo group were the second wave of migrants that came into the Eastern Delta Limit and settled with the Obolo. Owonaro (1949:1-66) recorded the blood relationship between the Ijo and the Obolo (Andoni). The ancestors of the Andoni, Kolokuma, Opokuma, Tarakiri, Mein, Ogboin and Olodiama who were the children of Ijo left Ile-Ife with their father. When they reached Benin City, they could not live there permanently but departed for the Niger Delta. Their father, whom they nicknamed "Indo", had named the ancestor of the Andoni after himself. As soon as Ijo passed away, his children started to call their Andoni brothers "Indo", and at later years "Ido" and "Idoni", a corruption of "Indo". Hence the name Andoni by which the Obolo came to be known to the outside world.

This second wave of migrants first settled at Ayama, now Peterside in Bonny, at a time when the ancestors of the present Bonny had not arrived. They moved to the Eastern Delta Limit, sojourned with the first set of Obolo at Egwede and Agana. Later, they founded Unyangala and other Obolo settlements like Oronija, Ilotombi and Iton (now extinct). Jones (1988:89-90) mentioned one Otuile, who founded Iton village, as the brother of Omuso, founder of Finima in Bonny. Otuile left Omuso to found Iton, while his grandson, Iramba, was the first settler at Oronija. According to Jones (1988:90), "they came there together from Ijo". It was this second wave of migrants that were the first settlers of the Rio Real, Asarama, Asaramatoru and Unyeada. They were assimilated by the first wave of migrants that established Egwede, Agana and other Obolo settlements. As a result, they lost their original Ijo language.

The founder of Ilotombi and Oyobumbi was among the second migrants from Ijo. Oyobumbi is said to have led five canoes to Ayama (Peterside). With him were Obah, the first settler of Abalama in Kalabari, Alama the first settler of Alabie (Agwut-Obolo) and Aba who founded Unyangala. They first sojourned

Nat Isiobozeng and Echirichong before moving to Egwede, Agana and Unyangala, respectively. To Jones (1988:96), they are all related to other Ijo groups, not with the Efik-Ibibio or with the Edo who had no idea of the existence of the Andoni and the Kalabari.

The third wave of migrants were also of Ijo stock. They came through Kalabari area of Ifoko to co-settle with the Obolo (Andoni). According to Jones (1963:29), they were from the Central Delta, moving eastwards towards Cameroon before retreating to Egwede. Prominent in this group was Ifop. He and Ekor from Cameroon co-settled at Alabie (Agwut-Obolo) with Alama, a son of Obolo. Thus, Alabie came to be named after the first settler, Alama. Ifop married Ekor's daughter and their son, Gogo, who founded Ngo Town, later called "Ngo" by Europeans who could not pronounce "Gogo" (Jones 1988:88-94). Presently, Ngo is the administrative headquarters of the Obolo. Like the second wave of migrants, they were also assimilated by the first Obolo settlers, and they only retained some words of their original Ijo language. Williamson (1988:65-119) says that the Obolo and other Ijo peoples share a basic vocabulary of only 17% .

However, the Obolo (Andoni) later expanded across the Imo river estuary and settled in the present Eastern Obolo and Ibeno Local Government Areas in Akwa Ibom State. Led by Ede and his assistants, they spread from the western bank of the Imo river estuary towards the Kwa Ibo estuary and established over forty settlements that constitute Eastern Obolo. Within the same period, the ancestors of the Ibeno also left Obolo central cluster for the Kwa Ibo and Cross River estuaries and created over twenty towns and villages. Among their settlements are Upenekang, which is their Local Government headquarters, Mkpanak where Exxon Mobil's Qua Iboe Terminal is located, as well as their premier town, Okoroutip, named in their original Obolo language (Enemugwem 1990:28-111). These two areas, Eastern Obolo and Ibeno, enrich Akwa Ibom State and Nigeria with petroleum resources.

The long distance separating the Ibeno from Obolo central cluster, and their proximity to non-Obolo speaking communities, reduced the depth of their relationship with their Obolo brothers in Rivers state. They were unable to retain the Obolo language and culture of their ancestors, except two villages, Ibra-Obolo (Opolom) and Ntafit. Faraclas (1984:2-5) states that they speak *Ibino*, a mixture of Obolo and Eket. The Ibeno memorandum to Jones (1956:1) summarized this predicament of losing the Obolo-Ijo civilisations as follows:

> when a people is broken into fragments from any cause and kept apart
> either by continued hostility, or by natural impediments to intercourse, it
> gradually loses its civilisation, and eventually even its literature dies out.

From the above, more than two hundred Obolo settlements emerged on the islands and mainland of the Eastern Delta Limit, between the Rio Real and the Cross River estuary. With every part of Obolo (Andoni) lying in the mangrove swamp and the Atlantic seaboard zone, their migrant fishing economy enabled them to contribute to the founding of some Ijo settlements.

Obolo Migrations into the Eastern and Central Delta

Obolo (Andoni) is the immediate homeland to some Central Delta and Eastern Delta communities. In the Central Delta, the Abureni communities of Abua, Odual, Ogbia, Kugbo, and Idema trace their ancestral blood relations and affinities to the Andoni. Centuries after the ancestors of the Obolo had left their Rio del Rey homeland, wars and insecurity drove the Abureni from the Rio del Rey into the Niger Delta. According to Sam (1982:1-12), they left what later became Cameroon and migrated in seven canoes between the seventeenth and eighteenth centuries into the Niger Delta and sojourned in Obolo (Andoni).

The Abua speak the Delta-Cross languages of the Niger-Congo family with the Obolo. This language family is identified with the northeast migrant group (Williamson, 1971; Williamson 1988:65-119). Agana, the son of Abua, is an Andoni name for one of the three Obolo earliest settlements. Furthermore, the sacred drum of the national religions of Abua and Andoni are called *Okama* and *Akama*, respectively. The Abua and Obolo languages are also similar.

In the Eastern Delta, Andoni migrants settled among the Ibani (Bonny and Opobo), Okrika, Kalabari and Nkoro. The Ibani and Nkoro are in the midst of the Obolo. According to Epelle (1964:39), "Bonny was first a settlement of fishermen from the Andony country; hence it was originally called Andony". Crowther (1882) suggested that some Andoni settlements at the Rio Real with a population of 300 may have been integrated into Grand Bonny. Outside Grand Bonny, Ayama (Peterside), Otuokolo, Finima, Abalamabie and the Asaramatoru villages were also first settled by the Obolo. According to Jones (1963:105), the national deity of the Ibani, Ikuba, "was derived from Andoni".

Ogan (1988:5) and Ejituwu (1991:28-41) state that the people of Okochiri, Okuru, Ogoloma, Bolo and Ogu mentioned Andoni as their immediate homelands.

According to Alagoa (1972:163), "several Kalabari towns have traditions of prior settlement in the Andoni country". Ibim (1983:1) states that Bille is from Andoni. Other Kalabari towns deriving founders from Andoni are Ido, Tombia, Abalama and Kula. Horton (1998:195-225) holds the view that except for the Endeme, the first settlers of the Akialame, Amabiame, Iturome and Bukome came from the Andoni area. To Jones (1963:21), "the Korome ward, as also some of the other groups in the Kalabari territory, is more likely to have been an Andoni than an Efik offshoot".

Ethnographic Relationship

The Obolo relationship with the Ijo is closer in terms of ethnography than in language. Alagoa (1972:163-165) used ethnographic data to authenticate the connection between the Ijo and the Obolo. He discovered identical place and personal names. Others include the Ijo loan words in Obolo language, such as "*Ama, Aya, Gogo, Obe* and *Igo*" for "village, old woman, namesake, pear and

527

eagle".The Andoni corpus of the Lower Niger Bronzes concretely demonstrate their relationship with the Ijo. On 6 September 1904, Commissioner A. A. Whitehouse told Charles H. Read of the British Museum that over seventy bronze objects were removed by the colonial officers from the shrine of the Andoni national god, *Yok-Obolo,* to the British Museum in 1904. Principal among them is the human figure of "an Ijo native" seated on a stool. A British government gazette of 1904 stated that this image is made of a copper nude figure, 11 ½ inches high.

Plate 22.1: Human Figure of an Ijo Native.

Source: A. A. Whitehouse to Charles H. Read of the British Museum, London,
Abstract from Government Gazette, No. 21 of 18 November 1904.

To Ejituwu (1991:168), this human figure was the bronze image of Obolo (Andoni), one of the children of Ijo.

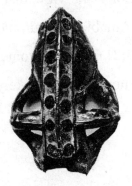 

Plate 22.2-22.3: Stylized canivore skull of a leopard from Obolo (Andoni)

Source: M.G. Anderson and P.M. Peek, *Ways of the Rivers (Los Angeles 2002), p. 51*

Two other Andoni bronzes of carnivore skulls of a leopard in the Royal Scottish Museum, Edinburgh, Plate 22.2 and 22.3 above, also suggest Obolo contacts with the Ijo. Peek and Nicklin (2002:52) noted their resemblance to the hyena bronzes at Okpoama and Odioma in the Nembe Ijo area.

Lorenz (1982: 52-53) recalled that the Lower Niger Bronze bell, shown as Plate 22.4, came from Andoni and is similar to the one at Sagbama in Bayelsa State.

Plate 22.4: Decorated bronze bell removed frm Obolo (Andoni)
to the British Museum in 1904
Source : A.A. Whitehouse to Charles H. Reed of the British Museum.
London, *Abstract from Government Gazette,*
No. 21 of 18 November 1904

So also are two Andoni Lower Niger Bronze swords. While Barley (1995:339) saw it as having the "Art Nouveau" style, Horton (1965:88) documented similar objects at Tema in Kalabari. However, Andoni traditions state that the bell was normally used in summoning warriors when the Obolo went to war, while the swords were part of their weapons.

Plate 22.5: Two Andoni Double-Edged Bronze Swords in the British Museum, 1904.

Source: M.G. Anderson and P. M. Peek, *Ways of the River,* (Los Angeles, 2002), p. 56

Other material evidence of cult objects found in Andoni and Ijoland are leopard skulls, and a house of skulls of over 2000 of their enemies killed in war as well as war gods. According to Alagoa (1972:16), like in Andoni, all Ijo groups have warriors and war-gods. These ethnographic relationships portray the ancestral affinity between the Obolo (Andoni) and their Ijo brothers.

The Obolo practice the big and small dowry marriages. The small dowry is friendship and its offspring belong to the matrilineal family. In the big dowry marriage, the woman and all the offspring enjoy patrilineal rights and privileges. Wubani (1935:28-29) noted that in the early period, inheritance rites in Andoni were matrilineal before the gradual change to patrilineal in modern times. This view first came from Jeffreys (1930: 100-102) that the Obolo practiced the matrilineal descent and dedicated their family shrines, *Isi Ebikan*, to both ancestral men and women. In ancient Obolo shrines, fish and animal skulls venerate Obolo male ancestors while decorated wooden figures commemorate female ancestors, as shown in Plate 22.6.

Plate 22.6: Andoni ancestral shrine, *Isi Ebikan*

Source: M.G. Anderson and P.M. Peek, *Ways of the Rivers.*)Los Angeles, 2002), p.302

The Obolo venerate their ancestors by naming their children after them as it is done in every Ijo community. Their group-dressing pattern is the Ijo ethnic costume. Male citizens wear *etibo* up, with a fathom of Indian george cloth, *nkpopu*, down, a cap, walking stick and a laceless shoe to match. Female citizens wear blouse up with four fathoms of Indian georg cloth, *nkpopu*, down; sown in two equal lengths with a piece of it as headtie. These are matched with earring, necklace and a handbag. Kings and chiefs wear *don* up and a fathom of Indian george cloth, *nkpopu*, down with a hat and staff of office to match. Large beads, *kalari*, are worn as necklace and small beads as hand bangles.

Like the Ibani and the Nkoro, the Obolo play the *Owuogbo* cult of mask dancing artists. In Okrika and Nembe, it is called *Sekiapu* and *Ekine* in Kalabari. The Obolo stage it twice annually with masquerades of carved headdresses. It includes mermaid (*egbelegbe*), species of fish and animals, lobster (*ikem*), crab (*uka*), as shown in Plate 22.7.

Plate 22.7:
Andoni *Owuogbo* headdress of a lobster (*Ikem*) with representations of fish traps *(uket)*, tilapia *(ikop)*, fishing canoe *(uji)*, periwinkle *(ntutut)* and crab *(uka)*.
Source: M. G. Anderson and P. M. Peek, *Ways of the Rivers* (Los Angeles, 2002), p. 303.

Nicklin (2002:305) maintained that the Andoni *Owuogbo* masquerades are within the range of their Ijo counterparts. Both chiefs and ordinary male in the community are members.

The *Owuogbo* cult is one of the instruments of preserving the culture history of the people and for acculturation. Secondly, members must be free from wickedness and other social vices; otherwise, they face the penalty of dismissal. This became a limiting factor to social vices in Obolo as in other Ijolands. Thirdly, if an initiate eventually finds himself in any Ijoland where he knows nobody, he can sojourn with any member of the cult there and enjoy the rights and privileges of Ijo society. The Owuogbo drum language is the instrument used in testing every initiate's understanding of the Ijo drum lore and culture history (Enemugwem 2003:33-50). Fourthly, the *Owuogbo* cult assists the *Ofiokpo* cult as the police arm of the traditional executive of the Andoni city-state in pre-colonial times.

Davidson (1977:222) noted Andoni as one of six city-states of the Niger Delta.

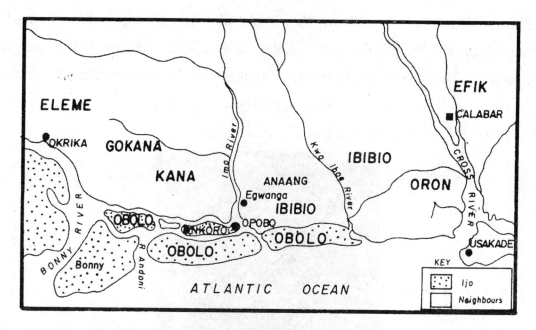

Fig. 22.1: The Ijo of the Eastern Delta Limit and their neighbours

Others were Warri, Nembe (Brass), Opobo, Kalabari (New Calabar), Bonny and Old Calabar. The Obolo (Andoni) city-state was a republic whose ruler was selected by valour. As recorded in Ejituwu (1991: 63), the king, *Okaan Obolo*, introduced a system of taxation that funded the centralized structure before the manila currency of the early Portuguese became the monetized medium of exchange in the sixteenth century. Barley (1999:399) puts it that the large spiral manila, Plate 22.8 below, found in Obolo was genuine bronze.

Plate 22.8:
Spiral manilla with trumpet-shaped ends removed from Andoni
to the British Museum in 1904
Source: A. A. Whitehouse to Charles H. Read of the British Museum, London, *Abstract from Government Gazette,* No. 21 of 18 November 1904.

They were not only in the currency units but also as an ornamental object worn as leg bangles by elderly women and around the neck by men as well as status symbols buried in the graves of leaders.

Other apparatus of government enabled the Andoni city-state to maintain the rule of law and the Atlantic commerce. The Atlantic trade introduced into Andoni: a monetized economy of manilla currency, *ekwe*, orange and rice which the Andoni and the Portuguese call *ulaja* and *laranja*; *orosi* and *araz*; respectively. Faraclas (1985) also noted manioc brought by the early Portuguese which the Andoni and the Portuguese call *mbitaka* and *mandioca*, respectively.

The English and the Dutch were also in Andoni trading with the Obolo from 1700 to 1800. Evidence of this is a large bronze Dutch bell that has the inscription "Otto Baker Rotherdam 1757". This bell was among the relics carried from Andoni by the colonial officers to the British Museum in 1904. More evidence of the trade between the Andoni and the Europeans is documented in Patterson (1969:132-133,142-143) who stated that in 1775 the slaves in the New World were 65 % Ibo, 20 % Ibibio and the rest came from other areas, "particularly the Andoni".

Before the Andoni went into the Atlantic Trade, they had pioneered an economic system of fish fence with screens. Other Ijo communities emulated them. According to Okorobia (1999:53), the Nembe and other Ijo groups call it, *Idoni*, after the Andoni. Jebbin (1984:24-31) says it takes between seventy and eighty-five screens to make an *Idoni* fence and not less than 14 anglers in the fishing crew.

In sum, the ancestors of the Obolo (Andoni) came from the Ijo and Cameroon areas into the Eastern Delta Limit. They sent out migrants that contributed to the founding of many Ijo settlements in the Niger Delta. As one of the city-states of the Niger Delta, they were in the Atlantic Trade and their ethnographic relation with their Ijo brothers, including the Nkoro and Opobo was close and generally cordial before the colonial era.

Obolo, Nkoro and Opobo Relations:

The Obolo (Andoni) live in the Eastern Delta Limit with other Ijo groups, including the Opobo (Ibani) and the Nkoro.

Alagoa (1972:165-169) and Jenewari (1983:3-98) cite Oboloma in Nembe as a possible place of origin of the Nkoro. They migrated from there to Okrika and finally to Andoni with their national deity, *Okwamboghu*, (*Okwamboku*), "related to *Fenibeso* of Okrika." Nkoro and Andoni were administered together in the Obolo County Council. They fought wars together, especially the Ibani and the Ogoni wars. In 1973 the Ogoni sacked the Nkoro fishing settlements close to Ogoniland because they supported Andoni.

In 1869, the European traders and Jaja came to Andoni, suggesting a tripartite alliance: the European traders, King Jaja and the Andoni. Apparently, they had discussed safe entry of Jaja and his people into Andoni because the Andoni escorted Jaja safely into Andoni. He was escorted to the shrine of *Yok Obolo* where he swore an oath (The Church Missionary Gleaner 1870, Tasie 1976:4-11). Evidence of this oath is the ritual necklace of *Yok-Obolo* worn by Jaja.

Colonial Era: The Period of Difficulty

In 1904, the British sent a punitive expedition against the Obolo and destroyed the House of Skulls at Alabie (Agwut Obolo). They divided Andoni into six parts and attached each part to one of six court areas in the neighbourhood: Ngo, the headquarters of Andoni, and Ikuru Town, were attached to Opobo Tcwn Court, Unyeada and its areas were attached to Ogoni Court, Ataba to Bonny, Okoroete and Okorinyong to Ukam and Elile to Ibeno. According to

534

Jeffreys, the intention of the British was to destroy the political and ethnic identity of the Andoni people. Nevertheless, the Andoni fought back. They rebuilt the shrine of *Yok-Obolo* with a new set of cultural artefacts. In 1931, the six parts of Andoni were brought together under the Agafor Native Court, Andoni.

Between 1870 and 1920, the Opobo had moved from the one Island (*Ijon Nkon*) given King Jaja to several other islands not given to him in 1869. It had become necessary to set up boundaries between the Andoni, Opobo and Nkoro. While Opobo people were given three islands and Nkoro one island, the Andoni were recognized as owners of all the rest. The Andoni were given the Andoni mainland from Oyorokoto in the west to Agbama on the Imo River. In 1955/58, this decision was confirmed by the West African Court of Appeal. Thus, apart from Queenstown, no Opobo settlement on this mainland was to be included in Opobo Town County Council (1958). In this way, it may be said that the colonial administration laid the foundation for the peace that has existed between the Andoni and Opobo since then.

Obolo (Andoni) in Post-Colonial Nigeria

Obolo (Andoni) entered the First Republic with jubilation. With two Obolo representatives in the Federal and Regional legislative houses, Andoni entered the golden era of Andoni political history. Hon. U.O. Ekenekot had defeaed Dr. Egbert Udo Udoma, on the platform of the NCNC to enter the Federal House of Representatives. Similarly, Hon. Rowland Oke had defeated Chief Iwarimie Jaja on the platform of the Action Group to enter the Eastern House of Assembly. Andoni came to the lime-light.

The Consequences of the Nigerian Civil War

The Andoni were not very troubled by the Civil War because of their location. For instance, they fished or produced salt from the seawater and survived. Where they had great difficulty was in the Eastern Obolo area where 105 indigenes were killed during the liberation of Okoroete Town. The Obolo also suffered the general effects of the Civil War. Andoni was placed in the South-Eastern State. Protest for merger with Rivers State soon found them placed in Bonny Local Government Area with a portion, the Eastern Obolo, left in Cross River State, and later Akwa Ibom State.

The Nasir Boundary Adjustment Commission of 1976 used the Imo River as the boundary between the then Cross River State and Rivers State, later Akwa Ibom State and Rivers State. In 1996, creation of more states and Local Government Areas (LGA) in Nigeria resulted in the creation of Andoni LGA and Opobo/Nkoro LGA from Bonny LGA and established the present political structures. In Akwa Ibom State, the eastern Obolo (Andoni) people were granted a Local Government Area, namely, Eastern Obolo LGA.

NKORO (KIRIKA)

Introduction

Nkoro is close to the coast not far from Andoni, Opobo and Ogoni and have two different languages, Defaka and Kirikaye. Defaka is spoken by the Afakani people and Kirikaye is the common *lingua franca* of the people. The Afakani use Defaka language when they do not want others to understand them. Nkoro was in the Andoni/Opobo Local Government Area until 1996 when it became part of Opobo/Nkoro Local Government with headquarters at Opobo.

Origin and History

The recorded traditions of Nkoro community state that their ancestral home was called "Gbelegbele Ama" in the present day Bayelsa State from where they migrated and settled in Ogoloma. Because of dispute between the Okrika and the Kirika (Nkoro), they withdrew and settled at their present site. The Nkoro people are found in three islands, Olom-ama, Iwoma Nkoro and Nkoro Town. Olom-ama is occupied by the Defaka or Afakani people, some of whom also live on the isolated island of Iwoma Nkoro near Kono, and others in the Afakani quarter of Nkoro Town. The Defaka are distinct from the Nkoro, but they have been assimilated into Nkoro culture to such a degree that their language remains the only evidence of a distinct Defaka identity. Defaka language is quickly receding in favour of the Nkoro language. The next most commonly used language among the Defaka is Opobo-Igbo owing to the political influence of Opobo since the period of the Oil Rivers trade.

The second group of settlers, led by Kirika, went to Ibiangafurutie. Nkoro tradition states that the need for foodstuff to supplement their fish, made Kirika's son Opu-Inyaba wander into Ogoni land where he met and became friendly with Yaakara. The riverside called Inyaba became a point of contact and exchange, and thus began the popular Inyaba market. Opu Inyaba and Yaakara are said to have entered into a blood pact not to kill each other.

The name Nkoro was acquired in a war against Bonny during the reign of their first monarch, Amanyanabo Otuagba 1700-1727. The Ibani marvelled at the stout resistance put up by this community in battle. Chief Oko Jumbo of Bonny called Nkoro "*Korika-ama*", meaning "a town that cannot be set on fire" (Alagoa 1972: 66).

After the death of Kirika, his brother Kereke became King and led the people to another settlement called Ayama or Ibiangafurutie (seize a point of vantage), (Alagoa 1972: 166).

King Kpokpo of Nkoro (1860-1875) hosted King Jaja of Opobo. Jaja was given a site at Olom Nkoro, from where he moved to *Kontoru* (fishing site) of the Andoni, now the present day Opobo.

Cultural Development

The Nkoro people observe a number of religious activities related to *Okwamboku* (the national deity) and a large number of deities such as *Okpoji, Ogomokiri* and *Ofiokpo* derived from Andoni. Nkoro masquerades and festivals are similar to those of their neighbours. For instance, *Okwamboku*; the national deity, and war god, is called upon for protection. Festivals are observed to appease the deity. The festival is presided over by a High priest, who pours libation at the shrine of *Okwamboku*, located at the original foundation spot of Nkoro.

Ofiokpo is a traditional masquerade dedicated to cleansing the society. It performs at mid-night in the month of August every year. Non-members are asked to stay in-doors between 10.00 pm to 6.00 am. Before the festivities of *Ofiokpo*, members of the society inform the community of their performance but warn that nobody should be seen during their period of performance. Any one caught would be sacrificed to the gods.

External Relations

Nkoro external relations have been characterized by conflicts with the Ogoni and Bonny. This necessitates constant vigilance, which is expressed in their drum language as follows:

Ofunguru toru munu munu:	The rat's eyes sleep
Beri munu na:	But not his ears.

Alagoa has shown that the Nkoro were desirous of a peaceful co-existence; this informs the entering into beneficial relations with the Andoni, Ogoni and Opobo. The trade pact with Wiyakara (Yakara) was to give the Nkoro a base to exchange their sea foods for agricultural products that the Ogoni readily supplied. Moreover, it became an opportunity for economic and cultural exchange with peoples of the hinterland.

Nkoro relations with Andoni and Opobo, their nearest neighbours have been friendly. There have been no traditions of conflict between the three communities. Rather there has been cultural borrowing. Thus, the Nkoro *Owuogbo* and *Ofiokpo* celebrated by three communities—Defaka, Pokoya and Oporokuno - were enriched with masks from Opobo and Andoni. But unlike the Opobo and Andoni, where *Owuogbo* performs annually, in Nkoro it is celebrated once in two years.

IBANI (OPOBO)

Introduction

The internal history of Opobo kingdom has received considerable scholarly attention (Cookey, 1972; Alagoa 1970; Jaja, J. 1995; Jaja S. 2000). It is now necessary to provide a more general analytical account. Developments are analyzed at three levels; the growth of the territorial structure and territorial organization, relations with other Nigerian peoples and states, and the cultural impact of such relations.

Political History

Four distinct periods can be identified in the history of the political development of Opobo. These are the early period 1870-1900, also known as the Jaja period. This was the Golden Age of Opobo history. The second period was the colonial period 1900-1960. This period coincided with the reigns of Prince Sunday Jaja, and Chief Frederick MacPepple Jaja and the early part of Chief Douglas Jaja's reign. It was a period of consolidation of King Jaja's achievements. The third period was the independence period 1960-1980 regarded as the Douglas period. This was a period of gradual decline of Opobo, and the final period is the period of crisis or the period of interregnum, 1980 – 2004.

The early period refers to the settlement period, when the early settlers from Bonny moved into the present site of Opobo. They were Ibani-Ijo with the original Ibani traditions and culture, including the Ibani language spoken by sixty percent of the early settlers. The radical population expansion policy altered the demographic and linguistic character of the fourteen initial Houses (compounds) that settled in metropolitan Opobo.

There were other early settlements established outside the metropolis, including Queen's Town (Queen Ama), Kalaibiama; and the *Kalama*, made up of

Epellema, Minimah and Iloma. These were followed by expansion into plantation settlements: Kalasunju, Okpukpu, Ozu Efere, Ikiriko, Abazibie, Opukalama, Ayaminimah and Ekeregborokiri. Some of the settlements were founded for King Jaja's warlords, like Ekeregborokiri; while other settlements were warehouses for the storage of goods, like Ozu Efere.

One tradition states that since King Jaja banned the hanging of fishing nets in any part of the metropolis, these settlements served as fishing settlements where fishermen could undertake their activities. These settlements had no independence of political action.

The central political calculation had been to maintain such balance in internal affairs that no two sections can combine effectively to undermine the political authority of the Jaja section. Thus, it was found necessary at the beginning of the nineteenth century to equip enterprising young men whose loyalty was not in doubt (Ejituwu 1991:153). Accordingly, Saturday Jaja and Ogolo were given their independence. Apparently, at the period, King Jaja wanted increased patronage of European traders on the Opobo River (Dike 1956; Anene 1960).

As Opobo kingdom became firmly established, it began to acquire leadership over a widening neighbourhood. Opobo economic supremacy, made possible by her new location, threatened Bonny economy and reduced oil palm exported from Bonny. Indeed, by the end of the nineteenth century, palm produce from Opobo division showed remarkable increase challenging that of Bonny. The implication was not just expanded produce business, but more capital and more labour requirement for Opobo merchants. It also meant considerable political authority for Opobo kingdom.

The towns of Iloma, Epellema, Minimah, Ozu Efere and Ekeregborokiri to the south of Opobo mainland occupy a stretch of solid land that could be effectively used for agriculture. These towns have traditions of migration from the mainland and are referred to collectively as *Kalama* (small town), they are under the administration of the *Alabo* in the metropolis.

The *Kalama* also play a vital role in defence, as stations for the storage of arms. Defence strategy does not allow armament to be stored mainly in the metropolis. Moreover, the plan or layout of the kingdom was such that strategic defence was emphasized. The Chieftaincy Houses were located in a way that residential houses formed a semi-circle with the *Alabo*'s home much bigger and centrally located. A central well and two gateways, one leading to the sea where the war-canoes and gig are housed for ease of launch in time of war, were provided. The war canoes were so crucial to the kingdom that by 1920 the initial fourteen war canoes had forty-three more added to bring the total to sixty-seven. The last was that of Ogolo in 1920.

In essence, the nineteenth century Ibani compound was planned to eliminate security risk. Opobo tradition maintains that security and political strategy was paramount in the creation of War-Canoe Houses. For instance, war-canoes houses of the Jaja section were planted strategically among others: Tom Jaja between Peterside and Ogolo, while Omubo Pepple and Saturday Jaja between Annie Stewart and Toby. This strategy informed the dominance of the Jaja section in the kingdom.

External Relations

The entry of Opobo community into the area expanded contacts and relations in the area.

The early diet of the first settlers consisted of fish and pounded cassava (*Utara* or *Akpakuru*). According to tradition, their agricultural foods were cassava (*Mpitaka*), yam (*Buru* or *Je*) and plantain (*Obirika*) which they got from the Ogoni and Ibibio. Opobo exchanged fish and salt from salt water. This profitable salt industry met the local demand of communities in the area. Salt making with the roots of the mangrove tree had little attraction for the Opobo;

rather salt extracted from salt water became major occupation of women who cooked them in clay pots bought from the Ogoni and Ibibio. Two rivers, controlled by Opobo traders, were the Imo and Qua Iboe rivers. Trade from the Qua Iboe River accounted for one third of the revenue derived from Opobo (Ofonagoro 1979:140). The Ibeno expedition of 1881, aimed at establishing Opobo monopoly of the Qua Iboe River, was stopped by the British.

Opobo markets were situated in three major areas, Ibibio, Ndoki and Ngwa. Opobo trade canoes went further up the Opobo River to the creeks of Qua Iboe into Ekparakwa, Ibeno, Etimekpo, Ndija, Essene and Egwenga. From Ibibio, cassava and yams were imported together with livestock.

The giant bell with the inscription "King Jaja of Opobo" found at Calabar also provides evidence of early trade in Ibibio hinterland. Although there are conflicting traditions regarding the bell, one tradition refers to the flight or immigration of Queen Ogbolo to Calabar after Ibinukpabi (Long Juju) acquitted her of witchcraft charges brought against her by Queen Osunju. Ogbolo and her followers were prevailed upon to settle in Calabar to avert a possible civil war with her accusers. It was speculated that Queen Ogbolo took the bell as a symbol of royalty to Calabar. The second tradition states that King Jaja imported goods from Britain and the bell was one of the consignments in the ship wrecked on the Calabar River. The bell was salvaged in 1885 but could not be returned immediately.

Trade with Ndoki, apart from vegetables, cocoyam (*ede*), pepper and plantain is suggested also by the spread of local cloth (*egere bite*) to Opobo through Azumini. Relations with the Ndoki were quite friendly, moreover, there are still traditions among both groups, which claim kinship of their founding ancestors. The Ibani claim to have come to their present location of Bonny directly from Ndoki country (Alagoa, 1972:150). Opobo traditions state that Opobo traders became middlemen bringing sea foods and European goods from the coast to sell at the Ndoki towns of Obehi, Ohambele, Akwete, Abala, Obete Ohanze,

Obohia, Asa, Umuogu Akanu, Umukalu Ikpoku Ohanko, Nchokoro among others.

Opobo markets also extended into the Ngwa area, where the main markets were located at Itu Ngwa, Umuaroma, Abayi, Umuokpara, Omuma, Osakwa, Umuagwu, Ovom, Osusu, Umuokoro Uku, Amandara Akpa, Iheorji Unugo Ozata and Umunta. Beaches were also developed along the Imo River for Opobo trade canoes. They included those of Chiefs Oko Jaja, Sam Oko Epelle and Ogolo (Abadist 14/1/49).

Some of these transactions were based on the "trust" system. According to Ofonagoro (1979:98), Opobo traders would solemnize loan transactions with hinterland customers by "swearing Juju" with the debtor to encourage fulfilment of the terms of the loan. Opobo entry into the overseas trade seems to have had a devastating impact on Bonny.

Opobo entered the mainstream Niger Delta economic activities in the 1870s. By 1900, the internationalization of trade, the monetary system brought Opobo into the world economic system. It was largely by offering the entire trade of Opobo to the firm of Miller Brothers that King Jaja succeeded in breaking the combination of firms, which had tried to impose low prices on Opobo middlemen (Ofonagoro 1979:334).

The case of Opobo kingdom presents an example of development of political institutions and structures in response to local and international circumstances. It would be faulty to interpret these developments solely to diffusion from their primary source of dispersal. There was local initiative and innovation, taking advantage of environment and circumstance.

Developments After Jaja

The palm oil trade, which became increasingly desirable, lifted individuals to commercial power and induced the rise of capital-owning and investing groups that given time, might have become a middle class of nation builders (Davidson 1992). But King Jaja and his kind were found inconvenient and intolerable to the colonising European powers. They were, accordingly, attacked, expropriated, exiled or otherwise done away with as Britain moved into the Niger Delta. King Jaja represented one such factor. The circumstances of his exit from Opobo have been well-documented (Cookey 1974; Alagoa 1970; Ikime 1977).

Trade rivalry and the scramble for palm oil markets seems to have intensified after Jaja's exit but his long shadow could not be so easily eliminated (Ofonagoro 1974: 334). Opobo depended on her hinterland connections with whom he was on good terms to stem the entry of the rival states of Bonny, Elem-Kalabari and Okrika. Opobo traders from the 1900s settled in the major towns and villages that produced palm oil and kernel in large quantities.

Some Opobo compounds because of the high concentration of compound members controlled particular trade routes. For example, the Azumini, Obete and Azu Ogu route, with a concentration of Ogolo traders who had collection centres along this area, controlled the route. Chief Atobera Ogolo, Chief Arlik Ogolo, Jonathan Ogolo and Chief Harry Ubani were major traders here. The Owerrinta, Abayi, Umuakpara Aro Ngwa routes had a number of Toby House traders who firmly controlled this route.

Trade and Cultural Interaction

Trade thus brought Opobo indigenes into contact with peoples of other cultures, especially the Igbo and Ibibio. The result of this unfettered interaction was that Opobo indigenes who settled at *Uzo Ahia* (trading settlements) returned from the 1930s, for Easter and Christmas holidays, "carrying some cultural traits" to Opobo.

In time, some of these new traits were imbibed and modified to suit the local environment. A good example is the festival of new crops (yam and corn) usually celebrated by predominantly farming communities such as the Igbo and Ibibio. It is not known when the *Amaiwo* (festival of new yam and new corn) was first celebrated, but Fanny S. B. Jaja states that it was introduced during the reign of Chief MacPepple Jaja (1920-1936).

> Two crops namely yam and maize are generally not allowed to be brought out in the market for sale until certain sacrifices or ceremonial rites have been performed by the *Owuogbo* from the Chiefs directive. The Amanyanabo and the Chiefs make arrangements for the festival and supply *Owuogbo* with all sacrificial animals and drinks.

It was usually a day's rite, accompanied by masquerades during which members of *Owuogbo* formally present the crops to the public, signifying formal admittance of the new crops into the kingdom, and the freedom to consume and openly exchange them in the market place.

The *Owuogbo* is a semi-secret society comparable with the *Okonko* of the Igbo, the *Epe* and highly exclusive *Mborko* of the Aro; the *Idion* and *Ekpe* of the Ibibio; the *Egbo* of the Efik, the *Ekine* of the Kalabari and the *Ofiokpo* of the Andoni.

Some scholars have studied the *Owuogbo* from within and have attested to its socio-cultural contributions to the kingdom before the 1980 interregnum (Cookey 1974; Macpepple, 1982 and Jaja 1995). Jaja (2004) has pointed out that the twenty-three years without a king dealt a devastating blow on the institution.

Another important cultural impact of trade interaction from the interior was the *Okonko* title society of the Ndoki Igbo. Ndoki traditions claim that *Okonko* was introduced to Opobo in 1898. According to Ofonagoro (1979: 38):

The success of *Okonko* members no doubt was associated to their role in the collection of trade tolls. Club members are known to plunder the goods and in many cases seize the owners, or drive them away.

In Opobo, membership was quite exclusive, but by 1916, the number of chiefs who showed active interest in *Okonko* was greatly reduced because of the British crack down on secret societies. In any case, the Opobo version did not confer economic benefits on its members.

A more significant cultural institution has been the *Nwaotam*, meaning child or masquerade of Otam, derived from Nkpajekiri in Ndoki where it was played once in seven years (Jaja 2004:87). It was introduced into Opobo in 1931 by a group of friends. The *Nwaotam* is now a popular carnival in Opobo, Bonny and other places in the Niger Delta in the Christmas season. Its entertainment value led to its introduction in Bonny in the late 1940s by Mr. Benstowe.

The Successors of King Jaja

The death of King Jaja in 1891 marked the end of an era. He had built and transformed the modest island into a powerful city-state, solid in its foundation, but much too dependent on the skilful manipulations of one man. His less fortunate successors were unable to rule absolutely or wisely and fell victim to new forces in the colonial and post-colonial period.

Prince Saturday his first son, on account of a debilitating illness could not ascend the throne. Consequently, Prince Sunday, his second son, was recalled from Britain where he was studying, to take up his father's throne. Prince Sunday (1891-1916) stepped into the shoes of his father which proved too large for him. He had no independent mind and had to govern with a body of advisers, including Chief Cookey-Gam. His association with the young Prince resulted in Cookey-Gam's appointment as political agent (Cookey 1972).

Arthur (1920-1936) became a war canoe chief in 1894, and succeeded to the headship of the royal Jaja House in 1916. The kingdom witnessed progress and vitality. He was able to project Opobo through the Niger Delta. Converted to Christianity and educated abroad under renowned scholars, Ada as he was fondly called, demonstrated considerable valour.

Arthur MacPepple's diverse diplomatic activities involved the safe-guarding of Opobo commercial interests, the preservation of political autonomy and above all, the expansion of Opobo political influence. His major political role was that of a peacemaker, a supreme arbiter in the endless feuds between groups and families. He was said to have negotiated successfully all disputes which broke out between Opobo, Andoni and Ogoni over plantation settlements.

Douglas Jaja (1936-1980), was an amiable gentleman who ascended the throne at the age of eighteen. He tried to effect changes. In 1938, he ordered that palm oil be sold only by the giant bell, not in the market or hawked around as it easily stains people. He was said to be highhanded, flogging individuals who misbehaved, even older chiefs. He was suspended in 1938 and recalled in 1940.

Douglas Jaja's career as monarch was marked by controversy. The civil war (1966-1970) truncated his reign. On his return he tried to rebuild his kingdom and cater for his subjects. His death in 1980 threw the kingdom into a succession dispute and crisis, which culminated in a long interregnum (Jaja, 2005). In 2004, his first son, Dandeson Jaja, was crowned after he won the contest to the throne in the Supreme Court of Nigeria.

Conclusion

The Eastern Niger Delta Limit is the home of the Obolo (Andoni), Opobo and Nkoro. These three communities have lived peacefully together. While the Obolo have lived almost permanently on fishing and trading, the Opobo prospered on the palm oil trade. The Nkoro have maintained a balance of allegiance between the Obolo and the Opobo.

CHAPTER 23
THE NORTHERN DELTA LIMIT
C. M. Sorgwe, O. C. Ama-Ogbari and M. P. Okonny

Introduction

The communities of the Northern Delta Limit identified in this chapter are the Epie-Atissa, Engenni (including Zarama), Degema (including Obonoma) and Ogbia (including Abureni), the Abua and Odual communities.

EPIE-ATISSA, ENGENNI, DEGEMA
Traditions of origin.

The Epie-Atissa, Engenni and Degema communities constitute a linguistic entity classified by linguists as Delta-Edoid (Elugbe 1979:82 – 101)

The traditions of origin of these three communities are tied up in what is known as the Okulogua Tradition (Sorgwe 2000:13). According to the Epie version of this tradition, their ancestral fathers took off from Benin and migrated southwards and settled somewhere in Isoko land. The founding fathers later crossed a wide river near Aboh town and wandered into the Engenni territory where they settled at Okulogua. According to this version, a man called Epie led the founding fathers into the Epie Creek from Okulogua.

The Engenni, while accepting the Okulogua tradition, trace the cause of the migration from Benin to a quarrel between Prince Ogun and Oba Ewuare (Owuore) of Benin (Nwokoma, 1982:2). The Engenni version also names Okpala as the Isoko town at which they stopped in the course of the migration. The version also states that the people lived at a place called Okpakio for many years before moving into their present location (Nwokoma, 1982:3).

The Degema version, like that of Engenni, dates the emigration from Benin to the reign of Oba Aware (Ewuare). This version states that one Khurobo led seven other families from Benin, namely, Ekebe, Ekeze, Ebilikiya, Nemia, Ogboloyai, Ozeri and Peika (Obibo, 1991:10-11). This tradition also names

Patani, Agbassa, Ogbolomini and Yenagoa as stopping points on the migratory route. The Degema tradition accepts Engenni ancestry and claims that the Degema first moved into the Epie Creek, and settled in Yenagoa before leaving for their present location (Phillips, 1991:3).

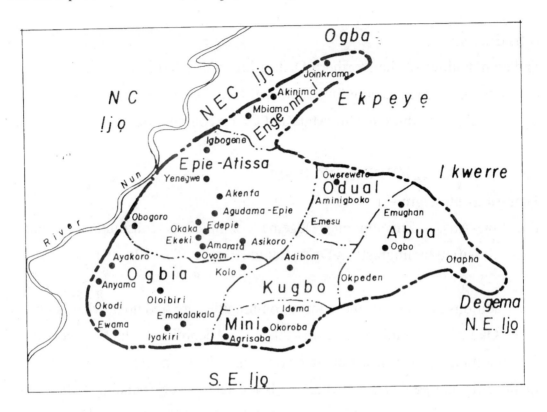

Fig. 23.1: The Northern Delta Limit

Social and Cultural Growth

The people of Epie-Atissa, Engenni and Degema have grown socially and culturally through contact with their neighbours and through western education and contact.

The people of Epie-Atissa are socially and culturally linked to their neighbours through inter-marriage, exchange of ideas, trade, in religion, and dance. Oyoyo market at Ovom in Yenagoa for several decades remained a major trading centre where the Epie-Atissa people met the Ijo, Ogbia and Engenni people. Swali market is today performing the same commercial service. Religious ties with the neighbouring communities exist in both the traditional and Christian sectors. Epie-Atissa people patronize such Ijo deities as Seibiri Ekine and

Benikurukuru. Many of the people are also associated with an Oshi-based deity in Engenni land. In the same way, the Anglicans and Roman Catholic Christians belong to common dioceses, archdeaconries and parishes with their Ijo neighbours. Similarly, the Baptist churches of Epie-Atissa, until very recent times, belonged to the Engenni Baptist Association (Sorgwe, 2000:6). The present Yenagoa Baptist Association also cuts across Epie-Atissa, Ijo and Ogbia communities.

The Engenni people have been positively affected by the Baptist presence in the area. The establishment of schools and mission hospital at Joinkrama in 1947 greatly enhanced the people's response to western education (Adu 1980:34).

Degema, like the Engenni community, received early influence of the Baptist mission. The presence of the Anglican and Baptist missions encouraged Western education among the people. Another agent of social growth in Degema was the location of the British Consulate in the community. In addition, the Government Teacher Training College and the Ministry of Agriculture were established in the community.

In spite of these external influences, the Epie-Atissa people have continued to observe their *Obunem-Epie* and *Uge Adiafa* festivals. Marriage according to the people's law and custom goes along side the wedding ceremonies in the churches. In the same way, the traditional religious practices exist in spite of the increasing number of Christian churches. What seems to have declined drastically are the traditional sports and games (Sorgwe, 2000:31). The Engenni people, like their Epie-Atissa neighbours practice the traditional religion together with Christianity. Some aspects of the traditional marriage and burial systems are also maintained to the present day. The Degema people similarly maintain the Aziba cult dedicated to a female deity (Phillips, 1991:14-16). The burial and marriage ceremonies of the Degema people have also retained much of the traditional elements.

Administration and Government

The earliest form of administration among the Epie-Atissa, Engenni and Degema was gerontocracy. The main units of administration in all three communities were the extended family lineage group called *iyeni* in Epie and Egenni and *afayn* in Degema. Although there are differences in detail, the basic lineage structure cuts across the three Delta-Edoid communities (Sorgwe, 2000:34, Okia, 1978:23, Obibo 1991:180).

The evolution of the administrative systems of the three are also largely identical. The Epie-Atissa abolished gerontocracy and adopted elected village heads or *obeneaken*. Each village head presided over a council of elected representatives of the lineage group. The Engenni communities also appointed village heads or *okilomakie* in the colonial era of the warrant chiefs (Okia, 1978:23). Similarly, the Degema people appointed council of chiefs under a head called *Onu-onyan-ekein* (Obibo, 1991:18).

Contemporary Nigerian Politics

The Epie-Atissa, Engenni and Degema have had significant taste of contemporary Nigerian politics. Each on her merit has made her position felt in the political history of the Niger Delta. Although they have always remained in the minority, they have never been insignificant in the scheme of things.

Yenagoa the traditional headquarters of the Epie-Atissa people was chosen as the administrative headquarters of the Central Ijaw Council in 1956 (Sorgwe, 2000:73). It was selected as the administrative headquarters of the Yenagoa Province in 1959 (Sorgwe, 2000:73). Yenagoa has remained a Local Government Area (LGA) headquarters since 1976. In 1996, it became the capital of the Bayelsa State of Nigeria and headquarters of Yenagoa Local Government Area.

Degema, another minority community in Rivers State of Nigeria, has continued to maintain a voice in the political scene of that state. The importance of

Degema as a political nerve centre in the Niger Delta dates back to the colonial period. The colonial authorities chose to place their consulate in Degema. It has continued to be an administrative headquarters of Degema province, Division and Local Goernment Area respectively over the years.

Relations of the Edoid Communities

There is a strong historical link among the three communities. In addition to the common traditions of origin is the close linguistic expression. The three languages are appreciably mutually intelligible.

The Degema, having been separated from Engenni and Epie-Atissa territories for centuries, have developed a language that is now different from the rest. The language now has a number of loan words from Kalabari and Abua. Epie, spoken by the Epie-Atissa people, and Engenni language have also developed significant differences due to long separation. From colonial times to the present, the Engenni have always been with the upland communities of Ekpeye, Ikwerre and Etche in the administrative structure. The Epie-Atissa people have, on the other hand, been administratively grouped with the Izon-speaking people, the Nembe and the Ogbia.

Consequently, both the Engenni and Epie have been largely influenced by the languages of their neighbours. The Engenni language has imbibed a lot of Igbo, Ekpeye and Ogba loans. The Epie language, on the other hand, has been very much affected by the Izon language. The evidence of Izon influence is most marked in the Epie spoken in the Atissa area.

Zarama is subsumed in Engenni ethnicity, yet Zarama has never been administered as part of Engenni. From colonial times to the present, Zarama has been administratively tied to the Epie-Atissa in Yenagoa or the Okordia, Biseni and Gbarain people of Taylor Creek. In spite of this administrative separation, the Zarama people accept the Okulogua tradition and her affinity with the Engenni, Epie and Degema.

OGBIA, ABURENI/MINI, ORUMA (Tugbene)

The Ogbia Sub-Groups

The Ogbia ethnic group settled in their present homeland, in the northern limit of the Central Niger Delta a long time ago. Ogbia possesses a distinctive culture, which has formed a bond of unity among the various sub-groups.

Migration and Settlement History

The abandoned forest site of Ebala, suggests ancient settlement in the region, possibly, prior to the current traditions of migration into the area. Ogbia traditions adopt the Benin stereotype and cite a migratory route through the Western Delta to the Brass River and up it to Ologoama in Okoroma local government area of Bayelsa State. It was from Otuokoroma that the sons and grandson of Ogbia and Okoroma dispersed in different directions and founded autonomous communities.

There are variations to this tradition from the Olei (Oloibiri), Okoroma, the Kolo, and the Odinade sub-groups. The Odinade sub-group comprising Akipelai, Emakalakala, Opume, Okoroba and Idema live close to the site of Ebala, and cite traditions of origin from east of the Niger Delta. Other communities remember traditions of migration into Ogbia territory from the Central Delta dispersal centre of Obiama.

Kay Williamson's linguistic studies suggest that the Ogbia belong to the Central Delta family of languages along with the Abua, Odual, Kugbo, Obronuagun, Obulom, and Ogbogolo. This classification points their ultimate places of origin in the direction of the Cross River Valley and beyond.

Ogbia in Inter-Group Relations

Ogbia relations with Nembe have been long standing in all spheres of human endeavour: in trade, political and cultural relations. In recent times they have been grouped in the same administrative units.

The Ogbia are geographically contiguous with Ijo groups, and have developed close ties with them. The Okoroma and other Ogbia, located along the Ekole Creek, are especially close to the Ijo. This has brought cross—cultural contacts in inter-marriages, commercial transactions, in traditional wrestling, songs and pattern of dance and drumming.

There are traditions relating the Ogbia to the Abuloma of Okrika, the Bakana of Kalabari, and the founder of the Amachree dynasty of Kalabari.

Oruma (Tugbene)

Traditions, recorded by E. J. Alagoa at Oruma, state that the founder of Oruma, Tu, left the Oboloma quarter in Nembe because of a disagreement, resulting from the sharing of game in a community hunting expedition. According to their tradition, Tu left Nembe to Ogbia through the Kolo Creek and migrated northward until he arrived at the present site. Tu noted that this site was comfortable for habitation, far from any intrusion and invaders.

According to Alagoa, Kolo Creek was wide when Tu arrived there. But since Tu was determined to prevent pursuit by his enemies in Oboloma, he sent for a medicine man from the Ibo country. A heavy object (*Ikuye*) and a light bamboo frond (*Pini*) were dropped into the river. The heavy object floated and the light one sank to the bottom; soon the creek silted up (Alagoa, 1972:183-185).

The other settlements which sprang from Oruma are Ibelebiri, Okordia and Buseni.

Abureni (Mini)

The Ebala tradition and culture which has influenced the Abureni group, is embedded in the celebration of the yearly *Iyal Ikai* festival among the Abureni and other members of the Odinade family.

The *Iyal Ikai* festival is celebrated between 27th February and 15th March each year. The date of the festival actually depended on when the tide at 9 a.m. corresponds with the ebb tide. It was a traditional rule that the *Iyal–Ikai* festival must not commence during the flow tide. *Iyal–Ikai* festival was celebrated during the dark period of the month. If the festival days correspond with the required tide but fall within the period of moonlight, the only remedy was that all the chiefs representing the ancestral group of Houses would abstain from raising their heads to see the sky throughout the festival period. If this was flouted, it was believed that the festival would be rejected by the gods of the land, and may lead to untimely death in the community (Tariwari, 2005:16).

Ogbia in Contemporary Times

The Ogbia people in contemporary times have made considerable progress. They have succeeded in maintaining and upholding their age-long historical identity. They have preserved the Ogbia language and culture, created Ogbia Town, and the traditional stools of *Obanobhan* and *Obanema*.

The Ogbia Language

The Ogbia language is an important part of Ogbia identity. Historical linguists have classified the Ogbia language as belonging to the Central Delta group of the Benue-Congo family, which belongs to the wider Niger–Congo language group in Africa (Williamson, 1987:1). Other languages in this sub-division include Abua, Odual, Kugbo, Bukuma, and Obulom.

The Ogbia Brotherhood

The Ogbia Brotherhood is a socio-cultural organization that came into existence in October 1940 at Oloibiri. The founding father was Rev. George Igabo Amangala. Its motto is: "*All for each and each for all*" (Ogbia Brotherhood: 1-13).

Besides the Ogbia language, the Ogba Brotherhood is: "One of the strongest institutions that had given the Ogbia man a common identity, direction, focus and relevance …. An umbrella body which provides the moving force for the progress of the Ogbia people".

Ogbia Town (Omemoma)

The establishment of Ogbia Town or Omemoma (New Town), was the result of a resolution reached by the Ogbia Brotherhood in 1971.

The philosophy of its founding fathers was the creation of a centre of Ogbia unity, a rallying point of socio-political and economic activities. Besides, the need for a neutral Ogbia headquarters became apparent when it was observed that Oloibiri could not accommodate the numerous projects earmarked for establishment by the Ogbia people.

The present site was chosen after due consultation with the landlord communities, including Otuabo, Otuogidi and Oloibiri. No money in form of compensation was paid to the communities. The appointment of Chief Melford Obiene Okilo as the Governor of the old Rivers State accelerated the development of Ogbia Town.

The Obenobhan and Obenema

The *Obenobhan* is the highest traditional political stool in Ogbia land. It is graded as a first class stool by the Bayelsa State government. *Obenema*, on the other hand is the "recognized ruler of a village or town in Ogbia" (Obanobhan Constitution: 1975).

Crude Oil at Itokopiri-Ogbia (Oloibiri Oil Wells)

The exploration and exploitation of oil at Itokopiri in Ogbia started in 1953 by Shell. Shell arrived at the Oloibiri District in 1953 through Okoroma. The company started operation in March 1954. This process continued until March 15th, 1956 when the first oil well in West Africa was struck at Itokopiri (Tarinyo: 2006).

It is important to note that the site of the first oil well is Itokopiri, a piece of forestland owned jointly by the communities of Otuabagi, Otuogidi and Opume. However the name Oloibiri was used by Shell as an operational name, because Oloibiri was the largest town and the district headquarters.

In 1958, the first crude oil load from Itokopiri entered the international market. At the peak of its exploratory activities, Shell was able to drill eighteen successful oil wells and one dry well.

The first oil spillage in Nigeria occurred in Itokopiri in 1973 (Tarinyo:2006), and adversely affected the environment and the landlord communities. Minimal compensation was paid to the communities, and by the mid-seventies, Shell had gone to other locations in the Niger Delta. Since then, a number of white elephant projects have been proposed for the area, such as a National Oil Museum, the Oloibiri Millennium Landmark project and a Research Institute.

ABUA
Origin, Migration, Settlement
Researchers have attempted to establish three main theories of Abua origin and migration, namely the autochthony, the Delta Cross movement and the Umake Egula tradition.

Talbot (1932) recorded a tradition that Abua "descended from heaven" and was the first man to settle on earth coming down to earth with his wife, Egula. Talbot states that Abua and Egula descended from heaven on a rope let down by Ake (the supreme God) and touched down at Olokpagha, a place which is currently forest and site of the central shrine of the Abua, also called Erugha Ogboko. According to this story, Abua had four sons: Agama, Emughami, Okpadien and Otami. The sons' dispersal led to the founding of the four Abua clans of Central Abua, Emughan, Okpeden and Otapha.

Murdock (1949), Nair (1972), Williamson (1987) classified the Abua language in the Central Delta group. They suggested Abua migration from the Bantu heartland through the Eastern Niger Delta. This theory postulates that the Abua, Odual, Kugbo, and Ogbia, referred to as the Central Delta group, migrated from the Bantu region of Cenral Africa through the Cross River to the Niger Delta. They possessed iron technology and superior agricultural knowledge and crops.

In the third theory of origin, Abua is tied to the Ogbia tradition of Benin origin, and migration through the Brass River.

The linguistic theory of movement from the east is the most acceptable at present. There is no basis for holding on to the Benin migration account. The tradition of autochthony is normal for a people who have been settled in a location for many years.

The closest neighbours to Abua on the northern axis are the Ekpeye and Ikwerre people. Because of the Ekpeye and Ikwerre contiguity with Abua all the three were jointly administered in the early colonial times from 1901. In 1991, Abua, Odual and Engenni became a local government area.

Degema (Udekema) is a close neighbour of Abua to the south. Abua and Degema share markets. In the olden days the trade between these neighbours was mainly by barter where sea foods were exchanged for food items such as garri, yam, coco-yam and palm oil; the Degema groups, though so close are of the Edoid group as the Epie and Engenni people (Greenberg, 1963).

The Kalabari communities to the south share boundaries with Abua; there has been a long relationship in trade from pre- colonial times. Bille and Bukuma located in the Eastern Delta also traded with communities of the Central Delta group.

The Struggle to Join Bayelsa State

The Abua, Odual and Kugbo people presented documents and request, to join Bayelsa State in the period of the struggle to create the new state. In their memoranda, the Abua, Odual, and Kugbo referred to the Ogbia, Nembe and other Ijo groups as their kith and kin.

CHAPTER 24
WILBERFORCE ISLAND:
A NIGER DELTA DISPERSAL CENTRE[†]

E. J. Alagoa
Emeritus Professor of History
University of Port Harcourt, Nigeria

- 1 -
Prologue

In Ijo number symbolism, three is male, four female, and seven, the sum of them, is spirit, sacred or divine. We intend to conduct a brief historical discussion of Wilberforce Island in three periods: Ancient, Modern, and Contemporary; in seven brief sections; leaving the most recent or current events to the politicians. Also, in terms of time dimensions, we would attempt to discuss matters of the Past and Present, make some effort to penetrate the Future, but would rather leave most of the Future and Eternity to God.

The periods and time dimensions are treated in a fluid and flexible fashion. But in the interest of the historians, I would adapt Derefaka's (2003: 4-5) five periods of Ijo history into my first and second, and adding a third:

4000 B.C. - 1400 A. D. Ancient times or Antiquity
1400 A. D. - 1900 A. D. Modem times
1900 A. D. - 2000+ A. D. Contemporary times

The times of the oral traditions, which reach back to ancient times, but are usually not deep enough to cover all antiquity, are treated early in section 2. The Ancient history revealed by linguistic studies and archaeology, follow in sections 3 and 4, to be followed by discussions of more Contemporary concerns related to the Environment and to Niger Delta studies. The approach is intended to be direct; and ideas are expressed in simple single-syllable words whenever possible.

---

† This Chapter was originally given as the First Public Lecture of the Centre for Niger Delta Studies, Niger Delta University, Wilberforce Island, Bayelsa State, in 2007.

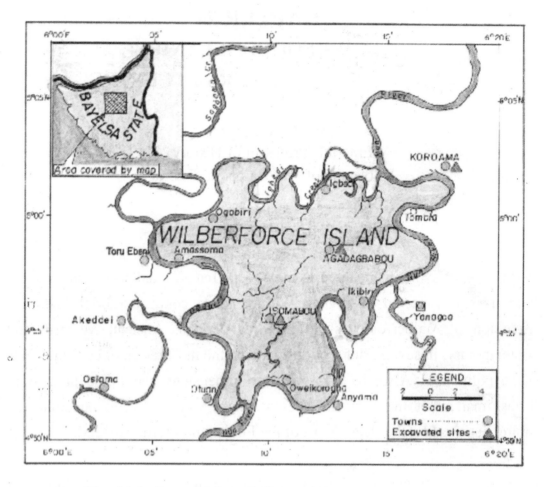

Fig. 24.1: Central Niger Delta showing excavated sites

At age seventy-plus, it would be futile to claim that I would present to you the results of new original research. The best you can hope for is a review of old data in the light of new work by others. The discussion that follows will be based on my own book, *A History of the Niger Delta: An Historical Interpretation of Ijo Oral Tradition* (Alagoa: 1972/2005), and on the new book by Professor Abi Alabo Derefaka, *Archaeology and Culture History in the Central Niger Delta* (Derefaka: 2003). You may note that I already have the title "Historian of the Niger Delta", conferred on me by my teacher, Professor Jan Vansina of the University of Wisconsin. I seize this opportunity to confer on Derefaka the title "Historian of the Central Niger Delta". I will, therefore, rely on him for guidance in this presentation. I will also rely on the authority of my late colleague, Professor Kay Williamson above all others. We begin our reliance on the Historian of the Central Niger Delta by taking our description of Wilberforce Island from him (Derefaka: 2003, 13/15):

"Wilberforce Island ...(circumscribed by the Nun River, Igbedi
Creek and Ogobiri River) is about 19 kilometres long (that is, from
the extreme northern to the extreme southern points) and about 21.5
kilometres wide (taking the extreme western and eastern points)."

The current Izon *ibe* residents of Wilberforce Island are the Ogboin at
Amassoma, Mein at Ogobiri, Kolokuma at Igbedi, the Ekpetiama at Agudama
and Bumodi, the lkibiri and others.

- 2 -
The Oral Tradition

When I did my research in the Niger Delta in the 1960s, I was very concerned
with identity: who are the Ijo, where did they come from, and what binds the
various *ibe* and polities together as Ijo. I had no ready-made answers. What I
intended to do was to seek answers from the people themselves, directly
through their oral traditions current at the time of my research, or from the
Intelligence Reports already recorded by the colonial authorities in the 1930s
and earlier. In the case of communities on Wilberforce Island, I was only able
to record the traditions of the Ogboin directly at Amassoma, as guest of "His
Royal Highness Zumoh Efeke V, the Ibenana-owei of Ogboin, and Crocodile of
the Rivers State." I was also guest of the Tombia community of Ekpetiama
across the Nun opposite Agudama on Wilberforce Island.

The answers I received from the Ijo communities around the Niger Delta
suggested a pattern of migrations from locations I named dispersal centres. A
majority of the dispersal centres lay in the Central Niger Delta. Wilberforce
Island appeared to be the most significant dispersal centre in the northern part
of the Central Niger Delta. The rest of the story comes from the people, my job
being to place it in historical context, and, as the subtitle of my book suggests,
interpret the traditions as historical documents.

When I first visited Amassoma in March 1964, the Amananawei, Z. A. Yeri (74), through the community spokesman, Mr. M. O. Nanakumo (62), recounted the history of **Ogboin** *ibe.* All Ogboin were the children of a common ancestor named Ogboin. According to him, all the major settlements were founded by sons or grandchildren of Ogboin. Amassoma, for example, was founded by Oboro, son of Ogboin, on a swampy site, hence the name, *amasuma;* each of the wards being founded by sons of Oboro: Alumu, Okpotu, and Ogoni. The origins of the Ogboin, however, featured Otuan very prominently. Ogboin was stated to have left his father, Izon (ljo), at Oruma on the North-Eastern Fringe of the Central Delta, and after wanderings, settled at a remote site named Orubiribaubolou, apparently, close to Otuan, and to Otuan from where his children dispersed to their separate locations.

My understanding of the traditions was, that the ancestral home of the Ogboin, Orubiribaubolou, was located at a site within Wilberforce Island. The tradition that Oko, founder of Okochiri (Okopiri) in Okrika, was son of Alumu of Amassoma, fields this location as a potential dispersal centre.

The Mein traditions of Ogobiri on Wilberforce Island clearly identify it as a major centre of dispersal. According to accounts derived from Ogobiri sources, the dispersal of the Mein from Ogobiri began in the generation of the sons of Kor, *Mein Okosuwei* (Elder of the Mein), son of Mein (P. V. Main, 1930). Three sons of Kor moved into the Western Delta, to sites along the River Forcados to found three new kingdoms: Kalanama founded the Akugbene Mein; Ngbile founded the Ngbilebiri Mein at Kiagbodo; and Ogbolu founded the Ogbolubiri Mein at Ogbodobiri.

The Mein thus became four polities at Ogobiri, Akugbene, Kiagbodo, and Ogbodobiri. While they maintained their loyalty to their common deity, Dirimoagbiya, each of the polities on the Forcados River sought new symbols of authority, and received bronzes from Benin, and took the title of *pere* to distinguish themselves from the *Mein Okosuwei* at Ogobiri.

Kolokuma and **Opokuma** traditions, first recorded in 1938 by Newington, stated that the two groups were founded by the two brothers, Opu-Okun and Kala-Okun, sons of Ndo/Indo/Ondo, who settled at Agadagbabou on Wilberforce Island, after a period of wandering. Opu-Okun, founder of Opokuma is claimed by some traditions to have first left Agadagbabou to settle along the Nun River. The Kolokuma, apparently, first moved to Orubou or Oruamatoru, before settling at various sites on the River Nun. Curiously, the Opokuma first worshipped the god Egbelekwe before switching to Opokuma Egbesu on the Nun; while the Kolokuma appear to have switched from the worship of a god named Okpotu at Agadagbabou to Kolokuma Egbesu from Orubou to the Nun.

Again, Agadagbabou on Wilberforce Island must count as a significant dispersal centre in the Central Niger Delta.

Two important towns of the **Ekpetiama,** Agudama and Bumodi, now stand on Wilberforce Island. The oral traditions of the group, now oriented to the Nun River, suggest origins inside Wilberforce Island, in the ancient site of Isomabou/Isomobou, near Ikibiri. Traditions at Ikibiri claim that Isomabou was not only the centre out of which the ancestors of the Ekpetiama migrated, but also Seimbiri *ibe* of the Western Delta; Ogoloma in Okrika in the Eastern Delta; Akaranbiri in Opokuma and Onopa in Epie-Atissa in the Central Delta; and Akiri in Aboh.

In 1964, I was informed by Pilisi Akuku (53) and others at Tombia, that Ekpetiamaowei or Ekpeti, had settled at a site they named Opuanbou, from which location his sons moved out to found Tombia, Bumodi, Agudama, Akabiri, and Gbarantoru. At Onopa I was informed that a man named Ewekere came from Yene-Iki (Ikibiri), first to a place named Aziokunumuvoazi, and, finally to Onopa in the Epie Creek. The settlement was first named Opuanbiri, after a lake on Wilberforce Island near Ikibiri. At Ogoloma in Okrika, Chief Ebenezer Opu-Ogulaya affirmed, that the founder, Opu-Ogulaya, had migrated from Isomabou. In 1981 the *amaokosuwei* (oldest man in Ikibiri) told Professor Derefaka that "Opugula is the main deity of the Ogbo".

The oral traditions at Ikibiri provide the most detailed account of Isomabou. The Ikibiri name their founding ancestor Ogbo, and, therefore, his community Ogbo *ibe*. After the outward migrations, and threats from other neighbours, Ikibiri increasingly sought the protection of their kinsmen in Ekpetiama. But the importance of Ikibiri and of the Isomabou dispersal centre is gradually becoming manifest. The Opuanbou cited at Tombia as dispersal centre of the Ekpetiama, and the Opuanbiri cited at Onopa are the same, and lead ultimately to Isomabou.

These oral traditions establish for me a central place for Wilberforce Island in the search for a homeland for the Ijo people. And the next step in the search would be to examine the results of Professor Derefaka's archaeological excavations at Agadagbabou and Isomabou on Wilberforce Island.

- 3 -
Archaeology

What does archaeology tell us about Wilberforce Island from the excavations done by Professor Derefaka at Agadagbabou and Isomabou/Isomobo?

At **Agadagbabou** Derefaka recovered a whole lot of broken bits and pieces of pots made in the locality, mostly for domestic use.The analysis of decorations suggested the making and/or use of cords, basketry, fish traps, and mats by the people who lived at Agadagbabou. The people also made smoking pipes, and may have smoked the dried leaves of the bush mango tree before the importation of tobacco from the Americas. A clay pendant was identified by the Kolokuma working with Derefaka as *kara,* "said to be worn around the neck by women during the period of circumcision rites or by priests. . . in the remote past"(Derefaka 2003: 90).

The people of Agadagbabou were farmers, fisher folk, canoe-carvers, hunters, and pot-makers, being also craftsmen and women. Some of them traded, as shown by the European imports of J. J. W. Peters gin bottles and the "two carnelian beads recovered", both being "cylindrical beads with green, red and yellow stripes"(Derefaka 2003: 90).

The dates obtained from the scientific analysis of charred palm kernel and charcoal samples place Agadagbabou in the Modem period "between 1640 and 1730 A. D." (Derefaka 2003: 99).

This late date has led Derefaka to doubt if the site excavated was, indeed, the ancient dispersal centre reported in Kolokuma and Opokuma oral traditions. He notes that the ancient site had become a burial place for priests of Kolokuma Egbesu, and, accordingly, "kept secret" (Derefaka 2003: 99). It is, therefore, possible, that we are yet to discover the ancient site in the "revered forest of Agadagbabou" (Derefaka 2003: 100). This is by no means strange. We had similar problems identifying the ancestral site of the Ogoni people in Nama Sii, even after several offerings to the local priests!

At **Isomabou/Isomobo,** Professor Derefaka recovered "an iron object (the tip of a fishing spear)", a large quantity of broken pottery (potsherd), charcoal, "post holes and ... fragments of house posts", animal and fish bones.

The people were farmers, fisher folk and hunters. They made canoes and used the oil palm tree, and could also work iron. Professor Derefaka notes that:

> "... the most significant aspect of the finds at the Isomabou site is
> the fact that all the artefacts recovered are locally made. There were
> no European or other external trade goods recovered from the four
> test pits that were fully investigated" (Derefaka 2003: 164).

The site had been undisturbed, and the scientific dates of 1030 A. D. to 1480 A. D. place Isomabou in the Ancient Period of Niger Delta history. These dates establish the status of a major dispersal centre suggested by the oral traditions for Isomabou. These dates agree with the dates from excavations in Ogoloma, Okrika, in the Eastern Niger Delta, which the oral traditions include in the Isomabou orbit of dispersals (Derefaka 2003: 227).

For Wilberforce Island, we may conclude that archaeology has produced support for its status as a significant location in the history of Ijo settlement from the evidence of Isomabou. And the expectation remains, that we may yet discover the authentic ancient site of Agadagbabou, and the site of Ogboin dispersal. The ancestral home of the Ogboin on Wilberforce Island is important, since Okochiri/Okopiri in Okrika claimed by Ogboin traditions as founded from Wilberforce Island is dated in the Ancient Period, A. D. 850 to A. D. 1500. And we are yet to excavate in the Ogobiri area.

A comparative analysis of the traditions of migration between the Central Delta and the Eastern Delta is yet to be done. The traditions of migration and settlement from Ogoloma, Okrika suggest that movements were not always direct between two points. We note that Ogoloma and Isomabou were of the same age. In addition, Ogoloma traditions also refer to a second Central Delta dispersal centre as ancestral home, namely, Obiama, in Okoroma/Tereke local government area. Although no excavations have been done in Obiama, excavations have been done at Saikiripogu (Ewoama, Okpoama), also populated, according to local traditions, by migrants from Obiama. The dates for Saikiripogu are also about the same as those for Isomabou and Ogoloma, "A. D. 1010 - 1640" (Derefaka 2003:227).

We may conclude that Archaeology has provided some answers to questions raised by the oral traditions concerning the history of Wilberforce Island and the Niger Delta, but new questions are raised; quite a few others, by the science of **Palynology**.

Professor Margaret Sowunmi, the palynologist, had accompanied the archaeologists to Onyoma and other sites to take soil samples at different levels, and to study the living vegetation. She eventually obtained a deep core sample from Shell from Ofuabo Creek near Onyoma, Nembe. It was from this material that she was able to define the changes in vegetation patterns in the Niger Delta over the past forty thousand years (Sowunmi 1988). She reports that the extent of the Niger Delta has increased and decreased over the past forty thousand years. Conditions for human occupation were changed from good to bad from the past 30,000 years, but have been generally good from about 5,600 to 5,300 years.

Evidence of human activity is recorded in the vegetation from about 3,000 years, according to the evidence of palynology, a period when the oil palm became "wide-spread and prominent" in the Niger Delta.

We can conclude that Archaeology and Palynology extend our knowledge of the Niger Delta beyond the limits of the oral tradition. The dating of Niger Delta history becomes firmer, and new issues are raised in the matter of origins and migrations, since the dates for Isomabou and places in the Eastern Niger Delta fall into the same period. The oral traditions had always indicated a number of dispersal centres, with the majority in the Central Niger Delta. Wilberforce Island is confirmed as a centre of dispersal at Isomabou, with other possible sites. What does Linguistics contribute to the discussion?

- 4 -

Linguistics

Professor Kay Williamson, the English lady who came to settle at Kaiama, among the Kolokuma, studied the languages of the Niger Delta, Nigeria, and Africa for almost fifty years. The government of Bayelsa State has acknowledged her remarkable contribution to the study and development of the languages of the Niger Delta by creating a special language institute in her memory at Kaiama. I am relying completely on Professor Williamson's work in the following discussion of language in the history of the Niger Delta.

Professor Williamson has compared all the languages of the Niger Delta, in relation to the neighbouring languages of the hinterland, using the techniques of the sciences of **lexicostatistics** and **glottochronology** and come up with the following ideas and conclusions (Williamson 1988).

First, the speakers of the language group she classified as Ijoid or Ijo-Defaka, have lived in relative isolation from the speakers of the neigbouring language groups, namely Igboid, Edoid, and Yoruboid, for "more than 7,000 years". That the other languages of the Niger Delta apparently moved into the region only in the last 2,000 years:

> the Abua-Ogbia arrived over 2,000 years ago, from an easterly direction; followed by the Ogoni group; and the Delta Edoid group from the west, namely the Degema (Udekama), Engenni, and Epie; and the Igboid group from a northerly direction, namely the Ogbah, Ekpeye, Ikwerre, Ukwuani, and the Ika.

According to Professor Williamson, the Itsekiri and Obolo (Andoni) arrived in the Niger Delta "less than 1,500 years ago".

Second, that the arrival of the Abua-Ogbia group caused a movement of Ijo speakers out of that part of the Niger Delta to the north-east and south-east, thus suggesting this part of the Niger Delta as another centre of Ijo dispersal or migration.

We have to accept Professor Williamson's own position that the dates she provides are not exact, and the conclusions on migration patterns are also tentative. However, the dates she supplies from language study are worthy of respect. The dates provide support for the antiquity of Ijo settlement in the Niger Delta, strengthening the same conclusion we derive from the evidence of archaeology and palynology. On the issue of centres of dispersal also, the linguistic studies support the suggestions of multiple centres.

In the matter of Ijo origins then, neither the oral traditions nor archaeology points us to a single location, centre, or site. On the other hand, Professor Robin Horton has used Professor Kay Williamson's linguistic data and his own interpretation of Ijo oral traditions to suggest two different possible locations (Horton 1998: 195 - 255), and proposing research to choose a single location.

First, he sees "Proto-Ijoid speakers coming down the Niger and entering the Delta through its apex". From this, Horton locates a single possible dispersal centre for all Ijo at a point at the Niger Delta apex.

Second, he locates a place of origin for all speakers of Ijoid languages at the eastern extremity of the Niger Delta beyond the Imo River.

Professor Horton estimates that it would take up to five years of linguistic research and "twenty five years at least" of archaeological work to decide between his proposed sites of origin (Horton 1998: 239).

We can only conclude that current evidence form all sources available to us places Wilberforce Island in the line of ancient settlement sites, along with other sites in the Central and Eastern Niger Delta.

- 5 -
Contemporary History

The contemporary history of Wilberforce Island is bound to be dominated by the story of Niger Delta University. Our discourse will necessarily end with Niger Delta University. Before we get there, we will briefly consider the relevance for our times of the lives of two figures from the colonial period and from the early independence period. What can we learn from the lives of Bebeke-Ola of Igbedi, son of Dubakemefa; and of Major Isaac Jasper Adaka Boro?

Bebeke-ola's story has been written by his grandson, Jones Ezekiel Ibenadeizi Bebeke-ola (Ibenah) while serving as a research assistant to Professor Kay Williamson at the University of Port Harcourt. Bebeke-ola was executed as a pirate by the colonial authorities at Sabagreia on the 3rd September 1903. Normally a trader and fisherman, he had been drawn into a life of violence. First to seek compensation from the people of Isiala near Aboh, who had given sanctuary to a slave of his father. Second, to seize the property of a Nembe trading canoe, in return for his own goods seized at Brass over a similar seizure of a Nembe man's property at Igbedi. Bebekeola became a household word for bravery in war for these and other violent exploits, and was believed to receive the blessing of Egbesu and the spiritual forces of the land. According to Ibenah,

> "He never attacked any Ijoman to exploit him, rather he would not
> allow others to exploit his people" (Ibenah, n. d. 31).

Yet, under pressure from a colonial expeditionary force, it was his own people who gave Bebeke-ola up. When approached to take away from Bebeke-ola the protection of Egbesu, the priest asked,

> "Has this man ever fought any person from your clan or killed any
> relative from the clan? To this they replied: NO. Then he said that
> as the whole of Kolokuma district had agreed ... he had no objection
> again, and so did remove the power He had vested in him
> accordingly." (Ibenah n. d. 27)

Bebeke-ola eventually surrendered:

> "...when Bebeke-ola was identified in the boat he was questioned
> about the allegations and so-called atrocities he was said to have
> committed. He did not answer any questions or make any statement.
> .. and after three days of questioning and torture when he did not
> open his mouth, the whole of Kolokuma people were invited to
> witness the FIRST ever execution at Sabageria (sic)" (Ibenah n. d.
> 29).

The story of **Major Isaac Jasper Adaka Boro** is better known to us. Like Bebeke-ola, he was led into violent struggle in the hopes of righting wrongs. Like Bebeke-ola, he surrendered himself on the basis of public demand, in the public interest:

> "On the 7th of March, 1966, I came to the village of Kalama from
> where I was handed over to the federal forces" (Boro 1982: 154).

Like Bebeke-ola, Boro was tortured, threatened, and sentenced to death:

> "Suffice it to say that all those arrested suffered innumerable hardships
> too extensive and pitiable to mention in these records. I was threatened
> with a swift military tribunal if I would not mention or expose persons
> behind my agitation. I did not yield to falsehood. For two weeks, I was

subjected to questioning and to sleeping on the bare floor. Tribal capitalist tycoons walked at pleasure into the police station to spit and rain abuses at me . . . Samuel Owonaru had one of his eyes almost blinded.." (Boro 1982: 155)

The vagaries of Nigerian history took Boro out of the Eastern region to Lagos, and gave him the opportunity to serve in the Nigerian Army, to liberate Rivers/Bayelsa State, to make the ultimate sacrifice of his life in the process.

These two brief biographies should provide sufficient material to the current militants of the Niger Delta to draw conclusions, and take decisions in the long term interest of the majority of the people.

Clearly, it is time to consider new strategies in our continuing struggle, learning lessons from the lives of men such as Bebeke-ola and Adaka Boro. **Chief Diepreye Simon Peter Alamieyeseigha J. P**, another remarkable son of Wilberforce Island, Governor of Bayelsa State (1999 - 2005), had the following to say on the subject.

". . . Adaka Boro left a legacy of dialogue as the best option for conflict resolution. The significance of his life was that, even though man can be pushed to the point of submission, there is little justifiable need to shed blood. This is a lesson for our youths and adults alike. And that is why there is every reason for us to develop Adaka Boro's legacy into a philosophy of development for the Izon nation." (Alamieyeseigha 2000: 15).

The call is for a new philosophy, new strategies and tactics in a struggle that continues unabated. And when it comes to fashioning weapons of peaceful combat and constructing tools for building cultural and spiritual institutions, we need persons such as the poet sage of Bumodi, Ekpetiama, Wilberforce Island, **Dr. Gabriel Imomotimi Gbaingbain Okara**.

Environment

We have taken a quick run down of the ancient, modem and contemporary history of Wilberforce Island. We move to the environment, which endures through all time and times, providing the conditions for life. The evidence of palynology suggests radical changes in the environment over the millennia. The archaeological evidence suggests stable conditions for human use of the resources of the land over recent millennia. This stability is threatened in the contemporary period by increasingly destructive methods in the use of the resources of the environment. In the words of Powell, "logging and forest conversion are out of control".

What is there in the Niger Delta that deserves to be conserved at the expense of logging, farming and development or used as a component of development?

The general aim of conservation, of course, is to preserve diversity in flora and fauna for the enjoyment and practical use of present and future generations. The Niger Delta as a whole must be one of the areas in Nigeria and the world with potentials for the preservation of species of plants and animals which have gone extinct in many parts of the world. Powell found the following in the area of mammals only (Powell 1997: 84):

Five mammals new to Nigeria, namely,

Delta red colobus, *Procolobus aff. pennantii* an endangered specie
Pygmy flying squirrel, *Idiurus cf. macrotis* a near threatened specie
Small green squirrel, *Paraxerus poensis*
Black tree squirrel, *Funisciurus sp. indet.*
Black-fronted duiker, *Cephalophus nigrifrons.*

Powell also discovered five mammals not previously known west of the Cross River, and six not previously reported in the Niger Delta. This shows the poor state of research in the environmental sciences over the Niger Delta. Our present call is for activity in Niger Delta University in its back yard in

Wilberforce Island. There have been calls for two forest reserves to the north in Taylor Creek, and to the south in Apoi Creek. For Wilberforce Island, logging has increased in volume, and getting out of control with the opening of the Tombia - Amassoma Road. And for the Niger Delta as a whole, the exploitation of crude oil and gas, and the pollution resulting from these activities quickly add up to loss of environmental resources. However, it should still be possible to follow the orthodox forest reserve approach over parts of Bayelsa State and the Niger Delta to escape the worst effects of environment loss. For Wilberforce Island, Niger Delta University may put pressure on the state government to pursue Powell's suggestion of

> "stop-gap measures to compensate landlord communities for preserving critical core areas of potential sanctuaries. The arrangements might be handled under Customary (traditional) Law with the approval of the State Director of Forestry. Such areas would cost as little as US$lOOO per sq. km. yearly and could also serve as much-needed teaching and research sites for local universities" (Powell 1997: 85).

Niger Delta University and its scientists cannot dodge the responsibility of making a difference on the environment and life of Wilberforce Island as a whole, and, eventually, on the whole of Bayelsa State and the Niger Delta.

- 7 -
Epilogue

This brief discourse places Wilberforce Island not only in the geographical centre of the Niger Delta, but also at the centre of its history. By building Niger Delta University on it, Chief Diepreye Alamieyeseigha has built an engine of change that should drive Bayelsa State and the Niger Delta into the main streams of development.

The university's founding instrument already has enshrined in it, a provision for an Institute/Centre of Niger Delta Studies, a unique provision in a university constitution. And Alamieyeseigha proceeded to commit the Bayelsa State government to endow a special Chair of Niger Delta Studies:

> ". . .the state will institute a chair on Niger Delta Studies at the Niger Delta Institute of the Niger Delta University, Wilberforce Island." (Alamieyeseigha 2000: 35).

This gives us assurance that Niger Delta University has the potential to develop into an institution, capable of protecting, promoting, and developing the languages, culture and traditions of the region. I place emphasis on cultural studies because these are easy to place on the back burner in development plans. Protection of the environment and development of its resources cannot be ignored, as well as science and technology in a space age. In order to take control of our oil and gas resources, for example, we have to master the relevant technologies and sciences. In the end, human resources development and prudent control of environmental resources provide the key to the future.

CHAPTER 25

THE ỊZỌN
AND THEIR
IGBOID NEIGHBOURS

**Ugwulor Eugene Nwala, Kingdom Orji
and Gamaliel Sokari-George**

Introduction

Contact between the Ijaw and their Igboid neighbours dates to very early times. Alagoa (1972:191) records that "the traditions indicate that yams, cocoyam and other root crops were purchased from the hinterland. Livestock such as sheep, goats, cow and dogs were also obtained in exchange for salt". The principal basis of this early contact was trade that sustained the economies of both groups. The present study reveals that these early contacts were not accompanied by settlement in each other's territory until the era of palm oil trade.

The river system of the Niger Delta linked the Ijaw to the markets and sources of production in the hinterland. Thus Dike (1956:19-20) quoted Sir Harry Johnson on this, that the Oil Rivers offered 'exceptional facilities for penetrating the interior by means of large and navigable streams and by a wonderful system of natural canalization which connect all the branches of the lower Niger by means of deep creeks'. Therefore, the long distance trade contacts at this period were generally achieved by the traditional canoe means of transport.

The slave trade era did not witness settlement of the Ijaw in the territories of their Igboid neighbours who at the time provided uninterrupted routes. However, with the suppression of the trade in men and the emergence of the era of legitimate trade in palm oil/kernel in 1807, the pattern of earlier trade soon changed.

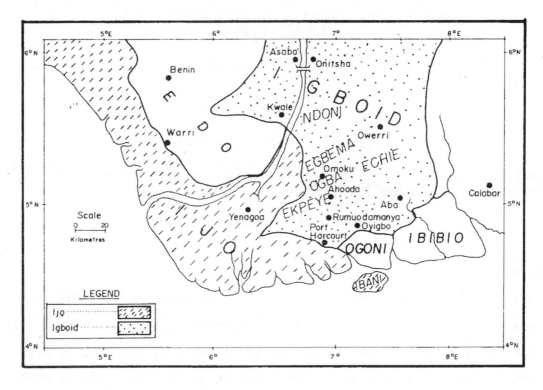

Fig. 25.1: The Ijo and their Igboid neighbours

The abolition of the slave trade created safe and conducive environment for the establishment of trading posts to meet the high demand of palm oil and kernel by the European merchants. From these early trading posts, Ijaw settlements gradually emerged in the territories of the Igboid peoples. The buying and selling of commodities was accompanied by contact of cultures, the exchange of ideas, the mingling of peoples and promotion of economic well-being.

The central focus of this Chapter, therefore, is the exploration of aspects of inter-group relations between the Ijaw and their Igboid neighbours. In the context of the present study, the ethnic nationalities that fall within the study are, the Ndoki, Etche, Ikwerre, Ekpeye, Ogba, Egbema, Ika-Ibo, and Ndoni (Aboh).

Ndoki

Background

The people of Ndoki are found in Oyigbo Local Government Area of Rivers State, Ukwa-East Local Government Area in Abia State; and the Uhuobu group of villages are part of Akwa Ibom State. Those in Rivers State include

Ayama, Okoloma, Umuosi and Obeakpu. From these early settlements, the people spread to Egberu, Afam-Ukwu, Afam-Nta down to Umuagbai, Azuogu, Maraihu, Okpontu Okwanku, Obunku and Obete. Those that later crossed the Imo River are found in Abia State and inhabit the following communities; Akwete, Azumini, Mkpuaejekere, Nkpunkpha, Nkpunkpule, Ogbuagu, Akirika-Ukwu, Akirika-Nta, Ohambele, Abaki, Akanu, Akiri-Obu, Eti, Obohia, Obozu, Obunku-Ugbor, Ohaobu, Ohandu, Ohanku, Ohanso, Uhuru, and Ubaku.

Traditions, collected recently from the Ndoki in Rivers State, cite Benin as a place of origin, and the Ibani (Ibani) as their companions in migration. The phrase, *Aminadokiari*, which they state as the folk etymology for the name Ndoki, is ofcourse, Eastern Delta Ijo for 'I am searching for my brother'. That is, that the Ndoki came searching for the Ibani in the course of their migration. Alagoa (1972:178) corroborates this when he observed:

> The traditions suggest that they migrated north and east-wards from the Central Delta along with the ancestors of the Ibani to their present location where they were affected by Ibo cultural influences.

The early Ndoki migrants in search of their Ibani brother passed through the Imo River to their present location, settling first at Obunku. On the other hand Alagoa (1976:337) states:

> "The Ibani (Bonny) say their ancestors came from the Central Delta through the Ibo hinterland. After a period of sojourn in Ndoki territory, they came down the Imo River through Andoni Country to the Coastal State".

These two accounts of the migration of the Ndoki and Ibani suggest that the two groups were closely related. Armoury Talbot (1967) the relationship as follows:

> "Indeed, it is now settled and well beyond argument that the people of Bonny came originally from the Ndoki ethnic group".

Ijaw Migration Routes

After the Bonny city-state was established, its traders used the same route to obtain the produce of the hinterland for the Atlantic trade. Bonny and Opobo traders established trading posts within Ndoki territories from the early 19th century. They traded in big canoes to Igwenga (Ikot Abasi) in the present Akwa Ibom State through the Neneobu River joining the Imo River at Akpala in Abia State. During the era of palm oil/kernel trade, the Ibani were in almost all the villages of Ndoki. But at the end of the Nigeria Civil War, many willingly withdrew from some of these villages. The Ibani are now concentrated in Azumini (their headquarters), Ahambele/Ohambele, Akirika-Ukwu, Akpala and Akanu communities.

The withdrawal was partly caused by the downward trend in palm oil and kernel trade in Nigeria after the Civil War following the emergence of crude oil as the major export commodity.

There is still a strong feeling of blood relationship among the Ndoki, Opobo and Bonny. Their greeting, *Ibani na-madu*, when they meet each other is a reminder of this kinship tie, meaning, literally, 'Ibani in person/blood'. Those early trading posts have developed into permanent settlements and are regarded as part of their respective Ndoki communities. The Ibani trading post at Azumini has developed into a big village known as Water-Side. This is because the Ibani are located along the River Neneobu.

Population

The population of Azumini Waterside Village has increased to about 7,000 people. Based on its numerical strength, the Water-Side village of Azumini boasts of the following institutions, namely, a primary school, health centre, Ibani na-madu market and many churches of different denominations.

Administration

Azumini Water-Side consists of the thirteen compounds that trace their origin to Opobo and Bonny, namely, Jaja, Ubani, Eppele, Brown, John Africa, Uranta, Peterside, Ogolo, Opusunju, Macpepple, Tobi, Cookey and Alaputa. Each of these compounds has a Chief or House Head that represents them in the Council of Chiefs of Water Side Village, headed by a Chairman.

The Chairman and Secretary of the Ijaw group are members of Azumini Council of Chiefs. The others resident in Ahambele, Akrika-Ukwu, Akpala and Akanu communities maintain Compound Chiefs who attend meetings at the headquarters at Azumini, and are loyal to the Chairman of Council of Chiefs at Azumini. This administrative arrangement promotes unity and understanding among the Ibani migrants in Ndoki.

The position of Chairman and Secretary of the Council of Chiefs are rotatory, and incumbents occupy them on the basis of merit. The present chairman of Ibani Council of Chiefs in Ndoki is Chief B. Ogolo.

Occupation and Culture

The occupation of the Ibani settlers remains mainly fishing, trading and farming. The absence of any level of discrimination encouraged cultural, political and social integration of the Ibani among the Ndoki. This has developed to a level that a visitor may not be able to discern any difference between the two groups, with extensive intermarriages between the two groups.

There are elements of Ibani traditional dances that have been adopted by the Ndoki such as Nwaotam society, Ogele Nokpa society, Iyeke society and Ofo-no-agu society. Exchange of cultural displays, particularly during festive periods takes place between Ndoki communities and Opobo and Bonny towns. The Ogu deity was brought from Ibani to Obeakpu but has been destroyed by Christianity. Alagoa (1972: 178) records:

> "The Ndoki have a strong sense of kinship with the Ibani,
> citing religious evidence. Early Ndoki worshiped Ikuba along
> with Ibani and the Otuburu, god of Azuogu Ndoki was also
> worshipped at the village of Ayambo near Bonny".

The Ibani settlers are known to speak Ibani language blended with the dialects of the Ndoki. The preponderant commercial language has been the language of the host group.

The migrant Ibani maintain close ties with the home front. They participate in the burial of members of their respective compounds at Opobo and Bonny, attend meetings and major functions at home as well as contribute to development projects.

The unlimited privileges accorded the Ibani immigrants by the Ndoki derive in part from the traditions of common ancestral heritage.

Ijaw Contribution

The early contact of the Ibani with Europeans exposed them to Western education and their approach to development in general. In order to step up development in the area, Ibani migrants built the first Anglican church of the Niger Delta Pastorate (NDP) at Azumini in 1912. In 1928 they built a primary school to provide western education. At present, Water-side area has attained the status of a village, and contributes to development projects in Azumini town like every other unit.

Etche

Background

Etche people of Etche and Omuma Local Government Areas of Rivers State tell several versions of the tradition of origin of Etche. Each of the migrant groups trace their pedigree and route of migration to represent the origin of the entire Etche ethnic nationality. The bottom line on the origin of the Etche people fits into the assertion made by Ikechi Nwogu (2003:2):

> "All the stories collected on this subject suggest a lengthy migration from outside, presumably from the central Delta to the fresh water swamp of the lower Niger, South-Eastern Nigeria, where the people of Etche now inhabit".

Another underpinning common element of the two main Etche traditions of Benin and Igbo origin and migration is the influence of Benin kingdom on the early migrants. Etche ethnic nationality consists of about 52 autonomous communities with a population of 242,000 people going by the 1990 population census. Our study identified Okrika plantation settlement at Umuebulu and some absorbed Okrika and Opobo migrants in Chokocho. The early contacts of Ijaw with Etche people predates trade in palm oil and kernel, but real trading posts and subsequent settlement commenced in the era of the palm oil trade.

The contacts extended as far as Orwu Town, at the North-western corner of Etche land. There were empty puncheons lying at Otamiri shores in Agbom village of Orwu in the early sixties. It was said by the late Duru Ozoemene Ezekiel Nwala that they used to paddle canoes of palm oil from Otamiri River through Imo River to Igwenga (Ikot Abasi) to sell. Also some of the commercial trips took them to Okumgba market in Okrika where they purchased fish and sold their goods, such as yams, cocoyams etc.

Besides trade, social and recreational ties encouraged good relationships between the Okrika and some towns in Etche. These relationships were sustained up to the late 20th century. For example, Kalio-Ama community of Okrika used to organize wrestling contests with Igbo town of Etche. These contacts led to inter-marriage.

Ijaw Migration Routes

Okrika traders used the Imo River which rises from Mbaise hills in Imo State, forming a confluence with Otamini river at Umuebulu where they purchased palm oil and kernel. According to Diebo Fiberesima, born at Umuebulu in 1944, the Umuebulu reported that they had previously given Bonny people a portion of their land as trading post. It was alleged that the Bonny traders later assisted Abam people in Abriba of the present Abia State to behead Umuebulu people for rituals and festivals.

The Okrika traders settled this matter through the District Officer at Bonny. They refunded to the Bonny traders the sum of 15,028 manilas, being the sum they had paid for the land. The Okrika traders, on their part, assisted to ward-off the intrusion of Abam head-hunters in Umuebulu. For this reason, the Umuebulu people compensated them with more lands. From this time the Okrika settlers are said to have lived in peace with their host, except for minor

Okrika settlers are said to have lived in peace with their host, except for minor disputes on land boundaries. According to Diebo (2006), negotiations began in 1888 and agreement was reached in 1911.

In 1935, the Umunwala group in Oyigbo laid claim to Umuebulu land including the area ceded to Okrika settlers. The settlers joined the Umuebulu people to wage legal battle that began from Ipu Customary Court in Ukwa to the Supreme Court in Lagos. The ruling was in favour of Umuebulu in 1962. According to Etche sources, Etche District used to collect tax up to the point in Oyigbo called "Ukwu-ube", later Slaughter Road. Today, the Etche Local Government is limited to the new Port Harcourt-Aba Express Way.

Population

The settlement known in official records as Okrika Plantation holds a population of about 300 Okrika people. The reason for this low population is that most of the early settlers migrated back to Okrika at the end of the Nigerian Civil War. Again, the Okrika man is said to find it difficult to settle outside the swampy mangrove environment of the Niger Delta. Consequently, some sold their parcels of land to the Igbo.

Administration

The Okrika Plantation has eight big compounds under the leadership of a Chairman, Mr. Alaya Rowlands from Obianime compound of Okrika Island.

The Chairman administers Okrika indigenes in this area, while each of them remains loyal to the chiefs of their respective compounds or War Canoe Houses in their Okrika ancestral home. The settlers also participate in the activities of their various Houses at Okrika, such as burials, festivals and development projects.

All the settlers in Umuebulu pay respects to Chief Sunday Njoku, the Ochimba 1 and oldest man in the community. Special recognition is accorded Okrika people at the palace of Chief Sunday Njoku.

Occupation and Culture

With urbanization rapidly spreading to the area, the inhabitants who are of Okrika stock are also modern traders, civil servant and business men. These are in addition to their traditional fishing, farming occupations and the initial palm oil/kernel trade. The settlers and their host community jointly bury deceased persons. Those from Okrika that wish to be buried at Umuebulu are interred there.

There are inter-cultural displays during ceremonies and festivals. The Okrika are requested to bring cultural troupes such as *pioru* dancers and war canoes. Most of their children speak the Etche language.

Ikwerre

Traditions from both the Ikwerre and Kalabari refer to early Kalabari settlement in Ikwerre country at Obuamafa. The migratory route to Obuamafa was a movement overland from the homeland of a wave of migrants from the Central Delta to the Eastern Delta (Alagoa 1972).

In the era of both the slave and palm oil trades, more migrations were made to Ikwerre land by their Kalabari neighbours, who for the purpose of convenience, chose to settle at certain Ikwerre water fronts, strategic to their businesses. There were Kalabari trading outposts at strategic points along the New Calabar/Obiatubu River. These settlements include, Iwo-fe, Isiodu, Elibrada, Oduoha, Ewveku, Rumuji and Ibaa. There were also temporary market camps at places like Ogbogoro, Choba and Nkarahia (Isiokpo). From the river front of Ogbakiri, Kalabari also established centres at Iku-Kiri and Adala (which Ogbakiri refer to as Eli-Ijaw i.e. Ijaw settlement). On the Sombreiro point of entry into Ikwerre territory, there were also market centres and temporary sites which facilitated economic as well as socio-cultural interaction amongst the two culture groups at Elele Alimini, Rumuekpe and Rumuji. These centres of trade or Ijaw settlements served as armouries or warehouses where arms and ammunitions were stored. Known to the Kalabari as *Igbe-kiri*, they also served as banking houses and treasuries where cash and other valuable treasures were stored.

The Okrika also established virile commercial and trade links with the neighbouring Ikwerre communities of Elelenwo, Rumuokwurusi, Rumuomasi, Woji, Elekahia, Rumueme and Oginigba, among others (Fiberesima, 1990:62). The creek leading to Diobu, provided access to the Ikwerre market of Mgbuoshimini and others for Okrika and Kalabari traders.

Today, most of the Ijaw settlements no longer exist, and those which do, do so as mere fishing camps for itinerant fisher folks and subsistent farmers. The decline is due mainly to collapse of the pattern of commercial activities that gave rise to them principal among which was the trade in palm oil and kernel. Ijaw and Ikwerre cultures have interacted as a result of the above contact history.

Cultural Influence

First, there is evidence of cross-cultural interaction between Ijaw and Ikwerre, taking Kalabari and Okrika with their Ikwerre neighbours for example. In the area of nomenclature, for instance, personal names, place names and names of things or objects reflect such age old cultural contact. Also loan words and phrases which depict borrowings from Ijaw from Ikwerre and vice versa occur in the lexis, structure and register of the groups involved. For instance, the case of two Ikwerre communities in Port Harcourt Local Government Area, Oroworukwo and Ogbunabali and Ogbogoro (Ozuoba) in Obio/Akpor Local Government Area, personal names like Wokogoloma, Ogbogbo, Kalagbor and Ogboro respectively suggest that these names are of Ijaw origin. Thus a name such as Wokogoloma in Ijaw means Ogoloma man, and Ogoloma is an Okrika– Ijaw community which has had long time of interaction with Ikwerre neighbours. Another Ikwerre name Worukwo also suggests Ikwerre link with Ijaw. For instance, Worukwo means in Ikwerre, 'rivers/waterside man'. As Nduka (1993) points out, the Ijaw are referred to, by their Ikwerre neighbours as *elerukwo,* meaning, 'people from the waterside or riverine area'. Kalagbor again in Ijaw, especially for Kalabari, Okrika and Ibani means Kalabo i.e. a diminutive of an older person which in colloquial terms is expressed as 'junior'. Also at Ogbogoro in Ozuoba territory of Ikwerre country, some traditions say that the present site of the community was initially occupied by a band of migrant Ijaw fisher folk who were known by the eponymous name of Ogboro, the name of the principal founding ancestor.

In the area of loan-words, however, there are words for items which suggest borrowings from Ijaw.

Table 25.1: Loan words—Ijaw-Ikwerre

Item	Ijaw	Ikwerre
Rice	arusun	arusi/erusin
Sugar	osikiri	osikiri
Farina	afenia	afenia

At the wake of modern times whose cardinal symbols are western education and Christianity, the cross-flow of Ijaw-Ikwerre relations is evident. During the early decades of the twentieth century, Ijaw from Bonny, Okrika and Kalabari remained the pivotal factor in the area of personnel used as teacher educators and Christian missionary leaders. By the fourth and fifth decades of the last century, Ikwerre elements, who had received the said 'light of the new age', were also qualified, and were deployed by their various employers and agencies to Ijaw land.

On the whole, the Ijaw–Ikwerre relationship has come a long way and over time, the phenomenon has progressed along the lines of change in the light of new realities. The relationship was an all encompassing one reflecting on several facets of the lives of the two cultures.

Administration

How were Ijaw settlements in Ikwerre organized? Taking the cases of Isiodu, Ibaa, Rumuji and Rumuekpe settlements, the study found that the Ijaw administered them in line with their socio-political cultures at home. The communities were sub divided into sections under section heads who in turn reported to the president of the council of section heads. The head of the council, *Kiri nyanabo,* ensures that there is cordial relationship between these settlements and their host communities, and sometimes to ensure stability and mutual trust, blood oaths were administered.

The Ijaw in these settlements were regularly in touch with their roots at home. According to testimonies from both Ijaw and Ikwerre informants, these settlements experience very low population during festive periods, when the Ijaw travel home. Also when an Ijaw resident dies, his corpse was taken home.

Ogbah

Location

The Ogbah are a group of people who are found in the Ogbah/Egbema /Ndoni Local Government Area of Rivers State. To the north of them lie the Egbema and Oguta clans. At the northwest lies the Ndoni while the Sombreiro River (known locally as Nkissa), which runs into parts of Ikwerre land, is found in the east. At the extreme northeast lie the Awarra and Asa ethnic groups. Some Ijaw communities are found located at the southwest. Ogbah land is bounded in the south by the Ekpeye.

Ogbah land occupies an area of about nine hundred and twenty four kilometers, of both dry and marshy land. The entire community is divided into three main groups, namely, the Usomini, Igburu and Egi with Omoku as the headquarters. The Ogbah in their tradition of origin claim to have migrated from Benin in about the second half of the 15th century. Their ancestor, Akalaka left Benin under the reign of Ewuare the Great (1440-1472) to found a new homeland.

Akalaka had two sons, Ekpeye and Ogbah. Currently Ogbah land has thirty-nine villages (Orji 1993:). The people engage in fishing, farming, hunting, crafts and trade as their means of livelihood. Recent archeological research has demonstrated that there is evidence of human settlement in Ogbah land as early as 3000 B. C (Derefaka 2002:270).

Contact

Some Ijaw communities are found in the southwest of Ogbah land. Ellah (1995:6) notes that the Sombreiro River which flows from the north to the south of Ogbah land runs through the Ogbah villages of Oboh, Okpurukpuali, Okansu, Ohiuga, Obiozimini to Abonnema (Kalabari Ijaw) where it rejoins the Orashi and empties itself into the Atlantic Ocean. The Ogbah and the Ekpeye have had long trading contacts with the Nembe, Kalabari and Bonny Ijo groups along the Orashi and Sombreiro Rivers (Alagoa and Kpone-Tonwe 2002: 177).

The commercial contact with the Ijaw revolved around the palm oil trade. The Royal Niger Company (later United Africa Company/UAC) established a trading station at Abonnema in the early 1880s, and a beach at Aligu, a village near Kreigani in Ogbah land in 1884 (Orji 1989: 60-65). The company made a treaty with the Alinso Okanu community of Aligu in 1884 (Nwabara 1977:79).

Settlement Pattern

The Ijaw settlers in Ogbah land are not known to be living in the same geographical location. Rather, they are scattered in various quarters of the community. The Dakoru family is found in the Obakata quarter, while Sunday Pedro settled in Obieti with Wokoma and Benibo families in Usomini. The Dakoru migrated from Tombia, while the Sunday Pedro and Wokoma came from Abonnema and Buguma respectively. These Ijaw families of the Kalabari stock maintain regular contact with their kith and kin. At Kreigani, there is a Braide family settled among the Ogbuanukwu family.

Cultural Integration

The Ijaw have inter-married with the Ogbah for a long period. Our informant, Gladson Dakoru got married to an Ogbah woman. Sunday Don Pedro got married to a wealthy Ogbah woman, Mrs. Dinah Pedro popularly known as Mama Ahiaorie, from the Orji family in Umuogidi lineage. These Ijaw settlers were fully integrated into various Ogbah lineages. In these families, they could share in the family farmland and could even be conferred with chieftaincy titles.

589

Indeed, the Dakoru, Pedro, Wokoma and Braide families are no longer seen as strangers but as full members of their various Ogbah lineages. The Dakoru are altached to the Umu-alinwa lineage (Obodo) while the Pedro belong to the Umuagburu.

The Ijaw settlers still retain some aspects of their culture. Notable is the Egwu Asawa dance which is now performed by most age grade groups in Ogbah land. The Egwu Asawa is borrowed from the Kalabari. This information proffered by Gladson Dakoru is corroborated in the work of Ellah (1995:136).

Contribution to Host Community

The Ijaw were known as Oru people among the Ogbah. Ellah (1995:129) notes that the famous Nkwo and Orie markets in Omoku were attended by the Aboh, Oru (Ijaw), Ndoni, Oguta, Awara (Ohaji), Ekpeye. In turn, the Ogba and the Ekpeye, Kalabari, Engenni, and Aboh patronized Emegi (Biseni) markets. From these market meetings, traders acquired new trading techniques, learnt new fashions, new songs, new dances and new ideas.

The instance of the *asawa* cultural dance that has become a household word in age grade ceremonies in Ogbah land has been highlighted. Ellah (1995:140) maintains that the *Egwu asawa* is sung by all age grades at their periodic meetings where singers and dancers spoke the Kalabari (Ijaw) dialect, often imperfectly. The drums and rythym, have been retained but the words are fast being turned into Ogbah by the new generation.

Another area where the Ijaw influenced the culture of the Ogbah is in dressing. The long *arigidi* attire which used to be in vogue has been replaced by the one fathom *george* round the waist with long shirts that reach to the knee. Older Ogbah men now prefer to wear the *don*, which are long dresses, in their imitation of the Kalabari. In fact the Kalabari fashion of *don* and *woko* have dominated the Nchaka and age grade celebrations in Ogbah.

590

There is no doubt that the palm oil trade, which the Ijaw promoted, impacted positively on the economy of the Ogbah.

EKPEYE
Background
The Ekpeye are currently found in two local governments areas namely, Ahoada-East and Ahoada West in Rivers State, located between latitude 4o461 N and 5o 151 N and longitude 6o 26 E and 6o 46 E. The Ikwerre are their closest neighbours to east, the Engenni to the west, while the Ogbah are found to the north with the Abua to the south. The population is about 636,205 (Amini-Philips 2002:47).

Ekpeye oral tradition state that they migrated from Benin under the leadership of Akalaka in the reign of Ewuare the Great. In their flight, they crossed the Orashi River, landed at Olakuma, and settled at Olube where the two sons of Akalaka, Ekpeye and Ogbah separated as a result of a feud. It was from this point that Ekpeye and his descendants moved eastwards to the banks of the Sombreiro River. The main economic activity of the Ekpeye is farming with limited forms of fishing, local industries and trade.

Migration Routes
Information gathered from Elder Godfrey Bull-Young Jack (2006) reveals that the Kalabari arrived Ekpeye land during the hey days of the palm oil trade, along with other Ijaw groups, Bonny and Nembe. The Kalabari from the Degema axis entered Ihuowo town through the Sombreiro River, while some others moved from other Kalabari towns. They brought seafood like fish and shell-fish, which they exchanged initially with palm oil and palm kernel.

Settler Community
One of the prominent Kalabari traders an palm produce was Chief Kio Young Jack. He settled at Iwokiri waterfront at Ihuowo. Eze (2000:26) states that 'at

Ihuowo, a town near Ahoada in his newly founded trading port, he built his own church and worshipped there till he left the place'. The descendants of the late chief Young Jack are still settled at Ihuowo where they have established a distinct community of their own. Alagoa (1976:358) confirms that the Kalabari expanded their trading network to as far as Oguta Lake and Orashi River in the 19th century.

Initially, the trade hinged around the concept of barter. Kalabari traders came with cloth, trinkets, gun and tobacco. With time, local currencies like the manilas, cowries (*Izege*), brass rod etc replaced trade by barter. It was only at the turn of the 20th century that the local economy became monetized with the introduction of British currency. This paved the way for the integration of the Ekpeye indigenous economy into the world capitalist system.

The Kalabari Ijaw are settled in their own quarter at Ihuowo, popularly known as Iwokiri. They have been integrated into the Umudhigwe lineage at Ihuowo. The Iwokiri land was given to them by late Chief Odukwu.

Occupation

It is obvious that Chief Kio Young Jack and other Kalabari Ijaw settlers were involved in the palm produce trade. This trade in palm oil is still on, even though the challenges of modern civilization, with the attendant pursuit for western styled education has impacted negatively on the volume. With the lull, the descendants of Chief Kio Young Jack have resorted to other means of economic endeavor. For example, Elder Godfrey Bull Young Jack (2006) reports that they are now engaged in sand mining.

Administration

Within the settler community at Iwokiri, the descendants of Chief Kio Young Jack under the leadership of Elder Godfrey Bull Young Jack, live like a single family. The Kalabari in Ihuowo are identified as an integral entity of the socio-political administration of the community. They belong to the Umudhigwe lineage. Other lineages in Ihuowo are Umuji, Idihuru and Uchi.

Cultural Integration

The Kalabari Ijaw in Ihuowo are a distinguished community within a larger one. The descendants of Chief Young Jack in their Iwokiri settlement still retain their Kalabari language while they also speak Ekpeye fluently.

Elder Bull Young Jack (2006) states that the Kalabari Ijaw stock still maintain their traditional dress like the *etibo, don, injiri* (*George* cloth) etc. On the economy, the change from palm produce trade to sand mining has produced some socio-economic consequences. The fact that sand mining has spread from Iwokiri in Ihuowo to other towns like Idoke and Ahoada meant that the economic benefits of the new trade would be reaped by the indigenous community.

During the palm oil trade, there was an incident that tended to threaten the peaceful relations between the Ekpeye and the Kalabari Ijaw. Amini-Philips (1994:13) observes that sometimes skirmishes ensued between the Kalabari and their Ekpeye partners. They disagreed on procedures, the adulteration of produce. But generally the atmosphere was cordial, and settlement land was provided without charge.

NDONI

Background

Ndoni is located in the present Rivers State and shares boundary with the Aboh in the present Delta State across the River Niger. His Royal Highness (HRH) Gabriel Okoyia Obi II, Awo of Ndoni, said that his people migrated from Benin to Igbogene in the present Bayelsa State before moving to their present site. The town consists of three principal villages namely, Ogbe-Ukwu, Umuojie and Ogbuebi.

The few Ijaw resident among the other inhabitants of the town hail from Biseni, Beyalsa State. Ndoni oral traditions maintain that the Ijaw have come to Ndoni markets to purchase and sell goods right from time immemorial.

Migration Routes

The earliest attempt of the Ijaw to settle in Ndoni was in 1968 at the peak of the Nigerian Civil War. Elder Chukwudeme Tombofa left Biseni with some members of his family to Animagwudi Island to take refuge.

The group trekked through Olombiri to Utu-Oga, crossing Obiofor to Ndoni. They settled at the Island till the war ended and Chudwudeme Tombofa according Charles, died in 1986. Chukwudeme Tombofa met Isoko people on the island with whom he lived in peace. Over time, the Island was renamed Chukwudeme Island when the Isoko people left.

The others remained after the death of their leader Chukwudeme Tombofa. As life in Biseni became more promising, the others returned home, leaving behind Charles Tombofa. In 1996, Charles Tombofa, and his family moved to Ndoni Town to enable their children attend school.

Occupation and Culture

The Ijaw at Animagwudi Island were fishermen. They sold fish to Ndoni people. When lakes are harvested, customers from Aboh and Omoku are also attracted to make purchases. In Ndoni town the Ijaw combine fishing with petty trading. The Ijaw communicate with their neighbours in Ndoni, but speak their own Ijaw dialect among themselves, and visit their native homes.

Administration

The Ijaw in Ndoni pay collective and individual respects to the Awo of Ndoni and his council of chiefs as well as to the leaders of the quarters in which they are domiciled.

THE IKA-IBO

Background:

The people assert that their ancestors migrated from Benin. Dike (1956:26) wrote:

> 'Although, they are Ibo speaking, they were not originally Ibos.Moreover, whereas the Ibos East of the Niger have no kings... yet these Ibo- speaking riverine towns to the west of the Niger have a society patterned after the semi-divine kingship of Benin'.

Our research located Ijaw in settlements mainly in the Oko communities of Oshimini Local Government Area of Delta State. There are five Oko Ijaw settlements viz; Oko-amakom (Power-line or Ukwu-bridge), Oko-Amala, found at Akwe Etiti (Central Island), Oko-Obiokpu, Oko-Ogbele located at Agwe-Obodo camp, and Oko-Odifulu. Those resident in Kwale and other communities are not in settlements but scattered among the people.

The Power-line settlement, the largest of them all, started as a fishing camp in about 1891 and blossomed into a fully fledged settlement in the 1940s. Initially, any one who had no fishing vessel was not allowed to settle in the area.

Mr. Pius Ifeagwu, aged sixty years (2006), who is the Vice Chairman of Power-line settlement, explained how the fishing group there pulled canoes to Mali, a journey that took over six months on fishing expedition. They also fished around the Kainji Dam. Today, the settlement with a metropolitan outlook at the outskirt of Asaba Township, hosts people from different areas: Ijaw, Igbo, Isoko, Yoruba, Mali, Ika-Ibo, Aboh. This development began after the Nigerian Civil War in 1970. One settler from Mali, Yakubu Yusuf, (aged 38 years) said he has lived in the area for twelve years and is married to an Isoko woman. This Malian claims to have come from Timbucktu, a similar environment on the River Niger.

Ijaw Migration Routes

Mr. Stephen Oruanare, an Ijaw settler in Power-line, an indigene of Tuomo in Bomadi Local Government Area of Delta State, explained that his father and others were trading in local gin along the River Niger. The voyage in hand-pulled canoes took up to eight days to accomplish. Today, with the use of engine boats, the distance takes only three days to cover. After sales the early traders bought food items, livestock, clothes, lamps and other goods. In the course of these trading trips, they saw a lot of fish, and decided to settle.

Occupation and Culture

The initial occupation of the Power-line settlers was fishing which included long distance fishing expeditions. It was customary and fashionable for some handy customers to provide fishing instruments in order for them to claim exclusive right of purchase on their catches. The scope of fishing declined due to the construction of Kainji Dam that impeded migration of fishes, for the hand pulled canoes made it increasingly difficult to move across the dam. The Ijaw located in the other Oko settlements are predominantly fishermen and farmers.

The rate of inter-marriage among the settlers is very high due to absence of discrimination. Every group is allowed, during their internal ceremonies, to display their cultural dances to entertain the people. The settlers also undertake burials together.

Population

The Ijaw noticed that the sharp decline of the fishes caught arose in part from water pollution. The decrease in daily income led to the resettlement of some Ijaw indigenes and many returned to their homelands. The overall implication of this drift is that only about fifty Ijaw adults are left in the Power-line village. In Kwale, the population is about 80, making a total of 200 in the area.

Administration

The Power-line village has an Executive Committee led by a chairman. At the time of our research tour, Mr. James Ibuebu was Chairman of the Village Welfare Union. In addition, every group has a chairman, who automatically becomes a member of the Executive Committee. It is from among them that the Chairman of the Council emerges. Each chairman informs his people of the decisions of the Central Council and ensures their implementation.

The settlers say they contribute to development projects of Oshimini Local Government and Delta State through the various levies they pay on sand mining and other business.

The Ijaw in Kwale operate under the umbrella of the Ijaw Progressive Union, officially recognized by the ruler, the Ezemu of Kwale.

Conclusion

This study of the relationship between the Ijaw and their Igboid neighbours underlines the following conclusions. First, almost all the Igboid speaking areas associate their origin with the Benin kingdom. Second, the early contacts with the Ijaw were induced by trade which gave rise to cultural exchange, cross-fertilization of ideas, mutual contribution to the economic and social development, and the evolution of Ijaw settlements in these areas. Third, Ijaw settlements are invariably located close to rivers, indicating the dexterity of the Ijaw in the management of riverine environments. Most of the settlers came by river, and lived by fishing. Fourth, there exists cordial and peaceful relationship between the settler communities and their hosts, except in the brief experience of the Ekpeye and Umuebulu of Etche. Most of the ancestors of the Ijaw used river routes in their movement to their host communities. Fifth, the Ijaw settlers sustained their affinity with their ancestral homes, and maintained contact where feasible.

CHAPTER 26

THE ỊZỌN
AND THEIR
OGONI NEIGHBOURS

Sonpie Kpone-Tonwe and Emma Gbenenye

Introduction

The Niger Delta has a span of over 70,000 square kilometers and four ecological zones. It is rated as one of the worlds largest expanses of wetland. The Niger Delta area is an ethnographic melting pot with over 25 distinct linguistic groups and a population of about seven million.

The territory of the Ogoni lies at the eastern mainland région of the Eastern-Niger Delta, between the Bonny and Andoni rivers and the southern bend of the Imo River. It is made up of four distinct clans. The Ogoni languages of Khana, Gokana, Goi and Eleme lie within the Delta-Cross sub-branch of the Cross River branch of the New Benue-Congo family of the Niger-Congo phylum (Williamson, 1988, 68, 91).

The neighbours of the Ogoni are the Igboid Ndoki to the north, the Ikwerre group to the north-west, the Annang/Ibibio, Andoni/Opobo to the east, and Bonny and Okrika groups to the south and south-west.

The Andoni, Opobo, Bonny and Okrika constitute the Ijo neighbours and the relationship that existed between the Ogoni and these Ijo neighbours is the main focus of this chapter. Such studies help to highlight the underlying unity of the people that eventually formed the Nigerian state.

This study is broadly divided into three eras, namely, the pre-colonial, the colonial, and the post-colonial or independence era.

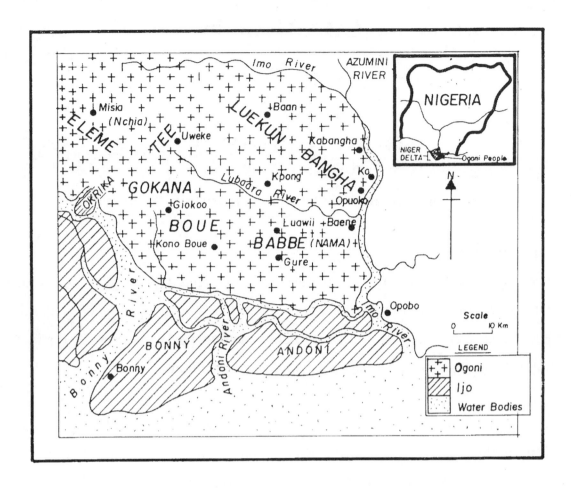

Fig. 26.1: The Ijo and their Ogoni neighbours

Internal Trade

Oral tradition provides evidence of an early trade relationship between the different communities before the 19th century. Trade in Ogoni was both local and external. Local trade refers to transactions which took place within a radius of about ten miles of the area of production. This was the range that could be covered by foot.

A classic example of this can be found between the Delta inhabitants and their main-land neighbours. It occurred naturally because of the Eastern Niger Delta economy based on fishing, salt-making exchanged these with forest products such as yams, palm oil, vegetables, palm wine, etc. from the hinterland.

Local Trade

Local trade in Ogoni was between the markets established in Ogoni which revolved around the five markets days—*Deemua, Deebom, Deezia, Deeson* and *Deeko*. The peak of trade with the neighbours was on *Deemua* at the water side, where all local communities came to exchange their produce. Such markets at Bodo, Kono Boue, Kaa, Duyaakara (Kpea), Gio, and Ko (Opuoko) brought the Opobo, Andoni, Bonny and Okirika closer to the Ogoni.

The internal trade within Ogoni became a vehicle of social mobilization. More significantly, trade during the period before the 19th century was mainly on the basis of satisfying local consumption needs. Thus, the productivity and exchange was essentially to satisfy local consumption or to obtain commodities necessary for subsistence.

The importance of these markets for Ogoni and her neighbours can be fully understood only if it is appreciated that they were social centres, and many social arrangements revolved around market days.

For instance, the practice of exogamy between the Ogoni and Ibibio in particular led to an intricate web of personal relationships and bound the village groups together.

Apart from trade, ritual brotherhoods, such as the type between the Ibani and Ogoni at Ko (Opuoko), festivals and periodic meetings, kept alive the solidarity of the village groups and their Ijo neighbours particularly the Ibani.

The range of contact and interaction between the Ogoni and their Ijo neighbours was made possible by the geography of the region. The geography of the area did not constitute a severe impediment to inter-group relations. There was none of the ethnic nationalities which constituted the Ijo neighbours whose frontiers were delimited in terms of natural barriers. The rivers, creeks and creeklets served as water ways, not barriers. The result was free movement of peoples, goods, services, and ideas out of and into Ogoni.

However, the life style and patterns of an agricultural society, like that of the Ogoni was such that the degree of contact with neighbours was limited.

There were wars in the relationship which built up between the Ogoni village groups on the coast and their Ijo neighbours, particularly the Andoni (Obolo) and Okrika who did not have the ritual blood pact of brotherhood with the Ogoni that the Ibani had with the Ko (Opuoko).

External Trade

Long-distance trade developed as a consequence of differences, or growing differentiation in ecological conditions leading to a situation in which one part produced more than one kind of goods that it could consume, and had to exchange the excess for those goods which it needed and could only get from its neighbours.

In the absence of large scale system or social formations in pre-19th century Ogoni land to ensure safety of travelers generally and traders, in particular, historians have wondered how trade and marketing could realize a high level of development among the Ogoni and her Ijo neighbours.

The relatively narrow range of Ogoni external contact was determined by two main factors. In the first place, a convention existed among the ancestors of the Ogoni forbidding inter-marriage with their non-farming neighbours, with the exception of the Ibibio/Annang whose women Ogoni men were free to marry. It was not based on any enmity between them and their neighbours but it served to preserve the purity and creativity of the Ogoni (Saro-wiwa, 2005:46). Secondly, the fact that the Ogoni were an agricultural people bound to their land by traditions and taboos, could have discouraged long distance marriages.

Only a small fraction of the population was made up of those who were fishers and felt the urge to travel by the water ways to the Ijo communities. There were also men of free status who moved out of their home communities temporarily in search of gainful employment as farmers, fishermen, carriers, craftsmen, oracle agents and diviners for which the Ogoni were noted. This migration was to bring the Ogoni into contact with their Ijo neighbours.

Thus, the needs of the Ogoni were limited, and they were content with what they had. Yet, the trade relations may have begun as soon as the Ijo settled in the region and as specialized fishermen. Thus the trade in the exchange of fish for agricultural produce could be said to be as old as the settlement of the Eastern Niger Delta itself.

Oral tradition has shown how the Ogoni and Bonny peoples were involved in an intricate system for ensuring safety of travelers. The Ogoni customs and morality forbade the molestation, let alone the wounding, killing, kidnapping, and enslavement of a fellow clansman. Traditionally, the Ogoni attached great importance to good moral living. In marriage contracts, for example, in-laws vow not to participate in anti-social behaviour towards each other. Relations undertaking business contracts vowed not to cheat each other. Hosts tasted food presented to their visitors in demonstration of the absence of poison.

In a society where people are in constant contact with each other, where relationships are on a personal intimate basis, a society which provided a generally secure system of checks and balances in behaviour, the culture of such society generally builds into its fabric a system of sanctions that limits overt deviant behaviour. Also built into the Ogoni way of life was the concept of status. Status was either achieved through personal efforts or ascribed. Secret society membership such as *Amanikpo, Kuetem, Okonkwo, Elutaa, Dooyan*, and of late *Efiokpo* cult, age and wealth, ensured peace and stability.

According to oral tradition in most cases, two villages had blood pact of long historic ancestry known as Buekobie. This was ritual brotherhood which forbade fighting, wounding or killing of fellow village groups bound by a covenant of ritual brotherhood. This brotherhood was extended to the Ibani of

Opobo and Bonny at Ko (Opuoko) Ogoni. This explains, in part, the absence of conflict or hostility between the Ogoni and the Ibani of Opobo and Bonny. Recently, this has been extended to the Nkoro people.

The Ogoni were among the Delta states that accorded diplomatic recognition to King Jaja of Opobo soon after he led the Annie Pepple House from Bonny in 1870. The Okrika and Kalabari chiefs who later arbitrated between Jaja and Bonny did so on the recognition of the sovereignty of Opobo (Jones, 1962:13-18). Given the foregoing, the Ibani, and even the Nkoro, have never been attacked by the Ogoni.

There were also rules which protected long distance travelers and business men. Knowledge of these rules and ability to abide by them distinguished *bona fide* business men and professionals from trouble makers and plain pirates. These included traveling in groups or in caravans and being armed in case of an attack by pirates.

In addition, traders had to purchase the protection of local patrons known for their wide-ranging influence, contacts, bilingualism, and familiarity with the passwords of secret societies, such as *Okonkwo, Kuegia* which operated along the trade routes. Payment of tolls which went into maintenance of young men who cleared the routes and patrolled them also enhanced trading expeditions and contacts with the Ijo.

This system was justified within the socio-cultural context of the people and their times. In David Northrup's (1978) book, *Trade Without Rulers*, we read the false claims of absence of rulers over a wide area of Nigeria. On the contrary, the Eastern Niger Delta before the arrival of Europeans had rulers and there were contacts between the Ogoni and their Ijo neighbours, such as Opobo, Bonny, Andoni and Okrika and Nembe. Professor Alagoa (1970:319), has uncovered some of the evidence which suggested that trade between the Ijo and their hinterland neighbours was already firmly established before the era of European trade. These commercial links seem to have been the most important

604

factors which brought about an exchange of ideas, inter-marriage, mingling of customs, tradition and culture between the coastal villages of Bodo, Boue, Bomu, Gbe, Nonwa and their Okrika, Bonny and Andoni neighbours.

The range of contacts and interactions between the Ogoni and their Ijo neighbours was made possible by the geography of the area. Geography was not a barrier to inter-group relations. It did not constitute a severe impediment to the ethnic nationalities, whose frontiers were delimited in terms of natural barriers, because there were rivers, creeks and rivulets, which served as waterways.

There were, in the Eastern Niger Delta, as many languages as there were ethnic groups, and, then within each ethnic group, almost as many dialects as there were autonomous village-groups or states. Did this fact impede inter-group relations between the Ogoni and their Ijo neighbours? The answer is no or, at least, not necessarily. The Ogoni and their Ijo neighbours found no difficulty in scaling the language barrier, as those villages at the borders were bilingual. However, the extent of the participation of the Ogoni in long-distance trade before the turn of the 20th century was not very substantial, although there were carvers, potters, smiths and weavers in Ogoni who did considerable business with neighbouring communities.

Agricultural products were in abundance and were traded for the marine products at the coastal markets, where the Andoni, Okrika and Bonny came to buy and sell. The Ogoni obtained tobacco and beads in exchange for agricultural produce such as yams, cassava, and maize.

The Ogoni traded on the Imo River confluence with the Ndoki communities of Ohambele, Keffe, as well as on the Kwa-Iboe River, with the Annang and Ibibio, Andoni, Ibani of Opobo and Bonny. Other trade routes were at Atabajo, located near Okrika with Gio and Mogho (Kpone-Tonwe, 1987). Several markets existed in Bodo. For instance there were markets at Kissala, Kisao and Ki-Gbee. Other markets were at Nonwa, and Bomu.

Ogoni-Bonny Relations

At the turn of the 19th century, the Ogoni traded on the Imo river confluence with the Ndoki communities of Azumini, Essene, Urata Keffe, Ohambele, Akwete and Obunku. They also had contact with the Ibani, Opobo and Bonny; and with the Annang and Ibibio on the Kwa-Iboe river.

The Ogoni people had, by this period, acquired a technology of producing palm oil. They produced in small quantity and brought them to the coast in calabashes. As the trade expanded, depots were established for the collection of palm oil in commercial quantities and since it was necessary to have a bulking point, the Opobo and Bonny middle men organized the palm oil trade by establishing depots at Kennwigbara and Egwanga in Ikot-Abasi, Akwa-Ibom state (Cookey, 1982).

The relationship between the Ogoni and the Ibani has been a long standing one based on a ritual blood pact between them. However, oral tradition has it that the Ogoni attacked some migrant Ibani fishermen during the early period of settlement at Ko (Opuoko). Nevertheless, peace and cordial relations subsequently prevailed as trade flourished.

The Ibani traders established trading posts both at the Koh and Boo-Koh riverside markets. The Ibani traders determined beforehand, while setting out for these markets, which of these towns they would berth their trading canoes. Because Boo-Koh was the smaller town (mainly the home of isolated twin parents), they distinguished these towns in their own language. They called the bigger town, "Opuoko" and the smaller Koh, Kala-Oko. These Ibani names eventually passed into the colonial records and stuck.

The relationship between Ogoni and the Bonny was political as well as commercial. In fact, Ogoni was part of the Bonny markets. This affirms the view of Jones (1963: 146) that Bonny dominated the Ndoki communities and Ogoni oil markets, as well as the mainland bordering Okrika, and sought to expand at the expense of the Kalabari.

Apart from the oil trade, Ogoni land was naturally blessed with agricultural produce, such as yams, cows, goats and sheep, which were sold in exchange for European goods such as tobacco, tools and cloth. Apart from trading, fishing on the Okoloma-toru (Bonny River) also brought the Ogoni, the Bodo people, in particular, to Bonny. The Ibani people, at one point according to Alagoa and Fombo (1972:1-5), "migrated from the central Niger Delta, whose ancient occupation was fishing".

Fishing settlements were a result of the migratory nature of some shoals of fishes. The Ogoni in course of the fishing expeditions settled at the various fishing villages of the Andoni, Okrika, Opobo and Bonny. Some of the prominent fishing settlements, where the Ogoni settled at Bonny were George-Kiri, Polo-Kiri, Kuruma,and Kala-ibiama. Other settlements between Bonny territory and Andoni, areas were Indontoru, Epelema, Mbabie, and Mgbekiri (Sokari-Green, 1984:43).

Oral tradition has it that the cast net (*igbo*) was part of the impact of Europeans on Bonny. The introduction of the cast net also brought about the use of cotton thread (*Iri)* by the Ibani for weaving, thereby replacing raphia palm types they were using. The Ogoni were to adopt this new type of net along with their Bonny neighbours. Apart from that, the *Telma* net was introduced to Bonny by the fishermen from Bodo, Ogoni in the 19th century. Some of the Ogoni dance styles and masquerades were also borrowed from their Ijo neighbours and vise versa.

Cultural Borrowing
The *Owu-ogbo* society, known in Bonny, Opobo and other delta communities, also came into Ogoni. The Nwatam cultural organization from Opobo was also borrowed by the coastal communities of Ogoni, namely, Bane, Duburo, Kpean, Kono and Boue. This cultural borrowing of Owuogbo and Nwatam has cemented the relationship between the Ogoni and the Ibani, as they participate in the dance during Christmas and New Year, when they meet in Opobo, Bori, Bonny, and in Port Harcourt.

The introduction of the drag net by the Europeans to Bonny brought about a revolution in the fishing industry. The new fishing gear attracted many Ogoni people to Bonny where they adopted this modern fishing equipment.

Another important part of the fishing industry was the making of dug-out canoes. The Bonny people were not good in canoe carving. They had to import most of their canoes from Egwema and Odioma in Nembe. The canoe industry developed along the coastal areas of Ogoni, namely Ko (Opuoko), Kalaoko, Baene, Limwa and Dubuo (Gbenenye, (1987:34). They sold their canoes to the Ibani traders at the Imo river confluence and Bonny river.

Fishing trade was usually dominated by women. The smoked fish were traded far into the hinter land of Ogoni. They sold the fish, and in exchange they bought palm oil, garri, cassava, coco-yams, from their Ogoni neighbours.

There was the use of oracles, a practice in which the Ogoni excelled. There was the *Gbenebeka* of Gwara, whose influence stretched to the Ijo neighbours. These gods had agents through whom they communicated to their adherents. They played a role in occupational stability. There is the belief by the Ogoni and Bonny that *Gbenebeka* and *Ikuba* controlled the water or river and the quantity of fishes caught by individuals. Sometimes, sacrifices were made by fishermen to these gods or deities, if they noticed that their catches were dwindling. The belief was so strong that if an Ogoni or Bonny fisherman experienced bad omen, he could equally invoke *Gbenebeka*, in the case of the Ogoni, or *Ikuba,* in the case of Bonny fisher men. Things offered for sacrifices included human beings, cows, he-goats, white fowls, eggs, gin, and other items. The cultural traits of dancing have also diffused into Ogoni as the fishermen from Ogoni borrowed the same dance steps and carnivals.

Ogoni-Andoni Relations
Unlike the Ibani traditions, the relationship between the Ogoni and the Andoni seems to be one of conflict and rivalry. The role of wars as a factor of contact

between the two groups has usually been misunderstood. Instead of peaceful coexistence, it is common to hear that wars were more endemic and that these wars created serious discontinuities in inter-group relations.

The wars between the Ogoni and Andoni did not create serious discontinuities in inter-group relations. These wars represent short interludes in the long history of peaceful co-existence and interchange of ideas and goods between the two groups.

It is difficult to trace the origin of conflicts between the Ogoni and Andoni. One account of a conflict is related in Nkoro tradition.

Alagoa, (2005: 166), recounts that as they arrived at their present location, they engaged the Ogoni and the Andoni in a fight. According to Alagoa, 2005:

> The little Nkoro community has been greatly influenced by its residence in the midst of the Andoni and by their proximity to the Ogoni.

In order to ensure a lasting peace between the Ogoni and Nkoro, Yaakara the Ogoni warrior and founder of Wiiyaakara town in Ogoni, met Opu-Inyaba the Nkoro leader, to negotiate for peace on behalf of the Nkoro. The result was the founding of Duyaakara (Yaakara market) also known to the Andoni as (Inyaba market) at the Ogoni water front near Kpean. Up to this day the Ogoni, Nkoro, Ibani, and Andoni are still using the market to exchange forest and marine products. Since then, the Nkoro living near the Ogoni have not had any conflicts. In the recent 1993 conflict between the Ogoni and Andoni, the Nkoro proclaimed neutrality. As a result of their neutrality, they were not attacked by the Ogoni.

Another tradition of conflicts between the Ogoni and Andoni has it that the Obolo attacked the Ogoni people who settled at Ekorikoi, probably, the present village of Kaa, opposite the Obolo village of Ajakaja.

Another war occurred when the Ogoni and Ibani (Bonny) formed an alliance to fight a common enemy, the Andoni at Unyeada. While the Bonny were attacking from the front, the Ogoni were also attacking from the rear.

The Andoni people reasoned that, but for the military assistance rendered to the Bonny by Ogoni people, Bonny could not have defeated the Andoni. The war took place by 1826 and since then the memory of the war has lingered.

The consequences of war varied from place to place. In that war, the Obolo (Andoni), were compelled to flee the theatre of the war to seek refuge in a more secure environment, namely a new Unyeada across the river. According to Ejituwu:

> It appears that this is the origin of the representation of the Ogoni as enemies of the Obolo.

Ever since 1826, the memory of the defeat of the Andoni by the Ogoni has lingered on and, again, the perception of the Ogoni as enemies has led to the situation that the Obolo cannot marry from Ogoni (Ejituwu, 1977:317).

The conflicts between the two groups persisted till the 1990s. The conflicts came every ten years in 1953, 1963, 1973, 1983 and in 1993.

Despite these conflicts, the Obolo (Andoni) and the Ogoni were in constant contact. The wars between the Ogoni and the Andoni did not create serious discontinuities in inter-group relations.

More significantly, the history of the relationships is underlined, not by the wars that have often been exaggerated, but by trade.

First, the range of contacts with the groups was determined by geography, which did not constitute a severe impediment to inter-group relations. The Ogoni/Andoni frontier has never been limited in terms of natural barriers. The result was that the movement of people, goods, services and ideas out of and into Ogoni land could take place easily and naturally. The Ogoni plains carried some of the major inland commercial routes of the area between Ogoni and Andoni. The Ogoni people were also linked with the Andoni through rivers, creeks and rivulets, all of which were carrying substantial volumes of traffic. The Saramatoro river was an important commercial water-way which helped to move peoples, materials and goods, including cultural ideas between Andoni, Ibani, and Ogoni.

The Ogoni, being predominantly farmers, provided the Andoni with yams, cassava, corn and several forest products in exchange for fish and other sea foods.

Indeed, the Ogoni and Andoni languages are more closely related than they are to any other languages in the region. An analysis of standard word lists of the two related languages, Ogoni and Andoni, could provide an estimate of the duration of their separation from their ancestral stock. The Ogoni call "cannon-ball", *Tigiri,* and the Andoni also call cannon *etiri*. Besides, the Ogoni name for manilla is *Kpugi* while the Obolo name for it is *Ikpoko*.

Besides, the Ogoni communities on the coast namely Sii, Gwaara, Kaa, and Bomu, which conducted their business of trading and fishing with the Andoni, were bilingual, or at times multi-lingual, speaking, both Ibani and Andoni.

Ogoni-Okrika Relationship
Okrika Island lies closer to the mainland than any of the other Eastern Delta states (Alagoa, 2005:5). Consequently, a long standing relationship was formed with the Ogoni, particularly, the Mboli (Eleme).

Alagoa and Fombo (1972) stress that the Ogoni, Okrika, and Bonny, traded on the produce of the hinterland. The points of contact of Bonny and Ogoni were through Ogu, the Imo River and Bodo city. The route between the Okrika and Ogoni was Nonwa, bordering Ogu/Bolo.

Several markets existed in Bodo in the pre-colonial era: for example, Kissala, Kisao, through K. Dere and KiGbee. At these markets, food stuffs, crafts and other essentials were exchanged for fish, and later, European goods, brought by the Okrika through their Bonny trading partners.

Jones, (1958: 43-53) has identified three main currencies in Southern Nigeria, cowries, the brass-rod and the manila that were widely in use in the Eastern Niger Delta.

Colonial and Post Colonial Periods

*nọ-ikosi*economic dispensation introduced by the colonial administration also dictated how the Ogoni related to their Ijo neighbours.

When King Jaja died in 1891 in exile, the monopoly he had in the palm oil trade was broken. As far as the Ogoni were concerned, it was the dawn of a new era. The Ogoni palm oil traders could deal directly with the merchants and companies at Egwanga (Ikot Abasi, near Opobo). Such companies were the British firm of John Miller, G. B. Olivant, and United Africa Company, and through these firms British currency was introduced into Ogoni in 1899. There was a revolution in palm oil production when Lever Brothers set up a crushing mill in 1910 at Egwanga with palm oil depots at Obunko, Omuosi, Obete, Keffe, Ohambele etc.

British penetration of Ogoni land came through Egwanga/Opobo to Kono, Ogoni in 1901.

The second prong of the British penetration of Ogoni came through Luuboo Sogho, Akwete-Ohambele-Obete axis into Gokana. The pacification process was followed by the establishment of a Native Court at Sogho in 1912. The violent reaction that followed led to its closure, but it was re-opened in 1914. The construction of roads, and wharfs at Egwanga, which was the administrative headquarters of the Ogoni under Calabar province, and another at Be Nnete, now Ke-Nwigbara, near Bane, a trading post, opened up Ogoni land.

In Ogoni, colonialism began with the total destruction of Gbenebeka shrine at Gwara in 1914. This shrine was the seat of the national goddess of the Ogoni. It was very important to the Ogoni and served as the religious and political centre of the people like Ikuba of Bonny and Yok-Obolo of Andoni. The British also fought the Kaani Teegbara war, the local name of the hero that fought the (war of resistance) in Ogoni.

From 1908-1947, Ogoni was administered as part of the Opobo Division, thereby forcing alien administrative structures on the Ogoni. Ken Saro-Wiwa has characterised the period as "crude and harsh".

Colonial Period

Paul T. Birabi, Finimale Nwika, Saronwiyo, Kemte Giadom, and others, put up a struggle through the forties to the fifties and founded, first, the Ogoni Divisional Union (ODU), and, later, the Ogoni State Representative Assembly (OSRA).

In 1942, a Representative Conference of Rivers People, mainly the Ogoni, Bonny, Okrika and Kalabari and other Ijo groups, had assembled in Lagos and formed the Ijo People's Congress to fight for the creation of a Rivers Province.

The constitutional amendment offered the Ogoni the opportunity to have a Division within the Rivers Province in 1947. The Ogoni were part of Opobo Division in Calabar Province, far from administrative headquarters at Calabar.

Other autonomous Divisions, such as Brass, Degema, Yenagoa, were created out of Owerri Province, and placed under Port Harcourt in 1947.

The Ogoni and their Ijo neighbours began the movement for a Rivers State. The movement gathered momentum after the constitutional conference of 1953, when the Rivers Council of Chiefs prepared a memorandum for the resumed conference of 1954.

Petroleum was discovered in Oloibiri in 1957, and in K. Dere, Ogoni (Bomu oil field) in 1958. Oil exploitation has turned Ogoni and her Ijo neighbours into a waste land. Lands, streams and creeks and the environment have been continually polluted. The atmosphere has been poisoned and charged with hydrocarbon vapours, methane, carbon monoxide, carbon dioxide, and soot emitted by continuous gas-flaring twenty-four hours everyday for thirty three years, in very close proximity to human habitation. In return for this, the Ogoni in particular, and the Niger Delta in general, have received nothing.

By 1960, when colonial rule ended, the British had consigned the Ogoni and her Ijo neighbours to a new nation. The nation which the British left behind was supposed to be a federal democracy.

Minorities such as the Ogoni and their Ijo neighbours, who were unable to mobilize large politically significant communities under the NCNC government of Eastern Nigeria, were denied self-representation, contracts, scholarships, loans, and such social amenities like electricity.

It was against the background of the discriminatory practices highlighted above that Isaac Adaka Boro embarked on a twelve-day revolution in 1966.

The Ogoni leaders of thought with their Ijo neighbours sent a delegation to lobby an ad hoc conference for a Rivers State and, on 14 September, 1960, they published a memorandum in Nigerian newspapers (Saro-Wiwa, 1989). While the Ogoni and their Ijo neighbours were lobbying for a Rivers State, the Eastern Nigeria Consultative Assembly, convened by Ojukwu, Military Governor of Eastern Nigeria, voted against any such states for the minorities. Instead, a new provincial system was worked out as a panacea for the minorities.

After the first military *coup d'etat* and counter *coup* in 1966, it became apparent that the creation of states was the only way of keeping the country together. Thus, Chief Dappa Biriye, Chief Edward Kobani, Barrister Nwaobidike Nwonodi, Mr. Graham Otoko, Mr. Robert P. G. Okara, Kemte Giadom and Finimale Nwika, signed a memorandum for the creation of Rivers State. Chief Dappa-Biriye led the delegation to present the document to the

Head of State, General Yakubu Gowon. Several persons, at the home front, supported the delegation which eventually brought about the successful creation of Rivers State in 1967.

The Ogoni and their Ijo neighbours had a common agenda for the development of the new Rivers State. The military Governor of Rivers State, Commander Alfred Diete Spiff appointed Ken Saro-Wiwa administrator of Bonny in November 1967. Shortly after, he was appointed Commissioner for Education in Rivers State when he awarded scholarships (local and abroad) to many sons and daughters of Rivers State. He later moved to the Ministry of Information and Home Affairs as commissioner, where he was instrumental in starting the *Nigerian Tide*, the first newspaper to be published by the Rivers State Government. This enhanced the relationship between the Ogoni and the Ijo. By 1974 a riverine/upland dichotomy had begun as a result of a demand for the creation of Port Harcourt State from Rivers State.

The minorities of the Eastern Region (Rivers, Bayelsa, Cross River and Akwa-Ibom State) suffered under rebel rule during the Nigerian Civil War. The Biafran soldiers often raided the homes of minorities, looting their property raping their women and girls and forcefully conscripting their young men, and manhandling their fathers and mothers. Young and old men were made to pass through forced labour known as "combing"—clearing the bush and mangrove forests to ascertain that the Federal troops were not there. The experience of the Ogoni also represents the sufferings of their Ijo neighbours.

Since oil was discovered in Oloibiri in 1957 and in Ogoni in 1958, basic amenities, health centres, hospitals, and clinics have been lacking, and transport in the region is both difficult and expensive. Thus most Ogoni people and their Ijo neighbours find it difficult to put their children through school.

In the absence of effective government regulations or monitoring of oil operations, Ogoni communities and their Ijo neighbours were faced with difficult barriers in defending their rights. Those who tried to assert their land rights faced a lengthy legal process in a congested court system. An example was the law suit brought by an Ogoni community in Eleme over an oil spill which occurred in 1970. SPDC appealed against the judgment requiring it to compensate the community with four billion naira.

For instance, the principle of derivation in revenue allocation has been consciously and systematically obliterated by successive regimes of the Nigerian state. There had been a drastic reduction of the derivation principle from the days of the Phillipson Commission of 1946, the Hicks Phillipson 1951, Chicks (1953), Binns (1964), Dina (1968), Aboyade Technical Committee (1977), Okigbo Committee (1980). Thus, it had fallen from 100% (1953), 50% (1960), 45% (1970), 20% (1975), 2% (1982), 1.5% (1984), to 3% (1992) and 13% (to date).

The political crisis in Nigeria is mainly about the struggle for the control of oil mineral resources, which accounts for over 80% of GDP, 95% of the national budget and 90% of foreign exchange earnings.

In 1940, a Minerals Act was passed by the colonial authorities. It said that all mineral discoveries belong to the governments, compensation was to be paid for disturbing the peace of the people but not royalty.

The Land Use Decree of 1978, while General Olusegun Obasanjo was Head of State, further nailed the fate of the oil producing areas of Ogoni and their Ijo neighbours. These common problems brought the Ogoni and their Ijo neighbours to a common understanding and awareness.

The Movement for the Survival of Ogoni People (MOSOP)
In October 1990, Chiefs and leaders of Ogoni submitted a Bill of Rights to the Nigerian President and his council. It was an attempt to transform the conflict of interests in the system through a Citizens' Charter. The Bill of Rights called for:

(a)   Political control of Ogoni affairs by Ogoni people

(b)   The right to control and use a fair proportion of Ogoni economic resources for Ogoni development.

(c)   Adequate and direct representation as of right in all Nigerian national institutions.

(d)   The use and development of Ogoni languages in Ogoni territory and;

(e)   The right to protect the Ogoni environment from further degradation.

Initially, some of the Ogoni neighbours did not understand that the Ogoni agenda postulates equity for all ethnic groups, big or small, within the Nigerian federation.

Later, matters came to a head at a public meeting that turned into a riot. Four illustrious Ogoni leaders were killed. Although Ken Saro-wiwa was nowhere near the scene of crime at Giokoo, he was charged with setting up machinery that led to the death of these leaders. Ken Saro-Wiwa and eight other Ogoni sons were sentenced to death at the prison in Port Harcourt on November 10, 1995.

The campaign Ken Saro-Wiwa led to hold Shell accountable for the pollution and devastation of lands has not been in vain. It has united the minority struggle of the Niger Delta people.

Conclusion

Ogoni land has heavy rainfall which is not destructive but encourages farming, the main occupation of the people, along with fishing and trading. The pre-nineteenth century trade in Ogoni was dominated by agricultural products, with some local crafts: pottery, carving, and weaving. The contact with their Ijo neighbours was complex, and stimulated economic changes that were of mutual benefit. The introduction of the slave trade proved to be a new factor in Ogoni external connections. During the period of legitimate trade in palm produce and other raw materials, new lines of communication were built. This trade involved many participants in Ogoni and the Ijo communities, as anybody who could work hard became a good trader. The effect of the palm produce trade created a class of entrepreneurs.

Colonialism, as a product of the pre-19th century trade, had pervasive influence on the lives of the Ogoni and their Ijo neighbours. Colonialism incorporated the traditional communal economy into the Western capitalist system and created a tendency to depend on imported goods.

The Ijo and their Ogoni neighbours have since been in political alliance. From 1942 they fought for the creation of a Rivers province, and, by 1954, they prepared a memorandum for a conference. The proposal they presented to Willink's Commission of 1957 was a clear manifestation of political alliance in which the Ogoni and the Ijo spoke with one voice under the leadership of Chief Dappa Biriye.

The exploitation of petroleum products has turned Ogoni and her Ijo neighbours into a wasteland as the principle of derivation in revenue allocation has been consciously and systematically obliterated by successive regimes of the Nigerian state. These events have produced new common causes.

The Ogoni, led by Ken Saro-Wiwa, rose up to protest their deplorable conditions. They formed the Movement for the Survival of the Ogoni People (MOSOP), a citizen charter as a Bill of Rights. The Bill of Rights serves as an agenda for the Ogoni, in particular, and other oil producing communities in the Niger Delta in their demand for "resource control".

The Ijo and the Ogoni remember Isaac Boro and Ken Saro-Wiwa as heroes and martyrs of the Niger Delta struggle for "resource control."

CHAPTER 27

THE IZON
AND THEIR NEIGHBOURS
OF THE CROSS RIVER VALLEY

Otu A. Ubi and Timipa Igoli

Introduction

The main emphasis of this study is to determine the extent of Ijaw impact on the Cross River valley and its peoples. While a great deal is now known about the active part played by the Ijaw of the Niger Delta in the history of southern Nigeria from the late seventeenth century through the nineteenth, the activities of the Ijaw in the Cross River valley during this period and thereafter have not been documented. Most of the documentation on the Ijaw has centred on the Ijaw as the leading city states on the Atlantic coast. Their active role as middlemen between the European supercargoes and the hinterland peoples of southern Nigeria has been the main thrust.

The Cross River Valley

The Cross River valley encompasses the area between the Qua Ibo River to the west and the Rio del Rey to the east. The area covers parts of Akwa Ibom, Abia, and Ebonyi states, and the whole of the Cross River State. It is the home of over thirty ethnic communities. The Efik, Ibibio, Annang, Oron, Eket, and Efut occupy the coastal littoral from the Bakassi peninsular in the east to Akwa Ibom state in the west, the domain of the Ibibio.

The people of the Cross River Valley

The Cross River Valley is peopled by very many ethnic groups who have migrated into the area in the dim past from different directions.

The following questions may be raised. What have been the historical impulses shaping the development of the territory? In the process, what significant impact has the Ijaw brought to bear in the historical shaping of the Cross River Valley? These are the issues we will be addressing in the rest of this chapter.

619

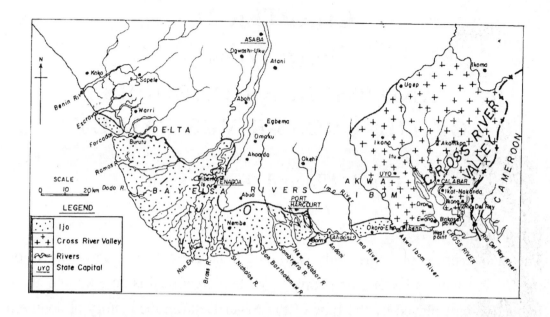

Fig. 27.1: The Ijo and the people of the Cross River Valley

The Cross River has been used in three different geographical contexts over the years. The first usage refers to the city states of Old Calabar. This is the sense in which E. U. Aye's widely read *Old Calabar through the centuries* (Aye, 1967) was used. This calls to mind the role of the Ijaw in city states building. The question is, whether or not the city state of Old Calabar developed independent of the Ijaw city states or was there exchange of ideas arising from commercial contact?

It is in the area of Ijaw institutional developments that Alagoa made his greatest contribution to Niger Delta studies. Before Alagoa, Niger Delta institutions were seen as having grown out of the Atlantic trade. Alagoa saw many of the institutions as having been in place before the start of the Atlantic trade. Long distance trade, for instance, existed before Europeans came to the Delta. Ijaw reasons for such internal long distance journeys were economic. Thus, unlike Dike and Jones, Alagoa derived the House system not from the Atlantic trade, but from the Ijaw political system. What the Atlantic trade did was to add the canoe house—the military arm, to the House system.

The Cross River was a navigable waterway, and it was part of a system very important in the economic history of Nigeria. A canoe could be taken from Badagry in the west coast of Nigeria to Rio-del- Rey in the east without going into the open sea. The extent of commerce during the era of the city states was from west of Lagos along the coast to the Camerouns and beyond. It stands to reason that the effect of commercial influence from Europeans whilst impacting first in the Ijaw city states to the west of Old Calabar must have contributed significantly to the economic and political development of Old Calabar.

A second conception is that Old Calabar is synonymous with the Efik. There is no doubt that the Efik are one of the most conspicuous historical groups in the Cross River Valley but even at the time of Old Calabar, the Qua (Ejagham/Etung/Efut) had a strong position in the city. The Ekpe institution is indigenous to the Qua, but the Efik utilized it as a governmental institution to facilitate coastal trade with the Europeans.

The third theory relates to the development of Efik imperialism. The concept developed following the expansion of Efik influence through trade, missionary activities and cultural contacts within the Cross River Valley and perhaps beyond. With these developments, the Efik, Efut, Ejagham (Qua), Ibibio, Annang, Oron, Agwagune (Biase), Yakurr, Bahumon/Agbo, Mbembe, Etung, Ofutop, Boki, Ekajuk, Bekwarra, Yalla, Atam, Bette and Sankwala became embodied in the concept of Old Calabar. In terms of Efik influence in the Cross River Valley, it has to be said that that influence did not go beyond 200 miles to the north of Calabar. The missionary influence that affected the region of Ogoja came from the west, i.e. Abakaliki. Thus, there is a marked cultural difference between the Ikom-Calabar axis, and the Ikom-Ogoja/Obudu axis.

Was the ideal of a city state derived from outside the Cross River region? In the entire Cross River valley, the House system, a fundamental structure of the city state concept, is to be found only in Calabar among the Efik. All other communities in the Cross River valley have not established the House system. Within the Cross River valley, it is only peculiar and applicable to the Efik. There is no evidence that the system existed in Efik society before the introduction of unbroken contacts between the region and the Europeans from about the sixteenth century. During the trade with Europeans in the sixteenth and seventeenth centuries, the Efik suddenly introduced the House system which was the key to the organization of city states in the Niger Delta. The Ekpe society was adopted by the Efik from the Qua/Ejagham, also about this period. The House system was, in all probability, derived from the Ijaw city states of the Niger Delta.

Efik trading contacts with the Niger Delta preceded the House system in Old Calabar. In Old Calabar, the House system was an institution which was developed in response to the trade with Europeans. The character of the Efik house is slightly different from the normal features of a House as a sub division of a family or lineage in the Niger Delta. Among the Efik of Old Calabar, the Canoe-house, according to Jones, was more compact and better organized for trading and fighting purposes. As Alagoa aptly expressed it, in respect of the Ijaw, the House system was both a military, commercial and kinship unit in the city state. The implication is, that the House system did not develop concurrently in all the city states at the same time. Rather, the system started in the Ijaw city states, and gradually found its way to the Efik of Old Calabar.

It is our considered opinion that the Ijaw developed the House system, because of their commercial interactions with European supercargoes, and because of their position as middlemen, standing between European traders and hinterland producers. The Efik adopted the House system following their commercial interactions with the Ijaw. In terms of control of their hinterland markets, the Efik were not as successful as the Ijaw in the Niger Delta. Hinterland markets, especially in the middle and upper Cross River, were under the control of local potentates such as Umon and Agwagune.

Umon is made up of fifteen villages, while Agwagune is made up of seven villages. Umon and Agwagune became very prominent throughout the eighteenth and nineteenth centuries, because they successfully controlled trade in the Middle and Upper Cross River from Umon in the south to Ogoja near the Benue Valley in the North. There were attempts by the Efik to break through the firm control of Umon territory in order to deal directly with the upper Cross River producers. Up to 1852 there appears to have been no success in that bid. D. M Macfarlan in his book, *Calabar: The C.S.M 1846-1946*, (1946, 45) states:

> "In 1846, the mission company had watched king Eyamba set out on
> an expedition to carry war into Umon country….."

As a matter of fact, up to about 1852, the Cross River was divided up into areas of influence between the Efik, Umon and Agwagune. The Efik controlled the area between the coast and Itu. Umon controlled the area between Itu and Ikot Ana, while Agwagune controlled the rest of the middle and upper Cross River areas. According to Afigbo, although Umon did not directly involve herself in the purchase and sale of goods, she benefited from the trade on the Cross River since she successfully made the Efik and Agwagune recognize her authority over her area of influence by extorting customs duty from them and forcing the Efik and Agwagune to use her territory as the centre of commerce in the hinterland. Up to 1852 Umon was the hinterland emporium. The trade treaty of 1852 between Consul Beecroft and Umon finally relaxed the militant posture of the Umon and so opened up trade in the Cross River to all people including the Efik and European firms.

The effect of the penetration of Efik and European firms to areas formerly under the exclusive control of local potentates was to render the services of these middlemen redundant. What applied to Umon and Agwagune soon applied to the Efik because the Efik, too, lost their middleman position to European firms, but, unlike Umon and Agwagune, the Efik picked up positions as agents of the European firms.

The effect of the economic change that took place largely as a result of the 1852 trade treaty was to force many Efik traders to develop plantations and fishing settlements such as Akpabuyo and Bakassi. According to Efik oral tradition, the Akpabuyo and Bakassi became influenced by their new environment and profession.

The city states were organized, not by consideration of kinship and descent, but by contiguity and residence. The Efik were a republic with single trading units/houses. Thus, whereas in the Niger Delta the term city state embraced not only the settlements on the coast but also their colonies in the hinterland, in Old Calabar, that was not the case. Eyo B. Ndem has argued that there was, rather, Efik cultural imperialism within the Cross River Valley. The Efik role was the disemination of Efik culture and system of thought, through the process of assimilation/acculturation, and total absorption of its less resilient neighbours.

The Ijaw in the Cross River Valley

The Ijaw have been in contact with the peoples of the Cross River Valley for many centuries. Their interactions in the area of commerce and culture has received scholarly attention. In this Chapter, our object is simply to locate the Ijaw resident in the Cross River valley, notably in the Akpabuyo and Bakassi Local Government Areas of the Cross River State of Nigeria.

In Akpabuyo Local Government Area, the Ijaw reside in twelve fishing settlements:

(i)	Akpairok	(v)	Esighi	(ix)	New Town
(ii)	Esuk Mba	(vi)	Efuta	(x)	Benebot
(iii)	Inua Esighi	(vii)	Efiang Camp Four	(xi)	Joshua Fishing Port
(iv)	Agamanga	(viii)	Agbamgba	(xii)	Ikang Ijo Camp

Joshua Fishing Port was formerly called Komotei Fishing Port. Komotei, according to our informants, was an Ijaw from Korokorosei, Southern Ijo Local Government Area, Bayelsa State. At the death of Komotei, his son Joshua, took over the leadership of the settlement. It was discovered that the name Komotei was resented by the Efik, from the idea that the name gave a false impression of the ownership of the land on which the settlement stood. Joshua's succession, thus provided an opportunity to effect a change of name from Komotei to Joshua. This happened before the Nigerian Civil War. .

In Bakassi, there are sixteen Ijaw fishing settlements:

(i) Ine Iban Iban	(vii) Koloni	(xiii) Zion Fishing Port
(ii) Bayelsa Fishing Port	(viii) Ine Koi	(xiv) Ine Hat Fishing Port
(iii) Ine Okpo	(ix) Inedu	(xv) Utang Iyak
(iv) Abuja Fishing Port	(x) Lemet Fishing Port	(xvi) Mission Fishing Port
(v) Enuya	(xi) Uruanyang 1,2 & 3	
(vi) Nwajo	(xii) Kanakure 1 & 2	

According to our informant, the newest, in terms of age, is Nwajo. According to our informants at Nwajo, their name is not Ijo. The name is Efik, meaning, Ijo quarters. The chief of the Ijaw in Nwajo, Chief Joseph Abel, from Liama, Brass Local Government Area, Bayelsa State, told us that most of the Ijaw in Nwajo were formerly residing in the Cameroun. According to this informant, by 1994, the relationship between Nigerians living in Cameroun and Camerounian *gendarmes* (police) became so bad that their security could no longer be guaranteed. For instance, one day, they went out fishing. By the time they returned, they found some of their houses pulled down. That was in 1994. They decided to migrate from Cameroun to Bakassi (Nigeria), and settled in Nwajo.

Within Akpabuyo and Bakassi Local Governments, the Ijaw reside in twenty eight Ijaw settlements. The oldest of these settlements is Koloni while the newest is Nwajo.

Ijaw Impact in the Cross River Valley

The first major impact the Ijaw have made on the Cross River valley is socio-political. A characteristic feature of the various peoples of the Cross River valley, from Calabar to Ogoja and from Eket (Ibibio land) to Bakassi, is that lineage borne out of biological descent dominate social relations. Such relationship could be maternal, paternal or both. In Yakurr, biological descent is both maternal and paternal. Amongst the Yakurr, maternal relationship is referred to as *Legimo* while paternal relationship is referred to as *Kepun*. This type of biological relationship is different from the House system that came to be established amongst the Efik. In the Efik House, many had been slaves who had become absorbed into the house. In Yakurr, slaves were absorbed into the maternal family of their purchasers. But even with time the mark of slavery was often indelible, since reference would continue to be made to it. Amongst the Efik and in their everyday life, the difference between members of the same house is not noticeable. However, it was when an Efik *Etubom* or *Obong* is to be picked from within a family (*Etubom*) or families (*Obong*), historical journeys to roots of potential nominees have to be made. In other words, even within a House, some members are more equal than others in that biological roots do determine the status and worth of members of each House.

It would appear that the House System was first established among the Ijaw city states of the Eastern Niger Delta. On the other hand, it is also known that throughout the Cross River valley, originally, none of the communities had the House System as an indigenous political institution. During the 16th Century trade with Europeans, the Efik adopted and adapted the House System in its socio-political and economic organization. The Efik also adopted the Canoe House as its military arm, but unlike the Ijaw, the Efik never made battle with any community. The only known attempt she made was on Umon. That attempt was abortive. Until the 1852 trade agreements between Beecroft and the hinterland peoples of Umon, Agwagune, Bahumono (Ediba), Yakurr etc, the Efik did not and could not have penetrated inland beyond Itu. The *status quo* of segmentalised control of the Cross River would still have persisted. What changed that scenario was the change of power, occasioned by Beecroft's treaties of 1852. Therefore, one can conclude that the House System, as found within the Efik society, was the only isolated pocket in the whole of the Cross River Valley. The idea, apparently, came to the Efik from the Ijaw of the Eastern Niger Delta with whom the Efik had been in contact over many centuries. The Efik also picked up the Ekpe institution from their neighbours to administer the trade with the Europeans.

There is also an economic/occupational influence that the Ijaw have made in the Cross River valley. In Akpabuyo and Bakassi, in locations lying east of the mouth of the Cross River and near the Atlantic Ocean, are clusters of fishing settlements occupied by Efik and Ijaw fishermen. From interviews conducted among these peoples, it is clear that these fishing settlements were established by the Efik fishermen who later absorbed the Ijaw. The ethnic composition of the area is, however, far more complex than the Efik/Ijaw reference would suggest. The ethnic composition shows diverse groups including the Ibibio, Oron, Efut, Qua/Ejagham and others. These various peoples are the riverine fishermen of the Cross River valley. These fishermen and women, too, have, in the past, carried out their occupation of fishing and exchanged their catch with other Cross River peoples for their products, such as yams, cocoyam, meat, salt, camwood and other products. With the displacement of the Efik/Ijaw African middlemen by the European powers, such Efik/Ijaw middlemen had to find alternative means of meeting the impending challenges.

Consequently, the Efik began establishing new settlements and plantations. The settlements in Akpabuyo and Bakassi are examples. The Efik sent most of their former canoe men and slaves to these new settlements. Akpabuyo and Bakassi are plantations and fishing settlements established by the Efik in response to the challenges of their dislodgement by Europeans from the Atlantic trade. But just as the Efik were battling with their resettlement, so too were the Ijaw. Apparently, a substantial number of Ijaw fishermen migrated to settle with the Cross River peoples in the coastal littoral settlements of Ibeno, James Town (Oron), Akpabuyo and Bakassi. These Ijaw migrants made fishing their fulltime occupation with consequences which have impacted greatly on the eating habit of the Cross River peoples. Thus seafood items of crayfish, smoked or fresh fish have now become a daily ingredient of Cross River meals from the coast to the northernmost parts and beyond. The domestic demand could not be met by indigenous fishermen's supply. The Ijaw participation in the supply helped to satisfy it. In fact, it is now known that the Ijaw fishermen supplied net traps and other output to the market both in terms of smoked fish, fresh and other sea foods.

Cross River and neighbouring Igbo now travel to Calabar, Ikang, Akpabuyo and Bakassi to buy fish food items for retail in other parts of Nigeria. This flourishing trade in seafood now engages both the riverine and upland peoples of the Cross River valley.   The Ijaw have been and are still very useful in the Cross River valley. The Ijaw undoubtedly strengthened the fishing industry in the Cross River valley.

There is the other side to the Efik reaction to their displacement. It is the establishment of plantations of oil palms, and kolanut trees.   The initiative which the Efik and other local communities took to better manage their forest and tree resources helped in rural empowerment through building income generating activities. In many cases the income generated from these resources acted as incentive for social stability, improved livelihood, thus supplementing incomes from other sources.

One other area which must be mentioned where the Ijaw have made an impact in the Cross River Valley is in the areas of dress fashion. Today, there is a pattern of dress that has been developed and worn by men and women which has become characteristic of the Cross River valley. In fact, the style of dress and hat is a recurrent motif in the Niger Delta. A brief glance at the history of the Efik will bring out a few salient points. The differences in the attire of the Ijaw and Efik derive, not simply from taste, but from decisive historical changes that have taken place within the various ethnicities of the Niger Delta. These changes which are due to historical circumstances or the ruling ideas and expectations of the time, are reflected in the people's attire. These two groups have extensively borrowed from each other. The bowler hat, a big wrapper or loin cloth, and beaded neck lace which are popular amongst the Ijaw and Efik are products of historical commercial interaction. Local adaptations are found among the Ibibio. Such variation only show the extent of dexterity and ingeniousness of the people of the Niger Delta and Cross River valley. The form of the Niger Delta attire has now been given the appellation "Resource Control" by local politicians. Nigerians have a flair for naming their costumes after specific contemporary events or issues. Thus for example, hair styles have been named "Nigeria drives right", "Eko bridge", and many more. Today, the burning issue, in the whole of the Niger Delta and the Cross River Valley, is "Resource Control". Consequently, the style of dressing favoured by politicians from the area is aptly named "Resource Control", which consists of an upper dress and a trouser.

Conclusion

This Chapter's focus is on the peoples of the Cross River Valley and the role the Ijaw have played in their historical development. While substantial knowledge is now available about the Ijaw in the Niger Delta from the 16th century down to the 19th century, the Ijaw activities in the Cross River Valley have never been sufficiently emphasized and documented. On the other hand, with regard to the peoples of the Cross River Valley, certain conclusions which have been held about them require reconsideration and revision.

On the contributions of the Ijaw in the Cross River Valley, the Efik House system was possibly a direct inheritance from the Ijaw. Economic activities of Cross River people, such as fishing and trading, have also benefited substantially from Ijaw participation. In terms of attire, there is evidence of substantial exchange between groups and local variations. There is now a unique attire, characteristic of the Niger Delta or what is now called South South geopolitical zone of Nigeria, which is called "Resource Control". The Ijaw have made great political, socio-economic and cultural impact in the Cross River Valley.

CHAPTER 28

THE IZON
IN NORTHERN NIGERIA

Ambily Etekpe and Joseph Kariboro

Introduction

In our effort to identify Ijaw settlements in Northern Nigeria, we visited nine states in the North to meet people and collect the empirical data presented in this report.

The fieldwork was guided by the following: to identify people who migrated on their own, not public servants on transfer; identify Ijaw villages/settlements, and to collate/analyse the data relating to their history of migration, occupations, governance and inter-ethnic relations.

In 1920, an Ijaw steward to a colonial official, came to Lokoja. Mr. Yoro, from Okoloba in Bayelsa State, founded an Ijaw community, known as Fakun in Kainji, Niger State, in 1955. Some Ijaw settled in Lake Chad in 1959 in their own distinct village. The Ijaw in the nine northern states with major rivers running through them live mainly as fishermen and traders, and are fully integrated in the local societies, contributing to the vitality of their host communities.

The realities discussed in this study raise very important questions that confront the Nigerian nation. The issues raised reflect a contradiction between the realities and what is represented and propagated by those responsible for providing national political leadership.

Benue State –Makurdi and Gboko
History of Migration

The Ijaw at Makurdi, Benue State, migrated mainly from Bayelsa, Delta and Rivers States in 1946. There are a few from Ondo State. They do not have separate villages of their own, but live among the local people. Nevertheless, they predominantly live at Demekpe area, Wadata; North Bank Garage (Park 1 & II); and by the bank of Benue River, but Gboko is the traditional headquarters of the Ijaw in Benue State. Ijaw are found also in Otukpo, Aliade and Kwande.

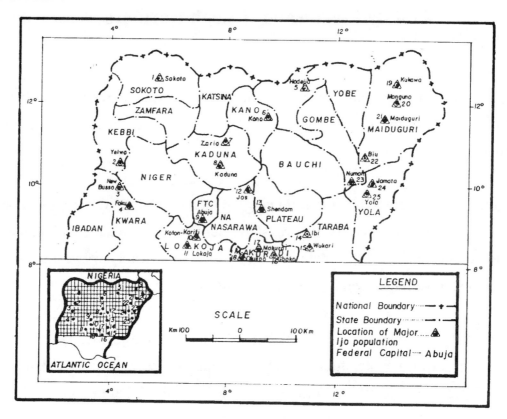

Fig. 28.1: Locations of major Ijo populations in Northern Nigeria

Mr. Edentu D. Oroso, from Okoloba in Delta State, Secretary of the Ijaw community in Makurdi, was born in Makurdi in 1966, his parents being among the first arrivals in 1946. The Ijaw in Benue state are mainly from Ondoro, Aleibiri, and Kolokuma/Opokuma in Bayelsa State; Okoloba, Bomadi and Burutu in Delta state; and Kalabari, Okrika and Bonny in Rivers State.

Occupation

The Ijaw are engaged in distilling and marketing *Ogogoro*, fishing, farming, especially in Gboko, Aliade and Otukpo areas. There are also some civil servants, especially retired military and police personnel, who have settled in Makurdi.

632

Governance and Inter-Ethnic Relations

The Ijaw are well organised and meet regularly at Local Government Area (L.G.A) level under elected officials. People from different LGAs meet at Gboko once a month. In Makurdi, the leader is Chief Odonikeme Bonke. He is recognised by the Makurdi L.G.A even though he is not paid stipends as other indigenous third class chiefs. In addition, within the Ijaw community, people from each of the Ijaw states have their separate meetings. The Ijaw are well integrated with other ethnic groups and intermarry with the Tiv, Idoma and Nupe.

Problems

As non-indigenes, the Ijaw are denied opportunities for employment or running for political office(s) like local government councillors. Recently, the Benue State government announced the retrenchment of non-indigenous teachers in public schools, and many Ijaw people were affected.

Kogi State – Lokoja and Koton-Karfi
History of Migration

Mr. Gbanton from Angalabiri in Bayelsa State was the first Ijaw settler in Lokoja in 1920. He was a steward to a colonial officer. According to Elder Arch. Onitsha Musu Miebaikedoh from Orua in Sagbama Local Government Area, Bayelsa State, he joined Gbanton in the early 1940s as a youth. He is now the patron of the Ijaw community in Kogi State, and an active community leader in Ijara quarters of Lokoja. From 1958 many Ijaw moved in and settled at Lokoja and its environs; most of them were staff of the Marine Department or fishermen. They settled along the waterfronts of Ijara and Adakolo quarters of Lokoja.

The Ijaw also migrated to the suburbs of Lokoja LGA, namely, Ijiho–Magajiya; Jamata (Hedeha) along present Murtala Muhammed Bridge; Koton-Karfi LGA, Igraya and Abayi; and Bassa LGA, especially Eshew. Mr. Afore Kerego from Peretorugbene in Bayelsa State, for example, migrated and settled at Koton-Karfi town, now headquarters of Koton-Karfi. He raised his family there, and his first son, Mr. Theophilus Afore-Kerego, has taken over his estate. Other migrants followed, and there is now an Ijaw settlement.

Many Ijaw people went back to their ancestral homes during the Nigerian Civil War in 1967; but some, along with new migrants, returned to Lokoja.

The Ijaw people who migrated to these areas are mainly from Sagbama, Peretorugbene, Amatolo, Odi and Opokuma in Bayelsa State; Okoloba, Ojobo, Patani and Akugbene in Delta State; Opobo in Rivers State; and Arogbo in Ondo State.

Occupation

The Ijaw are actively involved in the informal sector of the economy: tapping palm wine, distilling it to *ogogoro*, and distributing it through established trade networks. They also engage in crop farming, especially, in the rural areas; petty trading and restaurant business; and serving as civil/public servants in the urban centres.

Governance and Inter-Ethnic Relations

According to Elder Arc. O.M. Miebaikedoh, there are two divisions of Ijaw in Kogi state, namely: Bayelsa/Rivers community and community of other Ijaw. These units operate in five zones: Lokoja, Ajaokuta, Koton-Karfi, Dekina, and Idah.

Chief Ikposo from Odi is the Chairman of Bayelsa/Rivers Ijaw community while Elder Arc. Miebaikedoh is the patron of both organizations in Kogi State. Initially, both meetings were held in Elder Arc. Miebaikedoh's residence, but for the purpose of encouraging mass participation, the General Assembly meetings of the Ijaw community in Kogi State now rotate amongst the five zones. Each zone comprises several LGAs, and meetings rotate amongst the LGAs. The different villages organise their own regular meetings.

Elder Arc. Miebaikedoh tried to create an "Ijaw Camp" in the Ijara/Ndakolo quarters in the early 1970s. From the late 1990s the Ijaw people began to move into the camp. Apart from building houses here and there, there is no separate Ijaw neighbourhood or village in Lokoja and in Kogi State. Nevertheless, the Ijaw have occupied the Marine Road waterfront in large numbers, and this could be regarded as a major Ijaw settlement area.

The Ijaw relate very well with their neighbours. Elder Arc. Miebaikedoh, for example, is a key player in the Ajara community of Lokoja, and a member of the *Megari* Palace. The Ijaw are prominent in their callings and well known in the local communities. Mrs. Precilia's restaurant at Jamata (Hedeha), for example, is well patronised and Mrs. Agnes Afore Kerego is a renowned farmer.

Problems

Despite their long stay and integration into the local system, they are denied political appointments and opportunities for employment. This has created the urge to return home. The creation of Ijaw Camp would have addressed this, as the camp would have become a political unit or ward. The *ogogoro* business also cannot be carried out within strict Muslim neighbourhoods.

Niger State – Kainji and New Bussa Towns in Borgo LGA
History of Migration

Mr. Yabo Okporu from Okoloba, Delta State came to the Kainji area through Baro near Lokoja in 1955 by an outboard canoe, *Dogon-Gari*. He was a trader in search of new markets for his *ogogoro*, and the driver of the boat was Mr. Yoro Izon-Ebi from Isama town in Rivers State. They traded to Oshogbo, Ilorin and other parts of Yorubaland. Mr. Yoro Izon-Ebi later took over the business and decided to settle permanently at Fakun.

Yoro secured tenancy rights from the old Fakun people through the Emir of Borgu, Mokwa District, cleared the bush, and built his home in 1955. The old Fakun people were far away in the hinterland. Using Fakun as his trading base, the business (marketing of *ogogoro*, amidst hostilities), and the Ijaw people spread to other neighbouring communities: Sabon Pegi, Kpalagi, Ebi, Awuru, Zugurma up to Mokwa, and to Niki. Fakun is the only Ijaw village. The Ijaw live amongst the indigenes in the other villages.

When Kainji Dam was completed in 1964 and a motor road was constructed to Mokwa, Yoro went home and brought several more people to settle at Fakun for fishing, and there was plenty of catch. The fish was sold to distant markets, and the Ijaw community in Fakun became the main supplier of fish to

Ogbomosho and Ilorin, from where it was distributed to several parts of Yorubaland. Major fish distributors came to Fakun. In the process, some settled at Fakun.

As the *ogogoro* and fishing businesses flourished, more Ijaw people, and later, Urhobo, Isoko, Igbo and the Nupe also moved to Fakun. The settlement suffered out-migration during the Civil War, but at the end of the war in 1970, Yoro Izon-Ebi encouraged many more people to settle at Fakun and the neighbouring villages in Borgu LGA.

Prominent families that then migrated to the area were Mr. Ayapaye (Chief Carter's father) and Mr. Peter Nanakede in 1972. They both came from Enekorogha, Bayelsa State. Mr. Ayapaye, a retired World War II soldier, became a big-time fisherman. He brought his son, Chief Carter Ayapaye, to settle in 1983. The families of Aridanzi of Okoloba also settled here during this period. The Emir installed Izon-ebi as Sarki Ijaw in 1977. He thus became a member of the Emir's Council, representing also the Ijaw at New Bussa.

Occupation

The Ijaw settlers are involved in *ogogoro* business, fishing, petty trading, managing restaurants and serving as public servants.

Governance and Inter-ethnic Relations

The people are well organised in five zones: New Bussa, Fakun, Awuru, Sabon Pegi, and Kpalegi. During our visit, they announced Chief Carter as their new Sarki Ijaw.

Inter-ethnic relations between the Ijaw and their neighbours—Nupe, Yoruba, Urhobo—are good. It is as a result of this cordiality that the Emir appointed Yoro the Sarki Ijaw.

Problems

As in other locations, the Ijaw people are denied political rights—appointments and opportunity for employment. The Emir and Nupe people still look at the Ijaw as strangers.

The issue of citizenship rights for integrating the 250 ethnic nationalities as one remains to be tackled in Nigeria (Usman, 1999:34).

Kaduna / Zaria
History of Migration

The early settlers in Kaduna town were military personnel, who came either as Officers or trainees, especially in the Nigerian Air Force.

The second category of settlers were students who gained admission into Ahmadu Bello University (ABU) in the early 1960s; where, after their studies, about 10% usually remained behind to secure jobs. The third category comprised civil servants in Federal establishments, such as the Refinery, the Railway, and businessmen.

In Kaduna area, the Ijaw are predominantly found in the Air Force base, NDA quarters, Police Barracks, Kawo, Down Quarters (Railway Old and Extension Quarters), and Tundun Wada. Chief Ibibofori Iruenebere used to be the rallying point of the Ijaw community, but with his death, the coordination has shifted to Dr. Kalada D. Iruenebere, at Kwato Street. He has served as the Chairman of the Ijaw community in Kaduna, and is currently the Co-ordinator of the Ijaw National Congress in Northern Nigeria.

We went to Kaduna River bank and found there is no longer an Ijaw settlement there because of incessant religious and political crises. The Ijaw in Kaduna are predominantly from: Rivers State- - Kalabari, Okrika, Ibani, Andoni, Abua, Engenni; Bayelsa State- - Nembe, Kolokuma/Opokuma, Odi; and Delta State- - Okoloba, Bomadi, Patani, Burutu. Their population is as follows: Kaduna (800 families); Zaria (150 families) and Kafanchan (50 families), respectively. Of this number, Bayelsa State has 300 families.

There is the same pattern of settlement in Zaria, which is dominated by Nigeria Railway workers with a few private sector employees in the Nigerian Tabacco Company as well as students and staff of ABU and the School of Nursing. Within Zaria, the Ijaw are found at Samaru, Kongo, Sabon Gari and Tudun Wada quarters.

Occupation

The Ijaw people are public servants working in federal government establishments, mainly Nigerian Railways, ministries and military/police formations. The businessmen are in the health sector and three of them have their own hospitals and clinics, while the others are involved in trading and fishing.

Governance and Inter-Ethnic Relations

The Ijaw are well organised in separate Rivers and Ijaw communities meetings, especially after the creation of Bayelsa State in 1996. At present, the Ijaw in Kaduna State are operating under the umbrella of the Ijaw National Congress (INC). The different groups meet regularly, and, at the end of each month, members of the entire Ijaw community in Kaduna, under the auspices of INC, Kaduna Chapter, meet at different venues to deliberate on common issues.

Problems

The problems include non-employment opportunities into the state Civil Service, and denial of government scholarships.

Plateau State–Jos and Shendam
History of Migration

Like in Kaduna and Zaria, early Ijaw settlers came to Jos in the early 1930s principally as miners and workers in the colonial service. The second generation of settlers came between 1965 and 1969. In 1984, Ijaw migrated in large numbers to Jos through transfers from the Federal Civil/Public Service and private establishments.

In 2000, Mr. Goodleaf Obele from Agbura, Atissa, founded a distinct settlement, known as Kankan Village, near Dandin Kowa, Jos. Five Fulani and six Ijaw families are now living there.

There has been a large number of Ijaw in the military and para-military formations since the 1950s: Nigerian Army Barracks (Rukuba), Air Force Barracks (Bukuru) and Police College (Bukuru). The University of Jos and National Institute for Policy and Strategic Studies, Kuru, Jos, have also attracted Ijaw academics, non-academics and students.

The Ijaw, mainly from Opokuma, Odi, Nembe, Okordia, Zarama, Agbura, Atissa (Bayelsa); Ayakoromo, Bomadi, Burutu and Okoloba (Delta State); and Abua, Engenni and Ogoni (Rivers State), are located within the metropolis, predominantly settled in Dodin Kowa, Anglo-Jos, Alhari-Jos, Rayfield, Army Barracks at Rukuba, Air Force Base and Police College, Bukuru, Vom and Kuru. The population of Ijaw in Jos is about 300 families.

Occupation

Ijaw presence, therefore, is in the public service and the private sector. The business people are mainly in the informal sector: peasant farming and fishing. A few of them are in professional practice.

Governance and Inter-Ethnic Relations

The Ijaw in these States are well organised, especially from 1966, and they still have regular monthly meetings. The meetings rotate from house to house for purposes of familiarisation and mass participation. The Ijaw community comprise mainly Bayelsa, Delta, and Rivers State indigenes.

They form a part of an existing South-South Community (SSC) in Jos. The organisation comprises Cross River, Akwa-Ibom, Bayelsa, Delta, Rivers and Edo States, and each group is represented in the Plateau State Traditional Rulers Council (*Gwom Gwom Jos*). The representative of Bayelsans in the Council is Sir Ewarewah. The South-South Community has a Paramount

639

Ruler, Chief Zag Dome from Itsekiri, Delta State. He represents the SSC in all important meetings in the Plateau Council of Chiefs. There is also a President-General, Mr. Osoro from Akwa-Ibom State who oversees the welfare of South-South people in the Jos area. The SSC is recognised by the Plateau State government, and was formally inaugurated in August/September 2006.

There is cordial relationship between the Ijaw and the local people with whom they inter-marry. Sir Ewarewah's Iweeco Electrical Engineering Company Ltd. has trained over 300 persons from Plateau State who are now self-employed, and some are now even employers.

At Shendam, the early settlers were mainly there to sell *Ogogoro* and fish at the Dam, harassed by the Emir, they left for Ibi in Taraba State. The Deputy Emir often reported to NDLEA that *Ogogoro* is the same as *goskolo*, an illicit alcohol that is charming his subjects, especially youth, into criminality. The Ijaw community in Shendam and its environs has filed a law suit against NDLEA.

Ijaw also live in other neighbouring villages, such as Faju, Nabudi and Yamini. The total Ijaw population in the Shendam area was: Shendam (5 families), Faju (2 families), Mabudi (3 families) and Yamini (2 families), respectively.

Kano State – Bagauda Lake and Tiga Dam
History of Migration

There are several Ijaw people fishing along with the Jukun in Bagauda Lake. It was reported that the Ijaw migrated there from Ibi in Taraba State. They had left because of the frequent crises in Kano State. Ijaw settlers came in 1956 through the Nigerian Railways and defunct P&T. This was followed at independence by other public servants.

Population

There are over 500 Rivers and Bayelsa States indigenes residing in Kano. By geographical spread, the people are predominantly from: Kalabari, Degema, Okrika, Bonny and Ogoni in Rivers State; and Okordia, Nembe, Kolokuma in Bayelsa State. The Andoni are reluctant to join the community, and prefer to relate with the people of Akwa Ibom state.

Governance and Inter-Ethnic Relations

In Kano, the Rivers/Bayelsa Ijaw community meet regularly. Initially, each clan had its separate meetings, and the president, secretary and an elected representative of all the clans constituted a central delegates meeting held on the last Saturday of each month. The General Assembly, comprising every member of all the clans is held in December each year with cultural displays and social activities. In 2002, a new concept was introduced, allowing individuals to formally register. Over 400 heads of households have registered.

The people coexist peacefully with their neighbours, and participate actively in the Niger Delta Solidarity Forum. The Forum, chaired by Prince Ime Inwang of Akwa-Ibom discusses and champions the aspirations of the six oil producing states in the South-South zone.

Jigawa State - Hadejia
History of Migration

The Hadejia-Jamaare River Basin, 170 kilometres from Kano, was a major location of Ijaw fishermen. We met children and adults swimming in the river. Some Ijaw fishermen, who had come from Ibi, were returning to Ibi in Taraba state.

The Ijaw people cannot survive in Kano and Jigawa States due mainly to the frequent religious riots in which they are major victims. Under such conditions, they migrate to Ibi town in Taraba State.

Borno State - Maiduguri and Lake Chad

History of Migration

Ijaw fishermen on Lake Chad have suffered from the effects of desert encroachment of the Nigerian portion of the lake and the recent handing over of thirty three villages to Cameroon. So they have moved to the villages of Darrak and Sigiri to fish alongside Cameroon fishermen. In most villages, the Jukun are the dominant fishermen.

Lake Chad-Baga-Doro

At Shagara village, by Lake Chad, over fifty Ijaw fishing families have been living since 1959.

At Biu town, the Ijaw are mainly military people serving in the multi-national force in the Lake Chad area. The number of Ijaw rose from 60 families to 150 families in 1983 when NYSC was introduced and many former Youth Corpers remained there after their service years.

Governance and Inter-Ethnic Relations

The Ijaw community, comprising Rivers and Bayelsa States hold regular monthly meetings at Railway Station, an approved place for all meetings by non-indigenes in Maiduguri. There is also a Women Wing of the community that is very active.

The Ijaw Community is part of Niger Delta Forum, of which Chief Barr. Mark is the Acting Chairman. The Forum is about to metamorphose into South South Peoples Assembly, Maiduguri Chapter, where SSPA's membership forms are being bought at ₦1,000. The Forum meets at Zuwako's Hotel every last Saturday of the month.

There is cordial relationship between the Ijaw and the indigenes and other southerners. The Community's Chairman, Barr. Mark, married an indigene, a fellow lawyer in Maiduguri, and has even become a Moslem.

Adamawa State - Numan, Jimeta and Yola

History of Migration

Ijaw settlers in Numan came in 1958, mainly to serve the Christian missionaries, and to fish and market *ogogoro*. The influx increased in the 1980s. Ijaw settlers live in the other neighbouring towns of Demsa, Guyuk, Mayo-Lope, Lafia Lamude, Tino, Borrong and Balefi. In Numan, they are predominantly at Ahmadu Bello Way riverside.

The total population of Ijaw in Numan and its environs is 1,000 families, mainly from Odi, Opokuma, Sagbama, Ekeremor, Nembe of Bayelsa State; Okpokunu, Okoloba and Bomadi of Delta State; and Kalabari, Bonny and Okrika of Rivers State.

Chief Coastman Okubuama once mooted the concept of renaming the Riverside as Ijaw Community Riverside, Numan. In reaction, the Moslem Bachama destroyed Ijaw properties, and moved there to literally displace the Ijaw. They have even given quit notice to the Ijaw at the Riverside on the excuse that the distilling of *ogogoro* is an illegal business. But the Ijaw are still distilling and marketing *ogogoro,* fishing, and carrying on petty trade, and professional practice.

Governance and Inter-Ethnic Relations

The Ijaw Progressive Union in Numan controls those in the environs, except Yola, Jimeta and Mubi. The Emir of Bachama Kingdom in 1986 requested every non-indigene community to send a representative to his Council. The Ijaw Progressive Union elected Coastman E. Okubuama as the Paramount Ruler of the Ijaw Community in Numan and accredited him to the Emir's Council. In the last Moslem riot, several properties of the Ijaw were destroyed. About 50 Ijaw victims took refuge in Chief Okubuama's residence. He complained to the Emir's Council. After lengthy processes, Numan LGA released ₦40,000 and three bags of maize for the victims.

The local authorities have classified *Ogogoro* as an illegal drink, causing premature death for the elders and anti-social behaviour among youth who indulge in it. They therefore banned it, and the *Ogogoro* Market Association went to court, and eventually obtained judgement, but the local people have refused to accept. From time to time the youth of Bachama Kingdom, in particular, vandalise distilled drums of *ogogoro*, and harass the business.

The Nigerian Inland Waterways Authority (NIWA) also intercepts boats conveying *ogogoro* from one village to another along the river, and fishermen. The Ijaw Progressive Community meets on every first Sunday of the month to protect the interests and rights of its members..

The Ijaw in Jimeta, Yola and Mubi
There is a large population of serving and retired military and paramilitary personnel in Yola and Jimeta. Others have settled. In recent times, large numbers of public servants with federal establishments and private organisations have also moved in. Of these the Ijaw population is 80 families (Rivers) and 30 families (Bayelsa) in Yola and Jimeta, and 8 families in Mubi, who are mainly civil servants.

Governance and Inter-Ethnic Relations
There was a Rivers and Bayelsa Ijaw Community organization holding regular meetings up to 2003. Since then, no regular organization has been established.

Taraba State -- Wukari and Ebi Wukari Town
History of Migration
The Ijaw migrated to Wukari in 1964, left during the Civil War, and returnd from 1972. They are predominantly in the Shishi-Katon Section, along Ibi Road, Wukari. *Ogogoro* is brought in from Bomadi in Delta State. The population is 20 families in Wukari and 6 families in Gindi Dorwa town, mainly from Amassoma, Peretorugbene, Ekeremor in Bayelsa State and Toru-Orua and Bomadi in Delta State.

Governance and Inter-Ethnic Relations
There are village-by-village community meetings, but no general Ijaw community meetings.

The Jukun are very friendly to the Ijaw and other non-indigenes protecting them during the ethnic wars with the Tiv of Benue State.

Ibi Town

Ibi town contains the largest Ijaw settlement in Taraba State. The people are involved in fishing and *Ogogoro* business. The Ijaw who left Shendam, Bagauda Lake, Tiga Dam, and Hadeja in Plateau, Kano and Jigawa States respectively have eventually settled at Ibi town. They fish alongside the Jukun, Isoko, Urhobo and people from Akwa Ibom state. At Wukari and Ibi, the Ijaw are mainly from: Amassoma, Ekeremor and Peretorugbene in Bayelsa State, and Bomadi, Okoloba, Burutu in Delta State.

Summary and Conclusion

The Ijaw in Northern Nigeria have concentrated wherever there are major rivers, lakes and vast farmlands where they practice fishing, commerce (distilling and marketing of the native dry gin, known as *Ogogoro*), and peasant farming. As Andah (1995:20) found, when earlier Ijaw settled, they invited their kindred to live with them for purposes of protection and safety. Thus, the Ijaw have spread from the first settlement in Lokoja in 1920 to over nine states in the north.

The Ijaw people were concentrated in the Middle Belt region, because they are accepted there more than in the Hausa-Fulani states in Northern Nigeria. In these Middle Belt states, the Ijaw community leaders are even resource persons to the Emirate Councils. This enhanced their internal government and socio-economic integration. The co-operation between the people of the Middle Belt and the Ijaw is traced to the period of the struggle for self-determination, demand for separate states and minority politics. Chief Harold Dappa-Biriye received more support at the London Constitutional Conference of 1957/58, from the minorities of the Middle Belt than from any other group (Etekpe *et al* 2004:17). The historical tie between the peoples of the Middle Belt and the Oil Rivers from the pre-colonial period was also observed by Aminu Kano (Abba, A, 2006:13-26).

Notwithstanding the denial of political rights, the Ijaw settlers have contributed to the socio-economic development of the North through inter-marriage, fishing, petty business, technical and professional services.

The test of maturity and survival of the Nigerian political process remains the viability of the institutional arrangements or structures to accommodate every Nigerian in every part of the country.

CHAPTER 29

THE IZON
IN WEST AND
CENTRAL AFRICA

Saviour Nathan A. Agoro, Charles Asuk,
S.T. Olali and Ambilly Etekpe

Introduction

This is an overview of the migration of the Ijaw out of Nigeria into the various countries in West and Central Africa. The pattern of Ijaw migration differed from country to country. Whereas the Anglophone countries served as transit settlements, the people preferred settling in large communities in Francophone countries.

The reason for this pattern of settlement is not easy to determine. But the greater motivating factor behind all movements out of Nigeria was economic. People moved because they wanted greener pastures. But not all the people who left the traditional home land wanted to be associated with the occupation of their birth, which in most cases, was fishing.

Here a marked difference was noticed between the Ijaw who settled in Central Africa and those who settled in West Africa. Whereas the immigrants to Central Africa adopted the fishing solely as a means of livelihood, those who migrated to West Africa, who were more of urban dwellers, opted for the civil service and other professional vocations.

The Ijaw in Central Africa were able to establish little communities along the shores of the Atlantic Ocean while their counterparts in West Africa learned to get integrated into the cosmopolitan areas. The evidence in the disparity in the adoption of fishing as an occupation by the Ijaw in Central and West Africa could be seen in the response of people interviewed in the course of this study. Of all the people interviewed in this study in Ghana, Sierra Leone and The Gambia, only one person was associated with fishing as an occupation, whereas all the people interviewed in Gabon and the Cameroon were actively involved in fishing.

The Ijaw in Ghana, Sierra Leone and The Gambia

It is not easy to determine when the first set of Ijaw settlers migrated out of the homeland and settled in countries in West and Central Africa. Though precise dates are difficult to determine for all the countries involved, yet it will be safe to say that the Ijaw settled in these countries many years before some of the countries gained independence.

Some Ijaw had settled in Ghana before the first world war. One of the informants, Joel Nathan Tubonimi, reported that his grandfather had settled in Ghana from where he was recruited to fight for Britain in the First World War. Other Ijaw people had settled in Ghana at this period. Though precise figures are not available, it is obvious that the middle of the 19th century could likely be the time the Ijaw migrated to Ghana.

The story of the arrival of the Ijaw in Sierra Leone appears a little bit more complicated. Some Ijaw may have really been part of the Creole community which settled in Freetown. But due to the thinness of their number many have been assimilated into the Igbo and Yoruba which were the dominant groups.

It is the practice that most Creoles in Sierra Leone have an Igbo or a Yoruba first name as well as an English surname. The origin of the practice is related to the fact that many of the freed slaves identified themselves with the two predominant groups. But recent investigations have proved that other people apart from the Igbo and Yoruba groups from other parts of Nigeria, were part of the original group of settlers who have now metamorphosed into the present Creole group. It is a known practice too that some Nigerians who migrated into Sierra Leone have had to adopt Creole as a group to identify with, and similarly have either adopted an Igbo or Yoruba first name as well as an English surname. This is true of the Ijaw in Sierra Leone. Over the years, even some who bore Ijaw names might have taken Yoruba and Igbo names along with English names to become part of the Creole community. This position is borne out of the present experience of some Ijaw people whom this study revealed have adopted Yoruba names for their children in order to belong to the Creole community in Freetown.

But, apart from the possible dating of the first set of Ijaw settlers to the era of the freed slaves, we could date their arrival in Sierra Leone to the colonial and post colonial era. Two sets of immigrants are discernible: namely, those who came to look for employment opportunities or were transferred by their companies to Sierra Leone and those who left home to school at Fourah Bay College and stayed back to work in Sierra Leone on graduation. The peaceful nature of the country in those days must have been very alluring. And fruitful labour in an economy where the competition may not have been as stiff as it was in Nigeria may have encouraged people to remain behind.

Migration of the Ijaw into The Gambia appears to be more recent than in the other two Anglophone countries. Until recently, there was no university in the country, unlike the experience of Sierra Leone where some people were attracted to the country because of Fourah Bay College. The earliest possible time of known migration of Ijaw into The Gambia appears to be about fifty years ago. That puts the precise time of migration to slightly before independence. The nature of migration was dictated by economic considerations. Investigations revealed that The Gambia has provided a base for migration into other countries like Senegal, Guinea, Guinea Bissau and even some of the countries on the Atlantic Ocean. Since it has been somewhat of a transition camp for the Ijaw who have travelled abroad, the Ijaw population in The Gambia appears recent. Following independence, some Ijaw people have had to come to The Gambia as diplomats within the Nigerian diplomatic corps.

The Ijaw in the diaspora have not always retained the traditional occupation, fishing. This trend is noticeable among them in Ghana, Sierra Leone and even in The Gambia. It may be because, since fishing is mostly done as a family occupation, not many families have migrated together to the new environment. In most cases, even though other family members had joined the first émigré in the new country, since the foundation had not been earlier established, it may not have been easy to build on it. Besides, the Ijaw who migrated out to the new environment were better educated, and therefore better equipped to face life in the modern dispensation than their forebears. Many moved to the new environment with technical and professional skills to sell. Others learned to trade. Many were prepared to cope with the new work force that the new independent countries needed. For instance, in Ghana many Ijaw worked as porters in the University of Ghana, Legon. Others were employed as cooks in the university. Some combined civil service jobs with petty trading as well as fishing on a small scale.

This present study has revealed that Ijaw have been gainfully employed in the armed forces as well as in the police in Ghana and Sierra Leone. Some have risen to very high ranks in both countries. They have worked in the civil service of the three countries in various departments. But many have been self employed in a gainful manner. There are Ijaw in various fields of human endeavour in the countries they live in the Diaspora. Some have worked in professional areas like mining and aeronautical engineering, banking and insurance, pharmacy and medicine. As for the self employed, some are in the restaurant business. Others have stationery stores, while some have supermarkets. Still others have established construction firms and are into building of estates and roads. In fact, the Ijaw have adapted themselves to the economic environment in the countries in which they find themselves in the diaspora.

The Ijaw in diaspora in the countries covered in this project are familiar with their traditional religion, but like most of their counterparts at home, have opted for Christianity as a religion. If in the distant past they carried on practices associated with the traditional religion, in the present dispensation there is no semblance of any of those practices. The influence of Christianity has become predominant in their lives. The case is worth mentioning of The Gambia where an Ijaw man has the largest single congregation of Pentecostal believers. In fact, both in the physical infrastructure as well as in number, the church ranks first in the city of Banjul. Apart from Pastor S.J. Aganaba, who is the Senior Pastor of the Amazing Grace Victory Centre of the Redeemed Christian Church of God, Banjul, Gambia, there is also Dr. Tonye Romeo who is also a pastor in the church. Dr. Tonye Romeo combines pastoral responsibilities with the practice of medicine. It is obvious that as it is in The Gambia, Ijaw Christians in other countries of the diaspora too are into evangelism and church planting thereby enhancing the spread of Christianity.

It is easy to determine the extent of the degree of the survival and status of Ijaw culture in the diaspora. Since culture is the sum total of a people's way of life, the Ijaw in the diaspora have maintained many aspects of their way of life irrespective of the countries in which they have found themselves. For instance, the Ijaw in Diaspora still have respect and regard for the Ijaw language. Many still give names to their children in their language. They teach the Ijaw language to their children. So the distance from home has not hindered the young ones from learning and mastering their mother tongue.

Apart from the issue of language, the Ijaw have always shown interest in the music and dances of the homeland. Prior to the period of the Kofi Busia regime in Ghana, Ijaw women in Ghana used to form several performance groups which choreographed dances. These they exhibited during festive periods, either at the end of the year, or at some special occasions. Besides, they used to have wrestling competitions among Ijaw who lived in several Ghanaian towns.

Chief Tubonimi instituted a cup for which Ijaw from different towns competed each year. The competition was usually in Accra. The wrestling competition involved a lot of fanfare. The dance procession, *ogele,* was usually very colourful. Wrestling teams from different towns wore different costumes. And they used assorted paraphernalia in adorning themselves for the occasion. They usually tied two bells at the back of the waist as they danced along the streets and around the wrestling arena. Some times they even wore masks to symbolize the prowess of the particular champion. Wrestlers bore titles derived from fishes, birds, reptiles or animals. Some wrestlers called themselves sharks, tiger, python, boar, eagle, crocodile, elephant or lion as the case may be. Traditional wrestling is one aspect of Ijaw culture which endeared the people to Ghanaians.

The Ijaw in diaspora still wear dresses associated with the Ijaw at home. Even the Ijaw who live in cosmopolitan cities like Accra, Freetown and Banjul usually identify themselves not only as Nigerians but would by their attire like to show off their Ijaw heritage. Apart from sports and dressing, the Ijaw in diaspora still prepare and eat foods that are associated with the Ijaw at home.

There is no discernible political organisation among the Ijaw in the diaspora. In the countries covered in this study, they are found as part of a Nigerian union, either holding one office or another. In this present dispensation in Sierra Leone they are part of the South-South Association of Nigerians, while at the same time belonging to the Nigerian Union. In the Gambia they belong to the newly formed Union of Rivers and Bayelsa States Indigenes. This union does not have any political connotation. It is more of a welfare organisation which is formed to over see the overall well-being of its members. The Ijaw in diaspora pay allegiance to the governments in power in the countries in which they reside and relate to Nigeria through the Embassy or High Commission.

The Ijaw in diaspora are well received by their various host-countries. They are properly integrated into each of these countries. But that does not mean that all the policies put in place by these countries have been beneficial to the well being of the Ijaw. Since such policies are always general in nature we cannot say that any particular policy has been targeted against the Ijaw in particular. Be that as it may, the Ijaw like other Nigerian groups abroad, have suffered from some form of discrimination in some of these countries. The most glaring example of an inimical policy that is worth mentioning is the Aliens' Complaint Order of the Kofi Busia regime in Ghana. Till today the ill effects of that foreign policy and the way it affected other nationals in Ghana and the Ijaw in particular is still the subject of discussion in some quarters. Not too long ago other nationals were schemed out of the transport business in The Gambia by government fiat. The Ijaw suffered the fate of other ethnic groups badly affected by that national policy which sought to protect national operators in the transport sub sector of the economy.

The acceptance of Ijaw in the host countries could be seen as good neighbourliness that the Ijaw enjoy with nationals. Besides, there are several instances of intermarriages between Ijaw and nationals in Ghana, Sierra Leone and also in The Gambia. Some Ijaw have become so assimilated into communities in the host-countries that, for some of them, the idea of a return to the Ijaw homeland, one day in the future, sounds very distant if not strange. When confronted with the proposition of how they would feel in the face of a forceful eviction from these countries, all the people interviewed in this study were very resentful of the possibility of being asked out of the countries at any point in time. Some imagined that the prospect of being evicted from the host-countries was the figment of one's imagination until they were confronted with the reality of the Ghanaian experience. They were also reminded by the not too distant expulsion of some Nigerians from Libya and the Cameroon. It is believed that some Ijaw who managed to stay within Ghana, during the expulsion of other nationals from the country, adopted Ghanaian nationality.

For those categories of people their integration and assimilation have now become total. Some Ijaw speak the mother tongues of the region of their sojourn with ease and dexterity. Because of the rate of the fluency in the local languages they could be mistaken for nationals, other things being equal. Besides, a number of them, apart from being married to nationals of those countries, have built homes and established firms and other forms of business engagements.

Lastly, we shall consider the contribution of the Ijaw to the countries they live in the diaspora. At the rudimentary level, they live as law-abiding citizens of those countries and conduct the business of everyday living. They pay their taxes and contribute their own quota individually towards the development of those economies. Some Ijaw worked in the civil service in some of the countries, and have risen to enviable ranks. Several opt for the police force as well as the armed forces. Others are in paramilitary organisations.

On the whole, both in the public and private sectors the Ijaw have contributed to the countries in which they live. In the health sector, Ijaw doctors, nurses and pharmacists have worked hard in contributing their own quota to the well being of their host countries. Dr. Tonye Romeo was the Consultant Gynaecologist/Obstetrician at the Victoria Royal Teaching Hospital, Banjul, in The Gambia. From The Gambia. he went to East Timor, following that country's independence from Indonesia, to help build their health-care delivery system. As mentioned earlier, there are Ijaw in various fields of human endeavour in the countries where they live. They have worked creditably and contributed to the economies of their host countries in arious professional areas. In this way they have contributed to the well-being of the countries where they live. Not only have they been able to enhance their own standard of living, for those of them who have not lost their bearing, they still make wholesome contributions to their families and communities. Some have sent money home to take care of family and community needs. In this way, though they are far from home their impact is still felt as they are seen to be working towards the overall enhancement of the standard of living of their families and communities.

The Ijaw in the Republic of Cote D'Ivoire

The history of the Ijaw in Cote d'Ivoire dates back to the mid 20th century. As is the case with Ijaw in some parts of the West African Coast, the Ijaw in Cote d'Ivoire did not evolve settled communities but rather migrated to Cote d'Ivoire, as individual families, who are albeit closely knit under an Ijaw Association and Descendants Union in Cote d'Ivoire.

The current Ijaw represent the second generation of Ijaw migrants, most of whom were born and bred in Cote d'Ivoire, whose parents were the original migrants. The earliest Ijaw to come to Cote d'Ivoire came primarily for economic reasons. The Ijaw migrants may be divided into two broad categories, namely, those engaged in private business ventures and those who work in corporate organisations to earn a living.

Significant amongst Ijaw who migrated to Cote d'Ivoire for commercial reasons were Messrs Benson Manawa Okpounga and Adams Abraham Amafah.

Mr. Benson Manawa Okpounga was born on the 1st of January, 1918. A native of Abari town in Delta State, he was a caterer by profession. He migrated to Cote d'Ivoire in the mid 1950s, where he set-up a business in which he sold fish and *ifenia* (cassava meal, *farina*), in large quantities, from which he made a fortune and gained prominence as a businessman of repute in Cote d'Ivoire.

Mr. Adams Abraham Amafah is also from Abari Town in Delta State. He too went to Cote d'Ivoire in the 1950s, and established the *ifenia* and fish trade.

Adams Abraham Amafah prepared his *ifenia* (cassava meal) in such a fine manner that made it delicious and attractive to a lot of customers.

Some Ijaw migrated to Cote d'Ivoire to take up employment with corporate organisations as wage earners. Significant amongst them are Yebrifador Denyor Daniel of Sagbama town, Bayelsa State, who worked in the Obuasi Gold Mines in Ghana before going on to Abidjan with an American for whom he worked; and Omonika Owerikere of Amassoma in Bayelsa State who worked as a chef for the Transcap Shipping Company from the 1940s.

The Republic of Liberia

The Ijaw of Nigeria have had long standing contacts with the Republic of Liberia before the 19th century. Oral testimonies given by Ijaw sons who have lived in Liberia since the early and mid 20th century reveal that many Ijaw men served as cooks and sailors on board European ships and ocean-going vessels in the 19th century. The 20th century represents the era in which people of Ijaw stock actually began to settle in Liberia individually.

The first type of settlers may be described as "chance-settlers", because they came to Liberia and settled there unintentionally. The second type are the commercial settlers who came to Liberia to trade or engage in other businesses. The third category of settlers are people of Ijaw parentage who are in Liberia because they were born there by settler parents; and the fourth were, professionals who came to Liberia to work for their respective organisations.

The earliest Ijaw men, known and attested to have migrated and settled in Liberia went to that country in which they eventually lived for so many years afterwards, by chance. For example, Sampson Richards Sambo in the 1920s and Jones Wariebi in the 1940s, arrived in Liberia on ships bound for the United Kingdom, and dropped in Liberia. Both own private businesses in Monrovia.

Besides the first category of Ijaw who settled in Liberia by chance, are individuals who went to, and settled in Liberia for economic reasons, or to make a living.

In addition to the Ijaw who settled in Liberia by chance, and for economic reasons, are Ijaw who live in Liberia because they were born there, being heirs of the other categories of Ijaw settlers. The story of this generation of Ijaw descendants in Liberia will thus constitute another reliable index to the nature of Ijaw livelihood through the years in Liberia.

Ijaw in the Republic of Benin

We were unable to locate Ijaw settlers in the main cities of Benin, and none among the local fishing settlements inhabited by Fon, Yoruba and Akan.

However, a local historian, Martine de Souza (2000:35) records a migration from the Niger Delta to Whydah in the 15th century. The leader of the migrants, Ahobo, is credited with setting up the worship of the royal python, *dangbe*, in Whydah, a deity also worshipped at Nembe in Bayelsa State, and known there as *adagba*.

The Ijaw in Gabon, Cameroon, and Equatorial Guinea

The Ijaw first arrived in Central Africa in 1920, to search for a more profitable fishing environment. The arrival of Chief Oki and his household in Tiko, Cameroon, in 1920 marked the beginning of the influx of the Ijaw into the Tiko area of Cameroon, which subsequently became the hub of Ijaw dispersal into several other parts of Central Africa.

When Oki left Kulama, his hometown in present day Bayelsa State, he did not have the intention of going up to Tiko, Cameroon. He journeyed to a village called Atabong in the Bakassi Peninsula through the Calabar River and settled there for sometime. From Atabong he proceeded to Cameroon and settled in a village called Big Kombo in the Tiko area in 1920. A second group of Ijaw led by one Chief Isaac from Lobia arrived in Big Kombo to join Chief Oki. According to Mr Matthew Abaka, "if Oki and other Ijaw people had arrived Cameroon and there was no river for the fishing occupation or if the river was not conducive for the Ijaw traditional fishing occupation they would not have settled. This would have prompted an onward journey".

Chief Oki's arrival and settlement in Cameroon coincided with the placement of Southern Cameroon under the trusteeship of Britain, Nigeria's former colonial master. The indirect rule system of British colonial administration extended to Southern Cameroon as part of Nigeria. A prominent feature of the indirect rule system was the introduction of Warrant Chiefs to collect taxes from the people and remit to the colonial government. As the trend of the time, many Ijaw chiefs, starting from Chief Oki, came to acquire this status and perform the functions of overseeing the administration of an area of jurisdiction, collection of taxes and remitting same to the government. Others who acquired a similar status like Chief Oki of Kulama, were Chief Isaac of Lobia, and Chief Salmon Frank of Ezetu. They collected taxes from the people under their jurisdiction, whether Ijaw or non-Ijaw, within the Tiko District. Chief Salmon Frank, continued in this respected position into the post-colonial period, retiring only in 1986.

The settlement of Chief Oki in Big Kombo, Tiko District of South-Western Cameroon and the news of his presumed wealth from the Ijaw traditional fishing occupation signalled and prompted another wave of migration of Ijaw into Tiko. With the continuous inflow of Ijaw, the settlement of Big Kombo expanded and the population became too much for the place. Consequently, many Ijaw began to move out in various directions in search of convenient fishing grounds. It was in the course of this continuous movement that a son of Chief Oki, Didi Oki, and his group, made up of his household and friends, got to Gabon, and settled at a place called Akaungwa.

During this early period of Ijaw settlement in Cameroon, when anyone of them died in any part of Cameroon, the burial and funeral rites were done at Big Kombo. It is now almost a deserted settlement with a handful of Ijaw settlers.

There is some controversy concerning the earliest migrations to and settlement of the Ijaw in Gabon. It is about the first group of Ijaw to arrive Gabon, the probable date of arrival, and the first settlement founded. The first version came from Chief Boy Soubaikebula, the village head of Paediatric village, Gabon and one of the earliest Ijaw arrivals (with an arrival date of 1964). According to him, he was among the first Ijaw men to arrive and settle in Gabon in a place called *Owendo office du Bois*. The first group of Ijaw immigrants arrived in the same year (1964), though others probably came a few months earlier. He mentioned one Isamou from Ekeni as the first Ijaw man to settle in Gabon.

Another group while agreeing that it was Isamou who first arrived and settled in Gabon, state that he came in 1963 and settled in Akaungwa where he met a Gabonese who helped groups secure a plot of land, where they erected a CMS church building. The evangelist in-charge of the church was one Mr Jonathan Fawari (Snr) whose son, Chief Jonathan Fawari (Jnr), is one of the two Ijaw chiefs recognized by the government of Gabon. They continued their stay in Akaungwa till 1972 when the government of Gabon decided to build a harbour at Akaungwa. This resulted in the evacuation of the Ijaw from Akaungwa and their subsequent resettlement in Grand village.

The version concerning Didi Oki is stronger in Cameroon. It contends that Didi Oki opened Gabon for the Ijaw, and that his arrival and settlement predates 1963. Albeit, it is very interesting to note that all the movement to and settlement in Gabon, Equatorial Guinea and beyond, originated in the Tiko axis of Cameroon.

Our investigation in Equatorial Guinea revealed a different experience from Gabon and Cameroon. While the Ijaw have quasi-permanent settlements in Cameroon and Gabon, there was nothing to show as proof of settlement by the Ijaw in Equatorial Guinea. Both indigenous and official policies did not encourage the settlement of the Ijaw, even on the coastal lines of Equatorial Guinea. There were a few Ijaw in Bata, the second major city after Malabo. The consequence of this scanty settlement of the Ijaw in Equatorial Guinea is the attendant lack of any significant impact on the economy of the country. Foreigners, Ijaw inclusive, were not allowed to engage in the fishing occupation and other numerous economic endeavours.

In Gabon, the Ijaw are found in the following settlements viz: Alenakiri, Petit village, Akournam, Paediatric, Sovingab, Nede, Monkah, Ikendje, Libi, Bananier, Cocobeach. Others are the settlers in the cities of Libreville and Port Gentile.

In Cameroon, the Ijaw are found in the following settlements: Youpwe, Takele, Dongo, Campo, Kombo Dibo, Biobio, Passi, Ebikoro, Angalabiri, Mantanamasari, Gwapwe, Younwe, Kombo Mukoko, Kombo Wenge, Bouma, Ngotti I, II, III, IV, V, Bigekiri, Pouka I, II, III, Watchman Kombo, Akara Kombo, Beescool, Tende, Mangi, Big Kombo, Indikile, Ebikiri Zion, Kou, Mamanda, Cap Cameroon, Gbaple, Akponla Kombo, Ebonge, Kalanga, Sanje, Mbebelekume, Bousamba, Kakablanga, Musoko, Ngani, Ebeka, Isaki, Matimba, Epawpaw, Kumba, Tiko, Douala, etc.

The data presented above does not include those settlements that have been deserted either in Cameroon or Gabon.

It is clear that we do not have much to talk about Equatorial Guinea vis-à-vis Ijaw settlements and their impact. However, there was a prominent Ijaw man, Pastor Joel, who has a church, Christ Assurance Church, with a mixed population of over one thousand worshippers in Malabo, the capital city of Equatorial Guinea.

The early period of Ijaw arrival and settlement in Gabon and Cameroon was a period of fleeting success when the physical and social environment presented a conducive and favourable milieu for the conduct of their traditional fishing occupation. Therefore many Ijaw were attracted to fishing in Cameroon and Gabon, causing some sort of population explosion of the Ijaw in these countries and their continuous stay till this day. However, at present there is a deterioration and degeneration of the social and economic environment that has affected the Ijaw and their traditional occupation adversely.

It was the Ijaw who introduced the native population of the Cameroon and Gabon to the art of fishing beyond the subsistence level. The arrival of the Ijaw brought large-scale fish production, which served both the commercial needs of the economy and domestic consumption. The Ijaw were seen as hardworking and determined fishermen who, in the face of intimidating social problems, succeeded in making a living. According to Chief Ishmael Boufaghe, the Ijaw produce the greater portion of fish available in the Gabonese markets.

In response to and recognition of the fish production ability of the Ijaw, the Food and Agricultural Organization (FAO), a United Nations agency decided to provide grants and financial assistance to the Ijaw to improve on the fish production activities. Unfortunately, these incentives did not get to the poor Ijaw fishermen but were embezzled by officials of the government of Gabon. According to N.S. Dauda, Consular Officer, Nigerian Embassy, Gabon,

> "the Ijaw people control the coastal lines of Gabon and contribute about 70% of the total fish production in Gabon. During the unfortunate incident of mass repatriation of Nigerians in 1992, Gabon witnessed what could be regarded as a great depression in her economy. There was acute shortage of fish supply in the markets and the entire population fell back on meat consumption, which was grossly inadequate and costly."

Consequently, there was a reconsideration of the repatriation order to the extent that the Ijaw who avoided or escaped the repatriation exercise were encouraged to stay back and continue fish production. When those who were repatriated learnt of the "pseudo-acceptance" of the Ijaw again, some of them returned to Gabon. However, the return of the Ijaw resulted in molestation and harassment, such as the introduction of several obnoxious polices aimed at reducing the Ijaw people to the status of Gabonese "subjects". From 1992 till this day, the Ijaw are confronted with severe social problems.

These policies were intended to prevent the Ijaw from reaping the benefits of their fishing occupation. For instance, those Ijaw who used to take their fish to the markets themselves were subjected to a system whereby the Gabonese would have to come to the Ijaw settlements, particularly those at the coast of the metropolis, to buy the fish from the Ijaw. Tied to the above policy is the system of using scale, with a fixed price, introduced by the Gabon government, to sell Ijaw fish. The adoption of this marketing approach enhanced the ability of the government of Gabon to obtain semi-accurate statistics of the quantity of fish that enters the market on a daily basis.

The Gabonese established a fishing industry in Libreville at the wharf to undertake storage, preservation and processing of the fish from the Ijaw fishermen. The arrival of the Ijaw, which occasioned the emergence of deep-sea and large-scale fishing activities, also prompted the introduction of mechanized fishing and trawlers for industrial fishing in Gabon. Gabonese were sent out to study the art of fishing. Fishing vessels were imported and manned by those Gabonese trained overseas. Bilateral relations were negotiated with related companies in China. The new fishing company in Gabon and one of the first in Central Africa was commissioned in October, 2005.

The Ijaw in the fishing industry compete favourably. With their knack for creative traditional ingenuity in the area of fish preservation, they have crafted simple but effective methods of fish preservation. The fish is dissected, and salt is poured on the dissected surface and all over the body. The fish is then put in the sun for a period of two or three days depending on the intensity of the sun. On getting dried, the fish becomes solid like stock-fish and would remain in that state until it is used.

According to Chief Boy Soubaikebula, who arrived in Gabon in 1964, "before the arrival of the Ijaw the Gabonese knew very little about fish. The Gabonese depended solely on meat . The Ilaje, who arrived earlier than the Ijaw, restricted themselves to the production of *bonga* fish". The Ijaw who practised deep-sea fishing would stay for days, between five and seven days at sea. At first they got their fishing gear from Nigeria until a South Korean, Kavakas, started the importation of outboard engines, nets and introduced the fabrication of small boats in Gabon.

In July 2002, the Ijaw, who settled on the coast of Gabon, were forcefully evacuated from their coastal fishing settlements, like Grand village, and Petit village, and asked to merge with the natives. This constituted another horrible experience for the Ijaw who are predominantly fishermen residing with their fishing tools at the coast. But the people and government of Gabon were unhappy with the establishment of independent Ijaw settlements on the coast line. Some Ijaw settling in far away coastal communities like Monkah, Libi, Nede and Akenzeh, with distances from Libreville ranging between 65 km to 82 km sent several delegations, including prominent chiefs like Chief Peter Okegbe to the Gabon authorities for a consideration of the evacuation order. They were then allowed to remain in those settlements. Later a Nigerian government delegation, led by former Head of State, General Yakubu Gowon (Rtd), was received by the Vice-President of Gabon, and seen as an attempt to please the Ijaw.

In the past, Ijaw settlers lived in their own houses in quasi-independent settlements, without anything like rent-payment. But now they have been forced to live in houses owned by Gabonese and are confronted with the issue of rent payment. Reduced to the status of refugees, many Ijaw sent their children to attend school at home.

To what extent have the Ijaw been integrated into Gabonese society and its social milieu? Ijaw culture is at great variance with the cultures of the Central African republics of Cameroon, Gabon and Equatorial Guinea though there may be some identifiable similarities. It is also important to note that though there are flourishing inter-cultural exchanges between the Ijaw settlers and the natives of these countries, there was generally a limit to these interactions. The plethora of inter-cultural interactions did not, in any way, lead to a compromise in the observance of the Ijaw cultural practices and their retentions in the diaspora.

First, the aquatic environment necessitated and favoured the continuity of the Ijaw traditional fishing occupation and other traditional cultural practices. Closely related to the traditional fishing occupation is the art of canoe-carving. This important aspect of the cultural practice of the Ijaw people attracted serious attention due to the fact that it provides the principal support to the fishing occupation. The Ijaw people take seriously the art of canoe-carving in Gabon and Cameroon. While Ijaw in Gabon operate the canoe-carving industry clandestinely due to the hostile social milieu, in Cameroon the Ijaw canoe-carvers operate with greater freedom.

In Gabon, the Ijaw are not allowed free access, even to purchase timber. The Ijaw therefore go into negotiation with the forest guards who take them into the heart of the forest where they pay a levy when the timber is cut down. The Ijaw canoe-carver then remains in the forest to complete the canoe-carving processes. In the alternative, the Ijaw canoe-carvers get the timber from the sea. Often, there are floating timbers, which would have fallen into the sea during the process of loading. In this case, the Ijaw fishermen, who have access to the floating timber, bring it to the shore for the canoe-carving process.

In Cameroon, canoe carving is a thriving industry, dominated by the Ijaw. It constitutes an important economic contribution by the Ijaw to the development of their host countries.

Furthermore, while the social milieu in Gabon did not permit Ijaw producers of gin to carry out their trade, those Ijaw in Cameroon introduced and dominated the production of gin, although they were sometimes harassed, and their products seized. They were required to pay different kinds of taxes or their products were destroyed by the *gendarmes*.

The Ijaw are deeply interested in the retention and observance of their culture. This is evident in their traditional dressing code; the continuous speaking of the Ijaw language, which constitutes the vehicle or means of culture transmission to the new generation; the periodic or occasional display of the *owuugiri* and *owubene* dances; the observance of Ijaw traditional funeral and marriage rites, and many more of their customs. Indeed, many Ijaw men and women, who died in Cameroon and Gabon, were given Ijaw traditional burial.

There is also an example of a complete traditional marriage contracted between an Ijaw woman and a Gabonese man at Cocobeach, Gabon. In this particular instance, all Ijaw traditional marriage rites were observed. However, there are many casual relationships between the Ijaw and members of their host countries. The result of these unrecognized inter-cultural relationships are children with dual citizenship who share heritage from both cultures.

In Gabon, there has been a growing reduction of the display and practice of certain Ijaw traditions. Prior to the July, 2002 inter-settlement evacuation, which resulted in the destruction of their principal settlements, the Ijaw had tended to have quasi-independent settlement status, as those settlements had

100% Ijaw settlers. They could therefore observe their customs and traditions fully. But the evacuation and destruction of their settlements and their forceful incorporation into the midst of Gabon natives reduced their observance of Ijaw cultural practices.

The commitment of the Ijaw to the Christian religious faith resulted in the proliferation of churches, headed by Ijaw settlers and the emergence among them of many pastors, evangelists, missionaries and other workers. In Cameroon, there are as many churches as there are Ijaw settlements, particularly the Cherubim and Seraphim order. There are also a handful of other orthodox and Pentecostal churches with important Ijaw personalities, some headed by Ijaw. For example, Chief Jonathan Fawari (Snr), one of the earliest Ijaw to arrive in Gabon, rose to become an eminent evangelist in the CMS, Barak Mission, Libreville. In recognition of his achievements and contributions to the development of the mission, at his death he was buried in a reserved cemetery, meant for important personalities in Gabon. His son, Chief Jonathan Fawari (Junior), has stepped into his shoes and is doing wonderfully well to the extent that he has been offered Gabonese citizenship several times, which he has turned down. There are people like Pastor Godwin Joseph Abaka, founder of Triumphant Assembly Mission, Gabon; Pastor Joel, founder of Christ Assurance Church, Malabo; Pastor Livinus, who has been shepherding the flock of God in the Cherubim and Seraphim group in Cameroon since 1952.

In spite of limited inter-cultural exchanges, many contacts have been made between the Ijaw and the hosts. For example, while the Ijaw introduced the hosts to the art of deep sea fishing, they on the other hand, were introduced to new dishes and meals like *bobolo, mutoka, piodo,* and *gbundo.*

An official policy of alienation as against integration has reinforced nostalgic feelings in the Ijaw. Thus those of the new diaspora have a strong sense of attachment to their homeland. For example, the Ijaw in Gabon, when threatened by the Ilaje due to the recent skirmish between the two ethnic groups back home in Nigeria, quickly sent messages home for Supreme *Egbesu* assistance before the intervention by the Nigerian embassy ended in the signing of an undertaking to keep the peace.

In Cameroon, Equatorial Guinea and Gabon, these countries harass the Ijaw through *carte de sejour* (resident permit) and the imposition of several fishing taxes and levies.They are also attacked at sea by the *gendarmes*. Sometimes, the Ijaw communities are attacked at night and their houses looted. The cost of the *carte de sejour* in Cameroon is between CFA 100,000 and CFA 130,000 for two years, with a renewal fee of CFA60, 000; in Equatorial Guinea it is CFA 500,000 for 6 months with a renewal fee of CFA 100,000; and in Gabon it is CFA 600,000 for two years with a renewal fee of CFA 120,000.

A few Ijaw have been given employment as casual workers in the oil-rich province of Ponte Gentile in Gabon outside their traditional fishing occupation. They have not found their way into the civil service of the host countries or the organized private sector, and official policies of these host countries prevent Ijaw participation in the political system. Political campaigns, in fact, are not extended to Ijaw settlements, and polling booths and centres are not provided in their settlements. Consequently, Nigerian embassies in these countries have cautioned the Ijaw and other Nigerians against involvement in the politics of these countries. Human rights violations assume a record high proportion in Cameroon, Equatorial Guinea and Gabon. Ijaw and other Nigerians are imprisoned and brutalized without justice. Often those imprisoned die within a short period of time, while in prison custody. The Ijaw suffer the worst of the harassment and brutalization experiences, because their settlements are in the creeks.

A notable element about the Ijaw in Cameroon, Equatorial Guinea and Gabon is the political organizational structure of their communities. In their settlements, they practice the same system of political organization as at home.

667

Accordingly, in almost all the Ijaw settlements, there are two chiefs, a head chief and an assistant, who administer them.

The trend in Gabon is a little different, while there are Head chiefs for the various settlements, there are two prominent chiefs whose jurisdictions cover the whole Ijaw settlements in Gabon. Currently, these are Chief Jonathan Fawari and Chief Peter Okegbe, both recognized by the government of Gabon and the Nigerian embassy in Libreville. as the official representatives of the Ijaw people in Gabon. There is also the Ijaw Welfare Association, recognized officially. They collectively administer justice, law and order among the Ijaw in Gabon.

The Ijaw in Congo Brazzaville

Ijaw settlements exist in Mossaka in the north and in Pointe Noire in the south in the Republic of Congo.

Mossaka is the main port of call on the Congo River. Several rivers flow into the Congo at this point, making Mossaka a cross-roads town in the Cuvette region. The town was founded in 1912 by Colombe, a Frenchman. Ijaw fishermen arrived in the early 1950s along with other settlers from the Benin Republic. They are reported to have introduced improved fishing techniques, and gradually took over control of the fishing industry, with the use of nylon nets and the art of smoking fish.

Ijaw settlers spread from Mossaka to found the fishing villages of Sangha, Likouala and Ndeko. The host government set up a fish drying company, Usine de Mokalou de Mossaka in the early 1960s but this was shut down in 1979, and the fishermen have reverted to smoking fish. The ten Ijaw fishermen we met there reported that due to political crises in the region, most of their kinsmen had moved to Pointe Noire in southern Congo.

Pointe Noire is the main seaport. Ijaw fishermen arrived from Gabon and the Benin Republic in the early 1940s and founded a fishing village now known as Base Agip. Bobby from Peretorugbene in Bayelsa state is Chairman of the Ijaw community. He is engaged in deep sea fishing with a tug boat.

According to Bobby, Ijaw fishermen numbered up to a hundred in the 1960s when Base Agip was known as Izon-Ama. It gradually became cosmopolitan, with local Vili, Gabonese, Senegalese, and Ghanaians. Chinese commercial fishermen now dominate the business, making small scale fishing unviable.

In sum, Ijaw fishermen influenced the fishing industry in the Republic of Congo from the early 1940s at Mbamou, Kouilou lagoon, Mandingo Kayes, Mossaka and Pointe Noire. In each of these areas they founded their own settlements. Because of changing conditions, they have largely abandoned this region, and only a small number of Ijaw now remain in Mossaka and Pointe Noire.

CHAPTER 30

THE ỊZỌN IN BRITAIN

Benaebi Benatari Oguoko
and
Eva Ogbozimo Amgbare

Introduction

This documentation of the Ijo in European diaspora has concentrated on the United Kingdom as the centre of Ijo settlement. We have tried to document the Ijo living in other parts of Western Europe, namely, France, Italy, Germany and the Netherlands, to a limited extent. The focus also has been on recent times.

It is most probable that Ijo persons arrived in Europe from the beginning of the 15th century as part of the trans-Atlantic slave trade. We do know that from the 1450's onward the Portuguese transported thousands of enslaved Africans from the coastal regions of West Africa into Spain, Portugal and Italy to work as servants and in the fields. We know from the published accounts of Equiano (1777) that Africans were living in England as slaves and free persons. And that the free Africans organised themselves under the name of 'The Sons of Africa' in order to fight for the abolition of the trans-Atlantic slave trade. Ijo individuals may have been among them, considering the fact that Equiano himself had come from the Lower Niger region of Nigeria, and the Niger Delta was a hotbed of slaving activity. The Niger Delta was known as the 'Slave Coast' and its rivers the 'Slave Rivers', on account of the number of slave captives taken from this region and sold into slavery. This is noted by Ijo traditional history, the white slave dealers being identified as *omoni-beke* .

Liverpool, London and Bristol were the foremost slave trading cities of Europe, and Britain between 1700 – 1800 AD being a leader in the trade. The slave traders dealt directly with the Niger Delta slave trading city states of Elem Kalabari, Nembe, Ibani (Bonny) and Wakirike (Okrika). Infighting between the sectional interests within and between the city states, and slave raiding criminal gangs terrorising neighbouring communities allowed for the captivity of Ijo persons who were then sold into slavery. There is documentary evidence that Niger Delta people were taken over to Europe during this period. Africans certainly lived in Europe as slaves and as freemen during the period 1600 to 1850 AD.

Ijo in the United Kingdom

British trading interests were instrumental to the colonisation of the Niger Delta in the 19th century (known by this time as 'The Oil Rivers'). The Oil Rivers Protectorate was eventually incorporated into the emerging Nigeria by the British government. Liverpool and Bristol were the foremost slave trading cities of Europe and the UK followed by London. Liverpool shipping interests were directly responsible for the colonisation of the Niger Delta. Because of the colonial experience, a number of Ijo ended up either visiting or settling permanently in the United Kingdom.

London

Documentary evidence of Ijo persons visiting and living in the United Kingdom makes reference to some of the royal family of Ibani (Grand Bonny) Ijo. We can mention the early exile of King Dappa Perekule (also known as Willam Pepple) to London. Dappa Perekule was forced into exile by combined British and Ibani interests. He stayed in England for five years (1856–1861) with his wife and several children. Three of King William Dappa Pepple's children, namely Oruigbi Dappa-ye Perekule (George Pepple), Onu Perekule (Henry Pepple), and Charles Perekule (Pepple),stayed in England for up to eight years receiving an English education.

There are other references to an overseas educated class in 19th century Grand Bonny (Ibani) and the other city states of Elem Kalabari, Okrika and Nembe. Many of these educated citizens schooled in England.

Coming up to the more recent period, Ijo persons visited the UK as a part of the colonial armies that fought in World War I and II. Ijo who were not military men arrived in London in the 1920's and 1930's. They came as sailors and stowaways. Originally, many of these young men lived in Lagos or Ghana, before making their way to Britain in search of an education and better living. Britain was the colonial mother country, the source of the western education that was necessary to become somebody in the new dispensation.

The foundation nationalist and journalist, Ernest Ikoli, stayed in London for a few years. Ernest Ikoli was an early member of the United Negro Improvement Association (UNIA) in Lagos, led worldwide by the late Honourable Marcus Mosiah Garvey. Ernest Ikoli later became the local Nigeria Organising Secretary (Lagos Division Secretary) of the UNIA in 1922, a founding member of the Nigeria Youth Movement, and one of the pioneer nationalists who campaigned and fought hard for Nigeria's independence. Other Ijo arrived in the UK as soldiers serving in the British colonial armies of World War I and II. At this time, the Ijo community in London was not formally organised.

Many more pioneers arrived as sailors and stowaways in the 1930's and 1940's. These became the pioneering organisers of Ijaw communities in London, Liverpool, Birmingham and Manchester. They were joined later by students, who came to study in the late 1950's, and early 1960's. Many of these students were either on scholarship by the then regional governments, or on private sponsorship by foundations or personal family support. Later, quite a few returned to Nigeria. But others stayed and settled in the UK to establish the Ijaw community of London, pioneered by founders of the Ijaw People's Association in 1948.

The early Ijo community in London evolved around the Ijaw People's Association (IPA), which was founded in 1948 by the enlightened efforts of a few ordinary Ijo men. The main impetus came from Mr Young Kpiaye (Founding President of the IPA). He was not an educated man in the academic sense, but he had a keen sense of Ijo cultural and political awareness. He felt the need for an organisation that could bring the individuals and their families under one community umbrella. Thus was born the Ijaw People's Association (IPA) of the United Kingdom & Ireland. He went around rallying and convincing the few Ijaw men living in London at the time, on the need for an Ijaw organisation that could act as a cultural and social welfare centre.

It all started in Bethnal Green, East London, in the house of James Ingobor. The original foundation members who had joined before 1957 include Messrs H A Ofiniama (1st Secretary of the IPA from 1948-1965), Lawrence Okorodudu (18 years as President and 7 years as Vice President), A Zitubo, M B Oguoko (Chairman 1964), J K Okoro (foundation Treasurer till 1967), Y Kpiaye (foundation President till 1967), Y K Mieboh, W Oloula, D Appiah, Stephen Okpokpo, M Kantel (foundation Vice President till 1969, who was to later move to Manchester), M Suwari, I Alagoa, M Abeki, P Kalabeke, L Enekeme, L E Okudu, P Norman, J Ingobor and C Ijebu. Others who joined in the 1960's onwards include a wide cross section of Ijo drawn from the different parts of Ijawland.

During the 1930's and 1940s, British industry was rapidly developing, due to the impetus of the world wars and their after effects. Young Ijo men found ready employment in heavy industry. The various occupations of the individuals who came to the UK at this time ranged from railway workers (engineers, examiners, labourers), factory workers and clerical staff. Many sought to improve their education by going to night school and college. Many of these early pioneers married from the local white community or went back to Nigeria to bring Ijo wives. Most of the children of these marriages have grown up and become adults and form what is now known as the British-born Ijo community in London.

In the late 1950's and early 60's young Ijo began coming to the UK either as students or young professionals seeking a better life. They formed the Western Ijaw Students Union and the Rivers State Students Union in the late 1960s. They were followed by young professionals who came in the 1980's and 1990's. Some of them worked in Nigeria High Commission before seeking citizenship or dual nationality. More young Ijo people continued to arrive in the UK for various economic, educational and social reasons, especially during the massive flight of educated professionals during the later stages of the Babangida and Abacha regimes in Nigeria. The latest group of Ijo arriving in the UK for study and professional opportunities are students doing masters programmes sent by the Bayelsa State government of Nigeria.

The Ijaw People's Association developed from a small membership of about ten initial foundation members when it was established in the late 1940's, to about seventy plus members by 1968. Many students who came from Nigeria in the late 1950s and early 1960s returned to Nigeria and became government officials, university lecturers and business executives. The 1960s and 1970s records of the Ijaw People's Association show a wide cross-section of Ijo residing in London.

The Ijaw People's Association is a social, cultural, political non-governmental organisation (NGO). It has functioned in this capacity since its foundation from the late 1940s. The organisation played host to the great Nigerian and Ijaw nationalist leader, Chief Harold Dappa Biriye, as chief representative of the Ijaw and Niger Delta people during the 1957 constitutional conference held in London. Elders of the IPA recall that the late Pa L Okorodudu was sent to meet him at Victoria Station. They then hosted him at 40 Grove Road, London E3 (Tower Hamlets, East London), where he briefed them on the conference discussions, mainly 'why the Ijos should rise and claim their rights and the general underdevelopment of the whole of Ijo land'. He urged the Ijo in London to sit up. He was again hosted by the IPA in the early 1990s, when he came back from Brazil (Rio de Janeiro) where he attended an environmental conference.

Records dated 1966/68 show that during the 12 day revolutionary uprising in the Niger Delta effected by the late Isaac Jasper Adaka Boro, the Ijaw People's Association took a special interest. The Niger Delta Development Board, the detention and trial of Boro and his two lieutenant associates, Samuel Owonaro and Nottingham Dick were all matters of special interest. The IPA also raised funds for donations towards the appeal funds set up for the legal defence and assistance of Isaac Adaka Boro, Samuel Owonaro and Nottingham Dick. When Isaac Boro died on the war front, the IPA took a special interest in his death and all Ijo sons and daughters who had died as a result of the Nigerian civil war. Members thus held a wake-keeping for the late Major Isaac Boro on 3rd August 1968, in honour of his contribution to the emancipation of the Ijaw.

The Ijaw People's Association has functioned fairly consistently through the years in keeping the Ijo community together. It renders help during the celebration of births, and marking of death, funerals, marriages and weddings; and provides immigration advice and legal and, educational assistance.

The Ijaw House at 18 Strahan Road was let out to mostly Ijo persons, mostly students, at reduced rent. Ijo persons who found themselves homeless for various reasons were given temporary accommodation at Ijaw House, until they got themselves back on their feet. The IPA organises yearly fundraising, social awareness, seminars and general celebration events. Its members have taken part in the organising of events such as Ogele IPA Award Night in honour of the journalist Ms Ibiba Don Pedro (CNN Journalist of the Year), Boro Day in London, and other events to the delight and satisfaction of its members and visiting Ijaw dignitaries from Nigeria.

From the late 1960s to the creation of the Old Rivers State, the Ijaw People's Association has had a persistent problem of a division within the Ijo community in London between the Eastern and Western Ijo, but throughout its existence the Western Ijo played a dominant role in the affairs of the organisation. This was not intentional. Although the Western Ijo had a tendency of identifying with the whole Ijo ethnic nation, some Eastern Ijo identified more with the Rivers State Union, and did not feel the need to be members of the IPA. Records show that several Ijo and Niger Delta organisations existed in the 1960's, but again the records show that they all recognised the IPA as the main foundation body. Thus the bulk of the membership of the Ijaw People's Association in the London area derive from present day Bayelsa, and Delta States, with a minority from Rivers, Ondo and Akwa-Ibom States. The leadership of the IPA duly recognising this, reached out on a permanent basis to all the Ijo community organisations based on town or clan affiliation, to get a broad consensus when important decisions or matters affecting the Ijo nation are discussed and action taken. This takes the form of holding All-Ijaw conferences or meetings. Furthermore the IPA tries to keep an up-to-date database on all Ijo community organisations operational in the UK.

The official address of the Ijaw People's Association is 18 Strahan Road, Bow, London E3 5BD, a property owned by the IPA since the 1950's. IPA is in the process of acquiring more properties in order to fulfil its social housing obligations to the younger Ijo community in London.

The IPA, as a community based association organises fund-raising events. These include Foundation Members party, the End of Year celebrations and the Boro Day event. Among these are the 1st and 2nd Izon Conference held on 24 August 1996 at Dulwich Town Hall, London UK. The main aims of that conference were

1.   To highlight some of the problems Ijo face in the UK, in Nigeria, and elsewhere in the world, to the awareness of the public.

2.   To educate Ijo children born in the UK and some adults on aspects of Ijo culture.

3.   To encourage dialogue in order to moderate opposing views.

Seminar papers discussed include the following:

1.   The importance of the Izon language to the Ijo people, presented by Prof Kay Williamson.

2.   The traditional marriage customs of the Ijo, presented by Flora Oki.

3.   Is the Izon language becoming extinct? presented by Dr M Narebor.

4.   Izons (Ijos) in contemporary Nigeria, presented by Chief E K Clark.

From the late 1960's to the present, many other Ijo (Izon) community organisations have sprung into being e.g.: the Rivers State Union, from 1968 after the creation of Rivers State, and the Western Ijaw Students Union. All of them complement the Ijaw People's Association, and indeed many of the IPA members are also members of these other community organisations. We have the Izon (Ijaw) Women's Association, Kalabari Central Organisation, Opobo People's Association, Buguma Community of the United Kingdom, Buguma Internal Affairs, Wakirike (Okirika) Community of Great Britain, Wakirike Union, The Bonny Indigenes Association, Kaiama Community UK, Agbere Community UK, Esanma Community UK, Kabowei Ogbo UK, Arogbo

Community UK, Opobo Community Association, Ogbia Community Association, Nembe Ibe, Nyemoni (Abonema) Improvement Society, Bonny Community Association. The Ijo are also members of the following State Unions: Bayelsa State Union, Delta State Union and Rivers State Union. In the 1990s the ladies formed the Izon Women Association.

The Ijo Community in London has close links with the Ijo community in the USA, mainly through the organisational networks of the Ijaw National Alliance of the Americas (INAA), The Council of Ijaw Associations Abroad (CIAA) and others.

Liverpool

Ijo have been living in Liverpool from the 1930's. Most of them came as sailors and stowaways just like their counterparts in London. By 1945 the Ijaw People's Union was founded, later named the Ijaw Cultural Union. Later settlers came as students or seamen and various professionals.

From the 1960s, the Ijaw Cultural Union (ICU) has developed close cultural affiliation with the Ijaw People's Association of London and other cultural organisations of Nigerian origin, including the National Union of Nigeria, Yoruba Social Club, Urhobo Progressive Union, Ibo National Union, Calabar Friendly Society & Ibibio State Union. The ICU also had official contact with the Area Officer of the Nigeria High Commission. Members of the ICU such as the late Pa Agoro, have been patrons of the Nigeria National Union. The ICU operated on the basis of self help and collective welfare of its members. It maintained formal links with the Ijaw People's Association based in London. From time to time, the Ijaw People's Association organises visits to Liverpool to socialise with the few remaining Ijo in Liverpool.

Members of the Ijo community of Liverpool have actively participated in the life of Liverpool. For example, Mr Kenny Ebuwei is an active member of the Liverpool Labour Party, and is a member of the Board of Governors of his local primary school. Many of the original members of the Ijaw Cultural Union (ICU) and Ijo community have passed away or returned to Nigeria on retirement. Their children and grandchildren continue to live in Liverpool and other parts of the UK as active professionals contributing to the economic growth of the United Kingdom.

Manchester

During the 1960s the Ijo of Manchester formed the Ijaw Welfare Association to cater for the welfare needs of the small Ijo community.

The Ijaw Welfare Association started to wind up when members either returned to Nigeria or moved to other parts of the UK. Those who remained and were joined by students from Nigeria closed down the organisation, and founded, along with other Nigerians, the Nigerian Student Union of Manchester. Mr David Kentebe was instrumental in this and was very active in the new union. This union later changed its name to the Nigerian Community Association of Manchester.

The early Ijaw Welfare Association was in constant communication and cooperation with the Ijaw People's Association of London. The organisation cooperated fully, along with other Ijo organisations in raising funds for aid during the Civil War. Members attended the various meetings and All Ijaw meetings organised by the Ijaw People's Association of London. Many Ijo returned to Nigeria, and the Ijo community of Liverpool dwindled to a very small group of elders and their adult children. Since the late 1990s, Manchester has again become a destination of opportunity for young Ijo to better their lives and get a higher education. Many Ijo who recently arrived from Nigeria have begun settling in Manchester to study and make a living.

Other Major Cities

Ijo have also settled in Birmingham and Bristol. Other isolated Ijo persons live in smaller towns, such as Leeds, Leicester and Reading to name a few. These are individuals usually highly skilled professionals, namely, nurses, medical doctors, scientists and bankers.

Ijo Community Gatherings

Ijo living in the United Kingdom have created avenues for networking and meeting on a formal or informal basis to socialise and address issues affecting the Ijo community in the UK and Nigeria.

The various organisations and individuals, especially in London, attend each other's events such as births, deaths and funerals, launchings, fund-raisers, end-of-year parties, naming ceremonies and weddings. Though predominantly Christian, most have a cultural respect for traditional spirituality and belief systems. They try to preserve the beneficial culture and customs of the Ijo as much as possible.

Ijo in the Rest of Europe

In mainland Europe the Ijo presence is fluid and very fluctuating because many move to the United Kingdom as the preferred country of residence. There is an Ijo community in Germany scattered in various cities. Quite a few in number, they have formed the Ijaw People's Association, based in Berlin, the Ijaw National Congress of Germany, and the Ijaw Institute for Strategic Studies (Ijaw ISS). There are a few Ijo living in France, but the community is not formally organised. In Holland a few Ijo in the major cities, again, are not organised into a community. Not much is known about the few Ijo persons or their families living in Italy. Recently, the Nigerian Ambassador to France was Ijo, Godfrey Perewari.

Contribution to Political Events in Nigeria

The Ijo community in the United Kingdom, along with their counterparts in the USA and Europe, have directly and indirectly contributed towards political events in Nigeria. There was correspondence between the IPA and the pioneer government of Rivers State, led by Diete Spiff, and with the Federal Military Government then headed by Col Yakubu Gowon. Petitions were written to the Federal Military Government and the Midwestern Government. Members of the Ijo community in London also went on demonstrations against the creation of Biafra, and in support of the Federal Military government unity effort. There were frequent briefings and exchange of information between the Ijaw People's Association and the Western Ijaw Community in Lagos on the war situation in Nigeria.

In the 1970s, the Ijaw People's Association set up a Special Committee for Ijaw Action at home. From the early 1990s, the Ijo community in London and Liverpool were in constant interaction with Ijo and Niger Delta organisations back in Nigeria. The IPA has been in direct contact with the Ijaw National Congress since its inception. The IPA communicated with the Movement for the Survival of the Ijaw Ethnic Nationality in the Niger Delta (MOSIEND) and other Niger Delta youth movements. When the Ijaw Youth Council was established, its founding president, Mr Felix Tuodolo, visited London and was hosted by the Ijaw community and the IPA. The Ijaw People's Association was also actively engaged in the rehabilitation of victims of various community conflicts through an Ijaw Relief Fund. It sent relief materials and financial help to the Arogbo community, the Ogbe-Ijo community, Kaiama and Odi.

The IPA has written letters and petitioned the British Government to put pressure on the Nigeria government concerning the Niger Delta.

Thus, the Ijo community, mainly through the organisational efforts of the Ijaw People's Association, has been consistent in articulating the opinions and aspirations of the Ijo in diaspora.

Internationalising the Niger Delta Struggle

The Ijo community in Europe and the United States of America have made efforts to internationalise the Niger Delta struggle. They have been doing this by organising Boro Days in the UK and US, holding seminars and workshops, and communicating the plight of Niger Delta people to the governments of Britain and the US through elected representatives in both countries. The Ijo community in Europe is in a unique position with access to world-class centres of learning, libraries, information systems and telecommunications. It also has access to international media and voluntary NGOs, concerned with global environmental and social justice issues. This Ijo community has sought ways to contribute to the socio-economic development of Ijawland.

Ijo Youth

From the beginning of the 1960s, Ijo students formed themselves into associations to cater for their own welfare. Examples are the Western Ijo Student Union and the Rivers State Student Union, which no longer exist. But Ijo youth born in the United Kingdom, or on student visas from Nigeria, continue to access higher education facilities in the UK, remaining very much aware of their culture.

Indeed, Ijo youth, born in the United Kingdom, are beginning to reconnect with their Ijo culture and traditions. The increase in exchange visits between Ijo visitors from Nigeria, UK community cultural events, the access to satellite television, and their own visits to their parents' country have all contributed to this cultural awareness. They now see themselves as being dual citizens of Ijo (Nigeria) and Britain.

The Future

Some members of this younger generation of Ijo in Europe have already begun exploring ways of working with the Niger Delta State governments and the central government. With more interaction, these young Ijo born in Europe, can contribute effectively to the overall development of Ijawland through formal and informal exchange visits, educational opportunities and work experience in the private and public sectors.

CHAPTER 31

THE ỊZỌN IN NORTH AMERICA: HISTORY, POLITICS AND IDENTITY

Nimi Wariboko and Martha Anderson

Introduction

In this chapter, we will attempt to provide an overview of the Ijo Diaspora in North America. The Ijo presence in North America has, at least, four hundred years behind it, and we do not aspire to provide a detailed history of the Ijo throughout this period; rather we will give the reader a quick sense of their long past and a descriptive analysis of their activities from the 1990s. Thus, this chapter is divided into two parts: Part one dwells on the history of early Ijo settlers in North America and Part two focuses on contemporary Ijo political activities. While this chapter looks at the long presence of the Ijo in the Americas it does not give the impression that we are writing about the continuous history of Ijo in the Americas in the last four hundred years in the sense of the story of Ijo slaves and their descendants. Here we are basically narrating the stories of two sets of Ijo settlers. One set came as slaves about four hundred years ago; the other came as immigrants only decades ago. The two stories —arguably should be separated—give us a rough picture of the Ijo Diaspora past and present.

In Part one of our study, we used basic historical research methods to generate the data and perspective on the Ijo presence in North America. For the second part, we used a broadly ethnographic approach, using a range of qualitative methods. Specifically, we used participant observation, document reviews (hard and electronic), interviews with Ijo and leaders of Ijo ethnic organizations. For selected association leaders, we combined in-depth interviews and questionnaire survey. In general, the scope of our ethnographic endeavor was limited as it was only meant to be a preliminary first step to a full-scale

683

ethnographic study of Ijo in the United States. Certainly, the findings and conclusions of this chapter will be strengthened if the scope of the ethnographic study is broadened. This notwithstanding, our findings are comparable to other studies on Nigerian immigrants in the United States.

History of Ijo in North America

The Ijo have a long history in North America. There is evidence that they began arriving in North American colonies nearly four hundred years ago as slaves. Because efforts to establish the ethnicities of Africans who were sold into slavery have proved to be nearly as controversial as estimates of their numbers (e.g. Inikori 1987; Kolapo 1999; Eltis 1995), this essay can only suggest when, where, and how many early Ijo settlers arrived in North America. It will also highlight ongoing research that promises to add further details.

Scholars have traditionally designated the "hinterland" as the source of the slaves exported from the "Calabar Coast," but have argued about the extent of this vague region and the ethnicities it encompasses. Accounts dating to the era when the trade flourished often simply list the human cargoes as "Heebos" or "Eboes," meaning Igbo. Although many African–American historians have accepted the Igbo designation at face value (Littlefield 1991; Chambers 1997, 2005), others, especially Africanists, have countered that traders, slave owners, and others applied the word liberally to people of varying ethnic origins (Northrup, 2000:14; Hall, 2005: 129). For instance, during the nineteenth century in Sierra Leone, Africans from the Kalabari region, who had been liberated from slave ships caught by the British naval blockade, were designated "Ibo" (Northrup 2000: 13).

Some even question the accuracy of the ethnic origins the slaves claimed for themselves. "Calabar" could connote either New Calabar (Elem Kalabari) or Old Calabar, or serve as an ethnic designation. Gwendolyn Hall (2005: 133) proposes that Caribbean slaves who described themselves as Kalabari or Karabali may have been employing a broad coastal designation rather than an ethnic one. Even slaves who self-identified as "Igbo" may not have been Igbo in the way that we now use the word. Notions of "Igbo" or "Ijo" as an ethno-linguistic identity have developed only recently: slaves often identified themselves as members of smaller communities or defined their ethnicity in contrast to Africans from different cultural backgrounds (Northrup 2000: 1-3, 8; Inikori 2002: 78; Hall 2005: 129, 135). As Nwokeji and Eltis (2002: 365-366) point out, this situation has parallels in Europe, where notions of nationhood only existed in Spain, Britain, and France at the time the slave trade began.

Studies of the Atlantic slave trade have tended to focus on the role the Ijo played as middlemen, and have largely ignored their participation as slaves. Some Ijo slaves may have passed through Itsekiri or Efik hands, but the Ijo, like some of their neighbors, punished individuals for committing certain crimes, including murder, by selling them into slavery; they also raided other Ijo villages for slaves (Ume 1980: 8). Oral histories record infighting between Kalabari villages during the sixteenth century, where the most disruptive community, Bile under their ruler Agbaniye Ejika, "got its slaves by sacking neighboring Delta villages, rather than by trades with the hinterland." (Chambers 1997: 78, 93 n. 22, quoting Robin Horton). Central and Western Ijo communities continued this pattern of raiding into the twentieth century, keeping some of their captives as slaves and sacrificing or selling others. Those sold at interior markets could eventually be passed to coastal middlemen: inland buyers who purchased a Brass slave at an Igbo community later sold him to overseas traders, and he eventually became an interpreter for an 1841 Niger expedition (Nwokeji 2000: 643 n. 5).

Although they are at odds in other respects, two scholars agree about the prevalence of Ijo slaves in the early years of the trade. According to Chambers, the slaves who left the Bight of Biafra before 1650 were mainly Ijo and coastal non-Ijo, obtained by the pattern of raiding nearby villages mentioned above (1997: 75, citing Alagoa 1992: 10-16; and Jones 1963:12-13). Northrup (2000:8) concurs that in the early seventeenth century, most of the slaves came from Ijo communities located within a fifty mile radius of Elem Kalabari, supplemented by "a few Igbo and Efik-speakers." Noting that the trade was very limited during this early period. Chambers estimates that Igbo slaves gradually increased to represent 80% of the overall numbers from this region. In contrast, Northrup—who finds Chambers' figures to be grossly inflated—stresses diversity. He notes that in 1805, an agent of the African Association at "Old Calabar" mentioned Ijo slaves as well as those from various Efik, Igbo, and Cameroonian groups. He adds that Koelle, a Church Missionary Society (CMS) missionary, included Ijo among the 100 languages spoken by liberated Africans who were resettled in Sierra Leone in the early nineteenth century (Northrup 2000: 10).

Determining how many Ijo slaves arrived in North America proves extremely difficult. Calculations based on the number of ships carrying slaves between Africa and North America are not only controversial, but also misleading, because they do not cover voyages organized by slave owners or the transshipment of slaves from the Caribbean (Hall 2005: 136). For example, if Ouladah Equiano's account of his origins is authentic, as Paul Lovejoy and other prominent scholars continue to believe, he left an Ijo port for the Caribbean, but spent only a brief time in Barbados before being transported to Virginia by a new owner (Brooks 2004).

Linguistic evidence from the Caribbean and Central America verifies that Ijo-speakers entered those regions as slaves, but comparable traces have not been found in continental North America, where Ijo slaves would have been more widely dispersed and intermingled with slaves of very different—and widely assorted—origins. To complicate matters further, North American masters paid less attention to the ethnicities of their slaves than their counterparts in the Caribbean and Brazil, and rarely recorded their African names. Consequently, historians typically have to work with fragmentary evidence scattered in legal, penal, church, and family records to get even a vague idea of slave ethnicities (Chambers 2005:3-4). According to Hall (2005: 131, 136), American documents do record Ijo slaves, but they, as well as their Ibibio and Ekoi counterparts, appear to account for only a small percentage of the total slave population.

During the first half of the eighteenth century, the majority of African slaves shipped from ports in the Bight of Biafra ended up in the Chesapeake region, which included parts of the English-speaking colonies of Maryland and Virginia. Once there, they mixed with smaller numbers of slaves from West, Central, and East Africa to create a Creolized culture. Chambers (2005: 10-11, 1997: 84-87) finds this culture to be "informed by 'Eboe' or Igboesque principles and paraphernalia," but Northrup (2000:2) finds this analysis to be "Igbocentric," noting that it rests on inflated estimates of the number of Igbo slaves, the survival of a handful of stray words and the "curious" argument that "previously isolated Igbo-speaking groups not only coalesced into a cultural nation in the Americas, but they also 'Igboized' Africans of other origins." Because slaves from the Bight of Biafra included those of Ijo as well as Efik and Igbo origin, early Ijo immigrants must have contributed their own beliefs and practices to this Creolized culture.

Detailed slave lists from 1770 and 1827 suggest that Ijo slaves also formed a small fraction of the slaves imported to the French-speaking colony of Louisiana. Probate inventories dating from 1770-1789 list 81 Igbo, who represented 78.6% of all identified Africans from the Bight of Biafra; the remainder included Efik, Ibibio (including Moko, an Ibibio group), and quite possibly, Ijo. Hall's chart of "Africans from the Bight of Biafra Sold Independently of Probate in Louisiana, 1790-1820," from the *Louisiana Slave Database*, lists 75 Igbo, 10 Ibibio/Moko, and 15 "Calabar" slaves (Hall 2005: 136-40). Although Hall does not specifically include the Ijo on this chart, they may have been mistakenly identified as Igbo or "Calabar." Furthermore, Hall (2005:107) notes that "Northwest Bantu Speakers," the category in which she places the Ijo, "increased sharply" in both proportions and numbers during the 19th century, after the prohibition against trading in slaves and its enforcement by the British had altered the pattern of trade; she adds that some of the slaves smuggled into the north coast of the Gulf of Mexico after 1819 may have come from the Bight of Biafra (Hall 2005:163).

687

A project spearheaded by Nwokeji and Eltis focuses on this period. It draws on records kept by international courts in Sierra Leone and Havana; these contain African names and personal information for approximately 67,000 Africans who were liberated from slaving vessels between 1819 and 1844. Nwokeji and Eltis (2002) provided written and spoken lists of names to African-based scholars, including E. J. Alagoa, Robin Horton, Kay Williamson, A. O. Timitimi, and Eldred Green (Nwokeji and Eltis (2002), Nwokeji personal communication 2006). According to Alagoa (personal communication 2006), members of the team identified a number of Ijo names on the lists. Once the results of this data are published, more will be known about the ethnicities of slaves during this period, and this information can be correlated with the ships' intended destinations.

It may be difficult to trace the early Ijo slaves who arrived in North America through forced immigration, but visitors to Florida can view the *Henrietta Marie*, the oldest slave ship ever excavated; this English-owned vessel may well have carried Ijo slaves, because it set sail from Bonny in late January of 1700 with 206 captives. When it landed in Jamaica in May, buyers would have paid about 3000 British pounds—netting the sellers a profit of more than 600% and the equivalent of about US $400,000 in today's currency—for the 190 slaves who survived the arduous journey known as the Middle Passage. After filling the ship's holds with American products like cotton and indigo, the crew set sail for home in June of the same year, but storms caused the ship to founder on a reef off Key West, Florida and all hands were lost. Nearly three centuries later, in 1972, a team of treasure hunters discovered the wreck, but moved on to look for ships with richer cargoes. Scientists, however, soon realized that the *Henrietta Marie* was rich in history, if not in gold and jewels. The shackles, weapons, tableware, and beads from the wreck, as well as an ivory tusk, serve as touching reminders of the ship's human cargo (Burnside and Robotham 1997: 172-75; Tinnie 1995).

Ijo in North America: Politics and Identity

Earlier we attempted to document the presence of Ijo in pre-twentieth century North America. They came in as captives, as commodities for exchange, and as properties of other human beings. In the twentieth century, mainly from the 1980s, they came in as free men and women. There are other marked differences between these two periods. In the first period, they were not expected to keep their Ijo identity, but to blend into the American society as property and distinction-less blacks. Beyond the issue of survival, their concern and hope were in freedom, personal freedom, but not self-determination for the whole Ijo homeland.

There are differences and similarities in their plight with regard to ethnic identity. The two groups have to contend with the issue of what ethnic identity to keep in a foreign land. The slaves were not given a chance to define what it would mean for them to be Ijo people in North America. But the immigrants are confronting these identity-formation questions. "Who is an Ijo person in the context of the diverse, multiracial society of the United States? Who is an Ijo person in America in the light of the homeland being threatened by political oppression and ecological disaster? Put differently, what does it mean to belong to "Ijo community" in North America? Ijo immigrants do not want to be just Africans, Nigerians or blacks in North America. In addition to identity issues, they are confronted with the ongoing Ijo struggle for political autonomy or control over their natural resources.

Ijo immigrants are grappling with the modalities of building and sustaining an Ijo identity in a foreign land, and how best to support the socio-political struggles of the Ijo in Nigeria. In their dealing with the twin issues of identity formation and political struggle, the immigrants are dealing with the same problems as their Ijo brothers and sisters in Nigeria. According to Kathryn Nwajiaku (2005), the ongoing demand for resource control among the Ijo in the Niger Delta has forged a strong link between ethnic identity formation and political struggle. Although Ijo ethnic identity has existed long before the current political struggle, the conflicts over resources control since 1998 have helped to promote the identity of the Ijo as they have galvanized disparate members around a common plight.

In this second part of our study we will explore two related ethical and political issues. These are Ijo identity formation in a foreign land and identification with the struggle for self-determination in the homeland. In a sense the issue of identity formation is an ethical issue for the Ijo—what is the implication for behavior in forging a pan-Ijo national identity in America? The issue of struggle for self-determination is obviously political—not only in the sense of political activism, but also in the old-fashioned sense of politics as seeking the common good of one's *polity*. We combine these two aspects of Ijo life in this essay because we consider them to be closely related. One can only answer the question "What am I to do?" or "what good can I do?" if one can answer the prior question, "Who am I and what community or narrative do I find myself a part?" The good to be done in any given historical juncture is not a free floating, context-less good. It is always the good as done for, appropriated, and interpreted in a specific community. Aristotle considered *ethics* as a branch of *politics*. In his *Nicomachean Ethics,* he argued that ethics is the *science* of the good and politics is the *science* of the highest or supreme good of the polity.

The analysis of Ijo politics in this study will be limited to a discourse of selected political organizations and the kinds of reflection their leaders bring to bear on Ijo social practices and activism in the United States. It was Paul Lehman (1998:85) who stated that "politics is activity, and reflection upon activity, which aims at and analyzes what it takes to make and to keep human life *human* in the world." Owing to space limitations, the "ethical" in this study is limited to the description of the identity-formation practices which aim to develop "virtuous citizens" for the Ijo *polis*.

There are four sections in this part of the chapter. In section one, we will describe the structure of the political organizations of the Ijo. Next, we will describe the activities of these bodies as they relate both to building an Ijo identity and also to supporting the Ijo struggle. We will also attempt to delineate the nature of the struggle as seen through the eyes of Ijo Diaspora. In section three, we describe how the Ijo define their self-identity through the concept of community. For it is in the *community* that an individual comes in sight and find him or herself involved in *politics*. We bring the chapter to a close with concluding comments.

Structure of Ijo Political Organizations

These are often political, welfare, and cultural organizations wrapped into one. They work to foster unity among their members, create a sense of community within their members, offer welfare assistance to one another, promote Ijo culture as well as advance Ijo interests in Nigeria and the world. These organizations are at four interrelated levels, with their names often grounded in ethnic or geographic origins. The hierarchical structure reflects the political structures in traditional Ijo ethnic group. First there are compound or ward associations like Ikiri Johnbull (Erekosima) War Canoe House Inc. of Ikiri family members of Buguma resident in the United States. Second, there are the town associations like Bonny Island Foundation that cater for the political, economic, and social interest of the town indigenes in the United States. These local associations are springing up as a result of the increase in immigrants from the Niger Delta. These associations were formed primarily for the development of the towns or villages of origin of the immigrants. They are like the town associations in Nigerian cities working to improve the physical and social development of their members' places of origin. In the past some scholars have seen the town associations in Nigerian cities as "villagization" of the cities. We are attempted to see the town associations as "ijonization" of the alien American social space.

Our research showed that the motivation of Ijo immigrants to help their places of origin is not only driven by the impulse to "develop" their homeland, but also by a sense of guilt. Immigrants feel the urge to do something for their homeland because they are burdened by thoughts that they have abandoned their brothers and sisters in quagmire of poverty while they are "enjoying" the riches of the American economy. One Ijo woman said: "Our people are dying and our culture will eventually disappear if we do not do something for our people back home." Another Ijo female, a pharmacologist and health policy expert, Dr. Anne Medinus, who helped to found the *African Community Health Initiatives* (ACHI) lamented the radically poor state of medical facilities in Ijo towns and villages. The ACHI is set up "to support and improve the health of sub-Saharan Africans living in Massachusetts by promoting access to quality,

691

culturally competent health and social services through education, research and community partnerships." She said: It is very unfortunate that our people drop dead for diseases that can be easily cured here. If I can find honest and reliable medical organizations in Port Harcourt and in the local communities I would love to do what I am doing for Africans here in Boston for my own people at home.

At the next level of the four-layer hierarchical structure, we have the ethnic associations, like Kalabari National Association, Igbani Awo Associations, Ibani Furo Awo, Wakrikese, Izon Ebi Association, and Andoni Forum USA. There is often more than one association claiming to cater for the interest of an ethnic group's members in the United States. The town and village associations are integrated under the ethnic associations. Also integrated under the ethnic associations are chapters that cater for ethnic members living in the same location or region in the continental United States. Yearly, during annual conventions, members are integrated into one body in a physical locale. Usually during late spring and in the summer months members travel hundreds of miles to meet in one place to deliberate on the affairs of the association in the past one year, set the agenda for the next, discuss the history and traditions of their people, and treat themselves to heavy doses of cultural displays and revivals. In 1995 for instance, the *Oki* masquerade and *Iria* were on display in Baltimore, Maryland. The masks used were hand-carved by Ijo members of the Rivers Forum under whose aegis the masquerade festival took place.

At the apex, we have several organizations that draw membership from all Ijaw ethnic groups. Here we have Ijaw National Alliance of the Americas (INAA), Ijaw National Congress, and Ijaw Foundation, just to name a few. One of the motivating factors at this level—and it is by no means the only one—is human emotion. There is a combination of raw human emotions of both fear and hope. Ijo are afraid. Ijo are hopeful. They are afraid that the Niger Delta, if the present level of ecological disaster and neglect continue, will become a desiccated husk; like the remains of a once juicy orange sucked dry and left out in the African sun. They are afraid that with the increasing political marginalization their culture, lifestyle, and human worth will count for nothing in Nigeria. Ijo are afraid that the powerful military machinery of the Nigerian government is determined to crush them into silence. With each military intervention and killing, their trust in the Nigerian polity collapses into fear, and distrust engenders new quests for control over their future. Yet the Ijo are also driven by hope. They are hopeful that their struggle will lead to the elevation of the quality of life in their homeland, if not outright political autonomy. They are driven by hope for equality with freedom. The Ijo are motivated by what they see in America: citizens developing their own communities and stridently advocating for their political, civil, and economic rights and succeeding at it. The current struggle is a promise, even if, more deeply; its value rests on its being the pathway to control over Ijo natural resources and being a claim on future human flourishing (*eudaemonia*) in the homeland. In the words of Dr. Ebipamone N. Nanakumo, the president of Ijaw Foundation:

> In my view, an Ijaw man or woman in North America is someone in forced total or partial exile from his or her beloved Ijaw homeland that is being oppressed, plundered and destroyed by neocolonial Nigerian and international powers. The Ijaw person in North America or elsewhere in the Diaspora is praying and seeking for the emancipation of the Ijaw homeland so that he or she could return home to enjoy the beauty, bounty and very rich and unique Ijaw cultural heritage in peace and prosperity (personal communication, August 2007).

It has not been possible for all the Ijo to come under one unified central political body and speak with one voice. Even at the apex level as we have described it there are multiple organizations, each focusing either on an issue or drawing its members from a portion of the continental North America. Take for instance INAA which was founded in 1995, it is actually a regional organization. It is based in and draws its membership from northeastern United States. On the other hand, Ijaw National Congress is based in southwest USA. Recently, an Ijo organization has emerged to pull other Ijo organizations under a central umbrella: it is the Ijaw Foundation. It is one organization that is articulating the conflict between the Ijo on one hand and the federal government of Nigeria and the oil companies on the other on a pan-Ijo nationalist platform. We shall discuss it further in the pages below.

The four levels of segmentation or hierarchy we have described are also observable among the Igbo, Yoruba, and other Nigerian groups in the United States (James Ogundele 2005; Dennis Cordell and Garcia y Griego, 2005). When the first set of immigrants arrived, they tended to see themselves as Africans and then Nigerians. Later ethnic associations started forming in the 1970s. The ward, compound or extended family associations started in the 1990s. Common Ijaw associations did not start until the mid-nineties in general. This emergence of pan-Ijo associations was brought about, among other things, by the agitation for better oil revenue derivation formula and consciousness raised by the ecological devastation of the Niger Delta, the brutalities of the Abacha military dictatorship, and resentment against what the Ijo in North America see as the marginalization and oppression of the Ijo in Nigeria.

Given the degree of fragmentation, the building of a common identity would involve weaving these various levels and types of identity into a coherent whole. It is, therefore, not surprising to find that Ijo political leaders in their organizations' websites and in their speeches emphasize the need for unity among all Ijo. For example, the official website of INAA states that "Our mission is to promote unity and encourage the economic and socio-cultural advancement of Ijaw people...." It went on to emphasize the importance of nurturing dedication to the Ijaw struggle "through dedication to one another as members of a family." The good intentions of the leaders not withstanding, dedication to the struggle appears to be weakened, if not undermined, by the process of segmentation and fragmentation mentioned above. Mr. Dawari LongJohn, the president of INAA, states that "people tend to focus more on the towns, weakening the larger ethnic and national groups. The problem with central organizations like the Ijaw Foundation or INAA is the weakness of its component organizations. We are so fragmented at various levels".

694

The present reality of fragmentation has raised the question of how best to structure the quest for Ijo self-determination here in the Americas. Three views have emerged on this issue. There is one school of thought that says each individual can pursue the common good of Ijo by pursuing excellence in his or her own affairs. Another argues that one strategy is to strengthen the ethnic groups so long as they are pursuing individual and collective flourishing based on a common vision. The point being made is that a strong pan-Ijo nationalist identity needs to be rooted in strong ethnic identities. Still others argue for a strong and powerful central body to quickly pursue and realize the common good of all the Ijo. Leaders like Dr. Ebipamone Nanakumo, Mr. Dawari LongJohn, Dr. Matthew Sikpi (general secretary of INAA), and Dr. Tonye Erekosima who are strong advocates of common pan-Ijo leadership paradigm realize that there is a problem of Ijo consciousness. There are persons in the Ijo community who are yet to have a strong Ijo-nationalistic consciousness, to think of themselves as Ijo. The issue is how can the ordinary person grasp the meaning of pan-Ijoness? He or she, perhaps, first needs to grasp the meaning before it can grab him or her. The leaders' apparent frustrations are not being helped by the fact that many of the immigrants have to first learn to be Kalabari, Ibani, or Nembe not to talk of Kalabari-Ijo, Ibani-Ijo or Nembe-Ijo before they can become Ijo. As shown by studies of other immigrants in America, some persons become "Irish" or "Italians" for the first time when they are outside their provinces. It was after this stage that they became "Irish-Americans" or "Italian-Americans." It took them time to shed provincial identities in order to garb national identities (Northrup 2006).

Beneath each of these three options (individual, group/hyphenated Ijo, and pan-Ijo) there is a lively ferment of intellectual inquiry, self-critiquing, ethnic differences, and racial tensions. Implicit in the first option is the whole issue of the Ijo person—discriminated and marginalized first as a black person and second as a third-world immigrant—being compelled to prove his or her worth in the Americas. People are just so engrossed in the art of personal economic survival and staying ahead of racist putdowns that sometimes there is hardly any energy left for ultra-individual struggle. Added to this is a concern about freedom of individual Ijo to dissent or diverge from what those advocating pan-Ijo nationalism present as common Ijo-interests. The undercurrent of the second option is the ethnic and clannish tensions brought from the homeland. The impatience with the first two options is rooted in the recognition that adherence to anything less than pan-Ijo national identity has tended to ignore the grave problems of oppression which threatens to sweep the livelihood and civilization of Ijo into irrelevance.

Indeed, given the manifest and subterranean arguments, it is not an easy task to classify Ijo members and their leaders as to where they consistently and faithfully stand. There is no idealist stance, but only pragmatic attachment to any of these positions. Most, if not all, display ambiguous attachment to any one of the three positions. Actually, their practices often diverge from their legitimizing discourses and rhetoric. For example, those who promote the idea of membership in pan-Ijo group also actively participate in their compound, town, and ethnic associations. In fact, leadership in ethnic associations provides a stepping stone to offices in pan-Ijo groups. Those who express the individualist views also find good reasons to participate in ethnic association meetings and annual conventions of umbrella pan-Ijo organizations. The reasons often given are the need to introduce their children to Ijo culture and to meet with old friends from home. Kathryn Nwajiaku (2005: 491) who conducted a micro study of Ijo in Bayelsa state in 2002 also observed the ambiguity of attachment:

> Many of those engaged in the protests can be seen to display an ambiguous attachment to the idea of belonging to a pan-Ijaw group, preferring to reserve benefits of protest to oil producers, and when push comes to shove, to members of their village, and when really under pressure to members of their "community," family and so on.

Let us provide another perspective on these debates. Indeed, the various perspectives are not really irreconcilable if they are viewed from the deeper Ijo worldview that undergirds them. Rather than being seen as incompatibles, they should be viewed as tensions "promising resolution of outstanding differences as the ultimate state of affairs between them," to borrow a phraseology of Lehman (1998:251). Ultimately, the "individualistic" approach is not in conflict with that of the group, and both the group and individualist stances are not in any deep conflict with the pan-Ijo position. Indeed, the paramount goal of the traditional community is not just concerned with community well-being. The concern for the community's or group's well-being is simultaneously a concern for what the individual person *can do* and *can be* if such a person is not limited. There is the belief that every individual has been endowed by God with certain gift to bless his or her community, and the community needs to help the individual to fully realize this potential.

Even without looking deeper to highlight commonalities in the various positions, we could have discerned efforts underfoot to turn the fragmentation and segmentation process into a potent force for good. There is an ongoing debate on how to shape this process for the common good. The political and philosophical matter being addressed by the leaders is how to generate an ascending love of the compound, town, and ethnic groups for the pan-Ijo collectivity and how can the love of the higher express itself in care and love for the lower? As Dawari LongJohn stated, "you have to give something for persons to identify with and also ensure that there are material and emotional benefits from the object of identification. We pay visits to Ijos during bereavement and other life-changing events."

In section three, we will attempt to connect these debates to the issue of identity formation. In the interim let us focus attention on practical social, cultural, and political activities of Ijo organizations. For they provide *sites* for working out issues about political strategy and identity formation. It is within this kind of perspective that co-joins the search for personal identity and the identification with the political struggles of the homeland we will give an account of the activities of the Ijo. We will gaze at both directions at the same time or at least in rapid succession.

Socio-Political Activities

There are as many activities in Ijo political life as there are reflections on activities. Since the struggle is relatively new in the Americas and the dynamics are very fluid, praxis goes pari-passu with reflection on it. There are activities and activism and there are reflections on how to organize, reorganize, and position them for effectiveness. There appears to be no template and the leaders and their followers are inventing theoretical and practical paradigms as they go along. It is a running conversation between practice and theory, history and present, tradition and novelty.

It thus appears that a majority of the Ijo organizations in North America are Janus-faced. They invite and encourage their members to adopt the double vision of looking both to the past and to the future. They look to the past to recognize heroes and heroines and to the future for political liberation. They teach themselves about their past and present heroes, the culture and history of the homeland, as well as learning to draw lessons from the past to guide today's struggle. We see this penchant for amalgamating the past and present in the activities of INAA. This association came up with the Boro Day concept in 1998.14 It built on the activities, energy, and tradition of Isaac Jasper Adaka Boro's (1938-1968) friends and colleagues who were gathering every May to honor the memory of Boro and all that he and they fought for. The first five celebrations of Boro Day were done in Kaiama (1998 and 1999) and Yenagoa (2000-2002) in Nigeria and from 2003 it shifted to New Jersey, United States. It is now being celebrated in Britain as well. According to Dawari LongJohn, "to call it Boro Day was to build on those who were gathering in Kaiama to remember Boro at that time. We were looking for something that was symbolic that all Ijos can identify with. It is not intended to worship Boro, but only to say we need to acknowledge, recognize, and remember our heroes and to get Ijos to focus on themselves." The concept of Boro Day has been adopted by the government of Bayelsa state. In 2000, the then governor of the State, Dr. Diepreye S. P. Alamieyeseigha announced the Boro Foundation.

During the Boro Day celebrations in the United States, the annual "service and devotion" awards are given to "well-deserving Ijaws who serve Nigeria and humanity and have by that become ambassadors of Ijaws to the world." Past recipients of the INAA service and devotion award are Isaac Boro (1998), "Victims of the Crisis in Ijo land" (1999), Chief Alfred Diete-Spiff (2000), Brigadier-General George Kurubo (2003), Chief Edwin Clark (2004), Chief Joshua Fumudoh (2005), Chief Melford Okilo (2006), and Chief (Captain) Samuel Owonaro (2007). During these occasions there are masquerade displays and dancing, drinking, and eating to Ijo music. Members come out to these events in gorgeous traditional outfits, celebrating life, and renewing the élan vital for the struggle as well as old friendships.

The first Boro Day celebration in the United States in 2003 led to the establishment of the Ijaw Foundation. The Foundation with headquarters in Brooklyn, New York City, started as a platform to forge a common response to the oil-exploration induced ecological crisis in the Niger Delta. It describes itself as a "collaborative project of the Ijaws and Ijaw organizations in the Diaspora," and states its mission thus:

> Ijaws in the Diaspora hereby establish Ijaw Foundation to raise the much-needed Funds for the dire humanitarian needs of the fourteen (14) million Ijaw people of the Niger Delta region of Nigeria, who are amongst the world's most impoverished peoples despite their abundant God-given wealth of natural gas, crude oil, marine resources and forestry resources; and provide funding for projects that will protect, restore and preserve the Ijaw habitat that has been severely devastated and rendered barren by exploration for natural gas and crude oil."

Today, the Ijaw Foundation has moved into a platform for collective political and environment actions and has emerged as the umbrella voluntary organization for all Ijo (individuals, ethnic group associations, social clubs, and even pan-Ijo groups). The following America-based Ijo organizations are participating members of the Ijaw Foundation: Bayelsa State Associations (USA); Ibani Furo Awo; Igbani Awo Association, Inc. Kalabari National Association, Inc.; Wakirikese (USA); Ijaw International Alliance (Dallas,

Texas, USA); Ijaws of Northern California (USA); Izon Association of Southern California (USA); Ijaw United Fund (Texas, USA); Ijaw National Alliance of the Americas (INAA); Ijaw National Congress, North America (INCNA); Andoni Forum USA; Ijaw Women Association, Texas USA, Minnesota Ijaw Community Organization, USA, Ogele Club, Ijaw Institute of Strategic Studies (IJAWISS), Sons and Daughters of Buguma, Abonnema Foundation, and Izon Council for Human Rights.

According to the president of Ijaw Foundation, Dr. Ebipamone Nanakumo, one of the highlights of the struggle is the formation of the Foundation.

> It has been able to bring many disparate organizations together to pull resources and talents for the struggle here in the United States and in the United Kingdom. The Ijaw Foundation has waxed strong to be the platform for collective action by all Ijaws and Ijaw organizations in the Diaspora and the Ijaw homeland. Virtually all Ijaw organizations in the United States, United Kingdom, and Europe are member organizations of Ijaw Foundation" (personal communications, August 2007)

Further, Nanakumo pointed out that the transatlantic cooperation under the aegis of the Foundation led to the crafting and the adoption of the "Ijaw Agenda for Self-Government" during the 2006 Boro Day Celebration in New Jersey. During a teleconference on April 21, 2007 that drew participants from the United States, United Kingdom, and Nigeria the *Agenda* was inaugurated and commissioned. Also on that day four committees were set to pursue the implementation of the self-government agenda. One of the committees is working to formally present the *Agenda* to the United Nations; another is hard at work in seeking the endorsement and ratification of the *Agenda* by all Ijo communities in Nigeria.

The *Agenda* which came out before the new civilian Yar'Adua-Goodluck federal administration came to power used very strong language to express the call for self-government. For the sake of clarity, let us quote some of the statements:

Nigeria's proven intent to exterminate us is an absolute contraindication for us to continue to be part of Nigeria! It is a very strong warning for us to part ways with Nigeria before it is too late. By its ungrateful and evil actions against the Ijaws, Nigeria has made its separation with Ijaws inevitable.

The Ijaw Nation refuses to be part of a country whereby it is oppressed and marginalized by opportunists; whereby its development aspirations are subverted; whereby its resources are plundered; whereby its habitat is recklessly destroyed, and whereby its very survival is seriously threatened by ecocide and genocide....

Separation has become inevitable to eliminate oppression, suffering, animosity, and violence so that we can forge a new relationship based on love."

The strong language of the Agenda does not translate into a call for any forceful disengagement from the Nigerian polity. On page 9 under the section, "The Ijaws Want Peace," it states that "we the Ijaws...[are] engaged in a noble and heroic Struggle for Peace by protesting against this horrendous violence and terror that have robbed us of our peace." In the next page, it also states, "we want a peaceful disengagement. We urge our fellow Nigerians and the Nigerian government to support our peaceful agenda for self-government." It then calls on the United Nations "to establish a United Nations Committee for Self-determination for the Ijaws to: (a) mediate our negotiations with the Nigerian State for our peaceful separation from Nigeria; (b) provide us with the technical assistance to conduct our Referendum on Self-government; (c) oversee our transition to self-rule."

While there is some consensus on defining the struggle, there is yet no consensus on the possible ultimate goal of the struggle or even on how to proceed with the agenda for self-government. There is a serious reflection and discussion going on Ijo political activism. The conversations, according to Dr. Tonye Erekosima, have pointed up three principal foci of strategies, despite the common predicament. There is the view that the Ijo should work with the

701

Federal government to achieve Ijo goals gradually, believing that the Nigerian government can help the Ijo. There is the argument that the Ijo should demand to pull out of Nigeria immediately in order to attain autonomy and nationhood. The third group views any of these stances as flawed. Those in this group consider persons holding the first position as corrupt individuals looking for avenues to enrich their pockets. They also argue that there is not enough leverage to survive any retaliatory measures from the federal government if the second option is adopted. Their position is that the Ijo should work to set up the modalities for true federalism that will give maximum autonomy to the Ijo. According to Dr. Nanakumo, president of Ijaw Foundation:

> The overwhelming majority of Ijaws would agree to remain in Nigeria if Nigeria gives the Ijaws their self-governing geopolitical unit along with the power and responsibility to control the exploitation and management of their God-given resources and habitat. However, the Ijaws do not have any rights or power under the Nigerian system to obtain this concession that requires approval by up to two-thirds of the entire Nigerian political/electoral constituencies and/or National Assembly! (personal communication, August 2007)

A close reading and deconstruction of Ijaw Foundation's recent press releases revealed these tensions and internal debates about the struggle. All three positions seem to be reflected or alluded to in its public statements. Consider its press release of June 18, 2007, applauding the Nigerian federal government for the release of Muhajid Dokubo-Asari from detention. On page 2 of the release it calls for self-government:

> Dokubo-Asari's release is an important step in the right direction to resolve the Niger Delta Crisis. However, it cannot be over-emphasized that the only just and effective solution to the Niger Delta crisis is the granting of political autonomy of the Niger Delta people to enable them have control and responsibility for the exploitation of their natural resources, including oil and gas, as well as the protection of the Niger Delta habitat on which they depend for their survival.

Reflecting the position of those who argue that immediate pull-out will be disastrous for the Ijo, the June 18 press release calls for an immediate "sovereign national conference to restructure Nigeria to give political autonomy to every ethnic nationality with a view to enthroning true federalism." The writers of the press release later went on to take a swipe at Ijaw activists whose form of activism threatens their conception of the nature and purpose of the struggle. The June 18 press release added that:

> Ijaw Foundation takes this opportunity to request all our Ijaw Rights Activists in our creeks to follow the exemplary footsteps of Isaac Jasper Adaka Boro and Dokubo-Asari to uphold the Ijaw Heritage of Righteousness by acting with utmost integrity and refraining from any acts that will bring dishonor to the Ijaw Nation and the noble Ijaw struggle for Self Determination, socio-economic justice, environmental protection and survival. Furthermore Ijaw Foundation calls on our Ijaw Rights activists to eschew self-destructive factionalism and work together in indestructible solidarity and sincerity of purpose to actualize the ultimate goal of the noble Ijaw Struggle."

From the public statements and interviews with the Ijo leaders in the United States, we are able to tentatively decipher that emerging core solution appears not to be "separation" from Nigeria but some reconfiguration of Nigeria's federal system to give each of its ethnic nationalities or geographical units the control and management of its respective natural resources.

According to Dr. Erekosima, there is now emerging a fledging fourth focus of strategies, with aims which transcend the limitations of each of the three options as well as become immanent in their individual and collective strengths. He argues that this fourth perspective, which he calls the "integrative-organic approach," comes from a critical study of the civil rights movement in America. He elaborates extensively and it bears to quote him at length here:

> Each of these groups has a valid place within the agenda for self-determination. The extremists, those who have given up

703

on Nigeria, have a place but I am not part of them. There is a lesson to be learned from the American civil right movement. Had it not been for Malcolm X, the Black Panther movement, and the Black Muslims espousing violence the whites would have not done anything. The whites before then were only thinking of integration of select blacks into white structures. But for those extremists in the creeks who have shed their blood no one would have listened to us today or recognize us.

Martin Luther King, the nonviolence wing of black struggle generated public energy and commitment to civil rights. Thurgood Marshall and other legal luminaries translated the energies generated by Luther and Malcolm into law and legal instruments of the U.S. constitution. There were three streams that flowed into the ocean of liberation. And this is how we have to recognize the nature of the Ijo struggle—this is the way we have to see what is going on in Ijo land.

All three agree on the same goal: the liberation of Ijo people. So there is unity of purpose among them. The amalgamation of the current three approaches, each having its due place, and the movement of these three toward the final outcome is the way forward. It is not an either-or situation. We need to recognize and give place of value to each of the approaches. We need the three parallel lines of activism to flow together (personal communication, August 2007).

The political activism and the intellectual debates which are defining the nature, meaning, and strategies of the struggle are the manifest, formal part of the Ijo efforts at self-determination. There is a layer that is not so obvious, but is aimed at the same good of the *polis*. There is an undercurrent of the ceremonial and mundane that supports the manifest mission. Dr. Matthew Sikpi, the current general secretary and past president of INAA described his organization as not only political, but also cultural. According to him, the

INAA's flagship event, the annual Boro-Day celebration, is designed to bring the political and cultural dimensions of the struggle together.

> One of INAA's goals of the annual Boro-Day Celebration is to promote Ijaw culture. Therefore, Ijaw cultural dance and masquerade displays are major components of the celebration each year. Besides Americans and other nationalities, it is important that our children born in the United States (Ijaw-Americans) know about our culture. Therefore, we expose our children to the Ijaw culture during the Boro-Day (personal communication, August 2007).

The ceremonial aspect of Ijo culture has remained intact in two major ways, despite decades of sojourn in America for some of the Ijo. First, they have retained the symbolic cultural instruments of dress, music, masquerade, food, and dance to reinforce both their identity and the energy for the struggle. Second, they mark life transition situations like birth, graduation, wedding, and death. Listen to Erekosima: "We are supposed to be evolving into African-Americans, but it is not really happening. We have been here for 20-30 years and we are still dressing in our traditional clothes. A lot of people are getting Americanized, but we are doing a different kind of Americanization by retaining our identity at the cultural levels."

Becoming Ijo in the United States

The debates about political strategy reported in the previous sections overlay much more crucial debate about what it means to be an Ijo person in the United States. What does it mean to participate in Ijo community? The thinking is that if only they knew what it means to be an Ijo person in the United States or for that matter in a far-away foreign land, it would be easier to reach a consensus on political strategy. Undergirding this concern is an age-old question about the relationship between one's conception of human nature and one's political philosophy. But those in the midst of a struggle for self-determination like the Ijo leaders in the United States do not often have the time to sort out philosophical quandaries or treat matters sequentially. Ideas and issues are best worked out in praxis and attendant questions are worked on simultaneously. So while debates and thinking are going on about political strategy what it means to be Ijo in the United States is also being defined and contested.

In the midst of the struggle for self-determination, it is no longer enough to be born or culturally raised as Ijo in Nigeria to be Ijo in the United States. The Ijo in America is not one who is simply here in the United States. In the opinion of one of Ijo leaders, "the Ijaw person in North America or elsewhere in the Diaspora is praying and seeking for the emancipation of the Ijaw homeland so that he or she could return home to enjoy the beauty, bounty and very rich and unique Ijaw cultural heritage in peace and prosperity." Both the "prayer" and "seeking" parts of the Ijo involves communal efforts. In 2004, Ijo Christians in New York invited their fellow believers to pray for God's intervention in the Niger Delta crisis. There is also a branch of the Nigeria-originated Izon Prayer Network in the United States. This Christian group believes that the Niger Delta crisis is also a spiritual one and unless the spiritual aspect is dealt with the crisis will not be solved.

As we have already seen with other thoughts about strategy and solution to the crisis, there is also a searching inquiry about how to appropriate the spiritual to the Ijo cause or forge socio-spiritual framework for generation of solutions. Dr. Erekosima who is also a Christian minister maintains the "spiritual" is not only about praying to divinity, but also releasing the creative energies of the Ijo people to solve their own problems. He argues that "we need to get ourselves out of a mental block and generate an ideology of vision that is translatable into practical programs. We have to start recognizing the need to start from a different worldview. We have been so captivated by western worldview that we remain dwarfed and unable to use our creative energies for our development" (personal communication, August 2007).

The "seeking" also involves creating networks of members for support and pulling together of resources. An Ijo person participates in Ijo affairs and struggles; let him or herself be encountered and be counted. Ijo-ness cannot just be deduced by biology. The whole conception of Ijo-ness floats in the air until some aspects of the life of the individual is related to the collective flourishing of the people by participation in the common good. "A person is not one who feeds himself and his family, but who does that in addition to giving to his community," according to Dr. Erekosima. Ijo-ness—and for that matter an Ijo person—has no real presence in the foreign land apart from the fellowship-creating relationship in which one gives himself to another and receives the other in communal praxis. It is within this ethical reality of the community that an answer to the question: what am I, as a biological Ijo person and now residing in a foreign land, to do to create and sustain my Ijo identity? begins to come into view.

The idea of the *community* becomes both the melting pot within which the different groups can be forged to become ostensibly one nation (pan-Ijo national identity) and also serve as the vehicle for creating personal identity. Of course, individual identity is of multiform character, and it is often forged and expressed in communal practices as well as discourses and interactions. Every single identity, though it is personal and individualist, is of a particular community's identity. Identity is always formatted, reflecting traditions, social practices that define and sustain the traditions, and historical period. Identity which is completely free-floating and no particular community's identity is to be found nowhere. Ijo identity *qua* Ijo identity, as against say just being a black person or an African in the United States, is an expression of allegiance to a particular society and its tradition, values, and the experience of an Ijo person in the United States is the experience of the impact of that tradition on one's life. This experience is accessed and sustained through communal practices.

The Ijo are not just receiving American culture as an imposition; they are not acting as mere receptacles. They have used various cultural practices acquired at home to navigate the transition to civil life in America and fashion communities for themselves. There is cultural continuity through religion (indigenous and Christianity), food, language, dress, masquerade displays, and music, just to name a few. At most cultural events, whether organized by Ijo, Nigerians, Africans, even Americans, Ijo men and women and their children wear traditional Ijo attire (*dọni, wọkọ, etibọ, kịlalị sun, etc.*). They do this not only to acknowledge and remember where they come from, but also to pass

707

the culture to their children. Wearing ethnic clothes, they say, gives them a sense of pride and it is part of their struggle to keep their culture alive. Pastor Elsie Obed, a Kalabari woman living in New York City stated that she makes it a point of duty to take her children every year to Nigeria and to Rivers State so that they would not forget their roots and to instill in them a sense of pride as black persons. Just as in the homeland where women are custodial of the culture and primary agents in the reproduction of cultural identity, it is the same in the United States. Ijo women are very crucial in the reproduction of Ijo identity and defining cultural boundaries as they stand ready to correct and put right both men and children.

Another area of continuity is that at certain celebrations and gatherings, special ethnic Ijo foods are cooked and served. On such occasions, usually there is abundance of food. Ijo women coming to the occasions will make all efforts to bring foods to the occasion. Ijo men and women have been known in the United States to travel miles to buy fresh fish to make dinners (or *fulo*). During meetings when food and drinks are served, prayers are made: often libation will be poured to the ancestors and then supplications directed at the Christian God.

Masquerade displays are a staple part of Ijo cultural celebrations in Nigeria. Here in the United States they have also emerged as an invaluable part of annual conventions of various Ijo ethnic associations or pan-Ijo gatherings. Sometimes, the men hand-carve and decorate the headpieces from scratch to finish with materials procured in the United States; and at other times they are imported from Nigeria. The music, instead of being life, is supplied by electronic instruments. As part of its efforts to promote the cultural heritage of the Ijo in North America, the President of Ijaw Foundation, Dr. Nanakumo, informed us that there are plans to "organize tours in North America and Europe for various Ijaw musicians, the Bayelsa State cultural troupe and other Ijaw cultural troupes to promote pan-Ijo identity."

The Christian church in particular is one of the vehicles African immigrants have used to manage their transition into American society and maintain their cultural identity. The Ijo are not different. The Ijo participate actively in

708

churches. They are pastors of African churches and some even have Christian radio ministries in America. An Ijo male headed one of the biggest Redeemed Christian Church of God (RCCG) churches in North America for over nine years. He founded the RCCG, International Chapel in Brooklyn, New York in 1998 and later planted five other churches in the same city. He was also on the board of the coordinators (the highest decision-making body) of RCCG in North America and oversaw 14 churches in the states of New York and New Hampshire. Pastor Obed founded the Lilies International Christian Outreach (LICO). She organizes Christian music festivals ("Worship His Majesty") in world famous arenas like the Madison Square Garden and Waldorf Astoria Hotel in New York City. In such meetings, adorning Ijo *kilali sun* (coral-beaded hat in a crown shape), she would sing gospel songs in both Kalabari and English. In 2006, she even released a Christian CD, *Ibakam,* to communicate the Christian message in multicultural worship. Earlier on, she and her husband, Olusegun Obed, had opened RCCG churches in Tallahassee, Florida, and New York City. LICO also runs radio ministries in New York and an international Christian school for children. In the philosophy of contributing to the homeland, Pastor Elsie's school has a branch in Buguma, Rivers State. Pastor Biokpo Harry is another Ijo person who founded and is running a church ("Mountain of Prayer and Revival Ministry) in New York City.

Music in the church and at cultural gatherings has become a veritable instrument for the reproduction of ethnic identities or cultural continuity. Traditional Ijo music serves as a source of cultural inspiration and a lubricant of the limbs on the dance floor. At the 2007 Boro Day celebration in New York LaGuardia Airport Marriot Hotel, New York we observed as the dance floor too quickly and too long filled up when such old Rex Jim Lawson (1930-1969) tunes as *Jolly Papa, Love me Adure, Serre Nene, Osuala Oru Enene,* and *Aye Muba Udeaja* were played. As Lawson's voice filled the hotel's cavernous ballroom, an Ijo male on his way to the dancing floor whispered that there is a mysterious way that the home music gets into his spirit catapulting him into rapturous excitement. The atmosphere was almost spiritual; the dancing bodies were like those in contemplative activity such that any rational comment of their excitement and concentration would be like a profanation. In fact, in some

Ijo political circles, Lawson's memorable songs, *Bere Bote* and *Ene Bate* inspire mystery, awe, and fascination as they appear to be calling their Ijo listeners to wake up because *bere* (trouble) has come to them.

As part of the process of defining Ijo identity, Dr. Erekosima maintains that there is an urgent need to change the mentality of Ijo who think of themselves as a minority group in Nigeria. He stated that "we are not a minority. We are the fourth largest ethnic group in Nigeria and a people whose resources sustain the whole country cannot be termed a minority. We have been so mentally diminished, expropriated for so long". Important for this project of changing Ijo perception and conception of themselves and their place in the Nigerian polity are Ijo nationalist discourse and the creation of pan-Ijo ethnic associations around the common theme of Ijo oppression and marginalization. This project of identity formation by shirking off "the minority paraphernalia" is also taking place among Ijo in Nigeria (Nwajiaku, 2005: 470).

While the Ijo in Nigeria are only shirking off the minority label, those of their brethren in the United States also have to "shirk off" the terrorist label. Often Ijo organizations dealing with the government of the United States have to convince state agencies that they are not part of the so called "terrorist network" of the Niger Delta. The Ijaw Foundation was incorporated as a nonprofit charitable organization with the New York State on August 24, 2003. Between this period and 2006, it applied to the United States Internal Revenue for routine tax-exempt status. According to its leaders, they were put through rigorous investigation before the status was granted in April 2006. The words of Nanakumo: "the Foundation was put through a protracted process of clarifying questions and issues about terrorism, violence and hostage-taking regarding the Ijaw struggle. It was 'mission impossible' but we triumphed." Many of the Ijo leaders we talked to have several stories like this to narrate about their experience with government officials in America.

Narratives and story-telling are part of the cultural equipment used to create Ijo identity. The immigrants and their children have one more resource to access Ijo traditions and moral life in specific historical contexts. "There is no one to tell the Ijo story; inform the world about the Ijo plight. We have to do it," says LongJohn. So all gatherings and celebrations like Boro Day and Ijaw Foundation annual meetings, historians and other eminent personalities are usually invited to tell and retell the stories. The Ijaw are trying hard to tell their stories to the world. The stories they tell are crafted to reveal or disclose the truth about Ijo and its traditions and predicament; are meant to script the actions and words of their children, and educate them into salient virtues.

Concluding Statements

Our descriptions have simplified what is otherwise a very complex interplay of cultural resources imported from home and conditions the Ijo encountered in North America. They are constructing new identities that are shaped by traditions and solidarities, economic and political changes in Nigeria, imagined gains from control over their natural resources in the homeland, and socio-economic contexts of America within which they are emerging. As the Ijo are re-conceptualizing their Ijo identity in the United States, they are borrowing from cultures and adding new elements. The addition and constant re-juggling are done with an eye to survival under the physical and psychological circumstances in the host-land. It is an ongoing process of creation of group identities out of preexisting cultures. Our presentation is only an attempt to take a snapshot of a moving object.

In conclusion, this chapter has presented three descriptive analyses of the Ijo in North America. The first is a narrative of the presence of Ijo in North America. Studies of the Atlantic slave trade and even Ijo "collective memory" have tended to focus on the role Ijo played as middlemen, and have ignored their participation as slaves in the early years of the trade. Second, our research shows that Ijo immigrants are engaged in a struggle to control their own natural resources that is rooted in history and facilitated by current political organizations, ethnic forms of mobilization, identity-based politics, and emerging strategic discourses. Therefore, our third analysis is an examination of the techniques the Ijo are using to reconstruct their identities on a pan-Ijo nationalist platform to bolster their demand for resource control and increased political recognition in Nigeria.

CHAPTER 32

IẒỌN VISIBILITY IN THE CARIBBEAN NEW WORLD DIASPORA

Waibinte Wariboko, Otelemate G. Harry and Hubert Devonish

Introduction

As a consequence of the transatlantic slave trade, including other factors such as voluntary migration during and after the transatlantic trade, there are "between 70 and 100 million people of mainly black African descent" permanently residing outside of the ancestral continent today; and approximately 20 million of these persons "live in the West Indies and on the Caribbean mainland, including 5 million in Haiti, the main stronghold of African culture in the New World after Brazil." This population represents the African Diaspora in the New World. However, for a greater proportion of this population, their ancestors were enslaved and from diverse sociolinguistic groups in Africa, particularly West Africa, from about the end of the fifteenth to the middle of the nineteenth century. The Ijo-speaking peoples of the Niger Delta constituted one of the ethnic groups, among many others, that were enslaved and shipped out of the slave ports within the Bight of Biafra (now Bight of Bonny) on the West African coast: Bonny (Ibani), Old Calabar, New Calabar (Elem Kalabari), Cameroons, Gabon, Cape Lopez, Rio Bento (Brass), Rio Nun, and Bimbia. This Chapter, by focusing on the Ijo-speaking peoples, intends to make a very modest contribution to one of the "hotly debated" questions in the historical literature pertaining to "African ethnicities in the Americas": "Which ethnicities were shipped out of the Bight of Biafra, when, and in what proportions?"

Let us put the question slightly differently for the specific purpose of this Chapter: To what extent were the Ijo-speaking peoples of the Niger Delta represented among the slaves shipped across the Atlantic from the Bight of Biafra? Where were they located and what impact did they make on the socio-cultural life of the evolving Creole societies in the Black Atlantic,

713

particularly in the Caribbean? In order to put the issues revolving around these questions in historical perspective it is important to discuss, however briefly, the involvement of the dominant Eastern Niger Delta Ijo-speaking trading states—Bonny, New Calabar and Nembe-Brass in the trans-Atlantic slave trade.

The Eastern Delta Ijo States in the Transatlantic Slave Trade

Bonny, New Calabar, and Nembe-Brass were thriving centers for the internal long-distance trade between the peoples of the Niger Delta and their hinterland neighbours, particularly their Igbo- and Ikwerre-speaking hinterland neighbours. Traders from these states carried fish and salt to these hinterland farming communities in exchange for various vegetable and non-vegetable items. In 1668, for example, Olfert Dapper a Dutch traveler was impressed by the elaborate trade in yams, bananas, palm oil, pigs, buck and chicken which went on between New Calabar and the hinterland. This elaborate system of trade, according to Dapper, depended on an efficient mode of transport: "… the Negroes navigate the river Kalbarien [New Calabar River] in very large canoes with twenty oarsmen or paddlers on either side, in which sixty, even eighty, men can be carried." The canoe, which was the sole means of transportation in the Niger Delta, was also an important item of trade between the Eastern Delta consumers and producers in the Central Delta communities such as Apoi and Kugbo. Delta trading canoes mainly from Nembe-Brass and Bonny, according to David Northrup, traveled as far as the Igala bank and Idah on the Niger River to purchase, among others, the following manufactures: knives, hoes, spearheads, bolts, hinges and staples, cloth, baskets and pottery.

As E.J. Alagoa has argued, it was not difficult for the Ijo-speaking trading states in the Eastern Niger Delta to assume the role of middlemen in the trans-Atlantic slave trade because they were able to expand the pre-existing socio-political and economic structures in response to the demands of the new enterprise in slaves. For example, the canoes seen by Dapper were obviously deployed for the slave trade too. In some respects, in fact, the slave trade brought about an increase in the volume of the internal trade in other items. According to J. Barbot, a ship that takes in five hundred slaves

714

must provide about a hundred thousand yams to feed them. Barbot, for example, placed an order at New Calabar in 1699 for 50, 000 yams to be delivered at these rates:

> "sixty king's yams, one bar; one hundred and sixty slave's yams, one bar; .... A butt of water, two rings. For the length of wood, seven bars, which is dear; .... For a goat, one bar. A cow, ten or eight bars. A jar of palm oil, one bar and a quarter."

Up until the end of the seventeenth century, New Calabar was the dominant slave trading port in the Eastern Niger Delta. This period of dominance, as an anonymous Dutch manuscript entitled *West Africa in the Seventeenth Century* indicates, coincided roughly with the Dutch elimination of Portuguese trade monopoly in West Africa generally, and the growth of its trade "in the mouth of the Rio Real from 1638 to 1641" in particular. In 1668 Dapper also noted that New Calabar was "the most important place of trade for the Dutch." This view in 1699 was reechoed by J. Barbot thus: "New Calabar is the chief place for the trade of the Hollanders...." New Calabar's trade with the Dutch, according to the anonymous manuscript mentioned above, was dominated by the following middlemen described as "officers" in 1652: Caberyt, Foefera or Foufera, Niolate, Sioerse Grande and Sioerse Pequenine, Sware Grande and Sware Pequenine. These merchant "officers", we are told, were paid customs duty before any trade could begin between New Calabar and the Dutch traders—a practice that characterized Euro-African trade relations until the establishment of colonial administration by Sir Claude MacDonald in the Niger Delta in 1891.

The initial dominance of New Calabar over Bonny, for example, could easily be explained. It might well lie in the shorter distance which merchants had to travel in order to reach the hinterland supply markets. Barbot noted thus: " She [New Calabar] would get slaves much faster than Bandy [Bonny]; the Calabar Blacks being but two or three days out and home, to purchase them at inland markets: whereas the Bandy people, lying much lower, by the sea side, are eight or ten days out and home, to get them down." New Calabar's early success could be attributed to another factor. It would appear that before the rise of the famous [or infamous] *long-juju* at Aro Chukwu, which was to serve as the main supply source for slaves in the Igbo-speaking hinterland in the eighteenth century (a period coinciding with the growth of Bonny as the greatest slave market in West Africa) there existed an oracle at Ozuzu called *kamalu*. The oracle and its operators, located on the Otamiri River north of New Calabar, sold all those who came for the settlement of disputes to the New Calabar middlemen. In a sense *kamalu*, as a supply source, did for New Calabar in the seventeenth century what the *long-juju* did for Bonny in the eighteenth century. There is enough socio-linguistic evidence to show that, although a greater number of Igbo-speaking peoples were enslaved through the oracle at Ozuzu, those sold to the Dutch slave traders included, among other ethnicities, the Ijo-speaking peoples of the Niger Delta- all such relevant socio-linguistic data pertaining to the Ijo presence in Berbice Dutch and its significance in the formation of Atlantic Creole languages will be discussed later in this Chapter.

At the beginning of the eighteenth centur—a period roughly coinciding with the English dominance—New Calabar lost its dominant position to Bonny. In some oral traditions earlier recorded by Alagoa, New Calabar had attempted to explain why it lost its position to Bonny:

> After Oruyingi [mother of the gods] had given birth to all the gods of all *ibe* [communities] in the delta, she asked them to make requests for the benefit of their people. Owoamekaso [goddess of the Kalabari] asked for a book that would attract European ships to Elem Kalabari. After they left the presence of Oruyingi, Ikuba [god of Bonny] became jealous and tried to seize the book. In the ensuing struggle, Ikuba was able to make off with the larger fragment of the book, and so got the bigger ships calling at the port of Bonny, only smaller ships being able to go upstream to Elem Kalabari.

Having overtaken New Calabar in the Eastern Niger Delta, as shown in Table 1 below, Bonny also became the greatest slave market in the Bight of Biafra when it outpaced Old Calabar around 1740.

Table 32.1:
Identified slave departures from Ports in the Bight of Biafra [Bight of Bonny] [1676-1832]

Ports	Slaves	Percent	Ships	Percent
Bonny	384,000	52.8	1,048	46
Old Calabar	205,600	28.3	699	30.7
Elem Kalabari	66,800	9.2	238	10.4
Cameroons	26,800	4	166	5.1
Gabon	24,500	3.4	108	4.7
Cape Lopez	7,600	1	30	1.3
Rio Brass	4,700	0.6	16	0.7
Rio Nun	2,200	0.3	9	0.4
Bimbia	2,200	0.3	9	0.4
Other	1,200	0.2	6	0.3
Total Identified	**727,600**		**2,279**	

European visitors, traders and commentators to the West African coast after Barbot and Dapper in the seventeenth century—including Captain John Adams, who "carried out a scientific research into the West African trade and people" between 1786 and 1800—had emphasized the leading role and dominance of Bonny in the trans-Atlantic slave trade during the eighteenth and nineteenth centuries. According to the latter:

> This place [Bonny] is the wholesale market for slaves, as not fewer than 20,000 are annually sold here; 16,000 of whom are members of one nation, called Heebo [the Ibo/Igbo], so that this single nation ... during the last 20 years [exported no less] than 320,000; and those of the same nation sold at New Calabar [a Delta port], probably amounted, in the same period of time, to 50,000 more, making an aggregate amount of 370,000 Heebos. The remaining part of the above 20,000 is composed of the natives of the Brass country ... and also of Ibbibys [Ibibio] or Quaws.

The figures given in Table 32.1, including the comments of Adams, fully support the point made by G.M. Hall when she argued that "Well over 90 percent of the slaves from the Bight of Biafra [between 1676 and 1832] were exported from three ports: Elem Kalabari [New Calabar], Calabar [Old Calabar] on the Cross River, and Bonny, which arose as the leading port during the eighteenth century." Bonny enjoyed two competitive advantages over New Calabar. It had the advantage of being able to tap the resources of a wider supply market in the Igbo-, Ogoni- and Ibibio-speaking hinterlands of southern Nigeria; and its closer proximity to the sea, as compared to New Calabar, made it a more desirable and convenient embarkation port for European slave trading vessels.

Finally, according to Alagoa, Nembe-Brass procured "slaves from beyond the Igbo country down the Niger, from the Igala, and other northern Nigeria peoples. In the western delta, some western Igbo passed through Itsekiri middlemen, as well as Urhobo, Isoko and other groups from the regions under Benin influence. Some riverine Yoruba also came through the lagoon trade into the western delta."

All of the foregoing evidence indicates one thing: the political economy of the Niger Delta states during this period was heavily dependent on the transatlantic slave trade. It was therefore not surprising that the Bight of Biafra, and the Niger Delta in particular, came to be regarded during the eighteenth century as "the most important slave mart in West Africa". This was because the volume of trade from this area alone equaled "the trade of all West Africa put together." (Dike, 1956,28-29). So much on the general overview of the Eastern Niger Delta states in the transatlantic slave trade. Let us now turn our attention to the enslaved ethnicities, particularly the Ijo-speaking ethnicity, from the Bight of Biafra in the New World by addressing the question posed below.

To what extent were the Ijo-speaking peoples of the Niger Delta represented among those shipped across the Atlantic from the Bight of Biafra/Bonny?

We may begin by admitting that we neither have enough descriptive archival data nor concrete statistics to discuss this question effectively and exhaustively. We do know, however, that they constituted "a very small minority before the nineteenth century" both in the Caribbean and in the United States (Hall, 2006, 131). Within the Caribbean, as the socio-linguistic evidence derived from the study of Berbice Dutch Creole will show clearly, they were well represented in the Dutch colony of Berbice. In addition to the colony of Berbice, there are scattered references in other contemporary sources indicating the presence of Ijo-speaking peoples elsewhere in the Caribbean- for example, Jamaica. Unlike the Ijaw, both the oral and archival comments and testimonies pertaining to West African supply markets, including extant "Registration Lists" of enslaved African ethnicities in the West Indies, unequivocally support the view that the greatest victims of the transatlantic slave trade from the Bight of Biafra were the Igbo-speaking populations. Table 2, as given below, further strengthens and illustrates this point.

Table 32.2:
"African Ethnicities from the Bight of Biafra [Bight of Bonny] on British West Indies Registration Lists, 1813-1827" (Hall 2006, 139)

| Location | Ethnicity | | | | |
	Igbo	Moko	Ibibio	Other	Total
Trinidad [1813]	2,863 51.8%	2,240 40.6%	371 6.7%	21 .04%	5,520
St. Lucia [1815]	894 71.5%	291 23.3%	59 4.8%	6 .5%	1,250
St Kitts [1817]	440 72.4%	164 27.0%	Nil	4 .05%	608
Berbice [1819]	111 61.0%	64 35.2%	Nil	7 3.8%	182
Anguilla [1827]	4 66.7	2 33.3%	Nil	Nil	6
Total	4,312 57.9%	2,529 33.4%	371 [?] 5.0%	38 .005%	7,566

Generally speaking the slave traders of the delta, as Alagoa put it, "did not themselves raid for the slaves they sold to the ships but procured them from communities adjoining the delta or through the Aro and other trading communities of the hinterland." (1986, 127-130). However, Alagoa has also noted that "there is evidence of some raiding within the delta itself on weaker communities" for slaves. These raids, which were organized by the more powerful states of Bonny, New Calabar and Nembe-Brass against the numerically smaller and weaker delta communities, provided the tiny minority of enslaved Ijo-speaking Africans found in the colony of Berbice and elsewhere in the New World where they are virtually invisible. The towns of Egwema and Beletiema, both standing on the main river connecting Brass and Nun, were often raided by slavers from Nembe-Brass (Alagoa 1986). It is very likely that these enslaved persons were shipped to the New World slave-using societies through the ports of Rio Brass and Rio Nun.

C.G.A. Oldendorp, a Moravian missionary who worked in the Danish West Indies from 1767 to 1768, reported that he met and "interviewed five slaves who described themselves as members of the Kalabari [New Calabar] nation", and "that they lived far up the Calabar [New Calabar] River...." (Hall 2006, 113). This account is interesting because it could corroborate some New Calabar oral traditions pertaining to the slave trade during the period of king Amachree or Amakiri 1[ca1735-1835], the founder of the reigning Amakiri dynasty in New Calabar today. According to these traditions Agbaniye Ejika, the ruler of Bile [a delta community that had allied itself to Bonny against New Calabar], raided all vulnerable Kalabari-speaking communities for slaves until he was decisively subdued by Amakiri.

In addition to preying on the smaller, weaker communities, as these reported comments from a European commentator on Bonny suggest, defenseless and unsuspecting individuals were also captured within the trading states of the delta.

Mr. Douglas [the European slaver], when ashore at Bonny Point, saw a young woman come out of the wood to the water-side to bathe. Soon afterwards two men came from the wood, seized, bound ... and bringing her to him, Mr. Douglas, desired him to put her on board, which he did; the Captain's orders were, when anybody brought down slaves, instantly to put them off to the ship."

Some of those sold to Mr. Douglas at Bonny, according to the source just cited, were eventually resold to planters in Jamaica. The accounts of Oldendorp and

720

Douglas suggest that enslaved Ijo-speaking peoples were present in several Caribbean islands, but they constituted a small and invisible minority in many of these islands, except in the Dutch colony of Berbice where they have left an indelible imprint in the formation of the Creole language there.

Ijo Visibility in Berbice Dutch Creole and its Significance in the Formation of Atlantic Creole Languages

Within the substratum framework, a standard practice exists in the discussion of the role of West African languages in Atlantic Creole genesis. Scholars have proposed the influence of multiple West African languages in the formation of any one Atlantic Creole language. Proposals concerning this influence will either focus on groupings like Kwa or Mande, or cover the whole of Niger-Congo (Alleyne 1980). In addition, this influence is mainly assumed to be at the level of the syntax, and sometimes the phonology of these Creole languages since the bulk of their vocabulary, and usually almost all of their basic vocabulary, is of European origin. Saramaccan is a typical example which represents this general view of multiple African languages.

Saramaccan, which is usually considered to be the most "African" of these creoles, is claimed to have as much as 50 percent African vocabulary … this fact is intimately bound up with the high degree of cultural continuity exhibited by the speakers of Saramaccan. A recheck of a Swadesh 200-word list produced by Voorhoeve resulted in a score of 4.9 percent probably of African… This 4.9 percent is spread over various African languages such as Igbo, Kikongo, Yoruba, and Wolof…(Smith, Robertson, Williamson, 52).

In contrast it has been proven that Berbice Dutch originated from the contact between a European language, Dutch, and an African language, Ijo. In their study of Berbice Dutch N. Smith, I. Robertson and K. Williamson discovered that African retentions were much higher than that proposed for Saramaccan. African retentions are within 22.5 to 27.25 percent. Using two primary sources they effectively demonstrated that these figures come from only one African source, Ijo. Table 3.3 below illustrates the distribution of the lexical items in Berbice Dutch.

721

Analyses of Berbice Dutch sources (percentages)

	Robertson (1982)	Swadesh list
Dutch	67	60.58
Ijo	22.5	27.25
English	4	7.14
Amerindian	2.25	-
Others and doubtful	4.25	5.03

The word lists used in the comparison contain both basic and cultural vocabulary. 40% of the basic vocabulary comes from Ijo-related sources. Berbice Dutch is, therefore, special amongst Atlantic Creole languages since, not only can a significant portion of its vocabulary be demonstrated to come from West African language sources, but in addition, from a single linguistic source. From both linguistic and historical standpoints the data given above is very critical to the study of Ijo visibility in the Caribbean. To start with, because the source of West African language influence in Berbice Dutch is very obvious, a study of its origins and formation could provide some useful generalizations for other Creole situations where the sources of the West African language influence are less obvious.

In Table 32.3 it was clear that Ijo, besides Dutch, is the second major contributor to the lexicon of Berbice Dutch. However, it does not give us any information on the particular enslaved Ijo groups that contributed to the formation of Berbice Dutch. To deal with this problem Smith, Robertson and Williamson further examined Ijo items which have reflexes in Berbice Dutch. They compared reflexes of Ijo lexical items in Berbice Dutch with similar items from six Ijo lects; Kalabari, Bile, Okrika, Ibani, Nembe and Kolokuma. The first four are dialects of Eastern Ijo. Nembe is closely related to Eastern Ijo, while Kolokuma which is a dialect of Izon is distantly related to Eastern Ijo. Table 32.4 illustrates a summary of the comparison.

Eastern Ijo sources for Berbice Dutch lexical items

Berbice Dutch	Kalabari	Bile	Okrika	Ibani	Nembe	Kolokuma	Gloss
(a)bor?	b'?*ro*'	b'u'*ro*'	b'u'*ro*'	b'o'*ro*'	b'o'go'	b'o'*o*'	pass
abËk?	?b'?*kô'	?b'?*kô'	?b'?*kô'	?b'i*ô'	-	-	fowl
ap(u)	-apu'	-apu'	-apu'	-apu'	(-ongu)	(-otu)	plural
ba:m	-	-	-	ibi-b'a*-m	-	-	pretty
bol?	b'u'lo'(arch.	(fu*rô)	b'u'lo	(fu*rô)	-	-	belly
deki	do*kî, do*gî	do*kî	de*kî	Díí	-	-	carry
dekimu	do*kî mu*	do*kî mu*u	de*kî mu*	díí muí	-	-	carry
fori	o*fo*rí	o*fo*rî	o*fo*rí	o*fo*rí	(fa)	(faa)	absent
gaén(tå)	Ìòganiò	Ìòganiò	Ìòganiò	Ìòganiò	-	-	annoy
kånå	Kìòniò	Kìòniò	Kìòniò	Kìòniò	-	-	person
kori	koòriò(nama)	kiòniònama	(fiòriò)	(fiòriò)	(fiòriò)	(fiòriò)	work
ku	Kun	kuu*n	kuu*n	kuu*	-	-	catch

It is clear from the data above that the Berbice Dutch forms are more closely related to Eastern Ijo forms than they are to Nembe or Kolokuma. Given this comparison they suggested that most of the Ijo sources of items in Berbice Dutch came from Eastern Ijo. Nembe and Kolokuma are excluded as possible Ijo sources. In fact, some phonological comparisons reinforced the view that Eastern Ijo is the most likely source for Ijo elements in Berbice Dutch.

As a background to the interpretation of the data in Table 5 below, some details of the phonological structures are necessary here. The Berbice Dutch forms have their standard phonetic values. The Ijo lects have a nine vowel system with vowel harmony of the Advanced Tongue Root [ATR] type; four wide (advanced tongue root) /i e o u /, four narrow (retracted tongue root) /i$ e$ o$ u$/ and /a/, a neutral vowel which co-occurs with either set. /b d/ are implosives, /kp gb/ are labial-velars and /j/ is a postalveoalar affricate [d3].

Table 32.5:

Shared phonological innovation among Berbice Dutch and Ijo

	Berbice Dutch	Kalabari	Bile	Okrika	Ibani	Nembe	Kolokuma	Gloss
a	Bɪaka	?mb?aka*	?p?amgba*	?p?amgbaa*	mb?kpa	?mb?akpa*	(aka*)	Corn
b	Deki	do*kī, do*gī	do*kī	De*kī	díī	-	-	Carry
c	Feni	fe*ni*	fe*ni*	fe*ni*	fe*ni*	feni/ofoni	ofo*ni*	Bird
d	Mɪngi	minji	Minji	Mengi	mingi	mindi*	beni*	Water
e	mo$n?	mo*nō	mo*nō	Mo$*nō$	mu*nō	munu*	bu$*nu$*	Sleep
Total		4	3	5	4	3	0	

In (a), /k/ in Berbice corresponds historically to Kalabari /k/, ruling out the others with labial-velar consonants. (b) will also rule out Nembe and Kolokuma, as they do not have corresponding reflexes. Similarly, (c), (d) and (e) show some consistency between Berbice and Eastern Ijo lects. As noted by Smith, Robertson and Williamson, the phonological evidence might not be quite overwhelming, but it still points to Eastern Ijo as the most likely source.

H. Devonish and O. G. Harry, in a more recent study of the prosody (stress and tone) of Berbice Dutch, have proposed that speakers of Berbice Dutch seem to distinguish between items of Eastern Ijo origin and those of non-Eastern Ijo, mainly of Dutch origin. On the basis of pitch patterns observed in Berbice Dutch, the lexical items with mostly Eastern Ijo reflexes were divided into three: Class 1, Class 2 and Class 3, as illustrated in Table 32.6 a, b, and c below.

Table 32.6

A: Class 1, Items: Low-High-(Low) pitch pattern:
  pamba* 'wing'
  atɛ*tɛ 'grand mother'
  opro*po 'pig'
B: Class 2, Items: Falling-Low-High-(Low) pitch pattern:
  mângjapu* 'maroon'
  kâkaláka 'cockroach'
  shûkulu* 'A dress for children'
C: Class 3, Items: Falling-High pitch pattern:
  bjâká 'corn'
  kârá 'fish trap'
  bîtá 'clothes'
  lûku*bá 'tale'

Explanations for this tonal behaviour point to the fact that Berbice Dutch was probably created out of isolation forms from both Dutch and Eastern Ijo. In that sense, therefore, we are not dealing with either a form of Eastern Ijo heavily influenced by Dutch lexicon, or a form of Dutch heavily influenced by an Eastern Ijo lexicon. This seems to have been a language constructed from scratch using the lexicon of the two languages in contact, Dutch and Eastern Ijo. Perhaps, the ability on the part of speakers to keep prosodic distinctions between Dutch items and those of Eastern Ijo preserved Ijo forms over the period leading up to the abolition of the transatlantic slave trade and thereafter.

One important issue which arises, however, is the relationship between the Eastern Ijo dialects during the early stages of Berbice Dutch formation and evolution. Smith, Robertson and Williamson concluded that Kalabari '...formed the major basis for Berbice Dutch'. This conclusion was arrived at taking into consideration the degree of lexical correspondences between Berbice Dutch and the various Eastern Ijo dialects (see Table 32.4) and the shared phonological innovations within this body of lexical items (see Table 32.5). A consideration of the facts presented by them, however, shows the highest level of correspondence at the level of phonological innovation with Okrika (see Table 32.5 in particular). Devonish and Harry have taken an alternative approach by giving greater weight to the lexical correspondences. This approach was based on the findings of additional phonological features; these features examined at the prosodic level, tended to suggest a strong Okrika influence.

Conclusion

The prosodic analysis of Berbice Dutch, it has to be noted, does not refute previous claims in any significant way. In fact, it corroborates the high figure for Okrika and Berbice Dutch shared phonological innovations, thereby making Okrika the most prominent influence in Berbice Dutch. Finally, we were also able to propose an explanation of the relative contribution of various Eastern Ijo dialects, pointing to the special role of Okrika, not as the majority lect but one which, through an over-generalization of its features by other Eastern Ijo speakers, had a major influence on the prosody of Berbice Dutch. The small number of Africans involved in this early process illustrates one of the ways in which a minority group could have a major influence in the outcome of a new language. This latter proposal portrays some of the specifics of the relationships between African ethnic groups, here speakers of closely related dialects, in the formation of a Creole language.

CHAPTER 33

CONCLUSION:
WHAT FUTURE FOR THE IZQN
IN NIGERIA?[†]

Tekena N Tamuno

Two Foundation Platforms for Analysis

So far, in this study, Ijo communities would be seen more as victims than as victimizers in their ambient environment in the Niger Delta as described and analyzed from the various perspectives of the contributors, each of whom is a respected scholar in his or her field of specialization. Each analysis, as readers would also see and recollect, ably covered complex events and trends from pre-colonial times to the present as comprehensively as possible. Most of these we, therefore, take for granted in this Conclusion.

In the light of the above, the coverage, in this Chapter, would attempt to shed further light mainly on an issue of considerable importance: the political future of the Ijo, severely weakened not only by their status as an ethnic minority but also by their inability to unite effectively against formidable threats. Surely, the balance of advantage, in a conventional analysis of the category of "SWOT" (Strengths, Weaknesses, Opportunities, Threats), would not favour the Ijo in their disabling environment. Again, if, in place of SWOT, one were to use another standard of assessment, the results would not be quite different. In this context, I have in mind my standard parameters based on what I regard as key pillars of any useful historical analysis: those of Time, Circumstance, Leadership/Followership and Accident/Chance.

[†] An earlier version of this Chapter was presented as a lecture at a Conference of the Ijaw National Congress to celebrate its "2005 Ijaw National Day & Ijaw World Summit" with the Theme "The Ijaw Ethnic Nationality & the Nigerian State." It was held in Yenagoa, Bayelsa State, on 24-26 February 2005. Its title and text then have been considerably modified with necessary additions and subtractions to serve the purpose of this Chapter.

One would, therefore, emphasize demonstrable difficult relations between the Ijo and other major stakeholders and competing interests in the larger context of the development of the Nigerian state in an atmosphere of ethnic pluralism and multi-cultural proclivities. In these relationships, the strong tend to dominate the weak. This trend seems to be universal across frontiers of time and place.

But what reasonable response would any observer of sane mind expect of the Ijo under such circumstances of actual and potential threats to survival in their fatherland? As a well-known Nigerian proverb suggests: If you don't know where you are going, you know where you come from. Of course, it will not be reasonable, for anyone or group, to surrender easily without putting up a stout defence of their many-sided rights in the larger interests of aggrieved stakeholders, including succeeding generations. The long struggle of the Ijo for freedom, fairness, justice, equity, security, safety, stability, welfare and peace, in a sustainable way, can have no other meaning except in that context of continued attempts to be treated with the same standards as others enjoy in their own country. Discrimination of the kind which the strong meted to the weak the Ijo detested. To change that context of events to one of equal rights for all became, for the Ijo, and others in their League of the Weak, a gospel of Truth in which they firmly believed.

For this purpose, I humbly but honestly propose these two foundations or platforms for further analysis of the twists and turns in the protracted Ijo struggle for fundamental human rights, of the first, second and third generations, in respect of political, social and economic, and cultural dimensions, such as the United Nations and other relevant organizations recognized and espoused from 1948 to the present:

- "Big Fish eat the Small".
- "The Strong attack the Weak or the Weak attract attacks from the Strong".

The first of these two propositions would make much sense to fishermen and fish-eaters. The Ijo, therefore, have some clear advantages in knowing not only how small fishes defend themselves against big ones but also the art and science of how the former outsmart the latter in battles for survival in obviously hostile environments. Among seafarers and landsmen, the identity of contestants may differ; but the spirit of the contest or nature of the risk is the same: minnows in freshwater or jellyfish in the sea versus whales of the ocean or ants versus elephants in forests.

The second seems simple. Its composite side is this: All manner of Weakness invite Attack in the Animal and Plant kingdoms.

Concerning application, to the fate of the Ijo, locally, nationally and in the Diaspora, one would emphasize enlargement of size in agreed relationships to achieve desired goals. It is the type of strength one expects from a broom rather than from the separation of its composite sticks.

It can also be said that timely and effective adaptation to the grim logic of Change, in its widest possible dimensions, is another useful lesson for survival: one learning from the familiar fate of ancient dinosaurs. In their case, mere physical size of gargantuan proportions or conventional strength proved inadequate for the types of adaptation needed under changing conditions. Of course, changing times, changing circumstances plus more in that train would call for changing strategies as well as tactics, including goals and means, to secure these agreed ends against stiff competition or opposition from enemies known and unknown.

For example, and in the context of this chapter if not also of this entire work, would complete strangers who, for their own special national interests, promised protection of others who were demonstrably weak be expected to honour previous pledges and obligations, several decades later, when important changes, including interests and deaths of former *dramatis personae,* at home and abroad, occurred? Often, the weak discover too late serious implications and consequences of having or dealing with unstable friends whose loyalties and interests change from time to time. For the avoidance of doubt, the fate of compacts made in the 1880s and 1890s, with representatives of Oil Rivers Chiefs on one hand and officials of the UK government on the other, when the ambient political, commercial and diplomatic environment, between 1957 and 1958, dramatically changed, would fall into that class of crass opportunism and failed expectations in History.

Would that also make much sense to warring Ijo communities with powerful enemies all around them? Whose interests, one would ask, do obvious strategies and tactics of Divide-and-Rule in Ijoland serve? Hence, for purposes of defence and offence, one can bring to bear on several Ijo relationships, controversies, conflicts and crises the thrust of this familiar and apt saying: "United we stand, divided we fall".

With these observations in mind, one should examine next the state of readiness, for offence and defence, when phenomenal changes occurred in several parts of Ijoland at the beginning of the 19th century through factors of global proportions. How ready, one would also ask, were parts of Ijoland to absorb the inevitable shocks of Colonialism and the post-Colonial era in Nigeria? Were the Ijo then in the best possible position to adapt, quickly and well, to the multiple changes all around? Who, other than the Ijo, would accept the grave responsibility for their protection, locally, nationally and in the Diaspora? Did the Ijo have loyal friends, at all these levels, or did they let them down? If so, why? Beyond causation and explanation, whom would one blame for failure concerning that primary task of self-preservation?

Conflict-Resolution, on the other hand, walks along different pathways. Those who neither forget nor forgive the Past, riddled, as it were, with long or short lists of wrongs, resemble the familiar Bourbons of 19th century France, a well-known place of Revolution and Counter-Revolution. That is the same pathway of war and resultant bloodshed. The results, one will agree, are mind-boggling. But, that trend, with a careful, though difficult, turn of one's mind-set, one can change or transform into channels of Peace. So, from War, War and War one can go to Peace, Peace, and Peace. It is for this reason, a real Peace-Dividend, that I continue to admire the familiar UNESCO Motto: of seeing the Human Mind as the Prime Instrument of War and Peace. I do sincerely believe and recommend that the Ijo, old and young, can and do use that available instrument for Peace rather than War.

The last point I need to emphasize again here touches upon so-called Lessons one can learn from History. The challenge, as well as opportunity, here is for Self, Society and the State. Whether they are Pro-War or Pro-Peace would depend largely on one's mind-set. Because I am fully aware of these wide-ranging impacts on and implications for Self, Society and the State, it is my usual counsel, which I deliberately repeat here: Let the Past not mar the Present and the Future. The Past is irretrievable; but the Present and the Future one can change: for better rather than for worse.

Linguistic and Ethnic Dimensions

From a linguistic point of view, and from comprehensive evidence adduced in the preceding chapters of this work, the term "Ijaw" has had no standard spelling in available literature. No matter how others and native speakers spell or pronounce it -- as Ijaw, Ijo or Izon – the reference is to the same cluster of people with a distinctive language, dialects and value-systems. Earlier chapters of this study have, therefore, used all versions in references to the same groups of persons.   Spread along the coast and riverbanks, or not too far from them, these were and are the fishermen, farmers and traders whose life-styles Nature largely defined and new forces changed, from time to time.

In an Annual Lecture of the Ijaw National Congress at Yenagoa, Bayelsa state, on 23 February 2007, Professor JP Clark, NNOM, himself a native speaker, and national poet laureate, made a useful suggestion worth emphasizing here. Clark who then spoke on the subject "To be Izon today in Nigeria", said:

> "Above all, the Izon people must live by the strength of their name, Izon, not Ijo or Ijaw, all anglicized forms of that singular word which of course means truth, truth to themselves, and truth to their neighbours, so that, as Nigerians, they may all be members of a free, tolerant, and secure society."

Ijo clusters one would find in the Arogbo and Apoi areas of Ondo State and in some fringes. Ijo minorities also exist in Edo and Akwa Ibom States. Larger Ijo settlements abound in parts of Delta State, where bitter conflicts, with the Itsekiri, frequently occurred in the town of Warri, an active centre of commerce. Yet more Ijo groups compete and often clash with Ikwerre, Ogoni and Eleme interests in parts of Rivers State. After decades of agitation, Bayelsa, from 1996, became a mainly Ijo State in the centre of the Niger Delta. If there is any geographical divide, this can be only in respect of references to Western, Central and Eastern Ijo as well as others on the fringes as elaborately and competently defined in this entire work.

In the same lecture, Professor J P Clark, aware of current and recurrent dissatisfaction, among the Ijo, proposed:

> "All the Izon want from Nigeria are two more states of their own, namely, Toro Ebe in the west for the Izon now lost in Ondo, Edo and Delta (states) and to the east of Bayelsa, Oil Rivers State for those of them in Rivers and Akwa Ibom States. They will then be in a position, as one of the largest groups in the country, to control their own resources within the context of a federal structure fair to all its components."

Colonial Threats and Ijo Restiveness

In times out of mind, the Ijo environment was one of relative Peace. Ecological degradation and perennial pollution did not pose any serious threats to the Ijo then and their neighbours in the Niger Delta. Their simple lifestyles met their daily needs.

With the Trans-Atlantic Slave Trade, new threats occurred. With the Abolition of that trade, in 1807, and Emancipation, in 1833, Western Europeans became activists in the affairs of the Niger Delta communities. Soon, European traders and Christian Missionaries teamed up with Consular Officials to torment communities here. By the 1880s and 1890s, Treaties and Agreements, signed with "X-marks", featured in the relations between these communities on one hand and British authorities on the other. By 1893, the former Oil Rivers Protectorate gave way to the Niger Coast Protectorate. In the Niger Districts, a trading company, with a Charter, Royal Niger Company, from 1886, interfered with the internal affairs of the communities till its Charter was revoked in January 1900.

Among those communities in confrontation with new forces in the Oil Rivers (later Niger Delta) were those of Bonny, Okrika, Opobo, Benin and Nembe. Where diplomacy failed to settle issues in dispute, punitive expeditions (involving the use of British troops and lethal maxim guns) followed. With more bloodshed and destruction of physical property, on the African side, fierce resistance gave way to lukewarm accommodation.

That was also the era when British Colonial officials found nothing wrong whatsoever in breaking African eggs, as it were, to make their own delicious imperial omelets. They did so despite outcries from a few Humanitarian Societies and Members of Parliament in the United Kingdom.

Before the discovery of Crude Oil, in 1937, and its aggressive exploitation, from 1958, Palm Produce (Oil and Kernels) met the commercial and fiscal needs of the emerging Protectorate of Southern Nigeria. Gas, from the 1990s, entered this polluted field.

For our immediate purpose, it is important for one to recognize fully, at once, how the exploration and exploitation of Crude Oil, in parts of Ijoland and adjoining areas, brought about a Revolution, which helped to transform the thrusts of Politics, Economics and Ethics at the local, national and international levels. Few humanitarians, at home and abroad, came to the rescue of the Ijo and their neighbours at times of great need. Notions of national self-interest were such as most key players interpreted and applied only to their advantage without considering negative impacts on victims.

In that milieu occurred the twists and turns of British post-World War II policies and practices for dependencies, such as Nigeria. Yes, Ijo leaders, such as Ernest Ikoli, played prominent roles in Nigerian Politics, in the 1930s and 1940s, far away from home. As a leading journalist and politician, Ernest Ikoli made the Ijo voice heard, clearly and loudly, in Lagos politics.

"Treaty Rights" as Buttress for a New Political Order?
Outside Lagos but within the same context of national politics, Ijo contributions to national development, in the widest possible sense of this term, continued. One further example will be enough to validate and consolidate this conclusion.

There is no doubt whatsoever that Mr. (later Chief) Harold Dappa Biriye was far ahead of other leaders who fought against oppression and intimidation by their Ndi-Igbo neighbours in control of Eastern Nigeria in the era of Regionalism in Nigerian Politics. A Conference of Rivers Chiefs and People mandated Dappa-Biriye to fight on their behalf during the 1953 and 1957

734

Constitutional Conferences in London. In particular, these leaders sought protection of their people's interests and rights by virtue of their predecessors' Treaties and Agreements, with the British Crown, in the 1880s and 1890s. Rivers activists, led by Harold Biriye, did not oppose the general demand that Independence should come, after instalments of Regional Self-Government, in the late 1950s, would have been granted the governments that asked for it. But the Rivers Chiefs and People demanded that their pre-Colonial status be restored to them.

To appreciate fully what follows next, it is absolutely necessary to give readers immediate notice of a major source of later controversy over "Treaty Rights" and key differences concerning their interpretation and application by spokesmen, British and Nigerian, several decades after the deaths of those who signed them. In a tribute to a famous Tiv leader and crusader for ethnic rights, Chief Joseph S Tarka, Chief Harold Dappa Biriye, himself a robust Ijo freedom fighter, made a statement which seemed to have fallen outside the strict limits of available documentary evidence now made public, under extant rules, at the British National Archives in the United Kingdom. In his Tribute, on 15 May 1980, Biriye said:

> "It is no self praise to say that the one-man Rivers delegation to the London Constitutional Conference of 1957 was a prime factor in the processes leading up to Nigeria's Independence. Very few, if any, Nigerian Historians have written that there was a special conference in London between the British Government and Rivers Kings and Chiefs one week before the Nigerian Constitutional conference. It was held in the colonial office under the chairmanship of Sir John McPherson, then Under-Secretary for the Colonies. On his side were Mr. Eastwood and Sir Clement Pleas. On our Rivers side were myself and Sir Dingle Foot QC.

> The problem at issue in that forum was the nature of 'The separate Rivers State' which Rivers Kings and Chiefs were calling for and the status of the treaties between Her Majesty and the forebears of Rivers Chiefs in the light of changing circumstances. Had I opted for a Rivers State that would be separate from the rest of Nigeria so

would it have been. The situation in Kuwait came quickly to mind; but I stoutly resisted it. For early in the thirties of this century Britain and America discovered oil in Saudi Arabia in commercial quantity. Kuwait was then declared a special Area for development. Immediately arrangements were concluded to exploit her oil, Kuwait unilaterally declared her independence from Saudi Arabia. On that same day both Britain and the USA recognized Kuwait as an independent country.

By 1957 we in Bonny had known from Nigeria's premier oil company that the commodity existed in commercial quantity in the Rivers part of Nigeria. We had provided Shell-BP with some 1,200 acres of land for a tank farm and an oil terminal and I personally participated in no small degree in negotiations for the land fully and freely. My deliberate decision for a separate Rivers State that would be a unit of the Nigerian federation was a conscious consensus to go ahead with the experiment of one Nigeria for the good of all including myself. Ten years later when Colonel Ojukwu decided to carve out the oil-bearing part of Nigeria into a State of Biafra by force of arms and invited me specially to cooperate with him Rivers Chiefs and people under my leadership continued to stand by the course of one Nigeria and backed up General Gowon."

Any mature historian cannot and should not ignore what memory does or can do to actors in terms of exact recollection, not necessarily reconstruction, of events in which they played leading roles. Several factors, controllable and uncontrollable, may be involved in accounting for any discrepancy observed. It is, however, a professional historian's bounden duty to allow records, if available, to speak for themselves and let the reader alone determine the difference, if any, if much or less. The continuous search for the truth of any matter or subject of investigation demands nothing less, as necessary guidance, before conclusions, tentative or not, are reached. And this is done here without prejudice. It is in this respect that one has to construe significant differences in the accounts given by Biriye and that now available in the British National Archives. For this purpose, ample quotations of relevant sections will not be otiose.

736

Because of its significance, concerning the evolution of the Nigerian state, with the Niger Delta as an integral part thereof, one has to examine more closely tough arguments advanced by Biriye and Dr. Udo Udoma, leader of the Calabar-Ogoja-Rivers (COR) Movement, and counters by other stakeholders and speakers during the 1957 and 1958 Constitutional Conferences in London. While Dr. Udo Udoma was a brilliant lawyer (later, Justice of the Supreme Court of Nigeria), Biriye was not. The latter, therefore, relied on sound legal advice by eminent counsel of his choice with strong links to Whitehall and the Colonial Office, the relevant power houses for resolution of the conflict which involved the Rivers part of the Niger Delta on one hand and the UK government on the other. Biriye's counsel in London were Mr. (later Sir) Dingle Foot, Mr. RK Handoo, MP, and Mr. Graham Page, MP.

The briefs which Biriye took to London for discussion and resolution with senior staff of the Colonial Office, before and during these conferences, rested on solid homework done by other spokesmen in Nigeria. These included petitions and addresses. Rivers stakeholders were unanimous in their representations to the Governor, Eastern Region, on 17 August 1955 and 10 January 1956; to the Governor-General of Nigeria on 10 October 1955, 2 June1956, and 3 November 1956 as well as in an Address of Welcome to the Governor-General on 31 October 1955. In addition, at the Eastern Regional Summit Conference, in Enugu, on 9-11 July 1956, spokesmen of a proposed "Rivers State" included His Highness Mingi X, Amanyanabo of Nembe, Mr. I. Worrior-Osika, Mr. JA Nsirim, Hon. JHE Nwuke, MHA, and Hon. Kalada Kiri, MHA. Their candid views, in favour of the creation of a Rivers State, were tabled as Eastern House of Assembly Sessional Paper No. 5 of 1956.

In an informal and exploratory meeting on the Treaties with Rivers Chiefs, Eastern Region, at the Colonial Office, on March 1957, attended by Dingle Foot, Graham Page and others, some key issues were clarified. Those present were:

1. Mr. Eastwood (in the chair)

2. Mr. Dingle Foot

3. Mr. Graham Page

4. Mr. McPetrie

5. Mr. Williamson

6. Mr. MG Smith

7. Mr. Gordon-Smith

8. Mr. Pettitt.

One of the issues which only the above dealt with was the wish of Rivers Chiefs to be represented at the Constitutional Conference in 1957 to air their views on the creation of "a separate Rivers State" in the context of "their Treaty rights". The other key issue dealt with the identity of the state required.

Concerning the identity of a new Rivers State to be created, Dingle Foot clarified the intentions of his clients. For the avoidance of doubt, Dingle Foot said:

> "They wanted a separate Rivers State but they did not want the full status of one of the existing Regions. They wished for a strong central government with powers over some of the residual subjects now the responsibility of the Regions and wanted the existing Regions to be split into smaller states."

Mr. Dingle Foot, with Colonial Office representatives and others, met with Harold Biriye on May 1957. This meeting, the record disclosed, followed "arrangements made" at the earlier meeting on March 1957. There was no record of any other meeting held at the Colonial Office on the same subject; with the same members, but including Mr Harold Biriye.

Their agenda included "Treaty rights". In particular, Dingle Foot wanted to know how "the treaties would be affected by the grant of regional self-government to the Eastern Region". Biriye, on that occasion, made a singular contribution. According to the official Minutes:

> "Mr. Biriye said that the decisions of the (1950) Conference were not considered to be relevant to the relationship between the Rivers area and the UK Government and it was assumed that the treaties would remain valid. At the 1953 Conference the Rivers area was not directly represented but a Rivers delegate was a member of the UNIP Delegation and spoke only as a member of that Party. After the Conference they made representations to the Deputy Governor in connection with the Lagos Conference, 1954 but these were not accepted on its agenda. They had thus done all that was in their power to make clear their reservations about the new constitutional arrangements."

Meanwhile, Biriye and Udoma jointly reopened issues which they had raised on "Treaty Rights", on 4 June 1957, during a debate on the creation of new states by the Nigeria Constitutional Conference. Both issued a joint Statement on Treaty Rights on behalf of the Rivers Chiefs and Peoples' Conference on one hand and the United National Independence Party (UNIP) on the other. This was their Statement dated 6 October 1958, copy of which they made available to the Colonial Office. In it:

> "It was pointed out that the relationship between the people of the areas concerned and the British Crown was such that if there was a fundamental change in the exercise of sovereignty over Nigeria Her Majesty's Government should give the people the opportunity to choose whether to accept the new form of Government or to contract out of the Federation. Her Majesty's Government could not absolve themselves from their solemn responsibilities under the Treaties by abdicating power and handing over distinct people with distinct culture to a new sovereign Government.
>
> It was maintained at the Conference, at interviews with Representatives of the Colonial Office and before the Minorities Commission at the sittings in Calabar and Port Harcourt, that the Treaties of Protection concluded between Her Majesty's Government in the United Kingdom and representatives of the various Communities in the Province of Calabar, the non-Ibo areas of Ogoja Province and the Rivers Province whereby these areas

voluntarily place themselves under the protection of the British Crown, are still of full force and effect and cannot be terminated unilaterally.

We here and now insist that those Treaties, framed as they were, provide protection for the various Communities concerned against both foreign incursions and native tyranny, but cannot be held to authorize the transfer of sovereignty from the British Crown to any other authority in Nigeria without the prior consent of the Communities concerned.

As the British Government is about to transfer its sovereignty over Nigeria to a new government, namely, the Federal Government of Nigeria, these Communities, we submit, are entitled to decide what should be their relationship with the new sovereign power. They must be given opportunity to decide that issue."

With this firm stand of Biriye and Udoma, on the effects and serious political implications, of these Treaties, for the various communities, it was clear that the UK government was in a tight corner. At this point, Alan Lennox-Boyd, Colonial Secretary, on 8 October 1958, reported this weighty matter with copious enclosures reflecting comments of relevant actors, since the late 1880s, to the Right Hon. Viscount Kilmuir, GCVO, Lord Chancellor, for appropriate advice. It will be recalled that the joint statement made by Biriye and Udoma was dated 6 October 1958, two days earlier, indicating the urgency of this matter in dispute. In his letter, the Colonial Secretary described the matter in a historical setting reflecting the UK Government's point of view and chose his words carefully. This was how the Colonial Secretary put it:

'Stated briefly, the position is that between 1884 and 1888 a number of Treaties were made with the "Rivers Chiefs", whose areas are in the Eastern Region of Nigeria, extending to them the Queen's protection. The present Chiefs are claiming that it would be a breach of the treaties if HMG granted independence to Nigeria without making arrangements, acceptable to them, for themselves and their people, and they ask that a new Region should be created.

The matter was raised at the Constitutional Conference held in May and June, 1957, when the question of granting self-government to the Western and Eastern Regions was being considered, and (Sir Kenneth) Roberts-Wray wrote about it to Reggie (Sir Reginald) Manningham-Buller. In Reggie's view when the treaties were made with the Rivers Chiefs between 1884 and 1888 these Chiefs were not international persons and therefore it followed that the instruments in question were not "treaties" properly so-called. That being so, they did not create any legal obligations resting upon the Crown, and no legal problems were involved in the proposal to incorporate the Rivers area in the Eastern Region which was being given self-government. Reggie recognized that, it might be said that the incorporation was a breach of faith, but the question did not seem to him to be a question of law on which it would be for him to advise.

Whatever their status is as a matter of law, the Rivers Treaties are very highly valued by the Chiefs and peole of the area, and they certainly do not consider that HMG is free from legal obligation or that the treaties can be ignored or revoked unilaterally. I do not feel that, in view of the fact that they have raised both the position of the Queen and the question of moral (as well as legal) obligation, it would be right for me to meet the arguments advanced by their representatives at the present Conference simply by reiterating that in the view of HMG the Treaties are of no legal effect and will therefore be ignored. It would create a bad political effect to imply that the original Treaties themselves and HMG's word were of no real importance, whereas to them they are of great importance.'

So far, it would be seen that Biriye and Udoma, despite the respectable arguments which they advanced, did not succeed in making these compelling on the UK government at this critical stage in Nigeria's constitutional development. This is one further example of the strong attacking the weak. No matter how these two eloquent spokesmen tried, in pleading the cause of their respective Chiefs and people at the London Constitutional Conference, the odds were decidedly against them. Soon, these crusaders had to attempt convincing their own countrymen at the Conference; but there was no visible success.

There, too, their own countrymen's representatives demonstrated their power in opposing them, being the weak party. There was no doubt whatsoever that friends, tried and true, were few and far between as the available documents amply reveal and, for the avoidance of doubt, here fully demonstrate.

Despite these formidable obstacles, Biriye, in an eloquent testimony, again, argued the case for the Rivers Chiefs and People's Conference before an audience larger than the few who heard him in the sequestered rooms of the Colonial Office. Part of his stout defence, when attacked by some of his own countrymen, was before a full session of the Constitutional Conference on 7 October 1958, a day before Lennox-Boyd's historical presentation of the core issues in dispute to Lord Kilmuir. This was how the official record of proceedings reported Biriye's forceful arguments:

> "He drew attention in particular to chapter 7, paragraph 13 of the Minorities Report in which the Minorities Commission had commented on the treaties which existed between the Rivers Chiefs and Peoples and the British Crown. He said that the Commission had studied these treaties and had concluded that they imposed certain legal or moral obligations on Her Majesty's Government. The relevant treaties were treaties of protection and he quoted from a Foreign Office document of 1883 which affirmed that a Protectorate implied the existence of an obligation on the part of the stronger State to protect the weaker State against all its enemies. It might be asked whether the treaties were still valid. In answer to this, he did not think that it was necessary to look further than sub-section 2 of the Royal Instructions of 1948 which stated explicitly that nothing in any local ordinance could detract in any way from treaties of protection made by Queen Victoria and her successors. It was clear from this sub-section of the Royal Instructions that the treaties with the Rivers Chiefs and Peoples were recognized by Her Majesty's Government in 1948 as being valid; nothing had happened since then to alter the position. The United Kingdom Government had in the past made treaties with Nigeria of different kinds. There were those which ceded mineral rights or customs duties; and others which had been made by consuls. There was, finally, a third class of treaty, namely treaties of

protection. The terms of these treaties, and also the meaning of the word protection as used in them, were perfectly clear and he recalled the definition which he had given to the 1957 Conference. This was taken from a Foreign Office document of 1885 which stated that the word protection as used in the proposed treaty with the Rivers Chiefs and Peoples meant that the Queen did not wish to take the trade or the markets of the areas in question but that equally she undertook to ensure that no one else should take them. This made it clear that the treaties gave protection against native incursions as well as against foreign invasion.

The treaties had not been dissolved and could only be altered in one of two ways. First, the parties to the treaties could agree to meet again in order to conclude a new treaty. Secondly, when Nigeria became independent all existing treaties might be held automatically to lapse. There was, however, no doubt that the treaties could not be set aside unilaterally; and he cited the precedents of India and of Ghana.

In considering the treaties it was necessary to bear in mind the question of paramountcy. If the protecting power handed over its sovereign rights to a new sovereign body it was necessary to ensure that the rights previously ceded to the protecting power should revert to those units which had originally yielded them up. The chiefs and peoples with which he was concerned had handed over to Great Britain in the past certain paramount powers, namely the right of sovereignty, the right to make a constitution, the right of revenue and the right of making war. These rights belonged to the chiefs and peoples who had previously exercised them independently, as had been recognized by the Minorities Commission. The chiefs and peoples had not simply thrown away these rights but had ceded them to Great Britain under the terms of the treaties. Accordingly, if Great Britain intended to leave Nigeria, arrangements should be made for the rights ceded under the treaties to revert to the people who had originally yielded them up, so that they could then enter into fresh negotiations with the new sovereign power, the Federal Government of Nigeria."

Any dispassionate reader or listener would have agreed that Biriye's robust defence of Treaty Rights, as set out above, would have moved delegates present at that full session of the Conference to make necessary concessions to accommodate his point of view no matter whose ox was gored. But that was not so among some powerful Nigerian delegates. Yes, a few of them felt impressed and said so in their own contributions but not so in other quarters as the records showed. In practice, Politics, rather than Conscience, prevailed.

For example, Chief Obafemi Awolowo, Premier of the Western Region, leader of the Action Group delegation, and strong supporter of the Udoma-led COR Movement, aligned himself with the eloquent submissions by Biriye and Udoma. Dr. Nnamdi Azikiwe, Premier of the Eastern Region and leader of the NCNC delegation, saw the validity of treaties concluded with African chiefs as "a moot issue in international law" and expected the Secretary of State for the Colonies to make a pronouncement on it. Mr. (later Chief) DC Osadebay, a member of the NCNC delegation and subsequent Premier of the Midwest Region which was excised in 1963 from the Western Region, urged that "numerous other treaties covering all parts of Nigeria" should be considered along with the "Rivers treaties". Alhaji (later Sir) Abubakar Tafawa Balewa, Prime Minister, and member of the Northern Peoples' Congress delegation, made his opposition clear in strong terms. This was how the official record reported Balewa's reaction. He said:

> "... the NPC Delegation had been surprised to hear that Mr. Lennox-Boyd attached such importance to Dr. Udoma's statement. If the treaties were regarded as valid, then none of the major constitutional changes agreed upon at the Conferences since 1953 and brought into effect in Nigeria would have any legal effect: the division of Lagos and the Colony, the creation of Divisions, Provinces and, indeed, Regions, would all be invalidated. There had been thousands of treaties in the Northern Region, many of them made with very minor Chiefs and the majority of them of no significance. His Delegation felt bound to make it clear that they attached no importance to any of these treaties, or to the statement by Dr. Udoma."

Stung by what Balewa said, Udoma quickly and forcefully threw down the gauntlet. Careful in the use of distinctions to be made in the history of Colonial occupation of parts of the territories which later became known as Nigeria, and equipped with irrefutable references to aspects of British involvement in the first and second World Wars, Udoma retorted:

> "...his case could only be settled between himself, the people he represented, and Her Majesty. It was not within the competence of the Conference to make any decision on the validity of his case: this was a matter for him and the Government of the United Kingdom. A distinction should be drawn between territories in Nigeria which had been conquered and ceded, and territories whose rulers had invited the protection of the British Crown. The North had been conquered, Lagos had been ceded, and the treaties covering Asaba and Onitsha had been treaties of cession. His case, resting on the treaties of protection, applied only to the areas described by himself and Mr. Biriye. He said that according to his understanding it had always been the attitude of Her Majesty's Government that treaties were not scraps of paper to be discarded when they became inconvenient. The United Kingdom had twice gone to war in recognition of obligations imposed by treaties."

Fully aware of the thrusts and counter-thrusts of this bewildering array of arguments over a miscellany of treaties, made several decades ago, without any possible prediction of their likely effects on a future Nigerian state of variegated cultural colours and pluralistic ethnic preferences, the Colonial Secretary again sought sound legal advice. He, on 9 October 1958, referred these thorny issues to Lord Kilmuir who, on 13 October 1958, made his views known. These views Lennox-Boyd made available to delegates at this Conference. It would be clear, from a careful analysis of the advice given by Viscount Kilmuir, Lord Chancellor, that the UK Government avoided as much as possible the dimensions of international law and rested its case on convenience and *realpolitic* (pragmatism). Lord Kilmuir's views eventually became the bedrock of the stand of the UK government on this protracted controversy. Here, again, superior power and its effective use prevailed.

745

Immediate and long-term losers were the stakeholders and interests which Biriye and Udoma then represented in London. And this was what Lord Kilmuir said:

> 'In extending Her protection to the Chiefs and peoples concerned, Her Majesty cannot reasonably be regarded as having agreed to freeze conditions in the territory as they existed in 1884: this, indeed, is brought out specifically in the references in the longer version of the Treaty to "the general progress of civilization". It is also emphasized by all the steps which have been taken towards self-government in Nigeria in the past ten years or more, even though I should agree with the suggestion …that the Chiefs should not be regarded as being estopped by their participation in these constitutional developments. In assuming an obligation to extend Her protection to these territories, Her Majesty has surely become entitled to modify their relationship to the rest of Nigeria as part of an orderly process of development towards self-government. This is inconsistent with the contention that the Chiefs should in the last resort be entitled to have their sovereignty restored if the powers of the Crown are ultimately yielded up to a fully self-governing Nigeria (as argued by Mr. Biriye …) for this would tend towards anarchy and to the negation of the orderly progress of the territories which was assumed when the Treaties were made.'

To the best of my knowledge, based on what these deliberately copious citations from the available documents disclosed candidly, it would be fair to say that Biriye and Udoma, as representatives of their respective constituencies in Nigeria, fought a fierce but bloodless battle with key officials of the UK Government during this crucial phase of complex constitutional arrangements to facilitate a delicate transition to Independence. One could call the same contest the last major battle or obstacle before an otherwise bloodless struggle for Independence, with the 1914 map of Nigeria in tact not in tatters.

This battle demonstrated, among others, a prodigious resource-base of talents without which either side, in the combat zone of point versus counterpoint, would have lost much of what was at stake: good faith, security, safety, stability and peace. Yes, were there winners and losers? This bloodless battle could not be diplomatically described as the familiar one of "no victor, no vanquished," contrary to practice after the Nigerian Civil War. In the Constitutional battles, of 1957-1958, the stronger side, in terms of demonstrable power, won no more no less. For the same reason, the weaker side lost.

For the Ijo, in particular, this turn of sad events began with the era of Consular Jurisdiction which brought a plethora of so-called Treaties of Protection though these, as indicated above, failed to protect the weak when they needed such help most. The rest of the Colonial experience, which the Ijo shared with a few like them, further demonstrated weakness when Crude Oil, from the era of exploration in 1937 to that of commercial exploitation in 1958, opened up their fishing waters and farm lands to aggravated forms of environmental pollution and ecological degradation. The third phase was one of severe internal oppression which followed the post-Independence era as would be seen later.

That, of course, was the larger picture. The smaller one would still take one back to the struggle associated with Biriye and the resultant controversy, over a link with Kuwait, yet to be properly concluded.

Much of the preceding extensive and valuable documentation of the various technical and political aspects of the vexed "Treaty Rights" Question, particularly, in its 1957 and 1958 phases, was made possible by Dr. John Enemugwem, Senior Lecturer in History at the University of Port Harcourt, and Secretary, Ijaw History Project. Through painstaking research, he was able to unearth these extremely useful documents at the British National Archives in the United Kingdom. He made copies available to me in early January 2007. Before then, he and I were in considerable puzzlement over what one would call a "Kuwait Hypothesis" in dealing with these treaties and arguments based on them. One of these was contained in that already cited Tribute which Biriye paid Tarka in May 1980.

Some of the difficulties which Dr. Enemugwem and I encountered, in attempting to discover what interpretations and applications of these treaties to accept and project and what to reject with sufficient reasons, where necessary, will now be briefly identified. This kind of assessment was far from easy.

On the basis of the preceding documentation and analysis, so far, the British Government denied any such dramatic return to the *status quo ante* Consular Jurisdiction in the Bights of Benin and Biafra (later Bonny). The only concession it made, in 1957, was in respect of a Commission headed by Sir Henry Willink, Q.C., to allay the fears and anxieties of ethnic minorities before granting Nigeria Independence. Ijo representatives, among others, made their views on Self-Government, through limited statehood, known to the Willink Commissioners during their sessions in Nigeria. However, the Willink Report, 1958, disappointed all such hopes and aspirations.

First, the Willink Report failed to recommend a separate Rivers State, which would embrace all Ijo communities, East and West of the Niger. Second, it recommended instead the setting up of a Niger Delta Development Board (NDDB). Though this was done, in 1961, the NDDB proved too feeble to meet the needs of the Ijo and other ethnic minorities within its jurisdiction. Further, aggrieved Ijo and other communities, in the Niger Delta, felt that the Willink Commission denied them an appropriate and sufficient voice in the management of their affairs. To that extent, one would hesitate to call the Willink Report a watershed concerning the affairs of seriously marginalized ethnic minorities, including the Ijo communities of the Niger Delta. It saw much to be remedied; but did little.

Before and since the Willink Report, the Ijo of the Niger Delta remained a significant ethnic minority in the annals of Nigerian History. Their significance lay merely in providing the locale where Nigeria's golden eggs, through Crude

Oil, were laid and exploited for the benefit of avaricious politicians far away from the centres of despoliation and deprivation. The Ijo communities were also not significant in terms of population, though some observers still believe they constitute Nigeria's 5th or 6th highest ethnic group. That apart, excessive population-growth was not in favour of the Ijo communities because of the serious hazards to human health in their inclement environment.

Claim for a "Kuwait Model" for Rivers State

This seems the right time and place to throw more light than was possible before on any such "Kuwait Model" or Connection with the Niger Delta. In discussions with me, between August 2004 and 19 February 2005, some eminent academic colleagues suggested that some British policy-makers, during top secret talks in Whitehall, tried to lure the Rivers delegate, at the 1957 Constitutional Conference, into demanding a Kuwait Model for the Niger Delta communities with known reserves of Crude Oil discovered in 1938. British contacts, allegedly, offered, as it were, on a platter of gold, the Rivers delegate, Mr. (later Chief) Harold Dappa Biriye, a "Niger Delta Republic". Such an arrangement, if true, would have given British interests exclusive rights to Crude Oil exploitation, with handsome profits to the indigenes, in the future.

In 2004, an eminent Niger Delta historian, Professor Nkparom C. Ejituwu, had given some weight to aspects of the same story. In his Inaugural Lecture, at the University of Port Harcourt, on 8 April 2004, he observed that Niger Delta leaders and their people rejected a British offer of a "Niger Delta Republic" and opted for Nigerian nationhood which, then as now, turned out to be a frustrating tussle between various ethnic nationalities with irreconcilable special interests.

In the light of both these accounts, I began to ascertain their credibility. First, the Willink arrangements, as set out above, would suggest that, in the open sector, British officials did not favour any Kuwait Model for the Oil-bearing lands of the Niger Delta. Second, till Independence, the same officials refused to use their 19th Century Treaties and Agreements of Protection, with the Kings and Chiefs of the Oil Rivers (later, Niger Coast) as a basis for separate negotiations on a model in harmony with the idea of a "Niger Delta Republic". Moreover, other Nigerian delegates to those Conferences, as representatives of Nigeria's larger ethnic groups, would have opposed any such secessionist idea, if made openly or suspected to have been mooted. They had done so vehemently during earlier Secessionist Threats in 1953 and 1954. Such threats, then, had come from the Northern Region and Western Region respectively. It also did not seem plausible that the same Colonial Office, which had vehemently opposed the Secessionist bid of the Western Region, during the premiership of Chief Obafemi Awolowo, in 1954, would have shortly after that major threat to Nigeria's territorial integrity sponsored one in favour of a "Niger Delta Republic" in 1957.

So, as soon as I became a member of the Ijaw History Project, sponsored by the Ijaw National Congress, in the last quarter of 2004, I attempted to see and interview Chief Harold Dappa-Biriye. I was then told how sick he was at Port Harcourt. Moreover, an attempt to locate him in Port Harcourt to secure his consent for such a visit in order to clarify matters concerning what I would call a Kuwait Hypothesis ended in tragedy for reasons reported to members of the Ijaw History Committee during a session in Port Harcourt. Hence, that route of enquiry was postponed. Suddenly, on 17 February 2005, Chief Harold Dappa-Biriye passed away, aged 85. He died a hero to his people. The rest of Nigeria also honoured him and mourned his loss. Such recognition he duly deserved.

In his lifetime, he had fought doggedly for the rights of the various communities of the Niger Delta with intellectual power and rare political skill. By 1959, he had formed a political party, Niger Delta Congress (NDC), to pursue more vigorously his dreams for the communities there. He witnessed part success in the creation of three states in key parts of Ijoland: Rivers, Bayelsa and Delta. So, Biriye's place in Nigerian History, including its Ijo and Niger Delta components, is fully assured.

However, to put Biriye's Kuwait Model into proper perspective, one has to consider as well the following developments. Kuwait became a British Protectorate in 1914 (the same year of Nigeria's Amalgamation) and obtained Independence in 1961, one year after Nigeria's. The discovery of Oil in Kuwait, in 1938, its most outstanding asset of incomparable value then, followed Nigeria's in 1937. Moreover, Saddam Hussein's Iraq claimed Kuwait as part of its pre-Independence territory and so invaded and annexed it in August 1990. That invasion resulted in severe economic damage of Kuwait and extensive pollution of Gulf waters by oil. Before the resultant First Gulf War, in January-February 1991, Crude Oil provided 95% of Kuwait's national revenue. Thus, was Kuwait, though small in size, also beautiful in the eyes of British officials with other eyes on the Niger Delta with known Crude Oil deposits?

Surprisingly, a biography, titled *Harold Dappa-Biriye: His Contributions to Politics In Nigeria*, edited by Professor E J Alagoa, and launched, at Port Harcourt, on 10 February 2005, seven days before Dappa-Biriye's death, was silent on any possible Kuwait Connection. But the same book, in its Appendices II, III and IV, shed some useful, though familiar, lights on aspects of the background to the London Constitutional Conference in 1957.

It will be recalled that a Conference of Rivers Chiefs and People passed a key Resolution on 12 September 1956. In it, the Case for special treatment of the Rivers Area was powerfully articulated so that British authorities, in Nigeria and Britain, would take immediate notice as these were then actively engaged on granting Regional Governments which asked for such Self-Government to be followed by Independence at the earliest available opportunity. The Rivers Chiefs and People were then worried that their rights, as a people, with Treaties of Protection, concluded with the British authorities, in the late 19th century, would be neglected in favour of the larger ethnic groups in Nigeria. They, therefore, in this Resolution, amongst other things, asked for the immediate creation of a "separate Rivers State" or "Protected Rivers State of Nigeria." Significantly, their Resolution used the term "State" whereas the current term elsewhere in Nigeria then was "Region". The areas to be included in the State requested in the same Resolution were:

"the present Administrative Divisions of Aba, Ahoada, Brass, Degema, Ogoni, Port Harcourt, Western Ijaw, together with any Ijaw Districts adjacent to it, the Districts of Andoni, the legal territories of Opobo, and any Ikwerre and Etche Districts in the Owerri Division."

After consultations with British authorities, in Nigeria and Britain, the Rivers Chiefs and People Conference unanimously passed another Resolution, at Port Harcourt, on 23 May 1957. Through this, they mandated "Harold Jeneibiwari Rowland Biriye Esquire" (later Dappa-Biriye) to be their Sole Delegate at the next Constitutional Conference due in London in 1957. They then invested him " with all Power and Authority to do and perform all proper acts, matters and things which may be desirable or necessary for the promotion of our cause of a SEPARATE RIVERS STATE (*sic*)..."

Since not much came out of that enterprise, as the Report of the Willink Commission confirmed, disillusionment quickly followed. That climate of disgust and despair, among leaders of the Conference of Rivers Chiefs and People, neither the 1958 Constitutional Conference nor the prospect of Nigeria's Independence dispelled.

The next ray of hope seemed to lie in a promise, in 1958, to make the Rivers territory a "Special Area" with the possibility of carving it into another "Federal Territory" (in addition to Lagos). For that purpose, Biriye's Niger Delta Congress, formed in 1959, allied with the Northern Peoples' Congress. That dream also failed as the Western Region and Eastern Region vehemently opposed it. The latter, in particular, would have suffered not only loss of territory but also increasing royalties from the exploration and exploitation of commercial quantities of Crude Oil, since 1958, from Oloibiri and other fields in the area to be excised, if possible.

How much sense would all of the above make concerning a Kuwait Connection with the Niger Delta in 1957? First, the idea of a "Niger Delta Republic" then would not have been in consonance with well-established monarchical notions and institutions in Britain. Second, neither Eastern Nigeria nor any of the other Regions of the Nigerian Federation then would have supported such an idea without violence.

This set of facts would also not match Britain's decision to support Federal Nigeria during the fierce attempts by proponents of Biafra's attempted Secession and Civil war, 1967-70. Besides, in that confrontation, Ijo communities supported Federal troops in their bloody War against Biafra, which behaved like Iraq in her relations with Kuwait. Hence, until credible evidence becomes available, it is too soon to pin on the Ijo crisis of Identity, Equity and Justice, of the 1950s and since 1960, any attempted Kuwait Model, Connection or Hypothesis. Meanwhile, it is best to leave any such Model or Connection in the Cold Room of History, where most of the key actors of that era are now, until it is proved beyond any reasonable doubt.

If, indeed, Oil-rich Kuwait and Oil-rich Ijo Communities of the Niger Delta did not follow the same pathway, during the Colonial era, I humbly suggest the following reasons:

- Either British policy makers then did not actively and seriously canvass a so-called Kuwait Model (of unilateral excision),
- Either the official Rivers Delegate, in 1957, did not strongly press for it,
- Or both.

So, British officials, between 1957 and 1959, did not revoke the 19th Century Treaties and Agreements signed with the Kings and Chiefs of the Oil Rivers (later Niger Coast) Protectorate. That refusal sealed the fate of the Ijo and other communities of the Oil Rivers. Thereafter, their identification with the developing Nigerian State became inescapable. They had no viable alternative as their loyalty during the Civil War years amply demonstrated.

Post-Colonial Points of Friction with the Nigerian State
Moreover, the Ijo communities knew the same limits of planning a safe and sustainable course of action between the treble forces of micro-nationalism,

nationalism and internationalism (Globalism). They also knew how best to protect their interests in their epic struggle for survival against immense odds in the development of Nigeria's multi-national state from the Colonial era to the present.

As seasoned fishermen, farmers and traders, the Ijo communities knew the thrusts of the two hypotheses, propositions, foundations or platforms discussed earlier in this Chapter. Hence, their *modus operandi* was and should remain pragmatic. One and all, they should seek to optimize, not minimize, what are the best strategies and tactics, for defence and offence, in their ambient socio-political environment, which has been quite hostile to their interests. The Ijo, therefore, should not seek to eat the rest of Nigeria but the rest of Nigeria also should not attempt to eat the Ijo, despite the known fact that Big Fishes eat the Small. That way, it would also be possible for known elephants and ants to exist in an agreed atmosphere of "Live and let live": also the NDC's Motto. Accordingly, Alienation, though deep-rooted, should not be allowed by Ijo stakeholders and their neighbours to damage the undergrowth and superstructure of Nigeria's Stability Tree.

Ijo frustrations, in the post-Colonial era, discredited the leadership of elders in their Colonial struggle for survival on platforms of Justice, Equity and Equality with others in Nigeria. Youth leadership, through violence, no longer through failed peaceful ventures by elders, followed.

A new leader quickly announced his presence: Isaac Jasper Adaka Boro. This frustrated young Ijo undergraduate, of the University of Nsukka, assembled 159 Youths under the banner of the first Niger Delta Volunteer Service. On 23 February 1966, this formation began operations, in the creeks of the Niger Delta, against the rest of Nigeria. Its mission of Liberation of Ijoland, by force, quickly proved impossible. Their resistance collapsed within 12 days. They opposed better-equipped Federal troops.

With the collapse of dreams of a "Niger Delta Republic", Boro and two of his deputies – Samuel Owonaro and Nottingham Dick – were tried for treason in late March 1966. Found guilty, they were sentenced to death on 21 June 1966. Pardoned by Military Ruler, General Yakubu Gowon, in August 1967, Boro, Owonaro and Dick joined Federal troops in their efforts to liberate parts of Rivers State, then forcibly occupied by Biafran troops. Boro died on active service, on 20 April 1968. He, however, remained an undying hero and martyr in the hearts and minds of angry Ijo Youths decades after.

Here, some events and trends, during the 1980s and 1990s, in Nigeria and the rest of the world, which inflicted, at least, a few major demonstrable impacts on the Ijo Struggle, need attention. These included the following major events and trends worldwide:

- From the 1980s, the first century after the Berlin West African Conference on the Partition of Africa, 1884-85, international interest gradually shifted from earlier concentration on struggles for Independence to how the governed could combat recurrent disillusionment, crises and conflicts. Therefore, a painful search for peaceful resolution of conflicts, through other means, followed. These included measures to address and redress the claims of micro-nationalism against those of macro-nationalism.

- The end of the Cold War, in Europe, following the fall of the Berlin Wall and the era of President Mikhail Gorbachev in the former USSR, encouraged local freedom fighters to embark on their respective crusades without being labelled Communist sympathizers in Western circles.

- New NGOs sprang up, in Nigeria and elsewhere, from the 1980s, to advocate more vigorously than before the attainment and maintenance of Fundamental Human Rights.

- The era of Information and Communications Technology, (ICT) gave the widest possible and instant publicity to all manner of agitations and reactions to them worldwide.
- The UNO gave impetus to all such crusades by declaring the era, 1994-2004, its Decade of Indigenous Peoples.

In Nigeria, the era, since the 1990s, witnessed several episodes of micro-nationalism. The South-West had an Oodua Peoples Congress (OPC) in addition to cultural associations such as Afenifere and Yoruba Council of Elders (YCE). Northern Nigeria constantly espoused its interests through a powerful Arewa Peoples Congress (APC) and Arewa Consultative Forum (ACF). Before long, the Urhobo made decisions of their First Economic Summit a major feature of advancing their interests.

An Ogoni Bill of Rights (26 August 1990) and its Addendum (26 August 1991) hit national and international headlines with robust articulation of their "historic wrongs" and measures to redress them. More Declarations in the same spirit followed:
- Chikoko Movement, August 1997
- Kaiama Declaration, 11 December 1998.
- Oron Bill of Rights, 25 June 1999
- The Warri Accord, 25-29 June 1999

So, in the context of all the above, the renewed agitation for Ijo Rights, such as the Kaiama Declaration most eloquently articulated, to audiences at home and abroad, gave sufficient warning that the Old World in Nigeria needed change urgently. Failure to do so meant a refusal to discern the far-reaching consequences and impacts of what comparable events and trends elsewhere amply demonstrated. Indeed, several ardent advocates of freedom from oppression and fundamental human rights for all, including the hard-pressed Ijo communities, have held out the Kaiama Declaration, from 1998 to the present, as an effective summary of their hopes and aspirations in the foreseeable future.

Basically, approaches to Civil Rights and nationality crusades, such as the Kaiama and similar Declarations encouraged, though not as street-based and street-wise as those in post-1990 Eastern and Central Europe, adopted written Protests (and the like) as well as electronic media presentations. The Youth who led these activities were reasonably educated though the bulk of their followers came from school dropouts and un-employed graduates produced in Nigeria's Universities, Polytechnics and Colleges of Education. Other ranks included Civil Society's disgruntled wrecks (such as Trouble's Best Friends). Disillusionment, in their ranks, and among elders also, resulted from frustrations since the lukewarm recommendations concerning the Niger Delta, in the Willink Report (1958). From Independence, Nigeria's new rulers, drawn from her largest ethnic blocs (Hausa and Fulani, Yoruba and Ndigbo) had little or no regard for the General Welfare of smaller ethnic groups, such as the Ijo and their neighbours in the Niger Delta. Their world, one of oppressors, met all one would expect from the two guiding Hypotheses of this concluding chapter. Moreover, mere creation of new States, between 1967 and 1996, did not and could not sort out quickly the sores in the body politic from insults inflicted since the 1950s, if not much earlier, in the development of the Nigerian State based on multi-culturalism and ethnic pluralism.

Some of the sore points which caused perennial pains and groans, as far as the Ijo and their neighbours were concerned, were embedded in legislation during Nigeria's military era:

- The Minerals/Petroleum Decree, 1969.
- The Land Use Decree, 1991.
- The Oil Pipelines Decree, 1991.
- The Petroleum Decree, 1991.
- The National Inland Waterways Authority Decree, 1997.

Similarly frustrated were the Ijo and their neighbours over developments since the Willink Recommendations. These included:

- The Niger Delta Development Board (NDDB) 1961.
- The Niger Delta River Basin Authority (NDRBA) 1976.
- The Oil Mineral Producing Areas Development Commission (OMPADEC) 1992.
- The Niger Delta Development Commission (NDDC) 1999.

Superficially, the policies, practices, programmes and projects associated with all the above could be seen as Development–driven. But, basically, all, without exception, represented ideas dictated from the Top whereas most of the expected beneficiaries urged Bottom-Up types.

Moreover, at the national level, Ijo communities and their neighbours associated themselves with agitation for root-and-branch reforms concerning their General Welfare. These included controversies over items that resulted in victims and victimizers merely agreeing to disagree. Resultant crises, controversies and conflicts, in these respects and more, touched upon "Resource Control" or Fiscal Federalism (including liberal Derivation principles), Radical Review and Reform of Nigeria's system of Federalism as deformed by decades of Military Rule, Presidentialism and so-called "Power-Shift", Devolution of Powers, Poverty Alleviation (if not Elimination), Aggressive Crusades against epidemic Corruption, Crime and Indiscipline, among others. On these issues, Ijo advocacy did not always agree with preferences of other ethnic nationalities.

Youth and Adult disillusionment, elsewhere in the Nigerian Federation, resulted from grievances with local, national and wider inputs (including Nigeria's huge external debts and trans-national crimes of the "419", money laundering, counterfeiting and other related varieties). Glaring Adult involvement in such forms of malpractice really disappointed Youths, particularly, those in Nigeria's educational institutions, over the lack of Leadership credentials among national leaders and others in the private sector. Resultant Students Unrest nationwide included institutions in Ijoland.

In Ijo communities, local feuds, such as Chieftaincy and Land disputes, illegal "bunkering" and traffic in illegal firearms, aggravated an already intolerable climate of violence and counter-violence. In that milieu, political leaders and their followers truly led-by-example: by recruiting thugs with lethal weapons to ensure their continued success in controversial Party nominations and Nigeria's latest contribution to World Politics: "Carry-Go-Elections" in 2003 and "Do-and Die" types in 2007.

Hence, to a large extent, the phenomenon of Youth Militancy (involving indiscriminate resort to violence and counter–violence, including senseless hostage-taking) spread its tentacles within and outside Ijoland. Local factors encouraged miscellaneous organizations such as those led by Ateke Tom and Mujahid Dokubo Asari and others. Later, some of these took forms cast in a politics–driven mould. "Egbesu Boys", the main target of invading Federal troops in the Odi Massacre, November 1999, belonged to the same group of Youth intoxicated with the opium of politics. That type of vicious and much maligned Youth intoxication became more and more widespread, in the Niger Delta, from May 1999 to the present.

Even so, among leaders of militant youth organizations, Muhajid Dokubo Asari seemed unique. In his ideology, if not in other respects as well, Dokubo seemed a near perfect replica of Isaac Adaka Boro. Though, at first, treated as a common felon, Dokubo later gained immense respect, locally, nationally and internationally, including the Ijo Diaspora. Dokubo, as leader of the Boro-style Niger Delta Peoples Volunteer Force (NDPVF), and Ateke Tom, leader of a rival Niger Delta Vigilante Group, caused considerable mayhem and fear in the areas of their operations. Theirs and similar organizations, in the Niger Delta, helped to aggravate Terror nationwide.

Between 2006 and 2007, a new organization, known as Movement for the Emancipation of the Niger Delta (MEND), publicly expressed a strong desire to continue and win the protracted struggle for freedom as attempted by Boro and others. Most of its leaders and members, including University graduates and other professionals, unlike the predominance of school drop-outs in the preceding ranks of militants, were Ijo followers of Boro's idealism and heroic efforts before his sudden death. However, MEND ranks were soon infiltrated by hoodlums with criminal intent. For example, through incessant acts of terrorism, including hostage-taking and vandalization of oil pipes, among others, these infiltrators into MEND circles gave the Ijo struggle a bad name in parts of Rivers, Delta and Bayelsa states. These felons and others who aided and abetted them, indeed, commercialized Terror and derived huge sums, believed to run into several millions of naira per hostage. To combat these wanton acts, the Federal Government, first, under President Olusegun Obasanjo and, later, under President Umaru Musa Yar' Adua, deployed Joint Task Forces at sea, on land and in the air. However, success in such counter-terrorism efforts did not come quickly for reasons including the difficult environment and corruption in official and private quarters.

Miscellaneous matters arising from the above include how to put back into the bottle the genie that was allowed to come out of it: locally, nationally and internationally. It is no longer enough to put all the blame on the triangular conflicts between my category of 3 Cs: Communities, Corporations or Companies and Country. Poisons from those conflicts (through uncontrolled and, so far, uncontrollable bribery and corruption) have done their worst, just as Nigeria's conventional wicked have been known to do, in relations between all the 3Cs. Illegal Bunkering, of local, national and international dimensions, has also aggravated levels of corrupt practices in all Oil-producing outlets of the Niger Delta.

At the higher national level, social therapies needed would, in my view, include concerted efforts to ensure the reign of another set of 3Cs: Consultation, Consent and Co-operation. Without this extended family of three pro-Peace members, no lasting success can be guaranteed for Nigerians at the levels of macro-nationalism and micro-nationalism.

National Political Reform Conference or National Dialogue and its Alternatives

On 21 February 2005, an official or Presidential National Political Reform Conference (National Dialogue) began its sessions in Abuja with delegates or representatives selected, not elected, during Chief Olusegun Obasanjo's Presidency, from some specified bodies or organizations and respected individuals. Against it was an alternative preferred by its leaders, Chief Anthony Enahoro, a veteran politician and statesman, since the 1950s, and Nobel Laureate, Professor Emeritus Wole Soyinka: Pro-National Conference Organizations (PRONACO). While the former, National Dialogue, made Nigeria's territorial integrity and sovereignty as well as its system of Federalism "No-Go Areas", PRONACO's favoured a previous idea of a Sovereign National Conference (SNC) with no excluded zones. On the other hand, the official National Dialogue did not favour that line.

Though Nigerian Liberals and Conservatives took different positions on these two battle lines, public opinion generally favoured Dialogue, Now rather than Later and Never. Pessimists feared that, without that kind of timely intervention, Nigeria would most likely suffer from setbacks of an uncontrollable explosion or implosion with wide ranging continental and global impacts and implications.

Reactions to the above, among Ijo communities, took local and national dimensions. The Niger Delta States, including Ijo communities, complied with President Obasanjo's request to send six delegates each to the National Dialogue. The PRONACO line was one, which more radical-minded Nigerians, young and old, favoured. In particular, Muhajid Dokubo Asari, leader (since 2001) of his NDPVF, plus Ateke Tom of the Niger Delta Vigilante Group (former "Bush Boys" in Okrika) as well as leaders of the Ijaw Youth Council and Chikoko Movement hastily formed (in early February 2005) a Pan Niger Delta Action Conference (PANDAC). The representatives of PANDAC quickly met with Chief Enahoro and other leaders of PRONACO on goals and means for their preferred course of action. In the view of PANDAC's leaders, an

SNC, such as PRONACO espoused, was the only viable option in measures to promote peaceful co-existence of the country's numerous ethnic nationalities. For the avoidance of doubt, PRONACO's SNC claimed to represent Nigeria's estimated total number of 306 "ethnic nationalities". At the end of 2006, PRONACO leaders said they had worked out the lineaments of a new Constitution for Nigeria but its details were not made available for further discussion by members of the public.

What More Answers to the "Niger Delta Question"?

So, it is time now to put on President Umaru Musa Yar' Adua's table, for urgent political discourse, some ideas concerning ways to find viable answers to what most people term the "Niger Delta Question" since it still sets on fire innocent victims among the Ijo and other troubled communities in the Niger Delta. Before and since President Olusegun Obasanjo's National Dialogue, in 2005, attention on what most advocates and antagonists termed "Resource Control" considerably agitated minds in public and official circles. Earlier chapters of this book also referred to it as a possible solution of the long-standing three-pronged conflicts between the Ijo and other Niger Delta communities on one hand and relevant multi-national companies as well as country on the other. These I have always seen as the 3 Cs at the centre of the Niger Delta Crisis with difficult to dissect small and large intestines. In my view, control of such resources, including Oil and Gas, alone would not necessarily amount to a lasting solution of deeply felt injuries in the affected communities, nasty insults which have persisted for several decades since 1937, the year of encouraging Crude Oil exploration in the Niger Delta.

In my *Niger Delta Question* (2000), I had suggested the primacy of Education, among viable alternative options. I still believe so. My firm belief here rests on a sure foundation. Without doubt, Education, in its widest possible sense, and from the cradle to the grave, if well handled, is capable of producing and

762

reproducing a sufficient mix of multiplier effects which would constitute an essential engine for sustainable growth and development. Moreover, it is that kind of quality input, trigger or bullet which a people, such as the Ijo, still in their well-known predicament, would need most to secure their future: short-term, medium-term or long-term. Furthermore, whereas Oil and Gas are wasting assets or quite limited natural resources, for long-term Development, focused on sustainable General Welfare of a people, Education or the Knowledge-Industry based on it is not so limited. In addition, Education's total utility, across frontiers of time and place, makes it the ideal instrument for exploring and exploiting the best possible adaptations, as and when due, in an atmosphere of Change as earlier described. Indeed, this way and none other would it be possible for the Ijo and their neighbours in the Niger Delta, radically and effectively, to transform their current and recurrent status of comparative weakness into one of enduring strength.

Besides, concerning repeated and repeatable controversies, over the scale of and necessity for the so-called 13% Derivation formula, I am of the view that mere monetization of massive human suffering, through any form of Derivation principle, despite what others say to the contrary, may satisfy only advocates of compensation, in the short run, without bringing much needed security, safety, stability and peace of sustainable quality. Indeed, compensation amounts to what, in this case, I would regard as monetization of man's inhumanity to man in one's fatherland. Quite often, I have heard ardent Ijo youth deride the present (as of December 2007) Derivation figure of 13%, for Nigeria's Oil states, as "87% Deprivation". However, stronger voices in official and other circles continue to stick to this ignoble formula of little pro-Peace promise, particularly, as was amply demonstrated during the hot debates associated with it in the abortive mid-2005 Dialogue Exercise. In its place, one would easily draw sufficient wisdom from a familiar Latin adage: *"Bis dat qui cito dat"* (He gives twice who gives quickly). The dignity of man, which is ennobled further with every panoply of freedom and liberty, in my view, has no monetary equivalents whatsoever, anywhere, any time.

763

Moreover, where needless deaths have constantly occurred from Oil and Gas driven pollution and degradation, with serious threats of more and more lethal and fatal consequences, prevention, in these circumstances, as in others, is still better than cure. Often, advocates of Containment strategies and tactics, in preference to Prevention-driven measures, prove unwilling and unable to provide as well escalating costs which that approach to conflict-resolution entails.

Hence, in this ensuing battle of ideas, among an over-extended group of advocates and antagonists of measures to allay the fears and anxieties of the Ijo and their neighbours in seemingly unending distress, one finds that another eminent scholar has added his weighty voice on the side of sanity. Professor Ladipo Adamolekun, NNOM, a national laureate and specialist of great distinction in management studies, though in favour of giving Niger Delta communities more control of their resources, believed, like most of us, that the core issues in their long drawn crisis would be solved mainly through adoption of appropriate innovation and creativity-driven actions. Mere reliance on Resource Control, if based only on a, so far, politically unpredictable coalition of interests in a country yet to be sufficiently reconstructed for responses of the kind which Ijo and other Niger Delta communities continue to request, he further stressed, was not likely to succeed. So, in March 2007, he ruefully observed: "The Niger Delta (sic) is an extreme statement of the failure of the governance in Nigeria."

On the political plane, my own studies, over time, suggest that despite well documented cases of prolonged victimization, including miscellaneous impacts of weakness from myriad acts of commission and omission, on the part of the strong, the Ijo cause would be best served through continued membership of the Nigerian federal state, if reconstructed well enough to accommodate the hopes and aspirations of all citizens and residents through justice, equity, freedom and peace. It is a future whose broad frame and prospects should not be marred by the well-known errors of the Past, including injustice and all manner of discrimination. In that future, none would be seen as a slave or slave of a slave. So, anyone who escaped from one type of slavery, especially, that of Colonialism, should neither inherit nor be coerced into another form of servitude, called by other names, in his or her homeland. So construed, the Ijo and their counterparts, not only in the Niger Delta but elsewhere in Nigeria, would be entitled to enjoy all the first-fruits of citizenship and residency, particularly, those of security, safety, stability, general welfare and peace.

So far, it will be recalled that, in one chapter after another of this carefully constructed work, the dismal plight of the Ijo and their neighbours in the Niger Delta, including its fringes, has been honestly, comprehensively and authoritatively described and analyzed. Often, this enormous Ijo burden resembled an albatross on the shoulders of leaders and followers, before and since Nigeria's Independence. Their egregious acts of commitment and omission, inevitably, constituted part of this stubborn problem. Quite often too, their glib rhetoric, rather than demonstrable political skill and will to embrace radical reform and associated reconstruction, ruled the day. Being part of the problem, one would also expect them to be part of the solution. But, no quick answers of lasting value followed their uncertain steps in their combative arena of politics and governance.

Painfully, in circles of innocent victims, such as those of the Niger Delta, each and every misstep of a succession of Nigeria's top leaders before and since Independence, as these left much to be desired, brought instant dismay, disappointment and distrust. But, delay, here as elsewhere, could prove dangerous and should be best avoided.

Nevertheless, somehow, something tells me that a New Dawn, in the near future, should not be ruled out. One sincerely hopes that, if and when it comes, it would reveal not only promise but also fulfillment, one of desired change in goals and means for the ultimate good of Nigerians, particularly, those of the Niger Delta.

It does seem that a primary instrument, for that change, is most likely to be the new man at the helm of national policy-making and implementation. This would be no other than the former radical politician of NEPU and PRP fame, one well groomed in the School of a well-known reformist leader, Alhaji Aminu Kano, from Kano state. This new leader, Alhaji Umaru Musa Yar' Adua, former PDP Governor of Katsina state, and President, since 29 May 2007, has sufficient credentials and assets for a new role as a functional fulcrum of radical and bloodless change in the Niger Delta and elsewhere in Nigeria. Fortunately, he is also Commander-in-Chief of the Armed Forces of the Federal Republic of Nigeria with a Vice-President, Dr. Goodluck Jonathan, former Governor, Bayelsa state. Together, and with favourable trade winds, nationwide, both leaders should be able to guide the ship of state to safe ports with all the hitherto disaffected Ijo and neighbours on board. Both these top leaders would, thus, not only make desired change possible but also significant in terms of peaceable conflict-resolution for a long time to come. Thus, from 29 May 2007, a unique combination, at the top leadership, in Nigeria's Politics and Governance, which was never contemplated during the controversies surrounding the Constitutional Conferences of the era of the Willink Commission (1957-1958), came to assume responsibility for answering positively the over 50-year old Niger Delta Question. This combination is particularly unique in another sense. The Yar' Adua–Jonathan partnership represents not only North-South connectivity but also Fulani-Ijo understanding, both in political terms. Whether or not that rare opportunity would be taken in a statesmanlike fashion is another matter. In this regard, one need not rule out the doubts of avowed pessimists as well.

In the the light of all the above, readers would now be able to recall my earlier choice of some cardinal determinants of History which are also critical, in this case, for an urgent resolution of the long-standing Niger Delta crisis. For the avoidance of doubt, these are the key factors of Time, Circumstance, Leadership/Followership and Accident/Chance. Working in concert, they could provide the long-expected opportunity to ensure that the current and recurrent Niger Delta Question would be answered affirmatively.

Even so, I am not just a professional historian but also a realist, one not yet a converted prophet nor a star-gazing optimist. Yes, I fully recognize that Prediction and History are still poles apart. And so, I readily admit that, here too, there could be many a slip between the cup and the lip as sages of all ages still proclaim.

Before one gets crucified on such a needless cross, there is this irrepressible need to say here, and say it over and over, that calls for urgent change concerning Nigeria's latest major and widely acknowledged contribution to Globalization, the Niger Delta Question, have become more and more insistent, at home and abroad, for reasons not many vigilant observers would deny. Further delay could, therefore, injure severely domestic and international Oil and Gas interests. For example, dauntless MEND threats, incessant hostage-taking of innocent Nigerians (including most unfortunate children) and foreign citizens as well as spiralling increases in the price of Crude Oil (as much as $100 per barrel as of late November 2007) plus other forms of relentless distress nationwide have made it abundantly clear that the Niger Delta Question is now sufficiently globalized for all concerned to take due notice. Here, as elsewhere, a stitch in time could still save nine.

BIBLIOGRPAHY
(References Cited in the Chapters)

Jigekuma A. Ombu

Aaron, Uche E. 1994. *Tense and Aspect in Obolo Grammar and Discourse.* Ph.D. dissertation, University of California, Santa Barbara. [6]

Abam, A. S. 1999. *The Okrika Kingdom.* Owerri: The Author. [29]

Abam, A. S. 1988. *A History of the Eastern Niger Delta, 1885-1960: Challenges and Responses of a Society in Transition.* Unpublished PhD Thesis, University of Lagos, Nigeria [16]

Abangwo, D.S. 1996. *Reading and Writing Degema.* Fourth edition, revised by Daniel S. Okpara, Ethelbert E. Kari and Kay Williamson. Port Harcourt: Rivers Readers Project. [6]

Abasiattai, M. B. (Ed.). 1987. *Akwa Ibom and Cross River States: The Land, the People and Their Culture.* Calabar: Wusen Press. [23]

Abba, A. 2006. *The Politics of Mallam Aminu Kano.* Kaduna: Vanguard Printers and Publishers Ltd. [29]

Abia, O. T. 1988. *The Palm Industry and the Economic Transformation of the Lower Cross River Region.* PhD thesis, History Dept., University of Calabar. [23]

Abia, O. T. 2003. *Citation of His Royal Highness King Owen Sylvanus Ukafia-Ede VI, Paramount Ruler of Eastern Obolo LGA, Akwa Ibom State.* (Uyo: MSS) [29]

Achonwa, B. 1981. *Glimpse of Ōchichi: A Near-Extinct Language of Etche.* Unpublished Manuscript, School of Humanities, University Port Harcourt, Nigeria. [6]

Adams, J. 1822. *Sketches Taken During Ten Voyages to Africa Between the Years 1786 and 1800.* London: Hurst, Robinson & Co. [16]

Ade, R. M. 1980. *Baptist Work in Eastern Nigeria 1850-1980.* (An Unpublished Manuscript). [19]

Adelugba, D. (2005). 'Foreword', in Tamuno, T. N. *Lamentations of Yeske.* Ibadan: Stirling-Horden. [6]

Adelugha D., A. O. Ashaolu and S. O. Asein. 1986. J. P. Clark-Bekederemo Festschrift, *Review of English and Literary Studies* (Special Number). 3, 2. [6]

Ademola, A. 1987. Kings College, 1920-1924. In *Seventy-Five Years of King's College Lagos.* Lagos: King's College. [29]

Adesina, S. 1977. *Planning and Educational Development in Nigeria.* Lagos: Academy Press. [22]

Adeyinka, A.A. 1982. Traditional Education in Nigeria. (Unpublished Lecture Handout) [12]

Adu, G. C. 1980. *The Contributions of Rev. Dr. Mojola Agbebi to Missionary Work in Rivers State, Nigeria* (NCE Project Essay, Rivers State College of Education, Port Harcourt). [19]

Afigbo, A. E. 1965. Efik Origin and Migrations Reconsidered. *Nigeria. Magazine* No. 87. [23]

Afigbo, A. E. 1972. *The Warrant Chiefs: Indirect Rule in Southeastern Nigeria, 1891-1929.* London: Longman.   [17, 18]

Afigbo, A. E. 1980. The Eastern Provinces Under Colonial Rule. in Obaro Ikime (ed) *Groundwork of Nigerian History.* Ibadan: Heinemann Educational Books. [12, 19]

Afigbo, A. E. 1981. *Studies in Igbo History and Culture.* Ibadan. [23]

Afolabi, D. 1998. *The Nigerian Mangrove Ecosystem.* Third Regional Workshop of the Gulf of Guinea Large Marine Ecosystem (GOGLME). Lagos, Nigeria. [2]

Agbegha, C.B 2002. "Developing an Endangered Language: The Example" in O. Arohunmolase (Ed.) *The Development of the Minority Language in Nigeria.* Ondo: Complete Computer and Educational Service. [6]

Agbegha, M.L. 1961. *Ezon Mi Beke Mi Ten Eye Fun (Ijaw–English Vocabulary).* Warri: [The Author] Printed at Kagho Industrial Enterprises. [6]

Agbegha, M.L. 1968. *Izon Bibi Teghe Fun.* Warri: [the author] Kagho Ind. Enterprises. [6]

Agbegha, M.L. 1996. *Izon–English Dictionary Based on the Mein Dialect.* Port Harcourt: Riverside Communications. [6]

Agedah, D. B. 1984. *A History of Kolokuma: An unpublished B.A History Project,* University of Port Harcourt, Nigeria. [16]

Ajayi, J. F. A. 1965. *Christian Missions in Nigeria 1941–1891: The Making of a New Elite.* London: Longman Group Ltd. [12, 22]

Ajayi J. F. A. and Michael Crowder (Eds.) 1976. *History of West Africa,* Vol. I. Basingstoke, U.K.: Longman, Group Limited. [17, 21]

Ake, C. 1981. *A Political Economy of Africa.* London: Longman Group Ltd. [29]

Ake-Okahilian, O. 2002. "Ethnic Minorities and Marginalisation in the Niger Delta Region of Nigeria" Unpublished Ph.D Dissertation, University of Port Harcourt. [18]

Akpabot. S. E. 1985. *Football in Nigeria.* Ikeja: Nigeria Macmillan Publishers. [29]

Akpoghomeh, O.S. and A.M. Okorobia. 1999. Population Profile. in Alagoa, E.J. (ed) *The Land and People of Bayelsa State: Central Niger Delta.* Port Harcourt: Onyoma Research Publications. [3]

Akpoghomeh, O.S. and J. D. Atemie. 2002 Population Profile. in Alagoa, E.J. and A.A. Derefaka (Eds.) *The Land and People of Bayelsa State: Eastern Niger Delta.* Port Harcourt: Onyoma Research Publications [3]

Alagoa, E.J. 1964. Oporoza and Early Trade on the Escravos. *Journal of the History Society of Nigeria.* Vol. 5, No. 1, 152-156. [18]

Alagoa, E. J. 1964. *The Small Brave City-State: A History of Nembe-Brass in the Niger Delta.* Madison: University of Wisconsin Press. [16, 29]

Alagoa, E. J. 1966. Ijo Origins and Migrations. *Nigeria Magazine.* Vol 91, pp. 279-288. [16]

Alagoa E. J. 1967. Delta Masquerades. *Nigeria Magazine,* No. 93. [16]

Alagoa, E. J. 1967. Koko: Amanyanabo of Nembe. *Tarikh,* Vol. 1, No. 4. [23]

Alagoa, E. J. 1968. The *Ju* Festival. *Nigeria Magazine,* 96, 11-16. [17]

Alagoa, E. J. 1968. The Western Apoi: Notes on the Use of Ethnographic Data in Historical Reconstruction. *African Notes* (Ibadan), 5, 1, 12-24. [17]

Alagoa E. J. 1970. *A Slave Who Became a King,* London: Longman. [18]

Alagoa E. J. 1970. Long Distance Trade and States in the Niger Delta. *Journal of African History,* Vol. 11, No 3. [10, 17, 16, 22, 28]

Alagoa E. J. 1970. The Development of Institutions in the States of the Eastern Niger Delta. *Journal of African History.* Vol. 11, No 3. [10, 16]

Alagoa, E. J. 1971. Nembe: The City Idea in the Eastern Niger Delta. *Cahiers d'etudes Africaine.* Vol. 11, no 42. [16, 16]

Alagoa, E. J. 1971. The Development of Institutions in the States of the Eastern Niger Delta. *Journal of African History.* Vol. 12, No. 2, 269-278. [23]

Alagoa, E. J. 1971. The Niger Delta States and their Neighbours 1600-1800. In J. F. Ade-Ajayi and Michael Crowder (Eds.) *History of West Africa,* Vol. 1. New York: Longman Group Ltd. [25]

Alagoa E. J. 1971. The Slave Revolts: Nineteenth Century Revolutions in the Eastern Delta States and Calabar. *Journal of the Historical Society of Nigeria,* Vol. 5, No. 4. [16]

Alagoa, E. J. 1972. *A History of the Niger Delta: An Historical Interpretation of Ijo Oral Tradition.* Ibadan: Ibadan University Press. (Republished in 2005 by Onyoma Research Publication Publications, Port Harcourt). [1, 2, 3, 6, 18, 10, 16, 12, 17, 16, 17, 18, 19, 6, 21, 22, 24, 29, 25, 27, 28]

Alagoa, E.J. 1973. Oral Tradition and Archaeology: The Case of Onyoma. *Oduma* (Publication of the Rivers State Council for Arts and Culture). Vol. I No.1 October [10]

Alagoa, E.J. 1974. Terracotta from the Niger Delta. *Black Orpheus* Vol. 3, No. 2/3. [7]

Alagoa, E.J. 1975. The Inter-Disciplinary Approach to African History in Nigeria. *Presence Africaine* No. 94 (2nd Quarter): 171-183. [10]

Alagoa, E.J. 1976. Dating Ijo Oral Traditon. *Oduma.* Vol. 3 No. 1 April 1976, 19-21. [10]

Alagoa, E.J. 1976. The Niger Delta States and their neighbours to 1800. In J. F. A. Ajayi and M. Crowder (Eds.). *History of West Africa,* Vol. 1. London: Longman. [18, 21]

Alagoa, E.J. 1976. *Reconsttructing Ancient Times in the Eastern Niger Delta: The Contribution of Archaeology*. Paper presented to the 21st Annual Congress of the Historical Society of Nigeria, 7th-10th April. [10]

Alagoa, E. J. 1977. The Niger Delta States and their Neighbours to 1800. In J. F. Ade Ajayi and Michael Crowder (eds). *History of West Africa*; Vol. 1. Second Edition. New York: Colombia University Press and Longman. pp. 335-337 [16]

Alagoa, E. J. 1980. King Frederick William Koko of Nembe. In T. N. Tamuno and E. J. Alagoa (Eds.), *Eminent Nigerians of Rivers State*. Ibadan: Heinemann Educational Books. [29]

Alagoa, E.J. 1980. The Eastern Niger Delta and the Hinterland in the 19th Century. In Obaro Ikime (Ed.) *Groundwork of Nigerian History*. Ibadan: Heinemann Educational Books. [22]

Alagoa, E. J. 1986. The Slave Trade in Niger Delta Oral Tradition and History. In Ed. Paul E. Lovejoy (Ed.) .*Africans in Bondage: Studies in Slavery and the Slave Trade. Essays in honor of Philip D. Curtin.* Madison: African Studies Program, University of Wisconsin. [16, 27, 28]

Alagoa, E.J. 1988. Conclusion. In E.J. Alagoa, F.N. Anozie and N. Nzewunwa (Eds.) *The Early History of the Niger Delta.* Hamburg: Helmut Buske-Verlag.. pp. 232-249. [10]

Alagoa, E.J. 1988. Introduction. In Alagoa, E.J., Anozie, F.N. and Nzewunwa, N. (eds.). *The Early History of the Niger Delta.* Hamburg: Helmut Buske-Verlag. pp. 13-21. [6]

Alagoa, E. J. 1995. *People of the Fish and the Eagle: A History of Okpoma in the Eastern Niger Delta.* Lagos and Port Harcourt: Isengi Communications Ltd. [25]

Alagoa, E. J. (Ed). 1999. *The Land and People of Bayelsa State: Central Niger Delta.* Port Harcourt: Onyoma Research Publications [9, 16]

Alagoa, E.J. 1999 Traditions of Origin. In E.J. Alagoa (Ed) *The Land and People of Bayelsa State: Central Niger Delta.* Port Harcourt: Onyoma Research Publications. [3, 16]

Alagoa, E.J. 1999. *The Ijaw Nation in the New Millennium.* Port Harcourt: Onyoma Research Publications. [7, 12]

Alagoa, E.J. (2000). *Okpu: Ancestral Houses in Nembe and European Antiquities on the Brass and Nun Rivers of the Niger Delta.* Port Harcourt: Onyoma Research Publications. [16]

Alagoa, E.J. 2005. United by Rivers and Waterways: Efik-Kalabari-Bonny Relations. Okon E. Uya *et al. The Efik and their neighbours: Historical Perspectives,* Calabar. [17]

Alagoa, E.J. 2006. *Landmark Historical Events in the South-South Geo-Political Zone of Nigeria (1940-2006) in Rivers State.* Abuja: National Population Commission. [12]

Alagoa, E.J. 2006. *Oloibiri: Fifty Years After.* Isaac Adaka Boro Memorial Lecture., Yenagoa. [30]

Alagoa, E. J. and A. Fombo. 1972. *A Chronicle of Grand Bonny.* Ibadan: Ibadan University Press. (Republished in 2001 by Onyoma Research Publications) [16, 16, 18, 22, 26, 29, 30]

Alagoa, E. J., F.N. Anozie and N. Nzewunwa (Eds.). (1988). *The Early History of the Niger Delta,* Hamburg & Port Harcourt: Helmut Buske Verlag & University of Port Harcourt Press. [16, 19]

Alagoa E.J and S. Kpone-Towne. 2002. Traditions of Origin. In E.J. Alagoa E.J and A.A. Derefaka (Eds.) *The Land and People of Rivers State: Eastern Niger Delta.* Port Harcourt: Onyoma Research Publications. [17, 21]

Alagoa, E. J. and T.N. Tamuno (Eds.) 1980. *Eminent Nigerians of Rivers State.* Ibadan: Heinemann Educational Books Ltd. [22]

Alagoa, E.J. and Tekena N. Tamuno, (Eds.). 1989. *Land and People of Nigeria: Rivers State.* Port Harcourt. Riverside Communications. [18, 16]

Alale, M.M.E.K. 1994. *Discourse on Visual Art Practices.* [7]

Alamieyeseigha, D.S.P.. 2000. *The search for peace in the Niger Delta: The Isaac Boro example*Being the first Isaac Adaka Boro memorial lecture. Yenagoa. [24]

Alazigha, D. 1986. *Akiroro: Thought Currents In Poetry.* Sabagreia: Dagbo Cultural Academy. [6]

Aldred, C. 1949. A Bronze Cult Object from Southern Nigeria. *Man,* 47. [18]

Aleleye-Wokoma, I. P. and Hart, S. A. 1999. The Effect of Industrial Activities on the Primary Productivity in the Lower Bonny Estuary, Rivers State, Nigeria. *J. Appl Sci. Environ. Mgt.* 2: 39-42. [2]

Alex, I. 1987. *The Phonology and Word Structure of Bukuma.* BA Long Essay, University of Port Harcourt. [6]

Allen, J.R.L. and J.W. Wells. 1962. Holocene Coral Banks and Subsidence in the Niger Delta. *Journal of Geology* 70: 381-397. [10]

Allen, J.R.L. 1964. The Nigerian Continental Margin: Bottom Sediments, Submarine Morphology and Geological Evolution. *Marine Geology* Vol. 1 No.4, 547-600. [10]

Allen, J. R. L. and Wells J. W. 1962. Holocene Coral Banks and Subsidence in the Niger Delta. *Journal of Geol*ogy. 70 (4), pp. 381 -397. [16]

Allen, J.R.L. and J.W. Wells. 1965. Coastal Geomorphology of Eastern Nigeria: Beach Ridge Barrier Islands and Vegetated Tidal Flats *Geologie en Mijnbouw* 44:1-21. [10]

Allen, J.R.L. and J.W. Wells. 1970. Sediments of the Modern Niger Delta: A Summary and Review. In J. P. Morgan (Ed). *Deltaic Sedimentation:* 138-151. [10]

Alleyne, M. 1980. *Comparative Afro-American.* Ann Arbor, Mich.: Karoma Pressr. [28]

Amachree, A. W. 1980. A Historical Survey of the Growth of Formal Western Education in Degema Local Government Area of Rivers State. An Unpublished B.Ed Thesis,   Faculty of Education, University of Benin, Benin City. [12]

Amadi, E. and E.I. Green. 2002. The Literary Arts. In Alagoa E. J. and A. A. Derefaka (Eds.). *Land and People of Rivers State: Eastern Niger Delta.* Port Harcourt: Onyoma Research Publications. [6]

Amadi, K.O. The Ikwerre People. 1993. A Study of Their Origins and Migrations. In Otonti Nduka (Ed.) *Studies in Ikwerre History and Culture.* Vol.1. Ibadan: Kraft Books p. 34 – 48. [21]

Amangala, G.I. 1945. Short History of Ijaw with Appendix. Oloibiri: The Author. [18]

Ambakederemo, S. M. 1968. *Isaac Boro*. Port Harcourt: Beks Royal. [6]

Ambakederemo, S. M. 2004. *Justicia.* Yenagoa: Beks Royal. [6]

Amini-Philips, I. C. 1994. *King Iworisa of Ekpeyland, 1883-1899: His Life and Time.* Port Harcourt: Riverside Communications. [21]

Amini-Philips, I.C. 2002. Developing the History of Forbidden Bush in the Multinational Oil Companies Operational Areas in the Niger Delta: The experience of the Ekpeye people of Rivers State. In Amini–Philips (Ed.) *Historical and Cultural Perspectives of Rivers State.* Port Harcourt: ISCAP Enterprises Nigeria. [21]

Amini-Philips, Isaac. 2005. *A Synopsis of the Founding Fathers of Old Rivers State.* Port Harcourt: The Blueprint Limited. [29, 30]

Aminigo, E. R. and J C. Okoro. 2002. Microflora of Smoke-Dried Sea Foods Marketed in the Niger Delta: A Case Study of Port Harcourt, Rivers State. *Trans. Nig. Soc. Biol. Conserv.* (Special edition), 1-7. [2]

Amire, A. V. 2006. Monitoring, Measurement and Assessment of Fishing Capacity: The Nigerian Experience. <http: // www.fao.org> [2]

Andah, B.W. 1982. *African Development in Cultural Perspective* Ibadan: Ibadan University Press [10]

Andah, B.W. 1995. *The Epistemology of West African Settlements.* Ibadan: Ibadan University Press. [29]

Andah, B.W. and A.I. Okpoko. 1979. Oral Traditions and West African Cultural History: A New Direction. *West African Journal of Archaeology.* Vol. 9. [10]

Anene, J.C. 1966. Southern Nigeria in Transition, 1885-1906. Cambridge University Press. [18, 18, 22, 28]

Anene, J.C. 1970. *The International Boundaries of Nigeria.* London: Longmans. [23]

Anifowose, R. 1982. *Violence in Politics in Nigeria: The Tiv and Yoruba Experience.* Enugu: Nok Publishers International [16]

Anozie, F.N. 1976 The Archaeology of Niger Delta. Paper presented at the Archaeological Association of Nigeria Conference, Ibadan, December 1978. [10]

Anozie, F.N. 1987. Cultural Prehistory in the Niger Delta. In Alagoa, E.J., F.N. Anozie and N. Nzewunwa (Eds.) *The Early History of the Niger Delta:* 141-185. [10]

Anozie, F.N., N. Nzewunwa and A.A. Derefaka. 1987. Archaeological Fieldwork and Excavations in the Niger Delta. In Alagoa, E.J., F.N. Anozie and N. Nzewunwa (Eds.). *The Early History of the Niger Delta.* Bayreuth: Helmut Buske Verlag [10]

Aristotle. 1926. *Nicomachean Ethics* (Loeb Classical Library). New York: G. P. Putnam, 1926. [27]

Asein, S. O. 1988. J.P. Clark's Poetry. In Y. Ogunbiyi (Ed.). *Perspectives on Nigerian Literature: 1700 to The Present, Volume Two.* Lagos: Guardian Publishers [6]

Asiegbu, J. U. J. *1984. Nigeria and its British Invaders, 1851-1920: A Thematic Documentary History.* New York : Nok Publishers. [29]

Asseez, L.O. 1976. Review of the Stratigraphy, Sedimentation and Structure of the Niger Delta: Geology of Nigeria.. Lagos: Elizabethan Pub. Co. pp. 259-272 [10]

Atte, A. J. 1981. *A History of Eniwari from Foundation to 1960.* An unpublished B.A History Project, University of Port Harcourt, Nigeria. [16]

Avae, D.T.M. 1990. *The Essentials of Art.* Port Harcourt: Idodo Umeh Publisher Ltd. [7]

Awoala, E. B. A. P. *Culture of a People.* 1983. Port Harcourt: The Author. [29]

Awolowo, O. 1960. *Awo: The Autobiography of Chief Obafemi Awolowo.* Cambridge: Cambridge University Press. [29, 30]

Ayakoroma, B. 1997. *Dance On His Grave.* Port Harcourt: Dee Goldfinger. [6]

Ayakoroma, B. 1999. *A Matter of Honour.* Port Harcourt: Dee Goldfinger.[6]

Ayakoroma, B. 2002. *A Chance to Survive and Other Plays.* Yenagoa: Dee Goldfinger [6]

Ayakoroma, B. 2004. *Castles in the Air* Lagos: Mace. [6]

Ayakoroma, B. 2006. *Once Upon a Dream.* Lagos: Mace. [6]

Ayakoroma, B. 2006. *A Scar for Life*. Lagos: Mace. [6]

Ayakoroma, B. and A. Arikpo. 2000. *All for A Canoe and Other Plays*. Port Harcourt: Living Earth. [6]

Ayakoroma, B, A. Arikpo and L. Betiang. 2000. *Our Forest, Our Future and Other Plays*. Port Harcourt: Living Earth. [6]

Ayandele, E.A. 1966. *The Missionary Impact on Modem Education, 1842-1941*. London: Longmans. [12]

Aye, E. U. 1967. *Old Calabar Through the Centuries*. Calabar. [23]

Aye, E. U. [n.d.] Efik origins and migrations revisited. Calabar, [23]

Ayida, A.A. 1990. *Rise and Fall of Nigeria*. Lagos: Malthouse Press Ltd. [29]

Ayotamuno, Y. 2006. *The Contributions of King Alfred Diette-Spiff, Chief Melford Okilo, Chief Rufus Ada George and Dr. Diepreye Alamieyesiegha in National Development*. (Port Harcourt: Unpublished MS). [29]

Ayotamuno, Y. 2006. *Isaac Jasper Adaka Boro, Samuel Owonaru, Dick Nottingham and Captain Amangala*. (Port Harcourt: Unpublished MS). [29]

Ayres, J. C., J.O. Mundt, and W. E. Sandine. 1980. *Microbiology of Foods*. San Francisco, Freeman. [2]

Ayuwo, J.G.I. 1998. *A Socio-Semantic Study of Obolo Anthroponyms*. M.A. thesis, University of Ibadan. [6]

Baikie, W. B. (1856), *Narrative of an Exploring Voyage Up the Rivers Kwo'ra and Bin'ue ...* London: John Murray [19, 30]

Bakare, O.R. (1994); *Rudiments of Choreography*. Zaria: Pace Publishers Limited. [7]

Bamgbose, A. 1993. Deprived, Endangered and Dying Languages. *Diogenes.* Volme 4 No. 1. [6]

Banigo, Y. 2006. The State, Trans National Corporations and Indigenous Peoples: The Case of the Ijo-Speaking Peoples. A Ph.D Dissertation, University of Port Harcourt, Nigeria. [16]

Banigo, Y. 2006. *Chief Christopher 'Wari' Iwowari (1834-1897): His Life and Times.* Nembe: Unpublished MS. [29]

Barbot, J. 1732. A Description of the Coasts of North and South Guinea. Paris. contains James Barbot, "An Abstract of a Voyage to New Calabar River, or Rio Real in 1699". [18]

Barbot, J. 1732. An Abstract of a Voyage to New Calabar in the Year 1699. In Awnsham Churchill. *Collections of Voyages and Travels.* Vol. 5, London. pp. 455-466. [28]

Barley, N. 1995. Figure of a Woman. In Tom Phillips (Ed.), *Africa: The Art of a Continent,* London: Royal Academy of Arts. [18]

Barrett, A. I. 2005. *From Caves of Rotten Teeth.* Port Harcourt: Daylight Press [6]

Batubo, A. B. 1948. *The Dawn of Baptist Work in Eastern Nigeria* Port Harcourt: Goodwill Press. [12, 19]

Bebeke-Ola, J. E. I. 1979. *The Man Bebekala Dubakemefa of Igbedi.* Port Harcourt. [24, 30]

Bell-Gam, H. L. 1986. Ogole-Mkpa Movement and the Ritual Objects in Drama. *Nigeria Magazine.* [7]

Bell-Gam, H. L. 1991. *Orukoro.* Port Harcourt: Pam Unique. [6]

Bell-Gam, H. L. 1996. *King Jaja.* Port Harcourt: Gulf.   [6]

Bell-Gam, H.L. 1998. *No Sacrifice No Marriage*. Port Harcourt: Paragraphics. [6]

Bell-Gam, H.L. 2000. *The Hidden Treasure*. Port Harcourt: AGV Multi-Projects. [6]

Bell-Gam, H.L. 1999. *Une Calebasse d'Aubes*. Ile-Ife: Obafemi Awolowo Universtiy Press. [6]

Bell-Gam, H. L. 2000. *Ube Republic*. Port Harcourt: AGV Multi-Projects. [6]

Bell-Gam, H.L. et al. 2002. Fine and Performing Arts. In E.J. Alagoa and A.A. Derefaka (Eds.). *The Land and People of Rivers State: Eastern Niger Delta*. Port Harcourt: Onyoma Research Publications. [7]

Bell-Gam, H. L. 2004. *Longing for Another Dawn*. Port Harcourt: Pearl. [6]

Benike, J. 2002. How the Federal Government and the Multinationals underdevelop the Niger Delta. [18]

Benstowe-Onyeka, G. 2000. Bilingualism and Code Mixing in Izon as it Affects the Teaching and Learning of the Language. *Jolangs* 1,1-5. [6]

Bestman, A. M. 1998. *Textures of Dawn*. Ile-Ife: Obafemi Awolowo University Press. [6]

Binford, S.R. and L.R. Binford (Eds.). 1968). *New Perspectives in Archaeology* Chicago: University of Chicago Press. [10]

Blake, W. O. (Compiler). 1858. *The African Slave Trade and the Political History of Slavery in the United States*. Columbus, Ohio: J & H. Miller. Reprinted by Mnemosyne Publishing Inc, Miami, Florida. [28]

Bonchuki, O. M. 1997. *International Boundaries and Divided Peoples: A Case Study Of Boki and Ejagham Communities in the Cross River Area, 1884-1994*. PhD thesis, History Department, University of Calabar. [23]

Boro, I. A. 1982. *The Twelve-Day Revolution.* Benin City: Idodo Umeh Publishers [18, 24, 29, 33]

Bradbury, R.E. 1957. *The Benin Kingdom* (Ethnographic Survey of Africa, Western Africa). Part XIII. London. [18]

Briggs, D.A. 2004. Ethnic Militias Dilemma in Nigeria: A Case Study of the Egbesu Group. In D.A. Briggs and J.D. Sanda (Eds). *Issues of Peace and Security: Essays in Honour of Major General Charles B. Ndiomu*: Kuru: National Institute Publications. [12]

British Government Gazette No. 21 of 18th November 1904, Eth. Doc. 209. [18]

British National Archives,1958. Enclosure in Alan Lennox-Boyd, MP, to Viscount Kilmuir, GCVO, 8 October.. [33]

Brooks, J. (Ed). *2004. The Life of Olaudah Equiano: The Interesting Narrative of the Life of Olaudah Equino, or Gustavus Vassa, The African Written by Himself.* Chicago: Lakeside Press. [27]

Brown-West H. W. 1956. *A Short Genealogical History of Amachree I of Kalabari.* Enugu: The Author. (Printed by Sankey Printing Press, Yaba) [16]

Bunnett, R. B. 1979. *General Geography in Diagrams.* London: Longmans. [2]

Burns, A. 1963, A *History of Nigeria.* London: George Allen & Unwin [17, 30]

Burnside, M. and R. Robotham. 1997. *Spirits of the Passage: The TransAtlantic Slave Trade in the Seventeenth Century.* New York: Simon and Schuster. [27]

Calvocoressi, D. 1975. European Trade Pipes in Ghana. *West Aftican Journal of Archaeology.* Vol. 5:195-200 [10]

Calvocoressi, D. 1976. *Fish Remains in Archaeology and Paleo-Environmental Studies.* London: Academic Press. [10]

Carretta, V. 2005. *Equiano, the African: Biography of a Self-Made Man.* Athens, Georgia: University of Georgia Press. [27]

Chambers, D. B. 2005. *Murder at Montpelier: Igbo Africans in Virginia.* Jackson, Mississippi: University Press of Mississippi. [27]

Chambers, D. B. 1997. My own Nation: Igbo Exiles in the Diaspora. In Davis Eltis and David Richardson (Eds.) *Routes to Slavery: Direction, Ethniciy and Mortality in the Transatlantic Slave Trade.* London: Frank Cass. [27]

Clark J. D. 1970. *The Prehistory of Africa.* London: Praeger. [19]

Clark J. D. 1971. Three Kwa Languages of Eastern Nigeria. *Journal of West African Languages* 8 (1): 27-36. [19]

Clark–Bekederemo, J. P. 1961. *Poems.* Ibadan: Mbari Publications [6]

Clark–Bekederemo, J. P. 1964. *America, Their America.* London: Andre Deutsch. [6]

Clark–Bekederemo, J. P. 1964. *Three Plays*: *Song of A Goat, The Masquerade, The Raft.* Oxford: Oxford University Press. [6]

Clark–Bekederemo, J. P. 1965. *A Reed in the Tide.* London: Longman. [6]

Clark–Bekederemo, J. P. 1966. *Ozidi. Oxford:* Oxford University Press. [6]

Clark–Bekederemo, J. P. 1970. *Casualties.* London: Longman. [6]

Clark–Bekederemo, J.P. 1970. *The Example of Shakespeare.* London: Longman. [6]

Clark–Bekederemo, J.P. 1977. *The Ozidi Saga.* Ibadan: Ibadan University Press and Oxford.University Press. [6]

Clark–Bekederemo, J. P. 1978. *The Hero as a Villain*. Lagos: University of Lagos Press. [6]

Clark-Bekederemo, J. P. 1981. *A Decade of Tongues*. London: Longman. [6]

Clark–Bekederemo, J. P. 1981. *State of the Union*. London: Longman. [6]

Clark–Bekederemo, J. P. 1985. *The Bikoroa Plays: The Boat, The Return Home and Full Circle*. Oxford: Oxford University Press.   [6]

Clark–Bekederemo, J.P. 1988. *Mandela and Other Poems*. London: Longman. [6]

Clark–Bekederemo, J.P.   1991. *Collected Plays and Poems, 1958-1988*. Washington: Howard University Press. [6]

Clark–Bekederemo, J. P. 1991. *The Wives' Revolt*. Ibadan: Oxford University Press. [6]

Clark–Bekederemo, J.P. 2000. *A Peculiar Faculty*. Ibadan: Nigerian Academy of Letters. [6]

Clark–Bekederemo, J. P. 2001. *The Burden Not Lifted*. Lagos: ReDesign. [6]

Clark–Bekederemo, J. P. 2002. *The Poems: 1958 – 1998*. Lagos: Longman. [6]

Clark–Bekederemo, J. P. 2003. *Of Sleep and Old Age: New Poems*. Lagos: Crucible. [6]

Clark–Bekederemo, J.P.   2004. *Once Again a Child: More New Poems*. Ibadan: Mosuro. [6]

Coker, I. 1968. *Landmarks of the Nigerian Press*. Lagos: Nigerian National Press, 1968. [29]

Coker, I. (n.d.). *Seventy Years of the Nigerian Press*. Lagos: The Author. [29]

Coleman J. S. 1958 (Reprint 1971; 1986). *Nigeria: Background to Nationalism.* Berekely: University of California Press [26, 29, 30]

Comson, E. E. 1987. *The Phonology of Odual.* B.A. Long Essay, University of Port Harcourt. [6]

Cookey S.J.S. 1974. *King Jaja of the Niger Delta: His Life and Times 1821-1891.* New York: Nok Publishers. [18, 21, 22, 29, 30]

Cookey, S. J. S. 1980. Chief Cookey Gam: The Statesman of Opobo. In T. N. Tamuno and E. J. Alagoa (Eds.) *Eminent Nigerians of Rivers State.* Ibadan: Heinemann Educational Books. [22]

Cordell, D. D. and Manuel Garcia y Griego. 2005. The Integration of Nigerian and Mexicans Immigrants in Dallas/Fort Worth, Texas," *International Union for the Scientific Study of Population* (Tours), July. [27]

Costanzo A (Ed.). 2001. *The Interesting Narrative of the Life of Olaudah Equiano* [26]

Crowder, M. 1978. *The Story of Nigeria.* London: Faber & Faber. [12, 17, 30, 22]

Crowther, D.C. 1907. *The Establishment of the Niger Delta Pastorate Church, 1864-1892.* Liverpool: J.A. Thompson & Co. Ltd. [29]

Crowther, S. A. 1882. *Report on Bonny for 1882* (CMS G3/A3/36). [18]

Cyril, A. 2003. Imperialism and Economic Dependency in Nigeria. [Lagos]: Charismatic Forum. [22]

Da-Wariboko, R.A. 1989. The Impact of Western Education on the Culture of Kalabari People in Degema Local Government Area, Rivers State, 1874-1986. Unpublished MEd Thesis, Faculty of Education, University of Port Harcourt. [12]

Daget and Ligers. 1962. Pipes in Middle Niger. *IFA* [10]

786

Dahlin, J., S. Hess, P. Duncan and C.B. Powell. 1985. *Composition of Phytoplankton and Zooplankton Communities of the Niger Delta. Proceedings of Seminar on Petroleum Industry and the Nigerian Environment.* Lagos: Federal Ministry of Works and Housing and the Nigerian National Petroleum Corporation (NNPC). pp. 217-229. [2]

Daminabo, O. 2006. *Chief (Dr.) Isaac John Fiberesima of Okrika.* (Port Harcourt: MS). [29]

Dangana, J. A. 2002. Local Government System and the Development of Bayelsa State from an Historical Perspective. Unpublished Ph.D Dissertation, University Harcourt. [18]

Dappa, I. I. 2006. Professor E. J. Alagoa Distorts History of Bille Kingdom. *Weekly Star* (Port Harcourt), 25th -31st July. [16]

Dappa-Biriye, H. J. R. 1982. Tarka Tivism: A New Political Order. In Simon Shango, (ed.), *Tributes to a Great Leader, J. S. Tarka.* Enugu: Nwankwo Associates. [30]

Dappa-Biriye, H.J.R. 1995. *Minority Politics in Pre- and Post- Independence Nigeria.* Port Harcourt: University of Port Harcourt Press. [16, 30]

Dapper, O. 1975. Kalabari and the Eastern Delta. In *Nigserian Perspectives.* Oxford. [28]

Dathorne, O. R. 1976. *African Literature in the Twentieth Century.* London: Heinemann. [6]

Davidson, B. 1977. *A History of West Africa, 1000-1800.* Essex: Longman. [18]

Davidson, B. 1992. *The Black Man's Burden.* Ibadan: Spectrum Books. [18]

De Souza, M. de. 2000. *Regard Sur Ouidah: A Bit of History.* Ouidah: Imprime par B 3 P. [25]

De Lotbiniere, S. 1977. The Story of the English Gun Flint: Some Theories and Queries. *The Journal of the Arms and Armour Society.* Vol. IX, No. 1 (June). [10]

De Lotbiniere, S. 1979. Gun Flint Enquiry. *Chelsea Speleological Society Newsletter*, Vol. 20, No. 7 (April) [10]

De Cardi, *Comte* **C. N.** 1899. Andoni River and Its Inhabitants. In Mary Kingsely. *West African Studies.* London: Macmillan. [30]

Dema, I. 1980. King Ukwu of Abua. T.N.Tamuno and E.J. Alagoa (Eds.) *Eminent Nigerians of Rivers State.* Ibadan: Heinemann Educational Books. [19]

Derefaka, A.A. 1980. Cordage, Fabric, and Basketry of the Tichitt Tradition: A Late Prehistoric Complex of the South Western Sahara. *West African Journal of Archaeology* Vol. 10:117-153. [10]

Derefaka, A. A. 1998. Archaeological Research in the Niger Delta: Results, Problems and Prospects. In N. C. Ejituwu (Ed.). *The Multi-Disciplinary Approach to African History: Essays in Honour of Ebiegberi Joe Alagoa.* Port Harcourt: University of Port Harcourt Press. [18, 29]

Derefaka, A. A. 2003. *Archaeology and Culture History in the Central Niger Delta.* Port Harcourt: Onyoma Research Publications. [10, 24]

Derrick, J. 1975. *Africa's Slaves.* New York: Schecken Books. [28]

Devonish, H. and O. G. Harry [nd]. Eastern Ijo influence in Berbice Dutch Creole. *Nigerian Festschrift Series devoted to Professor Munzali Jibril.* Vol. 5. [28]

Dike K. O. 1956. *Trade and Politics in the Niger Delta, 1830-1895: An Introduction to the Economic and Political History of Nigeria.* Oxford: Clarendon Press London. [1, 10, 16, 16, 17, 18, 21, 22, 23, 25, 27, 28, 30]

Ebiwari, D. D. 1988. A Political History of Ogbia. Uunpublished B.A History Project, University of Port Harcourt [16]

Eboreime, O. J. 1992. Group Identities and the Changing Patterns of Alliances Among the Epie-Atissa People of Nigeria, 1890-1991. Unpublished Ph.D Dissertation of University of Cambridge. [16]

Edum, S. 2006. *Oral Interview on Ritual Objects and Masquerade Cults in Abua.* [7]

Efere, E. E. 2001. The Pitch System of the Bumo dialect of Izon. *Current Research on African Languages & Linguistics.* Vol. 4, 115-259. [6]

Efere E. E. and Williamson Kay. 1989. Languages. In E.J. Alagoa and Tekena N. Tamuno (Eds.). *Land and People of Nigeria: Rivers State.* Port Harcourt: Riverside Communications. [16, 19]

Efere E. E. and Williamson, Kay. 1999. Languages. In Alagoa E. J (ed) *Land and People of Bayelsa State: Central Niger Delta.* Port Harcourt: Onyoma Research Publications. [6, 16, 6]

Eferesuoa, J.B.E. 2003). *The Izon-English Dictionary of the Main Izon Dialects.* Benin City: J.E.B.E. Publishers. [6]

Egbuson, V. 2001. *A Poet is a Man.* Ibadan: Kraft Books. [6]

Egbuson, V. 2001. *Moniseks Country.* Ibadan: Kraft Books. [6]

Egbuson, V. 2002. *Love is Not Dead.* Ibadan: Kraft Brooks. [6]

Egbuson, V. 2006. *Womandela.* Ibadan: Kraft Books. [6]

Egharevba, J.U. 1968. A Short History of Benin. 4th Ed. Ibadan: Ibadan University Press. [18]

Ejituwu, N. C. 1980. Nna Biget of Obolo (Andoni). In T. N. Tamuno and E. J. Alagoa (Eds.), *Eminent Nigerians of Rivers State*. Ibadan: Heinemann Educational Books.. [29]

Ejituwu, N. C. 1991. *A History of Obolo (Andoni) in the Niger Delta*. Oron: Manson Press, in association with the University of Port Harcourt Press. [18, 19, 30]

Ejituwu, N. C. 1998. Old Calabar Rediscovered. In N. C. Ejituwu (Ed.), *The Multi-Disciplinary Approach to African History: Essays in Honour of Ebiegberi Joe Alagoa*. Port Harcourt: University of Port Harcourt Press. [18, 30]

Ejituwu, N. C. 1999. The Atlantic Trade. In E. J. Alagoa (Ed.), *The Land and People of Bayelsa State: Central Niger Delta*. Port Harcourt: Onyoma Research Publications. [16, 30]

Ejituwu, N. C. *et al.* 2003. Socio-Economic Impact Assessment Report FIMSCO Resources Nig. SPDC. Port Harcourt. [3]

Ejituwu, N.C. 2004. *Niger Delta Historiography in Time Perspective*. University of Port Harcourt Inaugural Lecture. [23]

Ejituwu, N. C and Sorgwe, C. M. 1999. The Nigerian Civil War. In E.J. Alagoa (Ed.) *The Land and People of Bayelsa State: Central Niger Delta*. Port Harcourt: Onyoma Research Publications. [16]

Ejituwu, N.C. [nd]. The Andoni-Bonny Treaty of 1846: A Diplomatic Curiosity" *Odu: West African Studies*. [18]

Ejituwu, N. C. [nd] The Political Economy of the Andoni-Bonny Treaty of 1846. In Y. A. Ochefu. *The Life and Work of Professor Erim O. Erim*, Makurdi: Aboki Publishers. [18]

Ekechi, F. K. 1972. Missionary Enterprise and Rivalry in Igbo Land (1857-1914. London: Frank Cass. [22]

Ekiyor, J.M.T. 1984. A History of Kabo-Ibe. An unpublished B.A History Project, University of Port Harcourt, Nigeria [16]

Ekpo, E. 1977. *Two Thousand Year Nigeria Art.* Lagos: Federal Department of Antiquities. [7]

Ellah F.J. 1995 *Ali–Ogba: A History of the Ogbah People.* Enugu: Fourth Dimension Publishing Co. Ltd. [21]

Eltis, D. 1995. The Volume and African Origins of the British Slave Trade before 1714. *Cahiers d'Études africaines.* Vol. 35 No. 2/3, 138-139; 617-27. [27]

Eltis, D., P. E. Lovejoy and D. Richardson. 1999. Slave Trading Ports: Towards an Atlantic Wide Perspective', in *Ports of the Slave Trade (Bights of Benin and Biafra).* Britain: Centre of Commonwealth Studies, University of Sterling. [28]

Eltis, D., D. Richardson, S. D. Behrendt, and Herbert S. Klein. 1999. (Eds). *The Trans-Atlantic Slave Trade: A Database on CD-Rom.* Cambridge: Cambridge University Press. [27]

Elugbe, B.O. 1979. Some Tentative Historical Inference from Comparative Edoid Studies. *Kiabara* (Port Harcourt). 2 (1): 82-101. [19]

Emenanjo, E.N. 1999. Language Endangerment, Native Speakers and Language Empowerment. In E.N. Emenanjo and Bleambo (Eds.) *Language Endangerment and Empowerment: Theory and Reality* Volume 1. Aba: National Institute for Nigerian Languages. [6]

Emuren, L. 2006. *Scenes of the Sinful Dancers.* Ibadan: Kraft Books. [6]

Encyclopaedia Britannica Premium Service. 2006. *Okara Gabriel.* 7 Sept. <http://www britannica. com/eb/article – 9056904> [6]

Enemugwem, J. H. 1990. A History of Eastern Obolo (Andoni). Unpublished BA Project, University of Port Harcourt. [18]

Enemugwem, J. H. 1992. Eyo Ita: A Nigerian Nationalist, 1903-1972. Unpublished MA (History) Thesis, University of Port Harcourt. [30]

Enemugwem, J. H. 2000. Ernest Ikoli: A Nigerian Politician, 1893-1960. *Ibom Journal of History and International Studies*, No. 8. [29, 30]

Enemugwem, J. H. 2000. *The Significance of the Niger Delta to the Political and Economic Development of Nigeria, 1849-1999.* Unpublished PhD (History) Dissertation, University of Port Harcourt, Nigeria.[3, 18, 30]

Enemugwem, J.H. 2003. Geoffrey Lysias Uzoño (1938-2001): A Revolutionary Genius from a Minority State in Nigeria. *Afe: Journal of Minorities Studies*, 5 (1). [29]

Enemugwem, J. H. 2003. The Nigerian Ethnic and Cultural Profile of Eastern Obolo (Andoni) of Akwa Ibom State (1700-2004). *Journal of Creative Arts*, 3 (1). [18]

Enemugwem J. H., M.N. Ediyeko and E.C. Assor. 2002. Colonial Rule. In Alagoa E.J. and A.A. Derefaka (Eds.). *The Land and People of Rivers State: Eastern Niger Delta*. Port Harcourt: Onyoma Research Publications. [21]

Enene, N.E. 1997. *A Comparative Morphology of Tense in the Obolo dialects.* M.A. Thesis, University of Port Harcourt. [6]

Ennals, G.T.C. 1934. Intelligence Report on the Ndoki Clan. An Unpublished Government Report [16]

Environmental Resource Managers Limited. 1997. *Niger Delta Environmental Survey: Phase 1 Report (Environmental and Socio-Economic Characte- ristics)*. Lagos: [16]

Epelle, E. M. T. 1955. *The Church in the Niger Delta* Port Harcourt: Niger Delta Diocese. [22, 29]

Epelle, E. M. T. 1964. *Bishops in the Niger Delta*, Aba: Niger Delta Diocese. [18, 22]

Erekosima, T.V, Lawson, W.H.K. and O. MacJaja (Eds). 1991: *Hundred Years of Buguma History in Kalabari Culture.* Lagos; Sibon Books Limited. [12]

Erim, E. O. 1990. The Early History of the Upper Cross River Region. In S. O. Jaja *et al* (Eds.). *History and Culture of the Upper Cross River.* Enugu. [23]

Esade, M. K. 1985. A History of the Timber Industry in Kugbo. B.A. Essay, University of Port Harcourt. [28]

Esang, M. 1984. *A Study of Oron Community of Calabar.* Paico [23]

Etekpe, A., Y.M. Ayotamuno. U.E. Nwala, M.C. Jumbo and J. Kariboro. 2004. *Harold Dappa-Biriye: His Contributions to Politics in Nigeria.* Port Harcourt: Onyoma Research Publications. [29, 29]

Eze, A.G. 2002. The Palm Produce Industry and Trade in Ekpeyeland 1800-1999. An Unpublished B.A. History Thesis submitted to the Department of History, University of Port Harcourt. [21]

Ezeomah, C. C. 1992. The Education of Migrants and Under-Served Children in the Society. In B. Ipaye (Ed). *Education in Nigeria: Past, Present and Future.* Lagos: Macmillan Publishers. [12]

Ezewu, E.E. and G.Tahir (Eds.). 1997. *Ecology and Education in Nigeria: Studies on the Education of Migrant Fishermen:* Onitsha; Tabansi Publications Ltd. [12]

Fafunwa, A. B. 1974. *History of Education in Nigeria,* London: George, Allen and Unwin Ltd. [12]

Faraclas, N. 1984. *A Grammar of Obolo: Studies in African Grammatical Systems.* Bloomington, Ind.: Indiana University Linguistics Club. [6, 18]

Ferguson, J. 1971. *Some Nigerian Church Founders.* Ibadan: Day Star Press [29]

Fiberesima, J. A. 1990. *Okrika in Search of Ancestry*. Ikeja: Evans Brothers (Nig.) Publishers Ltd. [21, 29]

Fiofori, T. and I. Ikeddy. 2003. *Nigeria and The All-Africa Games* (Lagos: Sun Arts/BEP. [29]

Flint, J. E. 1960. *Sir George Goldie and the Making of Nigeria*, London: Oxford University Press. [17]

Forcados, F.B. 1984. A History of Aleibiri. An unpublished B.A History Project, University of Port Harcourt, Nigeria. [16]

Frank-Opigo, N. A. 1997. *The Tiresome Trek to the Terminus: A Short History of the Struggle for a Homogenous Ijo State*. Port Harcourt: The Author. [30]

Frank-Opigo, N.A. 1980. Okolomobiri Ombu of Otuan. In E.J. Alagoa and T.N. Tamuno (Eds). *Eminent Nigerians of the Rivers State*. Ibadan: Heinemann Educational Books Nigeria Ltd. [16]

Gabel, C. 1967. *Analysis of Prehistoric Economic Patterns*. New York: Holt, Rinehart and Winston [10]

Gabriel, A.O.I. 1984. *Trends in the Development of Secondary School Education in the Rivers State of Nigeria: 1967-1983*. An Unpublished MEd Research Project, Department of Teacher Education, Faculty of Education, University of Ibadan. [12]

Gabriel, A.O.I. 2004. Beyond Policy: An Analysis of the Nomadic and Migrant Fishermen Education Programme in Nigeria, 1998-2002. *The Nigerian Academic Forum*. Vol. 6. No. 3. [12]

Gabriel, A.O.I. and J. Ezekiel-Hart. 2002. The Development of Migrant Fisher Folk Education in Rivers State of Nigeria: 1990-2002. *Otu-Ogal: Journal of Niger Delta Research, Vol. 4, No. 1*. [12]

Gabriel, A.O.I. and C.C. Zuofa. 2004. Education for all: Perspectives on the Migrant Fisherfolk in Bayelsa State of Nigeria, 1996-2002. *Journal of Education in Developing Areas, Vol. 13.* [12]

Gibbons, E. J. 1932. Intelligence Report on the Ogoni Tribe Within the Opobo Division. (NA/1,CS 26, File 29184. [22]

Gilbert, R. and W. McCarter. 1985. Living With Art. New York: Alfred A. Knopf Inc. [7]

Gillespie. 1986. *Radiocarbon User's Handbook.* Oxford University Committee for Archaeology, Monograph No. 3. [10]

Goldie, H. 1909. *Calabar and its Missions.* London. [23]

Goodwin,   A.J.H.   1946.   Prehistoric   Fishing   Methods   in   South Africa. *Antiquity.* 20:134-141. [10]

Graf, W. D. 1988. *The Nigerian State.* London: James Curry. [17]

Green, E. I. 2006. *Gabriel Okara : The Man and His Art.* Unpublished Birthday Lecture. [6]

Green, E. I. 2004. Maternal Influence and Ola Rotimi's Niger Delta Plays. In Koroye S. and N.C. Anyadike (Eds.). *Woman in the Academy*: *Festschrift for Professor Helen Chukwuma.* Port Harcourt: Pearl. [6]

Green, E. I. 2005. *Ogolo: Poems.* Port Harcourt: University of Port Harcourt Press. [6]

Green, E. I. [n.d.]   *Nostalgia in Selected Poems of Gabriel Okara.* Unpublished Paper. [6]

Green, S. E. 1985. *Fishing Industry in Bonny.* Unpublished Paper. [22]

Greenberg, J.H. 1955. *Studies in African Linguistic Classification.* New Haven, Conn.: Compass Publishing Co. [6, 19]

Greenberg, J.H. 1963. *Languages of Africa* The Hague: Mouton. [6, 19]

Guana, S. J. 1977. Liberian History up to 1847. Accra: Sedco Publishing Ltd. [25]

Hall, G. M. 2005; 2006. *Slavery and African Ethnicities in the Americas.* Chapel Hill, North Carolina: The University of North Carolina Press; Kingston: Ian Randle Publishers. [27, 28]

Hall, G. M. *Louisiana Slave Database*, 1719-1820. (Available with a search engine at: http://www.ancestry.com/search/db.aspx?dbid=7383 and with a search engine for the most important fields at: http://www.ibiblio.org/laslave/) [27]

Harry, O. G. 1989. *A Comparative Reconstruction of Proto-Koin Phonology.* Unpublished M. A. Dissertation, University of Port Harcourt. [28]

Hart, A. K. 1964. *Report into the Dispute over the Obongship of Calabar.* Enugu: Government Printer. [23]

Hartle, D.D. 1967. Archaeology in Eastern Nigeria. *Nigeria Magazine* No. 93. [10]

Heinecke, P. 1986. *Freedom in the Grave: Nigeria and the Political Economy of Africa.* Okpella, Nigeria: S. Asekome and Co. [29]

Henige, D. 1982. *Oral Historiography.* London: Longman Group Limited. [10]

Henrietta Marie websites: http://www.historical- museum.org/exhibits/hm/ henmarie.htm

Hill, M.H. 1976. Archaeological smoking pipes from Central Sierra Leone. *West African Journal of Archaeology.* Vol. 6:109-119. [10]

Hodder, B. W. and U.I. Ukwu. 1969. *Markets in West Africa.* Ibadan: Ibadan University Press. [21]

Hodgkin, T. *Nigerian Perspectives.* London: Oxford University Press, 1960. [17]

Hook, R.J. 1930. *Assessment (Intelligence) Report on the Ogula Clan of the Western Ijo Sub-Tribe, Forcados District, Warri Province.* [6]

Hopkins, A. G. 1975. *An Economic History of West Africa.* London: Longmans Group Ltd. [22]

Horton, Robin. 1965). A Note of Recent Finds of Brasswork in the Niger Delta. *Odu,* 2 (1). [18]

Horton, Robin. 1966. Igbo: An Ordeal for Aristocrats. *Nigeria Magazine,* XCI, 37-58 [16]

Horton, Robin. 1969. From Fishing Village to City-State: A Social History of New Calabar. In M. Douglas and P.M. Kaberry (Eds), *Men in Africa.* London:. [10, 16, 16]

Horton, Robin. 1970. Ikpataka Dogi: a Kalabari Funeral Rite. *African Notes* (Ibadan), 5, 3, 57-72. [17]

Horton, Robin. 1995. The Niger-Congo Diaspora: Language, Geography and History. In E.N. Emenanjo and O.M. Ndimele (Eds.). *Issues in African Languages and Linguistics: Essays in Honour of Kay Williamson.* Aba: National Institute for Nigerian Languages. pp. 306-338. [6]

Horton, Robin. 1998. Some Fresh Thoughts on Eastern Ijo Origins, Expansion and Migrations. Nkparom C. Ejituwu (Ed.). *The Multi-Disciplinary Approach to African History: Essays in Honour of Ebiegberi Joe Alagoa.* Port Harcourt: University of Port Harcourt Press. [17, 18, 24]

Ibeno. 1956. Ibeno Memorandum to G. I. Jones, Sole Commissioner of Inqiury into the Status of Chiefs in the Eastern Nigeria. Upenekang-Ibeno: MS. [18]

Ibim, O. 1983. The Phonology of Bille. Unpublished BA (English) Project, University of Port Harcourt. [18]

Ibomo, J.E, E.A. Allison-Oguru and A. Lazarus. 1999. Development Planning. In E.J. Alagoa (Ed.) *The Land and People of Bayelsa State: Central Niger Delta.* Port Harcourt: Onyoma Research Publications. [16]

Idobozi, V. 2000. A History of Okodia Ibe: From Settlement to 19996. An Unpublished B. A History Project, University of Port Harcourt Nigeria. [16]

Ifemeje, C.C. 1984. Evolution of Nigerian Education II. In B.O. Ukeje (Ed). 1994. *Foundations of Education.* Benin City, Ethiope Publishing Corporation. [12]

Ifie, J. E. 1994. *A Cultural Background to the Plays of J. P. Clark-Bekederemo.* Ibadan: End-Time Publishing House Limited. [6]

Ifie, J.E. 1988. *Kemefiere the Ogress.* Ibadan: Moba Printing and Publlishing Co. [6]

Igwe, S.O. 1987. *Education in Eastern Nigeria, 1984-1975: Development and Management: Church, State and Community.* London, Evans Brothers Limited. [12]

Ijaw People's Association of Great Britain & Ireland 1965 to present) *Association Archives.* [26]

Ijeoma, J. O. 1986. *Arochuku: History and Culture.* Enugu. [23]

Ijewere, G. 1999. *Accountability, Politics and Development in Colonial and Post-colonial Africa: A Case for Democracy and Federalism in Sub-Saharan Africa.* Lagos: Primary Limited. [29]

Ikeni, H. M. 2006. Oral Interview. [19]

Ikechi, N. N. O. *et al.* 2003. *History of Etche.* Port Harcourt: Springfield Publishers Ltd. [21]

Ikime, O. 1969. *The Fall of Nigeria.* London: Heinemann. [18]

Ikime, O. 1969. *The Merchant Prince of the Niger Delta*. New York: Macmillan [18]

Ikime, O. 1977. *Niger Delta Rivalry: Itsekiri-Urhobo Relations and the European Presence, 1884-1936*. London: Longman. [16, 18]

Ikime, O. 1980. The Peoples and Kingdoms of the Niger Delta Province. In Obaro Ikime (Ed) Ground work of Nigerian History. Ibadan: Heinemann Educational Books. [18]

Ikime, O. 1980. The Western Niger Delta and the Hinterland in the Nineteenth Century. In O. Ikime (Ed). *Groundwork of Nigerian History*. Ibadan: Heinemann Educational Books. [18]

Ikiriko, I. 2000. *Oily Tears of the Delta*. Ibadan: Kraft Books [6]

Ikonne, C. 2005. Foreword. In Green, E. I. *Ogolo*. Port Harcourt: University of Port Harcourt Press. [6]

Ilagha, N. 1998. *Apples and Serpents*. Port Harcourt: TMG. [6]

Ilagha, N. 1999. *Mantids*. Lagos: Mace. [6]

Ilagha, N. 2007. *A Birthday Delight*. Yenagoa: Treasure Books. [6]

Iloeje, N. P. 1987. *A new geography of Nigeria*. London, Longmans. [2]

Inikori, J. E. 1987. The Sources of Supply for the Atlantic Slave Exports from the Bight of Benin and the Bight of Bonny (Biafra). *Odu* 31 (Jan): 104-23. [27]

Inikori, J.E. 1982. The Import of Firearms into West Africa, 1950 to 1807: A Quantitative Analysis. In J. E. Inikori (Ed.). *Forces Migration* pp. 126-153; 300-306. [10]

Inikori, J.E. 2002. The Development of Entrepreneurship in Africa: Southeastern Nigeria During the Era of the Atlantic Slave Trade. In Allusine Jalloh and Toyin Falola, (Eds.). *.Black Business and Economic Power.* Rochester, NY: University of Rochester Press. pp. 41-79. [27]

Irele, A. 1991. Introduction. In J.P. Clark-Bekederemo. *Collected Plays and Poems, 1958-1988.* Washington: Howard University Press [6]

Isichei, E. 1983. *A History of Nigeria.* London: Macmillan. [16, 18, 30]

Isukul, C.M. 2002. *The Modernized Counting System of Ogbia.* Port Harcourt: Emhai Publishing Co. [6]

Isukul, C. M. 2006. *The Noun Class System of Agholo.* Unpublished Graduate Seminar, University of Port Harcourt. [6]

Jaja, J.M. 1995. *Opobo: A Cultural History 1870-1980.* Unpublished PhD Dissertation, University of Port Harcourt. [18]

Jaja, J. M. 2002. Women in Ibani Economic and Religious History. In N. C. Ejituwu (Ed.). *Women in Nigerian History: The Rivers and Bayelsa Experience.* Port Harcourt: Onyoma Research Publications. [29]

Jaja, J. M. 2005. Conflict Resolution and History: The Opobo Example in the Niger Delta," *Journal of Nigerian Languages and Culture.* Vol. 8. [18]

Jebbin, N. 1984. *Economic Change in Ataba-Andoni, 1800-1982.* Unpublished B. A. History Project, University of Port Harcourt. [18]

Jeffreys, J. O. 2006. *The Role of King Ukafia Ede VI in National Development.* Unpublished B. A. History Project, University of Port Harcourt. [29]

Jeffreys, M.D.W. 1930. *Intelligence Report on the Andoni Tribe, Opobo District, Calabar Province.* NA/E mm 10c [18, 22]

Jenewari C. E. W. 1983. *Defaka: Ijo's Closest Linguistic Relative.* Port Harcourt: University of Port Harcourt Press (Delta Series No 2). [6,10, 16, 18]

Jenewari, C. E.W. 1989. Ijoid. In Bendor-Samuel, John. (ed.). *The Niger-Congo Languages.* Lanham: University Press of America. pp. 105-118. [6]

John, B. 1989. *The Niger-Congo Languaes.* London: UPA [19]

John, M. P. 1979. *Africa.* London, Longmans. [2]

Johnson, S. 1921. *The History of the Yoruba From the Earliest Times to the Beginning of the British Protectorate,* Lagos: Church Missionary Society. [16]

Johnstone, P. and J. Mandryk. 2000. *Operation World: 21st Century Edition.* Cumbria, United Kingdom: Paternoster Lifestyle. [25]

Jones, A. (ed.). [nd]. *West Africa in the Seventeenth Century.* ASA Press. [28]

Jones, G. I. 1958. Native and Trade Currencies in Southern Nigeria During the 18th and 19th Centuries. *Africa.* [22]

Jones, G. I. 1963. *The Trading States of the Oil Rivers: A Study of Political Development in Eastern Nigeria.* London: Oxford University Press. [1, 18, 10, 16, 16, 17, 18, 21, 22, 27, 30]

Jones, G.I. 1988. The Background of Eastern Nigerian History: Oral Tradition. New Haven, Conn.: MS. [18]

Jones, W.O. 1957. Manioc: An Example of Innovation in African Economics, *Development and Cultural Change,* Vol. V No. 2. [18]

Kari, E.E. 2000. *Ogbronuagum: The Bukuma Language.* München: Lincom Europa. [6]

Kari, E. E. 2003. *Clitics in Degema: A Meeting Point of Phonology, Morphology, and Syntax.* Tokyo: Research Institute for Languages & Cultures of Asia and Africa. [6]

Kari, E. E. 2004. *A Reference Grammar of Degema.* Köln: Rüdiger Köppe Verlag. [6]

Kari, E. E. 2006. *Noun Class Vestiges in Odual.* A Paper Presented at the 20th Conference of the Linguistic Association of Nigeria (CLAN), Abuja, November 13-17. [6]

Kolapo, F. J. 1998. Trading Ports of the Niger-Benue Confluence Area, c. 1830-1873. *Ports of The Slave Trade (Bights of Benin and Biafra).* Papers from a Conference of the Centre of Commonwealth Studies, University of Stirling, June. Robin Law and Silke Strickrodt (Eds.). Occasional Paper Number 6 October. pp. 96-121. [27]

Kosemani, J.M. and A.K. Okorosaye-Orubite. 2002. *History of Nigerian Education: A Contemporary Analysis:* Port Harcourt: University of Port Harcourt Press. [12]

Kouwenberg, S. 1993. *A Grammar of Berbice Dutch Creole.* Berlin: Mouton de Gruyter. [6]

Kpone-Tonwe, S. 1987. The Traditions of the Ogoni of Nigeria. Unpublished MPhil Thesis, University of London. [18]

Krama, I.C. 2001. African Theatre and Drama: Themes and Perspectives. Port Harcourt: Akpokem International. [7]

Krauss, M. 1992. The World Languages in Crisis. *Languages.* 68: 3-10 [6]

Kumangu, W.A. 1984. British Imperialism in the Brass and Nun Rivers Estuaries and the Peoples Resistance, 1800-1914. Unpublished Long Essay, Department of History, College of Education, Port Harcourt. [30]

Kusemiju, K. 2004. The Sea and the Ocean: Towards a Sustainable Heritage. <http: // www.lead.org.ng> [2]

Lansing, K.M. [nd]. Art, Artists and Art Education. Toronto: McGraw-Hill Book. [7]

Latham, A.J.H. 1973. *Old Calabar, 1600-1891: The Impact of the International Economy upon a Traditional Society.* Oxford: Clarendon Press. [30]

Lee, J.D. and Kay Williamson. 1982. A Lexicostatistic Classification of Ijo Dialects. Paper presented at the Leiden Colloquium on African Linguistics. [10]

Lee, J. D. and Kay Williamson. 1990. Lexicostatistical Classification of Ijo Dialects. *Research in African Languages and Linguistics.* Vol. 1, No. 1, 1-10. [1, 10]

Legge, C.C. 1931. *Intelligence Report on the Seimbiri Sub-Clan of the Ogbo Clan of the Western Ijo Sub-Tribe, Forcados District, Warri Province,* (NA/1.CSO 26, 29181). [10]

Lehman, P.L. 1998. *Ethics in a Christian Context.* Eugune, OR: Wipf & Stock. [27]

Leis, P.E. 1972. *Enculturation and Socialization in an Ijaw Village.* New York: Holt, Rinehart and Winston, Inc. [16]

Lennox-Boyd, A. 1958. The British Colonial Secretary, Alan Lennox-Boyd, to David Dobson LCO 21 6953 of 8 October. [30]

Leonard, A.G. 1906. *The Lower Niger and its Tribes.* London: Macmillan & Co. 1906. [1, 10, 16, 17, 18]

Littlefield, D.C. 1991. *Rice and Slaves: Ethnicity and the SlaveTrade in Colonial South Carolina.* Urbana, Illinois: University of Illinois Press, 1991. [27]

Lloyd, P.C. 1963. The Itsekiri in the Nineteenth Century: An Outline Social History. *Journal of African History.* Vol IV No. 2, 121-214. [18]

Lorenz, C. 1982. Lower Niger Bronze Bells: Form, Iconography and Function. In M. T. Brincard (Ed.). *The Art of Metal in Africa*, New York: African-American Institute. [18]

MacPepple. 1982. Owuogbo of Opobo. Unpublished B.Ed. Long Essay, College of Education, Port Harcourt. [18]

Magi, J.M. 2002. Arogbo-Ijo/Ugbo-Ilaje Fratricidal Wars: An unnecessary Inter-Ethnic Conflict (My Memoires). [18]

McIntyre, A. 1984. *After Virtue.* Notre Dame: University of Notre Dame Press. [27]

Marida, H. and Philip Lei. 1989., *Becoming Nigerian in Ijo Society,* New Brunswick and London: Rutgers University Press [4]

Minima, M. 1997. *King Jaja or the Tragedy of a Nationalist.* Port Harcourt: Golden Productions. [6]

Minima, M. 1997. *Odum Egege.* Port Harcourt: Golden Productions. [6]

Minima, M. 2006. *The Referendum.* Port Harcourt: Golden Publishers. [6]

Moody, J.E. and H.L.B. Moody. 1966. Visit to Lake Chad. *Nigeria Magazine,* No. 88, March. [7]

Morel, E. D. 1968. *Affairs of West Africa.* London: Frank Cass. [17]

Movement for the Survival of Ogoni People (MOSOP). 1990. Ogoni Bill of Rights. Port Harcourt. Saros International Publishers. [22]

Nair, R. K. 1972. *Society and Politics in South Eastern Nigeria 1841-1906.* London. [18]

Ndem, E. 1990. Efik Cultural Imperialism. In S. O. Jaja *et al* (Eds.). *Old Calabar Revisited*. [23]

Nengi-Ilagha, B. 2003. *Crossroads*. Yenagoa: Treasure Books. [6]

Nengi-Ilagha, B. 2002. *Condolences*. Yenagoa: Treasure Books. [6]

Netherlands Enginnering Development Company (NEDECO). 1961. *The Waters of the Niger Delta: Report on an Investigation*. The Hague. [10]

Netting, E.M. 1977. *Cultural Ecology*. California: Commings Publishing Co. [10]

Newington, W. F. H. 1938. Eastern Ijo, Intelligence Report. (Unpublished Government Report), Enugu. [16]

Newns, A. F. F. P. 1935. An Intelligence Report on the Epie-Atissa Group in the Degema Division, Owerri Province. [17]

Ngugi wa Thiong'o. 1982. *Devil on the Cross*. London: Heinemann. [6]

Nicklin, K. 1971. Stability and Innovation in Pottery Manufacture. *World Archaeology* Vo. 3, No. 1:13-46. [10]

Nicklin, K. 2002. Obolo Arts. In Martha G. Anderson and Philip M. Peek (Eds.). *Ways of the Rivers: Arts and Environment of the Niger Delta*, Los Angeles: UCLA Fowler Museum of Cultural History. pp. 302-305. [18]

Nicklin, K. and S. J. Flemming. 1980. A Bronze 'Carnivore Skull' from Oron, Nigeria. *Masca Journal*, 1(4). [18]

Nicolson, F.F. 1979. *The Administration of Nigeria, 1860-1960*. Oxford: Clarendon Press. [17]

Nieketein P. B. 1941. *A Short History of Tarakiri Clan*. Ebedebiri: The Author. [26]

Niger Delta Development Commission (NDDC). 2005. The Niger Delta. <http: // www.nddconline.org/The Niger Delta/> [2]

Nigeria (Federal Republic of). 1979. *The Constitution of the Federal Republic of Nigeria.* Lagos: Government Printer. [12]

Nigeria (Federal Republic of). 1997. *Census 1991 Final Results: Rivers State.* Abuja: National Population Commission. [3]

Nigeria (Federal Republic of). 2004. *The National Policy on Education (Revised).* Lagos: Government Printers. [12]

Nkosi, L. 1981. *Tasks and Masks: Themes and Styles of African Literature.* Harlow: Longman. [6]

Nnoli, O. 1980. *Ethnic Politics in Nigeria.* Enugu: Fourth Dimension Publishers. [30]

Noah M.E. 1966. *Old Calabar: The City-States and the Europeans.* Uyo: Scholars Press. [12, 23]

Noah, M. E. 1970. *Ibibio Pioneers in Modern Nigerian History.* Uyo: Scholars Press. [23]

Noah, M.E. Ibibio Origins and Migrations in Historical Perspective: A Tentative Analysis. [23]

Northrup, D. 1972. The Growth of Trade Among the Igbo before 1800. *Journal of African History,* XII, 2. [28]

Northrup, D. 1978. Trade Without Rulers: Pre-Colonial Economic Development in Southern Nigeria. Oxford: Clarendon Press. [22]

Northrup, D. 2000. Igbo and Myth: Igbo Culture and Ethnicity in the Atlantic World, 1600-1850. *Slavery and Abolition* 21 (3), 1-20. [27]

Northrup, D. 2006. Becoming African: Identity Formation Among Liberated Slaves in Nineteenth-Century Sierra Leone. *Slavery and Abolition*, 27 (1), 1-21. [27]

Ntukidem, A. E. 1987. The Land and People of the Cross River Region. In Abasiattai, M. B. (Ed.). *Akwa Ibom and Cross River States: The Land, the People and Their Culture.* Calabar: Wusen Press. [23]

Numbere, N. E. 2002. *Greater Evangelism World Crusade: Landmarks in Her Vision and History.* Port Harcourt: GEWC Publications [29]

Nwabara S.N. 1977. *Ibo Land: A Century of Contact with Britain 1860-1960.* London: Hodder and Stoughton, 1977. [21]

Nwajiaku, K. 2005. Between Discourse and Reality: The Politics of Oil and Ijaw Ethnic Nationalism in the Niger Delta. *Cashier d'Etudes africaines,* XLV (2), 457-496. [27]

Nwajiaku, K. 2005. *Oil Politics and Identity Transformation in Nigeria: The Case of the Ijaw of the Niger Delta.* DPhil Dissertation, Nuffield College, Oxford. [17]

Nwokeji, G. U. 2000. The Atlantic Slave Trade and Population Density: A Historical Demography of the Biafran Hinterland. *Canadian Journal of African Studies* 34 (3) (Special Issue: On Slavery and Islam in African History: A Tribute to Martin Klein), 616-55. [27]

Nwokeji, G. U. and D. Eltis. 2002. The Roots of the African Diaspora: Methodological Considerations in the Analysis of Names in the Liberated African Registers of Sierra Leone and Havana. *History in Africa* 29, 365-79. [27]

Nwokoma, F. A. 1982. The History of Joinkrama in the Pre-colonial Era: An NCE Project Essay, Rivers State College of Education, Port Harcourt. [19]

Nyananyo, B. L. 1999. Vegetation. In: E.J. Alagoa (Ed.). *The Land and People of Bayelsa State: Central Niger Delta.* Port Harcourt: Onyoma Research Publications. pp. 44-57. [2, 18]

Nyananyo, B. L. 2002. Forest Resources. In E.J. Alagoa and A.A. Derefaka (Eds.). *The Land and People of Rivers State: Eastern Niger Delta.* Port Harcourt, Onyoma Research Publications. pp. 63-81. [2]

Nyananyo, B.L. 2006. Major Boardman Harrap Esinkuma Awo Nyananyo, M.A. (Mathematics, St. Andrews), Dip. Ed., MON-Posthumous. Port-Harcourt: MS. [29]

Nyananyo, B.L., C.U. Okeke and S.I. Mensah. 2004. *Rhizophora* L. (Rhizophoraceae) in the Niger Delta: Morphology and Distribution. *International Journal of Science and Technology (IJST).* 3 (I and II): 23 – 29. [2]

Nzewunwa, N. 1979. *Aspects of Economy and Culture in the Prehistory of the Niger Delta.* Ph.D. Thesis, St. Johns College, Cambridge. [10]

Nzewunwa, N. 1987. Economic Prehistory of the Niger Delta. In E.J. Alagoa, F.N. Anozie and N. Nzewunwa (Eds.) *The Early History of the Niger Delta:* Bayreuth: Helmut Buske Verlag. pp. 187-229. [10]

Nzewunwa, N. 1979. *Aspects of Economy and Culture in the Prehistory of the Niger Delta.* PhD. Thesis submitted at St. John's College, Cambridge. [10]

Nzewunwa, N. 1988. Extending the Chronology of the Eastern Niger Delta. *Nsukka Journal of the Humanities* Nos. 3/4 (June/December), 37-49. [10]

Nzewunwa, N. and A.A. Derefaka. 1989. Prehistoric Developments. In E.J. Alagoa and T. N. Tamuno (eds.) *Land and People of Nigeria: Rivers State.* Port Harcourt: Riverside Communications. [10]

Obi, S. *Tears in a Basket.* Ibadan: Kraft Books. [6]

Obibo, I. B. 1991. *The Origin of Degema.* An NCE Project Essay, College of Education, Port Harcourt. [19]

Obuoforibo, B.A. 1997. *History of Great Bishops.* Port Harcourt: CSS Press, [29]

Obuoforibo, B.A. 1980. *A History of the Niger Delta Diocese 1864-1980,* Port Harcourt: CSS Press. [29]

Obuoforibo, B.A. 1998. *History of Christianity in Bayelsa.* Port Harcourt: CSS Press. [29]

Obuoforibo, B.A. (Ed.). 2002. *Jubilee of the Niger Delta Diocese: The Odyssey of a Diocese, 1952-2002.* Port Harcourt: CSS Press. [29]

Obuoforibo, B.A. 2002. *Topics in Bonny Church History.* Port Harcourt: CSS Press. [29]

Obuoforibo, B. A. 2005. *The Church in Okrika,* (Port Harcourt: CSS Press. [29]

Obuoforibo, B.A. 2006. *Chief Daniel Oju Kalio (1857-1928) of Okrika.* Okrika: MS. [29]

Obuoforibo, B. A. 2006. *King Ibanichuka, Ado VI (1803-1896), Amanyanabo of Okrika.* Okrika: MS. [29]

Obuoforibo, B. A. 2006. *Chief Henry Buowari Brown (1881-1959) of Bonny.* Okrika: MS. [29]

Ockiya, D. O. 1988. *My Autobiography.* Akure: Idibiye Francis. [29]

Oduwole, A.D., K.D. Sales, G.V. Robins and D. R. Griffiths. 1983. *The Application of ESR Spectroscopy in Archaeology.* Invited Paper presented to the Pan African Congress, Jos, Nigeria, December. [10]

Ofonagoro, W. 1979. *Trade and Politics in Southern Nigeria 1881-1929.* New York: Nok Publishers. [18]

Ogan, E. S. 1994. *The Role of Chief Harold Dappa-Biriye in the Struggle for the Creation of a Separate Rivers State.* Unpublished B. A. History Project, University of Port Harcourt. [30]

Ogbowei, G. E. 1979. *The Fisherman's Invocation.* Benin City: Ethiope. [6]

Ogbowei, G. E. 1992. *Tonye and Kingfish.* Port Harcourt: Baron. [6]

Ogbowei, G. E. 2001. *Let the Honey Run and Other Poems.* Port Harcourt: Minson. [6]

Ogbowei, G. E. 2003. *The Towncrier's Song.* Port Harcourt: Minson. [6]

Ogbowei, G. E. 2005. *The Dreamer, His Vision.* Port Harcourt: University of Port Harcourt Press. [6]

Ogbowei, G. E. 2006. *The Heedless Ballot Box.* Ibadan: Kraft. [6]

Ogbowei, G. E.2006. *As I See It.* Port Harcourt: University of Port Harcourt Press. [6]

Ogundele, J. 2005. *Creating and Transferring Social and Economic Capital for Home Country Development: The Use of Ethnic Affiliation by Nigerian Immigrants.* Unpublished Paper, May 2005. [27]

Ojiako, J. O. 1981. *Nigeria; Yesterday, Today, and ...* Onitsha: Africana Educational Publishers. [17]

Okara, G. 1970. *The Voice.* London: Heinemann. [6]

Okia, C. D. 1978. The Village of Edagberi Joinkrama from Earliest Times to the Present. An NCE Project Essay, College of Education, Port Harcourt. [19]

Okoko, K.A.B and A. Lazarus. 1999. The Creation of Bayelsa State. In E.J. Alagoa, (Ed.). The Land and People of Bayelsa State: Central Niger Delta. Port Harcourt: Onyoma Research Publications. [16]

Okonkwo, R. 1985. *Heroes of West African Nationalism.* Enugu: Delta of Nigeria. [30]

Okonny, P. I., G. Ayologha and A.A. Dickson. 2002. Geology and Soils. In E.J. Alagoa and A. A. Derefaka (Eds.). *Land and People of Rivers State: Eastern Niger Delta.* Port Harcourt, Onyoma Research Publications. pp. 9-30. [2]

Okorobia, A. M. 1998. Draft Environmental Impact Assessment Report (Socio-Economic Component) on Idu 9 Oil Field of the Nigeria Agip Oil Company in Bayelsa State. [16]

Okorobia, A. M. 1999. A History of the Underdevelopment of the Eastern Niger Delta, AD 1500-1993. An Unpublished Ph.D Dissertation, University of Port Harcourt, Nigeria. [18, 16, 18]

Okorobia, A. M. 1999. The Impact of The Atlantic Trade. in E.J. Alagoa (Ed.). *The Land and People of Bayelsa State: Central Niger Delta.* Port Harcourt: Onyoma Research Publications. [18, 16]

Okorosaye-Orubite, A. K. 1990. Factors Responsible for Educational Underdevelopment in Rivers State; A Historical Analysis. Unpublished PhD Thesis, Faculty of Education, University of Port Harcourt, Port Harcourt. [12]

Okorosaye-Orubite, A.K. 1991. Local Community Initiative in the Introduction of Western Education in South-Eastern Nigeria. *Journal of Education in Development Areas. Vol. IV and V, 1991/1995.* pp. 71-80. [12]

Okorosaye-Orubite, A.K. 2000. The Universal Basic Education (UBE) Programme: Matters Arising. In J.M. Kosemani (Ed). *Nigerian Education: Matters Arising Vol. 1.* Port Harcourt: Abe Publications. [12]

Okosi, P. 1980. King Agbedi II of Amassoma. In T.N. Tamuno and E.J. Alagoa (Eds.). *Eminent Nigerians of the Rivers State*. Ibadan: Heinemann Educational Books, Nigeria Ltd. [16]

Okpewho, I. 1991. The Ozidi Saga: A Critical Introduction. In J.P. Clark-Bekederemo. *The Ozidi Saga*. Washington: Howard University Press. [6]

Olali, S.T. 2002. *From Indigenous Culture to the Introduction of Christianity*. Port Harcourt: Vicstol Ventures. [25]

Olsen, S.J. 1971. Zooarchaeology: Animal Bones and Archaeology and Their Interpretation. *Addison-Wesley Module in Anthropology.Vol.* 2, 1-30. [10]

Onduku, T.O. 1960. *Ezon Bibi Ge Brami. How to Write Ijo (Ijaw)*. Ibadan: Caxton Press (West Africa) Ltd. [6]

Onoh, S. O. 1994. *The Ejagham Nation in the Cross River region of Nigeria*. Ibadan: Kraft Books. [23]

Opara, I. I. 1997. *The Niger Delta Men in the Independence Movement, 1920-1960*. Abuja: MS. [30]

Opigo, E. 1999. *Frothy Facades*. Port Harcourt: Gratte-Ciel. [6]

Orji, K.E. 1989. The Impact of Colonial Rule on the Indigenous Economy of Ogbahland, an Unpublished MA thesis submitted to the Department of History, University of Port Harcourt. [21]

Orji, K. E. 1993. Landmarks in the Military History of Ogbahland. *Akwa* (an Ikwerre Socio-cultural Journal). [21]

Orji, K.E. 2003. The Changing Role of Women in the Development of Ogba/Egbema/Ndoni Communities. In N.C. Ejituwu and A.O.I. Gabriel (Eds) *Women in Nigerian History: The Rivers and Bayelsa States Experience*. Port. Harcourt: Onyoma Research Publications. pp. 237-249. [21]

Oruekpedi, C.A. 1995. *Izon Beeli Funbo.* Warri: GKS Press. [6]

Oruekpedi, C.A. 2000. *Izon Beeli Funbo Mamukaramo Fun.* Warri: GKS Press. [6]

Orugbani, A. 2005. *Nigeria Since the 19th Century.* Port Harcourt; Paragraphics. [18, 17]

Osaghae, E. E. 1995. The Ogoni Uprising: Oil Politics, Monetary Agitation and the Future of the Nigerian State. *African Affairs.* [22]

Oswald, A. 1975. *Clay Pipes for the Archaeologist.* Oxford: Oxford University Press *(British Archaeological Reports* No. 18) [10]

Otobotekere, A.J.T. 1986. Aspects of the Biology of Snout Fish (*Gymnarchus niloticus)* (Cuvier) from the Swamps of the Nun River, Rivers State. MPhil Thesis, Rivers State University of Science and Technology, Port Harcourt. [2]

Otobotekere, A. J. T. and F.D. Sikoki. 1999. Aquatic Fauna. In E.J. Alagoa (Ed.). *The Land and People of Bayelsa State: Central Niger Delta.* Port Harcourt. Onyoma Research Publications. pp. 58-71. [2]

Otobotekere, C. (2002). *Across the Bridge: Diadems Forever.* Port Harcourt: Newsfair. [6]

Otobotekere, C. 2005. *Around and About Book 1.* Port Harcourt: Newsfair. [6]

Otobotekere, C. 2005. *Around and About Book 2.* Port Harcourt: Newsfair. [6]

Otobotekere, C. [nd]. *Poetry World: An Introduction.* Port Harcourt. [6]

Ototo, L. 2004. *Ebiakpo the Orphan.* Port Harcourt: Alabaster Resources. [6]

Ototo, L. 2006. *Ovie and the Housefly.* Ibadan: Kraft Books. [6]

Ouirk, R. et. al. 1973. *A University Grammar of English.* London: Longman Group Ltd. [6]

Owonaro, S.K. 1949. The History of Ijo (Ijaw) and Her Neighbouring Tribes in Nigeria. Lagos: The Author [10, 16, 18, 16, 22, 29]

Ozanne, D. (1962) Review of Shaw's Dawu. *Trans. Hist. Soc. Ghana.* [10]

Ozanne, D. 1969. Diffusion of smoking. *Odu.* [10]

Ozanne D. 1962. Accra Plains. *Transactions of the Historical Society of Ghana.* [10]

Pacheco Pereira, D. 1508. *Esmeraldo de Situ Orbis.* Translated [into English] and edited by G.H.T Kimble. London. Printed for the Hakluyt Society in 1937. [1, 16, 16, 18]

Page, G. 1957. The Case for the Creation of a Rivers State: Memorandum E20 LCO 21 6953... [30]

Pamie-George, E. 1987. *Greater Evangelism World Crusade: A Pentecostal Church.* Unpublished NCE Thesis, Department of Religious Studies, College of Education, Port Harcourt [29]

Patterson, O. 1969. *The Sociology of Slavery: An Analysis of the Origins, Delopment and Structure of Negro Slave Society in Jamaica.* Rutherford. [18]

Payne, A. I. 1986. *The Ecology of Tropical Lakes.* Chichester: Wiley and Sons. [2]

Peek, P. M. and K. Nicklin.. 2002. Lower Niger Bronze Industries and the Archaeology of the Niger Delta. In M. G. Anderson and P. M. Peek (Eds.). *Ways of the Rivers: Arts and Environment of the Niger Delta.* Los Angeles: UCLA Fowler Museum of Cultural History. [18]

Phillips, U. U. 1991. *The Aziba Cult of Degema.* An NCE Project Essay College of Education, Port Harcourt. [19]

Porbeni, A. B. C. 2005. *Wise Mother Hen and Other Stories.* Lagos: BEC Wonder World. [6]

Porter, J. C. 1933. *Intelligence Report on the Okrika.* NAE. [29]

Porter, J.C. 1931. Oporoma Clan Intelligence Report. Unpublished Government Report. [16, 16]

Powell, C. B. 1993. Sites and Species of Conservation Interest in the Central Axis of the Niger Delta. A Report of Recommendations to the Natural Resources Conservation Council (NARESCON). Port Harcourt, Nigeria. [2]

Powell, C. B. 1997. "Discoveries and priorities for mammals in the freshwater forests of the Niger Delta", *Oryx,* 31 (2), 83-85...(Fauna and Flora International). [24]

Preboye, I.C. 1995. The Core Delta Iduwini Clan. Ibadan: Rural Development Nig. Ltd. [7]

Princewill, K. D. 1980. King Amachree I of Kalabari. In T. N. Tamuno and E. J. Alagoa (Eds.). *Eminent Nigerians of Rivers State.* Ibadan: Heinemann Educational Books. [29]

Raji, R. 2005. Foreword. In G.E. Ogbowei. *Let the Honey Run.* Ibadan: Kraft Books. [6]

Robert, A.L. 1982. *Celebration: A World of Art and Ritual.* Washington, D.C., Smithsoman Institution Press. [7]

Roberts-Wray, K. O. 1957. K.O. Roberts-Wray to Sir Reginald Manningham-Buller, Bart, Q. C. LCO 21 6953 of 8 May. [30]

Rotimi, O. 1983. *If: A Tragedy of the Ruled.* Ibadan: Heinemann Educational Books [6]

Rotimi, O. 1985. *Hopes of the Living Dead.* Ibadan: Spectrum Books. [6]

Rotimi, O. 2001. *Akassa You Mi.* Port Harcourt: Onyoma Research Publications and University of Port Harcourt Press. [6]

Rupert, E. 1965. *Akiga Story: The Tiv Tribe as Seen by One of Its Members,* London. [16]

Ryder, A.F.C. 1965. Dutch Trade on the Nigerian Coast During the Seventeenth Century. *Journal of the Historical Society of Nigeria.* Vol. 3 No. 2, 195-210. [18]

Ryder, A.F.C. 1980. The Trans-Atlantic Trade. In O. Ikimi (Ed). *The Groundwork of Nigerian History,* Ibadan: Heinemann Educational Books. [16]

Sam, K. I. 1982. A Brief History of Abua, 1600-1960: A Historical Survey of the Development of the Political, Economic, Social and Cultural Institutions of Abua. Unpublished BA Project, University of Port Harcourt. [18]

Saro-Wiwa, K. 1983. *Second Letter to Ogoni Youth.* Port Harcourt: Saros International. [22]

Saro-Wiwa, K. 1985. *Sozaboy: A Novel in Rotten English.* Port Harcourt: Saros International. [6]

Saro-Wiwa, K. 1989. *On a Darkling Plain: An Account of the Nigerian Civil War.* Port Harcourt: Saros International. [29, 22, 30]

Saro-Wiwa, K. 1994. Ogoni Moment of Truth. Port Harcourt: Saros International. [22]

Schmidt, P.R. 1978. *Historical Archaeology.* Westport: Greenwood Press. [10]

Schuyler, R.L. 1978. Historical and Historic Sites in Archaeology and Anthropology: Basic Definitions and Relationships. In M.P. Leone (Ed.). *Contemporary Archaeology.* [10]

Scott, J. S. 1966. *Report on the Fisheries of the Niger Delta Special Area.* Port Harcourt: Niger Delta Development Board. [2]

Shackley, M. 1981. *Environmental Archaeology* London: George Allen and Unwin [10]

Shango,S. {Ed.), Tributes to a great leader, JS Taka, Enugu. [33]

Shaw, T. 1960. Diffusion of Smoking. *Journal of the Royal Anthoropological Institute.* [10]

Shaw, T. 1970. Igbo Ukwu: An Ancient Archaeological Discovery in Eastern Nigeria. London: Thames and Hudson. [22]

Shaw, T. 1978. *Nigeria: Its Archaeology and Early History.* London: Thames and Hudson. [10, 23]

Shepherd. 1976. *Ceramics for the Archaeologist.* Washington, D.C: Carnegie Institution. [10]

Short, K.C. and A.J. Stauble. 1967. Outline Geology of the Niger Delta. *American Association of Petroleum Geologists Bulletin.* Vol. 51 No. 5, 761-779. [10]

Sikoki, F. D. and A.J.T. Otobotekere. 1999. Fisheries. In: E.J. Alagoa (Ed.). *The Land and People of Bayelsa State: Central Niger Delta.* Port Harcourt, Onyoma Research Publications. pp. 301-319. [2]

Sklar, R. L. 1983. *Nigerian Political Parties: Power in an Emergent African Nation.* New York: A. Knopf, [29]

Smith, N. S. H., I. E. Robertson and Kay Williamson. 1987. The Ijo element in Berbice Dutch. *Language and Society.* 16, 49-90. [1, 16, 16, 28]

Smith, S. R. 1976. Warfare and Diplomacy in Pre-Colonial West Africa. London: Methnen & Co. Ltd. [22]

Sogules, A. S. 1983. The Political Upheavals in Kalabariland (1870-1927). Unpublished B. A. History Project, University of Port Harcourt. [29]

Sorgwe, C. M. 1977. *A Textbook of Niger Delta History from Earliest Times to the Present.* Ibadan: Rescue Publications. [19]

Sorgwe, C.M. 1990. A History of Epie-Atissa: Oral and Ethnographic Dimensions. An Unpublished PhD Dissertation, University of Port Harcourt, Nigeria. [16]

Sorgwe, C. M. 1999. The Impact of Colonial Rule. in E.J. Alagoa (Ed.) The Land and People of Bayelsa State: Central Niger Delta. Port Harcourt: Onyoma Research Publications. [16]

Sorgwe C. M. 2000. *Epie-Atissa Since 1550: A history of an Edoid Community.* Ibadan: Rescue Publications. [19]

Sowunmi, M.A. 1981. Aspects of Late Quaternary Vegetational Changes in West Africa. *Journal of Biogeography.* 8 (4), 57-74. [10]

Sowunmi, M.A. 1981. Late Quaternary Environmental Changes in Nigeria in *Pollen et Spores.* Vol. XXII No. 1, 125-148. [10]

Sowunmi, M.A. 1981. Nigerian Vegetational History from the Late Quaternary to the Present Day. *Palaeoecology of Africa.* 13:217-234. [10]

Sowunmi, M. A. 1988. "Palynological studies in the Niger Delta", In Alagoa, E. J, F. N. Anozie, and N. Nzewunwa (eds.), *The Early History of the Niger Delta.* Hamburg. [24]

Sparks, B. W. 1977. *Geomorphology.* London, Longmans. [2]

Spaulding. 1971. Statistical Techniques for the Discovery of Artefact Types. In J. Deetz (Ed.). *Man's Imprint From the Past.* pp. 43-57. [10]

Stonely, R. 1966. The Niger Delta Region in the Light of the Theory of Continental Drift. *Geological Magazine.* 103:385-396. [10]

Taiwo, C.O. 1980. *The Nigerian Education System: Past, Present and Future.* Lagos: Thomas Nelson Ltd. [12]

Talbot, P.A. 1926. *The Peoples of Southern Nigeria: A Sketch of their History, Ethnology and Languages with an Abstract of the 1921 Census.* London: Oxford University Press. [16, 18, 19, 22, 23]

Talbot, P.A. 1932. Tribes of the Niger Delta, Their Religion and Customs. London: Sheldon Press (Reprinted in 1967 by Frank Cass) [1, 18, 18, 19, 21, 22, 29]

Talbot, P. A. [nd] *In the shadow of the bush.* [23]

Tamuno, T. N. 1966. *Nigeria and Elective Representatives, 1923-1947.* London: Macmillan. [29, 30, 33]

Tamuno, T. N. 1978. *The Evolution of the Nigerian State: The Southern Phase, 1898-1914.* London: Longman. [9, 16, 17, 30, 33]

Tamuno, T. N. 1982. *Songs of an Egg-Head.* Port Harcourt: Alafeni. [6]

Tamuno, **T.N. 1991. Peace and Violence in Nigeria.** Ibadan, 1991, [33]

Tamuno, T. N. 1999. *Festival of Songs and Drums.* Lagos: Newswatch. [6]

Tamuno, T.N. **2000. The Niger Delta Question,** Port Harcourt/. [33]

Tamuno, T. N. 2005. *Lamentations of Yeske.* Ibadan: Stirling-Horden. [6]

Tamuno, T. N. and E.J. Alagoa (Eds.). 1980. *Eminent Nigerians of the Rivers State.* Ibadan: Heinemann Educational Books. [19, 29]

Tanwari, E. 2005. *The Traditional Festival of Nembe people: A Case Study of the Iyal-Ikai Festival of Okoroba.* An unpublished Research Project. University of Port Harcourt. [19]

Tasie, G. O. M. 1976. King Jaja of Opobo and the Christian Mission under Bishop Samuel Ajayi Crowther: Aspects of the Clash Between Missionary Work and the Political and Economic Ambitions of a Nineteenth Century Niger Delta Nationalist. *Oduma*, 3 (1) April, 1976.[18]

Tasie, G.O.M. 1978. *Christian Missionary Enterprise in the NigerDelta 1864-1914.* London: E.J. Brill [12]

Tasie, G. O. M. 1980. The Prophetic Garrick Sokari Braide of Bakana. In T. N. Tamuno and E. J. Alagoa (Eds.). *Eminent Nigerians of Rivers State.* Ibadan: Heinemann Educational Books [30]

Thomas, E. 1978. A *Grammatical Description of the Engenni language.* (Publications in Linguistics 60). Dallas: Summer Institute of Linguistics. [6]

Thomas, E. and Kay Williamson (Eds.). 1967. *Wordlists of Delta Edo: Epie, Engenni, Degema*, Ibadan: Institute of African Studies. [16]

Tinnie, D. G. 1995. *A Slave Ship Speaks: The Wreck of the Henrietta Marie.* Key West: Mel Fisher Maritime Heritage Society. [27]

Traugott, E.C. and M. L. Pratt. 1980. *Linguistics for Students of Literature.* New York: Harcourt Brace Jovanovich, Inc. [6]

Trowell, M. 1952. Classical African Sculpture. [7]

Ubi, O. A. 1987. Biase Communities of Southeastern Nigeria: Melting Pot of Cultures? *Nigeria Magazine.* Vol. 55 No. 4. [23]

Ubi, O. A. 2004. *The Yakurr of the Middle Cross River Region, 1600-1950.* Calabar: Jamel Press. [23]

Udo, E. A. [nd]. The Ibo origin of the Efik by A. E. Afigbo: A Review. *The Calabar Historical Journal.* Vol. 1, No. 1. [23]

Udo, R.K. 1978. *A Comprehensive Geography of West Africa.* London: Heinemann Educational Books [10]

Udo, **R.K.** 1979. The *Human Geography of Tropical Africa*. Ibadan: Heineman Educational Books. [3]

Udoeyop, N. J. 1973. *Three Nigerian Poets*. Ibadan: Ibadan University Press. [6]

Ukafia-Ede VI, O. S. 2004. Welcome Address to His Excellency Chief Olusegun Obasanjo, President of Nigeria, On the Occasion of His Official Visit to Akwa Ibom State, August. Uyo: MS. [29]

Ukpohor, T. 2002. Dynamics 3D/4D Modeling of Natural Gas Reservoir: Resolving the Complexities of the Niger Delta Formation For Effective Gas. [2]

Ume, K. E. 1980. *The Rise of British Colonialism in Southern Nigeria 1700-1900: A Study of the Bights of Benin and Bonny*. Smithtown, New York: Exposition Press, 1980. [27]

Usman, Y.B. 1999. *History and the Challenges of the Peoples and Politics of Africa in the 21st Century*. Kaduna: The Abdullahi Smith Centre for Historical Research. [29]

Uya, O. E. 1984. *A History of Oron People of the Lower Cross River Basin*. Oron: Manson Press. [18]

Uya, O. E. 1984. *A history of Oron people*. Oron: Manson Press [23]

Vansina, J. 1965. *Oral Tradition*. London: Routledge and Kegan Paul. [10]

Vansina, J. 1967. The Use of Oral Tradition in Africa Culture History. In C. Gabel and N.R. Bennett (Eds). *Reconstructing African Culture History*. Boston: Boston University Press. [10]

Vansina, J. 1985. *Oral Tradition as History*. London: James Currey; Nairobi: Heinemann [10]

Wagner, R. 1975. *The Invention of Culture*. New Jersey: Prentice-Hall, Inc. [10]

Walker, I.C. 1975. The Potential Use of European Clay Tobacco Pipes. *West African Journal of Archaeology*. Vol. 5, 165-193. [10]

Wallwork, J.F. 1985. *Language and Linguistics: An introduction to the Study of Language*. London: Heinnemann. [6]

Walter, M.W. 1967. Length of the Rainy Season in Nigeria. In: J.S. Oguntoyinbo (Ed.). *A New Geography of Nigerian Development*. Ibadan: Heinemann EDucational Books. [2]

Wariboko, W. E. 1981. King Amakiri I of Kalabari: The Quest for Historical Truth in a Body of Politically Controversial Oral Tradition. Unpublished BA Essay, University of Port Harcourt. [28]

Wariboko, W. E. 1989. Social and Political Developments. In Alagoa, E .J. and Tamuno, T. N. (eds) *Land and People of Nigeria: Rivers State* Port Harcourt: Riverside Communications. pp. 125-128 [16]

Wariboko, W.E. 1991. *New Calabar and the Forces of Change ca. 1850-1945*. Unpublished PhD Dissertation, University of Birmingham. [28]

Wariboko, W.E. 1998. *Planting Church Culture in New Calabar*. San Francisco. [17]

West Equatorial Africa Church Magazine (WEACM): The Official Monthly Magazine of the Anglican Church in West Africa. 1926. [29]

Wewe, A.F. 1995. Oguberiberi Masks: the Ijo Stylistic Traits in Yoruba-Speaking Igbobini. *Kurio Africana: Journal of Art and Criticism*. (Ile-Ife), 2 (1), 34-39. [17]

Whitehouse, A. A. 1905. An African Fetish. *Journal of the African Society* London [18, 29]

Whitehouse, A. A. to Charles H. Read of the British Museum, London, 6 Sept. 1904. [18]

Williams, G. A. 1931. Intelligence Report on the Abua Clan. (26/3 File 28239 No. 146/36 NAI). [18]

Williamson, Kay. 1957. Notes taken on Okirika History. (cited in E.J. Alagoa: *A History of the Niger Delta*. Ibadan: Ibadan University Press, 1972. [22]

Williamson, Kay. 1965. *A Grammar of the Kolokuma dialect of Ijo*. West Africa Language Monographs No. 2. Cambridge: Cambridge University Press. [6]

Williamson, Kay. 1966. Ijo Dialects in the *Polyglotta Africana. Sierra Leone Language Review,* 5, 122- 133. [1,]

Williamson, Kay. 1968. Languages of the Niger Delta. *Nigeria Magazine* 97, pp. 124-130. [16]

Williamson, Kay. 1970. Some Food Plant Names in the Niger Delta. *International Journal of American Linguistics.* Vol. 36, No. 2 April. [10]

Williamson, Kay. 1971. The Benue-Congo Languages and Ijo. In T. A. Gebrok (Ed.). *Current Trends in Linguistics,* Vol. 7. [18]

Williamson, Kay. 1986. Foreword. In Alazigha, D. *Akiroro*. Sabagreia: Dagbo Cultural Academy. [6]

Williamson, Kay. 1987. The Pedigree of Nations: Historical Linguistics in Nigeria.. Inaugural Lecture, University of Port Harcourt. [19]

Williamson, Kay. 1988. Linguistic evidence for the prehistory of the Niger Delta. In Alagoa, E.J., Anozie, F.N. and Nzewunwa, N. (eds.). *The Early History of the Niger Delta*. Hamburg: Helmut Buske Verlag. pp. 65-119. [1, 6, 17, 16, 18]

Williamson, Kay. 1988. "The linguistic prehistory of the Niger Delta", in E. J. Alagoa, F. N. Anozie, and Nwanna Nzewunwa (eds.), *The Early History of the Niger Delta.* Hamburg. [24]

Williamson, Kay. 1989. Niger-Congo Overview. In J. Bendor-Samuel.(Ed.). *The Niger-Congo Languages.* Lantham: University Press of America. pp. 3-46. [6, 10]

Williamson, K. and A.O. Timitimi. 1983. *Short Izon-English Dictionary.* Port Harcourt: University of Port Harcourt Press. [6]

Willink, H. 1958. Report of the Commission Appointed to Enquire into the Fears of Minorities and the Means of Allaying Them. (Henry Willink Commission Report). London: Her Majesty's Stationary Office. [9, 22]

World Bank. 1995. Defining an environmental Development [2]

World Commission on the Environment and Development (WCED). 1987. *Our Common Future: Report of the World Commission on the Environment And Development.* Oxford, Clarendon Press. [2]

Woy, M.T. 1985. *A History of Abua Religion from 1880 to the Present.* Unpublished BA Project, University of Port Harcourt. [18]

Wren, R. 1984. *J. P. Clark.* Lagos: Lagos University Press. [6]

Wubani, M.N.W. 1935. A Small Beginning. *The Nigerian Teacher.* No. 5. [18]

Yeibo, E. 2003. *A Song For Tomorrow and Other Poems.* Ibadan: Kraft Books. [6]

Yeibo, E. 2004. *Maiden Lines.* Ibadan: Kraft Books. [6]

Zotora, Y. 1971. Jaja of Opobo: Fighter Against Colonialism. *New World Magazine.* [18]

INDEX

Hudron. K. Kari

B

Bagauda Lake (Kano State) 640

Baikie, William B. 481

Bakassi 625

Barrett, Igoni 217

Bassambiri 33, 470

Bassan (Basan) 465

Bayelsa State 30, 33, 34, 69, 110, 115, 290, 390, 490, 732

Bebeke-ola 571, 572, 573

Beecroft John 379

Bekederemo (Ambakederimo) 441

Beletiema 33

Balewa, Abubakar Tafawa 744, 745

Bell-Gam Henry Leopold 211

Benaaghe (Bush Spirit) 164

Benifei 408

Benin 412, 418, 438

Benin Empire 401, 405, 415, 432

Benin influence 437

Benin kingdom 86, 597

Benin Kingdom pull 8

Benin origin 427

Benin River 410, 419

Benin wave 362

Benue Congo 108, 373, 392

Benue-Congo languages 72, 73, 392

Berbice Creole of Guyana in the Caribbean 8

Berbice Dutch 9, 720, 722, 723-726

Berbice Dutch Creole 87, 719

Berlin West African Conference 755

Bestman Adiyi Martin 212

Biafra 490, 736, 752

Biafran troops 755

Bie masquerade of Cote d'Ivoire 178

Big-dowry 46, 47

Bight of Biafra 687, 713, 718, 719

Bight of Bonny 713, 717

Bille 371, 372

Bille Language group 80

Bini Kurukuru 121, 408

Bini pere (Rich man of the water) 166, 170, 410

Biosphere 12

Biseni 3

Biseni language group 81

Black African descent 713

Bolou Toru 93

Boma (Bumo) 465

Bomadi 31

Bonny 1, 364, 375-376, 714-719

Bonny Port 7, 33

Bonny River 7

Borno State 624

Boro day 698, 699, 705

Boro Foundation 698

Boro, Isaac Jasper Adaka 206, 220, 289, 291, 384-385, 489, 571-573, 675, 698, 699, 754, 759

Boro phenomenon 206

Boro's idealism 760

Bou gbee rite (pay the bush) 190

Bouomini 123

Brackish water swamp forest 281

Brass 403

Brass (Rio Bento) River 13

Brazil 508

Bride wealth 62

Bride wealth in Ebiama/Amakiri 43

British 380, 486, 515

British authorities 751

British-born Ijo 674

British colonial administration 204, 516

British colonial armies 673

British colonial rule 383

British colonialism 399

British consul 379

British consulate 423

835

R

S